MOON

TENNESSEE

MARGARET LITTMAN

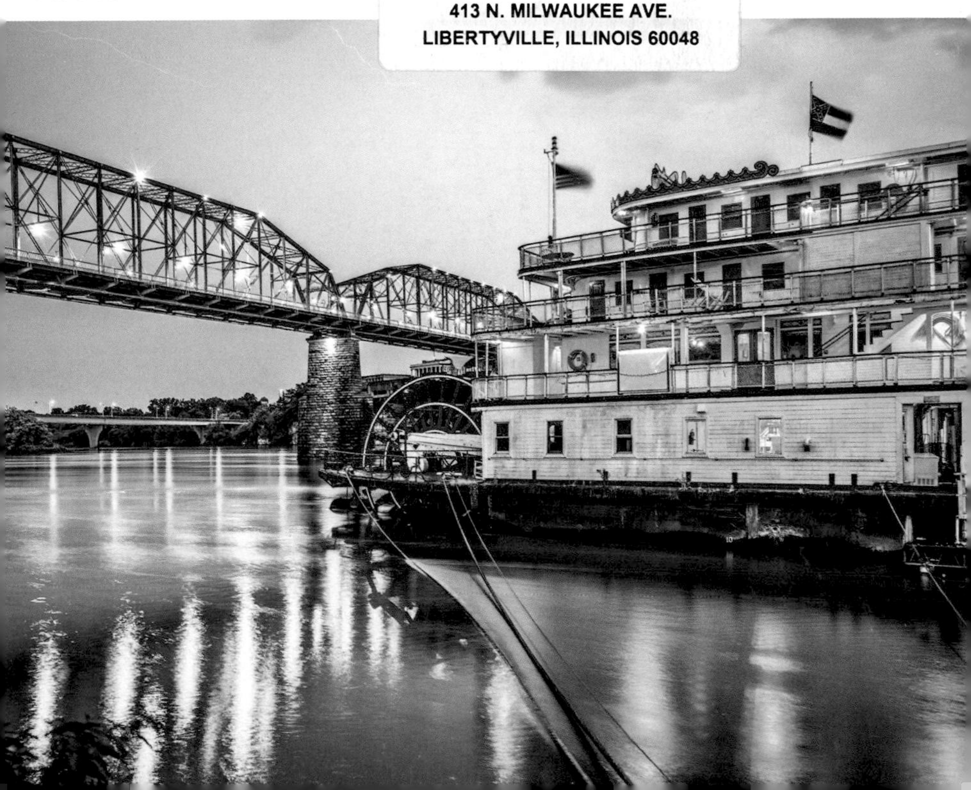

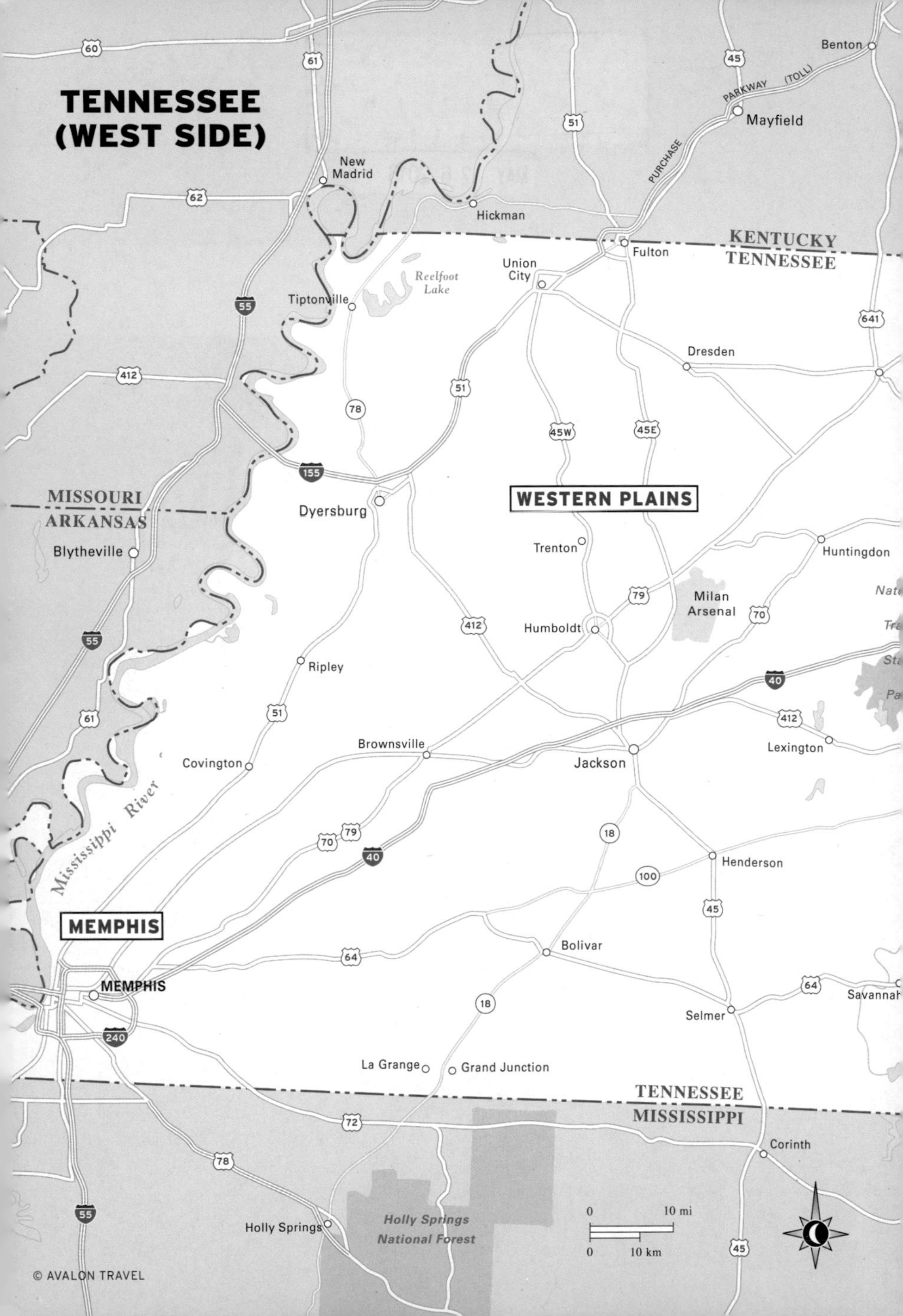
TENNESSEE (WEST SIDE)
KENTUCKY
TENNESSEE
MISSOURI
ARKANSAS
TENNESSEE
MISSISSIPPI
WESTERN PLAINS
MEMPHIS
Benton
Mayfield
PURCHASE PARKWAY (TOLL)
New Madrid
Hickman
Fulton
Union City
Reelfoot Lake
Tiptonville
Dresden
Dyersburg
Blytheville
Trenton
Huntingdon
Milan Arsenal
Humboldt
Ripley
Brownsville
Covington
Jackson
Lexington
Mississippi River
Henderson
Bolivar
MEMPHIS
Selmer
Savannah
La Grange
Grand Junction
Corinth
Holly Springs
Holly Springs National Forest
0 10 mi
0 10 km
60
61
45
51
62
55
412
641
78
155
45W
45E
79
70
40
18
100
64
240
72
© AVALON TRAVEL

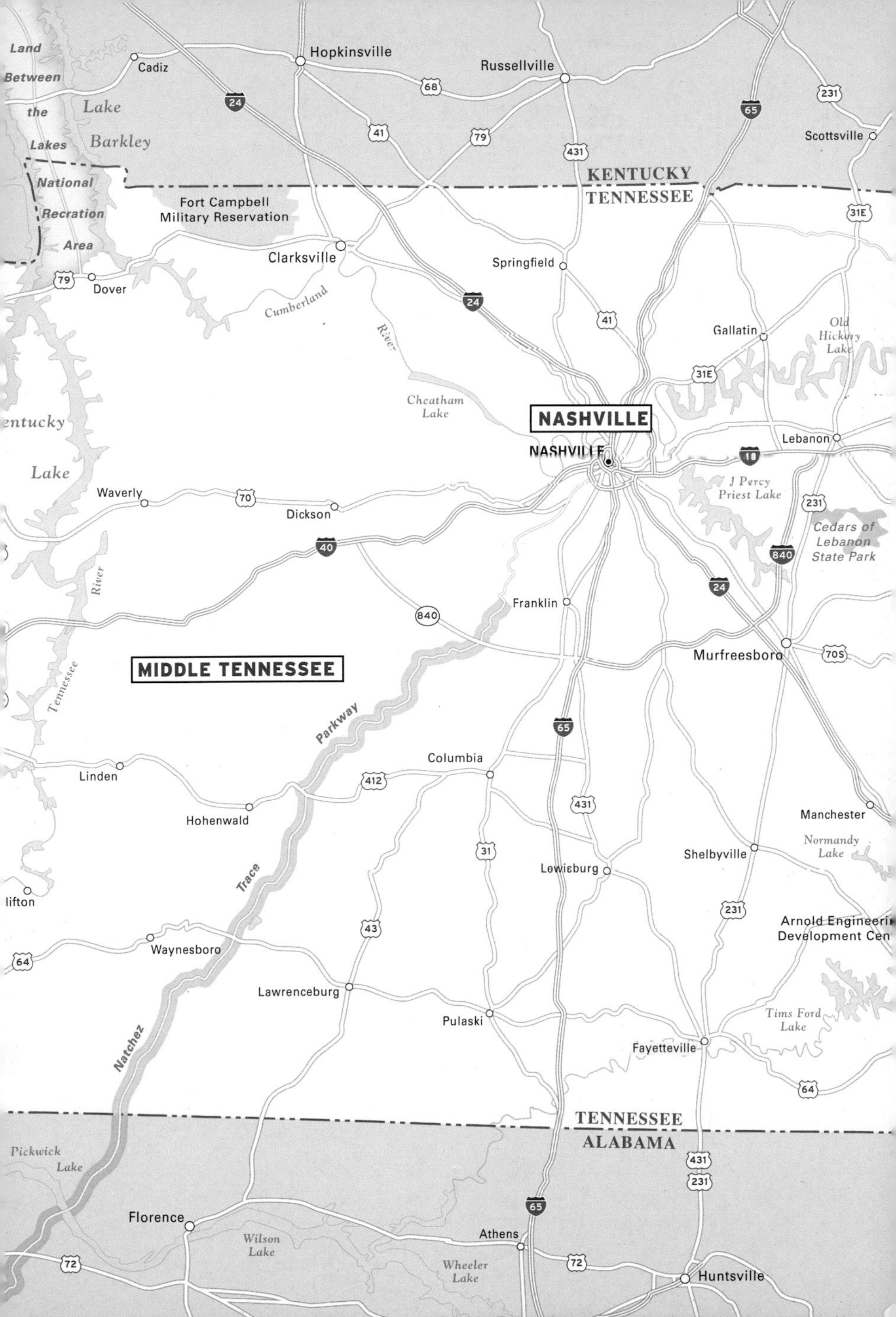

Land Between the Lakes National Recreation Area
Hopkinsville
Cadiz
Russellville
68
24
Lake Barkley
41
79
431
65
231
Scottsville
KENTUCKY
TENNESSEE
Fort Campbell Military Reservation
31E
Clarksville
Springfield
79
Dover
Cumberland River
24
41
Gallatin
Old Hickory Lake
31E
Cheatham Lake
NASHVILLE
Kentucky Lake
NASHVILLE
Lebanon
40
J Percy Priest Lake
Waverly
70
Dickson
231
Cedars of Lebanon State Park
40
840
Tennessee River
24
Franklin
840
Murfreesboro
70S
MIDDLE TENNESSEE
65
Natchez Trace Parkway
Columbia
Linden
412
Hohenwald
431
Manchester
Normandy Lake
31
Shelbyville
Lewisburg
Clifton
231
Arnold Engineering Development Center
43
Waynesboro
64
Lawrenceburg
Tims Ford Lake
Pulaski
Fayetteville
64
TENNESSEE
ALABAMA
Pickwick Lake
431
231
65
Florence
Wilson Lake
Athens
72
Wheeler Lake
72
Huntsville

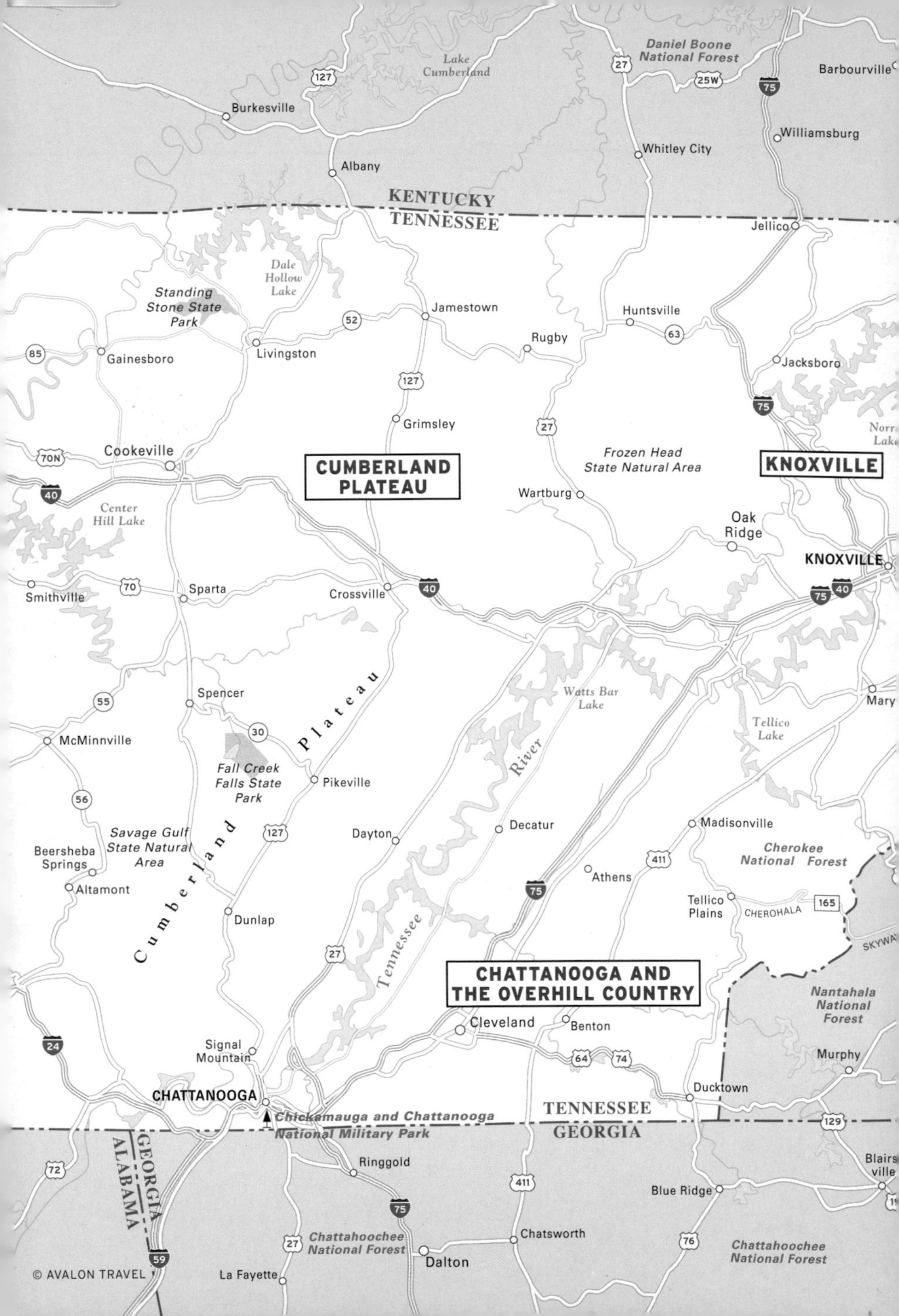

Lake Cumberland
Daniel Boone National Forest
Barbourville
Burkesville
Williamsburg
Whitley City
Albany
KENTUCKY
TENNESSEE
Jellico
Dale Hollow Lake
Standing Stone State Park
Jamestown
Huntsville
Rugby
Gainesboro
Livingston
Jacksboro
Grimsley
Cookeville
Frozen Head State Natural Area
CUMBERLAND PLATEAU
KNOXVILLE
Center Hill Lake
Wartburg
Oak Ridge
KNOXVILLE
Smithville
Sparta
Crossville
Spencer
Watts Bar Lake
Mary
McMinnville
Tellico Lake
Cumberland Plateau
Fall Creek Falls State Park
Pikeville
River
Decatur
Madisonville
Savage Gulf State Natural Area
Dayton
Cherokee National Forest
Beersheba Springs
Athens
Altamont
Tellico Plains
CHEROHALA
Dunlap
Tennessee
CHATTANOOGA AND THE OVERHILL COUNTRY
Nantahala National Forest
Cleveland
Benton
Signal Mountain
Murphy
CHATTANOOGA
Ducktown
Chickamauga and Chattanooga National Military Park
TENNESSEE
GEORGIA
GEORGIA
ALABAMA
Ringgold
Blue Ridge
Chatsworth
Chattahoochee National Forest
Chattahoochee National Forest
Dalton
La Fayette
© AVALON TRAVEL

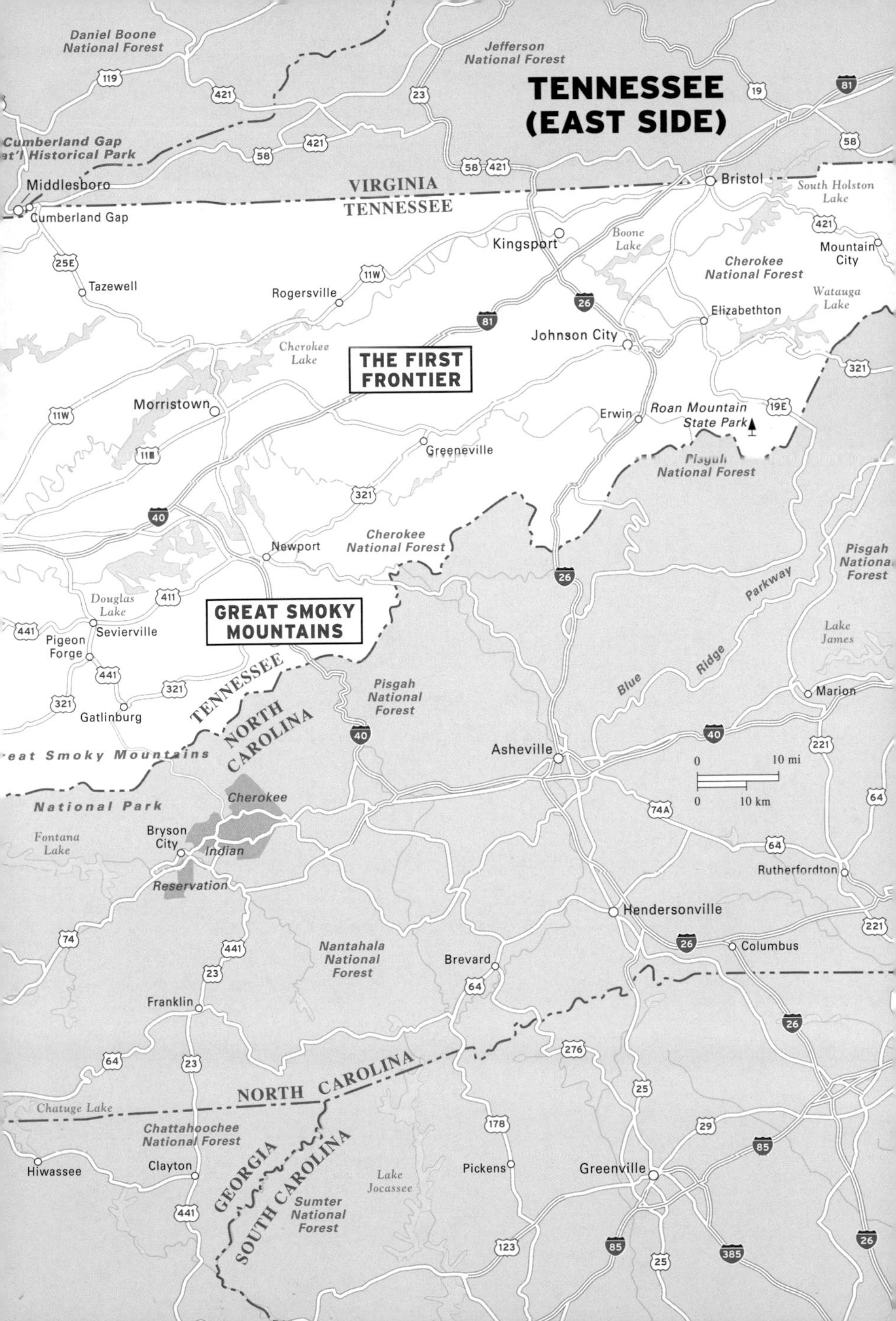

TENNESSEE (EAST SIDE)
THE FIRST FRONTIER
GREAT SMOKY MOUNTAINS
Daniel Boone National Forest
Jefferson National Forest
Cumberland Gap Nat'l Historical Park
VIRGINIA
TENNESSEE
NORTH CAROLINA
GEORGIA
SOUTH CAROLINA
Middlesboro
Cumberland Gap
Bristol
South Holston Lake
Kingsport
Boone Lake
Mountain City
Cherokee National Forest
Watauga Lake
Elizabethton
Johnson City
Tazewell
Rogersville
Cherokee Lake
Morristown
Erwin
Roan Mountain State Park
Greeneville
Pisgah National Forest
Newport
Douglas Lake
Sevierville
Pigeon Forge
Gatlinburg
Great Smoky Mountains National Park
Blue Ridge Parkway
Lake James
Marion
Asheville
Cherokee
Bryson City
Indian Reservation
Fontana Lake
Rutherfordton
Hendersonville
Columbus
Nantahala National Forest
Brevard
Franklin
Chatuge Lake
Chattahoochee National Forest
Hiwassee
Clayton
Sumter National Forest
Lake Jocassee
Pickens
Greenville
0 10 mi
0 10 km

Contents

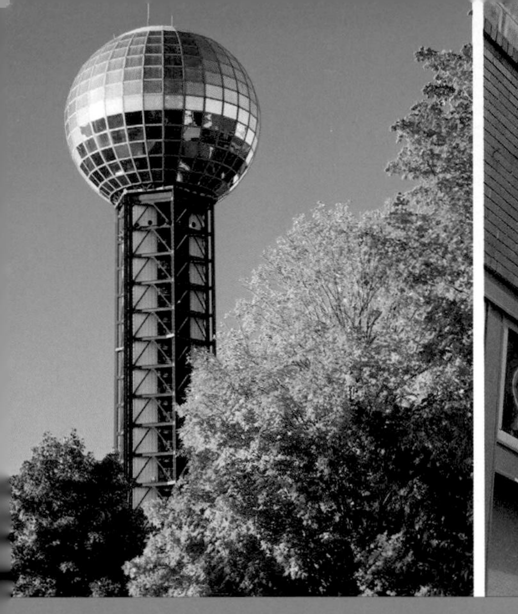

DISCOVER

Tennessee

My first visit to Tennessee was when I was a teenager. Back then I wasn't able to articulate what drew me to this Southern wonderland. But in the years since, I've moved away and come back, and now realize I have become quite verbose when it comes to the state where I make my home.

Tennessee offers a suggestion for every season, every mood, and every personality. It's the cradle of country music and the birthplace of the blues. It's produced Nobel laureates, Pulitzer Prize winners, and history-making statesmen. Creativity of all kinds seems to flow in the rivers and in the veins of the folks who call the Volunteer State home.

That creativity is evident even to visitors just passing through. It fosters an entrepreneurial energy that results in funky, offbeat music clubs for jamming, quirky boutiques for shopping, and one-of-a-kind roadside eateries for... well, eating. Allow us to introduce you to bluegrass, to Appalachian and African American quilts, to meat and three, hot chicken, and barbecue. You will soon become well acquainted with them all.

Clockwise from top left: Sunsphere in Knoxville; Robert's Western World, Nashville; Lake Winne amusement park, Chattanooga; carousel at Chattanooga Zoo; rhododendron at Roan Mountain State Park; canoe-kayak race at RiverRocks, Chattanooga.

The creative spirit seems to inhabit the landscape as well. East Tennessee has mountains—*real* mountains that climb up to cloud-covered peaks, and plunge down into valleys. Moving west through the state, the mountains become the rolling hills of Middle Tennessee and then the plains toward Memphis and the mighty Mississippi, Father of Waters.

Come to explore, to eat, to drink, to distill, to study, to shop, to hike and climb, to fish and run rivers, to hear music, to *play* music… it doesn't matter. No matter what brings you here, Southern hospitality assures that you'll feel at home minutes after your arrival. Just as Tennessee's geography, its arts, its history, and its people guarantee you can be here a lifetime and never be bored.

Clockwise from top left: Secret City Festival in Oak Ridge features car shows, live music, and more; Frozen Head State Park; Coolidge Park's interactive water fountain; Great Smoky Mountains National Park.

Planning your Trip

Where to Go

Tennessee is a long state: From tip to tip, the **Volunteer State** stretches 432 miles. That's eight hours on the interstate highway, though I don't recommend doing it like that: Get off the interstate and explore. Cultural and historical differences help define the state's three basic geographical regions: East, Middle, and West Tennessee. Here's an overview from west to east.

Memphis

Memphis may owe its physical existence to the mighty Mississippi, but it is music that gives this city its soul. The blues were born in Memphis, and they still call Memphis home in nightclubs on **Beale Street** and juke joints around the city. But the Bluff City isn't just the blues. It's gospel, **Elvis Presley,** Soulsville, Rev. Al Green, Isaac Hayes, and Sun Studio. And it's more than music. Memphis is an urban center with fine dining, parks, and art museums. It is a city where you can unwind by watching the ducks get the red-carpet treatment at the **Peabody Hotel** or fuel up with a plate of **barbecue.**

Western Plains

Look for bald eagles and wild turkeys amid the knob-kneed cypress trees at **Reelfoot Lake.** Hike and camp along the shores of Kentucky Lake at the **Land Between the Lakes.** Along the Tennessee River is the state's only **pearl farm,** the charming river town of **Savannah,** and **Shiloh,** the site of an epic Civil War battle. Don't miss outsider art masterpiece **Billy Tripp's** *Mindfield.*

the famous Beale street in Memphis

a model of Greece's Parthenon in Nashville's Centennial Park

The Smoky Mountains

Nashville

Even as Nashville grows, it is in no danger of losing its quirkiness. Nashville is the epicenter of **country music.** It is home of the **Grand Ole Opry,** the **Country Music Hall of Fame,** and hundreds of recording studios. It is the place where thousands of musicians and songwriters come to make it, and the city's **nightlife** is all the richer for it. Grand **antebellum homes,** fine arts, and excellent **dining** appeal to sophisticates. Museums, historic sites, and the grand Tennessee capitol recall the city's history, while expansive parks invite recreation in this leafy, livable city.

Middle Tennessee

Tennessee's midsection is a road trip waiting to happen. The landscape is rural and pure relaxation. This is **Walking Horse Country,** where picturesque horse farms dot the landscape and Tennessee sipping **whiskey** is made. In **Amish country** black buggies and old-fashioned homesteads litter the back roads. The **Natchez Trace** is a scenic highway that marks one of the oldest overland routes between New Orleans and Nashville. Explore the heartland in search of perfectly **fried chicken**, the world's largest **MoonPie**, and exciting **summertime festivals**. Don't forget to sip some of that Lynchburg lemonade.

Cumberland Plateau

The Cumberland Plateau is a breathtaking landscape of caves, waterfalls, gorges, and mountains. It is home to some of the state's best parks: the **Big South Fork** and **Pickett State Park** in the north, **Fall Creek Falls State Park** in the center, and **Savage Gulf** in the south. Come here for **outdoor recreation,** including hiking, biking, horseback riding, camping, and kayaking. The plateau offers destinations with fascinating history: the lost English colony of **Rugby,** the idealistic experiment of **Cumberland Homesteads,** and the **Children's Holocaust Memorial** at Whitwell.

Chattanooga and the Overhill Country

Nestled in a bend of the Tennessee River and

surrounded by the Cumberland Plateau and foothills of the Appalachian Mountains, Chattanooga is not called the **Scenic City** for nothing. It is a great place to bring the kids thanks to its excellent aquarium, children's museum, parks, zoo, caves, and other **family-friendly attractions.** East of the city lies the **southern Cherokee National Forest** and the **Ocoee River**—a destination for those interested in **white-water rafting** and other outdoor pursuits. No other region offers a better glimpse at the **legacy of the Cherokee,** who once populated the hills and valleys of this Overhill land.

Knoxville

Like the better-known Memphis and Nashville, Knoxville is emerging as a center for **live music** and **the arts.** Galleries, restaurants, nightclubs, and theaters on Gay Street, Market Square, and the Old City are funky, unpretentious, and fun. Of course, sports fans have been coming to Knoxville for years to watch the **University of Tennessee Volunteers** play football and basketball, and to tour the **Women's Basketball Hall of Fame.** Attractions such as the **East Tennessee History Center** and the gold-plated **Sunsphere** add to the city's draw.

Great Smoky Mountains

Tennessee's most picturesque wilderness is the Great Smoky Mountains. It is the **vistas** that first draw you in: the soft-edged peaks enveloped by wispy white "smoke," touched by brilliant red and orange at sunset, and crowned by crisp white snow in winter. Hike through **old-growth forest** and mysterious mountain balds. Camp next to a mountain stream. Hunt for **wildflowers.** Bicycle the **Cades Cove loop** to see historic cabins and churches. Outside the boundary of the park are gateway communities offering everything from the **Dollywood** theme park to quiet rural retreats.

The First Frontier

It was to the **eastern mountains** of northeast Tennessee that early settlers moved in the 1770s. More than 150 years later the descendants of these mountain folks brought forth modern country music during the **Bristol sessions.** This region of Tennessee is more closely linked to **Appalachia** than any other; this is a landscape of hills and hollers, small towns, and traditional ways. **Jonesborough** is the first city of storytelling, and the **Tri-Cities** draw race fans to **Bristol Motor Speedway.**

Know Before You Go

When to Go

Summer is the peak travel season for Tennessee. This is the season of hot weather and crowds at many popular sites, although it's also when some of the biggest music festivals and events are going on. If you can, avoid the crowds and the heat: **Spring and fall** are the best times to explore Tennessee. During spring, the weather is mild, flora is in bloom, and you can enjoy springtime festivals. During the fall, the trees change color and temperatures drop. The fall is a busy time in the Smokies, however, as "leaf peepers" come to see the foliage.

Visitors in **winter** may encounter cold weather and snow. If you're a skier, head to Gatlinburg. In other parts of the state, some attractions close or cut back hours November–February, but the cool months can also be a nice time to tour as you'll have many attractions to yourself.

Transportation

While visitors making a getaway to Memphis or Nashville may be able to subsist on public transportation, ride-hailing companies, and taxis, all others will need wheels to see this state. **A car is essential** if you are traveling in Tennessee. If it's

snowfall in Great Smoky Mountains National Park

the Tipton Cabin in Cades Cove, Great Smoky Mountains National Park

practical, bring your own car. If you're flying in, arrange a rental car ahead of time to save money and ease hassles. A good road map or GPS is helpful to have before you set out.

If you are flying to Tennessee, which airport you fly into will depend on your destination. Nashville and Memphis have **international airports** and generally the best airfare deals. Knoxville, Chattanooga, and the Tri-Cities regional airports are convenient if you're headed to East Tennessee.

What to Pack

A cell phone with a good roaming plan and Wi-Fi should cover your basic needs, but a **calling card** that will work at pay phones and hotels, particularly if you are likely to get off the interstate and out of the range of cell phone signals, isn't a bad idea.

Since your trip is likely to include a fair amount of driving, download a mess of **tunes.** Depending on your destination, pick up some classic country, bluegrass, blues, or Elvis albums to get you in the mood.

If you're planning on spending time in the Great Smoky Mountains, be sure to pack **rain gear** and several layers of clothes, including a jacket or sweater—even in the summer. If you think you may do some hiking, bring **good boots,** a **backpack,** and a **trail map.** Cowboy boots and a cowboy hat aren't required, but they're certainly always appropriate. Grab some stylin' sunglasses for all the photos you'll take.

The Best of Tennessee

Downtown and the Delta

Follow in the footsteps of the King (that would be Elvis), eat real Memphis barbecue, and explore the delta landscape that gave rise to the blues. Travel along the Tennessee River, stopping at a pearl farm, river towns, and the site of one of the bloodiest Civil War battles in Tennessee.

A Long Weekend in Memphis

DAY 1

Arrive in Memphis and check into a downtown hotel, such as the **Peabody** or **Big Cypress Lodge.** Grab some **Gus's World Famous Fried Chicken** and stroll down to **Beale Street** in the evening.

DAY 2

Take the Beale Street Walking Tour in the morning, stopping at the **W. C. Handy Home and Museum.** Take your picture with the Elvis statue, and go treasure hunting at **A. Schwab.** Eat lunch at the Little Tea Shop downtown, and then head over to **Mud Island** for the afternoon. Explore the Mississippi River Museum and the River Walk. Eat dinner at The Majestic Grill.

DAY 3

Go to the **National Civil Rights Museum** in the morning, eat lunch along South Main, and then go to the **Stax Museum of American Soul Music** and the **Blues Hall of Fame** that afternoon. Wash up and head to East Memphis to fine dine at **Erling Jensen, The Restaurant.**

Options

DAY 4

Make it Elvis Day. Start early at **Graceland** to

downtown Memphis

avoid the crowds, and then visit **Sun Studio,** where Elvis recorded his first hit. Eat a burger at Dyer's on Beale Street in memory of the King.

DAY 5

Start out at **Elmwood Cemetery** with the audio tour, and then drive east. Visit the **Memphis Brooks Museum of Art** and lounge in Overton Park. Tour **The Dixon** and eat dinner at the **Soul Fish** in Cooper-Young.

Excursions

MASON AND HENNING

Leave Memphis, driving northeast along Highway 70. Stop in Mason to pick up some of **Gus's World Famous Fried Chicken** for the road. Visit the **Alex Haley House Museum and Interpretive Center** in Henning, and then push on to Reelfoot Lake. Check into the Airpark Inn.

REELFOOT LAKE

Explore **Reelfoot Lake State Park.** Take a boat cruise or hike along the lakeshore. Eat fried catfish at Boyette's.

LAND BETWEEN THE LAKES

Drive east to Land Between the Lakes. Visit **The Homeplace** to see frontier life re-created and watch a celestial show at the **Golden Pond Visitor Center and Planetarium.** Overnight in a log cabin at Leatherwood Resort in Dover.

SAVANNAH

Drive south to historic **Savannah,** which you can enjoy on foot. Then tour the **Shiloh National Military Park.** Take the audio tour or hike to the Shiloh Indian Mounds. Overnight at the hotel at Pickwick Landing State Resort Park and eat dinner at the Broken Spoke.

PINSON MOUNDS AND JACKSON

Go to **Pinson Mounds State Archaeological Park** to stretch your legs and tour mysterious Indian mounds. Eat lunch in Jackson at Dixie Castle, see the ***Mindfield*** art installation, and then return to Memphis on the interstate.

Reelfoot Lake State Park

Nashville and Middle Tennessee

Start out in the state's capital, and then strike out through Tennessee's heartland to old railroad towns and quiet parks. See the stars on the Grand Ole Opry stage and make a pilgrimage to Lynchburg, home of that most famous Tennessee whiskey. Tour the sites of Civil War battles and hear the stories of those who fought and those who died.

A Week in Nashville

DAY 1

Arrive in Nashville. Check into a downtown hotel, such as the **Hermitage** or **Union Station.** Feast at Chauhan Ale & Masala House. Stroll **Lower Broadway** and enjoy dancing at the honky-tonks on your first night in town.

DAY 2

Visit the **Country Music Hall of Fame** in the morning and grab an early lunch at Arnold's Country Kitchen to fuel up. See the **Ryman Auditorium** and **Johnny Cash Museum**. See the **Grand Ole Opry** in the evening.

DAY 3

Head toward West Nashville. Drive through **Music Row** on your way to **Centennial Park** and **The Parthenon.** Eat lunch at Martha's at the Plantation at Belle Meade, and then spend the afternoon checking out the museum and gardens at **Cheekwood.** Eat dinner at the Capitol Grille downtown.

DAY 4

Go uptown to the **Tennessee State Capitol** and the **Civil Rights Room at the Nashville Public Library.** Then take one of **Walk Eat Nashville's** tours, where you can dine and learn at the same time. Visit **Fisk University** in the afternoon. Catch a songwriter's show at **The Bluebird Café** over dinner.

DAY 5

Drive east to Old Hickory and spend the day at **The Hermitage.** Explore the home and the grounds of this estate belonging to Andrew

Nashville War Memorial Auditorium and the state capitol

Top Festivals

In a state with nearly 1,000 annual festivals, how do you choose? One strategy: Start with a cross section of gatherings across the state and year, and then try some more.

- **National Cornbread Festival** (South Pittsburg, in April): A celebration of the iconic Southern side dish includes bluegrass music, cook-offs, and lots and lots of corn bread.
- **Bonnaroo** (Manchester, in June): What started as a jam-band festival on a Tennessee farm has grown into one of the most diverse and well-organized (albeit crowded) music festivals in the United States.
- **Elvis Week** (Memphis, in August): Elvis mania always exists in Memphis, but it reaches a fever pitch during the annual remembrance of the King's death.
- **Bristol Rhythm and Roots Reunion** (Bristol, in September): The beginnings of the music that made the state what it is are celebrated here.

crowds at Bonnaroo

Jackson. Grab takeout from **Prince's Hot Chicken Shack** on your way home and enjoy a quiet night in. Call Jake's Bakes to have warm cookies delivered to your hotel room.

Excursions

CLARKSVILLE

Take a day trip to Clarksville. Tour the **RiverWalk** park along the Cumberland and find the statue of Wilma Rudolph. Eat lunch at Silke's Old World Breads and explore **Dunbar Cave** in the afternoon. Return to Nashville for the night.

FRANKLIN

Depart Nashville. Drive south to Franklin and visit the **Carnton Plantation,** epicenter of the Battle of Franklin. Eat lunch at Puckett's Grocery and Restaurant, and then spend the afternoon shopping downtown and at The Factory. Eat dinner at Saffire and overnight in Franklin.

NORMANDY

Drive to Normandy and visit the **George Dickel Distillery.** Eat dinner at the Bell Buckle Café and overnight at the Walking Horse Hotel in Wartrace. This can be your home base for three nights.

SHELBYVILLE AND LYNCHBURG

Drive to Shelbyville for the **Tennessee Walking Horse National Celebration** and eat lunch at The Coffee Break. If it's not celebration season, then head to Lynchburg to tour the **Tennessee Walking Horse Museum** and the **Jack Daniel's Distillery.**

MURFREESBORO

Drive back to Nashville, stopping in Murfreesboro to visit **Stones River National Battlefield** on the way.

Knoxville and the Smokies

Start in Knoxville, and then head into the wilderness of the Great Smoky Mountains. Explore the rural reaches of the Cumberland Plateau and find the tallest waterfall east of the Rockies. Wind up in Chattanooga to tour the state's best aquarium and see Rock City, the South's most iconic attraction.

Knoxville

DAY 1

Arrive in Knoxville, and check into the **Oliver Hotel** downtown. Grab lunch to go from the **OliBea,** and listen to live music at the **WDVX Blue Plate Special** over the lunch hour. Visit the World's Fair Park and climb to the top of the **Sunsphere.** Eat dinner in downtown at **Five Bar.**

DAY 2

Drive to Oak Ridge and see the sights related to the **Oak Ridge National Laboratory.** Eat a Myrtle Burger at the Jefferson Soda Fountain at lunchtime and enjoy dinner with a view at Riverside Grille.

Great Smokies Road Trip

DAY 3

Charge the camera batteries and head to the Smoky Mountains. Drive to Gatlinburg and check into the Buckhorn Lodge or the Gatlinburg Inn. Drive to the top of **Newfound Gap** and enjoy the mountain views and cool air.

DAY 4

Get up early and take a picnic lunch to **Cades Cove** before the crowds strike. Look at old farmhouses and churches, and spy deer and cottontails. Hike to **Abrams Falls.**

DAY 5

Head north to the Cherokee National Forest and drive to the top of **Roan Mountain.** Take a stroll

summer bucks in Cades Cove

The Sunsphere is a Knoxville icon.

Lookout Mountain in Chattanooga

along the Appalachian Trail and look for the wild rhododendron. Overnight in Erwin.

DAY 6

Drive to **Historic Rugby** on the Cumberland Plateau and tour the Victorian English village. Stay in one of the historic bed-and-breakfasts and dine on authentic English fare at Rugby's restaurant.

DAY 7

Drive south to **Fall Creek Falls State Park** and hike to the falls, the tallest east of the Rockies. Visit the nature center and stay overnight in the park inn.

DAY 8

Drive down the Sequatchie Valley, stopping in Dayton to see the site of the Scopes Monkey Trial and Whitwell to visit the **Children's Holocaust Memorial.** Press on to Chattanooga, and check in to the Read House Hotel Historic Inn or another downtown lodging.

DAY 9

Visit the **Tennessee Aquarium** in the morning. If the skies are clear, drive to **Lookout Mountain** and tour Rock City and Point Park. Watch the sun set over Chattanooga. If the weather doesn't cooperate, visit the **Hunter Museum of American Art.** Eat dinner at Embargo 62.

DAY 10

Have breakfast at the Bluegrass Grill. Make your way back to Knoxville, stopping in Vonore on the way to tour a replica of the British **Fort Loudoun** and visit the **Sequoyah Birthplace Museum.**

The Great Outdoors

From the purple mountain majesty of the Smokies in the east to the dark mystery of Reelfoot Lake in the west, Tennessee is a land of surprising beauty. Wherever you are in Tennessee, you don't have to look hard for exceptional places to experience the outdoors.

- **Great Smoky Mountains National Park** (Gatlinburg): The most-visited national park in the United States offers lovely mountain vistas, miles of hiking trails, and hundreds of campsites.
- **Reelfoot Lake State Park** (Tiptonville): Formed during a massive earthquake, Reelfoot Lake is an unexpected landscape of knob-kneed cypress trees and flowering lily pads, with bald eagles flying overhead.
- **Land Between the Lakes** (Dover): You get two lakes for the price of one, plus bison, hiking, history, and more at this extensive recreation area.
- **Grundy Lakes State Park** (Tracy City): This small park is home to the remarkable vistas of the Fiery Gizzard Trail and the 60-foot drop of Foster Falls.

Great Smoky Mountains National Park offers outdoor opportunities for travelers of all kinds.

From Bluegrass to the Blues

Music is what many visitors to Tennessee want to experience more than anything else, and thanks to the broad spectrum of musical genres present in the state—bluegrass to the blues—music fans don't have to stick to what they know and love. Take a listen to something different; you're likely to discover a new favorite. At the very least, you will come to see the connections that exist between even the most varied musical forms.

Memphis

Beale Street is still the place to start if you want to find the birthplace of the blues. Visit the **W. C. Handy Home and Museum** to see where the father of the blues lived while he was in Memphis. After dark, stroll Beale Street to hear live blues and jazz at clubs like the King's Palace and B. B. King's.

The single best musical museum in Memphis is the **Stax Museum of American Soul Music.** Here you will learn not only about the remarkable story of Stax, but also soul's musical roots in gospel and country music. Stop at the **Blues Hall of Fame,** too.

No place in Memphis is more important to American musical history than **Graceland,** home of Elvis Presley. Here the King lived with his parents, wife, extended family, and his buddies, the Memphis Mafia. See his remarkable taste in decor and pay your respects over his grave in the Meditation Garden.

Sun Studio is where early blues records were made, where Elvis recorded his first hit, and where the likes of Jerry Lee Lewis and Johnny Cash laid down tracks. It's hallowed ground in musical history.

Any of Memphis's juke joints get kicking late on Friday and Saturday nights.

Western Plains

It was the landscape and hardship of country living that really gave birth to the blues. Drive the rural routes in Haywood County to breathe in the delta air. Stop in **Nutbush,** the childhood home of Tina Turner. Then stop in Brownsville at the **West Tennessee Delta Heritage Center** for exhibits about the singer (in **Flagg Grove School**), the music, and the culture of this region.

The **International Rock-a-Billy Hall of Fame** in Jackson has exhibits and tours, but the best deal is to come on Monday or Saturday night for the live music and dance lessons. Rockabilly never sounded so good!

Nashville

No part of Nashville says country music quite like Lower Broadway. It's one of the places both locals and visitors go, and colorful honky-tonks offer live music beginning at 10am. daily. For the more serious of mind, start at the **Country Music Hall of Fame** for an introduction to all things country. Visit the **Ryman Auditorium,** buy your new boots at one of the half-dozen clothiers on Lower Broadway, and stock up on CDs at Ernest Tubb. Admire the hardware at Gruhn Guitars and buy a retro-print poster at Hatch Show Print.

Then for something completely different, don your best duds (still with those boots) and enjoy a night at the **Nashville Symphony Orchestra.** The delightful sounds of one of the South's best symphonies will ease the mind and cleanse the musical palate.

Explore wax museums, souvenir shops, and the **Opryland Hotel** by day in Music Valley.

Historic Sun Studio in Memphis

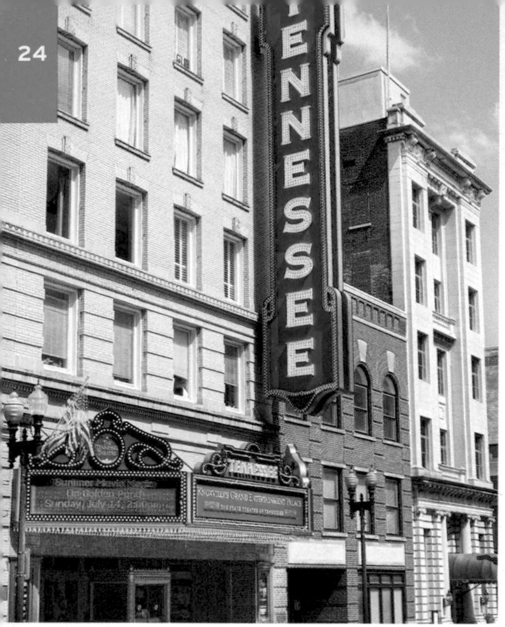

Tennessee Theatre, Knoxville

guitar sculpture at The Grand Ole Opry

Spend your evening at the **Grand Ole Opry** and your late-night at **Ernest Tubb's *Midnite Jamboree,*** still going strong.

Sandwiched between downtown and Hillsboro Village is Music Row, the business center of Nashville. While you're unlikely to see a star here, it's still worth the gamble. Take a stroll, and then grab a sweet treat at Fido for more star watching. At night, check out **The Bluebird Café** for the next big songwriter.

Knoxville

Listen to live music over lunch at the **WDVX *Blue Plate Special,*** and then take a walking tour of Knoxville's musical history. See the site of the last hotel where Hank Williams ever slept. Catch a live band in the Old City or on Market Square, or a concert in the historic **Tennessee Theatre.** Listen to modern roots music at the **Laurel Theater** in historic Fort Sanders.

Head out to Clinton and the **Museum of Appalachia** to tour its music room, with exhibits about Uncle Dave Macon and Roy Acuff.

Great Smoky Mountains

Experience the hillbilly side of music in Pigeon Forge. Visit **Dollywood,** a theme park owned and designed by East Tennessee native Dolly Parton. Get a ticket to the **Dixie Stampede** for a night of kitschy, over-the-top entertainment, or catch an Elvis tribute show. See a sunrise on the Smokies from Dollywood's DreamMore Resort hotel.

The First Frontier

Visit **Bristol**, the Birthplace of Country Music and the site of the historic Bristol Sessions. Visit the **Mountain Music Museum, the Birthplace of Country Music Museum,** and the home of Tennessee Ernie Ford. Head to **The Carter Family Memorial Music Center** for a Saturday-night concert.

In Johnson City, check in at the **Down Home** for bluegrass, folk, and country music. This venerable club has been nurturing music fans in upper East Tennessee since 1976.

Memphis

Look for ★ to find recommended sights, activities, dining, and lodging.

Highlights

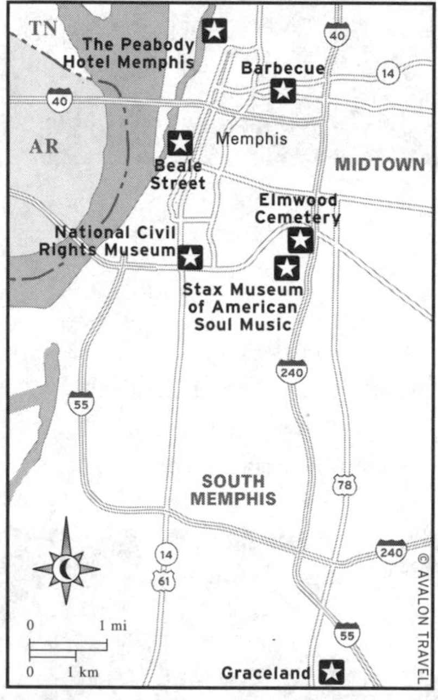

★ **Beale Street:** The street that gave birth to the Memphis blues celebrates its legacy every single night of the week (page 30).

★ **National Civil Rights Museum:** For years the Lorraine Motel merely represented the tragic assassination of Martin Luther King, Jr. Today, it tells the story of the African American struggle for civil rights, from before the Civil War to the present day (page 34).

★ **The Peabody Hotel Memphis:** Even the ducks in the fountain get the red-carpet treatment at this landmark hotel. The lobby is a must-visit (page 36).

★ **Stax Museum of American Soul Music:** Irresistible soul music is what made Stax famous in the 1960s, and it is what makes the Stax Museum sweet today. Exhibits bring to life the work of Otis Redding, the Staple Singers, Isaac Hayes, and more (page 43).

★ **Graceland:** The Elvis phenomenon is alive and well. Presley's south Memphis mansion is a testament not only to the King's music, but also his fans (page 43).

★ **Elmwood Cemetery:** Perhaps the most surprising attraction in Memphis, this is the final resting place of dozens of local characters: madams, blues singers, mayors, and pioneers of all types (page 44).

★ **Barbecue:** Tangy, juicy, and just a little sweet, Memphis barbecue at places like the **Cozy Corner** is the stuff of West Tennessee dreams (page 70).

Take away its music, and Memphis would lose its soul.

Memphis may owe its existence to the mighty Mississippi, but it is music that has defined this Southern metropolis. Memphis music started with the spirituals and work songs of poor Mississippi Delta cotton farmers who came to Memphis and created a new sound: the Memphis blues. The blues then spawned its own offspring: soul, R&B, country, and, of course, rock 'n' roll as sung by a poor truck driver from Tupelo, Mississippi, named Elvis Presley.

On any given night you can find joints where the music flows as freely as the booze, and sitting still is not an option. On Beale Street, music wafts from inside smoky bars out onto the street, inviting you to come inside for a spell. And on Sundays, the sounds of old-fashioned spirituals and new gospel music can be heard at churches throughout the city.

Memphis music is the backbeat of any visit to the city, but it by no means is the only reason to come. For as rich and complicated as Memphis's history is, this is a city that does not live in its past. Since the 1990s, Memphis has gone through a rebirth, giving new life to the region as a tourist destination. An NBA franchise (the Grizzlies) arrived, the National Civil Rights Museum opened on the grounds of the historic Lorraine Motel, a fantastic AAA baseball field opened downtown, and Memphis made its mark with films such as *Hustle & Flow, Forty Shades of Blue,* and *Black Snake Moan*. In 2014, more than 10 million people visited Memphis.

While you're here, you can sustain yourself on the city's world-famous barbecue, its fried chicken and catfish, and its homemade plate lunches, not to mention nouveau Southern eats. Eating may not be why you come, but it might be why you stay. Memphians are gregarious and proud of their city. Don't be surprised if someone invites you over for a Sunday fried chicken supper.

Memphis is a city of the South. More than just the largest city in Tennessee, Memphis is a hub for the entire Mid-South, which stretches from West Tennessee all the way down into Mississippi and Arkansas. As such, the city is a melting pot of cultural, musical, culinary, and economic influences from the entire Mississippi River delta.

PLANNING YOUR TIME

You can knock out Memphis's main attractions in a weekend, but it takes a bit longer

Previous: downtown Memphis; Beale Street. **Above:** Peabody Hotel's famous fountain—and ducks.

Memphis

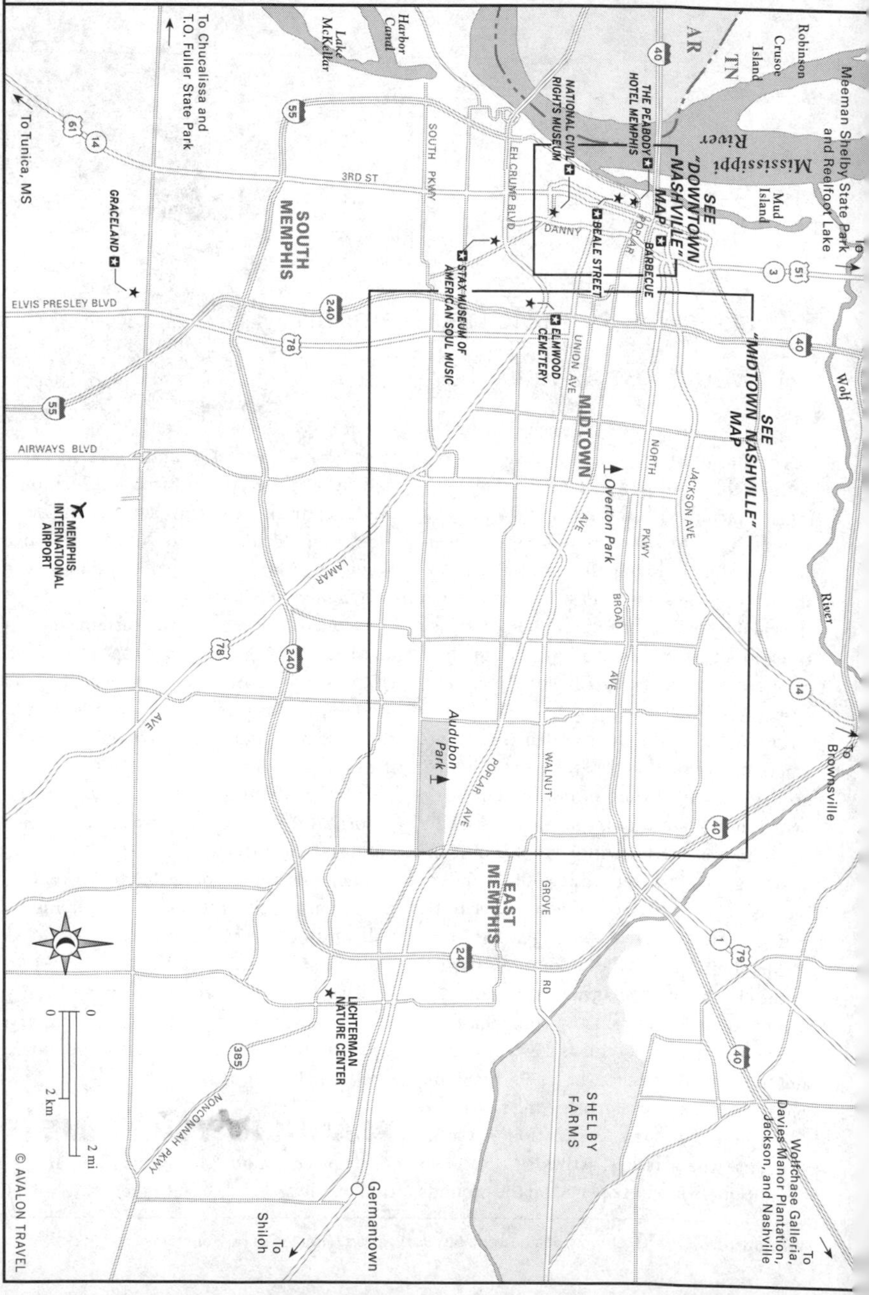

Meeman Shelby State Park and Reelfoot Lake
Robinson Crusoe Island
Mud Island
Mississippi River
TN
AR
Harbor Canal
Lake McKellar
To Chucalissa and T.O. Fuller State Park
To Tunica, MS
SEE "DOWNTOWN NASHVILLE" MAP
THE PEABODY HOTEL MEMPHIS
NATIONAL CIVIL RIGHTS MUSEUM
BARBECUE
BEALE STREET
DANNY
POPLAR
EH CRUMP BLVD
SOUTH PKWY
3RD ST
SOUTH MEMPHIS
GRACELAND
ELVIS PRESLEY BLVD
STAX MUSEUM OF AMERICAN SOUL MUSIC
ELMWOOD CEMETERY
UNION AVE
MIDTOWN
SEE "MIDTOWN NASHVILLE" MAP
NORTH PKWY
JACKSON AVE
Wolf River
Overton Park
BROAD AVE
AIRWAYS BLVD
MEMPHIS INTERNATIONAL AIRPORT
LAMAR AVE
Audubon Park
POPLAR AVE
WALNUT GROVE RD
To Brownsville
EAST MEMPHIS
LICHTERMAN NATURE CENTER
NONCONNAH PKWY
SHELBY FARMS
To Wolfchase Galleria, Davies Manor Plantation, Jackson, and Nashville
Germantown
To Shiloh
0 2 mi
0 2 km
40 51 3 55 61 14 240 78 1 79 385

to soak up the city's special mojo: the music, food, and laid-back attitude. In fact, if you want more than just a taste of Memphis's famous blues, its legendary barbecue, or its rich history, plan to stay at least a week.

Choose downtown Memphis as your home base. The city center is home to the best bars, restaurants, sports venues, live-music clubs, and, of course, Beale Street. Downtown is also the liveliest, and one of the safest, parts of Memphis after the sun sets.

While a lot of Memphis's attractions are downtown, others are located in the eastern and southern stretches of the city. A free shuttle is available to Graceland and Sun Studio from downtown, but for other attractions like the Stax Museum of American Soul Music and the Memphis Brooks Museum of Art, you will need a car or taxi. Take note that two of the city's best barbecue joints (a Memphis must), as well as its most famous juke joints, are not within walking distance of downtown.

WHEN TO GO

Memphis is a city with four seasons. The average temperature in January is 41°F, and in July it hits 81°F. Summer is certainly the most popular season for visiting—Elvis Week in August sees the most visitors of all—but the hot, humid Memphis summer is not for the faint of heart. Even in the South, where people are used to hot and humid, the Memphis humidity can be oppressive.

The best time to visit Memphis is May, when summer is still fresh and mild, and the city puts on its annual Memphis in May celebration. Memphis in May includes the World Championship Barbeque Cooking Contest, the Beale Street Music Festival, and the Memphis International Festival.

Fall is also a good choice. The Memphis Music and Heritage Festival held over Labor Day weekend is a great reason to come to Memphis, and probably the best choice for fans of traditional Memphis music.

But if you can't come when the weather is temperate, don't fret. Memphis attractions are open year-round, and the city continues to rock, day in and day out.

ORIENTATION

Memphis is perched atop a low bluff overlooking the majestic Mississippi River (hence one of its official nicknames, Bluff City). The center city district lies, roughly speaking, along the river. Main Street, a pedestrian-only mall (except for the trolleys) runs north-south, while Union, Madison, and Poplar Avenues are the main east-west thoroughfares.

While not compact, central Memphis is entirely walkable for people willing to use a little shoe leather. The Main Street Trolley makes it easy to see downtown and uptown attractions without a car.

In this guide, locations south of Union Avenue are considered **downtown,** while locations north of Union are **uptown.** Downtown's main attraction is Beale Street. Also contained within the downtown district is the area known as **South Main,** a three-block strip along southern Main Street that is home to trendy boutiques, art galleries, restaurants, and condos. South Main is about a 15-minute walk or a 5-minute trolley ride from Beale Street.

Another unique neighborhood in the city center is the **Pinch District,** located along North Main Street past the I-40 overpass. Originally settled by German immigrants, the Pinch is now a hub of restaurants and nightlife. It is also the gateway to gentrifying residential neighborhoods farther north.

Restaurants in the Pinch have been categorized as uptown in this guide. You can walk to the Pinch, but the best way to get there is to ride the Main Street Trolley.

In 1989, developers created **Harbor Town,** a New Urban community on Mud Island. The concept was to create a city community that offered amenities such as schools, gyms, entertainment, and restaurants within walking distance of each other. It was also designed to promote a sense of community; homes were built close together with low fences, front porches, and small yards so that residents would use community parks and green spaces.

In 2007, a boutique hotel opened in Harbor Town, putting the area on the accommodations map for the first time. A major draw for Harbor Town is that it is located right across the river from downtown Memphis but feels like a tight-knit residential community.

Memphis sprawls south, east, and north from the river. Head east from downtown, and you are in **midtown,** a district of strip malls, aging suburbs, and the city's best park and art museum. Poplar Avenue is the main artery of midtown, and it's a good point of reference when exploring by car (which is really the only way to get around midtown). The city's original suburb, midtown now seems positively urban compared to the sprawling burbs that creep farther eastward every year.

Located within midtown is **Cooper-Young,** a redeveloping residential and commercial neighborhood that lies around the intersection of Cooper Street and Young Avenue. Since the 1970s, residents of this neighborhood have fought the tide of urban decay by encouraging investment, good schools, and amenities like parks, art galleries, and independent restaurants, and generally fostering a sense of pride in the area. The result is a neighborhood where you'll find lots of restaurants, a great used-book store, record shops, and other attractions that draw the city's young and young at heart.

East Memphis is where you will find large shopping malls, major hospitals, the University of Memphis, and lots of traffic jams. There are also a few attractions out here, the Dixon and the Memphis Botanic Gardens among them.

Generally speaking, **north and south Memphis** are the most economically depressed areas of the city. Visitors beat a path to attractions like Graceland and Stax in southern Memphis during the day but tend to avoid those areas at night, at least unless they are with a local who knows the way around.

Sights

DOWNTOWN

Downtown refers to the area south of Union Avenue in the city center. It is the heart of Memphis's tourist district.

★ Beale Street

If you want to delve into the history and character of Memphis music, your starting point should be **Beale Street**, home of the blues.

A combination of forces led Beale Street to its place in musical history and popular culture. Named in the 1840s after a war hero, Beale Street was originally part of South Memphis, a separate city that rivaled Memphis during the 1840s.

Beginning in the 1850s, and continuing in greater numbers during and after the Civil War, African Americans began to settle along the western part of Beale Street. By the 1880s and 1890s, a middle class of black professionals began to emerge, and Beale Street became the center of commerce, entertainment, and life for many of them. Together with black-owned businesses on Beale Street were laundries, bars, restaurants, pawn shops, and more operated by immigrants from eastern Europe, Ireland, China, Greece, and Germany.

From the 1880s until the 1960s, Beale Street was the epicenter of African American life, not just for Memphians but also for the entire Mid-South region. It was here that blacks felt free from many of society's restrictions.

Beale Street's decline began in the mid-20th century, and by the 1970s it was a shadow of its former self. Investment during the 1980s and 1990s led to the street's rebirth as a destination for tourists and a source of pride for residents, who could now show off the street that gave birth to the blues.

Downtown Memphis

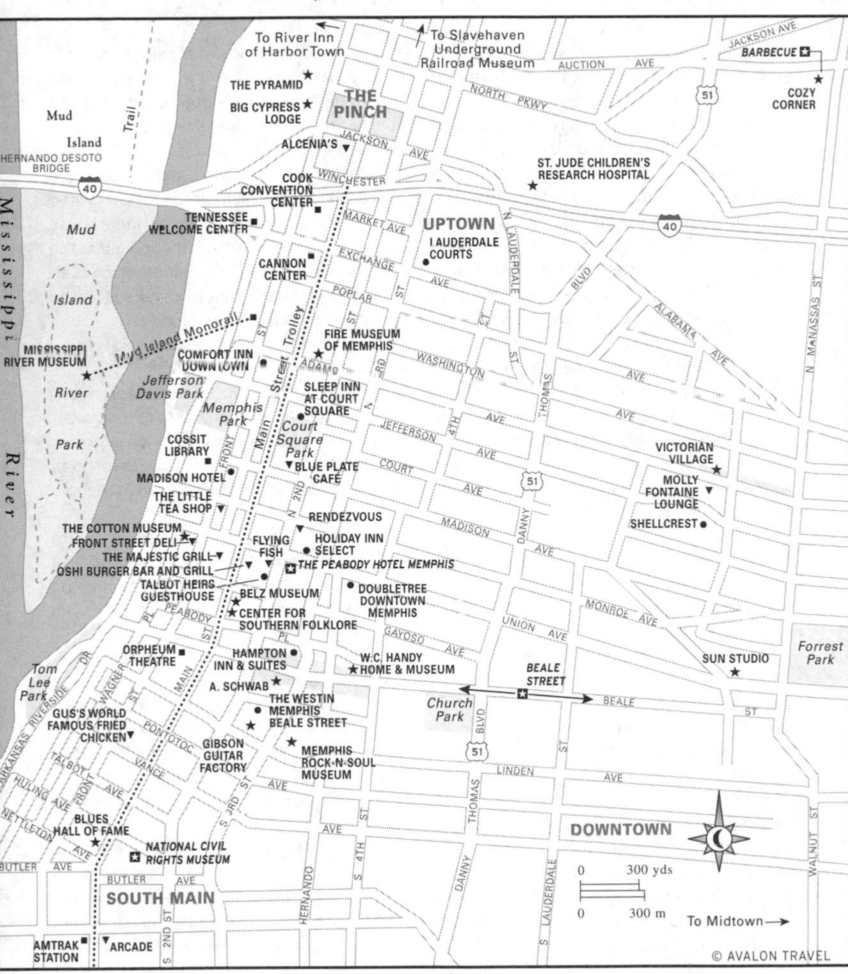

Today, Beale Street has two distinct personalities. During the day it is a laid-back place for families or adults to stroll, buy souvenirs, and eat. You can also stop at one of several museums and attractions located on the street. At night, Beale Street is a strip of nightclubs and restaurants, a great place to people watch, and the best place in the state, if not the country, to catch live blues seven nights a week.

W. C. Handy Home and Museum

The story of Beale Street cannot be told without mentioning William Christopher Handy, whose Memphis home sits at the corner of Beale Street and 4th Avenue. The building was originally located at 659 Jeanette Street, but it was moved to Beale Street in 1985. Now the **W. C. Handy Home and Museum** (352 Beale St., 901/527-3427, wchandymemphis.org, Tues.-Sat. 10am-5pm summer, Tues.-Sat.

Beale Street Walking Tour

Beale Street runs from the Mississippi River to Manassas Street in midtown Memphis, but it is the three blocks between 2nd and 4th Streets that really matter. In its heyday, the Beale Street commercial and entertainment district extended farther east and west, but today, it has been condensed into the half-dozen blocks from Main Street to 4th Street. This walking tour begins at the intersection of Beale and Main Streets, and heads eastward.

Near the corner of Beale and Main Streets is the **Orpheum Theatre** (203 S. Main St., 901/525-3000, www.orpheum-memphis.com). This site has been used for entertainment since 1890, when the Grand Opera House opened there with a production of *Les Huguenots*. Later, the opera house presented vaudeville shows and theater. Fire destroyed it in 1923, but in 1928 it reopened as the Orpheum, a movie theater and performing arts venue for the likes of Duke Ellington, Cab Calloway, Bob Hope, and Mae West. The Orpheum remains one of the city's premier venues for the performing arts, with Broadway productions, mainstream musical artists, and movies.

A block east of the Orpheum is a statue of Memphis's most famous native son, Elvis Presley. Depicting the King during his early career, the statue sits in **Elvis Presley Plaza.**

A. Schwab (163 Beale St., 901/523-9782, a-schwab.com, winter hours: Mon.-Weds. noon-6pm, Thurs. noon-7pm, Fri.-Sat. noon-9pm, Sun. 11am-6pm, may stay open later in the summer depending on crowds) has served Memphis residents for more than 140 years, although it focuses now on odd, out-of-date, and hard-to-find items rather than traditional general-store necessities. Stop in for a souvenir or to visit the A. Schwab "museum," a collection of old-fashioned household tools and implements.

A few doors down from A. Schwab, at the Irish pub Silky O'Sullivan's, you can see what remains of one of Beale Street's most magnificent old buildings. The facade of what was once the **Gallina Building** is held up by six steel girders. From the 1860s until 1914, this facade kept watch on the business empire of Squire Charles Gallina, who operated a saloon, restaurant, and 20-room hotel, as well as a gambling room.

Beyond 3rd Street is **Handy Park,** named for famous blues composer and musician W. C. Handy. Beale Street's Market House was torn down in 1930 to build the park. Since it opened, Handy Park has been a popular place for street musicians, peddlers, concerts, and community events, all of which are presided over by the life-size statue of W. C. Handy.

About midway up the southern side of the next block of Beale Street is the **Daisy Theater** (329 Beale St.), built in 1917 as a movie house. Much of the original interior remains today. The theater is closed to the public but may be rented for private events. Contact the Beale Street Development Corporation (866/406-5986) for information.

Across the street from the Daisy Theater is the **New Daisy Theater** (330 Beale St., 901/525-8981, www.NewDaisy.com), built in 1941 as another movie house. The New Daisy is one of Memphis's prime live-music venues, and it books rock and alternative acts from around the country.

Stately and old, the **First Baptist Beale Street Church** (379 Beale St.) was built between 1868 and 1885 and is home to one of the oldest African American congregations in Memphis. In the 1860s, the congregation started to meet under brush arbors at the present location, and the first temporary structure was erected in 1865. The cornerstone was laid for the present building in 1871. The First Baptist Beale Street Church was an important force in Memphis's African American history. It was here that black Memphians published their first newspapers, the *Memphis Watchman* and the *Memphis Free Speech and Headlight.*

Today, **Church Park** is a humble city park. But in 1899, when Robert Church built Church Park and Auditorium at the eastern end of the Beale Street commercial district, the park was something truly special. Church is said to have been the first black millionaire in the South. He was troubled that there were no public parks expressly for Memphis's African American residents, so in 1899 he opened Church Park and Auditorium on six acres of land along Beale Street. The park was beautifully landscaped and manicured, with bright flowers, tropical trees, and peacocks. The auditorium was a venue for black performers and speakers. Church Park remains a venue for community events, particularly the annual Africa in April event every spring.

W. C. Handy

W. C. Handy was born in a log cabin in Florence, Alabama, in 1873. The son and grandson of African Methodist Episcopal ministers, Handy was exposed to music as a child in his father's church. Handy was also drawn to the music of the black laborers of the area, and when he moved to Memphis in the early 20th century, he recognized the wealth of the blues music he heard in bars, on street corners, and in back alleys around Beale Street.

Handy was a trained musician, so he was able to set down on paper the music that had, up until then, been passed from one musician to another.

In 1909, Handy composed Memphis mayor Ed Crump's campaign song, "Mr. Crump," which he later published as the "Memphis Blues." But he is most famous for his composition "St. Louis Blues," published in 1914. Handy also created the "Yellow Dog Blues," "Joe Turner Blues," and "Beale Street Blues." Known as the Father of the Blues, Handy passed away in 1958.

11am-4pm winter, adults $6, children $4) is dedicated to telling the story of Handy's life. It was Handy who famously wrote, in his "Beale Street Blues": "If Beale Street could talk, married men would have to take their beds and walk, except one or two who never drink booze, and the blind man on the corner singing 'Beale Street Blues.' I'd rather be there than anyplace I know."

The Handy museum houses photographs of Handy's family, one of his band uniforms, and memorabilia of the recording company that he founded. You can also hear samples of Handy's music.

A. Schwab

During Beale Street's dark days of the 1970s and 1980s, when the clubs and restaurants closed and the pawn shops opened, one mainstay remained: **A. Schwab** (163 Beale St., 901/523-9782, a-schwab.com, winter: Mon.-Weds. noon-6pm, Thurs. noon-7pm, Fri.-Sat. noon-9pm, Sun. 11am-6pm, may stay open later in the summer depending on crowds). This landmark general store opened in 1876 and was owned and operated by the same family until 2011. Originally the source for household necessities for thousands of Delta residents, A. Schwab remains a treasure trove of goods. Here you will find practical items like underwear, hats, umbrellas, cookware, and tools, as well as novelties like old fashioned candy, incense, and actual cans of Tennessee whoop-ass. Upstairs is the A. Schwab museum, a hodgepodge of old-time tools, clothes, and memorabilia of the store's 130-plus-year history.

The new owners, who purchased the store from the Schwab family, added a turn-of-the-century-style soda fountain, a private event space, and spruced up this landmark for the next century.

Memphis Rock 'n' Soul Museum

Music fans should plan to spend several hours at the **Memphis Rock 'n' Soul Museum** (191 Beale St., 901/205-2533, www.memphis-rocknsoul.org, 10am-7pm daily, adults $12, children 5-17 $9), located right next to FedEx Forum, off Beale Street. An affiliate of the Smithsonian Institution, this museum tells the story of Memphis music from the Delta blues to *Shaft*. Start with a short video documentary, and then follow the exhibits with your personal audio guide, which includes recordings of dozens of Memphis-influenced artists, from B. B. King to Elvis. Exhibits are dedicated to Memphis radio stations; the influence of the Victrola, Sam Phillips, and Sun Studio; and, of course, all things Elvis, among others. It takes several hours to study all the exhibits in detail and to listen to all (or even most) of the music, so plan accordingly.

There is a free shuttle that runs between the Rock 'n' Soul Museum, Graceland, and Sun Studio. Look for the black van with the Sun label's distinctive yellow sun on the side.

Gibson Guitar Factory

Across the street from the Rock 'n' Soul Museum is the **Gibson Guitar Factory** (145 Lt. George Lee Ave., 901/544-7998, ext. 4075, www.gibson.com, tours every hour on the hour 11am-4pm Mon.-Sat., noon-4pm Sun., ages five and up $10, under five not admitted), one of three in the United States. The Memphis plant specializes in the semi-hollow-bodied guitar, and a wide range of models are for sale in Gibson's retail shop. On the hour-long tour of the factory floor you can see guitars being made, from the shaping of the rim and panels to the painting and buffing of the finished product. Tours sell out, so reservations are recommended, particularly during the busier summer months. Most factory workers leave by 3pm and have the weekends off, so plan ahead if you want to see the factory floor in full swing.

The story of Memphis music is told at the Memphis Rock 'n' Soul Museum.

★ National Civil Rights Museum

If you do nothing else while you are in Memphis, or, frankly, the state of Tennessee, visit the **National Civil Rights Museum** (450 Mulberry St., 901/521-9699, www.civilrightsmuseum.org, 9am-5pm Mon., Wed.-Sat., 1pm-5pm Sun., adults $15, students and seniors $14, children 4-17 $12). Built on the Lorraine Motel site, where Dr. Martin Luther King Jr. was assassinated on April 4, 1968, the museum makes a thorough examination of the American civil rights movement, from slavery to the present day. Exhibits display original letters, audio recordings, photos, and newspaper clippings from events including the Montgomery bus boycott, *Brown v. Board of Education,* Freedom Summer, and the march from Selma to Montgomery. Original and re-created artifacts, such as the bus where Rosa Parks made her stand in 1955 and the cell where Dr. King wrote his famous *Letter from a Birmingham Jail,* help to illustrate the story of civil rights.

When Dr. King visited Memphis in March and then again in April 1968, the Lorraine Motel was one of a handful of downtown hotels that welcomed African Americans. The room (and balcony and parking lot) where he spent his final hours has been carefully recreated, and a narration by those who were with King tells the shocking story of his death. Across Mulberry Street, in the building that was once the boardinghouse from where James Earl Ray is believed to have fired his sniper shot, exhibits probe various theories about the assassination, as well as the worldwide legacy of the civil rights movement.

Visitors to the museum can pay an extra $2 for an audio guide—a worthwhile investment. This is a large museum, and it is overflowing with information, so visitors who want to give the displays their due attention should plan on spending 3-4 hours here. A good way to visit would be to tour the Lorraine Motel exhibits first, take a break for lunch, and then go across the street for the second half of the museum when you are refreshed.

Spending half a day here is a powerful experience, and one that raises many thoughts about civil rights. Expect interesting conversations with your travel companions after coming here. The gift shop offers books and videos for more information on the topic.

Admission is free on Monday after 3pm to Tennessee residents. In June, July, and August the museum stays open until 6pm.

Belz Museum of Asian and Judaic Art

The **Belz Museum of Asian and Judaic Art** (119 S. Main St., 901/523-2787, www.belzmuseum.org, 10am-5:30pm Tues.-Fri., noon-5pm Sat.-Sun., adults $6, seniors $5, children $4), formerly Peabody Place Museum, houses one of the largest collections of artwork from the Q'ing dynasty. Forged from the private collection of Memphis developers Jack and Marilyn Belz, owners of the Peabody Hotel and the now shuttered Peabody Place mall, the museum features some 1,000 objects, including an array of jade, tapestries, paintings, furniture, carvings, and other artifacts. The museum is also home to the largest U.S. collection of work by Israeli artist Daniel Kafri.

The Belz Museum's new Holocaust Memorial Gallery includes portraits and testimonials from Jewish survivors of the Holocaust in the *Living On* exhibit.

Blues Hall of Fame

The **Blues Hall of Fame** (421 Main St., 901/527-2583, www.Blues.org, 10am-5pm Mon.-Sat., 1pm-5pm Sun., adults $10, students $8, children under 12 free) has existed as an entity—a project of the Blues Foundation—since 1980. But the physical building that you can tour and experience didn't open until 2015. The $2.9 million building is across the street from the National Civil Rights Museum at the Lorraine Hotel. It celebrates the music for which Memphis is famous and honors the musicians who make it.

More than 350 people have been inducted into the Blues Hall of Fame; of the 130 performers, 120 of them are African American. At the museum, you can learn about all of the inductees and listen to their contributions to the genre.

UPTOWN

Uptown refers to locations along Union Avenue and points north in the center city district. Here downtown workers are more common than tourists, and tall office buildings rise above the city blocks.

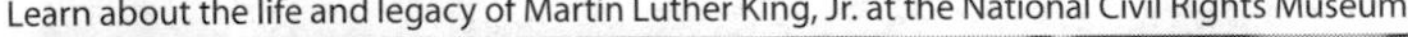

Learn about the life and legacy of Martin Luther King, Jr. at the National Civil Rights Museum.

The Cotton Museum

The **Cotton Museum** at the Memphis Cotton Exchange (65 Union Ave., 901/531-7826, www.memphiscottonmuseum.org, 10am-5pm Mon.-Sat., noon-5pm Sun., adults $10, seniors $9, students $9, military $8, children 6-12 $7) is located in the broad rectangular room that once was the nerve center of the Mid-South's cotton trade. The Cotton Exchange was established in 1873, and it was here that buyers and sellers of the South's most important cash crop met, and where fortunes were made and lost. Located just steps away from the Mississippi River, the Exchange was the trading floor of Cotton Row, the area of town that was defined by the cotton industry.

The Cotton Museum is home to exhibits about cotton's history, its uses, and the culture that its cultivation gave rise to in Memphis and the Mississippi Delta. There are several videos you can watch, as well as a live Internet feed of today's cotton exchange—now conducted entirely electronically. The nicest thing about the museum, however, is seeing the chalkboard where the prices of cotton around the world were written by hand. There is also a replica of the Western Union office, where buyers and sellers sent telegrams using an intricate system of abbreviations known only to the cotton trade. The museum expanded in 2010, adding more hands-on exhibits and an educational wing.

★ The Peabody Hotel Memphis

The Peabody Hotel Memphis (149 Union Ave., 901/529-4000, www.peabodymemphis.com) is the city's most famous hotel. Founded in 1869, the Peabody was one of the first grand hotels of the South, a place as well known for its elegant balls and big-band concerts as for the colorful characters who sipped cocktails at its famous lounge. Named in memory of the philanthropist George Peabody, the original hotel was located at the corner of Main and Monroe. It closed in 1923, and a new Peabody opened two years later in its present location on Union Avenue. It remained the place to see and be seen for generations of Memphians and Delta residents. It was historian and journalist David Cohn who famously wrote in 1935 that "the Mississippi Delta begins in the lobby of The Peabody Hotel."

Even if you don't stay here, you must stop by the elegant hotel lobby to see the twice-daily march of the **Peabody ducks** (a trip to Memphis is incomplete without this experience). The ducks live on the roof of the

The Peabody Hotel Memphis

hotel and make the journey—by elevator—to the lobby fountain every morning at 11am. At 5pm they march out of the fountain, back onto the elevator, and up to their accommodations on the roof.

The hotel employs a duck master who takes care of the ducks and supervises their daily trip downstairs. Watching the ducks is free, frenzied, and undeniably fun. It is also one of the most popular activities among visitors to Memphis, so be sure to get there early and secure a good vantage point along the red carpet to watch the ducks march.

Mud Island

In Memphis, it is sometimes easy to forget that you are just steps away from the great Mississippi River. A trip to **Mud Island** will cure this misperception once and for all. A narrow band of land in the river, Mud Island is home to the **Mud Island River Park and Museum** (125 N. Front St., 901/576-7241, www.mudisland.com, 10am-5pm Tues.-Sun., Apr.-Oct., adults $10, seniors $9, children $7), which has exhibits about early uses of the river, steam- and paddleboats, floods, and much more.

The park's **Mississippi River Museum** begins with a refresher course on European exploration of this region—de Soto, La Salle, and Marquette and Joliet—followed by information about early settlement. The highlight is being able to explore a replica of an 1870s steamboat. In the Riverfolk Gallery there are wax depictions of Mark Twain, riverboat gambler George Devol, and steamship entertainers. The museum also remembers the numerous river disasters that have taken place along the Mississippi.

Admission to the museum includes the **River Walk** at the Mud Island River Park, a five-block scale model of the entire Mississippi River—from Minnesota to the Gulf of Mexico. Walk along the model to see scale representations of cities along the river's path, and read placards about the river's history. On a hot day, wear your bathing suit so you can swim in the wading pool that is located at the end of the model of the river inside the park.

The River Park is also home to an outdoor amphitheater, which in summer hosts big-name concerts, a snack bar, outdoor tables, and restrooms. You can rent canoes, kayaks, and paddleboats to use in the still waters around the Mud Island harbor. Bike rental is also available. Mud Island is the site of the city's dragon boat races, which benefit the work of the Tennessee Clean Water

Mud Island River Park is a great place to take in views of downtown and the mighty Mississippi.

Network. These fundraising events, also held in Chattanooga, Oak Ridge, Knoxville, and Nashville, feature teams from local businesses and community organizations paddling 46-foot-long boats festooned with dragon heads in unison.

Admission to the River Park is free. You can pay $4 round-trip to ride the monorail to Mud Island, or you can walk across the monorail bridge for free (offering a great photo/selfie opportunity). The monorail station is on Front Street at Adams Avenue.

The Birth of Mud Island

Mud Island rose from the Mississippi River as a result of two seemingly small events. In 1876, the river shifted slightly about 20 miles south of Memphis, causing the currents that flowed past the city to alter course. And then, in 1910, the U.S. Navy gunboat, the USS *Amphitrite,* anchored at the mouth of the Wolf River for almost two years, causing a further change in silt patterns. When the ship left in 1912, the sandbar continued to grow, and Mud Island was born.

Residents initially disliked the island, since it was ugly and proved to be a danger to river navigation.

Beginning in the 1930s, poor Memphians squatted on Mud Island in ramshackle homes built of scrap metal and wood. Between 200 and 500 people lived on the island during this time.

In 1959, a downtown airport was built on the island, but the airport was closed in 1970 when the DeSoto Bridge was built. In 1974, plans were developed for what is the present-day Mud Island River Park, which includes a full-scale replica of a riverboat, a monorail to the island, and the signature 2,000-foot flowing replica of the Mississippi River.

Slavehaven Underground Railroad Museum

The legend of the Burkle Estate, a modest white clapboard house on North 2nd Street, has given rise to the **Slavehaven Underground Railroad Museum** (826 N. 2nd St., 901/527-3427, www.slavehavenundergroundrailroadmuseum.org, 10am-5pm Mon.-Sat. summer, 10am-4pm Mon.-Sat. winter, adults $10, youth $8). The museum here tells the story of slavery and the legendary Underground Railroad, which helped thousands of slaves escape to freedom in the North (and, after the 1850 Fugitive Slave Act, to Canada). Jacob Burkle, a German immigrant and owner of the Memphis stockyard, is said to have built the Burkle Estate around 1850. Escaping slaves would have hidden in a root cellar beneath the house before making the 1,500-foot trip to the banks of the Mississippi, where they made a further journey north.

Skeptics say that there is no evidence of this story and even point to documents that show that Burkle may not have purchased the property until 1871, well after the end of slavery. Advocates for the Underground Railroad story say that it was the nature of the railroad to be secret, so there is nothing unusual about a lack of concrete evidence.

Visitors today need not be too concerned with the details of the debate; the Slavehaven museum does a good job of highlighting the brutality of the slave trade and slavery and the ingenuity and bravery it took for slaves to escape. Perhaps the most interesting part of the exhibit are the quilts that demonstrate the way that slaves used quilting patterns to send messages to one another. Other displays show advertisements for Memphis slave auctions and images from the early 20th century that depict damaging racial stereotypes.

The museum is operated by Heritage Tours of Memphis, and staff is available to conduct guided tours of the property.

Fire Museum of Memphis

The **Fire Museum of Memphis** (118 Adams Ave., 901/320-5650, www.firemuseum.com, 9am-6pm Mon.-Sat., 1pm-6pm Sun. summer, 9am-4:30pm Mon.-Sat., 1pm- 4:30pm Sun. winter, adults $10, seniors $8, children $8, family pack for four is $30) is a good place to take children. There is a huge display of fire-engine toys, lots of firefighting paraphernalia, and a "fire room" that presents important lessons on fire safety. You can also see old-fashioned fire engines, and youngsters will enjoy playing in the kid-friendly fire truck. The museum is located in the old Fire Station No. 1 in downtown Memphis.

St. Jude Children's Research Hospital

The sprawling complex of **St. Jude Children's Research Hospital** on uptown's northern fringe has been saving lives and bringing hope to children and their families since 1962. St. Jude was founded by entertainer Danny Thomas in fulfillment of his promise to God to give back to those in need. Over the years and thanks to the success of its fundraising arm—the American Lebanese Syrian Associated Charities—St. Jude has expanded many times over and now leads the world in research and treatment of catastrophic childhood diseases, especially pediatric cancers. Programs with country music stars only expand the reach of St. Jude's and its work. The hospital never turns anyone away due to inability to pay, and it never makes families without insurance pay for their treatment.

Call in advance to tour a small museum about Danny Thomas and St. Jude in the **Danny Thomas ALSAC Pavilion** (332 N. Lauderdale St., 901/578-2042, www.stjude.org, 8am-4pm Sun.-Fri., 10am-4pm Sat., except when there are special events, free), located inside a golden dome on the hospital grounds. Just outside are the graves of Danny Thomas and his wife, Rose Marie. Hospital tours available Mon. through Fri. at 10am and 1pm.

The Pyramid

The Memphis **Pyramid** is the most physically dominating feature of the northern city skyline. Memphis's affiliation with all things Egypt began with its name and continued in 1897, when a large-scale replica of a pyramid was built to represent Memphis at the Tennessee Centennial Exhibition in Nashville. Pyramids were popular symbols on Memphis paraphernalia for many years.

The first serious proposal for a life-size pyramid to be built in Memphis was written in the 1970s, but the idea did not take off until the 1980s, when the city and county governments agreed to fund it. Denver developer Sidney Shlenker promoted the plan and promised

The Pyramid was revitalized by Bass Pro Shops Outdoor World.

restaurants, tourist attractions, and lots of revenue for the city. The 321-foot pyramid was built and opened in 1991, minus the money-making engines that Shlenker promised.

For years the $63 million "Great American Pyramid" sat empty. In spring 2015 this changed. Bass Pro Shops at the Pyramid (1 Bass Pro Dr., 901/291-8200, www.basspro.com, 8am-10pm Mon.-Sat., 8am-7pm Sun.) opened what it modestly calls "one of the most dynamic, immersive retail stores in the world." This outdoor gear store includes a cypress swamp, 10 aquariums holding 600,000 gallons of water, a Big Cypress Lodge 105-room hotel (800/225-6343, big-cypress.com) with treehouse cabins, a spa, Ducks Unlimited National Waterfowling Heritage Center, Uncle Buck's Fishbowl and Grill nautical-themed restaurant, a giant 28-story freestanding elevator, and more. Obviously, this isn't an average store. There are regular aquarium and fish feedings (10am and 5pm daily) and alligator feedings (2pm Tues., Thurs., and Sat.).

MIDTOWN

You'll need a car to explore the attractions in midtown, which sprawls along Union, Poplar, and Madison Avenues as they head eastward from the city center.

Sun Studio

It is well worth your time to drop by the famous **Sun Studio** (706 Union Ave., 800/441-6249, www.sunstudio.com, 10am-6pm daily, adults, $12, kids 5-11 free, under 5 not admitted), where Elvis Presley recorded his first hit, "That's All Right," and where dozens of blues, rock, and country musicians recorded during the 1950s. Founded by radioman and audio engineer Sam Phillips and his wife, Becky, the studio recorded weddings, funerals, events, and, of course, music. Phillips was interested in the blues, and his first recordings were of yet-unknown artists such as Rufus Thomas and Howlin' Wolf. In 1953, Elvis Presley came into the studio on his lunch break to record a $3 record of himself singing "My Happiness" for his mother. Phillips was not impressed with the performance, and it was not for another year—and thanks to the prodding of Phillips's assistant, Marion Keisker—that Phillips called Presley in to record some more. When Phillips heard Elvis's version of the blues tune "That's All Right," he knew he had a hit. And he did.

But the story of Elvis's discovery is just one of many that took place in the modest home-made Sun Studio, and this attraction is not just for Elvis fans. The one-hour tour of the studio leaves every hour on the half hour, and while you are waiting you can order a real fountain drink from the snack bar or browse the shop's collection of recordings and paraphernalia. The studio is still in business; you can record here for $75 an hour at night, and dozens of top-notch performers have, including Grace Potter, Beck, and Matchbox Twenty.

Tours start every half hour during business hours and take approximately 90 minutes. Children under the age of five are not permitted on the tours. There are free shuttles from Graceland and the Rock 'n' Soul Museum to Sun Studio.

Lauderdale Courts/ Uptown Square

Perhaps the least-known Elvis attraction in Memphis is **Lauderdale Courts** (252 N. Lauderdale St., 901/523-8662, $10 for adults, $7 12 and under, rent the room for the night $250), the public housing complex where Presley lived with his parents from 1949 to 1953, before his rise to fame. The handsome brick building was saved from the wrecking ball in the 1990s thanks to its history with the King, and the apartment where the Presleys lived has been restored to its 1950s glory. Most of the year, the Lauderdale Courts Elvis suite is rented out as a hotel room, but during Elvis's Birthday Week in January and Elvis Week in August it is open for public tours.

Victorian Village

Set on a tree-lined block of Adams Avenue near Orleans Street is Victorian Village, where a half-dozen elegant Victorian-era homes

Midtown Memphis

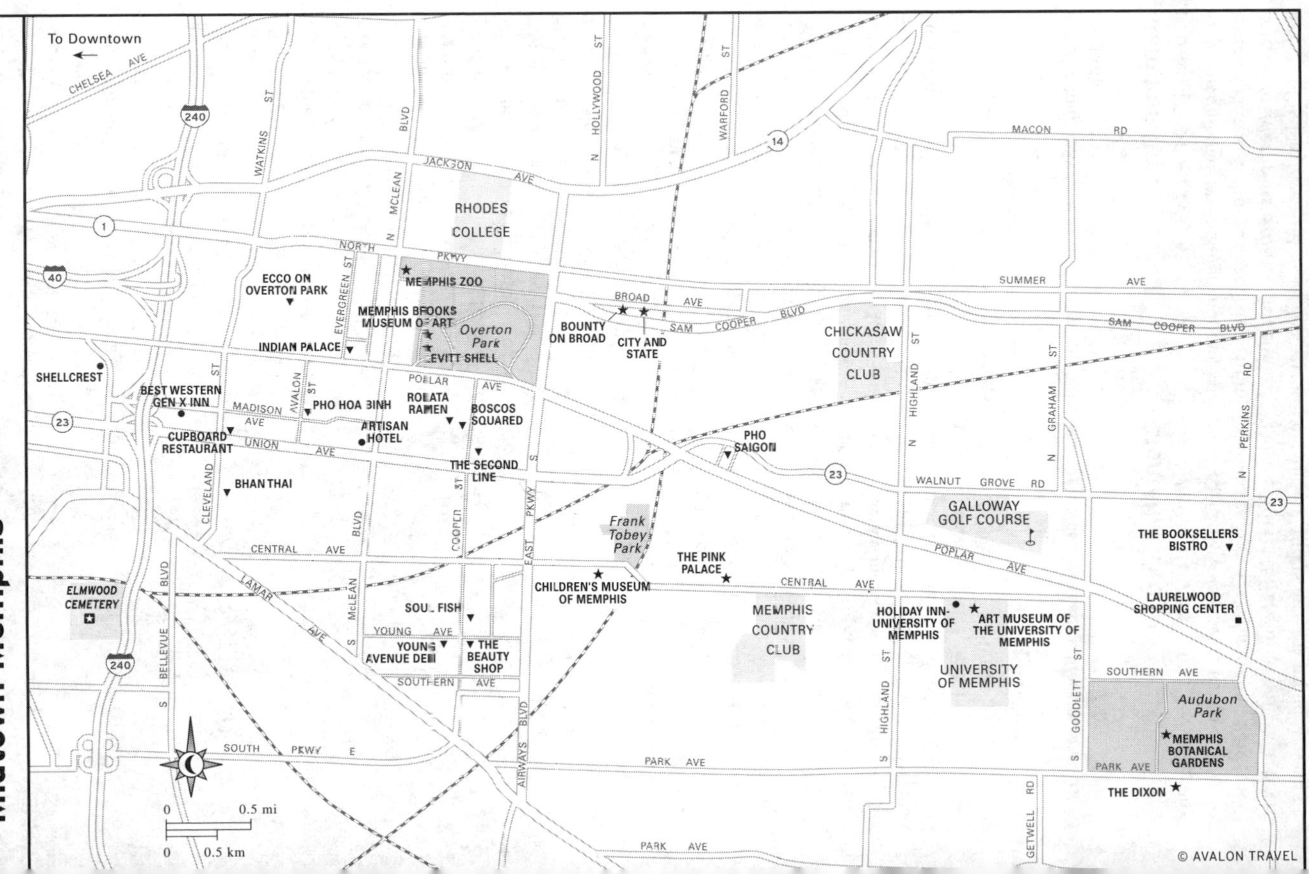

escaped the "urban renewal" fate of other historic Memphis homes.

Visitors can tour the **Woodruff-Fontaine House** (680 Adams Ave., 901/526-1469, www.woodruff-fontaine.com, noon-4pm Wed.-Sun., $10), one of the street's most magnificent buildings. Built in 1870 for the Woodruff family and sold to the Fontaines in the 1880s, the house was occupied through 1930, when it became part of the James Lee Art Academy, a precursor to the Memphis Academy of Art. When the academy moved in 1959, the building became city property and stood vacant. Beginning in 1961, city residents raised funds to restore and refurnish the house with period furniture and accessories, and it opened as a museum in 1964. This was during the period of urban renewal that saw to the demolition of many of Memphis's other old homes, and some of the house's furnishings were taken from homes that were later demolished. Tours include all three floors and the basement; there is no elevator to access the different levels. This is a good stop if you are interested in antiques.

The **Magevney House** (198 Adams Ave., 901/526-1484, free admission first Saturday of each month 1pm-4pm) and the **Mallory-Neely House** (652 Adams Ave., 901/523-1484, www.memphismuseums.org, 10am-4pm Fri.-Sat., adults $7, seniors $5, youth $5) are two other historical homes in the district. The Magevney House is the oldest middle-class residence still standing in Memphis. It was built in 1836 by an Irish immigrant to the city, Eugene Magevney. The Mallory-Neely House is of the same vintage and is notable for the fact that it was not refurnished in more than 100 years and so remains remarkably true to the era in which it was built.

Memphis Brooks Museum of Art

Memphis's foremost art museum is located in Overton Park in midtown, a short drive from downtown. **Memphis Brooks Museum of Art** (1934 Poplar Ave., 901/544-6200, www.brooksmuseum.org, 10am-4pm Wed. and Fri., 10am-8pm Thurs, 10am-5pm Sat., 11am-5pm Sun., adults $7, seniors $6, students and youth 7 and older $3) is the largest fine-art museum in Tennessee, and its permanent collection includes 8,000 works of art. This includes ancient African and Asian art, as well as 14th century-present European art and 18th century-present American art. There are 29 galleries at the Brooks, and special exhibitions have focused on the work of Annie Leibovitz, men's fashion in Africa, and the silver work of Paul de Lamerie, Activist Photographers of the Civil Rights Movement, and American Folk Art. There is also a museum shop and restaurant, as well as an auditorium often used to screen films.

A giant panda is one draw at the Memphis Zoo.

Memphis Zoo

The **Memphis Zoo** (2000 Prentiss Pl., 901/333-6500, www.memphiszoo.org, 9am-5pm daily Mar.-Oct., 9am-4pm daily Nov.-Feb., adults $15, children $10) has been expanding and is now the proud steward of two giant pandas, Le Le and Ya Ya; large cats; penguins; lions; tropical birds; and 3,500 other animal species. More hippos have been born here than at any other zoo. Its butterfly exhibit, open May-October, is a popular feature, and camel rides are available in the spring. The zoo is located on the grounds of Overton Park. Parking is an additional $5 and a point of some contention in the neighborhood. (Parking on the grass during zoo events upsets those who use the magnificent Overton Park for other events and purposes. Be mindful when you visit.)

Tennessee residents with ID can get in free on Tuesdays after 2pm, except in March; $3 fee for access to China/panda exhibit.

SOUTH MEMPHIS

★ Stax Museum of American Soul Music

Perhaps there is no place in Memphis that better tells the story of the city's legendary soul music than the **Stax Museum of American Soul Music** (926 E. McLemore Ave., 901/942-7685, www.staxmuseum.com, 10am-5pm Tues.-Sat. and 1pm-5pm Sun., additionally, 1pm-5pm Mon. Apr.-Oct., adults $12, seniors, students, and military $11, children 9-12 $9).

The museum tour starts with a short toe-tapping video that sets the scene for the musical magic that took place here during the 1960s. Exhibits include the sanctuary of an old clapboard Delta church, which illustrates the connection between soul and gospel music. You can also see Booker T. Jones's original organ, Otis Redding's favorite suede jacket, and Isaac Hayes's 1972 peacock-blue gold-trimmed Cadillac Eldorado, Superfly.

The museum also takes you through the studio's control room and into the studio itself, slanted floors and all. If you want to try your hand at singing, there is a karaoke machine, as well as a dance floor in case you can't help but move to the music. The Stax Museum is a must-see for music enthusiasts but also an educational journey for those who don't know the story behind some of America's most famous songs. It sits next door to the Stax Music Academy, a present-day music school that reaches out to neighborhood youth.

★ Graceland

Drive south from downtown on Elvis Presley Boulevard to reach the King's most famous home, **Graceland** (3717 Elvis Presley Blvd., 901/332-3322 or 800/238-2000, www.graceland.com or www.elvis.com, 9am-5pm Mon.-Sat., 9am-4pm Sun., Mar.-Oct., 10am-4pm daily Nov., 9 am-4pm Wed.-Mon. Dec., 10am-4pm Wed.-Mon. Jan-Feb., adults $36, seniors and students $32.40, children 7-12 $16, children 6 and under free). There is plenty of parking. Reservations are recommended.

Visitors can choose from five tour packages: The mansion-only tour takes about an hour and costs $36; the platinum tour includes the automobile museum, the Graceland Archives Experience and other special perks for $40. Platinum plus, at $45, adds Elvis's airplanes. Enthusiasts can choose one of the VIP packages, which give you "front of the line" access, an all-day pass, keepsakes, and access to exclusive exhibits, such as 60 Years of Elvis introduced to the VIP tour in 2014: $72 without a tour of Elvis's airplanes and $77 includes the airplanes.

Actor and Elvis fan John Stamos narrates an interactive multimedia digital tour that gives you access to archival audio, video, and photographs.

The Graceland complex blends into the strip malls and fast-food joints that line the boulevard in this part of Memphis. The ticket counter, shops, and restaurants are located on the west side of the boulevard, and here you board a shuttle van that drives across the highway and up the curved drive to the Graceland mansion. Graceland managers may have taken full advantage of the commercial opportunities presented by the home that Elvis left behind, but they have not overdone it. The operation is laid-back, leaving the spotlight on Elvis and, of course, his fans, who travel to Memphis from around the world to visit.

The mansion tour is conducted by audio guide. It includes the ground floor of the mansion (the upstairs remains closed to the public) and several outbuildings that now house exhibits about Elvis's life and career. High points include watching the press conference Elvis gave after leaving the army, witnessing firsthand his audacious taste in decor, and visiting the meditation garden where Elvis, his parents, and his grandmother are buried. There is also a plaque in memory of Elvis's lost twin, Jesse Garon. The audio tour plays many of Elvis's songs, family stories remembered by Elvis's daughter Lisa Marie Presley, and several clips of Elvis speaking. In 2015, Graceland opened two new exhibits: *Elvis: That's the Way It Is*, a documentary chronicling the legend's first Las Vegas performance, and "I Shot Elvis," which features photos from the early years of his career and encourages museum guests to take a photo with a larger-than image of the King.

The exhibits gloss over some of the challenges Elvis faced in his life—his addiction to prescription drugs, his womanizing and failed marriage, and his unsettling affinity for firearms among them. But they showcase Elvis's generosity, his dedication to family, and his fun-loving character. The portrait that emerges is sympathetic and remarkably human for a man who is so often portrayed as larger than life.

The automobile museum features 33 vehicles, including his pink Cadillac, motorcycles, and a red MG from *Blue Hawaii,* as well as some of his favorite motorized toys, including a go-kart and dune buggy. His private planes include the *Lisa Marie,* which Elvis customized with gold-plated seat belts, suede chairs, and gold-flecked sinks. Other special Graceland exhibits include "Sincerely Elvis," which chronicles Elvis's life in 1956, and "Elvis After Dark," which describes some of Elvis's late-night passions, like roller skating.

The Graceland mansion was declared a National Historic Site in 2006. It attracts more than 650,000 visitors annually. Expansion plans include the 450-room hotel/500-seat theater, Guest House at Graceland.

★ Elmwood Cemetery

Elmwood Cemetery (824 S. Dudley St., 901/774-3212, www.elmwoodcemetery.org, 8am-4:30pm daily), an 80-acre cemetery southwest of the city center, is the resting place of 70,000 Memphians—ordinary citizens and some of the city's most prominent leaders. It was founded in 1852 by 50 gentlemen who wanted the cemetery to be a park

Nothing, especially not the pool room, is understated at Graceland Mansion.

Soulsville

A lucky convergence of people, talents, and social forces led to one of Memphis's—and America's—most distinctive musical stories. **Stax Records** was founded in 1960 by Jim Stewart, an aspiring country fiddler, and his sister, Estelle Axton. The first two letters of the brother and sister's surnames came together to form Stax, a name now synonymous with the raw Memphis sound of performers like Rufus and Carla Thomas, Otis Redding, Sam and Dave, Isaac Hayes, Eddie Floyd, the Mar-Keys, the Staple Singers, and Booker T. & the MGs.

Stewart chose a closed movie theater in a working-class South Memphis neighborhood for his recording studio. He was on a tight budget, so he didn't bother to fix the sloped theater floor or angled walls, and the room's reverberating acoustics came to define the Memphis sound.

Motown was known as "Hitsville" for its smooth and palatable sound, so the artists at Stax began to call their neighborhood "Soulsville," a name that still refers to the area of South Memphis where Stax is located. The soul music that Stax recorded was raw and inventive, influenced by country, blues, gospel, and jazz.

The label's first hit was with WDIA-AM disc jockey Rufus Thomas and his daughter, Carla Thomas, who came in one day and recorded "Cause I Love You." The song became an overnight sensation.

Stax tapped into the talent of the neighborhood, and particularly the African American Booker T. Washington High School, which graduated such greats as the members of the Soul Children and the Mad Lads. As the Stax reputation developed, artists came from out of town to record, including a 21-year-old Otis Redding, who drove up from Georgia in hopes of making a record and made a career instead.

Stax also operated **Satellite Records,** right next door to the studio, and here Estelle Axton was able to quickly test-market new recordings on the neighborhood youngsters who came in for the latest music. Wayne Jackson, a member of the studio's house band, the Memphis Horns, recalls that Estelle and Jim would invite hundreds of young people from the neighborhood into the studio to listen to their newest recording. Based on the group's response, they would choose the single.

Stax was unique for its time as an integrated organization, where the love of music trumped racial differences. As the civil rights movement evolved, Stax artists turned to serious social themes in their music. In 1972, Stax artists organized **WattStax,** an outdoor black music festival in Los Angeles.

Between 1960 and 1975, when the Stax magic ran out, the studio produced 800 singles and 300 albums, including 243 Top 100 and 14 number-one R&B hits. Isaac Hayes's theme from the movie *Shaft* was the fastest-selling album in Stax history, and one of three Stax songs went to number one on the pop charts. Other big Stax hits were Otis Redding's "(Sittin' on) The Dock of the Bay," the Staples Singers' "Respect Yourself," and Sam and Dave's "Soul Man."

Sadly, Stax was destroyed financially by a bad distribution deal with CBS Records in 1975, and the studio was closed. Its rare master tapes were sold at auction, and the studio where soul was born was demolished.

Thankfully, the story of Stax has not been forgotten. In 2001, ground was broken for a new Stax story, one that grew into the present-day music academy and the **Stax Museum of American Soul Music.**

for the living as well as a resting place for the dead. They invested in tree planting and winding carriage paths so that the cemetery today is a pleasant, peaceful place to spend a few hours.

The cemetery is the resting place of Memphians like Annie Cook, a well-known madam who died during the yellow fever epidemic of 1878; Marion Scudder Griffen, a pioneering female lawyer and suffragette; and musician Sister Thea Bowman. Thousands of anonymous victims of the yellow fever epidemic were buried here, as were both Confederate and Union casualties of the Civil

War. Prominent citizens, including Robert Church Sr., Edward Hull Crump, and Shelby Foote, are also buried at Elmwood.

Visitors to the cemetery may simply drive or walk through on their own. But it is best to rent the one-hour audio guide ($10) of the cemetery, which takes you on a driving tour and highlights 50 people buried in the cemetery. Thanks to a well-written and well-presented narration, the cemetery tour comes closer than any other single Memphis attraction to bringing Memphis's diverse history and people to life.

The cemetery offers occasional lectures and docent-guided tours for $15. Call ahead or check the website to find out if any are scheduled during your visit. To find Elmwood, drive east along E. H. Crump Boulevard, turning south (right) onto Dudley, which deadends at the single-lane bridge that marks the entrance to the cemetery.

Tours are of the 1,500 trees in the Carlisle S. Page Arboretum are also available.

Church of the Full Gospel Tabernacle

A native of Arkansas and longtime resident of Michigan, Al Green first made his name as one of history's greatest soul singers, with hits like "Let's Stay Together," "Take Me to the River," and "Love and Happiness." Following a religious conversion in 1979, he dedicated his considerable talents to God and founded the **Church of the Full Gospel Tabernacle** (787 Hale Rd., 901/396-9192) in Memphis, where his Sunday sermons dripped with soulful gospel.

For almost 11 years, the Reverend Al Green left secular music, dedicating himself to God's music. He began his return to secular music in 1988 and in 1995 Green released the first of three new secular albums on Blue Note Records.

According to his official biography, *Take Me to the River*, Reverend Green faced some criticism when he returned to the secular scene. "I've got people in the church saying, 'That's a secular song,' and I'm saying, 'Yeah, but you've got Monday, Tuesday, Wednesday, Thursday, Friday, and Saturday to be anything other than spiritual. You've got to live those days, too!'" Reverend Green writes. In the book he says he has not neglected his duty to God: "The music is the message, the message is the music. So that's my little ministry that the Big Man upstairs gave to me—a little ministry called love and happiness."

Despite his rebirth as a secular soul

Elmwood Cemetery is the resting place of both famous and everyday Memphians.

performer, Al Green, now a bishop, still makes time for his church. He preaches regularly, but not every Sunday, and continues to sing the praises of God. The Sunday service at his Memphis church begins at 11:30am. Visitors are welcome, and you can come—within reason—as you are. Please show respect, though, by being quiet when it's called for and throwing a few bucks in the offering plate when it comes around. And don't forget that the church is a place of worship and not a tourist attraction. If you're not in town on Sunday, you can catch the weekly choir rehearsal on Thursday at 7pm.

National Ornamental Metal Museum

An unusual delight, the **National Ornamental Metal Museum** (374 Metal Museum Dr., 901/774-6380, www.metalmuseum.org, 10am-5pm Tues.-Sat., noon-5pm Sun., adults $6, seniors $5, students and children $4) is dedicated to preserving and displaying fine metalwork. Its permanent collection numbers more than 3,000 objects and ranges from contemporary American sculpture to works up to 500 years old. The museum hosts special exhibits several times a year, showcasing various aspects of metalwork. There is also a working metalwork studio, and the museum grounds on the bluff overlooking the Mississippi are an attraction in themselves. This is reputed to be the site where Spanish explorer Hernando de Soto and his men camped when they passed through the area in 1542. Demonstrations may be available on weekend afternoons; call the museum in advance to confirm.

C. H. Nash Museum at Chucalissa

A group of platform and ridge mounds along the Mississippi River are the main attraction at **Chucalissa Archaeological Site** (1987 Indian Village Dr., 901/785-3160, www.memphis.edu/chucalissa, 9am-5pm Tues.-Sat., 1pm-5pm Sun., adults $5, seniors and children $3). The mounds were once part of a Choctaw Indian community that existed AD 1000-1550. The village was empty when Europeans arrived, and the name *Chucalissa* means abandoned house.

The largest mound would have been where the chief and his family lived. The present-day museum, operated by the University of Memphis, consists of an exhibit about the Native Americans of the area and a self-guided tour around the mounds and courtyard area, where games and meetings would have been held. There is also a 0.5-mile nature trail along the bluff overlooking the river.

EAST MEMPHIS

East Memphis is home to old suburbs, gracious homes, and some excellent parks and other attractions.

The Dixon Gallery and Gardens

The Dixon Gallery and Gardens (4339 Park Ave., 901/761-5250, www.dixon.org, 10am-5pm Tues.-Sat., 1pm-5pm Sun., adults $7, seniors $5, children $3), an art museum housed inside a stately Georgian-style home, has an impressive permanent collection of more than 2,000 paintings, many of them French impressionist and postimpressionist style, including works by Monet, Renoir, Degas, and Cézanne. It also mounts a half-dozen special exhibits each year; previous ones have showcased the art of Lester Julian Merriweather, Rodin, and Brian Russell.

The Dixon is an easy place to spend several hours, immersed first in art and then in walking the paths that explore the house's 17 acres of beautifully tended gardens. There is a cutting garden, woodland garden, and formal gardens, among others.

Admission to the Dixon is free on Saturday between the hours of 10am-noon, and pay what you wish on Tuesday.

Memphis Botanic Garden

The 100-acre **Memphis Botanic Garden**

(750 Cherry Rd., 901/636-4100, www.memphisbotanicgarden.com, 9am-6pm daily summer, 9am-4:30pm daily winter, adults $8, seniors $6.50, children $5) is home to more than 140 different species of trees and more than two dozen specialty gardens, including a Sculpture Garden, Azalea Trail, and Iris Garden. Trails meander through the gardens, but for the greatest fun buy a handful of fish food and feed the fish and ducks that inhabit the pond at the Japanese Garden. The garden puts on a number of events, including blockbuster concerts, workshops, plant sales, wine tastings, and programs for children. **Fratelli's Café** (901/766-9900, 11am-2pm daily) is a good option for lunch onsite.

The Pink Palace

A good destination for families, the Pink Palace (3050 Central Ave., 901/636-2362, www.memphismuseums.org, 9am-5pm Mon.-Sat., noon-5pm Sun.) is a group of attractions rolled into one. The **Pink Palace Museum** (adults $12.75, seniors $12.25, children $7.25, free after 1pm Tues.) is a museum about Memphis, with exhibits about the natural history of the Mid-South region and the city's development. There is a full-scale replica of the first Piggly Wiggly supermarket, plus an exhibit about how health care became such a large part of the Memphis economy. The museum is housed within the Pink Palace Mansion, the Memphis home of Piggly Wiggly founder Clarence Saunders.

The Pink Palace is also home to the **Sharpe Planetarium**, which at this writing was closed for $1.5 million renovations. When complete it will include a newly upgraded 3D movie theater with daily screenings. Special package tickets are available for all the Pink Palace attractions.

The annual Enchanted Forest, a holiday-themed village and Christmas destination for families, is open mid-November through December 31. It has a separate or additional entry fee ($6 adults, $5 seniors and children under 12); proceeds benefit Le Bonheur Children's Hospital.

Art Museum of the University of Memphis

The **Art Museum of the University of Memphis** (142 CFA Building, 901/678-2224, www.memphis.edu/amum, 9am-5pm Mon.-Sat., free. Parking is free on weekends, otherwise $2 per hour in the parking garage) houses excellent but small exhibits of ancient Egyptian and African art and artifacts, and a noteworthy print gallery. There are frequent special exhibitions. The museum is closed during university holidays and in between temporary exhibits.

Children's Museum of Memphis

You will know the **Children's Museum of Memphis** (2525 Central Ave., 901/458-2678, www.cmom.com, 9am-5pm daily, $12) by the large alphabet blocks outside spelling its acronym, CMOM. Bring children here for constructive and educational play: They can sit in a flight simulator and real airplane cockpit, climb through the arteries of a model heart, climb a skyscraper, and more. The museum has 26 permanent exhibits and several traveling exhibits. Beat the Memphis summer heat at the museum's **H2Oh! Splash** park ($12 alone or $20 total combined with museum entry), which has 40 water sprayers in which children can frolic.

Davies Manor Plantation

Explore 32 acres of land and see the oldest log home in Shelby County open to the public at **Davies Manor Plantation**, (3570 Davieshire Dr., Bartlett, daviesmanorplantation.org, noon-4pm Tues.-Sat., Apr.-mid-Dec., adults $5, seniors $4, children and students $3, children 6 and under free) in suburban Bartlett. This historic plantation site includes a cotton patch, slave cabins, Civil War markers, and other artifacts left behind from a very different time in our nation's history. Davies Manor is likely not worth a trip on its own, but if you are traveling with kids to Western Plains attractions, it is worth a stop. Special events include quilt shows.

Lichterman Nature Center

Lichterman Nature Center (5992 Quince Rd., 901/636-2211, www.memphismuseums.org/lichterman-overview, 10am-3pm Tues.-Thurs., 10am-4pm Fri.-Sat., adults $6, seniors $5.50, children $4.50) is dedicated to generating interest and enthusiasm for the Mid-South's nature. The park encompasses some 65 acres, and visitors will enjoy seeing native trees and flowers, including dogwood, lotus, and pine. There is a museum about the local environment, picnic facilities, and pleasant trails. Environmental education is the center's mission, and this certified arboretum is a popular destination for families and school groups.

TOURS

History Tours

Heritage Tours of Memphis (901/527-3427, www.heritagetoursofmemphis.com, adults $35, youth 12-17 $27, children 4-11 $25,) is the city's only tour company dedicated to presenting Memphis's African American history. Operated by Memphians Elaine Turner and Joan Nelson, Heritage Tours offers black heritage, musical heritage, civil rights, and Beale Street walking tours. The company can also arrange out-of-town tours to area attractions, such as the **Alex Haley Museum and Interpretive Center** in Henning, Tennessee (adults $35, youth $30). Most local tours last about three hours.

The black heritage tour starts at the W. C. Handy Home and Museum and includes a stop at the Slavehaven Underground Railroad Museum plus narration that tells the story of black Memphians such as Ida B. Wells, Robert Church, and Tom Lee, and the events leading up to the assassination of Dr. Martin Luther King Jr. You will drive past the Mason Temple Church of God in Christ at 930 Mason Street, where Dr. King gave his famous "mountaintop" speech the night before his death.

River Tours

The **Memphis Queen Riverboat Tours** (901/527-2628, www.memphisriverboats.net, adults $20, seniors, college students, military, children 13-17 $17, children 4-12 $10, toddlers $5) leave daily at 2:30pm from the Port of Memphis, located at the foot of Monroe Avenue on the riverfront. The afternoon tour lasts 90 minutes and takes you a few miles south of the city before turning around. Commentary tells some of the most famous tales of the river, but the biggest attraction of the tour is simply being on Old Man River. The views of the Memphis skyline from the

Riverboat tours are one way to experience the Mississippi.

water are impressive. Concessions are available onboard. The riverboats also offer dinner cruises at 7:30pm with live music for about $45 per person. See website to check dates and times.

Music Tours

Music-themed tours are the specialty at **Backbeat Tours** (901/527-9415, www.backbeattours.com, $15-51, tickets must be reserved in advance). You will travel on a reconditioned 1959 transit bus and be serenaded by live musicians. Tours include the Memphis Mojo Tour (adults $28, students $26, children 7-12 $15), which takes you to Memphis music landmarks like Sun Studio and the Stax Museum, and the Hound Dog tour, which follows in Elvis Presley's Memphis footsteps. Backbeat can also take you to Graceland and offers two walking tours of Memphis—a Memphis Ghost Tour ($20 adult/$13 child) which explores the bloody and creepy side of history—and a Memphis historic walking tour (adult $15, child $9) both daily March-October and Saturdays only November and February.

Entertainment and Events

Memphis's vibrant, diverse personality is reflected in its entertainment scene. Blues, rap, R&B, and gospel are just some of the types of music you can hear on any given weekend. Alternative and indie rock finds a receptive audience in Memphis, as does opera, Broadway productions, and the symphony. There's always a good excuse to go out.

LIVE MUSIC AND CLUBS

Memphis may be the birthplace of the blues, but there's a lot more to the music scene than that. It's true that you can catch live blues at a Beale Street nightclub or in a city juke joint. But you can also find hard-edge rock, jazz, and acoustic music most nights of the week. The best resource for up-to-date entertainment listings is the free weekly ***Memphis Flyer*** (www.memphisflyer.com), which comes out on Wednesday morning and includes a detailed listing of club dates and concerts.

Keep in mind that big-name artists often perform at casinos in Tunica, just over the state line in Mississippi. Many of these shows are advertised in Memphis media outlets, or check out the upcoming events on the Tunica Convention and Visitors Bureau website, www.tunicamiss.com.

Blues

One of the first things you should do when you get to Memphis is to find out if the **Center for Southern Folklore** (119 S. Main St., 901/525-3655, www.southernfolklore.com, Sun.-Thurs. noon-8, am, 11am-11pm Fri.-Sat.) has concerts or activities planned during your stay. The center has been documenting and preserving traditional Memphis and Delta blues music since the 1970s. The free self-guided tour of all things traditional-Southern leads you through Heritage Hall. This is also the location of concerts, lectures, and screenings of documentaries; they offer group tours and educational programs, and host the annual Memphis Music and Heritage Festival over Labor Day weekend. It often has live blues on Friday afternoon and offers a variety of special shows. This is one of the best places to hear authentic blues. The folklore store sells folk art, books, CDs, and traditional Southern food, and often hosts live music on Friday and Saturday nights. A sign stating "Be Nice or Leave" sets the tone as soon as you step into this colorful and eclectic shop, one of the best gift shops in the city. The center is a nonprofit organization and well worth supporting. You'll find live music in the Folklore Store most Friday and Saturday nights starting around 8pm.

Beale Street is ground zero for Memphis's blues music scene. While some people lament that Beale has become a sad tourist shell of its former self, it can still be a worthwhile place to spend your evening. Indeed, no other part of Memphis has as much music and entertainment encompassing such a small area. On a typical night, Beale Street is packed with a diverse crowd strolling from one bar to the next. Beer seems to run a close second to music as the street's prime attraction, with many bars selling directly onto the street through concession windows. The "Big Ass Beer" cups used by many establishments say it all.

Nearly all Beale Street bars have live music, but one of the most popular is **B. B. King's Blues Club** (143 Beale St., 901/524-5464, www.bbkingclubs.com/memphis, Sun.-Thurs. 11am-midnight, Fri.-Sat. 11am-2am, on weekends typically there is a $3-5 cover, rarely on weekdays), owned by the legend himself. B. B. King performs here two or three times a year—keep your ear to the ground since the shows are not usually advertised. On other evenings, local acts and some nationally known performers take the stage. B. B. King's draws a mostly tourist crowd, and it is a chain, but with the blues on full throttle, you probably won't care too much.

Also on Beale Street, **Blues City Café** (138 Beale St., 901/526-3637, www.bluescitycafe.com, Sun.-Thurs. 11am-3am, Fri.-Sat. 11am-5am, cover $3-5,) books blues, plus a variety of other acts including doo-wop, zydeco, R&B, funk, and "high-impact rockabilly." The café-restaurant is one of the most popular on Beale Street, and its nightclub, **Rum Boogie Café** (rumboogie.com, 11am–2am daily, cover $3-5), has an award-winning house band, James Covan and the Boogie Blues Band, that performs most evenings.

Jazz

If you want a break from the blues, **King's Palace Café** (162 Beale St., 901/521-1851, Mon.-Thurs. 11am-10pm, Fri.-Sat. 11am-10:30pm, Sun. 11am-9:30pm, www.kingspalacecafe.com) specializes in jazz. Lots of wood paneling and red paint make the bar and Cajun restaurant warm and welcoming. This is an unpretentious place to have a meal or listen to live music. There is a $1 per person entertainment charge when you sit at a table.

Rock

Still on Beale Street, **Alfred's** (197 Beale St., 901/525-3711, www.alfredsonbeale.com, Sun.-Thurs. 11am-3am, Fri.-Sat. 11am-5am, cover $5 Fri. and Sat.) has rock acts five nights a week. On Sunday evening, the 17-piece Memphis Jazz Orchestra takes the stage. The dance floor at Alfred's is one of the best on Beale Street.

One of Beale Street's most historic concert venues, **The New Daisy** (330 Beale St., 901/525-8981, newdaisy.com, box office Tues. and Fri. 10am-6pm, Sat. noon-4pm, cover $10 and up, ticket costs vary) books rock 'n' roll, independent, and a few R&B acts. There are shows most nights of the week; call ahead or check the entertainment listings for a schedule. The Daisy is an all-ages club, and many shows attract a young audience.

Off Beale Street, the **Hi-Tone Café** (412-414 N. Cleveland, 901/490-0335, daily 5pm-3am, www.hitonememphis.com, cover varies, $2 charge for under 21) is probably the best place to see live music in town. The Hi-Tone books all kinds of acts, from high-energy rockers to soulful acoustic acts. They are really committed to bringing good live music to Memphis. The cover charge for local shows is a few bucks, but tickets for bigger-name acts can run $20 and more. The bar serves respectable burgers and finger foods, excellent martinis, and lots of beer.

Also in Midtown, **The Buccaneer** (1368 Monroe, 901/278-0909, daily 5pm-3am, cover varies) books rock acts most days a week. Cover charge rarely tops $5.

BARS

Downtown

You can head to Beale Street for a night out, regardless of whether or not you sing the blues.

Memphis Juke Joints

In Memphis, there are only two reasons to go to a juke joint full of blues: because you feel good or because you feel bad. Beale Street is a reliable source seven nights a week, and your visit to Memphis wouldn't be complete without checking out its scene. But if you want to sneak away from the tourist crowd and catch some homegrown talent, check out a real Memphis juke joint. Live music is typical on Friday and Saturday nights and sometimes Sunday, but it gets scarce during the week. Generally music starts late (11pm) and finishes early (3am). Don't be surprised if the person you've engaged in conversation sitting next to you gets called to the stage sometime during the evening and delivers a beautiful song.

Remember that it's in the nature of things for these clubs to come and go. The following listings were current as of this writing, but they are always subject to change.

- **Wild Bill's** (1580 Vollintine Ave., 901/207-3075): A legendary club in Memphis. The Patriarch himself passed away in the summer of 2007, but what he established will still carry on. The quintessential juke joint. Small, intimate, an open kitchen serving chicken wings, and ice-cold beer served in 40-ounce bottles. Home to Ms. Nikki and the Memphis Soul Survivors.
- **CC's Blues Club** (1427 Thomas St., 901/526-5566): More upscale. More mirrors. But a great dance floor, and don't you dare come underdressed. Security guards patrol the parking lot.
- **Mr. Handy's Blues Hall** (182 Beale St., 901/528-0150): New Orleans has Preservation Hall. Memphis has Handy's Blues Hall. Everyone bad-raps Beale Street and its jangly tourism scene, but if you catch it on a good night, when Dr. Feelgood warms up his harmonica and you look around the room at the memorabilia on the walls, you could be in a joint at the end of a country road in Mississippi.

The best place to grab a beer downtown is the **Beale Street Tap Room** (168 Beale St., 901/521-1851). With more than 30 beers on tap, this is a great choice for beer lovers. The service is friendly and low-key, and regulars have their own mug.

Off Beale Street, **The Peabody Hotel Memphis** (149 Union Ave., 901/529-4000, www.peabodymemphis.com) may be the best place to enjoy a relaxing drink. The lobby bar offers good service, comfortable seats, and an unrivaled atmosphere.

On Peabody Place, about a block from Beale Street, the **Flying Saucer Draught Emporium** (130 Peabody Pl., 901/523-8536, www.beerknurd.com) draws a lively happy-hour crowd. The bar offers more than 75 draft beers, plus cocktails and wine. Grab a seat along the windows and watch downtown Memphis come alive as the sun sets.

In the South Main district, **Ernestine and Hazel's** (531 S. Main St., 901/523-9754, earnestineandhazelsjukejoint.com) is one of Memphis's most celebrated pit stops for cold drinks and a night out. Once a brothel, Ernestine and Hazel's now has one of the best jukeboxes in town. Take a seat upstairs in one of the old brothel rooms and watch South Main Street below. Rumor is the joint is haunted, but folks come here for the jukebox, not the spirits.

If beer's your thing, check out the growler station at **Joe's Wine & Beer** (1681 Poplar Ave., 901/725-4252, joeswinesandliquor.com). Behind this iconic signage you'll find 20 beer taps and 10 wine taps.

Midtown

The **Young Avenue Deli** (2119 Young Ave., 901/278-0034, www.youngavenuedeli.com, daily 11am-3am, kitchen closes at 2am) is a friendly neighborhood bar that books occasional live acts. Located in the hip Cooper-Young neighborhood, Young Avenue Deli has hundreds of different beers on tap or in bottles. The bar attracts a diverse crowd, from young hipsters to older neighborhood denizens.

A favorite place for music, pool, and a night out in midtown is the **Blue Monkey** (2012 Madison Ave., 901/272-2583, www.bluemonkeymemphis.com, daily 11am-3am). Grab a pizza and a beer, shoot some pool, and then rock out to the live band. There's a second location downtown (513 S. Front St., 901/527-6665).

Murphy's (1589 Madison Ave., 901/726-4193, www.murphysmemphis.com, Mon.-Sat. 11am-3am, Sun. noon-3am) is a neighborhood bar with a nice patio.

Perfect for a business date or after-work pit stop, **The Grove Grill** (4550 Poplar Ave., 901/818-9951, www.thegrovegrill.com, Sun.-Thurs. 11am-9pm, Fri.-Sat. 11am-10pm) is popular with businesspeople and office workers.

Two of Memphis's best sports bars are found in the eastern reaches of the city. **Brookhaven Pub & Grill** (695 W. Brookhaven Cir., 901/680-8118, www.brookhavenpubandgrill.com, daily 11am-2am) has big-screen plasma televisions, great beer on tap, and lots of fans. Tuesday night is Team Trivia night.

There's more to do than just watch the game at **Rec Room** (3000 Broad Ave., 901/209-1137, recroommemphis.com, 4pm-midnight Mon.-Thurs., 4pm-2am Fri., 11am-2am Sat., 11am-midnight Sun.). In addition to oversized screens for sports-watching, you can also get your game on with vintage video games, board games, and tabletop games such as foosball and Ping-Pong. Though Rec Room doesn't have a menu of its own, food trucks regularly pull up to the patio to tend to customers' cravings. Kids are welcome before 5pm if escorted by an adult; after 5pm, it's 18 and up.

A modern reboot of a historic music venue, **Lafayette's Music Room** (2119 Madison Ave. 901/207-5097, lafayettes.com/memphis, 11am-10:30pm Mon.-Wed., 11am-midnight Thurs., 11am-2am Fri.-Sat., 11am-midnight Sun., $15-24) features live music every night, a two-story patio and Southern-inspired fare.

GAY AND LESBIAN NIGHTLIFE

Many Memphis gay and lesbian clubs don't get going until late night, after other clubs have closed.

Dru's Place (1474 Madison Ave., 901/275-8082, www.drusplace.com, Sun.-Thurs. 1pm-midnight, Fri.-Sat. 1pm-2am) is a welcoming bar that has weekly Drag Time and Beer Bust. The beer is cold and the liquor is BYO.

Club Spectrum Memphis (600-616 Marshall Ave., 901/292-2292, Fri.-Sat. 9pm-4am) is a gay-, lesbian-, and everyone-welcome dance club. This is a weekend-only spot to get your groove on.

The Pumping Station (1382 Poplar Ave., 901/272-7600, thepumpingstationmemphis.com, Mon.-Fri. 4pm-3am, Sat.-Sun. 3pm-3am) is one of the city's favorite gay bars, with a full bar, craft beers on tap, and an outdoor beer garden (called The Backdoor Lounge, which is the only place you can smoke). It is housed in a building that once allowed a Jewish couple, evicted from another location, to open a liquor store, and is proud of its inclusive historical roots.

THE ARTS

Memphis has a growing arts scene. **ArtsMemphis** (901/578-2787, www.artsmemphis.org) provides funding for more than 20 local arts groups and is a reliable source of information about upcoming events.

Major arts venues include the **Cannon Center for the Performing Arts** (255 N. Main St., 901/576-1200, www.thecannoncenter.com) and the **Orpheum Theatre** (Main and Beale Sts. 203 S. Main St, 901/525-3000, www.orpheum-memphis.com). They regularly book major artists and Broadway performances.

Theater

For theater, check out **Playhouse on the Square** (66 S. Cooper St., 901/726-4656, www.playhouseonthesquare.org). This dynamic Memphis institution serves as home to several of the city's acting companies and puts on 15-20 different performances every year. It also offers theater classes, school performances, and pay-what-you-can shows.

Theatre Memphis (630 Perkins Ext., 901/682-8323, www.theatrememphis.org) is a community theater company that has been in existence since the 1920s. It stages about 12 shows annually at its theater in midtown.

TheatreWorks (2085 Monroe Ave., 901/274-7139, www.theatreworksmemphis.org) and **Evergreen Theatre** (1705 Poplar Ave., 901/274-7139) encourage nontraditional and new theater with organizations, including Our Own Voice Theatre Troupe; Bluff City Tri-Art Theatre Company; Cazateatro, Emerald Theatre Company; FreakEngine; Inner City South; New; Threepenny Theatre, and others.

Music

The **Memphis Symphony Orchestra** (585 S. Mendenhall Rd., 901/537-2525, www.memphissymphony.org) performs on a varied calendar of works year-round in its home at the Cannon Center for the Performing Arts at 2155 North Main Street. The symphony was founded in 1952 and today has more than 850 musicians, staff, and volunteers.

Opera

Opera Memphis (6745 Wolf River Blvd., 901/257-3100, www.operamemphis.org) performs traditional opera at a variety of venues around town, including the historic Playhouse on the Square and the Germantown Performing Arts Centre. For the 30 days of September the company performs "pop-up" operas at different locations around the city.

Dance

Ballet Memphis (901/737-7322, www.balletmemphis.org) performs classical dance at the Playhouse on the Square, the Orpheum and other venues throughout the city. The **New Ballet Ensemble** (901/726-9225, www.newballet.org) puts on performances around the city with "dancers in do-rags as well as tights," in the words of the *Commercial Appeal*.

Cinemas

There are a half-dozen multiscreen movie theaters in and around Memphis. For independent movies, try **Malco's Paradiso** (584 S. Mendenhall Rd., 901/682-1754, www.malco.com) or **Studio on the Square** (2105 Court St., 901/725-7151, www.malco.com). In the summer, check out the **Orpheum** (203 S. Main St., 901/525-3000) for classic movies,

Catch a show at the Cannon Center for the Performing Arts.

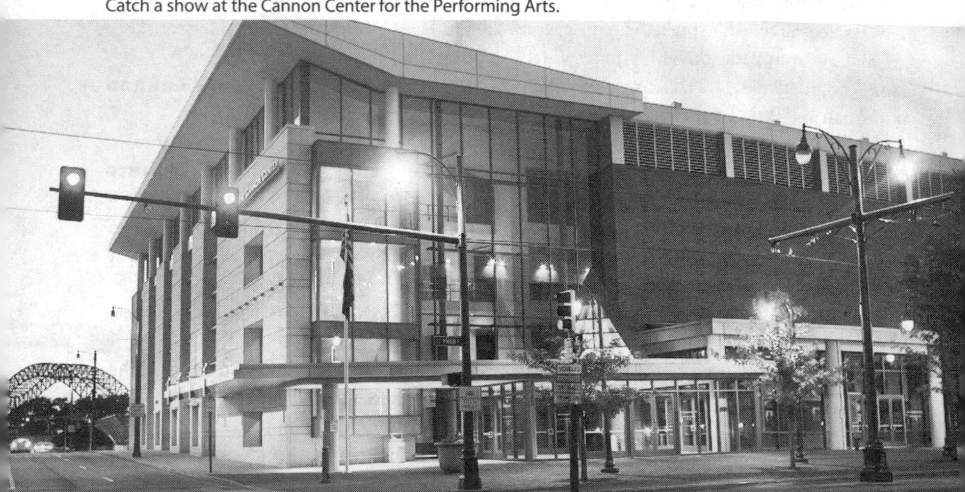

and the **Malco Summer 4 Drive-In** (5310 Summer Ave., 901/767-4320) for an outdoor movie-watching experience.

FESTIVALS AND EVENTS

Spring

Memphians celebrate their African heritage over a long weekend in mid-April. **Africa in April** (901/947-2133, www.africainapril.org) honors a specific country in Africa each year. Activities include cooking, storytelling, music, and a parade. The festival takes place at Church Park on the east end of Beale Street.

In early May, the Memphis-based Blues Foundation hosts the annual **Blues Music Awards** (www.blues.org), the Grammys of the blues world. Per the foundation, a nominee announcement, as well as ticket information for the event, is released each year in mid-December on their website.

Memphis in May (www.memphisinmay.org), the city's largest annual event, is really three major festivals rolled into one. The **Beale Street Music Festival,** which takes place at Tom Lee Park on the river, kicks things off with a celebration of Memphis music. Expect a lot of wow-worthy performers, plus many more up-and-coming talents. The festival has grown over the years, and it is now a three-day event with four stages of music going simultaneously. In addition to music, the festival offers excellent people-watching, lots of barbecue, cold beer, and festivity. You can buy daily tickets or a three-day pass for the whole weekend.

In mid-May, attention turns to the **World Championship Barbecue Cooking Contest,** a celebration of pork, pigs, and barbecue that takes place in Tom Lee Park. In addition to the barbecue judging, there is entertainment, hog-calling contests, and other piggy antics. If you're not part of a competing team (or friends with one), you can buy barbecue from vendors who set up in the park.

Finally, there's the **Memphis International Festival,** which pays tribute to a different country each year with presentations about its music, food, culture, and history.

A sunset symphony caps off the month-long festivities. Book your hotel rooms early for Memphis in May, since many hotels, particularly those in downtown, sell out.

Summer

Don't let the name fool you, **Carnival Memphis** (901/458-2500, www.carnivalmemphis.org) is a Mardi Gras-style celebration, not a fairgrounds-esque event. It features a parade, fireworks, a ball, and more. This festival, once called Cotton Carnival, was segregated for decades, but since the mid-1980s has been racially integrated. This celebration raises funds for local children's charities. Like carnivals elsewhere in the south, Carnival Memphis consists of several events, including the Crown & Sceptre Ball, Princess Ball, and a luncheon for businesses. Carnival members (who pledge $75-2500 in fees) get discounted tickets or tickets included in their membership, depending on their contribution. Public ticket prices are released annually on the website.

The annual candlelight vigil at Graceland on August 15, the anniversary of Elvis's death, has grown into a whole week of Elvis-centric activities throughout Memphis. More than 30,000 people visit Graceland during **Elvis Week** (www.elvisweek.com), and during the vigil his most adoring fans walk solemnly up the Graceland drive to pay their respects at his grave. Special concerts, tribute shows, and movies are shown during the week as the city celebrates its most famous son even more than usual.

Fall

Organized by the Center for Southern Folklore, the **Memphis Music and Heritage Festival** (901/525-3655, www.southernfolklore.com), held over Labor Day weekend, sticks close to the roots of Memphis music.

Performers include gospel singers, bona fide bluesmen and women, rockabilly superstars, and much more. Performances take place in the center's shop and concert hall on Main Street, making them more intimate than other blockbuster music festivals.

End-of-summer fairs are a tradition for Southern and rural communities all over the United States. The 10-day **Mid-South Fair** (901/274-8800, www.midsouthfair.org) in September is a bonanza of attractions: livestock shows, rodeos, agricultural judging, concerts, beauty pageants, exhibitions, carnival rides, funnel cakes, and cotton candy. The fair is held in northern Mississippi, about 30 miles south of Memphis.

In mid-September, the Cooper-Young neighborhood throws its annual jamboree at the **Cooper-Young Festival** (www.cooperyoungfestival.com). There is an arts and crafts fair, live music, and food vendors at this street carnival.

The annual **Southern Heritage Classic** (www.southernheritageclassic.com) is one of the South's big football games. But the match of two historically black college rivals, Jackson State University and Tennessee State University, is more than just a game, it is a serious citywide festival.

Forty-six-foot-long boats with dragon heads and tails race at Mud Island River Park each September during the **Duncan-Williams Dragon Boat Races** (www.memphis.racedragonboats.com). Proceeds benefit the work of the Tennessee Clean Water Network.

Winter

The colder weather welcomes a number of sporting events, including the **St. Jude Marathon and Half Marathon** (www.stjudemarathon.org, 800/565-5112) in December, which is a qualifying race for the Boston Marathon. The **AutoZone Liberty Bowl** (www.libertybowl.org, 901/795-7700) typically welcomes two of the National Collegiate Athletic Association's (NCAA) best football teams to town on New Year's Eve.

Taking place over the weekend closest to Elvis Presley's January 8 birthday, the **Elvis Birthday Celebration** (www.elvis.com) draws Elvis fans with special performances, dance parties, and a ceremony at Graceland proclaiming Elvis Presley Day.

The St. Jude Marathon gives runners a chance to run en masse on Beale Street.

Shopping

GIFTS AND SOUVENIRS

Any of the half-dozen shops along Beale Street sell gifts and souvenirs of the city. **Memphis Music** (149 Beale St., 901/526-5047, memphismusicstore.com) has a good selection of CDs and DVDs for music fans. For a unique gift or something practical for yourself, A. Schwab (163 Beale St., 901/523-9782, a-schwab.com) is your best choice and is lots of fun to boot.

Another good place for gift shopping is the **Center for Southern Folklore** (123 S. Main St., 901/525-3655), which has books, art, and music focusing on the region. All of the city's museums have good gift shops, including the **National Civil Rights Museum** (Sun. 1pm-5pm, Mon. and Wed.-Sat. 9am-5pm, closed Tuesday), **Stax Museum of American Soul Music** (Tues.-Sat. 10am-5pm, Sun. 1pm-5pm), and **Sun Studio** (daily 10am-6:15pm), where everything is emblazoned with the distinctive yellow Sun label.

If you have a car, head out to **Shangri-La Records** (1916 Madison Ave., 901/274-1916, www.shangri.com), one of the city's best record stores, which specializes in Memphis music. **Goner Records** (2152 Young Ave., 901/722-0095, Mon.-Sat. noon-7pm, Sun. 1pm-5pm, www.goner-records.com) is both a record store and a record label.

If the gift recipient in your life is a fashion maven, head to **Thigh High Jeans** (525 N. Main, www.thighhighjeans.com) where you can buy embroidered skirts and newly remade jeans created from recycled denim. A percentage of each purchase is donated to local, national and global charities. Or host a party with your friends and select the charity that is benefited.

ART

For art boutiques and galleries, head south to the South Main arts district, where you will find galleries, including **Robinson Gallery/Archives** (44 Huling Ave., 901/619-4478, Mon.-Fri. 10am-5pm, closed Sat. and Sun., www.robinsongallery.com), a photography gallery that houses the work of *Vogue* photographer Jack Robinson, Jr.

On the last Friday of each month the trolleys are free, the galleries stay open, and

Shopping at Goner Records is a Memphis must.

hundreds of arts-minded Memphians head to South Main to mingle into the night. For a directory of all South Main galleries, contact the **South Main Association** (www.gosouthmain.com). The event starts at 6pm and runs "'til the musicians go home."

Since 2003 the **Wings Gallery** (100 N. Humphreys Blvd., 901/322-2984, Mon.-Fri. 8:30am-5pm, closed Sat. and Sun.) has shown the work of artists whose lives have been impacted by cancer. Exhibitions change every six weeks.

ANTIQUES

Head out to Central Avenue between Cooper and East Parkway for the greatest concentration of antiques stores. **Flashback** (2304 Central Ave., 901/272-2304, Mon.-Sat. 10:30am-5:30pm, Sun. 1pm-5pm, www.flashbackmemphis.com) sells both vintage furniture and clothes, including a whole lot of Levi's jeans. **Palladio Antiques and Arts** (2169 Central Ave., 901/276-3808, Mon.-Sat. 10am-5pm, closed Sunday www.thepalladiogroup.com) works with more than 75 dealers to provide a cross-section of styles of finds.

THRIFT STORES

In a city where vintage never went out of style, you can expect excellent thrift stores. The biggest and best is **AmVets** (2526 Elvis Presley Blvd., 901/775-5010, Mon.-Sat. 9am-9pm, Sun. 10am-6pm). You can also try the Junior League of Memphis's **Repeat Boutique Thrift Store** (3586 Summer Ave., 901/327-4777, 10am-5pm Tues.-Sat.).

In a city of characters, the most colorful shopping experience in Memphis is found at **The Memphis Flea Market—The Big One** (in the AgriCenter, 7777 Walnut Grove Rd., 901/276-3532, www.memphisfleamarket.com), which takes place the third weekend of most months, the exceptions are the fourth weekend of February and an extra market the first weekend of December) at the Mid-South Fairgrounds. Between 800 and 1,000 vendors turn up each month with housewares, clothing, computers, jewelry, antiques, yard art, and so much more. Between 20,000 and 25,000 people come to shop. Admission is $3 for adults, free for kids. Parking is free.

SHOPPING MALLS

The most upscale shopping mall in the Memphis area is **Wolfchase Galleria** (2760 N. Germantown Pkwy., 901/372-9409). Located in Cordova, an east-lying suburb now consumed by Memphis sprawl, the galleria is approaching its 20th anniversary. It is now showing its age but still attracts shoppers with national retailers, including Victoria's Secret, Disney, Fossil, Gap, Coach, Abercrombie & Fitch, and Sephora. Department stores at the mall include Macy's, Dillard's, Sears, and JCPenney. You can take either exit 16 or 18 off I-40 to get to Wolfchase Galleria.

Also in Germantown, the swanky **Shops of Saddle Creek** (7509 Poplar Ave., 901/753-4264) has Anthropologie, Brooks Brothers, J. Crew, Vera Bradley, Talbots, Banana Republic, and an Apple computer store, among others.

Closer to the city center, **Oak Court Mall** (4465 Poplar Ave., 901/682-8928) was the location of the first Starbucks in Tennessee. It is also consistently voted Memphians' favorite mall, no doubt because it offers a good selection of stores in a pleasant atmosphere, and it's relatively close to town. Department stores at Oak Court include Macy's and Dillard's; the mall also has Godiva, JoS. A. Bank, Banana Republic, and dozens more stores.

And if that's not enough for you, head across the road to **Laurelwood Shopping Center** (Poplar Ave. at Perkins Ext., 901/682-8436), where you'll find bookstores, specialty clothing and shoe boutiques, as well as special events like free yoga classes.

In South Memphis, **Southland Mall** (1215 Southland Mall, 901/346-7664) is Memphis's oldest mall. Built in 1966 (it was the first enclosed mall in the Mid-South), Southland soldiers on. There is a Sears, as well as specialty shops, including Radio Shack and Bath & Body Works.

OUTLET SHOPPING

Opened in time for the 2015 holiday season, **Tanger Outlets** (5205 Airways Blvd., Southaven, MS, 662/349-1701www.tangeroutlet.com/southaven) has discounted outposts for more than 70 brands, including Michael Kors and LOFT.

Sports and Recreation

With a professional basketball team, excellent downtown baseball club, and lots of city parks, Memphis is a great city in which to both watch sports and get active yourself.

PARKS

Downtown

Named for the legendary blues composer W. C. Handy, **Handy Park,** on Beale Street, between 3rd Street and Rufus Thomas Boulevard, seems a tad out of place among Beale's nightclubs and restaurants. But the park is a site of historical importance, if only because of the statue of its namesake that guards its gates. The park hosts occasional outdoor concerts and festivals, and at other times you will find places to sit and a handful of vendors.

Uptown

Tom Lee Park, a long, 30-acre, narrow grassy park that overlooks the Mississippi, is a popular venue for summertime festivals and events, including the Memphis in May BBQ Festival. It is also used year-round for walking and jogging and by people who simply want to look out at the giant river. The park is named for Tom Lee, an African American man who saved the lives of 32 people when the steamboat they were on sank in the river in 1925. Lee, who pulled people out of the river and into his boat, "Zev," could not even swim. An outmoded monument erected at the park in 1954 calls Lee "a very worthy negro."

Located on the northern side of downtown Memphis, **Court Square,** three blocks from the waterfront along Court Avenue, is a pleasant city park surrounded by historic buildings. Court Square is one of four parks that was included when the city was first planned in 1819. There are benches and trees, and it is a wireless Internet hot spot.

Memphis Park, located on Front Street between Court and Jefferson Streets, commemorates Civil War soldiers who died in the Battle of Memphis. There is a statue of Jefferson Davis in the center of the park. This is where many Memphians gathered to watch the Battle of Memphis in 1862, and it remains a good place to view the river below.

Midtown

Located in midtown Memphis, **Overton Park** (1928 Poplar Ave.) is one of the best all-around parks the city has to offer. This 342-acre park has a nine-hole golf course, nature trails through the woods, bike trails, an outdoor amphitheater now called the Levitt Shell, and lots of green, open spaces. The park shares space with the Memphis Zoo and the Memphis Brooks Museum of Art, making the area a popular destination for city residents and visitors. Patience may be required when looking for a parking spot during an event at Overton.

The Madison Avenue trolley passes **Forrest Park,** along Madison Avenue, between North Manassas and North Dunlap Streets, an ample city park dedicated to the memory of the controversial Nathan Bedford Forrest. Forrest, a slave trader, Confederate, and the first grand wizard of the Ku Klux Klan, has an uncomfortable position of prominence in Memphis and the whole of western Tennessee. Both he and his wife are buried in the park.

South Memphis

Southwest of the city center, about 15 minutes' drive from the airport, is **T. O. Fuller State Park** (1500 Mitchell Rd., 901/543-7581). The visitors center here is open weekdays 8am-sunset. Amenities at the 1,138-acre park include sheltered picnic areas, tennis courts, a golf course, a swimming pool ($3), basketball courts, a softball field, six miles of hiking trails, and camping facilities. T. O. Fuller State Park was the first state park east of the Mississippi River open to African Americans, and the second in the nation. An outdoor Environmental Interpretive Learning Center is in the planning stages at T. O. Fuller State Park.

East Memphis

Located near the University of Memphis and Oak Court Mall, **Audubon Park** (4161 Park Ave.) has a golf course, tennis courts, walking trails, and other sports facilities. The Memphis Botanic Garden is located here.

Memphians celebrate the fact that their largest city park, **Shelby Farms** (www.shelbyfarmspark.org), is five times the size of New York's Central Park. But the fact is that Shelby Farms is underused, because most of its 4,500 acres are pleasantly undeveloped. There are plans to improve the park by adding more recreational facilities: a new visitors center, retreat center, event pavilion, boat kiosk, and wetland walk with new trails are envisioned. A zip line is also in the works.

More than 500,000 people come here annually to go mountain biking, horseback riding, inline skating, walking, or running along some of the many trails. You can also fish, raft, canoe, or sail on any of the park's six lakes. There is a wheelchair-accessible trail, areas for picnicking, and a shooting range. Shelby Farms was originally set aside to be the county penal farm, and although it was not used in this way, the county jail is found on the western edge of the park. Shelby Farms is located on the eastern side of the city, just outside the I-40/I-240 loop that circles Memphis. It is easily accessible from exits 12 and 14 off I-40, and exit 13 off I-240. Or follow Walnut Grove Road from midtown.

BIKING

Most cyclists in the city bike as a form of recreation, rather than transportation. The City of Memphis has established five bike routes that circle the city and various neighborhoods. These routes are marked and have

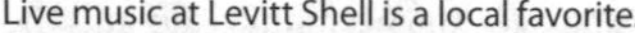
Live music at Levitt Shell is a local favorite.

designated parking and restroom facilities at the start. They are not bike paths—you share the road with cars—and normal safety measures are necessary.

The **Memphis Hightailers Bicycle Club** (www.memphishightailers.com) organizes frequent rides for various levels, with distances ranging 20-100 miles. Regularly scheduled Urban Bicycle Food Ministry rides are listed for people to help distribute food while riding 10-12 miles. For bike rentals, gear, and advice about riding in and around the city, go to **Peddler Bike Shop** (3548 Walker Ave., 901/327-4833, Mon.-Wed. and Fri. 9am-6pm, Sat. 9am-5pm, Sun. 1pm-5pm, closed Thurs., www.peddlerbikeshop.com), where owner Hal Mabray will happily help you get geared up to ride. A used-bike rental will cost about $35 for a half day, $50 per day. Peddler also has locations in Germantown, Tennessee, and Southaven, Mississippi. Opt for a long weekend rate for just $100.

There are a number of parks near Memphis that are bike friendly. **Meeman-Shelby Forest State Park** (910 Riddick Road, 901/876-5215), north of the city, has five miles of paved bike paths, and cyclists use the main park roads for more extensive riding. Bicyclists will also find trails and bike rentals at **Shelby Farms.**

It is also noteworthy that the **Mississippi River Trail,** a bicycle route that runs 3,000 miles from the headwaters of the Mississippi River in Minnesota to the Gulf of Mexico, runs through Memphis and on to Mississippi. For maps and details, go to www.mississippirivertrail.org.

GOLF

The City of Memphis operates award-winning 18-hole golf courses at **Audubon Park** (4160 Park Ave., 901/683-6941), with gently rolling hills; **Fox Meadows** (3064 Clarke Rd., 901/362-0232), which is easy to walk but has several challenging holes; **Galloway Park** (3815 Walnut Grove, 901/685-7805); **Davy Crockett Golf Course** (4380 Rangeline Rd., 901/358-3375); and **Pine Hill Park** (1005 Alice Ave., 901/775-9434), a great course for walkers.

There are two public nine-hole courses: one at **Riverside Park** (465 S. Parkway W., 901/576-4296) and one at **Overton Park** (2080 Poplar Ave., 901/725-9905). Greens fees on the public courses are under $20.

The semiprivate Audubon-certified **Mirimichi** (6195 Woodstock Cuba Rd., 901/259-3800, www.mirimichi.com) in Millington is part-owned by heartthrob Justin Timberlake, a native (and still sometimes) Memphian. Millington is about a 30-minute drive from downtown.

TENNIS

The city operates public tennis courts at several parks, including **Bert Ferguson Park** (8495 Trinity) four outdoor, **Gaisman Park** (4221 Macon) two outdoor, **Glenview** (1885 Highway 78) two courts, **Martin Luther King Jr. Park (Riverside)** (South Pkwy. at Riverside Dr.) four lighted, **University Park** (University at Edward) four outdoor, **Audubon** (4145 Southern Ave.) four indoor/eight outdoor, **Frayser Park** (2907 N. Watkins) eight outdoor, **Hickory Hill** (3910 Ridgeway Rd.) 4 lighted, and **Pierotti** (3678 Powers Rd.) eight lighted (www.tennismemphis.org).

There are also four public indoor/outdoor tennis complexes: **Bellevue at Jesse Turner Park** (1239 Orgill Rd., 901/774-7199, Mon.-Thurs. 3pm-9pm, Fri. 3pm-7:3pm, Sat.-Sun. 9am-3pm); **Leftwich** (4145 Southern, 901/685-7907, Mon.-Fri. 7:30pm-9pm, Sat.-Sun 7:30am-7:30pm); **Whitehaven,** also called **Eldon Roark Tennis Center** (1500 Finley Rd., 901/332-0546, indoor courts Mon.-Thurs. 3pm-9pm, Fri. 3pm-7:30pm, Sat. 9am-6pm, Sun. noon-6pm, outdoor courts Mon.-Thurs. 9am-noon and 3pm-9pm, Fri. 9am-noon and 3pm-6pm, Sat. 9am-3pm, Sun. noon-6pm); and **Wolbrecht** (1645 Ridgeway, 901/767-2889, Mon.-Fri. 7:30am-9pm, Sat.-Sun. 7:30am-7:30pm). Fees vary per facility; call in advance for information and court reservations.

GYMS

Out-of-towners can get a day pass to the **Louis T. Fogelman Downtown YMCA** (245 Madison Ave., 901/527-9622, 5am-10pm Mon.-Thurs., 5am-8pm Fri., 7am-5pm Sat., noon-5pm Sun., day pass $10 to use the indoor pool and track, and extensive gym facilities). City residents can buy one of the membership packages.

SPECTATOR SPORTS

Basketball

In 2001, Memphis realized the dream of many in the Mid-South when the Vancouver Grizzlies announced they would be moving south. The National Basketball Association (NBA) team played its first two seasons in Memphis at the Pyramid before the massive $250 million FedEx Forum opened for the 2004-2005 season. The arena is one of the largest in the NBA and hosts frequent concerts and performances by major artists.

The **Grizzlies** have yet to achieve any major titles, but their finals and playoffs rankings keep fans coming back. Ticket prices range from under $20 to several hundred dollars. For ticket information, contact the **FedEx Forum box office** (191 Beale St., 901/205-2640, www.fedexforum.com, 10am-5:30pm Mon.-Fri.) or purchase through Ticketmaster. The NBA season runs October-April.

The **University of Memphis Tigers** surprised many in 2008 by making it all the way to the men's NCAA Championship. The team's remarkable 38-2 season brought new energy and excitement to the university's basketball program that continues today.

You can watch Tigers basketball November-April at FedEx Forum. Tickets are available from the FedEx Forum box office, or contact University of Memphis Athletics (www.gotigersgo.com) for more information.

Baseball

From April to October, the **Memphis Redbirds** (901/721-6000, www.memphisredbirds.com, $6-26) play AAA ball at the striking **AutoZone Park** in downtown Memphis. The stadium is bounded by Union Avenue, Madison Avenue, and 3rd Street, and is convenient to dozens of downtown hotels and restaurants. The Redbirds are an affiliate of the St. Louis Cardinals. Cheap tickets ($6) buy you a seat on the grassy berm, or you can pay a little more for seats in the stadium or boxes.

The Memphis Redbirds play at Autozone Park.

The Redbirds are owned by a nonprofit organization that also operates a number of community and youth programs in the city.

Racing

The **Memphis International Raceway** (550 Victory Ln., 901/969-7223, www.racemir.com) is located a short drive from downtown Memphis in Millington, northeast of the city center. The park includes a 0.75-mile NASCAR oval, a 0.25-mile drag racing strip, and a 1.77-mile road course. It hosts more than 200 race events every year, including a stop in the annual Busch Series races.

Millington is located about 30 minutes' drive north of Memphis. From the west, take I-40 E toward Nashville. From the east, take I-40 W toward Memphis.

Ice Hockey

The **RiverKings** (662/342-1755, www.riverkings.com, $5-30, Oct.-Apr.) play minor-league ice hockey at the **Landers Center** (4650 Venture Dr., Southaven, MS), about 20 miles south of Memphis off I-55.

Accommodations

There are thousands of cookie-cutter hotel rooms in Memphis, but travelers would be wise to look past major chains. If you can afford it, choose to stay in downtown Memphis. With the city at your doorstep, you'll have a better experience both day and night. Downtown is also where you'll find the most distinctive accommodations, including fine luxury hotels, charming inns, and an antebellum guest home.

Budget travelers have their pick of major chain hotels; the farther from the city center, the cheaper the room. Beware of very good deals, however, since you may find yourself in sketchy neighborhoods. There is a campground with tent and RV sites within a 15-minute drive of downtown at T. O. Fuller State Park.

DOWNTOWN

$150-200

The ★ **Talbot Heirs Guesthouse** (99 S. 2nd St., 901/527-9772, www.talbotheirs.com, $130-275), in the heart of downtown, offers a winning balance of comfort and sophistication. Each of the inn's eight rooms has its own unique decor—from cheerful red walls to black-and-white chic. All rooms are thoughtfully outfitted with a full kitchen and modern bathroom, television, radio and CD player, sitting area, desk, and high-speed Internet. Little extras, like the refrigerator stocked for breakfast, go a long way, as does the cheerful yet efficient welcome provided by proprietors Tom and Sandy Franck. Book early since the Talbot Heirs is often full, especially during peak summer months.

Over $200

In 2007, Memphis welcomed the **Westin Memphis Beale Street** (170 George W. Lee Ave., 901/334-5900, $195-369), located across the street from FedEx Forum and one block from Beale Street. The hotel's 203 guest rooms are plush and modern, each with a work desk, high-speed Internet, MP3-player docking station, and super-comfortable beds. The location can be noisy when Beale Street is in full swing. Expect to pay $18 a day for parking.

The **Hampton Inn & Suites** (175 Peabody Pl., 901/260-4000, www.bealestreetsuites.hamptoninn.com, $199-320) is less than a block from Beale Street. The Hampton Inn has 144 standard rooms with high-speed Internet and standard hotel accommodations. The 30 suites ($250) have kitchens and separate living quarters. The entire hotel is nonsmoking. Add $17 per day for parking.

UPTOWN

$100-150

The most affordable downtown accommodations are in chain hotels. One of the best choices is the **Sleep Inn at Court Square** (40 N. Front St., 901/522-9700, $119-299), with 124 simple but clean and well-maintained rooms. Guests have access to a small fitness room, free parking, and a free continental breakfast. For those with a bigger appetite, the excellent Blue Plate Café is just across the square. It's a five-block walk to Beale Street from Court Square, but the trolley runs right past the front door of the hotel. Parking will run you $12 each day.

Even closer to the action is the 71-room **Comfort Inn Downtown** (100 N. Front St., 901/526-0583, $150-184). This hotel is within easy walking distance of all the city-center attractions. Rooms aren't anything special, but the staff is often quite friendly; guests get free breakfast, Internet access, and indoor parking; and there's an outdoor pool. Ask for a room facing west, and you'll have a nice view of the Mississippi River. Parking is $10 a day.

$150-200

Near AutoZone Park and a lot of restaurants is **Doubletree Downtown Memphis** (185 Union Ave., 901/528-1800, $134-299). A 272-room hotel set in the restored Tennessee Hotel, the Doubletree maintains a touch of the old grandeur of the 1929 hotel from which it was crafted. Rooms are large, and there's an outdoor swimming pool and fitness room. Valet parking is $22 or more per night.

If you want to be in the middle of things but can't afford to stay at the swanky Peabody, consider the **Holiday Inn Select** (160 Union Ave., 901/525-5491, www.hisdowntownmemphis.com, $139-199). Located across the street from the Peabody and near AutoZone Park, this Holiday Inn routinely gets good reviews from travelers.

Over $200

★ **The Peabody Memphis** (149 Union Ave., 901/529-4000 or 800/732-2639, www.peabodymemphis.com, $219-2,500 for a presidential suite) is the city's signature hotel. Founded in 1869, the Peabody was the grand hotel of the South, and the hotel has preserved some of its traditional Southern charm. Tuxedoed bellhops greet you at the door, and all guests receive a complimentary shoeshine. Rooms are nicely appointed with plantation-style furniture, free wireless Internet, and in-room safes, as well as all the amenities typical of an upper-tier hotel. Several fine restaurants are located on the ground floor, including the lobby bar, which is the gathering place for the twice-daily red carpet march of the famous Peabody ducks.

One of Memphis's newer hotels is the **River Inn of Harbor Town** (50 Harbor Town Sq., 901/260-3333, www.riverinnmemphis.com, $257-625). A 28-room boutique hotel on Mud Island, the River Inn offers great river views and a unique location that is just minutes from downtown. Set in the mixed residential and commercial New Urban community of Harbor Town, the River Inn provides guests with super amenities like a fitness center, reading rooms, free wireless Internet, free

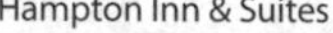
Hampton Inn & Suites

parking, modern decor and furniture, two restaurants, a 1.5-mile walking trail, and spa. Even the most modest rooms have luxurious extras like 32-inch flat-screen televisions, chocolate truffle turndown service, and full gourmet breakfast at Currents, one of two restaurants on the property. The River Inn offers the best of both worlds—a relaxing and quiet getaway that is uniquely convenient to the center of Memphis.

The decor at the **Madison Hotel** (79 Madison Ave., 901/333-1200, www.madisonhotelmemphis.com, $200-2,500) is modern, with a touch of art deco. Guests enjoy every perk you can imagine, from valet parking to room service from one of the city's finest restaurants, Grill 83. The daily continental breakfast and afternoon happy hour are an opportunity to enjoy the view from the top floor of the old bank building that houses the hotel. The 110 rooms have wet bars, Internet access, and luxurious bathrooms.

It is hard to describe the **Big Cypress Lodge** (1 Bass Pro Dr., 800/225-6343, bigcypress.com, $225-1,475) without making is sound a little crazy. First of all, this 103-room hotel is inside a giant pyramid that houses a Bass Pro Shop retail store. Opulent rooms are designed to look like treehouses and duck-hunting cabins. Rooms overlook the cypress swamp filled with alligators and fish and the retail shopping of the Bass Pro Shop. But for all its quirkiness, this hotel, which opened in 2015, is a luxury resort, with all the associated amenities, including a spa and a bowling alley. Expect to pay a $20 resort fee plus $20 per day for parking.

MIDTOWN

Midtown hotels are cheaper than those in downtown. By car, they are convenient to city-center attractions as well as those in midtown itself.

Under $100

There are a few budget hotels within trolley distance of downtown. The **Quality Inn** (42 S. Camilla St., 901/526-1050, $72) is about two blocks from the Madison Avenue trolley and has an unremarkable but free breakfast. The **Motel 6** (210 S. Pauline St., 901/528-0650, $50-72) is about three blocks from the trolley. These choices are certainly not ritzy, but they're acceptable and welcome a large number of budget travelers.

$100-150

The **Best Western Gen X Inn** (1177 Madison

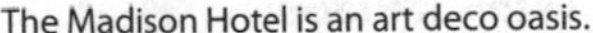

The Madison Hotel is an art deco oasis.

Ave., 901/692-9136, $100-200) straddles downtown and midtown Memphis. Located about two miles from the city center along the Madison Avenue trolley line, Gen Xers can get downtown on the trolley in about 15 minutes, with a little luck. The hotel, which has free parking and breakfast, is also accessible to the city's expansive medical center and the attractions around Overton Park. These rooms are standard hotel style, enhanced with bright colors, flat-panel plasma TVs, and a general aura of youthfulness. The whole hotel is nonsmoking, and guests enjoy a good continental breakfast and a special partnership with the downtown YMCA for gym use. This is a good choice for travelers who want to be near downtown but are on a budget, particularly those with a car. No pets are permitted here.

$150-200

The **Holiday Inn-University of Memphis** (3700 Central Ave., 901/678-8200, $132-165) is part of the university's hospitality school. All rooms are suites, with a wet bar and microwave, sitting room, and spacious bathrooms. The lobby contains an exhibit on Kemmons Wilson, the Memphis-born founder of Holiday Inn, who is credited with inventing the modern hotel industry. It is located about six miles from downtown Memphis.

Over $200

The five rooms available in **The James Lee House** (690 Adams Ave, jamesleehouse.com, 901/359-6750, $245-450) may be in one of the most opulent homes you've had the pleasure to stay in. The building may have been built in the 19th century, but the inn's amenities, such as wireless Internet and private gated parking, are 21st century.

You can sleep where Elvis slept at ★ **Lauderdale Courts** (252 N. Lauderdale St., 901/523-8662, $250). The onetime housing project where Elvis and his parents lived after they moved to Memphis from Mississippi is now a neat midtown apartment complex. The rooms where the Presleys lived have been restored to their 1950s greatness, and guests can use the working 1951 Frigidaire. The rooms are decorated with Presley family photographs and other Elvis memorabilia. You can rent Lauderdale Courts No. 328 for up to six nights. It sleeps up to four adults. The rooms are not rented during Elvis Week in August or his birthday week in January, when the suite is open for public viewing for $10 per person.

SOUTH MEMPHIS

There are two reasons to stay in south Memphis: the airport and Graceland. But even if you are keenly interested in either of these places, you should think twice about staying in this part of town. You will need a car, as some of these neighborhoods are seedy and south Memphis is not within walking distance of anything of interest.

Under $100

If you need to be close to the airport, the **Holiday Inn Memphis Airport Hotel & Conference Center** (2240 Democrat Rd., 901/332-1130, $100-160), which caters to business travelers, gets points for location, if not much else. There is a guest laundry, free airport shuttle, room service, a business center, and a decent fitness room.

You can't sleep much closer to Graceland than the **Days Inn at Graceland** (3839 Elvis Presley Blvd., 901/346-5500, $55-110), one of the most well-worn properties in the venerable Days Inn chain. The hotel has amped up the Elvis kitsch; you can tune into free nonstop Elvis movies or swim in a guitar-shaped pool. There is a free continental breakfast. Book early for Elvis Week.

The renovated **Kings Signature Hotel Airport/Graceland** (1471 E. Brooks Rd., 901/332-3500, www.cedarstreethospitality.com/thecedarhotel.php, $54-80) is a tidy, safe oasis in an otherwise unappealing part of town. Before its remodel, being close to Graceland and the airport were the only draws of this budget hotel. It remains affordable, but now it has the added perk of being clean, with updated rooms and bathrooms, plus a new restaurant and bar. There's a nice outdoor pool, a small fitness room, and a lovely lobby. Book early for Elvis Week.

$100-150

For the most Elvis-y Graceland digs, why not give in and stay at the **Elvis Presley Heartbreak Hotel** (3677 Elvis Presley Blvd., 901/332-1000, www.heartbreakhotel.net, $115-155)? This 128-room hotel has special Elvis-themed suites ($555-605), and the lobby and common areas have a special Elvis flair. Elvis enthusiasts should check out special package deals with the hotel and Graceland.

CAMPING

You can pitch your tent or park your RV just a 15-minute drive from downtown Memphis at **T. O. Fuller State Park** (1500 Mitchell Rd., 901/543-7581, tnstateparks.itinio.com/t-o-fuller, $20). The park has 45 tent and RV sites, each with a picnic table, fire ring, grill, lantern hanger, and electrical and water hookups.

On the north side of Memphis, **Meeman-Shelby Forest State Park** (910 Riddick Rd., Millington, 901/876-5215, $20) is a half-hour drive from downtown. Stay in one of six lakeside cabins, which you can reserve up to one year in advance; book at least one month in advance to avoid being shut out. The two-bedroom cabins can sleep up to six people. Rates are $85-100 per night, depending on the season and day of the week. There are also 49 tent/RV sites, each with electrical and water hookups, picnic tables, grills, and fire rings. The bathhouse has hot showers.

Food

Eating may be the best thing about visiting Memphis. The city's culinary specialties start—but don't end—with barbecue. Plate-lunch diners around the city offer delectable corn bread, fried chicken, greens, fried green tomatoes, peach cobbler, and dozens of other Southern specialties on a daily basis. And to make it even better, such down-home restaurants are easy on your wallet. For those seeking a departure from home-style fare, Memphis has dozens of fine restaurants, some old established eateries and others newcomers that are as trendy as those in any major American city.

Not sure where to start? Try a **Tastin' 'Round Town** food tour (901/310-9789, tastinroundtown.com). Choose from barbecue for $65 or Taste of Memphis for $48. These walking tours are multi-restaurant experiences that let you sample some of the city's best.

Memphis also has a decent food truck scene. Find one of the 45 trucks out and about (memphisfoodtruckers.org).

CAFÉS AND DINERS

Downtown

You can order deli sandwiches, breakfast plates, and a limited variety of plate lunches at the **Front Street Deli** (77 S. Front St., 901/522-8943, 7am-3pm Mon.-Fri., 8am-3pm Sat., $4-9, frontstreetdelicatessen.com). The deli, which claims to be Memphis's oldest, serves breakfast and lunch on weekdays only. One of its claims to fame is that scenes from *The Firm* were filmed here.

For the best burgers on Beale Street, go to **Dyer's** (205 Beale St., 901/527-3937, www.dyersonbeale.com, 11am-1am Sun.-Thurs., 11am-5am Fri.-Sat., $7-12). The legend is that Dyer's Burgers' secret is that it has been using the same grease (strained daily) since it opened in 1912. Only in Tennessee could century-old grease be a selling point. True or not, the burgers here are especially juicy. Dyer's also serves wings, hot dogs, milk shakes, and a full array of fried sides.

For coffee, pastries, and fruit smoothies,

Bluff City Coffee (505 S. Main St., 901/405-4399, www.bluffcitycoffee.com, 6:30am-6pm Mon.-Sat., 8am-6pm Sun., $2-7.50) is your best bet in this part of the city. Located in the South Main district of galleries and condos, the shop is decorated with large prints of vintage Memphis photographs, and it is also a wireless Internet hot spot.

Midtown

No restaurant has a larger or more loyal following in midtown than **Young Avenue Deli** (2119 Young Ave., 901/278-0034, www.youngavenuedeli.com, 11am-3am Mon.-Sat., noon-3am Sun., $4-8), which serves a dozen different specialty sandwiches, grill fare, including burgers and chicken sandwiches, plus salads and sides. The Bren—smoked turkey, mushrooms, onions, and cream cheese in a steamed pita—is a deli favorite. The food is certainly good, but it's the atmosphere at this homey yet hip Cooper-Young institution that really pulls in the crowds. There is live music most weekends, and the bar serves a kaleidoscope of domestic and imported beer, including lots of hard-to-find microbrews. The deli serves lunch and dinner daily.

For a good cup of coffee in the Cooper-Young neighborhood, head to **Java Cabana** (2170 Young Ave., 901/272-7210, www.javacabanacoffeehouse.com, 6:30am-10pm Tues.-Thurs., 9am-midnight Fri.-Sat., noon-10pm Sun., $4-7). Java Cabana serves light breakfast fare, including pancakes and omelets, all day. For lunch or later, you can order simple sandwiches or munchies like apple slices and peanut butter, potato chips, or Pop-Tarts.

Coffee shop and general store **City & State** (2625 Broad Ave., 901/249-2406, cityandstate.us, 7am-6pm Mon.-Fri., 8am-6pm Sat., 8am-2pm Sun., $1.50-9) peddles tea, coffee, pastries and sandwiches alongside locally made goods for retail sale, right in the heart of the Broad Avenue Arts District. Note: Credit cards only, no cash.

Restaurant Iris chef Kelly English also runs a more casual restaurant **The Second Line** (2144 Monroe Ave., 901/590-2829, secondlinememphis.com, 5pm-10pm Mon.-Thurs., 5pm-11pm Fri.,11am-11pm Sat., 11am-10pm Sun., $15-18) right next door. The kitchen rolls out New Orleans-inspired classics such as fried oyster po'boys and barbecue shrimp alongside southern dishes with a global twist, like roasted beet and feta shawarma or oyster rangoon.

the outdoor seating at Young Avenue Deli

East Memphis

Porcellino's Craft Butcher (711 W. Brookhaven Circle, 901/762-6656, porcellinoscraftbutcher.com, 7am-9pm Tues.-Sat., $10-28) is first and foremost a butcher shop selling cuts from local farms. It also doubles as a coffee shop in the morning and a sandwich shop come lunchtime, serving meaty options such as roast beef with giardiniera and horseradish aioli on a hoagie. When the sun sets, the space morphs into a cocktail bar serving small plates and heartier entrees centered around fresh cuts from the butcher case.

SOUTHERN

Downtown

Tucked inside an unassuming storefront across from the valet entrance to the Peabody Hotel is **Flying Fish** (105 S. 2nd St., 901/522-8228, 11am-10pm daily, $8-20), your first stop for authentic fried catfish in Memphis. If cat fish isn't your thing, try the grilled or boiled shrimp, fish tacos, frog legs, or oysters. The baskets of fried seafood come with fries and hush puppies, and the grilled plates come with grilled veggies, rice, and beans. The tangy coleslaw is a must. The atmosphere here is laid-back; place your order at the window and come and get it when the coaster they give you starts to vibrate. The checkered tables are well stocked with hot sauce and saltines.

It would be a grave mistake to visit Memphis and not stop at ★ **Gus's World Famous Fried Chicken** (310 Front St., 901/527-4877, 11am-9pm Mon.-Thurs. and Sun., 11am-10:30pm Fri.-Sat., $6-12) for some of their delicious fried bird. The downtown location is a franchise of the original Gus's, which is a half-hour drive northeast out of town along U.S. 70, in Mason. It is no exaggeration to say that Gus's cooks up some of the best fried chicken out there: It is spicy, juicy, and hot. It's served casually wrapped in brown paper. Sides include coleslaw, baked beans, and fried pickles. The restaurant also serves grilled-cheese sandwiches. The service in this hole-in-the-wall establishment is slow but friendly, so come in with a smile on.

The **Arcade** (540 S. Main St., 901/526-5757, www.arcaderestaurant.com, 7am-3pm daily, $5-10) is said to be Memphis's oldest restaurant. Founded in 1919 and still operated by the same family (with lots of the same decor), this restaurant feels like a throwback to an earlier time. The menu is diverse, with pizzas, sandwiches, and plate-lunch specials during the week, and breakfast served anytime. The chicken spaghetti is a stick-to-your-ribs favorite.

Uptown

★ **The Little Tea Shop** (69 Monroe, 901/525-6000, 11am-2pm Mon.-Fri., $4.95-7.50) serves traditional plate lunches through the week. Choose from daily specials like fried catfish, chicken potpie, and meat loaf with your choice of vegetable and side dishes by ticking off boxes on the menu. Every meal (except sandwiches) comes with fresh, hot corn bread that might as well be the star of the show. This is stick-to-your-ribs Southern cooking at its best, so come hungry. If you have room, try the peach cobbler or pecan ball for dessert. The staff's welcoming yet efficient style makes this perfect for a quick lunch. Not to be missed.

The **Blue Plate Café** (113 Court Square S., 901/523-2050, 8am-2pm daily, $4-10) serves hearty breakfasts, plate lunches, and traditional home-style cooking. Its newsprint menu imparts wisdom ("Rule of Life No. 1: Wake up. Show up. Pay attention.") and declares that every day should begin with a great breakfast. It's not hard to comply at the Blue Plate. Eggs come with homemade biscuits and gravy, and your choice of grits, hash browns, or pancakes. For lunch, try a meat-and-three or vegetable plate, slow-cooked white-bean soup, or a grilled peanut butter and banana sandwich. Locals swear by the fried green tomatoes. There is also a Blue Plate Café in an old house in midtown (5469 Poplar Ave., 901/761-9696).

Alcenia's (317 N. Main St., 901/523-0200, www.alcenias.com, 11am-5pm Tues.-Fri., 9am-3pm Sat. , $9-11), located in the Pinch

District, is among Memphis's best Southern-style restaurants. Known for its plate lunches, fried chicken, and pastries, Alcenia's has a style unlike any other Memphis eatery, witnessed in its offbeat decor of '60s-style beads, folk art, and wedding lace. Proprietor B. J. Chester-Tamayo is all love, and she pours her devotion into some of the city's best soul food. Try the spicy cabbage and deep-fried chicken, or the salmon croquette, and save room for Alcenia's famous bread pudding for dessert. Chicken and waffles is the Saturday morning specialty.

Midtown

Just follow the crowds to the **Cupboard Restaurant** (1400 Union Ave., 901/276-8015, www.thecupboardrestaurant.com, 7am-8pm daily, $6-10), one of Memphians' favorite stops for plate lunches. The Cupboard moved from its downtown location to an old Shoney's about a mile outside of town to accommodate the throngs who stop here for authentic home-style cooking. The Cupboard gets only the freshest vegetables for its dishes like okra and tomatoes, rutabaga turnips, steamed cabbage, and green beans. The meat specials change daily but include things like fried chicken, chicken and dumplings, hamburger steak with onions, and beef tips with noodles. The corn bread "coins" are exceptionally buttery, and the bread is baked fresh daily. For dessert, try the lemon icebox pie.

The Women's Exchange Tea Room (88 Racine St., 901/327-5681, www.womans-exchange.com, 11:30am-1:45pm Mon.-Fri., $8-15) feels like a throwback to an earlier era. Located one block east of the Poplar Street viaduct, the Women's Exchange has been serving lunch since 1936, and the menu has not changed much over the years. The special changes daily and always includes a choice of two entrées, or a four-vegetable plate. Classics like chicken salad, salmon loaf, beef tenderloin, and seafood gumbo are favorites, and all lunches come with a drink and dessert. The dining room looks out onto a green garden, and the atmosphere is homey—not stuffy. The Exchange also sells gifts, housewares, and other knickknacks.

In the Cooper-Young neighborhood, **Soul Fish** (862 S. Cooper St., 901/725-0722, www.soulfishcafe.com, 11am-10pm Mon.-Sat., 11am-9pm Sun., $8-16) offers traditional plate lunches, vegetable plates, and several varieties of catfish. You can get the fish breaded and fried or blackened with a potent spice mix. Soul Fish is owned in part by Tiger Bryant, owner of the venerable Young Avenue Deli, and it has the hallmarks of a well-conceived eatery. The atmosphere is open and cheerful, with a few touches of subtle sophistication. In this case, the main attraction is good food at a good price—a combination that can be hard to find elsewhere in Cooper-Young. Soul Fish also has locations in East Memphis and Germantown.

South Memphis

Gay Hawk Restaurant (685 Danny Thomas Blvd., 901/947-1464, 11am-3pm Mon.-Fri., noon-5pm Sun., $6-10) serves country-style food that sticks to your ribs and warms your soul. Chef Lewis Bobo declares that his specialty is "home-cooked food," and it really is as simple as that. The best thing about Gay Hawk is the luncheon buffet, which lets newcomers to Southern cooking survey the choices and try a little bit of everything. The Sunday lunch buffet practically sags with specialties like fried chicken, grilled fish, macaroni and cheese, greens, and much, much more. Save room for peach cobbler.

★ BARBECUE

Barbecue is serious business in Memphis, unlike anywhere else in the state. On the northern fringe of downtown Memphis is one of the city's most famous and well-loved barbecue joints: ★ **Cozy Corner** (745 N. Parkway, 901/527-9158, www.cozycornerbbq.com, 11am-9pm Tues.-Sat., $9-20). Cozy Corner is tucked into a storefront in an otherwise abandoned strip mall; you'll smell it before you see it. Step inside to order barbecue pork, sausage, or bologna sandwiches. Or get a two-bone, four-bone, or six-bone rib dinner plate, which comes with your choice of baked beans, coleslaw, or barbecue spaghetti, plus slices of Wonder bread to sop up the juices. One of Cozy Corner's specialties is its barbecued Cornish hens—a preparation that is surprising but delicious. Sweet tea goes perfectly with the tangy and spicy barbecue.

Jim Neely's **Interstate Bar-B-Que** (2265 S. 3rd St., 901/775-2304, www.interstatebarbecue.com, 11am-10pm Mon.-Wed., 11am-11pm Thurs., 11am-midnight Fri.-Sat., 11am-7pm Sun., $5-23) was once ranked the second-best barbecue in the nation, but the proprietors have not let it go to their heads; this is still a down-to-earth, no-frills eatery. Large appetites can order a whole slab of pork or beef ribs, but most people will be satisfied with a chopped pork sandwich, which comes topped with coleslaw and smothered with barbecue sauce. Families can get the fixings for 6, 8, or 10 sandwiches sent out family style. For an adventure, try the barbecue spaghetti or barbecue bologna sandwich. If you're in a hurry, Interstate has a drive-up window, too, and if you are really smitten, you can order pork, sauce, and seasoning in bulk to be frozen and shipped to your home.

Although aficionados will remind you that the ribs served at the **Rendezvous** (52 S. 2nd St., 901/523-2746, www.hogsfly.com, 4:30pm-10:30pm Tues.-Thurs., 11am-11pm Fri., 11:30am-11pm Sat., $8-20) are not technically barbecue, they are one of the biggest barbecue stories in town. Covered in a dry rub of spices and broiled until the meat falls off the bones, these ribs will knock your socks off. If you prefer, you can choose Charlie Vergos's dry-rub chicken or boneless pork loin. Orders come with baked beans and coleslaw, but beer is really the essential accompaniment to any Vergos meal. The door to Rendezvous is tucked in an alley off Monroe Avenue. The smoky interior, decorated with antiques and yellowing business cards, is low-key, noisy, and lots of fun.

Central BBQ (2249 Central, 901-272-9377, cbqmemphis.com, 11am-9pm daily, $5-25) appeals to both those who love dry rub and those who want their sauces. Can't decide between the pulled pork, the brisket, and other local favorites? Easy solution: Get the combo platter. Central has several locations around town.

A Memphis chain, **Gridley's** (6842 Stage Rd., 901/377-8055, 11am-8pm Sun., Mon., Wed., Thurs., 11am-9pm Fri.-Sat., $4-18) serves wet-style barbecue ribs, pork shoulder plates and sandwiches, plus spicy grilled shrimp. The shrimp is served with a buttery and delicious dipping sauce. Try the half-pork, half-shrimp plate for a real treat. Meals here come with baked beans, slaw, and hot, fresh bread. Sometimes Gridley's closes on Wednesdays, so call ahead if you are headed there on hump day.

The mustard slaw at **Leonard's Pit Barbecue** (5465 Fox Plaza Dr., 901/360-1963, www.leonardsbarbecue.com, 11am-2:30pm Sun.-Thurs., 11am-9pm Fri-Sat., $5-20) is an essential side dish to complement the classic Memphis barbecue.

CONTEMPORARY

Downtown

The Majestic Grille (145 S. Main St., 901/522-8555, www.majesticgrille.com, 11am-10pm Mon.-Thurs., 11am-11pm Fri., 11am-2:30pm and 4pm-11pm Sat., 11am-2:30pm and 4pm-9pm Sun., $8-48) serves a remarkably affordable yet upscale menu at brunch, lunch, and dinner. Located in what was once the Majestic Theater, the restaurant's white tablecloths and apron-clad waiters lend an aura of refinement. But with main courses starting at just $8-9, this can be a bargain. Flatbread pizzas feature asparagus, spicy shrimp, and smoked sausage, and sandwiches include burgers and clubs. Specialties include pasta, barbecue ribs, grilled salmon, and steaks. Don't pass on dessert, served in individual shot glasses, such as chocolate mousse, key lime pie, and carrot cake, among others.

It is impossible to pigeonhole **Automatic Slim's Tonga Club** (83 S. 2nd St., 901/525-7948, automaticslimsmemphis.com, 11 am-11 pm Mon.-Thurs., 11 am-1am Fri., 9 am-1am Sat., 9am-11pm Sun., brunch $8-14, lunch $9-14, dinner $16-27), except to say that this Memphis institution consistently offers fresh, spirited, and original fare. Named after a character from an old blues tune, Automatic Slim's uses lots of strong flavors to create its eclectic menu; Caribbean and Southwestern influences are the most apparent. Take a seat and in two shakes you'll be presented with soft, fresh bread and pesto-seasoned olive oil for dipping. Start with Lobster Tater Tots or Coconut Shrimp, or come for brunch and an Oreo Waffle. A meal at Automatic Slim's would not be complete without a famous Tonga Martini or one of the kitchen's delectable desserts: Pecan tart and chocolate cake are good choices. Automatic Slim's is a welcome departure from barbecue and Southern food when you're ready. Its atmosphere is relaxed, and there's often a crowd at the bar, especially on weekends, when there's live music on tap.

Long the standard-bearer of fine French cuisine, **Chez Philippe** (149 Union Ave., 901/529-4188, 6pm-10pm Wed.-Sat., $78-100, three-course afternoon tea 1pm-3:30pm Wed.-Sat., $30-40/$24 kids), located in the Peabody Hotel, now offers French-Asian fusion cuisine. The Asian influences are noticeable in the ingredients, but the preparation of most dishes at Chez Philippe remains traditional French. Entrées include grouper, bass, pork chop, and venison. Chez Philippe offers a prix fixe menu: Three-course meals are $80 and five courses, $105.

Midtown

In 2007, Memphis's foremost restaurateur, Karen Blockman Carrier, closed her fine-dining restaurant Cielo in Victorian Village, redecorated, and reopened it as the **Molly Fontaine Lounge** (679 Adams Ave., 901/524-1886, molliefontainelounge.com, 5 p.m.-"'til the spirits go to sleep" Wed.-Sat., $8-11). Carrier's vision was an old-fashioned club where guests can order upscale cocktails, relax with live music, and eat tasty Mediterranean- and Middle Eastern-inspired tapas. The restaurant has an upmarket but cozy atmosphere, with equal measures of funky and fine. The live piano jazz is the perfect backdrop for the restaurant's artistic small plates.

Surprisingly good for a bookstore café, **The Booksellers Bistro** (387 Perkins Ext., 901/374-0881, thebooksellersatlaurelwood.com/bronte-bistro, 8am-9pm Mon.-Thurs., 8am-10pm Fri.-Sat., 9am-8pm Sun., $10-17), offers salads, soups, and sandwiches, as well as daily meat and fish specials. The soup-and-sandwich combo is filling and good. Breakfast may well be the best meal on offer, however. The morning menu features specials designed by celebrity chefs, including omelets, baked goods, and crepes.

One of Memphis's most distinctive restaurant settings is an old beauty shop in the Cooper-Young neighborhood. ★ **The Beauty Shop** (966 S. Cooper St., 901/272-7111, www.thebeautyshoprestaurant.com, 11am-2pm Mon.-Sat. and 5pm-10pm Mon.-Thurs., 5pm-11pm Fri.-Sat., 10am-3pm Sun., lunch $6.50-10, dinner entrées $23-26) takes advantage of the vintage beauty parlor decor to create a great talking point for patrons and food writers alike. The domed hair dryers remain, and the restaurant has put the shampooing sinks to work as beer coolers. At lunch, the Beauty Shop offers a casual menu of sandwiches and salads. For dinner, the imaginative cuisine of Memphis restaurateur Karen Blockman Carrier, who also owns Molly Fontaine Lounge and Automatic Slim's Tonga Club, takes over.

If you enjoy your beer as much or more than your meal, then head straight for **Boscos Squared** (2120 Madison Ave., 901/432-2222, www.boscosbeer.com, 11am-2am Mon.-Thurs., 11am-3am Fri.-Sat., 10:30am-2am Sun., lunch $10-15, dinner $11-24). Boscos is a brewpub with fresh seafood, steak, and pizza. Its beer menu is among the best in the city, and many of the brews are made on the premises.

Bolstering the craft butchery trend is **Bounty on Broad** (2519 Broad Ave. 901/410-8131, bountyonbroad.com, 5pm-9:30pm Tues.-Thurs., 5pm-10pm Fri.-Sat., 11am-2pm. Sun.,

$14-25), a restaurant and boutique butcher shop. On the restaurant side, expect family-style dishes with a farm-to-table slant. Note: Cash is not accepted, just credit cards.

East Memphis

To many minds, Memphis dining gets no better than ★ **Erling Jensen, The Restaurant** (1044 S. Yates Rd., 901/763-3700, www.ejensen.com, 5pm-10pm daily, $33-50). Danish-born Erling Jensen is the mastermind of this fine-dining restaurant that has consistently earned marks as Memphians' favorite restaurant. Understated decor and friendly service are the backdrop to Jensen's dishes, which are works of art. The menu changes with the seasons and is based upon availability, but usually it includes about six different seafood dishes and as many meat and game choices. Black Angus beef, elk loin, and buffalo tenderloin are some of the favorites. Meals at Jensen's restaurant should begin with an appetizer, salad, or soup—or all three. The jumbo chunk crab cakes with smoked red-pepper sauce are excellent. Reservations are a good idea at Erling Jensen, and so are jackets for men. Expect to spend upwards of $80 for a four-course meal here; $60 for two courses. Add more for wine.

Memphis's premier steak house is **Folk's Folly** (551 S. Mendenhall Rd., 901/762-8200, www.folksfolly.com, 5:30pm-10pm Mon.-Sat., 5:30pm-9pm Sun., $35-70), located just east of Audubon Park. Diners flock here for prime aged steaks and seafood favorites. For small appetites, try the 8-ounce filet mignon for $32; large appetites can gorge on the 28-ounce porterhouse for $65. Seafood includes lobster, crab legs, and wild salmon. The atmosphere is classic steak house: The lighting is low, and there's a piano bar on the property.

Some say **Acre Restaurant** (690 S. Perkins, 901/818-2273, www.acrememphis.com, lunch: 11am-2pm Mon.-Fri., dinner: 5pm-10pm Mon.-Sat., $22-35) is Memphis's best. Certainly, it has one of the best wine lists in town. The menu combines southern and Asian traditions with locally grown and raised ingredients in a modern setting.

Where else in the world can you enjoy the offbeat combination that is **Jerry's Sno-Cone and Car Wash** (1657 Wells Station Rd., 901/767-2659, 11am-7pm Mon.-Sat.)? Choose from more than 70 varieties of shaved ice.

INTERNATIONAL

Downtown

For sushi, try **Sekisui** (Union at 2nd Ave., 901/523-0001, www.sekisuiusa.com, noon-3pm and 6pm-11pm daily, where a roll costs $2.50-8, and a filling combo plate will run you about $15). Sekisui is a Memphis chain, and there are other locations in midtown (25 S. Belvedere Blvd., 901/725-0005, 11:30am-2pm and 5pm-9:30pm Mon.-Thurs., 11:30am-2pm and 5pm-10:30pm Fri., 5pm-10:30pm Sat., 5pm-9:30pm Sun.) and the suburbs, as well as in Chattanooga.

Lively, funky **Oshi Burger Bar** (94 S. Main St., 901/341-2091, oshiburger.com, 11am-10pm Sun.-Thurs., 11am-midnight Fri.-Sat., $7-12) specializes in burgers and hot dogs with an Asian twist: think toppings such as kimchi slaw or nori flakes and sides such as tempura onion rings. Milkshakes with additions like Pop Rocks, sake, bacon dust, or bourbon are a fun treat.

Midtown

The **India Palace** (1720 Poplar Ave., 901/278-1199, www.indiapalaceinc.com, lunch: 11am-3pm Mon.-Fri., dinner: 5pm-9:30pm Mon.-Thurs., 5pm-10pm Fri.-Sun., $9-17) is a regular winner in readers' choice polls for Indian food in Memphis. The lunchtime buffet is filling and economical, and the dinner menu features vegetarian, chicken, and seafood dishes. The dinner platters are generous and tasty.

Pho Hoa Binh (1615 Madison, 901/276-0006, 11am-9pm Mon.-Fri., noon-9pm Sat., $4-9) is one of the most popular Vietnamese restaurants in town. You can't beat the value of the lunch buffet, or you can order from the dizzying array of Chinese and Vietnamese dishes, including spring rolls, vermicelli

Piggly Wiggly

Memphian Clarence Saunders opened the first **Piggly Wiggly** at 79 Jefferson Street in 1916, thus giving birth to the modern American supermarket. Until then, shoppers went to small storefront shops where they would ask the counter clerk for what they needed: a pound of flour, a half-dozen pickles, a block of cheese. The clerk went to the bulk storage area at the rear of the store and measured out what the customer needed.

Saunders's big idea was self-service. At the Piggly Wiggly, customers entered the store, carried a basket, and were able to pick out prepackaged and priced containers of food that they paid for at the payment station on their way out.

Suffice to say, the Piggly Wiggly idea took off, and by 1923 there were 1,268 Piggly Wiggly franchises around the country. Saunders used some of his profits to build a massive mansion east of the city out of pink Georgia limestone, but he was never to live in the Pink Palace, which he lost as a result of a complex stock loss.

Today, **Saunders's Pink Palace** is home to the **Pink Palace Museum,** which includes, among other things, a replica of the original Piggly Wiggly supermarket.

noodle bowls, rice, and meat dishes. There are a lot of vegetarian options here.

The atmosphere at **Bhan Thai** (1324 Peabody Ave., 901/272-1538, www.bhanthairestaurant.com, 11am-2:30pm Tues.-Fri., 5pm-9:30pm Sun.-Thurs., 5pm-10:30pm Fri.-Sat., $14-23) in midtown is almost as appealing as the excellent Thai food served there. Set in an elegant 1912 home, Bhan Thai makes the most of the house's space, and seating is spread throughout several colorful rooms and on the back patio. Choose from dishes like red snapper, masaman curry, and roasted duck curry. The Bhan Thai salad is popular, with creamy peanut dressing and crisp vegetables.

It's the regulars who are happy at the **Happy Mexican Restaurant and Cantina** (385 S. 2nd St., 901/529-9991, www.happymexican.com, 11am-10pm Sun.-Thurs., 11am-11pm Fri.-Sat., $7-15). Serving generous portions of homemade Mexican food for lunch and dinner, Happy Mexican is destined to become a downtown favorite. The service is efficient and friendly, and the decor is cheerful but not over the top. It's located just a few blocks south of the National Civil Rights Museum. There are three other locations in the greater Memphis area.

Ecco on Overton Park (1585 Overton Park, 901/410-8200, eccoonovertonpark.com, 11am-2pm and 4:30pm-9pm Tues.-Thurs., 11am-2pm and 5:30pm-9:30pm Fri., 10am-2pm and 5:30pm-9:30pm Sat., $12-28) channels all the comforts of a European café with dishes such as cassoulet, pasta puttanesca and burgundy-sauced beef short ribs. Drink as the Italians do with an Aperol spritz or sip a bit of Spain with a bottle of rosé from Rioja.

Robata Ramen & Yakitori Bar (2116 Madison Ave. 901/410-8290, robatamemphis.com, 5pm-midnight daily, $7-15) is equal parts fun and affordable, with an array of yakitori (bite-size meats and veggies that are skewered, then grilled) sold by the piece and a create-your-own ramen menu.

East Memphis

Andrew Michael Italian Kitchen (712 W. Brookhaven Circle, 901/347-3569, andrewmichaelitaliankitchen.com, 5pm-10pm Tues.-Sat., $10-30) is home to chefs Andrew Ticer and Michael Hudman—who were honored as finalists in the Best Chef: Southeast category for the 2015 James Beard Foundation Awards. They learned the nuances of Italian cooking from their grandmothers as well as travels throughout Italy. Ticer and Hudman also own Porcellino's.

VEGETARIAN

Midtown

Raw and vegan food delivery service **Raw**

Girls Memphis (raw-girls-memphis.myshopify.com) also runs two food trucks that dole out cold-pressed juices, snacks, soups, salads and sandwiches. Eats are as clean as it gets—free of gluten, dairy, and refined sugar, a boon for those navigating food allergies or sensitivities—featuring organic, locally grown produce to boot. Look for the trucks parked in Midtown (242 S. Cooper, 10am-6pm Wed.-Sun., $7-9) and East Memphis (5502 Poplar Ave., same hours).

MARKETS

The closest gourmet grocery is located in Harbor Town, the residential community on Mud Island, where **Miss Cordelia's** (737 Harbor Bend, 901/526-4772, www.misscordelias.com, 7am-10pm daily) sells fresh produce, bakery goods, and staples. A deli in the back serves soups, salads, sandwiches, and a wide variety of prepared foods.

For a full-service grocery store in midtown, look for the **Kroger** at the corner of Cleveland and Poplar.

The **Memphis Farmers Market** (901/575-0580, www.memphisfarmersmarket.com, Sat. 7am-1pm Apr.-Oct., rain or shine) takes place in the pavilion opposite Central Station in the South Main part of town.

For liquor and wine, go to **The Corkscrew** (511 S. Front St., 901/523-9389, www.corkscrewmemphis.com, 10am-11pm Mon.-Sat.).

Information and Services

INFORMATION

Visitors Centers

The city's visitors center is the **Tennessee Welcome Center** (119 Riverside Dr., 901/543-6757), located on the Tennessee side of the I-40 bridge. The center has lots of brochures and free maps and staff who can answer your questions. It is open 24 hours a day, seven days a week. The center assists more than 350,000 travelers annually.

Although it is not designed to be a visitors center per se, the **Memphis Convention and Visitors Bureau** (47 Union Ave., 901/543-5300, www.memphistravel.com, 8:30am-5pm Mon.-Thurs., 8:30am-4pm Fri.) is a resource for visitors. You can collect maps and ask questions here. The bureau also produces videos highlighting city attractions and restaurants, which are available on many hotel televisions. Other locations are on Riverside Drive and State Route 385 at I-40.

Hand-out maps that highlight key attractions are available from visitors centers in Memphis. If you are only interested in Beale Street, Graceland, and the interstates, these will be fine. The free maps provided at the concierge desk of the Peabody Hotel are particularly well marked and useful.

If you want to explore further, or if you plan to drive yourself around the city, it is wise to get a proper city map or GPS. Rand McNally publishes a detailed Memphis city map, which you can buy from bookstores or convenience marts in downtown.

Media

The daily ***Commercial Appeal*** (www.commercialappeal.com) is Memphis's major newspaper, available all over the city. The ***Memphis Flyer*** (www.memphisflyer.com) is a free alternative weekly, published on Wednesday, with the best entertainment listings.

Memphis magazine (www.memphismagazine.com) is published monthly and includes historical anecdotes, restaurant reviews, features on high-profile residents, and lots of advertising aimed at residents and would-be residents.

There are two independent radio stations of note: **WEVL 89.9 FM** is a community radio station that plays blues, country, and other Memphis music. **WDIA 1070 AM,** the historical Memphis station that made the blues famous, still rocks today. Another noteworthy station is **WRBO 103.5 FM,** which plays soul and R&B.

SERVICES

Fax and Internet

Send a fax at the **FedEx Office** (50 N. Front St., 901/521-0261), located across from the Peabody's valet entrance.

Most of the major hotels and attractions have wireless Internet access.

Postal Service

There is a postal retail center, which sells stamps and offers limited postal services, at 100 Peabody Place (800/275-8777, 8:30am-5pm Mon.-Fri.).

Emergency Services

Dial 911 in an emergency for fire, ambulance, or police. The downtown police department is the **South Main Station** (545 S. Main St., 901/636-4099). Police patrol downtown by car, on bike, and on foot.

Several agencies operate hotlines for those needing help. They include: Alcoholics Anonymous (901/726-6750), the Better Business Bureau (901/759-1300), Emergency Mental Health Services (855/274-7471), Deaf Interpreting (901/577-3783), Rape Crisis/Sexual Assault Hotline (901/272-2020), and Poison Emergencies (901/528-6048).

Hospitals

Memphis is chockablock with hospitals. Midtown Memphis is also referred to as Medical Center for the number of hospitals and medical facilities there. Here you will find the **Regional Medical Center at Memphis** (877 Jefferson Ave., 901/545-7100), a 325-bed teaching hospital affiliated with the University of Tennessee; and the **Methodist University Hospital** (1265 Union Ave., 901/516-7000), the 617-bed flagship hospital for Methodist Healthcare.

In East Memphis, **Baptist Memorial Hospital** (6019 Walnut Grove Rd., 901/226-5000) is the cornerstone of the huge Baptist Memorial Health Care System, with 771 beds.

Laundry

Try any of these two laundries, which are located near downtown: **Crump Laundry Mat and Dry Cleaning** (756 E. Ed Crump Blvd., 901/948-7008) or **Jackson Coin Laundry** (1216 Jackson Ave., 901/274-3536).

Libraries

Memphis has 18 public libraries. The city's main library is **Hooks Public Library** (3030 Poplar Ave., 901/415-2700, 10am-8pm Mon.-Thurs., 10am-5pm Fri.-Sat., 1pm-5pm Sun.), a modern, new public library with 119 public computers, an extensive book collection, community programs, meeting rooms, a lecture series, and more. The central library is located on a busy thoroughfare in midtown and would be a challenge to visit without a car.

The downtown branch library, **Cossit Library** (33 S. Front St., 901/415-2766, 10am-5pm Mon.-Fri.), has a good collection of new releases, and staff there are happy to help visitors looking for information about Memphis. The current building was constructed in 1959, but the Cossit Library was founded in 1888 as the Cossit-Goodwyn Institute.

Getting There and Around

GETTING THERE

Air

Memphis International Airport (MEM, 901/922-8000, www.mscaa.com) is located 13 miles south of downtown Memphis. There are two popular routes to Memphis from the airport. Take I-240 north to arrive in midtown. To reach downtown, take I-55 north and exit on Riverside Drive. The drive takes 20-30 minutes.

The airport's main international travel insurance and business services center (901/922-8090) is located in ticket lobby B and is open daily. Here you can exchange foreign currency, buy travel insurance, conduct money transfers, send faxes and make photocopies, and buy money orders and travelers checks. A smaller kiosk near the international arrivals and departures area at gate B-36 is open daily and offers foreign currency exchange and travel insurance.

There is wireless Internet service in the airport, but it is not free.

AIRPORT SHUTTLE

TennCo Express (901/645-3726, www.tenncoexpress.com) provides an hourly shuttle service from the airport to many downtown hotels. Tickets are $20 one-way and $30 round-trip. Look for the shuttle parked in the third lane near column number 14 outside the airport terminal. Shuttles depart every half hour 7:30am-9:30pm. For a hotel pickup, call at least a day in advance.

Car

Memphis is located at the intersection of two major interstate highways: I-40, which runs east-west across the United States, and I-55, which runs south from St. Louis to New Orleans.

Many people who visit Memphis drive here in their own cars. The city is 300 miles from St. Louis, 380 miles from Atlanta, 410 miles from New Orleans, 450 miles from Dallas, 480 miles from Cincinnati and Oklahoma City, and 560 miles from Chicago.

Bus

Greyhound (800/231-2222, www.greyhound.com) runs daily bus service to Memphis from around the United States. Direct service is available to Memphis from a number of surrounding cities, including Jackson and Nashville, Tennessee; Tupelo and Jackson, Mississippi; Little Rock and Jonesboro, Arkansas; and St. Louis. The Greyhound station (3033 Airways Blvd., 901/395-8770) is open 24 hours a day.

Train

Amtrak (800/872-7245, www.amtrak.com) runs the City of New Orleans train daily between Chicago and New Orleans, stopping in Memphis on the way. The southbound train arrives daily at Memphis's Central Station at 6:27am, leaving about half an hour later. The northbound train arrives at 10pm every day. It is an 11-hour ride overnight between Memphis and Chicago, and about 8 hours between Memphis and New Orleans.

The Amtrak station (901/526-0052) is located in Central Station at 545 South Main Street in the South Main district of downtown. Ticket and baggage service is available at the station daily 5:45am-11:15pm.

GETTING AROUND

Driving

Driving is the most popular and easiest way to get around Memphis. Downtown parking is plentiful if you are prepared to pay; an all-day pass in one of the many downtown parking garages costs about $12. Traffic congestion peaks, predictably at rush hours and is worst in the eastern parts of the city and along the interstates. But traffic isn't the problem it is in Nashville; Memphis commutes are considered more reasonable.

Public Transportation

BUSES

The **Memphis Area Transit Authority** (901/274-6282, www.matatransit.com) operates dozens of buses that travel through the greater Memphis area. For information on routes, call or stop by the North End Terminal on North Main Street for help planning your trip. The bus system is not used frequently by tourists. A daily pass is available for $3.50 or $16/week.

TROLLEYS

Public trolleys (or hybrid bus shuttles when the trolleys are being serviced) run for about two miles along Main Street in Memphis from the Pinch District in the north to Central Station in the south, and circle up on a parallel route along Riverfront Drive. Another trolley line runs about two miles east on Madison Avenue, connecting the city's medical center with downtown. The Main Street Trolleys run every 10 minutes at most times, but the Madison Avenue trolleys run less often on weekends and evenings after 6pm.

Fares are $1 per ride. You can buy an all-day pass for $3.50, a three-day pass for $9, or a monthlong pass for $25. All passes must be purchased at the North End Terminal at the northern end of the Main Street route.

The trolley system is useful, especially if your hotel is on either the northern or southern end of downtown or along Madison Avenue. Brochures with details on the routes and fares are available all over town, or you can download one at www.matatransit.com. The trolleys are simple to understand and use; if you have a question, just ask your driver.

SUN STUDIO FREE SHUTTLE BUS

Sun Studio runs a free shuttle between Sun Studio, the Rock 'n' Soul Museum at Beale Street, and Graceland. The first run stops at the Graceland Heartbreak Hotel at 9:55am, Graceland at 10am, Sun Studio at 10:15am, and the Rock 'n' Soul Museum at 10:30am. Runs continue throughout the day on an hourly schedule. The last run picks up at Heartbreak Hotel at 5:55pm, Graceland Plaza at 6pm, and Sun Studio at 6:15pm.

The shuttle is a 12-passenger black van painted with the Sun Studio logo. The ride is free, but consider tipping your driver. The published schedule is a loose approximation, so it's a good idea to get to the pickup point early in case the van is running ahead. You can call 901/521-0664 for more information.

Taxis

Memphis has a number of taxi companies, and you will usually find available cabs along Beale Street and waiting at the airport. Otherwise, you will need to call for a taxi. Some of the largest companies are **Yellow Cab** (901/577-7777), **City Wide Cab** (901/722-8294), **Arrow Transportation Company** (901/332-7769), and **Metro Cab** (901/322-2222, ridememphis.com). Expect to pay $25-35 for a trip from the airport to downtown; most fares around town are under $10. Taxis accept credit cards. App-based ride-sharing services like Uber and Lyft (approximately $17 from the airport to downtown) operate in Memphis and have agreements with the local government to allow them to make stops at the airport and other destinations.

Western Plains

Look for ★ to find recommended sights, activities, dining, and lodging.

Highlights

★ **Alex Haley Museum and Interpretive Center:** See the home where Alex Haley, one of the country's most celebrated writers and author of *Roots*, first imagined his ancestors (page 87).

★ **Discovery Park of America:** Explore art, history, and science at this mega-museum (page 90).

★ **Reelfoot Lake State Park Visitors Center:** Knob-kneed cypress trees, abundant wildlife, and fresh air are elixir for those who come to this quiet corner of the delta (page 93).

★ **Tennessee River Folklife Center:** Explore the forgotten past of Tennessee River pearls, steamships, and houseboats at this museum (page 100).

★ **Fort Donelson National Battlefield:** The scene of one of the Civil War's most significant battles is also a picturesque park (page 103).

★ **The Homeplace:** Located in beautiful Land Between the Lakes, this living-history museum depicts the farmer's way of life at the midpoint of the 19th century (page 107).

★ **Pinson Mounds State Archaeological Park:** These sprawling and mysterious mounds are a reminder of those who lived here centuries before (page 116).

★ **Shiloh National Military Park:** See one of the country's best Civil War landmarks (page 119).

From the Tennessee River to the Mississippi, Tennessee's western plains are perhaps more like the Deep South than other parts of the state.

The landscape is spare; in the heart of the delta all you see for mile upon mile are cotton fields—flat with neat rows of the bushy plants. In the south, near the Mississippi state line, piney woods give rise to the state's largest timber industry. Along the Tennessee River, manmade lakes present unmatched opportunities to fish, boat, or simply relax.

Of course, life here was not always peaceful or idyllic. West Tennessee had the largest plantations and the greatest number of slaves before the Civil War. This was Confederate territory. The war touched just about every town in Tennessee's western plains, but none more than the quiet, rural community of Shiloh along the Tennessee River. On April 6 and 7, 1862, an estimated 24,000 men were killed or wounded on this bloody battlefield. Emancipation brought freedom, but not justice to thousands of African Americans who now struggled as sharecroppers and remained the victims of discrimination and worse.

Out of the hardship of life in the Tennessee delta emerged some of the state's most gifted musicians, including "Sleepy" John Estes, Tina Turner, and Carl Perkins.

The knobby knees of Reelfoot Lake and cypress swamps of other natural areas, including Big Hill Pond and the Ghost River, are a landscape unseen in other parts of Tennessee, if not the United States. These habitats give rise to exceptional bird-watching, fishing, and hunting. Come in the spring or fall to see the area at its best (and avoid the worst of summer's heat). Late summer is the season of county fairs and other festivals, and the time when the people of West Tennessee retreat to the nearest lake, river, or stream to cool off.

PLANNING YOUR TIME

A road trip is the best way to experience the western plains; get off the interstate and give small-town restaurants and inns a try. Fresh catfish from the nearby rivers and lakes are served in traditional style—dusted with cornmeal and deep fried. Sample the varieties of hush puppies between Reelfoot Lake and

Previous: The Homeplace; Fort Donelson National Battlefield. **Above:** Reelfoot Lake.

Western Plains

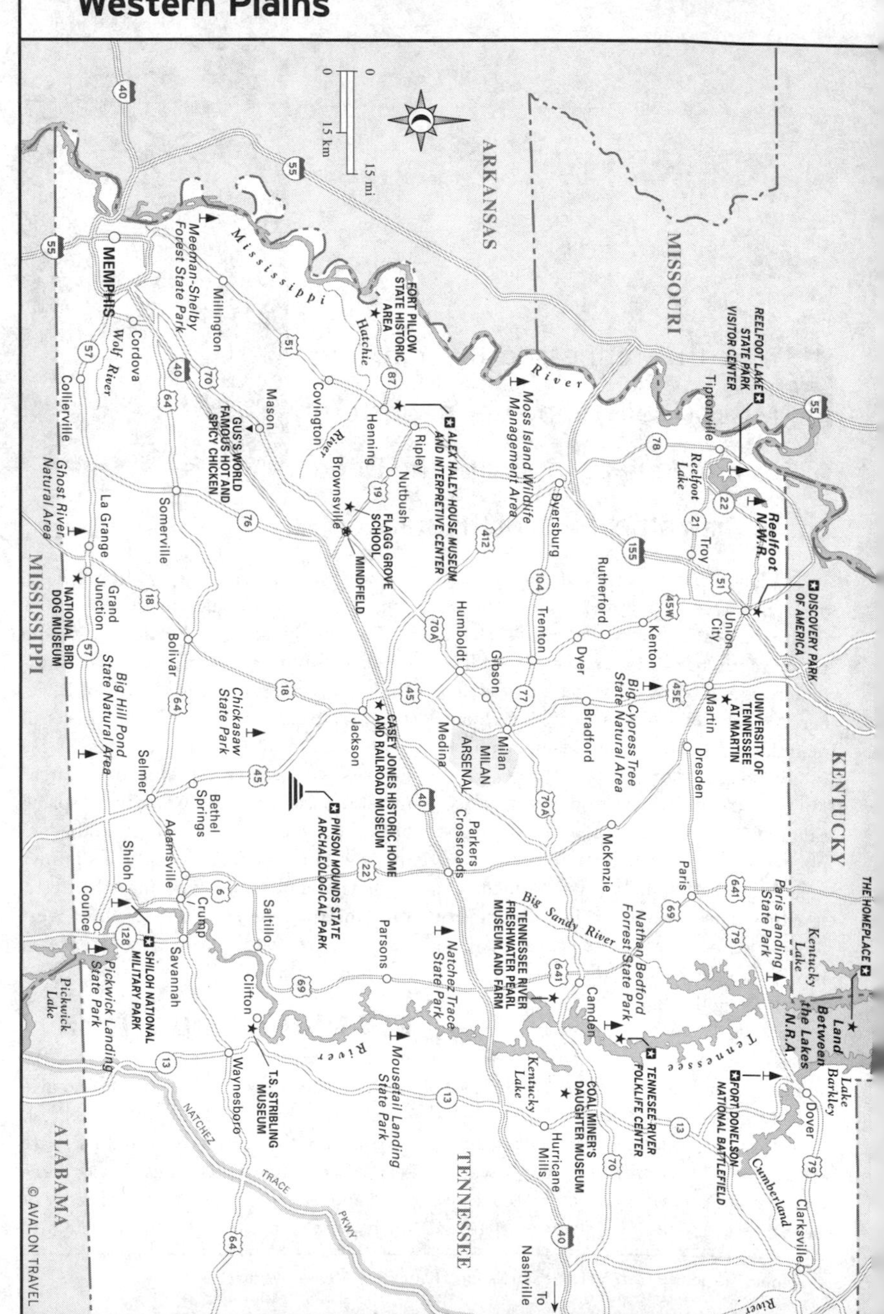

Shiloh. Campers will find numerous options for shelter in state parks.

The western plains can be toured in about a week, although outdoors enthusiasts often want to budget more time to hike or fish. If you are interested in the cultural and musical attractions of the region, choose Jackson or Brownsville as your home base. If you are interested in Shiloh and the natural attractions along the southern Tennessee River, Savannah is a good choice. For a tour along the Mississippi River, the best accommodations are found around the picturesque Reelfoot Lake in the northwest corner of the state. Paris Landing State Park is a good home base for exploring the Kentucky Lakes region.

Driving is the best—honestly, the only—way to get around the western plains. Even in the largest city, Jackson, attractions, restaurants, and accommodations are spread out. A good road map or updated GPS is all you need to find your way around, and residents are friendly and helpful if you get lost.

The Delta

Flat, spare, and rural, the delta region of West Tennessee was, and still is, the state's largest producer of cotton. Cotton fields in cultivation spread out between small towns and farmhouses. Drive through these areas in the fall, and you'll see fields of silvery white blowing in the wind. County seats of the delta have stately courthouses, enclosed by classic courthouse squares. While the region is home to the cities of Jackson and Brownsville, the delta remains rural, and the way of life is laid-back and traditional.

The delta countryside is fertile soil not only for farming, but for music, too. Blues musicians "Sleepy" John Estes, Hammie Nixon, and Yank Rachell are from Brownsville.

The best way to explore the area in your car (or rental car) is by starting in Brownsville and ending up north in Union City.

BROWNSVILLE

The county seat of the largest cotton-producing county in Tennessee, Brownsville was founded in 1824 and quickly became the home to many of West Tennessee's most affluent settlers. Early leaders carefully mapped out the city lots, and they were sold to doctors, lawyers, and merchants who helped the town develop quickly during its first decades.

Brownsville's first newspaper was founded in 1837, its first bank in 1869, and in its heyday it also boasted an opera house and several hotels and restaurants. It lost hundreds of its residents to the yellow fever epidemic of 1878, and hundreds more fled to avoid becoming ill. A marker in the town's Oakwood Cemetery designates the resting place of the yellow fever victims. Brownsville is 40 miles west of Jackson via I-40, which turns into Route 1 as it heads straight into the center of town.

West Tennessee Delta Heritage Center

Half welcome center, half museum center, the **West Tennessee Delta Heritage Center** (121 Sunny Hill Cove, 731/779-9000, www.westtnheritage.com, 9am-5pm Mon.-Sat., 1pm-5pm Sun., free) is your best stop for understanding the special music, culture, and history of the delta region. The exhibits in three of its museums—the West Tennessee Cotton Museum, the West Tennessee Music Museum, and the Hatchie River Museum—examine the musical heritage of the region, the ecology of the nearby Hatchie River, and cotton, the region's most important crop.

The cotton exhibit illustrates the process from cultivation to baling. A huge basket of picked cotton is there for you to touch, as well as the cotton both before and after being ginned. After driving past miles of cotton fields, visitors will welcome the illustration and explanations.

The heritage center also has displays about each of the counties in the region, with visitor information on each. There is also a gift shop stocked with some locally made goods.

Right next to the heritage center's museums is the **"Sleepy" John Estes Home,** a faded clapboard house that was relocated here so tourists could see where the blues legend was living when he died in 1977.

But the newest addition to the museum complex is the one that is getting international attention. The ★ **Flagg Grove School** was the childhood one-room schoolhouse of Anna Mae Bullock, better known as **Tina Turner.** Turner attended the African American school while growing up in nearby Nutbush (hence the title for her hit, "Nutbush City Limits"). The museum houses costumes, platinum and gold records, fan mail, an old yearbook and other artifacts in sleek, modern displays in contrast with old wood floors, chalkboards, and wooden desks. The gift shop features quirky items that remind you of the uber-star's rural roots: kudzu- and cotton ball-scented candles, for example.

Estes was born in Ripley, Tennessee, in 1904 but lived most of his life in Brownsville. A blues guitarist and vocalist, Estes had a distinctive "crying" vocal style and sounded like an old man, even on his early recordings. Estes made his recording debut in Memphis in 1929, and he recorded regularly until the United States joined World War II in 1941. Estes spent the end of his life blind and living in poverty.

The heritage center is located at exit 56 off I-40.

Historic Brownsville

It is pleasant to drive or walk around historic Brownsville, a leafy area of antebellum homes and buildings. Each home is marked with a brown-and-white sign in the yard that is visible from the road and gives the approximate date of construction. For a more detailed guide, visit the Brownsville-Haywood Chamber of Commerce (121 West Main St, Brownsville, 731/772-2193, 8am-5pm daily) for a copy of its historical guidebook of Haywood County prepared by the historic society and sold for $10, which includes a walking tour of Brownsville.

Two of the city's most noteworthy old homes are the **Tripp Home** at 420 Main Street, a two-story Greek Revival home built in 1824 (it is not open to the public but worth a

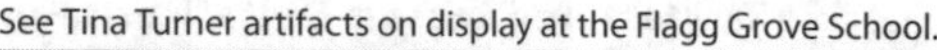

See Tina Turner artifacts on display at the Flagg Grove School.

drive-by), and the **Christ Episcopal Church** at the corner of West College and North Washington, organized in 1832. Brownsville is also home to the oldest Jewish temple in continuous service in Tennessee, the **Temple of Adas Israel,** at 18 North Court Street, built in 1882.

Historic Brownsville surrounds the College Hill Center, where you will find the **Haywood County Museum** (127 N. Grade Ave., 731/772-4883, 2pm-4pm Sun., free), housed in the old Brownsville Baptist Female College. This museum is home to a remarkable collection of Abraham Lincoln artifacts and papers, donated by Brownsville native Morton Felsenthal. The museum is open limited hours, so plan accordingly or call ahead to inquire whether someone can open it for you.

The attractive red brick College Hill Center, which houses the museum, was built in 1851 as the Brownsville Baptist Female College. After 1900, it became the Ogilvie Training School for boys, and later it was the Haywood County High School, from 1911 to 1970.

The area has three different historic districts on the National Registry of Historic Places: College Hill Historic District, North Washington Historic District, and the Dunbar Carver Historic District.

Mindfield

Tucked next to a payday-loan storefront and convenience store near downtown Brownsville is the unexpected ***Mindfield***, a collection of steel sculptures created by local artist Billy Tripp. At first glance it looks like an electrical transformer station, but this acre of creations is a remarkable work of outsider art, that is, art produced by self-taught artists. Begun in 1989, the sculptures will continue to grow and change until Tripp's death, at which point the site will be his place of internment. Tripp works on the piece more often in the summer than in the rest of the year.

Today it stands seven stories tall in places and includes messages of optimism and open-mindedness from the artist. There's an opportunity to leave comments about your impressions of the works, which are largely made from reclaimed steel and other materials. Find the *Mindfield* off U.S. 70, one block away from the town square on the south side of West Main Street/Highway 54, next to Sunrise Inn motel.

Hatchie River National Wildlife Area

Just south of Brownsville is the **Hatchie River National Wildlife Area** (731/772-0501), a 12,000-acre preserve along the Hatchie River. Established to protect the more than 200 species of birds that winter or migrate on the Hatchie, the wildlife area presents excellent opportunities for bird-watching. You can also fish in many areas. Hunting of deer and birds is allowed, with restrictions; be sure check for updated information with your license (www.fws.gov/hatchie). Camping is not allowed. For more information, contact the Refuge Office located at the intersection of Highway 76 and I-40.

Festivals and Events

Brownsville honors its most famous daughter during the annual **Tina Turner Heritage Days** (731/779-9000). Fans descend on the city the fourth weekend of September for three days of tours, music, and more. The area also hosts the **Hatchie Fall Festival** (www.hatchiefallfest.com) on the third Saturday in October by on the courthouse square in Brownsville, which offers live music, including lots of blues, and family-oriented fun.

Accommodations

Brownsville has the greatest concentration of hotels in this part of Tennessee. Most of these are located along I-40, a five-minute drive from downtown Brownsville, some even within walking distance of the West Tennessee Delta Heritage Center and fast-food restaurants. Chain hotels located here include **Econo Lodge** (2600 Anderson Ave., 731/772-4082, $50-60) and **Days Inn** (2530 Anderson

Ave., 731/772-3297, $50-65). An independent option is the spartan **Sunrise Inn** (328 Main St., 731/772-1483, $50-60).

In the historic downtown, try **Lilie's Bed and Breakfast** (508 W. Main St., 731/772-9078, $100). Gail Carver has two rooms in this elegant 1855 home, each with its own private bath.

Food

Southern Living magazine lauded **Helen's BBQ** (1016 N Washington, 731/779-3255) as one of the region's best; no small feat when you think about the amount of barbecue in the south. Owner Helen Turner worked at several local restaurants before hanging out her shingle. This is open pit style, fall off the shoulder pulled pork.

Otherwise, Brownsville has fast-food restaurants, a few barbecue joints, a classic Italian joint, and several Mexican restaurants. **Las Palmas** (27 S. Lafayette, 731/772-8004, daily 10 a.m.-9 p.m., $8-15) is on the courthouse square and serves combination plates, fajitas, and grilled seafood.

Information

The **West Tennessee Delta Heritage Center** (121 Sunny Hill Cove, 731/779-9000, www.westtnheritage.com, 9am-5pm Mon.-Sat., 1pm-5pm Sun., free), near the interstate at Brownsville, has comprehensive information about visiting not only Brownsville, but all the counties in West Tennessee. Make this your first stop for information about the area. There is also a better-than-average gift shop and free public Internet access.

The **Brownsville-Haywood Chamber of Commerce** (121 W. Main St., 731/772-2193, www.haywoodcountybrownsville.com) can also help with information about the region.

MASON

Along Highway 70 near Mason, one landmark restaurant attracts not only Memphians and residents of the delta, but also visitors statewide. ★ **Gus's World Famous Fried Chicken** (505 Hwy. 70, 901/294-2028, 11am-5:30pm Mon., 11am-7pm Tues.-Thurs., 11am-8:30pm Fri.-Sat., 11am-6pm Sum., $8-14) has been heralded by the likes of *GQ* magazine and celebrity chef Emeril Lagasse as *the* place for good fried chicken. Gus's is set in an old frame house, modified over the years to accommodate the thousands of loyal patrons who can't get enough of Gus's hot and spicy fried chicken. Coated in batter and a special seasoning paste, Gus's chicken is fried so that the crust is crispy, the meat juicy, and the taste just spicy enough to be perfect with a cold beer. Just when you think it can't get any better, someone drops a quarter in the old jukebox and the blues fill the air. Wise diners get two orders: one to eat now and one to eat on the way home. Don't miss the quirky signage and ambience.

NUTBUSH

This rural farming community would be a mere speck on the map were it not for R&B superstar Tina Turner, who was raised in and around **Nutbush** from her birth in 1936 until she moved to St. Louis at age 16. Turner penned the semiautobiographical tune "Nutbush City Limits" in 1973, which gave rise to a popular line dance called the Nutbush. Turner rereleased the song in 1991.

Reality is that Nutbush is too small to even have city limits; it feels much like a ghost town today. But the lone business, the Nutbush Grocery and Deli on State Highway 19 (renamed in 2001 the Tina Turner Highway), proclaims its association with the R&B megastar with a sign. But the home where Tina Turner once lived in Nutbush was torn down long ago, the lumber used to build a barn elsewhere in town.

HENNING

The tiny sawmill town of **Henning** is a half-hour drive through the cotton fields from Brownsville. It would be unremarkable except for the fact that it nurtured one of Tennessee's greatest writers, Alex Haley.

★ Alex Haley Museum and Interpretive Center

The **Alex Haley Museum and Interpretive Center** (200 S. Church, 731/738-2240, www.alexhaleymuseum.org, 10am-5pm Tues.-Sat., by advance arrangement for groups of 15 or more Sun., $6, Seniors $5, children $4) illustrates the early childhood of the Pulitzer Prize-winning author Alex Haley. This is where Haley spent his first 10 years, and he later returned here during the summers to stay with his maternal grandparents, Will and Cynthia Palmer.

Visitors tour the kitchen where Cynthia Palmer told Haley stories of her ancestors, which he later used as inspiration for his masterwork, *Roots.* The museum has artifacts of the period, as well as family pictures and heirlooms. You also hear a recording of Haley describing Sunday dinners served in the family dining room.

The museum was established with Haley's help, and he was buried here in 1991.

FORT PILLOW STATE HISTORIC PARK

The drive along Highway 87 to **Fort Pillow State Historic Park** (3122 Park Rd., 731/738-5581) takes you through almost 20 miles of rolling cotton fields and past the West Tennessee State Penitentiary, making it unlike any other wilderness area where you might choose to camp or hike. The park, which perches atop a bluff overlooking the Mississippi River, offers group, tent, and small RV camping (however, there aren't electrical or water hookups; the second camping area is a five-mile hike that requires a permit), picnic areas; 15 miles of hiking trails; wildlife viewing; and fishing in Fort Pillow Lake. There is also a **museum** (8am-4pm daily, free) that tells the controversial story of the 1864 Battle of Fort Pillow, which many historians say is more aptly referred to as the Fort Pillow Massacre for the brutality displayed by Southern troops under the command of Nathan Bedford Forrest.

There's a boat ramp on a no-wake lake, but no boat rentals, so you must bring your own. Get a state fishing license to try to catch bass, bream, and crappie.

Visitors to modern-day Fort Pillow can hike to the remains of the fort itself and see the area where the battle took place. The museum's exhibits and a short video are dated, but an interested visitor will find a great deal of information contained in them. There are reenactments of the battle in April and November. The Mississippi River Bike Trail passes through the park.

CHICKASAW NATIONAL WILDLIFE REFUGE

More than 130,000 people visit the 25,000-acre **Chickasaw National Wildlife Refuge** (731/635-7621) annually. The refuge, located 10 miles north of Ripley, along the Mississippi River, is home to dozens of species of birds, including bald eagles. The refuge is a popular area for hunting and fishing—the fall squirrel hunt is one of the largest. You can also bike or hike along the reserve's 20 miles of paved and gravel roads, looking at acres of hardwood trees. The refuge was established in 1985 and occupies land once owned by a private timber company.

Find the refuge by driving east along Highway 87 (back toward Henning) and head north onto Lightfoot Luckett Road. Follow that road until you reach Highway 19. Continue on Highway 19, heading west. Exit Meadow Road/Walnut Grove Rd. Continue northwest along Barr Rd to Watkins Rd.

RIPLEY

Ripley's famous tomatoes take center stage at the annual **Lauderdale County Tomato Festival,** which takes place the weekend after July 4 every year. In addition to tomato tasting, cooking contests, and exhibitions, there is live music, a carnival, and a beauty contest. The event is organized by the Lauderdale County Chamber of Commerce (731/635-9541, www.lauderdalecountytn.org) and it takes place at Ripley City Park (200 Mary Robert Drive); admission is free. Ripley is

"Remember Fort Pillow!"

The earthworks at Fort Pillow along the Mississippi River were built by the Confederates in 1861, but the fort was soon abandoned so that the rebels could consolidate their troops farther south. Union forces occupied the fort for several years, owing mainly to its strategic position at a sharp bend in the Mississippi River. On April 12, 1864, there were more than 600 Union troops stationed at Fort Pillow—200 of them were newly freed African Americans who had volunteered to join the Union cause.

By 1864 it was clear to many, if not most, that the South would lose the war, so when legendary Confederate general Nathan Bedford Forrest attacked Fort Pillow on April 12, it was not a battle of strategic importance but instead a fight for supplies and pride.

Accounts are that the Confederates quickly overcame the fort by land, but that an inexperienced Union commander, Maj. William Bradford, twice declined to surrender. Whether he finally surrendered or not is a matter of debate. Regardless of whether the Union formally surrendered, there was never any question which force would prevail. Forrest had more men and the advantage of surprise. With such a clear-cut victory at hand, it is no wonder that as news of the massive Union casualties emerged, the immediate cry was of massacre.

Forrest reported that a mere 14 Union men were killed in the battle, but Union records say that 300 men lost their lives, 200 of whom were black. Even Confederate soldiers writing home described the events as "butchery" and told of savagery so great that Forrest himself rode through the ranks and threatened to shoot any Confederate who stopped killing.

The U.S. Congress immediately ordered an investigation, and after reviewing a number of accounts and interviewing witnesses, declared the battle a massacre. The Confederates dismissed this as propaganda and blamed the heavy bloodletting on poor command. The precise nature of what happened at Fort Pillow remains a matter of debate.

For Union soldiers, and particularly African American soldiers, there was no ambiguity in their minds over what took place at Fort Pillow. Recognizing that official retribution may never come, black soldiers used Fort Pillow as a rallying cry in battle. "Remember Fort Pillow," they yelled on advance.

Poet Paul Laurence Dunbar immortalized the incident in his poem "The Unsung Heroes," which reads in part: "Pillow knew their blood, That poured on a nation's altar, a sacrificial flood."

just outside of Chickasaw National Wildlife Refuge. Use Barr Rd. and travel approximately 13 miles southeast, just past Highway 51.

HALLS

American Pickers fans will be delighted with interesting antiques at a number of stores tucked away in small towns in this part of Tennessee. Perhaps the most interesting is **Murray Hudson's Antiquarian Books and Maps** (109 S. Church St., 731/836-9057, www.antiquemapsandglobes.com, 9am-5pm Mon.-Sat.). Hudson has been collecting for more than 30 years and has a remarkable collection of old globes, some of them dating back to the early 1700s. He also sells old maps, books, and historic prints.

Halls is just 13 miles north of Ripley, along Highway 51.

ALAMO

The county seat of Crockett County, Alamo was named for the Alamo Mission in Texas, where Davy Crockett died. Its population is about 2,500.

You can see exotic animals including zebras, wildebeest, oryx, and water buffalo at the **Tennessee Safari Park at Hillcrest** (Hwy. 412, 731/696-4423, www.tennesseesafaripark.com, open daily early spring-late fall, cars admitted 10am-4:30pm Mon.-Sat. and noon-4:30pm Sun., call for appointment to visit in winter, adults $12, children $8) just outside of town. The park is the creation of the Conley family, who have been collecting and raising exotic animals on their farm since 1963. The farm has more than 250 animals, and visitors can drive a two-mile loop through the farm safari style. Free-roaming animals come up to your car window to visit. At the barn there is a petting zoo, where you can feed and touch more animals. While the Conleys have been raising exotic animals for decades, the park has been open to the public only since 2007. The park is 16 miles up Highway 412 from I-40 at exit 78.

Old West Tennessee has been lovingly re-created at **Green Frog Village** (Hwy. 412, 731/663-3319, www.greenfrogtn.org, 10am-4pm Tues.-Sat., $6 adult, $3 child), located between Alamo and Bells, just north of I-40. The village includes an antique cotton gin, 1830s rural church, antique log cabin, one-room schoolhouse, railroad station, and country store. It is also an arboretum. The mission of the village is to preserve the rural culture of the Tennessee delta, and it has been the life's work of emergency-room doctor John Freeman and his wife, Nancy. It is open from April until "it is too cold to be out in the elements."

Alamo is easy to reach from Halls. Head east on TN-88 for approximately 20 miles.

HUMBOLDT

Humboldt was chartered in 1866 at the site where the Louisville and Nashville Railroad and the North-South Mobile and Ohio Railroad crossed. It was named for German naturalist and explorer Baron Alexander von Humboldt. Farmers around Humboldt grew cotton and, after the 1870s, diversified into strawberries, rhubarb, tomatoes, cabbage, lettuce, sweet potatoes, and other crops. Agriculture remains an important industry, but manufacturing is increasingly important. Companies including Wilson Sporting Goods, ConAgra, and American Woodmark have plants in Humboldt. Humboldt is about 14 miles northeast of Alamo, just off of Highway 152.

Sights

The **West Tennessee Regional Art Center** (1200 Main St., 731/784-1787, www.wtrac.tn.org, 9am-4:30pm Mon.-Fri., free; donations encouraged. The center has just one staffer, so call ahead) is located in the city's restored city hall building. It houses the Caldwell Collection of oil paintings, sculpture, watercolors, prints, and lithographs—the only permanent fine-art museum between Nashville and Memphis. The downstairs gallery is free; the upstairs gallery charges admission. The center also showcases memorabilia from the West Tennessee Strawberry Festival, and staff can answer your questions about the area.

Humboldt's **Main Street** is home to barber shops, real estate agents, banks, and a Mexican grocery. It also has a downtown movie theater, **The Plaza** (1408 Main St., 731/784-7469, www.plazatheater.net).

Festivals and Events

Humboldt is best known for the annual **West Tennessee Strawberry Festival,** which celebrates one of this region's sweetest crops. Established in 1934 to encourage the growing, packing, and consumption of strawberries, the festival takes place in early May at the height of the strawberry harvest. It includes a parade, car show, foot races, beauty pageants, cooking contests, and good old-fashioned fireworks. For details and specific dates, contact the Humboldt Chamber of Commerce (1200 Main St., 731/784-1842, www.humboldttnchamber.org).

Accommodations

The pet-friendly **Deerfield Inn** (590 Hwy. 45 Bypass, 731/824-4770, $45-55) is a standard roadside motel, with single and double rooms, cable TV, and in-room refrigerators.

Information

The **Humboldt Chamber of Commerce** (1200 Main St., 731/784-1842, www.humboldttnchamber.org) can help with information about the town.

DYERSBURG

This town of 20,000 people was mentioned in the Arrested Development song *Tennessee*: "Outta the country and into more country / Past Dyersburg into Ripley / Where the ghost of my childhood haunts me / Walk the roads my forefathers walked / Climbed the trees my forefathers hung from."

The county seat of Dyer County, **Dyersburg** has a handsome redbrick-and-white courthouse, built in 1912. The courthouse square is home to several antiques shops, professional services, the **Downtown Dyersburg Development Association** is housed within the Chamber of Commerce (2000 Commerce Ave. 8am-5pm Mon-Thurs., 8am-4pm Fri.). Dyersburg is just east of the Mississippi River on I-55.

You may not need any farming implements, vegetable plants, or fertilizer, particularly while traveling, but you may still want to check out **Pennington Seed and Supply** (214 S. Main, 731/285-1031, 7am-5pm Mon.-Sat.) for its pecans and vintage look.

From Humboldt, head west on Highway 152 and merge onto US-412 west to reach Dyersburg.

Accommodations

Dyersburg has a handful of chain hotels in the delta, outside of Brownsville. They include a **Best Western** (770 Hwy. 51 Bypass, 731/285-8601, $75-85) and **Days Inn** (2600 Lake Rd., 731/287-0888, $80-90).

Information

The Chamber of Commerce (8am-5pm Mon-Thurs., 8am-4pm Fri.) is the best source of information about the town.

BIG CYPRESS TREE STATE NATURAL AREA

You won't find *the* namesake tree at **Big Cypress Tree State Natural Area** (295 Big Cypress Rd., Greenfield, 731/235-2700, summer: 8am-sunset, winter: 8am-4:30pm); the 1,350-year-old tree, which measured 13 feet in diameter, was struck by lightning and died

Much of the town of Dyersburg harkens back to another time.

in 1976. But there are bald cypress and other flora and fauna here. A short hiking trail has signage that identifies many of the trees.

The 330-acre park, which is near Greenfield, is for day-use only and has a picnic area, covered pavilion, and a short nature trail. There's a lovely arts and crafts festival each October.

Approximately 36 miles northeast of Dyersburg, Big Cypress Tree State Natural Area is located off of TN-445 east.

★ DISCOVERY PARK OF AMERICA

Thanks to an $80 million initial private donation in 2013 (and $2-3 million in continuing funds), the **Discovery Park of America** (830 Everett Blvd., 731/885-5455, www.discoveryparkofamerica.com, 10am-5pm Tues-Sat, adults $13.95, seniors $11.95, children $10.95; two-day passes are $19.95, $16.95 and $14.95, respectively), is a well-funded educational center and museum in Union City. That's a remarkable achievement for a town with a population of just 11,000. The idea was to bring the kind of tourism that Dollywood brought to East Tennessee to a section of West Tennessee that has faced financial hardship.

There's something for everyone, including more than 70,000 square feet of exhibits focused on nature, science, technology, history, and art. Favorites include a 20-foot-tall generator, a giant "human" with a slide down its leg, and a World War II airplane that hangs from the ceiling. Learn about Native American tools and traditions from a hologram who gives a lecture. Journals from the Civil War make for fascinating reads.

The Park sits on 50 acres, and there's a lot to explore, including log cabins and gardens. If you're traveling with kids , it can be worth planning to stay for two days (and buying the two-day passes). Wear comfortable walking shoes; you'll cover a lot of ground.

The park is located in Union City, northwest of Big Cypress Tree State Natural Area, off of US-45.

Reelfoot Lake

Tennessee's "earthquake lake" is a hauntingly beautiful landscape of knob-kneed cypress trees, gently rippling water, and open spaces. **Reelfoot Lake** is a flooded forest, eerie looking and peaceful. With some 13,000 acres of water, the lake is also a sportsman's dream: 54 species of fish live in Reelfoot, including bream, crappie, catfish, and bass. From January to March—the best fishing season—the lake sees a steady stream of visitors who come to troll its waters. The cypress tint the water a clear but dark color, contributing to the magical feel of the place.

Reelfoot Lake is home to thousands of wintering and migratory birds. Visitors cannot help but notice the daily symphony of bird calls, not to mention the sight of ducks, herons, wild turkeys, eagles, and geese around the lake. Bird-watchers have identified some 238 species of birds in Reelfoot Lake, and the April turkey hunt in the area is excellent.

Bald eagles are the most iconic of the bird species that winter at the lake, and spotting

Discovery Park of America

Reelfoot Lake

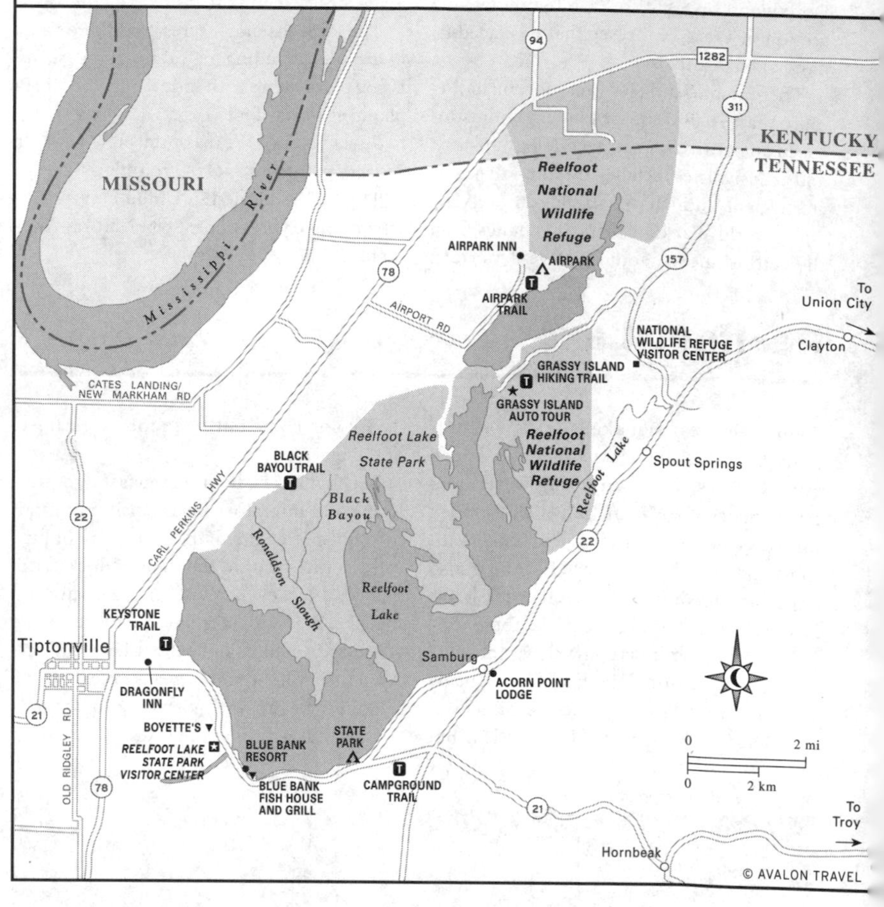

these majestic creatures is a popular pursuit January-March. Normally, the winter eagle population on the lake numbers 100-200 birds. Bald eagles had virtually disappeared from the area in the 1960s due to the effects of DDT contamination of their nesting grounds, but thanks to a nesting project started in 1988, they have returned.

ORIENTATION

Reelfoot Lake sits in the extreme northwestern corner of Tennessee, which makes it a little bit hard to get to. Its northernmost finger nearly touches the Kentucky state line, and the Mississippi River is only a mile to the west. Two-lane state highways circle the lake; the entire loop is about 35 miles. The southern portion of Reelfoot is a state park, and the northern half of the lake is a national wildlife refuge. Several thousand residents live in lakefront communities that dot the area.

The closest town to the lake, Tiptonville is a cluster of homes and businesses at the southwestern corner of Reelfoot. The boyhood home of Carl Perkins is found here; look for a sign on Highway 78, south of town, to find it.

Seasonal Wildlife

There are distinct variations in the type of wildlife you will see in and around Reelfoot Lake throughout the year.

In January and February, the wintering eagle and Canada goose populations peak, and cold water crappie fishing is good. In March, the eagles begin their northward migration, while osprey return from South America. Wild turkeys are often visible in March.

Spring comes to the lake in April and May, with wildflowers in abundance and the best season for bird-watching. This is also the best season to listen for frogs. By June, you may see deer fawns, and the floating aquatic plants are in bloom.

July and August are the hottest months at Reelfoot Lake, and therefore the season of mosquitoes and deerflies. By September, it has cooled off. Fall fishing for crappie and bass begins.

During the fall, migrating and wintering birds begin to return. Short raccoon and archery deer hunting seasons take place in October; the deer gun hunt takes place in November. December is one of the best months to view ducks, geese, and eagles.

Most accommodations, restaurants, and provisioning locales are found along the southern shore, just a few minutes' drive from Tiptonville. There are a few private camps and inns, which are set on the lake's western shore, about 10 miles from Tiptonville. The trails and visitors center maintained by the U.S. Fish and Wildlife Service are located on the more isolated northern shore of the waters. New cabins are planned for the south end of the lake.

SIGHTS

★ Reelfoot Lake State Park Visitors Center

The **Reelfoot Lake State Park Visitors Center** (2595 State Rte 21E, 731/253-9652, 8am-4:30pm Mon.-Fri., free) provides the best introduction to the lake, with exhibits on its history, wildlife, legends, and ecology. You can see a traditional Reelfoot Lake boat and read the story of the local vigilantes who took matters into their own hands when the lake

The cypress trees on Reelfoot Lake are breathtaking.

The New Madrid Earthquake

A series of powerful earthquakes struck the central United States between December 1811 and February 1812. At the time there was no way of measuring magnitude, but modern scientists now say that at least three of these temblors exceeded magnitude 8.0.

The first major quake struck on December 16, 1811, and caused the ground to split open around New Madrid, Missouri. A sulfurous gas filled the air, and witnesses saw thousands of birds flying away from the area. On this day the *New Orleans*, one of the nation's first steamboats, was voyaging down the Mississippi River. The crew was no doubt alarmed to find that as they entered the earthquake-stricken area, riverbanks were shaking and waves were rocking the boat. The steamboat weathered the effects of temblors on December 19, and on December 21 the crew woke to find that the mooring that they had cast the night before was no longer secure because the very island they had anchored to had disappeared under the water.

The final quake struck on February 7, 1812, and gave birth to what is now Reelfoot Lake. The most violent of all the quakes, it caused dishes to shake in Montreal, Quebec, Canada, and rang bells in Boston. The Mississippi riverbed rose and sank; boats capsized or were sucked into fissures that appeared suddenly in the earth. The quake was so powerful that it caused the Mississippi River to flow northward for a period, and it diverted a large amount of water onto once-dry land, creating Reelfoot Lake.

was threatened with development. This is also the place to sign up for popular lake cruises, free guided canoe trips, and sightseeing tours.

Outside the museum are a couple of mesh cages where you can see bald eagles, owls, and red-tailed hawks. A half-mile boardwalk trail extends out over the lake at the rear of the visitors center and is a must for anyone who wants to experience the special beauty of the lake.

Reelfoot National Wildlife Refuge

As of December 2015 the physical refuge center (4343 Hwy. 157, 731/538-2481, 8am-4pm daily, free) is closed while a new one is under construction, but the resources to visitors remain. Take note that the **Reelfoot National Wildlife Refuge**, which is, essentially, the northern half of the lake, is only open to the public for fishing and wildlife observation March 15-November 15 every year, Contact the visitors center for specific rules about fishing, hunting, and public access to the refuge. When the center reopens there will be exhibits about the flora and fauna of the area.

The wildlife refuge maintains the **Grassy Island Auto Tour,** a three-mile self-guided auto tour, year-round. The tour leads to an observation tower overlooking the Grassy Island part of the lake and is worth the detour required to reach it.

SPORTS AND RECREATION

Boating

If you can do only one thing when you visit Reelfoot Lake, get out on the dark, lily-pad-filled water in a boat. The best cruises are provided by the state park; reservations are required. One-hour cruises are offered on weekends for $6/person; The **three-hour cruises** (731/253-9652, adults $10, children 5-15 $6) take place May-September and depart daily at 9am. from the visitors center on the south side of the lake. Your guide will point out fish, birds, and other distinctive features of the lake. It is a good idea to bring drinks (a cooler with ice is provided) and snacks.

In March and April, the park offers a deep-swamp canoe float that departs on weekends at 8am and 1pm. The cost is $10. From January to March, special bald eagle tours are offered daily at 10am.

Fishing

Fishing is the most popular recreational

activity at Reelfoot Lake. With 13,000 acres of water and an average depth of just over five feet, the lake is a natural fish hatchery. An estimated 54 species of fish live in the lake. The most common fish are bream, crappie, catfish, and bass. The fishing season generally runs March-July, although some species are plentiful into the fall.

Because Reelfoot Lake is so shallow, and because of the cypress knees that lurk beneath the surface, most anglers use a specially designed Reelfoot Lake boat. If it's your first time boating, sign up with a local guide, who can help make arrangements for a boat rental and will share local fishing knowledge. Experienced guides include Jeff Riddle (731/446-7554), Craig Vancleave (731/592-2223), and Mark Pierce (731/538-2323). For a complete and current listing of local guides, check with the visitors center or tourist council. Boat rentals usually cost $50 and up per day, and guides charge $150 and up per day.

Several hotels catering to anglers offer special packages that include room, a boat and motor, bait, ice, and fuel for as little as $120 per night.

Hiking

Campground Trail: A 0.5-mile trail that begins in the spillway area and ends at the state park campground on the southern tip of the lake. The trailhead is located on Highway 21/22.

Keystone Trail: This 1.5-mile path skirts the edge of the lake along part of its southern shore. Hikers should wear shoes or boots that can withstand the sometimes-muddy path. Birds are common. The trailhead is located off Highway 21/22 and is adjacent to a large picnic area.

Black Bayou Trail: This two-mile walk through the cypress swamp follows the Black Bayou Slough. The trailhead is located along Highway 78 on the western shore of the lake.

The Airpark Trail: This 1.5-mile trail winds through cypress and hardwood forest as well as open fields. The trailhead is next to the old Airpark Inn site off Highway 78.

Grassy Island Hiking Trail: Part of the national wildlife refuge at Grassy Island, this 0.5-mile path cuts through lowland forest and over swampy wetlands. A portion follows the paved auto-tour road through Grassy Island.

Biking

The terrain around Reelfoot Lake is flat, and traffic is relatively light. **Biking** is a good way to get around and explore what the lake has to offer. Bring your own bike, however, since no rentals are available.

ACCOMMODATIONS

The **Blue Bank Resort** (813 Lark Dr, Hornbeak, 877/258-3226, www.bluebankresort.com, $109-179) has a traditional motel as well as cabins that stand over the lake, with expansive decks and a 12-person hot tub. The cabins can sleep 3-16. All rooms have a lot of exposed wood, giving the resort the feeling of a hunting lodge. The Blue Bank offers fishing packages that cost $200-300 per person for up to four nights and include gear—boat, motor, bait, and ice—for fishing. If you're just interested in a room without the add-ons, call at the last minute to find out if there is a vacancy.

The **Acorn Point Lodge** (Hwy. 22 and 1685 Lake Dr., Hornbeak, 731/538-9800, www.acornpointlodge.com, $59-89) has 12 rooms, half of which have lake views. Rates vary according to season and include breakfast. There are packages for hunters and groups.

For the most intimate accommodations at Reelfoot Lake, try **Dragonfly Inn** (365 Sunkist Beach Rd., 731/253-0206, www.dragonflyinnreelfootlake.com, $60), formerly Miss Pauline's Bed-and-Breakfast. Set in an old farmhouse, this friendly bed-and-breakfast is just one mile from Reelfoot Lake but feels removed from the crowds that exist during peak season. The four rooms are homey, and each has a private bath, individual heating and air-conditioning, and a queen-size bed. Host Marianne serves a full breakfast and accommodates anglers with early breakfasts, freezer space, and lots of boat parking in the driveway. Rates are higher during the October arts and crafts festival.

New cabins are planned for the south end of the lake, but no date has yet been announced by Tennessee State Parks.

Camping

Reelfoot Lake State Park (2595 State Route 21E, Tiptonville, 731/253-9652) runs two campgrounds for RVs and tents, although at press time the north campground was under construction. A larger campground is on the southern shore near the visitors center. Rates at both campgrounds are $25 for an RV site and $8 for a tent site. Sites are given on a first-come, first-served basis; no reservations are accepted.

FOOD

Catfish and other lake fish are the food du jour around Reelfoot Lake. ★ **Boyette's** (Hwy. 21, 731/253-7307, 11am-9pm daily, $10-18) is located across the road from the Reelfoot Lake State Park Visitors Center. The catfish platter is the specialty here, and it comes with generous portions of French fries, onion rings, hush puppies, coleslaw, and green beans. If you've worked up an appetite after a day of fishing, go for the all-you-can-eat catfish dinner, a steal at $16. You can also get frog legs, steaks, and burgers.

A little bit farther east along the lakeshore road you will find **Blue Bank Fish House and Grill** (813 Lake Dr., 877/258-3226, 11am-9pm daily, $6-24). The Blue Bank menu is sure to have something that will please everyone. In addition to all-you-can-eat catfish, fried quail, and country ham, you can choose from pasta, shrimp, steak, loaded potatoes, and burgers. The dinner menu is $8-20, and lunchtime entrées are $6-14. Blue Bank also serves breakfast. The kitchen closes 2pm-4pm on weekdays.

INFORMATION

Stop at the **State Park Visitor Center** (Hwy. 21, 731/253-7756, 8am-4:30pm daily) or the **Reelfoot Lake Tourism Council** (4575 Hwy. 21 E., 731/253-6516, www.reelfoottourism.com, 8am-5pm Mon., 9am-5pm Thurs., 9am-6pm Fri.-Sat., 1pm-6pm Sun.) for visitor information. The Reelfoot Lake State Park Auto Tour guide, a single-sheet handout available at any of these offices, is the most useful map of the area.

Kentucky Lake

The part of the Tennessee River that runs from the striking Land Between the Lakes region near the Kentucky-Tennessee line to Decatur County is commonly referred to as **Kentucky Lake**. The name reflects the river's breadth and its lake-like calmness, thanks to river dams built in the 1930s and 1940s.

The lake provides opportunities for recreation and is home to a one-of-a-kind pearl farm. Off the water, this region includes Fort Donelson National Battlefield, a significant and picturesque Civil War site, and Hurricane Mills, the town known as the home of country music superstar Loretta Lynn.

ORIENTATION

Kentucky Lake is the largest artificial lake east of the Mississippi by surface area, with approximately 2,064 miles of shore, located along the southwest border of the Land Between the Lakes National Recreation Area and just north of Tennessee National Wildlife Refuge. Nearby communities include Buchanan to the west, Big Sandy to the south, and Dover to the east.

HURRICANE MILLS

Loretta Lynn, the mega country music star, recalls going for a Sunday drive in the countryside west of Nashville in the early 1960s.

Kentucky Lake

That was when she and her late husband, Oliver Lynn, also known as "Doolittle" or "Doo," first saw the 1817 plantation home where they would eventually raise their family. "I looked up on this big ole hill and said, 'I want that house right there,'" she is reported to have said.

Lynn, who moved to Tennessee in 1960 at the beginning of her music career, is one of the most influential female artists in the genre. During the height of her career in the 1970s, she published her autobiography, *Coal Miner's Daughter,* later made into a film. In 1979 she was named Artist of the Decade by the Country Music Association. With the help of hipster/music guru Jack White, her music was introduced to a new generation with 2004's "Van Lear Rose."

The mansion that Lynn bought in 1966 is now just one of a half-dozen Lynn-inspired attractions in **Hurricane Mills** (931/296-7700, www.lorettalynnranch.net), a town that time would have forgotten were it not for Loretta Lynn. First buying just the mansion, Lynn now owns the whole shebang: Even the U.S. Postal Service rents the Hurricane Mills Post Office from Lynn.

The town is located seven miles north of I-40, along Highway 13. Waverly and Dickson are the closest large towns.

Sights

Visitors to Hurricane Mills can tour the antebellum mansion Lynn bought in 1966, as well as a replica of her childhood home in Butcher Holler, Kentucky, and a simulated coal mine, made to look like the one in which her father worked. Guided tours, which cost $12 for adults and $6 for children 6-12, last about an hour and depart daily at 9:30am, 10:30am, 11:30am, 1pm, 2pm, 3pm, and 4pm.

The **Coal Miner's Daughter Museum** (931/296-1840, 9am-4pm daily, adults $10, children 6-12 $5) is an 18,000-square-foot exhibit hall packed with items from Lynn's personal and professional life. Opened in 2001, the museum includes her tour bus, pictures, clothing, portraits, and gifts from celebrity friends. There is also **Loretta's Doll and Fan Museum** (free), located in a beautiful red 1896 gristmill.

The museums and plantation tours are open April-October and are generally closed during the winter. Call ahead to confirm.

Practicalities

The **Loretta Lynn Ranch** (44 Hurricane Mills Rd., 931/296-7700, www.lorettalynnranch.net) has an RV park, campground, and cabin rentals. There are also canoe rentals, paddleboats, and occasional concerts by Lynn herself. For something a little different, book a night on Lynn's old tour bus. For $125-150 per night, up to four people can sleep tour-bus-style, with television, a microwave, refrigerator, and coffeemaker. The ranch is open March-October.

For food, entertainment, and shopping, head to **Cissie Lynn's Country Store and Music Barn** (8000 Hwy. 13 S., 931/296-2275, 6am-6pm daily). Operated by Loretta Lynn's daughter Cissie, the restaurant and music hall serves sandwiches and country-style food ($7-15). In the evenings there are writers' nights, live music, and special events.

Closer to the mansion, **Rock-a-Billy Cafe** (Stage Coach Hill, 931/296-1840, 9am-5pm Fri.-Sun.) is a casual restaurant located in the old gristmill.

MOUSETAIL LANDING STATE PARK

Located on land once occupied by an eponymous river town, **Mousetail Landing State Park** (Linden, 731/847-0841, tnstateparks.com/parks/about/mousetail-landing) was dedicated in 1986. This 1,247-acre park lies on the east bank of the Tennessee River in the rural and picturesque Western Valley. The town acquired its name from the large number of rodents that once took shelter in the town's tanning factories. Tanned hides were shipped northward to markets up the river, including Paducah, Louisville, and St. Louis.

The park contains several ruins from the historic era, including the original pier, a blacksmith shop, and the old community cemetery.

Recreation

There is a three-mile day-use hiking trail through the woods, as well as an eight-mile loop with two overnight shelters along the way. The shelters are well maintained and provide lovely protection from the elements. The hike is relatively easy; you could complete the entire loop in a day and camp at the park campground.

One-half-mile south of the main entrance to the park there is a boat launch and courtesy pier. Fishing is popular and permitted anywhere in the park. Bass, bream, crappie, striper, and catfish are among the most frequent catches.

Also near the boat dock is a small swimming beach. There is no lifeguard on duty. A small, cold creek near the entrance to the park is ideal for wading and exploration.

Families enjoy the playgrounds, archery range, horseshoes, basketball, and volleyball court.

Camping

There are two campgrounds at **Mousetail Landing** (Rt. 3, Linden, 731/847-0841). Rates are $8-25 per site. The main campground, located in a woodland forest, has 25 sites, including 20 with electricity and water. There is a modern bathhouse and laundry facilities, plus picnic tables and grills. There is also a dump station.

Spring Creek Campground has 21 sites along the banks of the Tennessee River, located at the public boat dock.

Both Campgrounds are open year-round.

TENNESSEE NATIONAL WILDLIFE REFUGE

The **Tennessee National Wildlife Refuge** encompasses more than 51,000 acres along the Kentucky Lake, divided into three units. The Big Sandy Unit is just south of Paris Landing State Park; the Duck River Unit is farther south, near Eagle Creek and where I-40 crosses the river; the Busseltown unit is farther south still, near Perryville and Mousetail Landing State Park.

The refuge was established in 1945 as a safe haven for waterfowl. Today it consists of several different habitats, including open water, bottomland hardwoods, upland forests, freshwater marshes, and agricultural lands. As a refuge, the first priority is to protect animal species rather than provide a space for human recreation.

Fishing and hunting are allowed in certain parts of the refuge at certain times of the year. There is an observation deck at the entrance to the Duck River "bottoms" area, where you can see a variety of waterfowl, especially in fall and winter. There is another observation deck at the V. L. Childs Overlook at the Big Sandy Unit off Swamp Creek Road. There is a 2.5-mile hiking trail here, too.

A new **refuge headquarters and visitors center** (1371 Wildlife Dr, Springville, 731/642-2091, 8am-4pm Mon.-Sat.) opened in 2014.

NATCHEZ TRACE STATE PARK AND FOREST

Named for the famous old road from Natchez to Nashville, this is one of the largest state parks in Tennessee. The park (24845 Natchez Trace Rd., Wildersville, 731/968-3742, tnstateparks.com/parks/about/natchez-trace, park office 8am-4:30pm Mon.-Fri.) has four lakes, including Pin Oak Lake, which offers fishing, boating, and swimming. Historically the Natchez Trace has offered horseback riding through the **Natchez Trace Equestrian Center** (731/967-5340, 9am-5pm Fri.-Sat., 1pm-5pm Sun. Mar.-Memorial Day and Labor Day-late Nov., 9am-5pm Tues.-Sat., 1pm-5pm Sun. Memorial Day-Labor Day) for adults and children as young as three years. An hour's guided ride costs $24. The center can be closed unexpectedly, so it is best to call ahead if horseback riding is your primary motivation for going to the park.

There are 13.5 miles of hiking trails at the park, as well as a museum about the natural history and wildlife of the area. Tennis courts, baseball fields, a basketball course, and an archery and shooting range round out the facilities.

The park also has cabins, a campground, a resort inn, and group lodge.

CAMDEN

The town of Camden is the seat of Benton County, whose eastern edge is bounded by the Tennessee River.

Patsy Cline Memorial

Country music star Patsy Cline, together with Hawkshaw Hawkins, Cowboy Copas, and Randy Hughes, died in an airplane crash about three miles northwest of Camden on March 5, 1963. The Grand Ole Opry stars were heading back to Nashville after playing a benefit concert in Kansas City. The Piper Comanche airplane that they were in stopped in Dyersburg to refuel and took off shortly after 6pm, despite high winds and inclement weather. The plane crashed at 6:20pm in a forest west of Camden, just 90 miles from Nashville. Cline was 30 years old.

The site of the plane crash remains a memorial to Patsy Cline, maintained over the years by her loyal fans. There is a memorial stone, bulletin board, and mailbox where fans can leave their personal sentiments about the star. The memorial is located 2.8 miles northwest of town along Mount Carmel Road.

Near Camden

North America's only freshwater pearl-culturing farm is located a few miles south of Camden on Birdsong Creek, an inlet of the Tennessee River. The **Tennessee River Freshwater Pearl Museum and Farm** (255 Marina Rd., 731/584-7880, www.tennesseeriverpearls.com, 8am-5pm Mon.-Sat., 1pm-4pm Sun., free) is the unlikely result of one family's passion for pearls. John and Chessie Latrendressee founded the farm in 1979 and made their first successful harvest in 1984. Wild pearls were harvested from mussels fished from the bottom of the Tennessee River for years, but the Latrendressees were the first to successfully farm the gem.

The small museum explains the culturing process, the history of the Tennessee River pearl farm, and the history of pearls. You can also watch a *CBS Sunday Morning* segment produced about the Tennessee River Pearl Farm. There is a gift shop that sells some of the homegrown pearls; others are exported around the world. For a more detailed look, sign up for one of the farm's tour packages. There are several tour options ranging from the one-hour ($15) "Tour Bus Tweener Tour" to the full 3-5-hour tour ($55) that includes lunch and a visit to the farm itself, where you can see the phases of pearl culturing. Tours require at least 15 people, but small groups can often add onto tours that have already been booked. Call ahead to check the schedule.

The pearl farm is located at **Birdsong Resort** (www.birdsong.com), which is also a favorite place for boaters and anglers, as well as group getaways. There are dozens of cabins, 50 campsites, a marina, catering facilities, and a pool.

NATHAN BEDFORD FORREST STATE PARK

Dedicated in 1929 to Nathan Bedford Forrest, the controversial Confederate Civil War general, this 2,500-acre state park offers camping, cabins, hiking, swimming, group pavilions, and fishing. There are eight cabins ($85-125, minimum two-night stay), each of which can sleep up to eight people, plus a group lodge that accommodates up to 64 people. The campgrounds can accommodate tents or RVs.

There are more than 30 miles of hiking trails, ranging from easy to rugged. Swimming is good at Eva Beach, a rough sandy beach on Kentucky Lake.

The **park office** (1825 Pilot Knob Rd., Eva, 731/584-6356, tnstateparks.com/parks/about/nathan-bedford-forrest) is open 8am-4:30pm daily.

★ Tennessee River Folklife Center

Located at Pilot Knob overlooking the Tennessee River, the **Tennessee River Folklife Center** (1825 Pilot Knob Rd., 731/584-6356, 8am-4:30pm daily, free) lovingly depicts the traditional ways of river folk. The centerpiece of the museum is *Old Betsy*, a traditional riverboat built from old farm equipment in the 1960s by T. J. Whitfield. Exhibits include photographs of a houseboat family and displays about river mussels, the pearl industry, and traditional foods and music. The museum is comprehensive but not too large to be overwhelming.

Just steps from the doors to the folklife center is a monument to Nathan Bedford Forrest and his cavalry, which defeated a federal supply depot at Old Johnsonville, near the park, in 1984. There are impressive views of the Tennessee River from the porch outside the museum, including several manufacturing plants that emit distinctly industrial smells at certain times of the day.

JOHNSONVILLE STATE HISTORIC AREA

This 600-acre park (90 Nell Beard Rd., New Johnsonville, 931/535-2789, tnstateparks.com/parks/about/Johnsonville) is the site of Johnsonville before the creation of the Kentucky Lake, and this is where the battle of Johnsonville took place during the Civil War. The November 4, 1864, battle is noteworthy because it was the first time that a naval force was engaged and defeated by a cavalry.

The day-use park has picnic pavilions, playgrounds, and 10 miles of hiking trails.

PARIS

Paris, the largest town in the Kentucky Lake region, was founded in 1823 and named after the French capital in honor of the Marquis de Lafayette. Not long after, tourists were traveling to this Paris to drink and soak in a nearby sulfur well, which was believed to have health benefits. The well was submerged by

The Legacy of Nathan Bedford Forrest

Nathan Bedford Forrest is both one of the most celebrated and reviled historical figures in Tennessee. An accomplished Confederate cavalry commander and the first grand wizard of the Ku Klux Klan, Forrest has come to symbolize the Old South.

Forrest was born in 1821 in Chapel Hill, a small town in Marshall County in Middle Tennessee. At the age of 16, Forrest's blacksmith father died, and the young man became the head of his family. He had a mere six months of formal education in his lifetime, yet he became a successful businessman, primarily as a plantation owner and slave trader.

Forrest was a staunch believer in the Southern cause, and when Tennessee seceded from the Union in 1861, he enlisted as a private in the Tennessee Mounted Rifles, together with his younger brother and 15-year-old son.

In a peculiar twist, Forrest offered freedom to his 44 slaves at the outbreak of the Civil War if they would fight for the Confederacy. All agreed, and 43 reportedly served faithfully until the end of the war.

Forrest was daring on the battlefield, often taking great risks to avoid capture and defeat. Historian Brian S. Wills wrote: "His ferocity as a warrior was almost legendary. . . . Forrest understood, perhaps better than most, the basic premise of war: 'War means fighting and fighting means killing.'"

Forrest was involved in dozens of battles—small and large—during the war. In February 1862, he led his men out of Fort Donelson rather than surrender. He was wounded at Shiloh and fought at Chickamauga. In May 1863, he outmaneuvered a stronger Union force in northern Alabama by fooling Colonel Abel Streight into believing that Forrest had more men than he did.

Forrest's victory at Fort Pillow in April 1864 was tarnished by the deaths of so many black Union soldiers, allegedly killed after they surrendered.

His victory at Brice's Cross Roads, in Mississippi, where Forrest defeated a much larger force of Union infantry and cavalry in June 1864, is believed by many to be his greatest success.

Forrest ended the Civil War as lieutenant general in command of cavalry in Alabama, Mississippi, and east Louisiana. His last battle at Gainsville, Alabama, in May 1865 ended in surrender.

Following the war, Forrest struggled to adapt to the changes it had brought. He supported the Ku Klux Klan in hopes of restoring the conservative white power structure that existed prior to the war and served as the Klan's first grand wizard.

His business dealings floundered. Forrest lost a fortune in the railroad industry, and he spent his remaining years running a prison farm and living in a log cabin.

In his last years, Forrest seemed to reconsider many of his views on racial equality. In 1875, he spoke to a local group of freedmen, saying, "I came to meet you as friends, and welcome you to the white people. I want you to come nearer to us. When I can serve you I will do so. We have but one flag, one country; let us stand together. We may differ in color, but not in sentiment." Forrest kissed the cheek of an African American woman who handed him a bouquet of flowers, a gesture of intimacy unknown in that era.

Forrest died in Memphis in October 1877. He was buried at Elmwood Cemetery but later reinterred at Forrest Park, built in his honor, in midtown Memphis.

In the years since the civil rights movement, many people have questioned Forrest's legacy. In 2005, there was an effort to move the statue over Forrest's grave and rename Forrest Park, and others have tried to get a bust of Forrest removed from the Tennessee House of Representatives chamber: Both efforts failed.

Kentucky Lake in 1944 when TVA dammed the Tennessee River.

In keeping with its name, Paris has a model of the Eiffel Tower, donated to the city in 1992 by Christian Brothers University of Memphis. Located in Memorial Park on the outskirts of the city, the model tower is surrounded by a playground, ball field, and walking trails. Don't expect to see it towering over the town, however, as the model is only 60 feet tall.

To learn about the history of Paris and Henry County, visit the **Paris-Henry County Heritage Center** (614 N. Poplar St., 731/642-1030, www.phchc.com, 10am-4pm Tues.-Fri., 10am-2pm Sat.), located in the Cavitt Place, a 1916 Italian Renaissance-style two-story home. The center houses exhibits about the history of Henry County and can provide an audio walking guide to historic Paris. There is also a gift shop.

Festivals and Events

More than 12,500 pounds of catfish are served at the **World's Biggest Fish Fry** (www.worldsbiggestfishfry.com), which takes place in Paris in late April every year. The tradition evolved from the annual Mule Day, when farmers traveled to the town to trade their mules and other farm equipment ahead of the summer growing season. In 1953, the fish fry was established, and it has grown in popularity every year, once the organizers started using local fish. Today, the fish fry is a week-long event with rodeos, races, a parade, and four days of fish dinners, available for $10 a plate at the Bobby Cox Memorial Fish Tent.

Accommodations

In Paris, there are several serviceable chain hotels, but the option that allows you to really experience the area at its best is to choose from the many cabins and lakeside resorts nearby.

On U.S. 641 one mile outside of Paris, the **Terrace Woods Lodge** (1190 N. Market St., 731/642-2642, www.terracewoodslodge.com, starting at $40) is not as rustic as it sounds, with free wireless Internet, flat-screen televisions, and views of the woods. This is a standard motel, but the rooms are clean and the service acceptable.

Two guest rooms are available in the renovated 1909 **Home Sweet Home B&B** (108 N College St, 731/642-8135, homesweethomebandb.com, $60-110). You'll be well fed during your stay, thanks to the large country breakfast in the morning and the cocktail hour snacks at night.

Food

Downtown Paris has a bona fide coffee shop, with espresso, cappuccino, latte, and other specialty coffee drinks. **Jack's Java** (116 N. Market St., 731/642-4567, 7:30am-5pm Mon.-Fri., 9am-noon Sat.) doubles as a bookstore and paint your own pottery studio, providing a great kids' activity if your camping trip gets rained out. Jack Jones Flowers and Gifts is next door.

Enjoy homemade soups and sandwiches before you dig in to decadent cupcakes at **A La Mode Sweet Shoppe**,(112 Market St,, 731-641-1222, 11am-5pm Mon.-Fri., 10am-4pm Sat.).

French-themed **Paulette's** (200 S Market St., 731/644-3777, 10:30am-2pm Mon.-Fri.) is a favorite of locals who celebrate birthdays, with quiche and other house specialties.

For a sit-down dinner, try **Lepanto Steak House** (1305 E. Wood St., 731/641-1791, 11am-9pm, $10-24 Mon.-Sat.), where you can get seafood, pasta, and chicken as well as steaks.

Information and Services

Get visitor information from the **Paris-Henry County Chamber of Commerce** (2508 E. Wood St., 731/642-3431, www.paristnchamber.com) in Paris.

Also in Paris, the **W. G. Rhea Public Library** (400 W. Washington St., 731/642-1702, 9am-5pm Mon.-Sat.) has 50,000 volumes as well as computers with Internet access. The library is open until 7pm on Tuesday and Thursday evenings.

NEAR PARIS

The most laid-back accommodations in the area are found at **Mammy and Pappy's B&B** (7615 Elkhorn Rd., Springville, 731/642-8129, www.mammy-pappysbb.com, $95), a 1900-era farmhouse in Springville. Located about 13 miles from Paris in rural countryside, this is a real getaway. Dannie and Katie Williams manage this family property, which has been lovingly cared for over the years. Each of the four bedrooms

The outcome of the Civil War was determined at Fort Donelson National Battlefield.

has hardwood floors and private baths. Breakfasts include homemade biscuits, and guests are also provided an evening snack. Additional nights' stays are $80 (rather than the initial $95).

PARIS LANDING STATE PARK

One of Tennessee's "resort parks," **Paris Landing** (16055 Highway 79 N., Buchanan, 731/642-4311) is an 841-acre park on the banks of Kentucky Lake. The 130-room park inn is located next to a large conference center and dining room, all with views of the lake. There is also an award-winning public golf course and swimming pool.

Day-trippers gravitate to the lake itself. Fishing is the most popular activity; catfish, crappie, bass, sauger, walleye, bluegill, and striper are some of the most common catches. The park maintains two fishing piers and one launch ramp for public use. There are also more than 200 open and covered slips for rent.

The park has a public swimming beach, hiking trails, tennis, basketball and baseball facilities, and pavilions for picnics and parties.

Accommodations

For accommodations on the lake, you cannot beat **Paris Landing State Resort Park** (16055 Hwy. 79 N., 731/641-4465), which has hotel rooms, cabins, and campground facilities on the water. The 130-room inn ($58-176) looks like a concrete goliath, but the rooms are comfortable, and all have beautiful views of the lake. The three-bedroom cabins ($170-180) can sleep up to 10 people and are set on a secluded point overlooking the lake. The campground ($11-20) has both RV and tent sites, a laundry, bathhouse, and dump station.

As its name suggests, **The Reel Inn** (2155 Hwy. 119 N., Buchanan, 731/232-8227, $99) caters to anglers. The lakeside offerings here include two-bedroom cabins with washer/dryers, daily maid service, full-size kitchen appliances, and other comforts of home.

Buchanan Resort (Hwy. 79, west of Paris Landing State Park, 731/642-2828, www.buchananresort.com, $69-210) has a place to rest your head, no matter what your preference. Choices include a motel, lodges that accommodate up to 20 people, and waterfront suites and cottages.

There is no shortage of welcoming resorts with lakeside cabins in the area. Another good option includes **Mansard Island Resort and Marina** (60 Mansard Island Dr., Springville, 731/642-5590, www.mansardisland.com, $84-147, with a two-night minimum), which has town houses and cottages for lake-goers, and lots of amenities, including a swimming pool. There are discounted rates for extended stays. Pets are not permitted.

★ FORT DONELSON NATIONAL BATTLEFIELD

On Valentine's Day in 1862, Union forces attacked the Confederate Fort Donelson on the banks of the Cumberland River. **Fort Donelson National Battlefield** (Hwy.

79, 931/232-5706, www.nps.gov/fodo) is now a national park, making this site a good choice for both history buffs and those who are more interested in the great outdoors. A visitors center with an exhibit, gift shop, and information boards is open 8am-4:30pm daily. The 15-minute video does a good job describing the battle and its importance in the Civil War.

A driving tour takes visitors to Fort Donelson, which overlooks the Cumberland River and may be one of the most picturesque forts in Tennessee. The earthen fort was built by Confederate soldiers and slaves over a period of about seven months.

You are also directed to the **Dover Hotel** (Petty St., 931/232-5706, 8am-4:15pm), which was used as the Confederate headquarters during the battle. The hotel, built between 1851 and 1853, is a handsome wood structure and has been restored to look as it did during the battle. It contains self-guided exhibits about the Battle of Fort Donelson and film about the discussions that led to the surrender in 1862. It is located a few blocks away from downtown Dover on a bucolic property near the Cumberland River.

The **National Cemetery,** established after the war, was built on grounds where escaped slaves lived in a so-called contraband camp during the Civil War. The camp was established by the Union army to accommodate slaves who fled behind Union lines during the war. The freedmen and freedwomen worked for the Union army, often without pay. It was not until 1862 that the Union army allowed blacks to join as soldiers.

There are more than five miles of hiking trails at Fort Donelson National Battlefield, including the three-mile River Circle Trail and four-mile Donelson Trail. Both hikes begin at the visitors center. Picnic tables are located next to the river near the old fort.

Unconditional Surrender

It was the day after Valentine's Day 1862, and things were bleak for the Confederate army at Fort Donelson. The fort, located on the banks of the Cumberland River, was under attack from Federal forces, and generals feared a siege.

Southern generals John B. Floyd and Gideon Johnson Pillow slipped away overnight, leaving General Simon B. Buckner, a former friend and schoolmate of General Ulysses S. Grant, in command. On the morning of February 16, Buckner wrote to Grant asking for the terms of surrender.

In Grant's famous reply, he said no terms other than "unconditional and immediate" surrender would be accepted. Buckner surrendered, and 13,000 Confederate men were taken prisoner. The path to the heart of the Confederacy was now open, and Grant earned a new nickname: "Unconditional Surrender" Grant.

DOVER

A small town set at the southern shore of the Cumberland River, **Dover** is Tennessee's major gateway to the Land Between the Lakes. It is also the place where General Ulysses S. Grant earned the nickname "Unconditional Surrender" during the Civil War.

Dover has a reputation for being a speed trap, so obey posted speed limits when driving here.

Accommodations

Just west of the entrance to Land Between the Lakes, the **Dover Inn Motel** (1545 Donelson Pkwy., 931/232-5556, $60-70) has both traditional motel rooms and modern cabins with full kitchens. All rooms have telephones, cable TV, air-conditioning, and coffeemakers. The motel caters to hunters and anglers who are going to Land Between the Lakes but don't want to camp. There is a swimming pool on the property.

Choose from a private campground or log cabins at **Leatherwood Resort** (753 Leatherwood Bay Rd., 931/232-5137, www.leatherwoodresort.com, $35 campground, $104-210 cabins). The cabins have a minimum four-night stay. Leashed pets are permitted, and there are discounts for weekly rates.

Food

For something sweet, head to the **Dip Dairy Freeze** (610 Donelson Pkwy., 931/232-5927, 10am-7pm Mon-Wed, 1pm-8pm Thurs.-Sun., $4-8), a casual, but iconic, restaurant serving burgers, hot dogs, and ice cream that's located just west of downtown Dover.

Located downtown, **The Dover Grille** (310 Donelson Pkwy., 931/232-7919, 7am-9pm daily, $5-12) serves burgers, dinner plates, Southwestern platters, pasta, and salads.

Several miles east of the town is the **Log Cabin Café** (1394 Hwy. 79, 931/232-0220, 5am-9pm Mon.-Sat., 5am-3pm Sun., $6-12). The café serves traditional Southern food in a modern log cabin. It is a popular pit stop for workers; the café's breakfast will fuel you all day long.

Information

The **Stewart County Chamber of Commerce** (117 Visitor Center Ln., 931/232-8290, www.stewartcountychamber.com) provides visitor information.

CROSS CREEKS NATIONAL WILDLIFE REFUGE

Four miles east of Dover is the 8,862-acre **Cross Creeks National Wildlife Refuge** (643 Wildlife Rd., 931/232-7477, www.fws.gov/crosscreeks, refuge: daylight hours daily Mar. 16-Nov. 14, visitors center: 7am-3:30pm Mon.-Fri. year-round). Established in 1962, the refuge includes 12.5 miles of bottomlands along the Cumberland River, plus nearby rocky bluffs and rolling hills. There is also a marsh, brush, and farmland. The refuge is an important habitat for geese, ducks, raptors, shorebirds, wading birds, and neotropical migratory birds. In January, when the bird population is at its peak, as many as 60,000 birds may be in the refuge. Mallard ducks make up the majority. American bald eagles and golden eagles also live in the refuge, along with great blue herons, wild turkeys, muskrats, coyotes, and bobcats. Farms within the refuge grow corn, soybeans, grain sorghum, and wheat; a portion of each harvest is left in the field for wildlife to consume.

A network of paved and gravel roads along the southern shore of the Cumberland are the best places to view the refuge. Rattlesnake Trail is a one-mile hiking path through the refuge. While hunting is allowed at certain times of year, camping and campfires are prohibited.

To find Cross Creeks, drive about four miles east of Dover on Highway 49. Look for Wildlife Drive on your left.

Land Between the Lakes

This narrow finger of land that lies between the Cumberland and Tennessee Rivers is a natural wonderland. Comprising 170,000 acres of land and wrapped by 300 miles of undeveloped river shoreline, the **Land Between the Lakes National Recreation Area** (Golden Pond Visitor Center, 238 Visitor Center Dr, Golden Pond, KY 270/924-2233, www.landbetweenthelakes.us, 9am-5pm daily) has become one of the most popular natural areas in this region of the country. Split between Tennessee and Kentucky, the area provides unrivaled opportunities to camp, hike, boat, play, or just simply drive through quiet wilderness.

The area lies between what is now called Kentucky Lake (the Tennessee River) and Lake Barkley (the Cumberland River). At its narrowest point, the distance between these two bodies of water is only one mile. The drive from north to south is 43 miles. About one-third of the park is in Tennessee; the rest is in Kentucky. It is managed by the U.S. Forest Service, an agency of the U.S. Department of Agriculture.

HISTORY

Land Between the Lakes was not always a natural and recreational area. Native Americans settled here, drawn to the fertile soil, proximity to the rivers, and gentle terrain. European settlers followed, and between about 1800 and the 1960s the area, then called Between the Rivers, saw thriving small settlements. Residents farmed and traded along the rivers, which were served by steamboats.

In many respects, settlers in Between the Rivers were even more isolated than those in other parts of what was then the western frontier of the United States. They did not necessarily associate with one state or another, instead forming a distinct identity of their own. During the Civil War, it was necessary to finally determine the border between Tennessee and Kentucky, since this line also marked the border between the Union and the Confederacy.

It was during another period of upheaval in the United States that the future of the Between the Rivers region changed forever. In the midst of the Great Depression, Congress created the Tennessee Valley Authority, which improved soil conditions, eased flooding, brought electricity, and created jobs in Tennessee. One of TVA's projects was the Kentucky Dam, which was built between 1938 and 1944 and impounded the Tennessee River. In 1957, work began on Barkley Dam, which impounded the Cumberland River and put an end to floods that damaged crops and destroyed property along the river.

About 25 years later, president John F. Kennedy announced that the U.S. government would buy out residents of the land between the Cumberland and Tennessee Rivers to create a new park, which would serve as an example of environmental management and recreational use. The project was to bring much-needed economic development to the area by attracting visitors to the park.

The project was not without opponents, who objected to the government's use of eminent domain to take over lands that were privately owned. Residents lamented the loss of unique communities in the lake region. More than 2,300 people were removed to create Land Between the Lakes (LBL). In all, 96,000 of the 170,000 acres that make up LBL were purchased or taken from private hands.

Over time, however, the controversy of the

Land Between the Lakes National Recreation Area

creation of the park has faded, and the Land Between the Lakes has become well-loved. It is the third most-visited park in Tennessee, behind only the Smoky Mountains and Cherokee National Forest.

PLANNING YOUR TIME

Some of the best attractions at Land Between the Lakes charge admission. If you are planning to visit all or most of them, consider one of the packages offered by the Forest Service. The discount package allows you to visit each attraction once over a seven-day period at a 30 percent discount. Another option is the $35 LBL Fun Card, which gives you 10 admissions to any of three attractions. It does not expire. You can buy packages at either the north (Kentucky) or south (Tennessee) welcome station or the Golden Pond Visitor Center.

During certain summer weekends there are free two-hour tours of Lake Barkley's **Power Plant and Navigation Lock** (270/362-4236). You must call in advance to reserve a spot and complete a registration form.

SIGHTS

Driving south to north along the scenic main road, or trace, that runs along the middle of the park, you will find the major attractions within Land Between the Lakes.

GREAT WESTERN IRON FURNACE

About 11 miles inside the park is the Great Western Iron Furnace, built by Brian, Newell, and Company in 1854. If you have traveled around this part of Tennessee much, you will have come to recognize the distinctive shape of the old iron furnaces that dot the landscape in the counties between Nashville and the Tennessee River. Like the Great Western Furnace, these plants were used to create high-quality iron from iron ore deposits in the earth.

The Great Western Furnace operated for less than two years. By 1856, panic over reported slave uprisings and the coming of the Civil War caused the plant to shut down. It would never make iron again.

★ THE HOMEPLACE

Just beyond the furnace is **The Homeplace** (10am-5pm Wed.-Sun. Mar. and Nov., 10am-5pm daily Apr.-Oct., ages 13 and up $5, ages 5-12 $3, children 4 and under free), a living-history museum that depicts life in Between the Rivers in about 1850. At the middle of the 19th century, Between the Rivers was home to an iron ore industry and hundreds of farmers. These farmers raised crops and livestock for their own use, as well as to sell where they could. In 1850, about 10,000 people lived in Between the Rivers, including 2,500 slaves and 125 free blacks.

The Homeplace re-creates an 1850s farmstead. Staff dress in period clothes and perform the labors that settlers would have done: They sow seeds in the spring, harvest in the summer and fall, and prepare the fields for the next year in the winter. The farm includes a dogtrot cabin, where you can see how settlers would have lived, cooked, and slept. Out back there is a small garden, a plot of tobacco, pigs, sheep, oxen, and a barn. You may see farmers splitting shingles, working oxen, sewing quilts, making candles, or any other of the dozens of tasks that settlers performed on a regular basis.

The Homeplace publishes a schedule that announces when certain activities will take place, such as canning, sheering of sheep, or harvesting tobacco. Even if you come when there is no special program, you will be able to see staff taking on everyday tasks, and you can ask them about any facet of life on the frontier.

ELK AND BISON PRAIRIE

Archaeological evidence shows that elk and bison once grazed in Tennessee and Kentucky, including the area between the rivers. Settlers quickly destroyed these herds, however. Both bison and elk were easy to hunt, and they were desirable for their meat and skins. By 1800, bison had been killed off, and about 50 years later elk were gone, too.

When Land Between the Lakes was created, elk and bison were reintroduced to the area. The South Bison Range across the road from the Homeplace is one of the places where bison now live. The bison herd that roams on about 160 acres here can sometimes be seen from the main road, or from side roads bordering the range.

You can see both bison and elk at the Elk and Bison Prairie, a 700-acre restoration project located near the midpoint of the Land Between the Lakes. In 1996, 39 bison were relocated from the south prairie here, and 29 elk were transported from Canada. Since then, the population of both animals has grown.

Visitors may drive through the range along a one-mile loop. Admission is $5 per vehicle. You are advised to take your time, roll down your windows, and keep your eyes peeled for a sign of the animals. The best time to view elk and bison is in the early morning or late afternoon. At other times of day, you may just enjoy the sights and sounds of the grassland. Pay attention to the road as well as the animals, as the car in front of you may slow to take photos of one of these magnificent creatures. You may also see some bison from the trace en route.

GOLDEN POND VISITOR CENTER AND PLANETARIUM

For the best overview of the history, nature, and significance of the Land Between the Lakes, stop at the **Golden Pond Visitor Center and Planetarium** (Golden Pond Visitor Center, 238 Visitor Center Dr, Golden Pond, KY 270/924-2233, www.landbetweenthelakes.us, 9am-5pm daily, visitors center free, planetarium shows ages 13 and up $5, children 5-12 $3, children 4 and under free). The visitors center is home to a small museum about the park, where you can also watch a video about the elk that have been restored on the Elk and Bison Prairie. There is also a gift shop, restrooms, and a picnic area.

The planetarium screens at least four programs daily about astronomy and nature, with more during the holidays. On Saturday and Sunday at 1pm you can get a sneak peek at the night sky above.

Golden Pond was the name of Land Between the Lakes's largest town before the park was created. Golden Pond, also called Fungo, was a vibrant town that, at its peak, had a hotel, bank, restaurants, and other retail outlets. During Prohibition, farmers made moonshine in the woods and sold it in Golden Pond. Golden Pond whiskey was sought after in back alley saloons as far away as Chicago. When Land Between the Lakes was created in 1963, Golden Pond had a population of about 200 people. Families moved their homes and relocated to communities outside the park. In 1970, when the historic society unveiled a marker at the site of Golden Pond, the strains of "Taps" rang out over the hills.

You can visit the site of Golden Pond by driving a few miles east of the visitors center on Highway 80. There is a picnic area.

WOODLANDS NATURE STATION

The final major attraction in Land Between the Lakes is the **Woodlands Nature Station** (north of the visitors center on the Trace, 270/924-2020, 10am-5pm daily Apr.-Oct., 10am-5pm, Wed.-Sun. Mar. and Nov., closed Dec.-Feb., ages 13 and up $5, children 5-12 $3, children 4 and under free). Geared to children, the nature station introduces visitors to animals, including bald eagles, coyotes, opossum, and deer. There are also opportunities for staff-led hiking trips. Special events and activities take place nearly every weekend, and during the week in summertime.

CENTER FURNACE

You can see the ruins of what was once the largest iron furnace in the Land Between the Lakes along the Center Furnace Trail. Along the short (0.3 mile) walk you will see signs that describe the process of making iron and explain why it was practiced in Between the Rivers.

Center Furnace was built between 1844 and 1846. It continued to operate until 1912, much longer than any other furnace in the area.

RECREATION

Promoting outdoor recreation is one of the objectives of Land Between the Lakes. Visitors can enjoy hiking, biking, paddling, or horseback riding; hunting and fishing; and camping. There is even an area specially designated for all-terrain vehicles.

Trails

There are 200 miles of hiking trails in Land Between the Lakes. Some of these are also open for mountain biking and horseback riding.

The **Fort Henry Trails** are a network of 29.3 miles of trails near the southern entrance to the park, some of which follow the shoreline of the Kentucky Lake. The intricate network of trails allows hikers to choose from a three-mile loop to something much longer.

Access the trails from the south welcome station, or from the Fort Henry Trails parking area, at the end of Fort Henry Road. These trails crisscross the grounds once occupied by the Confederate Fort Henry. They are for hikers only.

The **North-South Trail** treks the entire length of the Land Between the Lakes. From start to finish, it is 58.6 miles. Three backcountry camping shelters are available along the way for backpackers. The trail crosses the main road in several locations. Portions of the trail are open to horseback riders. The area from the Golden Pond Visitor Center to the northern end is also open to mountain bikers.

The 2.2-mile **Honker Lake Loop Trail** begins at the Woodlands Nature Station. This trail is open to hikers only. Sightings of fallow deer and giant Canada geese are common along this trail. The banks of nearby Hematite Lake are littered with bits of blue stone, remnants of slag from Center Iron Furnace.

Finally, at the northern end of the park are the **Canal Loop Trails,** a network of hiking and bike trails that depart from the north welcome station. These trails meander along the shores of both Kentucky Lake and Lake Barkley. The entire loop is 14.2 miles, but connector trails enable you to fashion a shorter hike or ride if you want.

A detailed map showing all hiking, biking, and horseback trails can be picked up at any of the park visitors centers. You can rent bikes at Hillman Ferry and Piney Campgrounds.

Off-Highway Vehicles

There are more than 100 miles of trail for off-highway vehicles (OHVs). OHV permits are available for $20 for one to three days, and $75

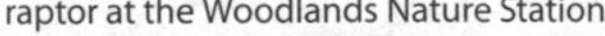
raptor at the Woodlands Nature Station

for an annual pass; passes may be purchased at any Land Between the Lakes visitors center. Call 270/924-2000 in advance to find out if any of the trails are closed due to bad weather or poor conditions.

Fishing and Boating

Land Between the Lakes offers excellent fishing. The best season for fishing is spring, April-June, when fish move to shallow waters to spawn. Crappie, largemouth bass, and a variety of sunfish may be caught at this time.

Summer and fall offer good fishing, while winter is fair. A fishing license from the state in which you will be fishing is required; these may be purchased from businesses outside the park. Specific size requirements and open dates may be found at any of the visitors centers.

There are 19 different lake access points where you can put in a boat. Canoe rentals are available at the Energy Lake Campground, which is over the border in Kentucky. Energy Lake is a no-wake lake.

Hunting

Controlled hunting is one of the tools that the Forest Service uses to manage populations of wild animals in Land Between the Lakes. Hunting also draws thousands of visitors each year. The annual spring turkey hunt and fall deer hunts are the most popular.

Specific rules govern each hunt, and in many cases hunters must apply in advance for a permit. Hunters must also have a $25 LBL Hunter Use Permit, as well as the applicable state licenses. For details on hunting regulations, call the park at 270/924-2065.

CAMPING

There are nine campgrounds at Land Between the Lakes. All campgrounds have facilities for tent or trailer camping.

Most campgrounds are open March 1-November 1, although some are open year-round. There's a complicated formula for figuring out the price of campsites, based on the exact campground and campsite location, the time of year, and the length of stay. In general costs range $12 basic site; RV sites range $22-40, depending on whether there is access to electricity, water, and sewer services.

Reservations are accepted for select campsites at Piney, Energy Lake, Hillman Ferry, and Wrangler Campgrounds up to six months in advance. Call the LBL headquarters in Kentucky at 270/924-2000 or visit the website at www.lbl.org to make a reservation.

PINEY CAMPGROUND

Located on the southern tip of Land Between the Lakes, **Piney Campground** is convenient to visitors arriving from the Tennessee side of the park, and, as a result, can be one of the most crowded campgrounds in LBL. Piney has more than 300 campsites; 281 have electricity; 44 have electricity, water, and sewer; and 59 are primitive tent sites.

There are also nine rustic one-bedroom camping shelters with a ceiling fan, table and chairs, electric outlets, and a large porch. Sleeping accommodations are one double bed and a bunk bed. Outside there is a picnic table and fire ring. There are no bathrooms; shelter guests use the same bathhouses as other campers. Camp shelters cost $35-37 per night and sleep up to four people. Piney all offers basic four-person cabins ($50), which have air-conditioning and heat.

Piney's amenities include a camp store, bike rental, archery range, playground, swimming beach, boat ramp, and fishing pier.

ENERGY LAKE CAMPGROUND

Near the midpoint of Land Between the Lakes, **Energy Lake Campground** has tent and trailer campsites, electric sites, and group camp facilities. It tends to be less crowded than some of the other campgrounds and has nice lakeside sites, with a swimming area, volleyball, and other kid-friendly activities.

HILLMAN FERRY CAMPGROUND

Located near the northern end of Land Between the Lakes, Hillman Ferry has 380 tent and RV campsites. It is nestled on the shores of Kentucky Lake, between Moss Creek and Pisgah Bay.

Electric and nonelectric sites are available. There is a dumping station, bathhouses with showers and flush toilets, drinking water, a camp store, swimming area, coin-operated laundry, and bike rentals.

Boat and Horse Camping

In addition to the campgrounds already listed, Land Between the Lakes operates five lakeside camping areas that are designed for boaters who want to spend the night. Rushing Creek/Jones Creek is the most developed of these camping areas; it has 40 tent or RV sites and a bathhouse with showers and flush toilets. Other campsites, including Birmingham Ferry/Smith Bay, Cravens Bay, Fenton, and Gatlin Point, have chemical toilets, tent camping sites, and grills.

LBL also has Wrangler's Campground, designed for horseback riders. In addition to tent and RV sites, there are camping shelters and horse stalls. Amenities include a camp store, bathhouses, coin laundry, and playground.

Backcountry Camping

Backcountry camping is allowed year-round in Land Between the Lakes. All you need is a backcountry permit ($7 for 3 days or $30 annually) and the right gear to enjoy unlimited choices of campsites along the shoreline or in the woodlands.

FOOD

There are no restaurants in Land Between the Lakes. There are vending machines with snacks and sodas at the Homeplace, Golden Pond Visitor Center, and the Woodlands Nature Station. Picnic facilities abound.

There is a McDonald's at the southern entrance to the park. Dover, five miles east, has a number of fast-food and local eateries. Twenty miles to the west, Paris has dozens of different restaurants.

INFORMATION AND SERVICES

The Forest Service maintains a useful website about Land Between the Lakes at www.landbetweenthelakes.us. You can also call 270/924-2000 to request maps and information sheets. The park headquarters is located at the Golden Pond Visitor Center.

When you arrive, stop at the nearest welcome or visitors center for up-to-date advisories and activity schedules. Each of the welcome centers and the visitors center are open 9am-5pm daily.

The **Land Between the Lakes Association** (800/455-5897, www.friendsoflbl.org) organizes volunteer opportunities and publishes a detailed tour guide to the park, which includes historical and natural anecdotes.

Jackson

The largest city between Nashville and Memphis, **Jackson** is the center of commerce and business for rural West Tennessee. Every Pringles potato chip in the world is made in Jackson, which also hosts a number of events, including a Division One women's basketball tournament, the Miss Tennessee pageant, and the West Tennessee State Fair.

Jackson owes its existence to the railroads, and the city has preserved this history at a top-notch museum set right next to the railroad tracks. Jackson is also home to a museum dedicated to the life and death of famous railroad engineer Casey Jones, and another that zeroes in on that endearing art form, rockabilly.

SIGHTS

Jackson's city center is about five miles south of I-40, and the roadways between the interstate and downtown are cluttered with strip malls, motels, and traffic. Most of the attractions, with the exception of Casey Jones

Jackson

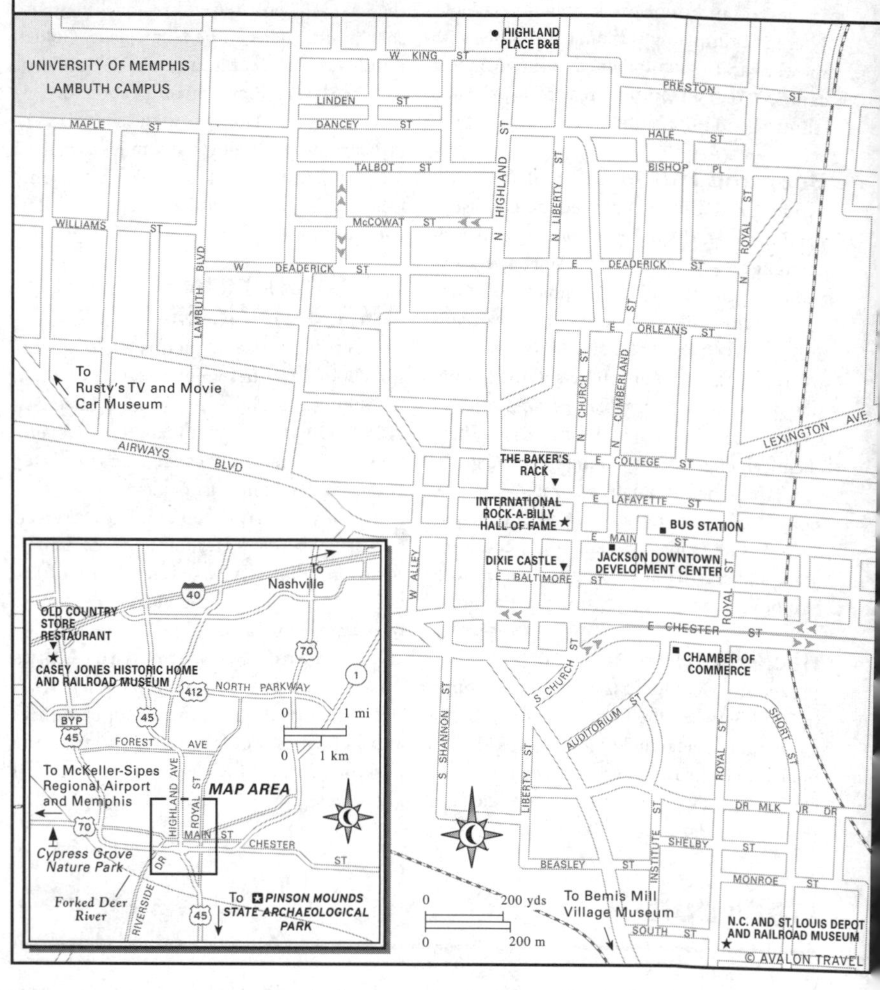

Village, are downtown on the blocks surrounding the stately courthouse square.

CASEY JONES HISTORIC HOME AND RAILROAD MUSEUM

In 1980, the home of the legendary railroad engineer was moved from the city of Jackson to Casey Jones Village, a plaza of shops and restaurants just off the interstate north of Jackson. The museum includes Jones's white clapboard home and a replica of the engine that he rode to his death in 1900. The home and engine form the centerpiece of the **Casey Jones Historic Home and Railroad Museum** (56 Casey Jones Ln., 731/668-1222, www.caseyjones.com, 9am-5pm Mon.-Sat., noon-5pm Sun., adults $6.50, children 6-12 $4.50, children under 6 free), which tells the story of Casey Jones's life and the legend that surrounds him to this day. Exhibits document every detail of the deadly 1900 crash that took his life, but some of the most fascinating parts of the museum deal with the legend of Casey Jones that evolved after his death. There are also elaborate model train sets that you can run for just a few quarters. An 1837 antebellum mansion, Providence House, was moved to the property in early 2011. The traditional southern farm features a barn, cotton gin, and tenant housing. The farm will produce vegetables for a farm-to-table restaurant in the works.

N. C. & ST. LOUIS DEPOT AND RAILROAD MUSEUM

Jackson owes its existence to the railroads that passed through the town, and the **N. C. & St. Louis Depot and Railroad Museum** (582 S. Royal St., 731/425-8223, 10am-3pm Mon.-Sat., free) documents much of the city's railroad history. Located inside Jackson's oldest railroad station a few blocks south of downtown, the museum walls are covered with photographs and memorabilia of the railroads. There is a large model train in the rear of the station and, outside, visitors can explore a dining car and engine.

Over the railroad tracks from the museum is a covered well whose waters once drew thousands of people to Jackson. The **Electro Chalybeate Well** (604 S. Royal St.,731/425-8333) was discovered in the late 1800s, and its waters were reputed to cure a host of ailments. In recent years the city of Jackson built the fountain, gazebo, and benches around the well. You can drink the water from a circle of water fountains if you like.

INTERNATIONAL ROCK-A-BILLY HALL OF FAME

As the city that lays claim to Carl Perkins, Jackson is home to the **International Rock-a-Billy Hall of Fame** (105 N. Church St., 731/427-6262, www.rockabilly.org, 10am-5pm Mon.-Thurs., 10am-2pm Fri.-Sat., $10). This storefront museum features exhibits about a number of the genre's famous performers. There is also a room of Elvis memorabilia and a performance space for concerts and dancing. A tour with enthusiastic guide Linda McGee costs $10 and is best suited for hard-core rockabilly fans. There are line-dancing lessons Monday and Tuesday beginning at 6pm and live music on Friday night starting at 7pm.

BEMIS MILL VILLAGE MUSEUM

The history of Bemis, a cotton mill town established in 1900, is recorded for the ages at the **Bemis Mill Village Museum** (2 N.

The legend of Casey Jones lives on in Jackson.

The Legend of Casey Jones

Casey Jones was born John Luther Jones, but he was better known as Casey after his hometown, Cayce, in Kentucky. He started as a telegrapher for the Mobile and Ohio Railroad in Kentucky and worked his way up to brakeman, fireman, and eventually engineer. Casey had a reputation for running the trains on time, no matter what.

In the early morning hours of April 30, 1900, Jones was running a passenger train from Memphis to Canton, Mississippi, when he crashed into the tail end of a freight train that was blocking a portion of the track near Vaughn, Mississippi. Jones died when his engine, No. 382, collided with the freight train and veered off the tracks. Jones was the only person killed in the accident.

The story of Casey Jones did not end with his death, however. An African American engine wiper, Wallace Saunders, started to sing a song that he composed about the dead engineer, and soon "The Ballad of Casey Jones" was a well-known folk song. The professional songwriting team Sibert and Newton copyrighted the song in 1909, and it became one of the most famous songs in America. Neither the Jones family nor Wallace Saunders ever received a penny from its success. The engineer's story also became the inspiration for an eponymous song by the Grateful Dead in 1970.

The story of Casey Jones's life and death was immortalized on television, film, and stage. His widow, Janie Jones, and accident survivor Simeon Webb remained minor celebrities for the rest of their lives.

The story of Casey Jones is told at the Casey Jones Home and Railroad Museum in Jackson.

Missouri St., 731/424-0739, www.bemishistory.org, by appointment only, donations encouraged). The museum is housed in the Bemis Auditorium, a large, imposing building constructed in 1922 to be the focal point of community life for the townspeople. The building is an elegant, sophisticated example of Beaux Arts design. It houses exhibits about the Bemis Brothers Bag Company, as well as life in an early-20th-century company town. Additional exhibits, with recently acquired artifacts, are in the works.

RUSTY'S TV AND MOVIE CAR MUSEUM

If you care more about the car than the star, head to **Rusty's TV and Movie Car Museum** (323 Hollywood Dr., 731/267-5881, www.rustystvandmoviecars.com, 9am-5pm Fri.-Sun., other days by appointment, $5, kids under five free). This offbeat museum just off I-40 has more than 25 cars that have been used on the big and small screens, as well as other memorabilia. In many cases, these are the real deal—cars from *The Fast and the Furious* and one of many General Lees, not just reproductions.

FESTIVALS AND EVENTS

Jackson hosts three major annual events. **The Shannon Street Blues MusicFest** (www.downtownjackson.com) brings blues, jazz, and other music to the West Tennessee Farmers Market in June. The Rock-a-Billy Hall of Fame organizes an **International Rock-a-Billy Festival** (731/427-6262, www.rockabillyhall.org) every August, and the Casey Jones Village puts on an **Old Time Music Fest** (731/668-1223, jacksonareaplectralsociety.webs.com, www.caseyjonesvillage.com) in September.

In addition, every September sees the **West Tennessee State Fair** (731/424-0151, wtsfair.com), a week of competitions, amusements, performances, and rides at the Jackson Fairgrounds Park.

The Tennessee Clean Water Network brings the **Wild and Scenic Film Festival** (www.tcwn.org), a collection of movies on environmental issues, to town in November.

SHOPPING

The **Casey Jones Village** (www.caseyjones.com) is home to both their Old Country Store complex and independently owned shops.

The **West Tennessee Farmers Market** (91 Market St., 731/425-8310, www.cityofjackson.net, 7am-4pm Tues.-Sat.) operates Tuesdays-- Saturdays, but it is Saturday mornings when you'll find locals. In addition to the standard food and produce fare, there are shopping vendors, such as Nashville's Haus of Yarn's mobile yarn bus.

SPORTS AND RECREATION

Parks

A few miles southwest of downtown Jackson is **Cypress Grove Nature Park** (Hwy. 70 W., 731/425-8316), a pleasant park with boardwalks, picnic facilities, walking paths, and an observation tower.

Spectator Sports

The **Jackson Generals** (4 Fun Pl., 731/988-5299, www.jacksongeneralsbaseball.com, $6-10) play in Pringles Field just off I-40 in Jackson. A farm team for the Seattle Mariners, the Generals put on a good show for fans during their season, April-October.

ACCOMMODATIONS

For the most luxurious accommodations in Jackson, if not the region, choose ★ **Highland Place Bed & Breakfast** (519 N. Highland Ave., 731/427-1472, www.highlandplace.com, $119.50-185). Set in a stately redbrick historic home along central Highland Avenue, a five-minute drive from downtown, the inn has four rooms ranging from a three-room suite to single rooms. Each room has a private bath, cable television, and wireless Internet access. The rooms are decorated with antique and modern handmade furniture. All guests have the run of the numerous public rooms, including a living room, library, and breakfast room. It sure beats a standard hotel room. Pets are not permitted.

Get away from it all at the 36-acre **Peaceful Oaks Bed-and-Breakfast** (636 Barnes Rd., Medina, 731/ 616-7921, www.peacefuloaks-bandb.com, $125). The bed-and-breakfast has three well-appointed rooms, one with a hot tub, plus great views of the Western Plains.

FOOD

★ **Dixie Castle** (215 E. Baltimore, 731/423-3359, 10am-2pm Mon.-Fri., 5pm-9pm Mon.-Sat., $6-14) attracts a large local crowd for lunch and dinner. This diner-style restaurant serves plate-lunch specials, burgers, and sandwiches. The food is home style, with large portions. You'll be hard-pressed to find a table at the peak of the lunch rush. At dinner, Dixie Castle offers steaks, pork chops, and chicken dinners. It does a brisk takeout trade as well, and the servers are some of the friendliest in town.

Also downtown, **The Baker's Rack** (203 E. Lafayette, 731/424-6163, 7am-5pm Mon.-Fri., $3-10) serves a diverse menu of hot and cold sandwiches, baked potatoes, plate lunches, and a famous strawberry salad. It also makes decadent desserts: Try the red velvet cake or "better than sex" cake. For breakfast, choose from biscuits, eggs on toast, oatmeal, French toast, or a generous breakfast platter with all the fixings.

In Casey Jones Village, off I-40, the **Old Country Store Restaurant** (56 Casey Jones Ln., 731/668-1223, www.caseyjones.com, 6:30am-9pm daily, $7-12) serves specials such as country ham, smothered chicken, and fried catfish, plus burgers and barbecue. The breakfast bar is a popular choice for those with a big appetite. It also has a fruit bar and the usual breakfast choices of eggs, biscuits, pancakes, and omelets. The Village's Ice Cream Parlor and Fudge Shoppe was included in a USA Today list of top-50 ice-cream parlors.

The **West Tennessee Farmers Market** (91 New Market St., 731/425-8310, www.cityofjackson.net) takes place under shelters in downtown Jackson 6am-5pm Tuesday-Saturday.

Locals love the ribs, sides, and more at South Jackson's **Diddy's Bar-B-Que**, (2384 US 45, 731/736-3460 10:30am-7pm Tues-Sat).

INFORMATION AND SERVICES

Maps and general information on Jackson can be found at the **Jackson Downtown Development Corporation** (314 E. Main St., 731/935-9586, www.downtownjackson.com) or the **Jackson Area Chamber of Commerce** (197 Auditorium St., 731/423-2200, www.jacksontn.com).

The **Jackson-Madison County Library** (433 E. Lafayette St., 731/425-8600, www.jmcl.tn.org, 10am-8pm Mon.-Thurs., 10am-5pm Fri.-Sat.) is one of the nicest public libraries in West Tennessee.

GETTING THERE AND AROUND

Jackson is located about midway between Nashville and Memphis along I-40, and most people drive there. The regional **McKellar-Sipes Airport** (731/423-0995, www.mckellarsipes.com) has on-and-off commercial air service, subject to the ups and downs of the airline industry. Check with airport officials to find out if commercial service is available.

Photographers have been known to make a detour to photograph the iconic **Jackson Main Street Greyhound bus terminal** (407 E. Main St., 731/427-1573), with its retro art deco style. The station is convenient to several attractions and restaurants but not close to any hotels. There is daily service to Memphis and Nashville; Paducah, Kentucky; and Jackson, Mississippi.

While trains still travel on Jackson's famous tracks, there is no passenger service to or from the city.

★ PINSON MOUNDS STATE ARCHAEOLOGICAL PARK

One of the largest complexes of mounds ever built by Woodland Indians is found 10 miles south of Jackson. **Pinson Mounds** (460 Ozier Rd., 731/988-5614, tnstateparks.com/parks/about/pinson-mounds, museum open 8am-4:30pm Mon.-Sat. and 1pm-5pm Sun., remainder of park open until dusk, free,), now a state park, is a group of at least 17 mounds believed to have been built beginning around 50 BC. The mounds were discovered in 1820

Pinson Mounds State Archaelogical Park

by Joel Pinson, part of a surveying team that was mapping new territory bought from the Chickasaw in 1818. Early archaeological digs were carried out in the late 1800s, but it was not until 1961 that the first major investigation of the site was completed (by scientists from the University of Tennessee).

Despite continuing archaeological study on the site, many mysteries remain. Among them is the significance of the design and arrangement of the mounds and why the mound builders abandoned the site around AD 500. Some scientists believe that the mounds were arranged as markers for the summer and winter solstices.

Visitors to Pinson Mounds begin within a 4,500-square-foot mound replica, which houses a museum and bookstore. The museum is dedicated to telling the story of what is known about the mysterious mounds and the people who built them. The mounds themselves are spread out along six miles of hiking trails that meander through the archaeological park. Many of the trails are across open fields, and walking can be hot during the summer months. A bike is an ideal way to get around, but you'll need to bring your own as there isn't a rental facility.

FESTIVALS AND EVENTS

Archaeofest is a family-friendly festival celebrating Native American culture. It takes place every September and includes artistic demonstrations, food and craft vendors, storytelling, flintknapping, and more. Contact the park office for more information.

CAMPING

Pinson Mounds has a **group camp facility** with lodge and cabins that can accommodate up to 32 people. There is also a day-use picnic area.

BETHEL SPRINGS

About 30 miles south of Jackson on Highway 45, near the community of Bethel Springs, is **Ada's Unusual Country Store** (9653 Hwy. 45, 731/934-9310, 8am-5pm Mon.-Sat.) which is unusual indeed. The shelves are packed with organic and natural food items, including grains, flour, pastas, and snacks. You can buy fresh local eggs, honey, and milk; Amish cheese and cookbooks; and homemade breads and sweets. For a meal on the go, you can get cold drinks, fresh-made sandwiches, and ice cream.

South Along the Tennessee

The Tennessee River flows by Clifton and southward to the state line. It passes Tennessee's most lovely river town, Savannah, and the site of the state's bloodiest Civil War battle, Shiloh. Clifton is about 115 miles southwest of Nashville International Airport (along I-40 to US-641) and 150 miles east of Memphis Internationl Airport (along I-40). Savannah is about 20 miles southwest of Clifton (along TN-128 and US-64).

CLIFTON

Pulitzer Prize-winning author T. S. Stribling was born in the river town of **Clifton** in 1881. His works include the 1,479-page trilogy *The Forge, The Store,* and *Unfinished Cathedral,* which portray the history of a Florence, Alabama, family from the Civil War to the 1920s. He won the Pulitzer Prize for fiction in 1933 for *The Store.* Stribling was one of the first Southern writers to speak out about issues of social conscience. He also wrote formulaic adventure novels and detective stories. His autobiography, *Laughing Stock,* was published posthumously in 1969.

A museum dedicated to Stribling and his life's work is located in a building that shares space with the Clifton Public Library. This 1924 Craftsman bungalow is where Stribling and his wife, Lou Ella, lived in their

The Death of General Johnston

Gen. Albert Sidney Johnston, the Confederate commander of the western department of the army, was concentrating all available forces at Corinth, Mississippi, in early April 1862. His objective was to launch an offensive against the Union army under the command of General Ulysses S. Grant at Pittsburg Landing, Tennessee, before Union reinforcements arrived.

On April 3, Johnston ordered his troops to march north, toward the engagement. Heavy rains and bad roads slowed their progress, and the Southern troops lost a day on their journey, a delay that would prove significant in the coming days.

The Confederates arrived at their camp south of Pittsburg Landing on the late afternoon of April 5, and Johnston decided to delay the attack until morning. During the evening, he and his second-in-command, P. G. T. Beauregard, disagreed about the coming fight; Beauregard argued against the attack, saying that the Union army would not be surprised. But Johnston would not be deterred. He wanted to attack the Union forces before reinforcements from Nashville arrived.

As it turned out, the Union army was surprised by the Confederate attack in the early morning hours of April 6. Soldiers described the disorder and chaos of the Union camps as word was quickly spread about the advancing fighters. General Grant, who was breakfasting at the **Cherry Mansion** in Savannah, a few miles north of Shiloh, was surprised by the sound of gunfire and rushed to the scene.

General Johnston would not live to see the outcome of the battle that he orchestrated. Midafternoon on the first day of fighting, just before the Confederates reached the high-water mark of their efforts, Johnston was struck in the leg by a minié ball. At first his companions did not realize the seriousness of his injury, and neither did Johnston. But at 2:45pm on April 6, the Confederate general died, passing command to Beauregard.

Johnston was the highest-ranking officer on either side of the Civil War to be killed in active duty.

retirement. The museum includes Stribling's typewriter, Bible, papers, and other personal articles. The **T. S. Stribling Museum** (300 E. Water St., 931/676-3678, 11:30am-6:30pm Tues.-Fri., free) is operated by the City of Clifton. The museum/library has an ongoing book sale to raise funds for its work.

SAVANNAH

A quaint town on the eastern bank of the Tennessee River, **Savannah** has historic homes, a good museum, and the greatest selection of restaurants and accommodations in this part of the state. You can guess what is on the menu as it is known as the catfish capital of the world.

In its early life, the town was Rudd's Ferry, named for James Rudd, who operated a ferry across the river. The ferry was taken over by David Robinson, whose wife is said to have renamed the town Savannah after her hometown in Georgia. In 1830, Savannah became the seat of Hardin County and soon developed a reputation as a wealthy, cultured town.

TENNESSEE RIVER MUSEUM

Savannah is a river town, and the mighty Tennessee River is one of its main attractions. The **Tennessee River Museum** 495 Main St., 731/925-8181, 9am-5pm Mon.-Sat., 1pm-5pm Sun., adults $3, kids free) documents the history of the region and the river. Exhibits detail the prehistoric peoples of the region and include an original red stone effigy pipe found inside one of the Shiloh Indian Mounds a few miles south. There are also exhibits on Shiloh and the river during the Civil War, riverboats, and the economic uses of the river, including pearl farming and mussels. One of the most interesting exhibits features receipts issued by Savannah merchants to the U.S. Army party that was escorting 2,500 Cherokee Indians down the river on the Trail of Tears in 1838.

The museum is an informative first stop

for visitors to the area, and staff can provide information about other area attractions. Through a partnership with Shiloh National Military Park, guests who show their Shiloh parking pass receive free entry to the museum.

HISTORIC HOMES

David Robinson built the **Cherry Mansion** (265 W. Main St.) on the riverbank, on top of what historians believe was an Indian mound. Robinson gave the mansion to his daughter when she married William H. Cherry, for whom it was named. The house, which is closed to the public, is where U.S. general Ulysses S. Grant stayed during the days leading up to the Battle of Shiloh. Cherry was a noted Union sympathizer, and the mansion remained a Union headquarters and a field hospital during the war. Although the house is privately owned, visitors are welcome to stop and look. There is a river overlook next door.

Savannah was settled between 1830 and 1850, but many of the old houses were damaged or destroyed during the Civil War. However, beautiful homes were rebuilt, and many of these remain in the leafy residential area just north of Savannah's Main Street. The homes are elegant examples of fine homes of the late 19th century.

Pick up a **Savannah Historic Guide** at the Tennessee River Museum (495 Main St., 731/925-8181).

HALEY MEMORIAL

Savannah is where the paternal grandparents of Pulitzer Prize-winning author Alex Haley are buried. Alex Haley Sr. operated Rudd's Ferry, and his wife, Queen Haley, worked in the Cherry Mansion for the Cherry family. Haley's novel *Queen* was inspired by his grandmother's life. The couple's shared tombstone is located in the Savannah Cemetery. To find the Haley Memorial, take Cherry Street from downtown Savannah and over a small bridge and enter the cemetery. Take the first gravel road to your right, and then walk over the hill, taking a right at the *Y*. The Haleys, as well as Alex Haley Sr.'s first wife, Tennie, share a gravestone.

Accommodations

You can get a clean, comfortable bed at the **Savannah Lodge** (585 Pickwick St., 731/925-8586, www.savannahlodge.net, $35-55), a motel that boasts the basics for its guests, as well as amenities like a swimming pool. Pets are allowed. Several national chains also have locations in Savannah.

Food

A good choice for home-style cooking in Savannah is **Toll House Restaurant** (610 Wayne Rd., 731/925-5128, 5am-9pm Mon.-Sat., 5am-2pm Sun., $4-9), whose home fries and eggs draw a crowd in the morning. At lunch and dinner, there is an ample buffet with traditional favorites like macaroni and cheese, fried catfish, and beef tips.

You can't help but have a good time at somewhere called **The Porky Rooster** (120 Water St., 731/412-5032, 11am-8pm Thurs.-Sat., 11am-3pm Sun.). Grab chicken (including a boneless wing option), barbecued brisket, and the area's famous slugburgers (deep-fried grain burgers).

Information

Stop at the **Tennessee River Museum** (495 Main St., 731/925-8181, 9am-5pm Mon.-Sat., 1pm-5pm Sun.) to pick up maps and other information about Savannah.

You can also contact the **Hardin County Convention and Visitors Bureau** (731/925-8181, www.tourhardincounty.org) for information.

★ SHILOH NATIONAL MILITARY PARK

The **Shiloh National Military Park** (1055 Pittsburg Landing Rd., 731/689-5696, 8am-5pm daily, 8am-4:30pm daily in winter, closed Christmas Day, free) is set along the western shore of the Tennessee River about eight miles south of Crump. The Battle of Shiloh is one of the most remembered of the Civil War; it was the battle that demonstrated to both the North and South that the war would be a longer and harder fight than either had imagined. Shiloh today is a landscape of alternating open fields and wooded forest, populated by hundreds of monuments to soldiers who fought and died at Shiloh on April 6-7, 1862. The peacefulness of the present brings into even greater focus the violence of the battle that took place here more than 150 years ago and claimed nearly 24,000 casualties.

You can drive around the battlefield, but some of the most important sites are a short walk from the road. At the visitors center there is a small museum where you can watch a film, *Shiloh-Fiery Trial*, about the battle.

Sights within the park include the peach orchard, now being regrown, where soldiers described the peach blossoms falling like snow on the dead and injured; the "bloody pond," where injured men crawled for water and, in some cases, to die; and the Hornet's Nest, the site of some of the most furious fighting.

The 10-acre **Shiloh National Cemetery** is located next to the visitors center. Two-thirds of the 3,695 bodies interred here are unidentified. Most are Union soldiers killed at Shiloh, but there are others from nearby battles, the Spanish-American War, both World Wars, and the Revolutionary War. The Confederate dead were buried in five trenches around the battlefield and remain there today.

Nearly 800 years before the Civil War, the riverbank near present-day Shiloh was home to a mound-building Mississippian Indian community. The **Shiloh Indian Mounds** that they left behind sit along the west bluff of the riverbank and are one of the largest mound groups in the country. A remarkable effigy pipe was discovered here in the 1890s and is on display at the Tennessee River Museum in Savannah. The mounds are accessible on foot from two points in the park.

Practicalities

A printed guide and map to the battlefield is available at the visitors center, and it takes about an hour to follow its path. For a more detailed examination, you can buy an audio tour from the park bookstore for $12. This tour takes about two hours to complete and includes narratives by soldiers, historians, and civilians.

The bookstore is one of the best in the area and has an extensive collection of books on the Civil War, Tennessee, Native Americans, and African American history.

There are snack and drink vending machines at the visitors center and a picnic area in the park. The closest restaurants are in Shiloh, Savannah, and Counce. For accommodations, look in Savannah.

With its miles of flat roads and restrained traffic, Shiloh is a good place to bicycle. There are no rental facilities nearby, however, so bring your own wheels.

SHILOH

There is not much to the modern town of Shiloh, except a few souvenir shops and one excellent catfish restaurant that has been serving visitors since 1938. The "world famous" ★ **Hagy's Catfish Hotel Restaurant** (1140 Hagy Lane, 731/689-3327, 11am-9pm Tues.-Thurs., 11am-10pm Fri.-Sat., 11am-9pm Sun., $12-29, www.catfishhotel.com) is set off by itself in a beautiful clearing overlooking the Tennessee River. You can stretch your legs with a walk down to the water's edge. Hagy's menu has fried and grilled catfish, plus other favorites like chicken and steak. But choose the catfish, which is nicely seasoned and expertly fried. It comes with hush puppies and coleslaw. This will be a meal to remember.

Find Hagy's by looking for the large sign for the turnoff along Highway 22 on the northern side of Shiloh National Military Park.

PICKWICK LANDING STATE PARK

Pickwick Landing State Park was a riverboat stop from the 1840s until the 1930s, when Pickwick Dam was built and the lake formed. Pickwick Lake was created in December

1937 when the Tennessee Valley Authority dammed the Tennessee and flooded farmland in the valley. The lake was dedicated in 1940, and a crowd of 30,000 people attended the services on the southern earth dam. Today it attracts vacationers from around the region who enjoy the laid-back atmosphere and top-flight bass fishing.

The lake lies in Tennessee, Alabama, and Mississippi and is one of the premier spots for recreation in the area. Boating, fishing, and swimming are especially popular. There are several nearby golf courses and opportunities to camp, hunt, and hike.

Pickwick Landing State Park (Hwy. 57, 731/689-3129) is one of Tennessee's resort parks, with a modern hotel, conference center, golf course, and marina.

Hiking

There is an easy three-mile hiking trail that meanders along the lakeshore.

Golf

The Pickwick Landing State Park golf course is a par 72 champion's 18-hole course. The pro shop rents clubs and carts, and sells golf accessories. Use the online reservations tool (tnstateparks.com/parks/about/pickwick-landing) to grab your tee time. Greens fees range from $13-22, depending on the season and day of the week.

Boating

Pleasure riding, sailing, waterskiing, paddling, and fishing are all popular activities on Pickwick Lake. There are three public boat-launch ramps at Pickwick Landing State Park, and marine fuel and other boating items are available from the park marina.

You can rent a pontoon boat from **Pickwick Boat Rentals** (731/689-5359, www.pickwickboatrentalsinc.com), starting at $225.

Fishing

Fishing on Pickwick Lake is best in the spring and fall. Conditions here include shallow stump flats, well-defined channels, active feeder creeks, steeply falling bluffs, rocky ledges, and long grass beds.

Pickwick Outdoors, Inc. (731/689-8000, www.pickwickoutdoors.com) organizes fishing vacations for groups. For a fishing guide, contact **Big Orange Guide Service** (731/689-3074) or **Rick Matlock's Guide Service** (731/689-5382).

Swimming

Pickwick Landing State Park has three swimming beaches. Circle Beach and Sandy Beach are in the day-use area; Bruton Beach is in the primitive area, which is located across the lake from the main park.

Accommodations

★ Pickwick Landing State Resort Park (Hwy. 57, 731/689-3135, rooms $74-230, cabins $100-125, campsites under $8-25) is the home of one of Tennessee's newest state park inns and conference centers. The modern hotel has 119 rooms, each with a balcony looking out over the lake and the dam. Cabins and campsites are also available. There is a pool and a 135-seat restaurant at the inn, which serves three meals a day, with an emphasis on Southern cuisine.

COUNCE

This humble town is the western gateway to Pickwick Lake. It is also a hub in the region's hardwood timber industry, and you will smell the distinctive scent of the local paper plant at certain times of the day.

Accommodations

If you're planning to stay more than a few days at Pickwick Lake, consider renting a cabin. **Pickwick Lake Cabin Rentals** (11268 Hwy. 57, 731/689-0400, www.pickwicklakecabins.com) represents the owners of two dozen one-, two-, and three-bedroom cabins on and around the lake. Lakefront cabins will cost $300-550 per night, water-view cabins will cost $175-350, and cabins off the water cost $100-200. Many lakefront cabins come with a private dock and can accommodate large groups.

Food

It is clear by the name what owners Quentin and Betty Knussmann serve at **Pickwick Catfish Farm Restaurant** (4155 Hwy 57, 731/689-3805, pickwickcatfishfarm.com, 5pm-9pm Fri.-Sat., 4pm-7pm Sun.). Once a fish-processing plant, the restaurant specialized in smoked catfish, which you can take to go, or dine in and grab traditional Southern sides such as hush puppies or slaw.

Southwestern Tennessee

The southernmost stretch of West Tennessee spans Adamsville in the east to La Grange in the west. Here you'll find a museum dedicated to Sheriff Buford Pusser, another dedicated to bird dogs, and one of the loveliest small towns in all of Tennessee.

INFORMATION

Seven Tennessee counties have come together to form the **Tourism Association of Southwest Tennessee** (731/616-7474, www.visitswtenn.com), which produces brochures and stocks information stands at interstate rest stops and other crossroads. Their guide to the region has helpful listings and a map. The nearest airport to southwestern Tennessee is Memphis International Airport. Adamsville is 109 miles east of Memphis International Airport on US 72. Selmer, La Grange, and Grand Junction can be reached in succession by continuing west from Adamsville on US-64 and south on TN-18.

ADAMSVILLE

Famed McNairy County sheriff Buford Pusser worked in Selmer, the McNairy County seat, but he lived in Adamsville, a small town a few miles down Highway 45. Fans of Pusser and the movies that his legacy inspired, starting with the 1973 film *Walking Tall,* can learn more about his life at the **Sheriff Buford Pusser Home and Museum** (342 Pusser St., 731/632-4080, www.bufordpussermuseum.com, summer: 10am-5pm Mon.-Fri., 9am-5pm Sat., 1pm-4pm Sun., hours vary off-season, call ahead, $8 adults, $5 seniors, $3 children over 5). Pusser earned a reputation as a no-nonsense lawman during his eight-year career as sheriff. He was famous for raiding moonshine stills and for fighting criminals, with little regard for his own personal safety. In 1967, his wife, Pauline, was killed in an ambush when she was riding along with him in his patrol car. Seven years later, Pusser was killed in a single-car accident while he was driving home from the McNairy County Fair in Selmer. When Pusser died, hundreds of people came to his funeral. Elvis Presley visited the family privately to offer his condolences.

The home and museum features a video about Pusser's life, family memorabilia, and two cars that Pusser used.

Shiloh Golf Course and Restaurant (2915 Caney Branch Rd., 731/632-0678) in Adamsville is a par 71 course and driving range.

Continue west from Adamsville on US-64 to reach Selmer.

SELMER

In **Selmer**, the McNairy County seat, you can see the courthouse where Buford Pusser worked, and where Mary Winkler was put on trial in 2007 for the murder of her preacher husband, Matthew Winkler.

This quiet town is also home to the **McNairy County Historical Museum** (114 N. 3rd St., 731/646-0018, 10am-4pm Sat., 1pm-4pm Sun., free), nestled in the old Ritz theater. Exhibits are dedicated to schools, the Civil War, churches, the healing arts, business, and agriculture.

Don't miss two music-themed murals painted by Nashville artist Brian Tull. These public art landmarks now help mark the

Rockabilly Highway (the stretch of 55 miles of U.S. Highway 45 between Madison County and McNairy County to the Mississippi state line were named as such in 2008).

Selmer is also famous for its slugburgers, deep-fried grain burgers that are sold at lunch counters around town.

Continue north on US-45 and then southwest on TN-100 to find Chickasaw State Park.

CHICKASAW STATE PARK

Named for the Indians who once lived and hunted in this part of Tennessee, **Chickasaw State Park** (20 Cabin Ln., Henderson, 800/458-1752, tnstateparks.com/parks/about/Chickasaw, 8am-10pm daily) encompasses Lake Placid. The 14,400-acre park lies midway between Jackson and Bolivar. There are more than four miles of roads for hiking or biking, plus tennis courts, an archery range, horseback riding, campsites, and an inn. Horses, rowboats and pedal boats are available for rental here, or you can bring your own horse, kayak or paddleboard. A 100-seat restaurant serves Southern specialties (Thurs.-Sun., 731/989-6807).

Bear Trace at Chickasaw (9555 State Rte. 100, 731/989-4700, www.beartrace.com) is par 72 Jack Nicklaus golf course with natural beauty and challenging holes.

Follow TN-100 west to catch TN-18 south and find La Grange.

LA GRANGE

La Grange, a mere speck of civilization 50 miles east of Memphis, feels like the town that time forgot. Old homes—some elegant, some ramshackle—line narrow drives. The post office, town office, and an old-fashioned country store constitute the business district.

La Grange, named in honor of the Marquis de Lafayette's ancestral home in France, seemed destined for great things when it was chartered in 1829. Its population quickly swelled to more than 3,000. The first Episcopal church in West Tennessee was founded here, and in 1835 stockholders chartered the La Grange & Memphis Railway. The plans for a railroad faltered, however, and La Grange suffered from Union occupation during most of the Civil War. A tornado destroyed part of the town in 1900, and La Grange lost its telegraph station and express mail delivery to nearby Grand Junction. Hopes for La Grange to grow into a city dwindled.

Despite its size, La Grange was and is known for a special refinement and pursuit of the arts and education. In 1855, the La Grange Female College and the La Grange Synodical College for Men were chartered. The town's local newspapers, *The Monitor* and, later, the *Spirit of the Age,* were respected in the region. During the Civil War, La Grange native Lucy Pickens was depicted on the face of the Confederate $1 note and three different $100 notes. Pickens, whose childhood home at 290 Pine Street is still standing, was known as the Queen of the Confederacy.

Sights

In 1998, La Grange dedicated a 2.5-ton bronze and limestone monument to the nearby Wolf River. The **Wolf River Monument,** located near the post office and fire department, was rendered in the shape of a wolf's head and was created by Memphis sculptor Roy Tamboli.

Unfortunately, since the closure in 2007 of Cogbill's Store and Museum, there is not much to do here except look. If you come by on Saturday morning, stop at the La Grange General Store, which is part of the **La Grange Inn** (240 Pine St., 901/878-1000). Both are open by appointment. The town office is open weekday mornings.

Despite the dearth of outright attractions, La Grange, also called La Belle Village, delivers an experience unlike any other town in this part of Tennessee. Its lovingly preserved antebellum homes, rural landscape, and charming people are unique and worth seeing.

GHOST RIVER STATE NATURAL AREA

The Ghost River is a 14-mile section of the Wolf River that meanders through bottomland forest, cypress-tupelo swamps, and open marshes. The river got its name from the loss of river current as the water flows through marshes and swamps.

About a three-mile drive south of La Grange you can hike or canoe in the **Ghost River State Natural Area**. To find the 600-foot boardwalk and hiking trail, drive south from La Grange on Yager Road, and then turn west on Beasley Road. The parking area is about 1.5 miles down the road. There is another parking area and a place to put in a canoe along Yager Road, and a marked canoe path so you don't get lost in the swamp. There is another parking area at the canoe take-out on Bateman Road. Grab a map from the La Grange town office or from the State of Tennessee website (www.state.tn.us).

Information

La Grange City Hall (20 Main St., 901/878-1246, www.lagrangetn.com, 8am-noon Mon.-Fri.) is the best source of information about the town. Staff can provide you with a large fold-out map of the town's historic homes.

Grand Junction is approximately 4 miles east of La Grange along TN-57.

GRAND JUNCTION

A few miles east of La Grange on Highway 57 is the **National Bird Dog Museum** (505 Hwy. 57 W., 731/764-2058, 9am-2pm Tues.-Fri., 10am-4pm Sat., 1pm-4pm Sun., free). The collection includes paintings and photographs of champion sporting dogs, plus lots of taxidermy. There's a gift shop for souvenirs for the dog lover in your life. The National Field Trials take place just down the road at the Ames Plantation.

Continue east on TN-57 (back toward Selmer) for almost 30 miles to find Big Hill Pond State Park.

BIG HILL POND STATE PARK

Big Hill Pond was created in 1853 when dirt was removed from a borrow pit to build a levee across the Tuscumbia and Cypress Creek bottoms for the Memphis to Charleston Railroad. Over the years, a grove of cypress trees has grown in and around the 35-acre pond.

The centerpiece of the state park (1435 John Howell Rd., Pocahontas, 731/645-7967, tnstateparks.com/parks/about/big-hill-pond) is the boardwalk through the scenic swamp and the observation tower, which provides views of the swamp and lake. There are 30 miles of hiking trails, 14 miles of horseback riding and mountain bike trails, a campground with 30 sites, a picnic area, and opportunities to fish and hunt.

There's no backcountry camping allowed here, but there are four camp shelters.

Nashville

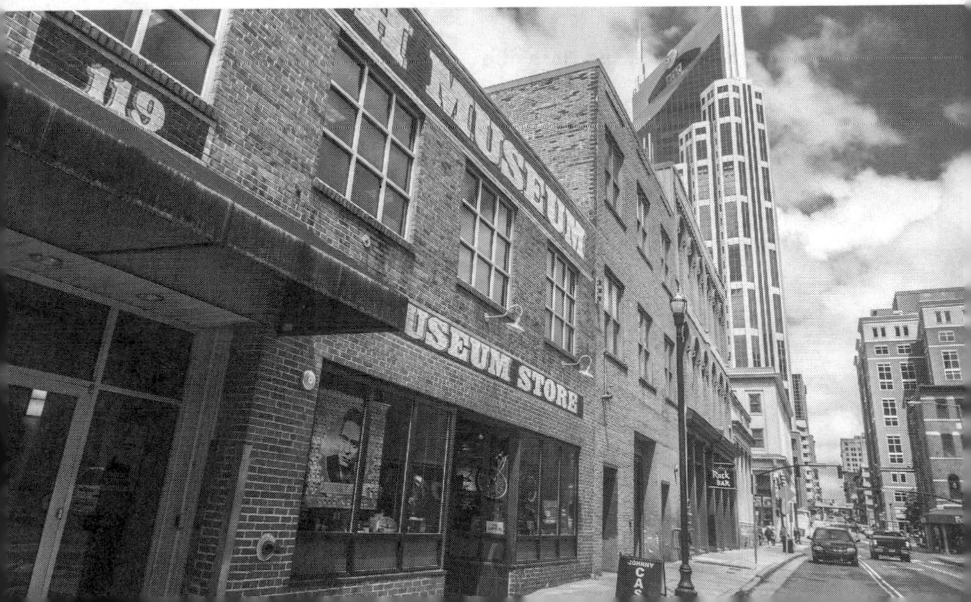

Look for ★ to find recommended sights, activities, dining, and lodging.

Highlights

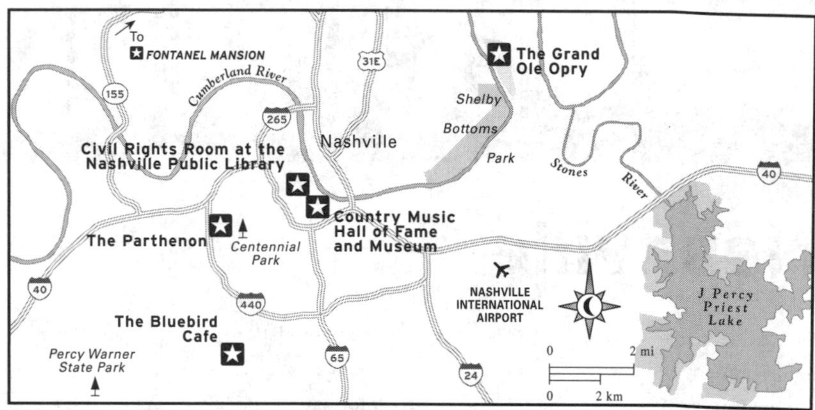

★ **Country Music Hall of Fame and Museum:** Learn about the genre's complex roots and then be ready to explore the city's live music bounty (page 132).

★ **Civil Rights Room at the Nashville Public Library:** The public library houses the best exhibit about the historic Nashville sit-ins of 1960 and their role in the U.S. civil rights movement (page 138).

★ **The Parthenon:** This life-size replica of the Greek Parthenon, complete with a statue of Athena, is a gathering place, a museum, and one of the reasons Nashville is called "the Athens of the South" (page 141).

★ **Fontanel Mansion:** Music and nature come together at the former home of Barbara Mandrell, now a museum and music venue with acres of hiking trails (page 155).

★ **The Grand Ole Opry:** Get an introduction to the depth and breadth of country music (page 157).

★ **The Bluebird Café:** The quintessential Nashville listening room hosts intimate music sessions with the people who really do write the songs (page 160).

Nashville is where America goes to make music.

This city of more than 659,000 (and growing) on the banks of the Cumberland River is where tomorrow's hits are written, performed, and recorded, and where you can hear them performed on the stage of the longest-running live radio variety show, the Grand Ole Opry.

There is a song in the air all around the city—in the honky-tonks along lower Broadway, on the streets of downtown Nashville, in the studio along Music Row, and in Music Valley, modern home of the Opry. During the annual Country Music Association (CMA) Festival in June, the whole city is alive with the foot-tapping rhythm of country music. But locals like Jack White, Robert Plant, and the Kings of Leon have done their part to make Music City's sound more than just twang.

Nashville is also the city where performers and songwriters come to make it in the music business. Listening rooms and nightclubs all over the city are the beneficiaries of this abundance of hopeful talent, and their creativity and energy seeps into almost everything in this city.

It is wrong to think that music, country or otherwise, is all there is to Nashville. After the Civil War and Reconstruction, Nashville became known as the Athens of the South because it was a center for education and the arts. Still today, Nashville offers visitors much more than a night at the Opry (not that there's anything wrong with that). Art buffs love the Frist Center for Visual Arts and Cheekwood Botanic Garden and Museum of Art, not to mention neighborhood and downtown gallery districts. The Nashville Symphony Orchestra plays in the elegant, acclaimed, and renovated Schermerhorn Center downtown.

Come to watch the NFL's Tennessee Titans play football, or to play golf at one of the award-winning courses nearby. Admire the Parthenon in Centennial Park, or drive to the southern outskirts of the city for a hike at Radnor Lake State Natural Area.

For a city that is populated by so many transplants (there's often a double take when one meets an actual native Nashvillian, with all the relocated musicians, university students, and health-care executives in town), Nashville has a strong sense of community. This was never as evident as it was in May

Previous: the Parthenon in Centennial Park; the Johnny Cash Museum. **Above:** The Stage.

2010 after the Cumberland River crested more than 12 feet above its flood stage. Downtown, Music Valley, and other parts of the city were underwater, causing an eventual $2 billion in damage. Major sights, including the Gaylord Opryland Resort, the Grand Ole Opry, and the Schermerhorn Center were temporarily shuttered. But folks pitched in, as is fitting in a place called the Volunteer State, and most of the public damage was repaired. Some sights are even better than they were pre-flood. Estimates are that the metro area will see an additional 1 million residents by the year 2020, so the community keeps growing.

Downtown is dominated by tall office towers and stately government buildings, including the state capitol. Meat-and-three restaurants serve irresistible Southern-style meals, East Nashville welcomes award-winning chefs, while eateries along Nolensville Pike reflect the ethnic diversity of the city.

Nashville is a city that strikes many notes but sings in perfect harmony.

PLANNING YOUR TIME

Nashville is within a one day's drive for much of the U.S. population, and as a result it is a draw for weekend getaways. In just two days you can see a few of the city's attractions and catch a show at the Grand Ole Opry. Musical pilgrims, history enthusiasts, and outdoors enthusiasts should plan to spend more time in Music City. Even the most disciplined explorers will find themselves happily occupied if they choose to stay a full week.

Downtown is a good home base for many visitors. Hotels here are within walking distance of many attractions, restaurants, and nightclubs. They are also the most expensive accommodations in the city. Visitors who are primarily interested in seeing a show at the Grand Ole Opry or shopping at Opry Mills can shack up in Music Valley, where there is a wide cross-section of affordable hotel rooms, as well as the luxury of the Opryland Resort.

Visitors with a car can opt for accommodations outside of the city center. There are affordable hotels in midtown and smaller bed-and-breakfasts in Hillsboro and East Nashville. All these neighborhoods have their charms but are less tourist centric than downtown and Music Valley. The city's lone hostel is in midtown and is a good choice for budget travelers.

WHEN TO GO

Summer is the most popular time to visit Nashville. The CMA Music Festival in June draws thousands to the city. Temperatures in August top out around 90°F, although it can feel much hotter, thanks to the humidity and a thermometer that doesn't dip when the sun sets.

Spring and fall bring mild temperatures and may be the best time to visit Nashville. You will avoid the largest crowds but can still sample all that the city has to offer. In spring you will enjoy sights of tulips, dogwoods, and magnolias in bloom. Beginning in mid-October, foliage around the city starts to turn blazing red, brown, and yellow.

In winter, temperatures range 30-50°F. During November and December, holiday concerts and decorations liven up the city. Many attractions cut back hours during winter, and some outdoor attractions are closed altogether, particularly in the post-Christmas slack of January.

ORIENTATION

For a city of its size, Nashville takes up a lot of space. In fact, Nashville has the second-largest footprint of any major American city. But don't picture a scene of concrete: Nashville is a leafy, suburban city. Outside downtown is a patchwork of traffic lights, strip malls, and tree-lined residential neighborhoods, several of which are incorporated towns with their own elected officials, city halls, and police.

Nashville's attractions are spread out among the city's various neighborhoods. Learn the locations and identities of a few parts of town, and you are well on your way to understanding Music City.

Nashville

City Center

Nashville straddles the Cumberland River, a waterway that meanders a particularly uneven course in this part of Tennessee. Downtown Nashville sits on the west bank of the river, climbing a gradual incline from Broadway to the Tennessee State Capitol. It is defined by landmarks including the AT&T Building, the tallest building in Tennessee, better known by many as the "Batman Building" for the two tall antennae that spring from the top. (The building was designed to be evocative of the shape of the top of a desk phone, where you place the receiver . . . in the days before cell phones.)

Downtown is where you will find major attractions like the Country Music Hall of Fame, the Ryman Auditorium, and lower Broadway, a Bourbon Street-like strip of clubs and bars. Downtown includes the traditional business zone, where you'll find office buildings, the Tennessee State Museum, and city parks.

Grab the good walking shoes and leave the car in the garage in central Nashville. Traffic and parking are what you would expect in a downtown area of a city of this size. But remember: Nashville is built on a hill. Walking between Broadway and the state capitol is perfectly doable, but on a hot summer day, or with small children in tow, you may need to take plenty of breaks (or hop on one of the free Music City Circuit buses).

East Nashville

The John Seigenthaler Pedestrian Bridge spans the Cumberland River, taking you from Riverfront Park to the heart of East Nashville. Now dominated by Nissan Stadium, home of the NFL's Tennessee Titans, the eastern reaches of Nashville are also home to some of the most charming residential neighborhoods. **Edgefield,** Nashville's oldest suburb, was a separate city when it first sprang up in the 19th century. Many of its most elegant homes were destroyed in the great East Nashville fire of 1916, but it still boasts a lovely mix of Victorian, Princess Anne, and Colonial Revival homes. Farther east is **Lockeland Springs,** and farther north is **Inglewood.**

While East Nashville is short on tourist-magnet attractions, visitors should consider the growing number of bed-and-breakfast accommodations here. The neighborhoods are close to downtown but also boast their own unique nightlife, restaurants, and character.

North Nashville

North of the state capitol and Bicentennial Mall is **Germantown,** a compact historic neighborhood now home to a few shops, galleries, restaurants, and studios, once the home of European immigrants. On the edge of Germantown, just outside downtown, is First Tennessee Park, home to the minor league Nashville Sound baseball team. Heading west from Germantown, **Jefferson Street** takes you past several of Nashville's African American landmarks, including Fisk University and Meharry Medical College.

A neighborhood created entirely for the tourist trade, **Music Valley** is the zone of hotels, restaurants, and retail that has popped up around the Opryland Hotel and the Grand Ole Opry House. Located inside a narrow loop of the Cumberland River, Music Valley lies northeast of downtown Nashville. It is a quick drive from the airport along Briley Parkway.

If Music Valley is actually a valley, you wouldn't know it. The strip of hotels, restaurants, souvenir shops, and malls is just about as far removed from the natural environment as you can get. But you overlook the neighborhood to get to the Grand Ole Opry, the Gaylord Opryland Resort, and the discount shopper's paradise that is Opry Mills. Music Valley is also home to a wide variety of hotel accommodations, including some budget-friendly choices, plus family-friendly restaurants.

West Nashville

Perhaps the most famous neighborhood in

all of Nashville, **Music Row** is where country music deals are done. The tree-lined streets of 16th and 17th Avenues, a few blocks southwest of downtown, shade dozens of different recording studios, record labels, and producers.

Lying just west of downtown, **Elliston Place** is a block of nightclubs, restaurants, and two famous Nashville eateries: Elliston Place Soda Shop and Rotier's.

The neighborhood is surrounded by medical complexes and is a few blocks from the city's only downtown hostel. Centennial Park, Nashville's best urban park, is a few blocks farther west.

The youthful energy of nearby Vanderbilt and Belmont Universities keep **Hillsboro Village** one of the most consistently vibrant neighborhoods in Nashville. Hillsboro is home to one of Nashville's finest used-book stores, stylish and pricey boutiques, and notable restaurants, including the down-home Pancake Pantry, and Fido, a restaurant/coffeehouse where record contracts are signed and hit songs are written. Hillsboro is also where you will find the alternative movie house the Belcourt, which screens independent and arts movies, plus hosts live music concerts.

Together, Hillsboro and Elliston Place are Nashville's **Midtown.**

Sylvan Park, once a suburb of the city, is located between Charlotte Avenue and Murphy Road, just west of the city center. Noted for neat homes and state-named roads, the neighborhood is quiet and residential, with a growing number of shops and restaurants. Along Charlotte Avenue, facing Sylvan Park, you will find antiques and thrift stores, the Darkhorse Theater, and Rhino Books, specializing in used and rare books. Farther out along Charlotte is a burgeoning number of international eateries.

West End refers to the neighborhoods along West End Avenue. It includes Belle Meade, an incorporated city and one of the wealthiest in the whole state. Head in this direction to find beautiful homes, the Belle Meade Plantation, and Cheekwood.

South Nashville

South of the city center are several distinct neighborhoods. **8th Avenue South,** close to downtown, is the antiques district. Restaurants like Arnold's Country Kitchen and the Jackalope Brewery, and clubs, including the Mercy Lounge, draw people to this neighborhood.

Follow 12th Avenue as it heads south from downtown to find **the Gulch.** Rising from what was once a railroad wasteland, the Gulch is now the city's hot spot for high-rise housing and urban condos.

A few miles farther south along 12th Avenue is **12 South,** another of Nashville's most popular gentrified neighborhoods. An influx of young professional property owners has given rise to new restaurants, boutiques, and coffee shops.

You have to leave the main drag to find the greenery left in **Green Hills,** a retail hot spot south of Hillsboro Village. If you can tolerate the inevitable traffic jam (particularly after school gets out on weekdays), follow 21st Avenue south to find the tony Mall at Green Hills, the even more upscale Hill Center, media darling Parnassus Books, and the venerable Bluebird Café, tucked away in a strip mall a few blocks farther south.

Sights

BROADWAY

This is the entertainment and tourism hub of Nashville. Walk along lower Broad, as the blocks from 5th Avenue to the river are called, and you will pass dozens of different bars (honky-tonks), restaurants, and shops catering to visitors. Second Avenue, near where it crosses Broadway, is a neighborhood where old warehouses have been converted to more restaurants, shops, office space, and loft condominiums. The vibe of Lower Broadway has become more like Bourbon Street in recent years.

★ Country Music Hall of Fame and Museum

The distinctive design of the **Country Music Hall of Fame and Museum** (222 5th Ave. S., 615/416-2001, www.countrymusichalloffame.com, 9am-5pm daily, $24.95 adults, $22.50 seniors, $14.95 children) is the first thing you will notice about this monument to country music. Vertical windows at the front and back of the building resemble piano keys, the sweeping arch on the right side of the building portrays a 1950s Cadillac fin, and from above, the building resembles a bass clef. The Hall of Fame was first established, in 1967, and its first inductees were Jimmie Rodgers, Hank Williams, and Fred Rose. The original hall was located on Music Row, but in 2002 it moved to this signature building two blocks off Broadway in downtown Nashville.

Country music fans are drawn by the carload to the Hall of Fame, where they can pay homage to country's greatest stars, as well as the lesser-known men and women who influenced the music. Those who aren't fans when they walk in generally leave with an appreciation of the genre's varied roots. The hall's slogan is "Honor Thy Music."

The museum is arranged chronologically, beginning with country's roots in the Scotch-Irish ballads sung by the southern mountains' first settlers, and ending with displays on some of the genre's hottest stars of today. In between, exhibits detail themes, including the rise of bluegrass, honky-tonk, and the world-famous Nashville Sound, which introduced country music to the world.

The Country Music Hall of Fame and Museum is a monument to the music that made Nashville famous.

Downtown Nashville

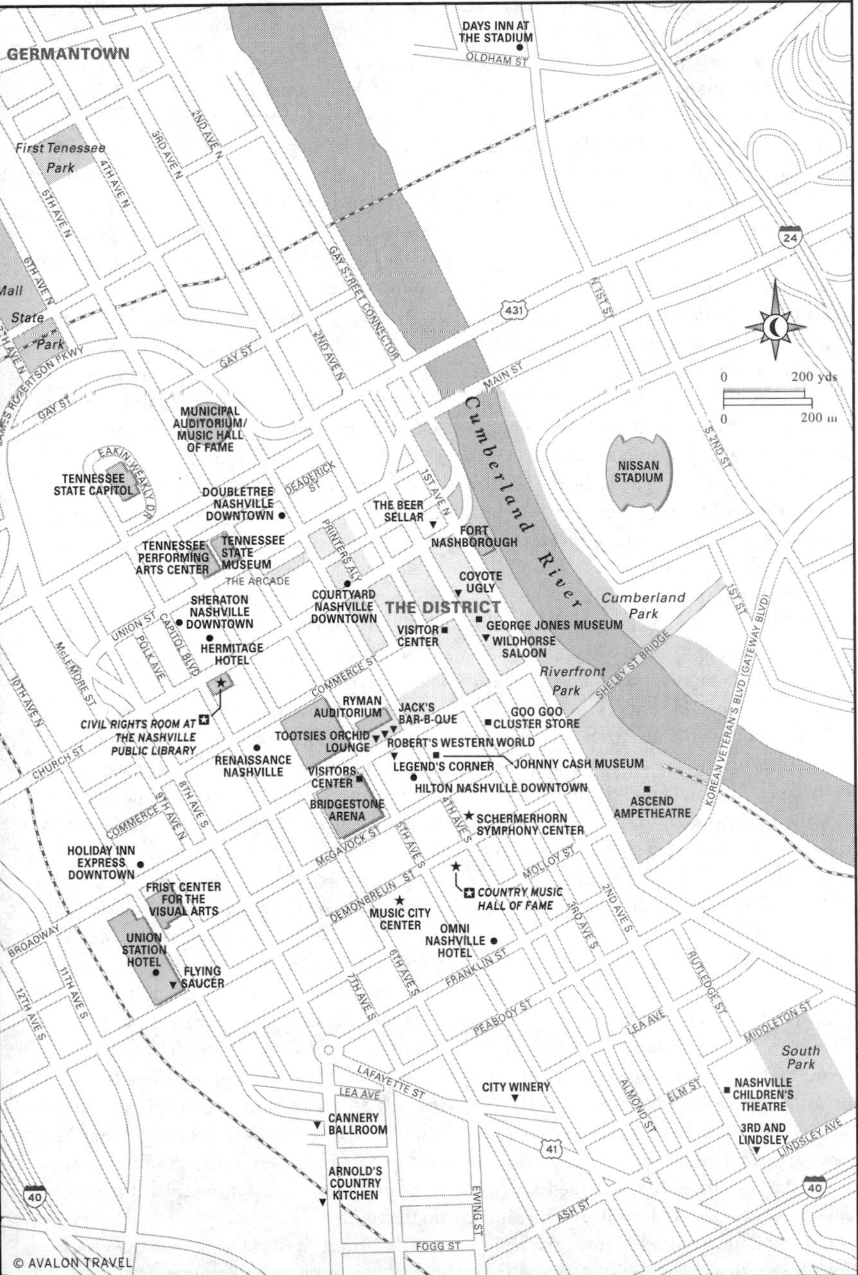

There are a half-dozen private listening booths where you can hear studio-quality recordings of seminal performances, as well as a special display of a few of the genre's most famous instruments. Here you can see Bill Monroe's mandolin, Maybelle Carter's Gibson, and Johnny Cash's Martin D-355.

If you are interested in learning something about country music while you're here, splurge on the $5 audio guide, which adds depth to the exhibits, and really immerse yourself in the music.

The hall of fame itself is set in a rotunda. Brass plaques honor the 100 inductees, and around the room are the words *Will the Circle Be Unbroken?*, from the hymn made famous by the Carter Family.

The only way to visit Music Row's famous **Studio B,** where Elvis once recorded, is to buy your ticket at the museum box office and hop on the Hall of Fame's guided tour bus. The tour takes about an hour, including the 10-minute drive to Music Row and back. The Studio B tour is an additional fee to your admission, but you can buy it as a package all at once. The Platinum Package is adults $39.95, children $29.95 total, for the audio tour, museum admission, and Studio B.

The Taylor Swift Education Center is an interactive space where kids and parents can learn to play instruments and think creatively about songwriting and music making. The museum has several gift shops, one of which is chockfull of much of the music you hear in the museum. The iconic Hatch Show Print store, art gallery, and printing facility is now in the Hall of Fame complex as well.

The Ryman Auditorium

Thanks to an $8.5 million renovation in the 1990s, and another $14 million in 2015, the historic **Ryman Auditorium** (116 5th Ave. N., 615/889-3060, www.ryman.com, 9am-4pm daily, adults $13, children $6.50) remains one of the best places in the United States—let alone Nashville—to hear live music. Built in 1892 by Capt. Thomas Ryman, the Union Gospel Tabernacle, as the Ryman was then called, was designed as a venue for the charismatic preaching of Rev. Samuel P. Jones, to whom Ryman owed his own conversion to Christianity.

Managed by keen businesswoman Lula C. Naff during the first half of the 20th century, the Ryman began to showcase music and performances. In 1943, Naff agreed to the Ryman hosting a popular barn dance called the Grand Ole Opry. The legacy of this partnership gave the Ryman its place in history as the so-called Mother Church of Country Music.

The Opry remained at the Ryman for the next 31 years. After the Opry left in 1974, the Ryman fell into disrepair and was virtually condemned when Gaylord Entertainment, the same company that owns the Opry, decided to invest in the grand old tabernacle. Today, it is a popular concert venue, booking rock, country, and classical acts, plus comedy and more. Performers still marvel at the fabulous acoustics of the hall. Performers like to show them off, playing a number or two without a mic. The Opry returns here during the Christmas season, and in the summer there's a weekly bluegrass series.

Seeing a show at the Ryman is by far the best way to experience this historic venue, but if you can't do that, pay the admission fee to see a short video and explore the auditorium on your own, which includes museum-style exhibits about the musicians who have performed here through the ages. You can sit a few minutes on the old wooden pews and even climb on stage to be photographed in front of the classic Opry backdrop. A guided tour that takes you backstage (adults $27.50, children $22.50) isn't just for die-hard fans. It gives lots of insight into how stars behaved when they were behind these famous walls. The guides tend to throw in an extra tall tale or two. Plus, you get to walk on the storied stage yourself. More than one marriage proposal has taken place at this point on the tour.

The 2015 renovation improved the visitor experience, with more exhibits in its tours, easier ticket booth areas, and the addition of Café Lula (8am-5pm daily, with extended hours during events) if you need a snack. None of the original 1892 architecture was changed during the expansion.

John Seigenthaler Pedestrian Bridge

Built in 1909, the Sparkman Street Bridge was slated for demolition in 1998 after inspectors called its condition "poor." But citing the success of the Walnut Street Bridge in revitalizing downtown Chattanooga, Tennessee, advocates succeeded in saving the bridge. The now-named **John Seigenthaler Pedestrian Bridge** reopened in 2003 as a footbridge and bike bridge.

Today, the John Seigenthaler Pedestrian Bridge connects East Nashville neighborhoods with downtown. It is frequently featured on ABC's *Nashville* because of its great views of the city, and many folks get their iconic Music City photos taken there (including this author). It is named after the civil rights crusader and journalist. At the base of the east side of the bridge is **Cumberland Park** (592 S. 1st St., 615/862-8508, www.nashville.gov/parks), and the East Bank Landing's kayak, canoe, and paddleboard launches.

Johnny Cash Museum

Opened in April 2013, the **Johnny Cash Museum** (119 3rd Ave. S., 615/256-1777, www.johnnycashmuseum.com, 9am-7pm Mon.-Sun., $17, $16 seniors and military, $13 youth) looks like a small storefront with a tiny gift shop. But back behind the cash register is a wealth of information on all things Johnny Cash. The collection was amassed by one fan-turned-collector, and features interactive listening booths, the jumpsuit the Man in Black wore when he flipped the bird in public, and other memorabilia from a varied and lauded career. Locals are crazy for the rebuilt stone wall that was taken from Cash's fire-destroyed suburban home. In just a few years this has become one of the city's most visited attractions.

George Jones Museum

Known as "the Possum," George Jones was a country music great who passed away in 2013 at the age of 81. He struggled with alcohol abuse: He famously drove a John Deere tractor to the liquor store once because his brother-in-law hid his car keys, and was known for being a "no show" for performances. His wife devoted her time to helping him get better. Now she's devoting her time to preserving his musical legacy. The

The Johnny Cash Museum celebrates the Man in Black.

George Jones Museum (128 2nd Ave. N., 615/818-0128, georgejonesmuseum.com, 10am-10pm daily, adults $20, seniors and military $18, youth $15) is filled with artifacts from his life and career, from stage costumes to awards to, yes, a replica of that John Deere tractor. Some exhibits include a hologram of Jones, to give the experience of seeing the legend. A rooftop bar looks out at the Cumberland River.

Tennessee Sports Hall of Fame

Sports fans will enjoy the **Tennessee Sports Hall of Fame** (Bridgestone Arena, 501 Broadway, 615/242-4750, www.tshf.net, 10am-5pm, Tues.-Sat., $3). Located in a state-of-the-art 7,500-square-foot exhibit space inside Bridgestone Arena, the hall chronicles the history of sports in Tennessee from the 1800s to today's heroes.

Customs House

Located at 701 Broadway, the old Nashville **Customs House** is a historic landmark and architectural beauty. Construction on the Customs House began in 1875, and President Rutherford B. Hayes visited Nashville to lay the cornerstone in 1877. The building is an impressive example of the Victorian Gothic style. It was designed by Treasury architect William Appleton Potter and was completed in 1916. Although it is called a customs house, the building served as the center of federal government operations in the city: Federal government offices, courts, and treasury offices were housed in the building.

Hume Fogg

Located across Broadway from the Customs House is **Hume Fogg** Magnet School. It sits on land formerly occupied by Hume School, Nashville's first public school. The four-story stone-clad 1912 building was designed by William Ittner of St. Louis in the Norman Gothic style with Tudor Gothic details. Today, it is a public magnet school with a reputation for high academic standards.

The Frist Center for the Visual Arts

Nashville's foremost visual art space is the **Frist Center for the Visual Arts** (919 Broadway, 615/744-3247, www.fristcenter.org, 10am-5:30pm Mon.-Sat., 10am-9pm Thurs. and Fri., 1pm-5:30pm Sun., adults $12, seniors, students, and military $9). The Frist is located in a stately building that once housed the 1930s downtown post office (and there's still a working post office in the basement). High ceilings, art deco finishes, and unique hardwood tiles distinguish the museum. Look carefully in the hallways, and you can see the indentations in the walls from folks who leaned here while waiting for their turn in line at the post office.

With no permanent collection of its own, the Frist puts on about 12 different major visiting exhibitions annually. At any given time, you will see 3-4 different exhibits, many of which are regional or national premieres. There are typically plenty of ongoing educational activities paired with the exhibitions. ArtQuest, a permanent part of the Frist, is an excellent hands-on arts activity room for children and their parents. The Frist's café serves better-than-expected salads and sandwiches, and has a nice outdoor patio for alfresco dining.

DOWNTOWN

The greater part of downtown is dominated by large office buildings and federal, state, and city government structures. From Commerce Street northward to the state capitol, you will find historic churches, museums, and hordes of office workers.

Tennessee State Capitol

Set on the top of a hill and built with the formality and grace of classic Greek architecture, the **Tennessee State Capitol** building (505 Deaderick St., 615/741-2692, 10am-5pm Tues.-Sat. 1pm-5pm Sun., free) strikes a commanding pose overlooking downtown Nashville. Construction of the capitol began in 1845, two years after the state legislature finally agreed that Nashville would be the permanent capital city. Even with the unpaid labor of convicts and slaves, it took 14 years to finish the building.

The capitol is built of limestone, much of it from a quarry located near present-day Charlotte and 13th Avenues. In the 1950s, extensive renovations were carried out, and some of the original limestone was replaced. The interior marble came from Rogersville and Knoxville, and the gasoliers were ordered from Philadelphia. The capitol was designed by architect William Strickland, who considered it his crowning achievement and is buried in a courtyard on the north end of the capitol.

Visitors are welcome at the capitol. Ask at the information desk for a printed guide that identifies each of the rooms and many of the portraits and sculptures both inside and outside the building. If the legislature is not in session, you can go inside both the House and Senate chambers, which look much as they did back in the 19th century. In the 2nd-floor lobby, you can see two bronze reliefs depicting the 19th and 14th amendments to the U.S. Constitution, both of which were ratified by the State of Tennessee in votes held at the capitol.

Guided tours of the capitol depart hourly 9am-4pm Monday-Friday. Ask at the information desk inside for more information.

Other important state buildings surround the capitol. The **Library and Archives** sits directly west of the capitol and next to the **Tennessee Supreme Court.** The **Tennessee War Memorial** is a stone plaza on the south side of the capitol and a nice place to people-watch (and where, in 2000, Al Gore told supporters he would fight on in the election against George Bush). This is where Occupy Nashville protesters gathered in 2011. A number of state office buildings are nearby, and state employees can be seen walking to and fro, particularly at lunchtime.

Tennessee State Museum

If you are used to the flashy multimedia exhibits found in many of today's top museums, the **Tennessee State Museum** (505 Deaderick St., 615/741-2692, www.tnmuseum.org, 10am-5pm Tues.-Sat., 1pm-5pm Sun., free) might seem like a musty throwback to the past. The displays are largely straightforward combinations of text and images, and they require visitors to read and examine on their own. There are but a few video presentations. But for patrons with enough patience

the state capitol

to give the displays their due, the museum offers an excellent overview of Tennessee history from the Native Americans to the New South era of the 1880s.

Exhibits detail the state's political development, explore the Revolutionary and Civil Wars, and profile famous Tennesseans including Andrew Jackson and Davy Crocket. They also cast a spotlight on the lifestyles and diversions of Tennesseans of various eras, from the early frontiersmen and frontierswomen to a free African American family before emancipation. Special artifacts include the top hat worn by Andrew Jackson at his presidential inauguration, a musket that belonged to Daniel Boone, and the jawbone of a mastodon.

The **Military Branch Museum** (Legislative Plaza, 615/741-2692, 10am-5pm Tues.-Sat., free) is associated with the Tennessee State Museum and highlights America's overseas conflicts, beginning with the Spanish-American War in 1989 and ending with World War II. The exhibits examine the beginnings of the wars, major battles, and the outcomes. There is a special exhibit about Alvin C. York, the Tennessee native and World War I hero. The military museum is located in the War Memorial Building on the south side of the capitol.

★ Civil Rights Room at the Nashville Public Library

The Nashville Public Library (615 Church St., 615/862-5800, 9am-8pm Mon.-Thurs., 9am-6pm Fri., 9am-5pm Sat., 2pm-5pm Sun., free) houses a powerful exhibit (615/862-5782, www.library.nashville.org/civilrights/home.html) on the movement for civil rights that took place in Nashville in the 1950s and 1960s. Nashville was the first Southern city to desegregate public services, and it did so relatively peacefully, setting an example for activists throughout the South.

The story of the courageous men and women who made this change happen is told through photographs, videos, and displays in the **Civil Rights Room at the Nashville Public Library**. The library is a fitting location for the exhibit since the block below on Church Street was the epicenter of the Nashville sit-ins during 1960.

Inside the room, large-format photographs show school desegregation, sit-ins, and a silent march to the courthouse. A circular table at the center of the room is symbolic of the lunch counters where young students from Fisk, Meharry, American Baptist, and Tennessee A&I sat silently and peacefully at sit-ins. The table is engraved with the 10 rules of conduct set out for sit-in participants, including to be polite and courteous at all times, regardless of how you are treated. A timeline of the national and Nashville civil rights movements is presented above the table.

Inside a glass-enclosed viewing room you can choose from six different documentary videos, including an hour-long 1960 NBC news documentary about the Nashville sit-ins. Many of the videos are 30 minutes or longer, so plan on spending several hours here if you are keenly interested in the topics.

The centerpiece of the Civil Rights Room is a glass inscription by Martin Luther King Jr., who visited the city in 1960 and said, during a speech at Fisk University: "I came to Nashville not to bring inspiration, but to gain inspiration from the great movement that has taken place in this community."

Nashville is planning a new and much-needed museum dedicated to its African American history and culture, which will be located at the corner of Jefferson and 8th Avenues, near the farmers market. Until this museum is built, the Nashville Public Library is the best place to learn about the city's racially segregated past and the movement that changed that.

The Civil Rights Room is located on the 2nd floor of the library, adjacent to the room that houses its Nashville collection.

The Arcade

One of Nashville's most distinctive urban features is the covered arcade that runs between 4th and 5th Avenues and parallel to Union Street. The two-story arcade with a gabled

The Nashville Sit-Ins

Greensboro, North Carolina, is often named as the site of the first sit-ins of the American civil rights movement. But, in truth, activists in Nashville carried out the first "test" sit-ins in late 1959. In these test cases, protesters left the facilities after being refused service and talking to management about the injustice of segregation. In between these test sit-ins and the moment when Nashville activists would launch a full-scale sit-in campaign, students in Greensboro took that famous first step.

The Nashville sit-ins began on February 13, 1960, when a group of African American students from local colleges and universities sat at a downtown lunch counter and refused to move until they were served. The protesting students endured verbal and physical abuse, and were arrested.

Community members raised money for the students' bail, and black residents of the city began an economic boycott of downtown stores that practiced segregation. On April 19, the home of Z. Alexander Looby, a black lawyer who was representing the students, was bombed. Later the same day, students led a spontaneous, peaceful, and silent march through the streets of downtown Nashville to the courthouse. Diane Nash, a student leader, asked Nashville mayor Ben West if he thought it was morally right for a restaurant to refuse to serve someone based on the color of his or her skin. Mayor West said, "No."

The march was an important turning point for the city. The combined effect of the sit-ins, the boycott, and the march in 1960 caused Nashville to be the first major Southern city to experience widespread desegregation of its public facilities. The events also demonstrated to activists in other parts of the South that nonviolence was an effective tool of protest.

The story of the young people who led the Nashville sit-ins is told in the book *The Children* by David Halberstam. In 2001, Nashville resident Bill King was so moved by the story of the protests that he established an endowment to fundraise for a permanent civil rights collection at the Nashville Public Library. In 2003, the Civil Rights Room at the Nashville Public Library was opened. It houses books, oral histories, audiovisual records, microfilm, dissertations, and stunning photographs of the events of 1960. The words of one student organizer, John Lewis, who went on to become a congressman from Georgia, are displayed over the entryway: "If not us, then who; if not now, then when?"

glass roof was built in 1903 by developer Daniel Buntin, who was inspired by similar arcades he saw in Italy.

From the moment it opened, the **Arcade** was a bustling center for commerce. Famous for its peanut shop, the Arcade has also been the location of photo studios, jewelers, and a post office for many years. Today, restaurants (including Manny's House of Pizza) crowd the lower level, while art galleries, artists' studios, and professional offices line the 2nd floor. Don't miss the bustling activities here during the monthly Art Crawl on the first Saturday of the month.

Downtown Presbyterian Church

William Strickland, the architect who designed the Tennessee State Capitol, also designed the **Downtown Presbyterian Church** (154 5th Ave. N., 615/254-7584, www.dpchurch.com), a place of worship now on the National Register of Historic Places. Built in 1848 to replace an earlier church destroyed by fire, the church is in the Egyptian revival style that was popular at the time. It is, however, one of only three surviving churches in the country to be built in this style.

Downtown Presbyterian, which added the word *Downtown* to its name in 1955, was used as a Union hospital during the Civil War, and it is where James K. Polk was inaugurated as Tennessee governor in 1839. Visitors are welcome to come for a self-guided tour 9am-3pm Monday-Friday; groups of five or more can call in advance. The church's **Waffle Shop** brunch, held in December, is a local tradition.

Musicians Hall of Fame & Museum

Not to be confused with the Country Music Hall of Fame, the **Musicians Hall of Fame & Museum** (MHOF) (401 Gay St., 615/244-3263, www.musicianshalloffame.com, 10am-5pm Mon.-Sat., adults $18.95, seniors and military $15.95, youth $10.95) honors the people who pick and strum. Not necessarily the stars and not the songwriters, but the guitar players and drummers and others, regardless of genre or instrument, who make a song something to which we want to tap our toes. The MHOF was displaced when the city built the mammoth Music City Center. Located in Municipal Auditorium—once the city's leading concert venue—since 2013, the MHOF displays memorabilia and instruments from the unsung heroes of the industry. Inductees are nominated by current members of the American Federation of Musicians and others. A 8,500-square-foot Grammy Museum Gallery expansion is in the works.

MUSIC ROW

Home to the business end of the country music industry, Music Row can be found along 16th and 17th Avenues south of where they cross Broadway. While there are few bona fide attractions here, it is worth a jaunt to see the headquarters of both major and independent music labels all in one place (this might be your best chance for a celebrity sighting).

Music Row's most famous, or infamous, landmark is ***Musica,*** the sculpture at the Music Row traffic circle. The sculpture, by local artist Alan LeQuire, caused a stir when it was unveiled in 2003 for the larger-than-life anatomically correct men and women it depicts. Regardless of your views on art and obscenity, it is fair to say that *Musica* speaks more to Nashville's identity as the Athens of the South than as Music City USA.

RCA Studio B

As a rule, the music labels in Music Row are open for business, not tours. The lone exception is Historic RCA Studio B (Music Square W., 615/416-2001, www.countrymusichalloffame.com, $29.95-33.95). The RCA studio was the second recording studio in Nashville and the place where artists including the Everly Brothers, Roy Orbison, Dolly Parton, Elvis Presley, and Hank Snow recorded hits. Also called the RCA Victor Studio, this nondescript studio operated from 1957 to 1977. Visitors on the one-hour tour, which departs from the Country Music Hall of Fame downtown, hear anecdotes about recording sessions at the studio and see rare footage of a 1960s Dottie West recording session.

Tours can only be purchased in conjunction with admission to the Country Music Hall of Fame. Tours depart hourly 10:30am-2:30pm Sunday-Thursday. On Friday and Saturday, tours leave every half hour 10:30am-2:30pm.

The Upper Room

Three million Christians around the world know the *Upper Room Daily Devotional Guide,* a page-a-day pocket devotional available in 106 countries and 40 languages. Headquartered in Nashville, the Upper Room Ministry has established a bookstore, museum, and chapel to welcome visitors. **The Upper Room Chapel and Museum** (1908 Grand Ave., 615/340-7207, http://chapel.upperroom.org, 8am-4:30pm Mon.-Fri., free, $4 suggested donation) features a small museum of Christian-inspired art, including a wonderful collection of Nativity scenes from around the world made from materials ranging from needlepoint to camel bone. Visitors may also tour the chapel, with its 8- by 20-foot stained-glass window and 8- by 17-foot wood carving of Leonardo da Vinci's *Last Supper.* A 15-minute audio presentation discusses features of the carving and tells the history and mission of The Upper Room.

MIDTOWN

Encompassing the neighborhoods of Elliston Place, Hillsboro Village, and Green Hills, midtown refers to the parts of Nashville between downtown and the West End.

the statue of Athena at the Parthenon

★ The Parthenon

In 1893, funds began to be raised for a mighty exposition that would celebrate the 1896 centennial of the state of Tennessee. Though the exposition would start a year later, in 1897, it would exceed all expectations. The old West Side Race Track was converted to a little city with exhibition halls dedicated to transportation, agriculture, machinery, minerals, forestry, and African Americans, among other themes. There were Chinese, Cuban, and Egyptian villages; a midway; and an auditorium. The exposition attracted 1.7 million people between May 1 and October 31. While the event turned only a modest profit for its organizers, it no doubt contributed in other ways to the local economy and to the stature of the state.

When the exposition closed in the fall of 1897, all the exhibition halls were torn down except for a life-size replica of the Greek Parthenon, which had housed an art exhibit during the centennial. The exposition grounds were made into a public park, aptly named Centennial Park, and Nashvillians continued to admire their Parthenon.

The Parthenon replica had been built out of wood and plaster, and it was designed only to last through the centennial. Remarkably, it survived well beyond that. But by the 1920s, the Parthenon was crumbling. City officials, responding to public outcry to save the Parthenon, agreed to restore it, and they hired a contractor to rebuild the replica. The contractor did so using tinted concrete.

Today, the Parthenon remains one of Nashville's most iconic landmarks. It is a monument to the creativity and energy of the New South, and also to Nashville's distinction as the Athens of the South.

You can see and walk around the Parthenon simply by visiting Centennial Park. It is, in many respects, most beautiful from the outside, particularly when lit dramatically at night.

As breathtaking as it is from the exterior, it is worth paying to go inside the **Parthenon** (Centennial Park, 2600 West End Ave., 615/862-8431, www.nashville.gov/parthenon, 9am-4:30pm Tues.-Sat., Sun. only 12:30pm-4:30pm June-Aug., adults $6, seniors and children $4). The landmark has three gallery spaces; the largest is used to display works from its permanent collection of 63 pieces of American art. The other two galleries host interesting, changing exhibits. But upstairs is the remarkable 42-foot statue of Athena, by local sculptor Alan LeQuire. Athena is designed as a replica of what the statue would have looked like in ancient Greece, in all her golden glory. In ancient Greece the doors of the Parthenon would have been open, and she would have been seen from a distance. In Nashville her scale and gilded loins are front and center.

Vanderbilt University

Named for philanthropist "Commodore" Cornelius Vanderbilt, who donated $1 million in 1873 to found a university that would "contribute to strengthening the ties which should exist between all sections of our

Midtown Nashville and West End

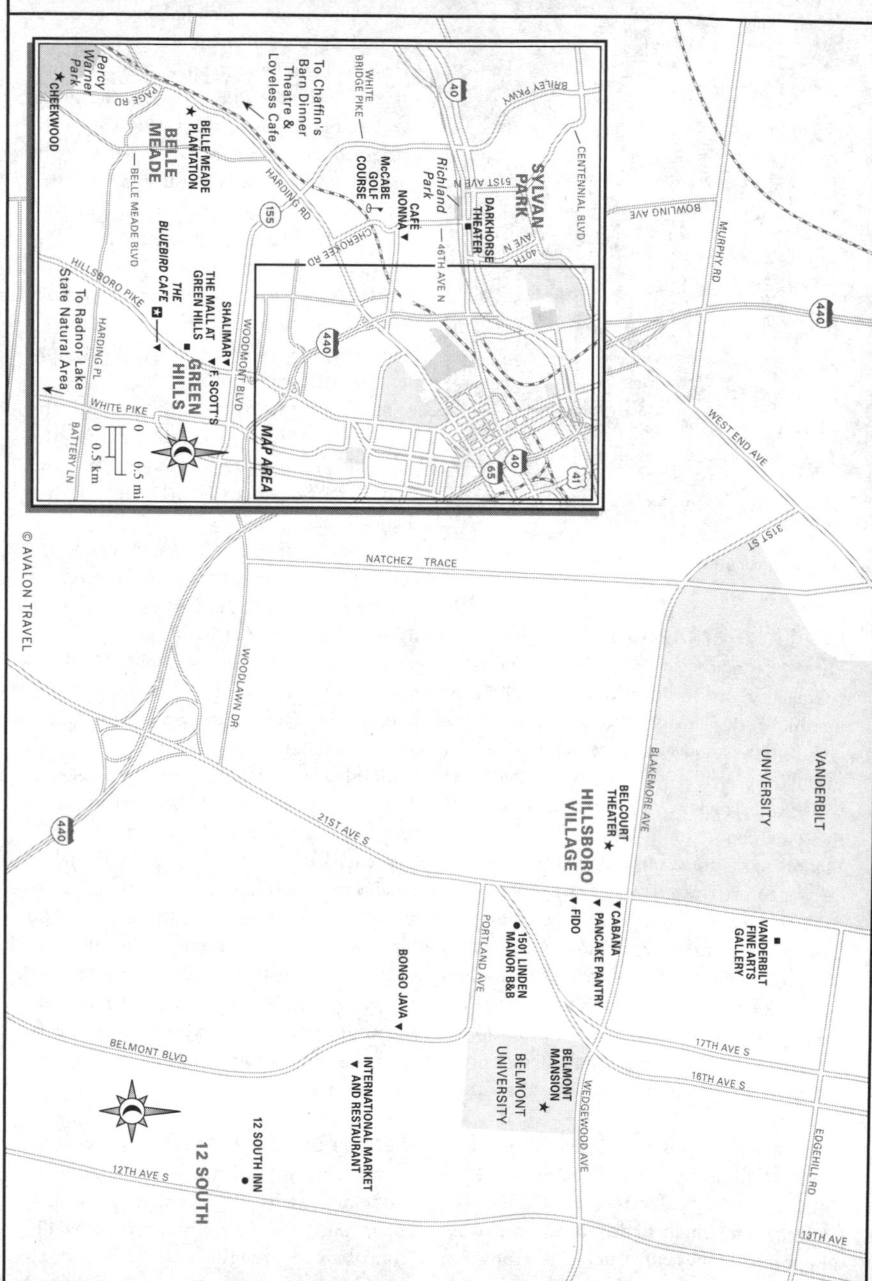

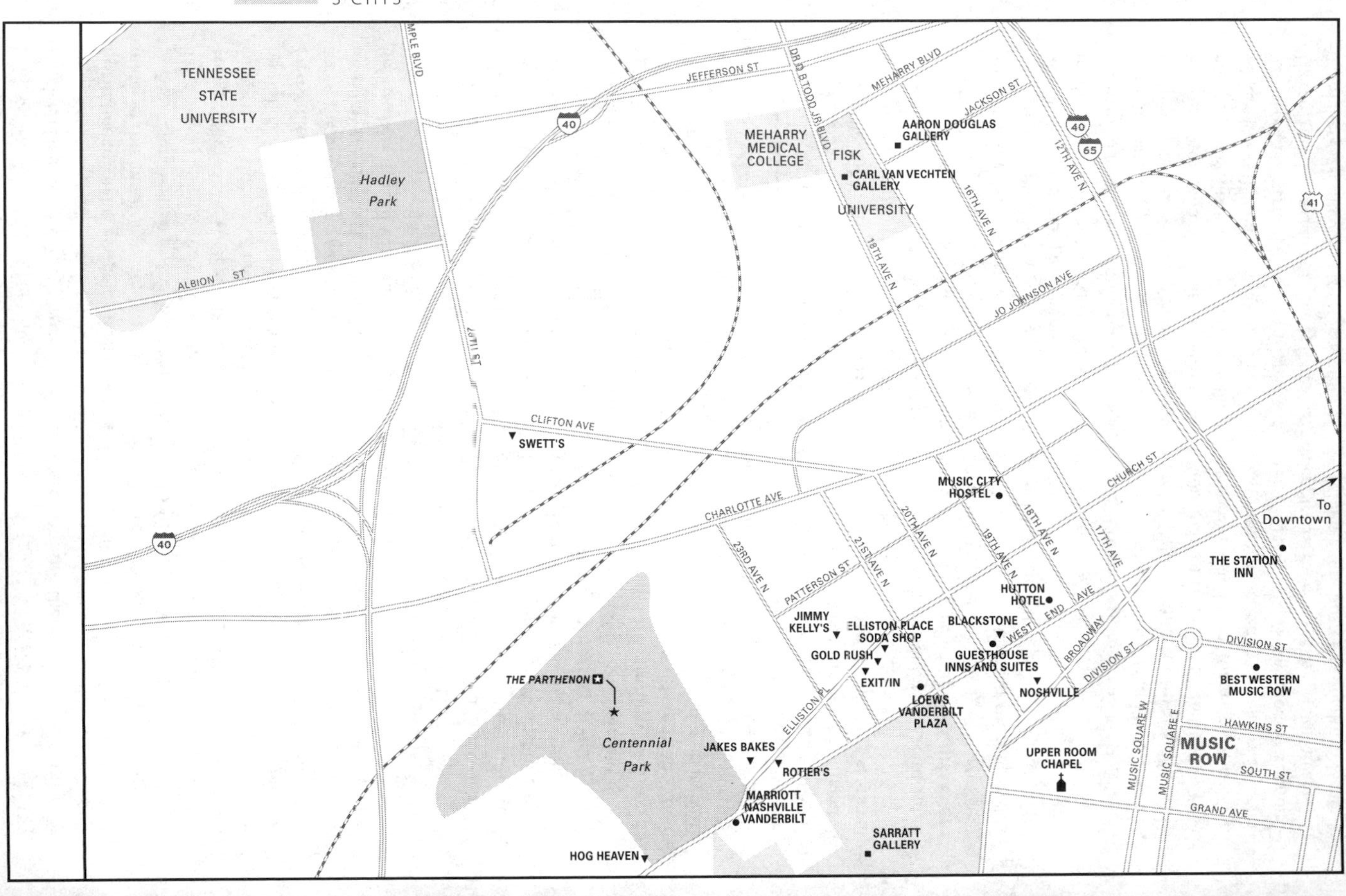
TENNESSEE STATE UNIVERSITY
ALBION ST
Hadley Park
TEMPLE BLVD
40
28TH ST
SWETT'S
CLIFTON AVE
THE PARTHENON
Centennial Park
HOG HEAVEN
JAKES BAKES
MARRIOTT NASHVILLE VANDERBILT
ROTIER'S
ELLISTON PL
23RD AVE N
CHARLOTTE AVE
JEFFERSON ST
MEHARRY MEDICAL COLLEGE
DR D B TODD JR BLVD
FISK UNIVERSITY
CARL VAN VECHTEN GALLERY
AARON DOUGLAS GALLERY
MEHARRY BLVD
JACKSON ST
18TH AVE N
16TH AVE N
JIMMY KELLY'S
PATTERSON ST
21ST AVE N
ELLISTON PLACE SODA SHOP
GOLD RUSH
EXIT/IN
SARRATT GALLERY
LOEWS VANDERBILT PLAZA
20TH AVE N
MUSIC CITY HOSTEL
BLACKSTONE
GUESTHOUSE INNS AND SUITES
HUTTON HOTEL
19TH AVE N
18TH AVE N
WEST END AVE
NOSHVILLE
BROADWAY
JO JOHNSON AVE
12TH AVE N
65
17TH AVE
CHURCH ST
UPPER ROOM CHAPEL
DIVISION ST
MUSIC SQUARE W
MUSIC SQUARE E
MUSIC ROW
GRAND AVE
SOUTH ST
HAWKINS ST
BEST WESTERN MUSIC ROW
THE STATION INN
To Downtown
41

common country," Vanderbilt University (211 Kirkland Hall, 615/322-7311, www.vanderbilt.edu) is now one of the region's most respected institutions of higher education (and the alma mater of this author).

A private research university, Vanderbilt has an enrollment of 6,700 undergraduates and 5,200 graduate students. The university comprises 10 schools, a medical center, public policy center, and The Freedom Forum First Amendment Center. Originally just 75 acres, the university had grown to 250 acres by 1960. When the George Peabody School for Teachers merged with Vanderbilt in 1979 another 53 acres were added.

Vanderbilt's campus life is vibrant, and there is a daily roll call of lectures, recitals, exhibits, and other special events for students, locals, and visitors alike. Check http://calendar.vanderbilt.edu for an up-to-date listing of all campus events.

Prospective students and their parents can sign up for a campus tour. Vanderbilt also offers a self-guided tour of the campus's trees, which form the Vanderbilt Arboretum. Most trees on the tour are native trees common to Nashville and Middle Tennessee. This is a nice activity for people who want to hone tree identification skills. Download a podcast or print a paper copy of the tour from the website or contact the university for more information.

Vanderbilt University also has two excellent art galleries: The **Sarratt Gallery** (Sarratt Student Center, Vanderbilt Place near 24th Ave., 615/322-2471, 9am-9pm Mon.-Fri., 10am-10pm Sat.-Sun. Sept.-mid-May, 9am-4:30pm Mon.-Fri. mid-May-Aug., free), which has a more contemporary bent, and the **Vanderbilt Fine Arts Gallery** (1220 21st Ave. S., noon-4PM Mon.-Fri., 1pm-5pm Sat.-Sun. Sept.-early May, noon-4pm Tues.-Fri. 1pm-5pm Sat. early May-mid-June, may be open longer hours during homecoming and special events on campus, free), which includes works that demonstrate the development of both Eastern and Western art, plus six different traveling exhibits annually. The Fine Arts Gallery is located near the intersection of West End and 23rd Avenues. Both galleries are closed or limit their hours during university holidays and semester breaks, so it's a good idea to call ahead.

There is designated visitor parking in several lots on the Vanderbilt campus. Look on the eastern edge of the sports facilities parking lot off Natchez Trace, in the Wesley Place parking lot off Scarritt Place, or in the Terrace Place parking lot between 20th and 21st Avenues, north of Broadway. Pay attention to these signs, as the university parking monitors do ticket those who park in prohibited areas.

Belmont University

The school for girls founded in the Belmont Mansion in 1890 evolved in 1913 to the Ward-Belmont School for Women and in 1951 to coed Belmont College. Since 1991, it has been **Belmont University** (1900 Belmont Blvd., 615/460-6000, www.belmont.edu), a higher-education institution with links to the Tennessee Baptist Convention. Today Belmont is a fast-growing university with highly respected music and music business programs. In 2011, the school opened the first new law school in the state in the last century. Belmont, which hosted one of the 2008 presidential debates, has a student enrollment of 6,400. Campus tours are available twice a day on weekdays.

Several Belmont facilities are of interest to the public, including the **Curb Event Center** (2002 Belmont Blvd., 615/460-8500). The Curb Event Center hosts sporting events, concerts, and lectures.

Belmont Mansion

The elaborate "summer home" of Adelicia Acklen was constructed in 1853 and was named Belle Monte. **Belmont Mansion** (1900 Belmont Blvd., 615/460-5459, www.belmontmansion.com, 10am-4pm Mon.-Sat., 1pm-4pm Sun., adults $12, seniors $11, children 6-12 $3), as it is known today, is a monument to the excesses of the Victorian age.

Adelicia was born to a wealthy Nashville

McKissack and McKissack, Architects

The oldest African American architectural firm in Tennessee can trace its roots to **Moses McKissack** (1790-1865), a member of the West African Ashanti tribe. He was sold into slavery to William McKissack of North Carolina. Later, McKissack moved to Middle Tennessee. Moses became a master builder, and he passed his knowledge on to his son, Gabriel Moses McKissack, born in 1840. Gabriel Moses passed his knowledge of the building trade to his own son, Moses McKissack III, born in 1879.

Moses McKissack III was born in Pulaski, where he received a basic education in the town's segregated schools. In 1890 he was hired by a local white architect. Until 1905, McKissack designed and built homes throughout the area, including many in Mount Pleasant in Maury County. He developed a reputation as an excellent architect and tradesman.

In 1905, McKissack moved to Nashville, where he started his own construction company. Within a few years, he was working on major projects. He built a home for the dean of architecture and engineering at Vanderbilt University and the Carnegie Library at Fisk University. In 1922, Moses's brother, Calvin, joined him, and they opened McKissack and McKissack, Tennessee's first black architectural firm.

The McKissacks continued to distinguish themselves in the building industry, and they have also kept the business in the family. Since 1991 the company has been led by Cheryl McKissack, a fifth-generation McKissack. The firm employs more than 100 people and has corporate offices in Philadelphia and New York City.

family in 1817. When she was 22, Adelicia married Isaac Franklin, a wealthy bachelor 28 years her senior. When Franklin died seven years later, Adelicia inherited his substantial wealth. Adelicia remarried to Joseph Acklen, a young lawyer, and together they planned and built Belmont Mansion. The home was built in the Italian style, with touches of Egyptian revival style.

The home boasted 36 rooms and 16,000 square feet of space, including a grand gallery where the Acklens hosted elaborate balls and dinner parties. The property included a private art gallery, aviary, zoo, and conservatory, as well as a lake and acres of manicured gardens. After the Civil War, Adelicia traveled to Europe, where she purchased a number of paintings and sculptures that are now on display in her restored mansion.

Shortly before her death, Adelicia sold Belmont to two female educators who ran a girls school from the property for 61 years. Later, it was purchased by the founders of Belmont College.

Visitors to the mansion are given a 45-minute guided tour of the property, which includes the downstairs sitting and entertaining rooms and three of the upstairs bedrooms.

WEST END

Nashville's most posh neighborhood, Belle Meade, is actually a city with its own government. Named after an antebellum plantation, Belle Meade, the city, is home to Nashville's elite, and it famously possesses one of the most wealthy zip codes in America. Drive through to spy on mansions that look more like museums and lawns that look like botanical gardens.

Around Belle Meade are other nice neighborhoods where Nashville's professionals and the upper class live. West End Avenue, the area's thoroughfare, is home to lots of nice restaurants. As you head westward, you pass Cheekwood, the Warner Parks, and eventually meet up with the Natchez Trace Parkway.

Belle Meade Plantation

The mansion at the former **Belle Meade Plantation** (5025 Harding Pk., 615/356-0501, www.bellemeadeplantation.com, 9am-5pm Mon.-Sat., 11am-5pm Sun., adults $18, seniors

$16, students $12, youth $10) is the centerpiece of present-day Belle Meade Plantation and one of the finest old homes in the city. Its name means beautiful pasture, and indeed it was Belle Meade's pastures that gave rise to the plantation's fame as the home of a superb stock of horses. Purchased as 250 acres in 1807 by Virginia farmer John Harding and his wife, Susannah, the estate grew to 5,400 acres at its peak in the 1880s and 1890s.

Belle Meade was never a cotton plantation, although small amounts of the cash crop were grown here, along with fruits, vegetables, and tobacco. Instead it was the horses, including the racehorse Iroquois, that made Belle Meade famous. The mansion was built in 1820 and expanded in 1853. Its grand rooms are furnished with period antiques, more than 60 percent of which are original to the house. The estate also includes outbuildings, including a smokehouse, dairy, and the original log cabin that Harding built for his family when they moved to Belle Meade in 1807.

The plantation also includes a slave cabin, which houses an exhibit on Belle Meade's enslaved population, which numbered more than 160 at its peak. Two of these slaves are described in detail. Susanna Carter was the mansion's housekeeper for more than 30 years, and she remained with the family even after the end of slavery. On her deathbed, Selena Jackson, the mistress of Belle Meade for many years, called Susanna "one of the most faithful and trusted of my friends." The other African American who features prominently at the museum is Bob Green, whose skill and experience as a hostler earned him one of the highest salaries ever paid to a horse hand of the day.

Visitors to Belle Meade are given a one-hour guided tour of the mansion and then visit the outbuildings and grounds on their own.

Cheekwood

Plan to spend a full morning or afternoon at **Cheekwood** (1200 Forrest Park Dr., 615/356-8000, www.cheekwood.org, 9:30am-4:30pm Tues.-Sat., 11am-4:30pm Sun., adults $14, seniors $12, students and children $7-10) so you can experience the full scope of this magnificent art museum and botanical garden. Galleries in the Cheekwood mansion house the museum's American and European collections, including an excellent contemporary art collection. Cheekwood has the largest public collection of works by Nashville artist William Edmondson, the sculptor and stoneworker. Cheekwood usually displays items from its permanent collection as well as traveling exhibitions from other museums. Many exhibits have special ties with Nashville.

But the Cheekwood is far more than just an art museum. The mansion overlooks hundreds of acres of gardens and woods, and it is easy to forget that you are near a major American city when you're at the Cheekwood. Walk the mile-long **Carell Woodland Sculpture Trail** past works by 15 internationally acclaimed artists, or stroll past the water garden to the Japanese garden. There are dogwood gardens, an herb garden, a delightful boxwood garden, and much more. Wear comfortable shoes and pack a bottle of water so you can enjoy the grounds in comfort.

The Cheekwood owes its existence to the success of the coffee brand Maxwell House. During the 1920s, Leslie Cheek and his wife, Mabel Wood, invested in the new coffee brand being developed by their cousin, Joel Cheek. Maxwell House proved to be a success and earned the Cheeks a fortune, which they used to buy 100 acres of land in West Nashville. The family hired New York residential and landscape architect Bryant Fleming to create a 30,000-square-foot mansion and neighboring gardens. Cheekwood was completed in 1933.

Leslie Cheek lived in the mansion just two years before he died, and Mabel lived there for another decade before deeding it to her daughter and son-in-law, who later offered it as a site for a museum and garden. Cheekwood opened to the public in 1960.

Visitors pay admission at a guard gate at the entrance; parking is $3 per car. Once inside, drive to parking lot B so you can explore

The Sculpture of William Edmondson

The first African American artist to have a one-man show at the Museum of Modern Art in New York was Nashville-born sculptor William Edmondson (1874-1951).

Edmondson was born in the Hillsboro area of Nashville. He worked for decades as a laborer on the railroads, a janitor at Women's Hospital, and in other similar jobs before discovering his talent for sculpture in 1929. Edmondson told the *Nashville Tennessean* that his talent and passion were God given: "God appeared at the head of my bed and talked to me, like a natural man, concerning the talent of cutting stone He was about to bestow. He talked so loud He woke me up. He told me He had something for me."

Edmondson was a prolific sculptor. He worked exclusively with limestone, and he created angels, women, doves, turtles, rabbits, and other "varmints." He also made tombstones. Edmondson never learned to read or write, and he called many of his works "mirkels" because they were inspired by God.

In the 1930s, Louise Dahl-Wolfe, a photographer for *Harper's Bazaar* magazine, brought Edmondson and his work to the attention of Alfred Barr, the director of the Museum of Modern Art. Barr and other trustees of the museum admired what they termed as Edmondson's "modern primitive" work, and they invited him to display a one-man show at the museum in 1938. In 1941, the Nashville Art Museum put on an exhibit of Edmondson's work.

Edmondson continued to work until the late 1940s, when he became ill with cancer. After his death in 1951 he was buried in an unmarked grave at Mt. Ararat Cemetery in Nashville. The city park at 17th Avenue North and Charlotte Avenue is named in honor of Edmondson.

There is an exhibit of some of Edmondson's work at the Cheekwood Museum.

the art museum and grounds. Parking lot A is for the museum shop and restaurant.

SOUTH NASHVILLE

Head south on 4th Avenue, which becomes Nolensville Pike, toward a diverse array of attractions.

Fort Negley

Early in the Civil War, the Union army determined that taking and holding Nashville was a critical strategic link in their victory. So after Nashville fell in 1862, the Federals wasted no time fortifying the city against attacks. One of the city's forts was **Fort Negley**, built between August and December 1862 on St. Cloud Hill south of the city center.

Fort Negley owes its existence to the 2,768 men who were enrolled to build it. Most were blacks, some free and some slave, who were pressed into service by the Union army. These men felled trees, hauled earth, and cut and laid limestone for the fort. They slept in the open and enjoyed few, if any, comforts while they labored. Between 600 and 800 men died while building the fort, and only 310 received payment.

When it was completed, Fort Negley was the largest inland masonry fortification in North America. It was never challenged. Fort Negley was abandoned by the military after the war, but it remained the cornerstone of one of Nashville's oldest African American communities, now known as Cameron-Trimble. During the New Deal in the 1930s, the Works Progress Administration rebuilt large sections of the crumbling fort, and it became a public park.

In 2007, the city opened a visitors center to tell the story of the fort. **Fort Negley Park** (Fort Negley Dr., 615/862-8470, noon-4pm Tues.-Thurs., 9am-4pm Fri.-Sat. June-Aug., noon-4pm Tues.-Fri., 9am-4pm Sat. Sept.-May, free) includes a museum about the fort and Nashville's role in the Civil War. There is a short, paved loop trail around the base of the fort, plus raised boardwalks through the fortifications themselves. Historic markers tell the story of the fort's construction and detail its military features.

South Nashville

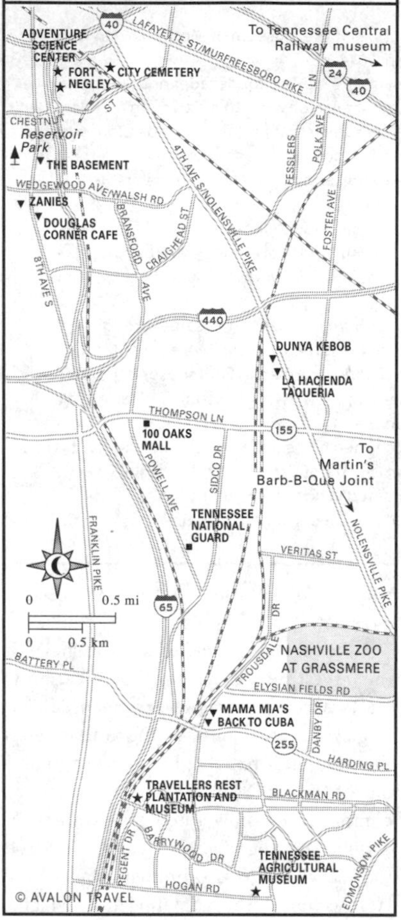

During the Civil War, the cemetery was contracted to bury more than 15,000 Union and Confederate dead, although they were later reinterred in different cemeteries.

Visitors are welcome 8am-5pm daily. Consult the information board in the Keeble Building for help with your self-guided tour. Guided tours and special events, such as living history tours, garden tours, and historical lectures, take place on the second Saturday of each month. The events are aimed at telling the history of Nashvillians who are buried at this historical cemetery.

Adventure Science Center

Children and their caretakers will enjoy the hands-on science education available at the **Adventure Science Center** (800 Fort Negley Blvd., 615/862-5160, www.adventuresci.com, 10am-5pm Mon.-Sat., 12:30pm-5:30pm Sun., adults $14, children $11). Interactive exhibits explore how the body works, the solar system, and other scientific areas. There's a multistory climbing tower in the building's center that features a giant guitar and other instruments.

The center's **Sudekum Planetarium** (www.sudekumplanetarium.com, additional $6) is the largest planetarium in Tennessee. The 164-seat planetarium offers a variety of space-themed shows. There are also star-viewing parties, gravity-suspending rides, and other exhibits about space flight, the moon, the solar system, and other things found in space.

City Cemetery

Right next to Fort Negley Park, off Chestnut Street, is the old **City Cemetery**. Opened in 1822, City Cemetery (1001 4th Ave. S., www.thenashvillecitycemetery.org) was the final resting place of many of Nashville's most prominent early citizens, including founder James Robertson; William Driver, the U.S. Navy captain who named the flag "Old Glory"; Mabel Lewis Imes and Ella Sheppard, members of the original Fisk Jubilee Singers; and 14 Nashville mayors.

Tennessee Central Railway Museum

Railroad enthusiasts should make a detour to the **Tennessee Central Railway Museum** (220 Willow St., 615/244-9001, www.tcry.org, 9am-3pm Tues., Thurs., and Sat., free). This institution is best known for its special railroad excursions, but it also collects railroad equipment and paraphernalia, which are on display at the museum. The museum is located in an otherwise industrial area between the interstate and the railroad tracks, one block north of Hermitage Avenue and east of Fairfield Avenue.

Nashville Zoo at Grassmere

See familiar and exotic animals at the **Nashville Zoo at Grassmere** (3777 Nolensville Pike, 615/833-1534, www.nashvillezoo.org, 9am-6pm daily Apr. 1-Oct. 15, 9am-4pm daily Oct. 16-Mar. 31, adults $15, seniors $13, children ages 3-12 $10, children under 3 free, free parking). Many of the zoo's animals live in beautiful habitats like Lorikeet Landing, Gibbon Islands, and Bamboo Trail. The zoo's meerkat exhibit, featuring the famously quizzical and erect animals, is one of its most popular. The Wild Animal Carousel is an old-time carousel with 39 different brightly painted wooden animals.

The zoo is located at Grassmere, the onetime home and farm of the Croft family. The historic Croft farmhouse has been preserved and is open for guided tours in October and December.

Travellers Rest Plantation and Museum

Travellers Rest Plantation and Museum (636 Farrell Pkwy., 615/832-8197, www.travellersrestplantation.org, 10am-4pm Tues.-Sat., 1pm-4pm Sun., ages 12 and older $12, seniors $11, children ages 7-11 $10, children 6 and under free, family of four, $40) was the home of John Overton, a Nashville lawyer who helped found Memphis, served on the first Tennessee Supreme Court, and was a trusted advisor to Andrew Jackson, the seventh U.S. president and the first from Tennessee.

Overton was born in Virginia and studied law in Kentucky before he decided to move to Middle Tennessee, what was then the western frontier of the United States. When workmen were digging the cellar for the original home in 1799, they uncovered Native American skeletons and artifacts—Overton had chosen a Mississippian-era Indian mound for the site of his home. But the archaeological finds did not stop Overton, who initially named his home Golgotha, or hill of skulls. The name did not stick, however; tradition has it that Overton later renamed the home Travellers Rest because it was his place of rest between long trips as a circuit judge in Middle and East Tennessee.

Travellers Rest underwent two major expansions in its lifetime: one in 1808 and another 20 years later. The additions allowed Overton first to accommodate a growing number of young law students who wished to study law with him; later his wife, Mary, and their children; and, finally, the elaborate parties that Overton hosted to further the political career of Andrew Jackson.

John Overton was many different things in his lifetime. Among them was slave owner. Records show that 30-80 slaves lived at Travellers Rest before emancipation. While Overton's plantation was not the primary source of his wealth, it no doubt contributed to his status and prominence. Sadly, when the L&N Railroad purchased the Overton property in the 1940s, the company destroyed not only the Overton family burial ground and peach orchard, but also the slave cabins that remained at the rear of the house.

Visitors to Travellers Rest may choose to skip the mansion tour; admission to the grounds alone is just $5 for everyone over the age of 4. But to get the full story and flavor of the property, choose the 45-minute guided tour.

Tennessee Agricultural Museum

The **Tennessee Agricultural Museum** (Ellington Agricultural Center, 615/837-5197, www.tnagmuseum.org, 9am-4pm Mon.-Fri., adults $10, seniors, students, and military $7, self-guided tour free) celebrates the ingenuity and dedicated labors of farm life from the 17th to the 20th century. Operated by the Tennessee Department of Agriculture and set on the department's pleasant south Nashville campus, the museum depicts various facets of Tennessee farm life. There are exhibits about clothes washing, blacksmithing, coopering,

The Battle of Nashville

During most of the Civil War, Nashville was occupied by Federal forces. After Fort Donelson, 90 miles northeast of Nashville, fell in mid-February 1862, Nashville was in Union hands. The Federals turned Nashville into an important goods depot for the Northern cause and set strict rules for city residents during occupation.

As the war drew to a close in late 1864, Nashville was the site of what war historians now say was the last major battle of the Western Theater.

The Battle of Nashville came after a string of defeats for the Confederate army of Tennessee, commanded by John Bell Hood. After his bloody and humiliating losses at Spring Hill and Franklin a few miles south, Hood moved north and set up headquarters at Travellers Rest, the home of John Overton. His plan was to set up his troops in an arc around the southern side of the city. Union major general George H. Thomas did not plan to wait for Hood's attack, however. He devised to attack first and drive the Confederates away from Nashville.

A winter storm and frigid temperatures delayed the battle. For two weeks, from December 2 to 14, 1864, the two armies peered at one another across the no-man's-land between the two lines. Then, at dawn on December 15, 1864, the Union attack began. Union troops on foot and horse, including at least four U.S. Colored Infantry brigades made up of African American soldiers, attacked various Confederate posts around the city. By the close of the first day of fighting, Hood withdrew his troops two miles farther south from the city.

The dawn of the second day of battle augured more losses for the Confederates. Unable to hold their line against the Union assault, they fell back again. As darkness fell, Union major general Thomas wired Washington to announce his victory. Pursued by a Union cavalry commanded by Major General James Wilson, what remained of the Confederate army of Tennessee marched south, and on the day after Christmas they crossed the Tennessee River into Alabama. Four months later, the war was over.

The **Battle of Nashville Preservation Society, Inc.** (www.bonps.org) offers tours of the battlefield sites.

plowing, weaving, and more. Outside, there is a small kitchen garden with heirloom vegetables, and replicas of a log cabin, one-room schoolhouse, and outdoor kitchen. There is also a short self-guided nature trail illustrating the ways that settlers used various types of native Tennessee trees.

JEFFERSON STREET

Jefferson Street runs from downtown through northwestern Nashville, past several of the city's African American landmarks.

Bicentennial Mall

Tennessee celebrated its 100th anniversary in 1896 with the construction of the beloved Centennial Park, so it must have seemed like a good idea to celebrate its 200th anniversary in much the same way. The **Bicentennial Capitol Mall State Park** occupies 19 acres on the north side of the capitol building. It offers excellent views of the capitol, which towers over the mall. The mall and the capitol are separated by a steep hill and more than 200 steps, which may look daunting but are worth the climb for the views and access to downtown.

The mall has dozens of features that celebrate Tennessee and Tennesseans, including a 200-foot granite map of Tennessee embedded in concrete; a River Wall with 31 fountains, each representing one of Tennessee's rivers; and a timeline with Tennessee events, inscriptions, and notable quotes from 1796 to 1996. A one-mile path that circles the mall's perimeter is popular with walkers and joggers, and a 2,000-seat amphitheater is used for special events. The park may be a civics lesson incarnate, but it is also a pleasant place to pass the time. Ninety-five carillon bells (for the state's

Fisk's Stieglitz Collection

When photographer **Alfred Stieglitz** died in 1946, his wife, **Georgia O'Keeffe**, herself one of the most important artists of her generation, was left with the responsibility of giving away his massive art collection. Stieglitz had collected more than 1,000 works by artists who included Arthur Dove, Marsden Hartley, O'Keeffe, Charles Demuth, and John Marin. He also owned several African sculptures.

Stieglitz's instructions regarding this art collection were vague. In his will he asked O'Keeffe to select the recipients "under such arrangements as will assure to the public, under reasonable regulations, access thereto to promote the study of art."

O'Keeffe selected several obvious recipients for parts of the collection: the Library of Congress, the National Gallery of Art in Washington, the Metropolitan Museum of Art, the Art Institute of Chicago, and the Philadelphia Museum of Art. Nashville's Fisk University was a surprise, and Carl Van Vechten, a writer, photographer, and friend of Stieglitz and O'Keeffe, is credited with making the suggestion. Van Vechten was keenly interested in African American art and was close friends with Fisk president Charles Johnson.

O'Keeffe and Fisk were not an easy partnership. According to an account by C. Michael Norton, when she first visited the university a few days before the Carl Van Vechten Gallery would open on campus, O'Keeffe ordered major changes to the gallery space, eventually flying in a lighting designer from New York on the day before the opening. At the opening ceremony on November 4, 1949, held at the Memorial Chapel at Fisk, O'Keeffe declined President Johnson's invitation to the lectern and spoke from her chair, saying curtly: "Dr. Johnson wrote and asked me to speak, and I did not answer. I had and have no intention of speaking. These paintings and sculptures are a gift from Stieglitz. They are for the students. I hope you go back and look at them more than once."

The Stieglitz Collection at Fisk consists of 101 remarkable works of art, including 2 by O'Keeffe, 19 Stieglitz photographs, prints by Cézanne and Renoir, and 5 pieces of African tribal art.

Cash-strapped Fisk has sought to sell parts of the collection to raise funds. A proposal to sell a 50 percent share in the collection for $30 million to Walmart heiress Alice Walton's Crystal Bridges Museum in Bentonville, Arkansas, has been rejected by a court, but Fisk continues to press its case. Several alternative proposals have been made, including one to house the collection in the planned museum of African American culture, art, and history, to be located near the Bicentennial Mall. But that idea offered no immediate financial relief for Fisk and raised many unanswered questions. Meanwhile, Fisk reopened the Van Vechten Gallery in October 2008 so that the legendary collection is once again accessible to the public, as the will directed.

95 counties) play "The Tennessee Waltz" every hour on the hour.

To the west of the mall is the amazing **Nashville Farmers Market,** where you can buy fresh produce, flowers, gourmet breakfasts and lunches, and locally made crafts. Locals often picnic in the mall with goodies from the market. There's plenty of free parking here, but don't speed. Because this is a state park, tickets come from the state police, and they're pricier than metro Nashville tickets.

Fisk University

Founded in 1866 to educate newly freed slaves, **Fisk University** (1000 17th Ave. N., 615/329-8500, www.fisk.edu) has a long and proud history as one of the foremost U.S. black colleges. W. E. B. Du Bois attended Fisk, graduating in 1888, and Booker T. Washington married a Fisk alumna and sent his own children to Fisk. In more modern times, Knoxville native and poet Nikki Giovanni attended Fisk. Fisk sits at the corner of Jefferson Street and Dr. D. B. Todd Jr. Boulevard, about 10 blocks west of downtown Nashville. The campus is a smattering of elegant redbrick buildings set on open green lawns, although a few more modern buildings, including the library, detract from the classical feel. One of the oldest Fisk buildings is **Jubilee Hall,** on the north end of the campus, which is said to be the first permanent building constructed for the education of African Americans in the country. It was built with money raised by the Fisk Jubilee Singers, who popularized black spirituals during a world tour 1871-1874. Another notable building is the **Fisk Little Theatre,** a white clapboard building that once served as a Union hospital during the Civil War.

At the corner of Jackson Street and Todd Boulevard is the **Carl Van Vechten Gallery** (615/329-8720, 10am-5pm Tues.-Sat., adults $10, seniors and college students $6, children free), named for the art collector who convinced artist Georgia O'Keeffe to donate to Fisk a large portion of the work and personal collection of her late husband, Alfred Stieglitz. The college still retains much of this collection, although it has sought to sell parts of it to raise funds for the cash-strapped private school, and the legal battle has waged in courts for years. The collection includes works by Stieglitz and O'Keeffe, as well as acclaimed European and American artists, including Pablo Picasso, Paul Cézanne, Pierre-Auguste Renoir, Diego Rivera, Arthur Dove, Gino Severini, and Charles Demuth. It is truly a remarkable collection and one worth seeing, but call ahead to confirm hours, particularly when school is not in session. Ring the bell to the right of the door to be let in.

The **Aaron Douglas Gallery** (Jackson St. and 17th Ave. N., 11am-4pm Tues.-Fri., 1pm-4pm Sat., 2pm-4pm Sun., free) houses Fisk's collection of African, African American, and folk art works. It also hosts visiting exhibits and others by Fisk students and faculty. It is named after painter and illustrator Aaron Douglas, who also established Fisk's first formal art department. The gallery is located on the top floor of the Fisk library. **Cravath Hall** houses several Aaron Douglas murals that are worth seeing.

Fisk welcomes visitors, but there is no central information desk or printed guide. A map is posted just inside the library, and this is the best place to go to start your visit. Historical markers provide details of each of the main campus buildings. To see the famous painting of the Jubilee Singers, enter Jubilee Hall and bear right to the Appleton Room, where it hangs at the rear.

Meharry Medical College

Just across Dr. D. B. Todd Jr. Boulevard from Fisk is **Meharry Medical College** (1005 Dr. D. B. Todd Jr. Blvd., 615/327-6000, www.mmc.edu), the largest private, comprehensive, historically black institution educating medical professionals. It was founded in 1876 as the Medical Department of the Central Tennessee College of Nashville, under the auspices of the Freeman's Aid Society of the Methodist Episcopal Church.

Meharry was at one time responsible for graduating more than half of all African American doctors and nurses in the United States. Today it has an enrollment of almost 800 students.

Marathon Village

This "new" neighborhood is actually one that dates back to 1881. A former auto factory, **Marathon Village** (www.marathonvillage.com) now houses sleek urban condos, restaurants, the Corsair Artisan Distillery, Bang Candy Company, and shops, including Antique Archaeology Nashville, owned by Mike Wolfe of *American Pickers* TV fame. Marathon Village's gentrification has been slow, and it still has a ways to go to be a bustling destination. But the 2011 addition of live music venue Marathon Music Works is bringing out the locals, and architecture and history buffs love the buildings' bones.

Hadley Park

Founded in 1912, **Hadley Park** (1037 28th Ave. N., 615/862-8451) is believed to be the oldest public park developed for African Americans in the South and, most likely, the United States. The park got its start when Fisk University president George Gates requested that the city buy land and create a park for its black citizens. This was in the era

The Jubilee Singers

Jubilee Hall on the Fisk University campus was paid for with the proceeds of the Fisk Jubilee Singers.

In 1871, Fisk University needed money. Buildings at the school established in old Union army barracks in 1866 were decaying while more and more African Americans came to seek education.

So, in what might later be considered a very Nashville-style idea, the school choir withdrew all the money from the university's treasury and left on a world tour. The nine singers were Isaac Dickerson, Maggie Porter, Minnie Tate, Jennie Jackson, Benjamin Holmes, Thomas Rutling, Eliza Walker, Green Evans, and Ella Sheppard. Remembering a biblical reference to the Hebrew "year of the jubilee," Fisk treasurer and choir manager George White gave them their name, the Fisk Jubilee Singers.

The choir struggled at first, but before long audiences were singing their praises. They toured first the American South, then the North, and in 1873 sailed to England for a successful British tour. Their audiences included William Lloyd Garrison, Wendell Phillips, Ulysses S. Grant, William Gladstone, Mark Twain, Johann Strauss, and Queen Victoria. Songs like "Swing Low, Sweet Chariot" and "Nobody Knows the Trouble I've Seen" moved audiences to tears. The singers introduced the spiritual to mainstream white audiences and erased negative misconceptions about African Americans and African American education.

In 1874, the singers returned to Nashville. They had raised enough money to pay off Fisk's debts and build the university's first permanent structure, an imposing Victorian Gothic six-story building now called Jubilee Hall. It was the first permanent structure built solely for the education of African Americans in the United States.

Every October 6, the day in 1871 that the singers departed Fisk, the University recalls their struggle and their triumph with a convocation featuring the modern-day Jubilee Singers.

of segregation, so other city parks were not open to blacks. The request was granted, and the park opened in July 1912. An old farmhouse was converted into a community center, and benches and a playground were installed. It is now home to a state-of-the-art gym and fitness center, computer labs, meeting rooms, and tennis courts.

Tennessee State University

Founded in 1912 as a normal school for blacks, **Tennessee State University** (3500 John A. Merritt Blvd., 615/963-5000, www.tnstate.edu) is now a comprehensive university with more than 9,000 students. In 1979, as a result of a court order to desegregate the state's universities, TSU merged with the Nashville campus of the University of Tennessee. Today, TSU's student body is 75 percent African American.

MUSIC VALLEY

A collection of tourist attractions separated from the rest of Nashville by the Cumberland River, **Music Valley** is most known for being the new home of the Grand Ole Opry. The area was one of those hit hardest by the 2010 flood, leading to some significant improvements and upgrades, and some closures. This strip of motels, restaurants, and country music "museums" is tourist-centric. It is more campy than authentic, although it does offer some fun, affordable ways to explore Music City's kitsch.

If you're game, however, head straight for **Cooter's Place** (2613 McGavock Pk., 615/872-8358, www.cootersplace.com, 9am-7pm Mon.-Thurs., 9am-8pm Fri.-Sat., 9am-6pm Sun., free), a gift shop and museum dedicated to the *Dukes of Hazzard* television show. The museum features a mind-boggling array of toys, ornaments, and model cars manufactured in the 1970s and 1980s to profit off the Dukes' wild popularity. You can also see one of the bright-orange Dodge Chargers that became the Dukes' icon. In the gift shop, buy a pair of "official" Daisy Dukes or any number of General Lee souvenirs. Cooter's Place is operated by Ben Jones, who played Cooter, the affable sidekick mechanic, in the original television series. In recent years, Jones has been one of the forces behind DukeFest, a wildly popular annual celebration of fast cars and the General Lee held at the Nashville Motor Speedway. Jones has been determined to keep the signature Confederate flag as part of the art associated with the *Dukes of Hazzard*, despite controversy over the flag.

A few doors down from Cooter's Place, you will find **Willie Nelson and Friends Museum and General Store** (2613 McGavock Pk., 615/885-1515, 8:30am-9pm Mon.-Sat., 8:30am-9pm Sun., $8), which showcases a number of things that once belonged to Willie Nelson, including his golf bag, a replica of his tour bus, and the guitar he played during his first performance at the Grand Ole Opry. Many of the Willie Nelson items were purchased by museum operators Jeannie and Frank Oakley at an IRS auction.

The Grand Ole Opry

Since 1974, the **Grand Ole Opry** (2802 Opryland Dr., 615/871-6779, www.opry.com) has been most often staged at the specially built Grand Ole Opry House in Music Valley.

the tasting bar at Corsair Artisan Distillery

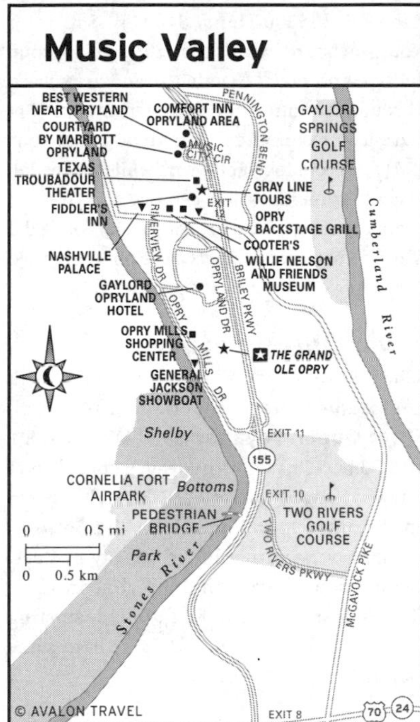

This is the Opry's sixth regular home, and it was completely renovated after it was shuttered due to the 2010 flood. The Opry House may have been closed, but the Opry went on. The show still made the airwaves for every scheduled performance, playing at different venues around town while construction went on around the clock.

The Opry performs at least two times a week, Friday and Saturday, with additional shows on Tuesday night most weeks. The **Grand Ole Opry Museum** is still shuttered since the flood (it is unclear if it will reopen), but with the renovated Opry came a renovated backstage tour. Daytime tour tickets go on sale two weeks in advance and are generally offered every 15 minutes; if you are buying tickets to a show, you can also purchase postconcert backstage tours. On this docent-led tour you'll get to see dressing rooms, learn lots of Opry history, and hear plenty of juicy stories about performers and their backstage behavior. One of the highlights of the guided tour is to get to go on stage and have your photo taken under the lights. If you book a postshow tour, you'll see a performer or two. Tickets are $25 for adults, $20 for children; VIP tour $125 after a show; daytime tours are $22 adults, $17 children.

NORTH NASHVILLE

★ Fontanel Mansion

The former estate of country music icon Barbara Mandrell, **Fontanel Mansion** (4225 Whites Creek Pk., 615/727-0304, www.fontanelmansion.com, 9am-3pm daily, adults $24, seniors $22, children $14) has become a surprising draw for locals and tourists alike since it opened in 2010. These 136 acres include walking trails, a music venue, a restaurant with its own live music, an art gallery, and a gift shop. But the main attraction is the mansion, a 27,000-square-foot log cabin, which is the city's only country music mansion tour. Fans get to see how the most famous of the Mandrell sisters once lived. Tours are sometimes given by Mandrell's daughter, who throws in lots of personal tidbits. Even those who don't love "I Was Country When Country Wasn't Cool" will appreciate the music history, artifacts such as Gretchen Wilson's "Redneck Woman" Jeep, the indoor shooting range, and the bucolic scenery.

TOURS

Nash Trash Tour

Nashville's most notorious tour guides are Sheri Lynn and Brenda Kay Jugg, sisters who ferry good-humored tourists around town in a big pink school bus. The **NashTrash Tours** (615/226-7300 or 800/342-2123, www.nashtrash.com, $33-36) is a raunchy, rollicking, rib-tickling tour of city attractions, some of which you won't even find in this guidebook. Be prepared to be the butt of some of the jokes yourself. Its "I Got Trashed" T-shirts have a double meaning. You'll snack on canned cheese, and there's a pit stop to buy beer. Not appropriate for children or adults who aren't comfortable laughing at themselves and others. As Sheri Lynn says, "If we haven't offended you, just give us some time." NashTrash Tours sell out early and often. If you think you want this perspective of the city, make your reservation now. Tours depart from the Nashville Farmers Market.

Gray Line Tours

Nashville's largest tour company, **Gray Line** (2416 Music Valley Dr., 615/883-5555 or 800/251-1864) offers more than 12 different sightseeing tours of the city. The three-hour Discover Nashville tour costs $49 per adult and includes entrance to the Ryman Auditorium and the Country Music Hall of Fame, and stops at other city landmarks.

The three-hour Homes of the Stars tour takes you past the homes of country stars, including Alan Jackson, Vince Gill, Dolly Parton, and the late Tammy Wynette for $35. There is also a one-hour downtown trolley tour for $15 and a 90-minute downtown walking tour for $20. Gray Line also offers a one-hour downtown trolley tour and a downtown walking tour, plus an option to see the sights featured on ABC-TV's Nashville drama.

General Jackson Showboat

Gaylord Opryland's **General Jackson Showboat** (2812 Opryland Dr., 615/458-3900, www.generaljackson.com, tickets $65-135, depending on time of day and year) offers campy, big-budget-style musical shows on the stage of a giant riverboat as it lumbers down the Cumberland River. Show dates and times vary by season, but typically there are midday lunch and evening dinner cruises. A smaller boat, the *Music City Queen,* offers tailgating cruises before Tennessee Titans NFL football games. Because of the meal and the live entertainment, these cruises aren't necessarily the best way to see the river, as you're focused on the stage rather than the scenery.

Nashville Pedal Tavern

Have 15 friends and a taste for beer? Then the **Nashville Pedal Tavern** (1516 Demonbreun St., 615/390-5038, www.nashvillepedaltavern.com, 11:30am-11pm daily, $380 Sun., $350 Mon.-Wed., $300 Thurs., $400 Fri.-Sat.) is for you. You board what is basically a giant group bicycle and pedal together to move forward through downtown or Midtown, stopping at various pubs on the route. Members of your party pass out food and drink while you pedal. Each tour includes between two and five pub stops; at each spot there's a special for Pedal Tavern customers. Expect to be photographed by people on the street as you ride by.

River Queen Voyages

Choose between several different kayak tours down the Cumberland River with **River Queen Voyages** (1900 Davidson St., 615/933-9778, www.rqvoyages.com, hours vary by day, May-Oct., $29-59). The three-mile guided tour starts in Shelby Bottoms Greenway, winding under railway bridges, ending downtown with the skyline in sight. The eight-mile tour is self-guided, starting further up the river, but ending with the same payoff.

Walk Eat Nashville

Former *Tennessean* editor Karen-Lee Ryan started her **Walk Eat Nashville** (East Nashville and Midtown, locations disclosed when tour booked, 615/587-6138, www.walkeatnashville.com, 1:30pm-4:30pm Thurs., 11am-2pm Fri., 1:30-4:30pm Sat., $49) walking culinary tours as a way to show off her neighborhood of East Nashville. They were so popular, she soon expanded to Midtown, with other 'hoods in the works. The walking tours include food tastings at six restaurants and artisan food shops. Ryan and her guides narrate as you walk (and taste) and you get the benefit of her considerable knowledge of the city. You'll leave satisfied, but not full.

Tennessee Central Railway

The **Tennessee Central Railway Museum** (220 Willow St., 615/244-9001, www.tcry.org) offers an annual calendar of sightseeing and themed railway rides in central Tennessee, including kids' trips, Old West shoot-outs, and murder mysteries. Excursions include fall foliage tours, Christmas shopping expeditions, and trips to scenic small towns. All trips run on the Nashville and Eastern Railroad, which runs east, stopping in Lebanon, Watertown, Cookville, or Monterrey. Prices vary based on the trip, but run between $46-135 for adults.

These tours are not just train rides, but well-organized volunteer-led events. You might get "robbed" by a Wild West bandit (the cash goes to charity) or taken to a scenic winery. The volunteers know their railroad trivia, so feel free to ask questions. The cars vary depending on what is available, but there is a car that doubles as a gift shop and another that is a concession stand, although you are welcome to bring your own food on the train. Trips sell out early, so book your tickets well in advance.

Entertainment and Events

From live music to theater, Nashville offers visitors plenty of diversions. Even if you are not a fan of country music, you will find plenty to do in Music City.

LIVE MUSIC VENUES

No trip to Nashville is complete without listening to some live music. Music City overflows with musicians and opportunities to hear them. So whether you catch a show at the Opry, stake out a seat at The Bluebird Café, or enjoy a night at the symphony, be sure to make time for music during your visit.

Even before you arrive in the city, you can plan out your nights, thanks to the Nashville Convention and Visitors Bureau (www.nashvillecvb.com). Through a handy feature on the bureau's website you can check out upcoming concerts a month or more in advance. Many venues will let you buy tickets in advance over the phone or online. But don't panic if you can't plan ahead. One of the benefits of being in Music City is that there is always a show worth seeing somewhere. And because there are so many shows, there is always something that hasn't sold out.

Published on Wednesday, the *Nashville Scene* always includes detailed entertainment listings and recommendations. The *Nashville Tennessean*, the city's daily paper, publishes its entertainment insert on Friday. Now Playing Nashville (www.nowplayingnashville.com), an initiative with the Community Foundation of Middle Tennessee, is a great resource for both entertainment listings and discounted tickets. Now Playing Nashville has a kiosk in the Nashville airport.

★ The Grand Ole Opry

If there's any one thing you really must do while in Nashville, it's go to see the **Grand Ole Opry** (2802 Opryland Dr., 615/871-6779 or 800/733-6779, www.opry.com, $32-72). Really. Even if you think you don't like country music. For more than 90 years this weekly radio showcase of country music has drawn crowds to Nashville. Every show at the Opry is still broadcast live on WSM, a Nashville AM radio station. Shows are also streamed online, and some are televised on cable. But nothing beats the experience of being there.

The Opry runs on Friday and Saturday nights, with two 2.5-hour shows each night. The early show starts at 6:30pm, and the late show starts at 9:30pm. Often there is an additional Tuesday evening show. Since this is a radio broadcast, shows start and end right on time.

Every Opry show is divided into 30-minute segments, each of which is hosted by a different member of the Opry. This elite country music fraternity includes dozens of stars that you've heard of and others you haven't. The host performs two songs; one at the beginning of his or her half-hour segment and one at the end. In between the host will introduce two or three other performers, each of whom will sing about two songs. In between segments, the announcers read radio commercials and stagehands change around the stage set.

All in all, it is a fast-paced show that keeps your toes tapping. Even if there's an act that you don't like, they won't be on the stage for too long. Of course, the flip side is that if it's an act you love, well, they're only on the stage for two songs, too. Even when the biggest stars appear on the Opry stage, they rarely sing more than a few numbers. Fans are welcomed, and even encouraged, to walk to the front of the seating area to take photographs during the performances.

The Opry usually releases the full lineup for each show about a week in advance. Some fans wait until then to buy their tickets so they're sure to catch a big-name artist. My advice is to forget about bragging to your friends back home about who you saw at the Opry and buy tickets to any show at all. Each show is carefully balanced to includes bluegrass, classic country, popular country, and, sometimes, gospel or rock. It is a true showcase that music and Americana fans will enjoy.

Most Opry shows take place in the Grand Ole Opry House, a 4,400-seat auditorium in Music Valley that was renovated after the 2010 flood. A circle of the original stage from the Ryman Auditorium was cut out and placed in the center of the Opry House stage, and it is here that artists stand when they perform. During the Christmas season the Opry returns to its Ryman roots (and the Radio City Rockettes take the Opry House stage).

One advantage of shows at the Opry House is that you can buy tickets for a guided backstage tour. Tickets go on sale two weeks in advance; times vary based on the time of year and time of day. The tours include a peek at the Green Room, Opry stars' mailboxes, and other behind-the-scenes treasures. If you book one of the evening tours, you're likely to see performers jamming in folding chairs after a show. Glitzy costumes, juicy stories, and a chance to walk on that stage are all part of the tour offerings.

Tours are $17.50 for adults and $12.50 for children. You can also book combination packages that include the backstage tours, an Opry performance, and hotel rooms and meals at the Gaylord Opryland Resort.

Ascend Amphitheatre

This open-air concert venue offers the chance to rock out by the river in Metro Riverfront Park. Between folding seats, box seats and the lawn, it can hold 6,800 concert-goers, all of whom get a view of the skyline and great sightlines of the stage. **Ascend Amphitheatre** (1st Ave. S, 615/999-9000, www.ascendamphitheater.com, hours vary by event, cost varies by event) is the place to see a big show, with big-name national acts on the schedule as well as the Nashville Symphony. Locals have been known to picnic nearby (or paddleboard or kayak on the river) during shows because they can hear the sounds without being inside.

Texas Troubadour Theatre

Known as the Texas Troubadour, Ernest Tubb started a tradition when he set up a live radio show at the back of his Broadway record shop. The **Ernest Tubb's *Midnite Jamboree*** was broadcast after the Opry shut down across the street, and it lived up to its name. The *Jamboree* continues, now broadcast from the **Texas Troubadour Theatre** (Music Valley Village, 2416 Music Valley Dr., 615/889-2472, www.ernesttubb.com, no cover). Located across the street from the Gaylord Opryland Resort, the *Jamboree* gets started early in the evening, while the Opry is still on, but things really get swinging after midnight.

The Texas Troubadour Theatre is also home to the **Cowboy Church** (2416 Music Valley Dr., 615/859-1001, www.nashvillecowboychurch.org). Every Sunday at 10am, locals and tourists dressed in anything from shorts to Stetsons gather here for a lively praise-and-worship country gospel church service led by Dr. Harry Yates and Dr. Joanne Cash Yates. The church was founded in 1990 with just six souls; today it attracts hundreds to its weekly services. Country and gospel music legends make cameo performances now and again, but the real star is Jesus.

Presenting The Grand Ole Opry

Nashville's most famous broadcast can trace its roots to October 1925, when Nashville-based National Life and Accident Insurance Company opened a radio station in town. Its call letters (then and now), WSM, stood for "We Shield Millions," the company's motto.

WSM hired George D. "Judge" Hay, a radio announcer who had worked in Memphis and Chicago, to manage the station. Hay—who, while in Chicago, had announced one of the nation's first live country radio shows—planned to create a similar program in Nashville.

On November 25, 1925, Hay invited a 78-year-old fiddler, Uncle Jimmy Thompson, to perform live on Saturday night over the radio airwaves. The response was electric, and WSM continued to broadcast live old-time music every Saturday night. In May 1927, the program developed the name the Grand Ole Opry, practically by chance. Hay was segueing from the previous program of classical opera to the barn dance. "For the past hour, we have been listening to music taken largely from Grand Opera. From now on, we will present the Grand Ole Opry," he said. The name stuck.

During the first few years, most Opry performers were unknowns who worked day jobs in and around Nashville. But as the show gained popularity, some acts were able to make it professionally, including Uncle Dave Macon, the Vagabonds, and the Delmore Brothers. By 1939, the Opry gained a slot on the nationwide NBC radio network, allowing it to reach a national audience every week.

Always a live audience show, the Opry was performed in several different venues over the years. It started in the WSM studio, then moved to the Hillsboro Theater (now the Belcourt), the Dixie Tabernacle on Fatherland Street, and the War Memorial Auditorium downtown. In 1943 it moved to the Ryman Auditorium, where it remained until 1974, when National Life built a new 5,000-seat auditorium in a rural area north of Nashville. The first show from the new Opry House in Music Valley was broadcast on March 16, 1974. President Richard Nixon attended. In 1983, the Opry was acquired by Oklahoma-based Gaylord Broadcasting Company. After the 2010 Nashville flood, the Opry House was gutted and renovated by Gaylord Entertainment, who still owns all the Opry properties.

The music that flows from the Opry's stage on a Saturday night (and now, Tuesday and Friday, too) has changed since the first fiddler took the airwaves. Just as country music broadened its appeal by softening its hard edges, the Opry has evolved with its audience. Today it is a showcase for all types of country and country-inspired music, including bluegrass, gospel, honky-tonk, and zydeco. It remains, however, one of the most esteemed and celebrated institutions in American music.

The Ryman Auditorium

The most famous music venue in Nashville, the **Ryman Auditorium** (116 5th Ave. N., 615/889-1060, www.ryman.com, cover varies) continues to book some of the best acts in town, of just about every genre you can imagine. On the good side, the hall still boasts some of the best acoustics around. On the bad, the pew-style bench seats are just as uncomfortable as ever. But seeing the reverence performers have for this venue makes it hard to notice anything else. Musicians love to show off the acoustics here, often playing a song or two without a mic.

Country Music Hall of Fame

The **Country Music Hall of Fame** (222 5th Ave. S., 615/416-2100, www.countrymusichalloffame.com) hosts concerts, readings, and musical discussions regularly in an auditorium located inside the hall. These daytime events are often aimed at highlighting one type of country music or another, but sometimes you'll find big names playing. Admission is free with your paid admission to the hall, so it is a good idea to plan your trip to the hall on a day when there's a concert scheduled (separate admission to concerts is not available). Check the website for a listing of upcoming events.

Carl Black Chevy Woods Amphitheater

Opened in 2010, this 4,500-seat outdoor concert venue is nestled, as its name suggests, in the woods at Fontanel, a spot that used to be the home of country star Barbara Mandrell. The **Carl Black Chevy Woods Amphitheater** (4225 Whites Creek Pk., 615/727-0304, www.woodsamphitheater.com) has space for picnicking on the lawn during a concert and VIP boxes, as well as folding chairs for a more traditional concert experience. Fontanel often operates free shuttles to and from downtown, for those who don't want to drive to Whites Creek for a concert. This can be a bonus, as the driveway to the parking lot can get congested.

Marathon Music Works

The 14,500 square feet **at Marathon Music Works** (1402 Clinton St., 615/891-1781, www.marathonmusicworks.com, ticket prices vary depending on the performing artist) are some of Nashville's most progressive when it comes to concert-going. Located in the historic Marathon Village, this venue has exposed brick, a swanky VIP loft area, multiple bars, and plenty of space for cutting the rug. Musical acts booked run the gamut from The Black Belles to the Yonder Mountain String Band.

★ The Bluebird Café

In some ways, no other music venue is as quintessentially Nashville as **The Bluebird Café** (4104 Hillsboro Pk., 615/383-1461, www.bluebirdcafe.com, cover varies). It is intimate and homey. It books some of the best up-and-coming country and acoustic acts in the business, as well as the songwriters who penned the lyrics you are used to hearing other people sing. Its shows start as early as 6:30pm. There is no talking during the acts and virtually none of the usual bar pickup scene. In short, The Bluebird is a place where music comes first and everything else is a far second.

Opened in 1982 by Amy Kurland, The Bluebird is located next to a dry cleaner in a nondescript shopping mall a few miles south of Hillsboro Village. While it started out as a casual restaurant with live music, over the years it evolved into a destination for music lovers who appreciate its no-nonsense take on live music, and who hope that they just might stumble in on the next big thing. The Bluebird is famous as an early venue for the then-unknown Garth Brooks, but its stage has also

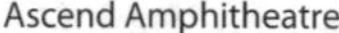
Ascend Amphitheatre

Let's Go Honky-Tonkin'

It may be known locally as honkytonk, honky tonk, or honky-tonk and it may be used as a noun (a bar that plays Western swing, where people dance), a verb (dancing to Western swing), or an adjective (a descriptor of the type of music), but one thing is for sure, in Nashville honky-tonk is what makes Music City sing.

These bars are across the city, but the main strip is found along Lower Broadway in the heart of downtown. They play a specific strain of Country and Western swing music, with a live band. Small or large, these venues all have some empty space to cut the rug, because dancing is an essential part of Nashville honky-tonk.

The best places to go honky-tonking include: Tootsie's, The Wheel, Legends Corner, and Robert's Western World. Most of these establishments are open to all ages during the day, but convert to 21 and over after 6 pm. They typically don't have a cover charge, although when the cowboy hat is passed for the band, don't forget to drop a few dollars in.

hosted the likes of Emmylou Harris, Kathy Mattea, Gillian Welch, Trisha Yearwood, and Steve Earle, among many more. In 2008, it was sold to the Nashville Songwriters Association International, a deal that has improved the venue by streamlining some of the booking and ticket-buying processes.

The Bluebird is open every night of the week, and most evenings the entertainment starts at 6:30pm. Cover is usually under $15. There are just 20 tables and a few additional seats at the bar, so, depending on the show, you have to be on your toes to get a spot in the house. Reservations are only taken online (not by email or by phone), and some shows are first come, first seated only.

Once you've successfully nabbed a seat at The Bluebird, sit back and enjoy some fine live music (but really, no talking—you will be shushed). Nashville is the city where anybody can become a somebody, and it's places like The Bluebird that make that happen.

Lines have always been long, but since the ABC-TV show *Nashville* first aired, they're even longer.

CONCERT SERIES

Thursday nights in September and October transform downtown's Public Square Park for **Live on the Green** (www.liveonthegreen.net, free). The outdoor concert series tends to attract a lot of indie rock acts, and the crowd is young, hip, and socially aware. Food and arts and crafts vendors line the sidewalks under tents.

Also taking place on Thursday nights in the summer, **Bluegrass Nights at the Ryman** (116 5th Ave. N., 615/889-3060, www.ryman.com/bluegrass, 7:30pm Thurs. late June-late July, $28.50, or $155.50 for a season pass) is a concert series that features some of the best pickers in the country. Starting in June and ending in July, this Ryman Auditorium series is always popular.

Held in early summer and early fall, **Musicians Corner** (2500 West End Ave., musicianscornernashville.com, 11am-5pm Sat. May-June and Sept.-Oct., free) is a concert series in its own location inside Centennial Park. There's some permanent seating in the form of stone benches, but most people bring blankets and camp chairs and hang for the day. Since 2010, more than 750 artists of all genres have graced this stage . Food trucks and kids activities are on site, but the focus is the music.

CLUBS

Venues here are categorized by their predominant music type, but keep in mind that variety is the name of the game. Most bars and clubs (except for honky-tonks) charge a cover when there is a band or performer, while songwriter nights and open mics are usually free.

Country

Nashville's most colorful country music establishments are the honky-tonks that line Broadway. Once places where country boys and girls would come to shake a leg or meet a sweetheart, these all-day, all-night bars and music clubs now cater to visitors. After the Opry moved to Music Valley in the late 1970s, taking with it the customers who kept Broadway businesses afloat, the street's honky-tonks subsisted first on local barflies and later on the tourist trade. But now they've bounced back, and locals and visitors alike take advantage of the high energy, cheap beer, and talented musicians found here. Whether you're looking for a place to drown your sorrows or kick off a night on the town, Broadway's honky-tonks are a good place to go. They are always open and typically free, although you are encouraged to participate when the hat is passed for the band.

Tootsie's Orchid Lounge (422 Broadway, 615/726-0463, no cover) is painted purple and exudes classic country every day of the week beginning as early as 10am. Three doors down from Tootsie's is **Robert's Western World** (416 Broadway, 615/244-9552, www.robertswesternworld.com, no cover), voted the city's best honky-tonk. Originally a store selling boots, cowboy hats, and other country music regalia, Robert's morphed into a bar and nightclub with a good gift shop. Another choice is **The Stage** (412 Broadway, 615/726-0504, no cover), with a large dance floor and music seven nights a week.

The **Wildhorse Saloon** (120 2nd Ave. N., 615/902-8200, www.wildhorsesaloon.com, cover varies) is a boot-scootin', beer-drinkin' place to see and be seen, although almost exclusively by tourists. When the Wildhorse opened in 1994, promoters drove a herd of cattle through the streets of downtown Nashville. The huge dance floor is often packed with cowboys and cowgirls line dancing to the greatest country hits. Free dance lessons are offered every day (6:30pm-8:30pm Mon.-Thurs., 6pm-9:30pm Fri., noon-9:30pm Sat., 2pm-7:30pm Sun.). The Wildhorse books big-name acts many nights of the week, including country music, roots rock, and classic rock stars. The Wildhorse opens Thursday-Sunday at 11am and on Monday at 5pm. When there is a show on, doors normally close at 6pm and reopen at 7pm for people with tickets. On other nights the cover charge is $4-6. From 10pm on, the Wildhorse is a 21-and-up club. The Wildhorse is owned by Gaylord, the same folks who own the Ryman, Opryland, and the Opry, and often offers deals for hotel guests. There is a shuttle back to the Opryland Hotel for folks staying there.

Doyle & Debbie parody (and praise) Nashville at the Station Inn.

It doesn't look like much (or anything) from the outside, but inside this cinder-block box is the city's most popular venue for bluegrass and roots music, **The Station Inn.** There is no cover for the Sunday-night bluegrass jam. Monday nights feature the Time Jumpers, a world-class Western swing jam band. Most Tuesday nights the hilarious parody **The Doyle and Debbie Show** (www.doyleanddebbie.com, $20) takes the stage. (402 12th Ave. S., 615/255-3307, www.stationinn.com, cover varies) is perhaps the country's best bluegrass club, and it showcases fine artists every night of the week. This homey and casual club opens nightly at 7pm, with music starting about 9pm. This is a 21-and-over club, unless you come with a parent or guardian. There is no cover for the Sunday-night bluegrass jam. The **Nashville Palace** (2400 Music Valley Dr., 615/889-1540, no cover) is a restaurant, nightclub, and dance floor across from the Opryland Hotel. Live music is on tap daily starting at 5pm, and talent nights on Tuesday and Wednesday always draw a crowd.

Jazz and Blues

If you need to get that country twang out of your head, a good dose of the Memphis blues will do it. **B. B. King Blues Club** (152 2nd Ave. N., 615/256-2727, www.bbkingclubs.com, cover varies) is a good place to start for a night of the blues. The club is a satellite of King's original Beale Street club in Memphis, and it books live blues every night. The cover charge is usually under $10, unless B. B. King himself is making one of his rare appearances.

In Printer's Alley, the **Bourbon Street Blues and Boogie Bar** (220 Printer's Alley, 615/242-5867, cover varies) is a hole-in-the-wall nightclub that specializes in New Orleans-style jazz and blues.

While not a club per se, the **Nashville Jazz Workshop** (1319 Adams St., 615/242-5299, www.nashvillejazz.org, cover varies) has live performances in its Jazz Cave as well as at special events around town. Ticket prices are typically modest.

Eclectic

Clubs listed here may book a rock band one night and folk the next. Always check the free weekly *Nashville Scene* for the latest entertainment listings.

The **Exit/In** (2208 Elliston Pl., 615/321-3340, www.exitin.com, cover varies) has been a favorite rock music venue for years, although it also books alternative country, blues, and reggae. Located on Elliston Place, the club is convenient to Vanderbilt and downtown.

Coffee shop by day, bar and live music venue by night, **Café Coco** (210 Louise Ave., 615/321-2626, www.cafecoco.com, cover varies) in Elliston Place is the best of both worlds. Monday is songwriter's night, Tuesday is open-mic poetry, and Thursday is open-mic music. Jazz and rock bands play other nights, when the cover is $2-5.

The Basement (1604 8th Ave. S., 615/254-8006, www.thebasementnashville.com, cover varies) calls itself a cellar full of noise, but it's a good kind of noise. Indie rock is the most common art form here, but it books other types of acts, too. The Basement's New Faces Night on Tuesday is a popular place to hear singer-songwriters. Admission is 21 and over, unless accompanied by a parent or guardian. The brick walls and subterranean feel give the Basement its cool atmosphere. It is nestled under **Grimey's New and Preloved Music,** one of the city's best record stores. Park behind the club and on side streets.

Located in an old warehouse that has housed a flour mill, jam factory, and country music concert hall, **Cannery Ballroom** (One Cannery Row, 615/251-3020, www.mercylounge.com, cover varies) and its derivative **Mercy Lounge** are two cool venues for live music. Cannery Ballroom is a large, somewhat cavernous space with lots of nice cherry-red touches, hardwood floors, and a shiny red bar. It can hold up to 1,000 people. The Mercy Lounge upstairs is a bit more intimate, with a capacity of up to 500 people. The Mercy Lounge hosts 8 off 8th on Monday nights, an open-mic event, where eight different bands get to perform three songs. Both venues book rock, country, soul, and all sorts of other acts. It is located off 8th Avenue South.

3rd and Lindsley (818 3rd Ave. S., 615/259-9891, www.3rdandlindsley.com, cover varies) is a neighborhood bar and grill that showcases rock, alternative, progressive, Americana, soul, and R&B music. Over the years it has developed a reputation for booking good blues acts. It serves a full lunch and dinner menu, the bar is well stocked, and the club offers a great atmosphere and sound quality.

The **Douglas Corner Café** (2106-A 8th Ave. S., 615/298-1688, www.douglascorner.com, cover varies) offers a Tuesday open-mic night and country and other acts the rest of the week. It is known as a place where singer-songwriters are discovered, and it is laid-back in both attitude and ambience. An intimate setting, full menu, and good acoustics make this a popular choice for music listening. Several live albums have been recorded here.

BARS

Barhopping is best enjoyed downtown, where there is the greatest concentration of nightclubs, restaurants, and bars. Even on weeknights lower Broadway and its side streets are crowded with people, some dressed in designer cowboy boots and fringed shirts, others in Preds jerseys, others in business suits. This is the official entertainment district of Nashville, and it is well patrolled by police and cruisers alike. Outside of downtown, there are several other enclaves of nightlife that cater more to residents than visitors.

Nashville won't issue a liquor license unless the establishment also serves food, so all of the following bars double as restaurants.

Downtown

The honky-tonks along Broadway, Wildhorse Saloon, and B. B. King Blues Club are several of the most popular nightclubs downtown. Right next to the Wildhorse Saloon, **Coyote Ugly** (154 2nd Ave. N., 615/254-8459, www.coyoteugly.com) draws a youthful, raucous crowd. Drinking beer and making friends are the two primary pursuits here, and for many visitors, there's no better place to do either.

Memorabilia of Nashville's past adorns the walls at **Legends Corner** (428 Broadway, 615/248-6334), a popular and more authentic club for live music and rollicking crowds. There is never a cover, but, as always, be sure to put in a few bucks when they pass the hat for the performer.

A few blocks from downtown, near the Frist Center for the Visual Arts, you'll find one of the city's best beer bars. Behind the Union Station Hotel on the west side of downtown, the **Flying Saucer** (1001 Broadway, 615/259-7468, www.beerknurd.com) has one of the best selections of beer in town. Monday is pint night, when you can get $2.50 pints of just about any of the beers on the wall.

Yes, **The City Winery** (609 Lafayette St., 615/324/1010, www.citywinery.com/nashville, ticket prices vary) restaurant/wine bar/live music venue is a chain (it has locations in Chicago, New York and Napa, California, too). But this chain is the brainchild of Michael Dorf, who created the iconic Knitting Factory club earlier in his career. That means even in a city like Nashville, where everyone is a musician or knows a musician, the musical lineup is impressive. Tickets typically include seating, so you can eat and drink and not crane your neck to see the act. This isn't a place where people generally get up and dance.

Midtown

Elliston Place is home to several live music clubs, plus a few neighborhood bars and college hangouts (Elliston is just blocks from the Vanderbilt University campus). The Exit/In and The End have live bands most nights of the week. **The Gold Rush** (2205 Elliston Pl., 615/321-1160, www.goldrushnashville.com) is a time-worn but beloved late-night mellow hangout.

Also in Hillsboro Village, **Cabana** (1910 Belcourt Ave., 615/577-2262, www.cabanannashville.com) is a popular, if trendy, place to people-watch and unwind. It is a bar/restaurant/late-night hangout that attracts a youthful and well-dressed crowd. Lounge at the bar or in the expansive backyard. Choose from dozens of beers, wines, and some excellent martinis.

Blackstone Restaurant and Brewery (1918 West End Ave., 615/327-9969, www.blackstonebrewery.com) is a local favorite, with its own brand of craft beers, a cozy fireplace, and a laid-back vibe. The menu features better-than-bar food.

There's no sign on the exterior, but that hasn't kept people across the country from discovering **Patterson House** (1711 Division St., 615/636-7724, www.thepattersonnashville.com). Cocktails here are mixed with care, and there's no standing room. You must have a seat in order to be served, both of which contribute to a civilized cocktail hour.

Near the Mall at Green Hills, **The Greenhouse** (2211 Bandywood Dr., 615/385-3357) offers specialty drinks, beers, and lots of hanging plants. To find it, look for the Green Hills Kroger and take a left. Its location means you'll find more locals than tourists.

East Nashville

Edgefield Sports Bar and Grille (921 Woodland St., 615/228-6422) is a no-frills watering hole that caters to East Nashville residents.

No. 308 (407 Gallatin Ave., 615/650-7344, www.bar308.com) is a sleek, mod, hipster hangout with hand-crafted drinks. Come during happy hour, when these custom cocktails are more budget friendly.

Another Nashville mixology house that has received national attention, **Holland House Bar and Refuge** (935 W. Eastland Ave., 615/262-4190, www.hollandhousebarandrefuge.com) specializes in handmade, old-fashioned cocktails. The bar stocks an impressive selection of whiskey and bourbon, and it hires bartenders who know how to use them.

You might think you're south of the border at the **Rosepepper Cantina** (1907 Eastland Ave., 615/227-4777, www.rosepepper.com), a Mexican restaurant and bar. Choose from 30 different variations of the margarita, and enjoy the house band on weekend nights.

12 South

The gentrified neighborhood on 12th Avenue South has attracted new residents, and they like to hang out at a number of neighborhood bars.

Snag a seat on the crowded patio outside **Mafiaoza's Pizzeria and Neighborhood Pub** (2400 12th Ave. S., 615/269-4646, www.mafiaozas.com), a popular neighborhood hangout known for its pizza, which you watch be slid into the giant ovens.

The extensive list of brews on tap has earned **12 South Taproom and Grill** (2318 12th Ave. S., 615/463-7552, www.12southtaproom.com) a loyal following. The above-average bar food includes several vegetarian-friendly options.

GAY AND LESBIAN NIGHTLIFE

You don't have to be gay to enjoy **Tribe** (1517-A Church St., 615/329-2912, www.tribenashville.com), but it helps to be beautiful, or at least well dressed. The dance floor here is one of the best in the city, and the atmosphere is hip. Martinis and other specialty drinks are the poison of choice at this standard-setting club, which stays open until the wee hours.

Right next door to Tribe is **Play** (1519 Church St., 615/322-9627, www.playdancebar.com), the city's highest-energy gay club, with drag shows and performances by adult-film stars.

Women outnumber men at the **Lipstick Lounge** (1400 Woodland St., 615/226-6343, www.thelipsticklounge.com), a cool yet homey club in East Nashville. Live music, pool, and great food attract a crowd nearly every night. Across the street is **Mad Donna's** (1313 Woodland St., 615/226-1617, www.maddonnas.com), where the second floor is home to drag queen bingo, karaoke, and other festivities.

COMEDY

Nashville's only dedicated comedy club is **Zanies** (2025 8th Ave. S., 615/269-0221), where you can hear stand-up comics every weekend and some weeknights. But there's much to amuse you all over town, including **The Doyle and Debbie Show** at **The Station Inn** (402 12th Ave. S., 615/255-3307, http://www.doyleanddebbie.com) and the **NashTrash Tour** (615/226-7300 or 800/342-2123, www.nashtrash.com, $32). Check out comedy listings at **Nash Comedy** (www.nashcomedy.com).

THE ARTS

Before Nashville was Music City, it was the Athens of the South, a city renowned for its cultural, academic, and artistic life. Universities, museums, and public arts facilities created an environment for artistic expression unparalleled by any other Southern city. It has an opera company of its own, not to mention an award-winning symphony (and symphony center), an innovative arts scene, and ample opportunities to sample contemporary and classic music, film, and theater.

Theater

The **Nashville Repertory Theatre** (505 Deaderick St., 615/782-4000, www.tennesseerep.org) is Tennessee's largest professional theater company. It stages five big-name shows and three off-Broadway productions annually. The Rep performs in the Tennessee Performing Arts Center, located in the James K. Polk Cultural Center in downtown Nashville. This is the same building that houses the Tennessee State Museum, plus some Nashville Opera performances, and the Nashville Ballet. Some of its productions have included *The Crucible, I Hate Hamlet,* and *Doubt*. The season runs October-May.

Artists' Cooperative Theatre (ACT 1, 615/726-2281, www.act1online.com) is an organization dedicated to bringing theatrical gems, both classic and modern, to Nashville audiences. Founded in 1989, ACT 1 has presented productions of more than 90 of the world's greatest plays. Each year the theater puts on four or five productions. ACT 1 performs at the Darkhorse Theater at 4610 Charlotte Avenue.

New theatrical works are given the spotlight by the **Actors Bridge Ensemble** (1312 Adams St., 615/341-0300, www.actorsbridge.org), a theater company for new and seasoned actors. The Ensemble brings provocative and new plays to Nashville, often performing at the Belmont Black Box Theater in midtown.

Circle Players (www.circleplayers.net) is the oldest nonprofit, all-volunteer arts association in Nashville. As a community theater, all actors, stagehands, directors, and other helpers are volunteers. The company stages four or five performances every year at a variety of theater locations around the city. Performances include classic theater, plus stage adaptations of popular cinema and literature.

Nashville's leading experimental theater group is the **People's Branch Theatre** (615/254-0008, www.peoplesbranch.org). Founded in 2000, the group brings together local actors to produce bold and innovative professional theater. They perform at the Belcourt Theatre in Hillsboro Village.

Children's Theater

Nashville Children's Theatre (724 2nd Ave. S., 615/254-9103, www.nashvillechildrenstheatre.org) is the oldest children's theater company in the United States. During the school year, the company puts on plays for children from preschool to elementary-school age in its colorful theater. In the summer there are drama classes for youngsters, plus lots of activities that include Mom and Dad.

Teenagers own and operate the **Real Life Players** (615/297-7113), a stalwart theater company that produces original plays written by Nashville teens. Profits are donated to teen-related community organizations. Plays are performed at the Darkhorse Theater at 4610 Charlotte Avenue.

Don't miss the **Marionette Shows at the Nashville Public Library** (615 Church St., 615/862-5800). Using marionettes from the collection of former library puppeteer Tom Tichenor, plus others acquired from Chicago's Peekabo Puppet Productions, the library's children's room staff put on excellent one-of-a-kind family entertainment.

Dinner Theater

Chaffin's Barn Dinner Theatre (8204 Hwy. 100, 615/646-9977, www.dinnertheatre.com, adults $60, students 13-18 $40,

Famous Nashvillians

Nashville is used to celebrity, what with all the big-name music stars around. But it's not just musicians who call, or called, Nashville home:

- **"Jefferson Street Joe" Gilliam,** one of the first African American quarterbacks in the National Football League, played college ball at Tennessee State University. The former quarterback for the Pittsburgh Steelers died in 2000 in his hometown of Nashville, five days before his 50th birthday.
- **Madison Smartt Bell** was born and raised in Nashville. The novelist's works include *All Souls Rising, Ten Indians,* and *The Year of Silence.*
- **Oprah Winfrey** was raised in Nashville by her father, Vernon. In her second year at Tennessee State University she was hired as Nashville's first female and first African American TV news anchor at WTVF-TV.
- **Julian Bond,** civil rights activist, political activist, and the chairman of the NAACP, was born in Nashville and lived here until he was five years old.
- **Bobby Jones,** host of BET's *Bobby Jones Gospel,* was once a professor at Tennessee State University. The program is the longest running show on cable television and is taped in Nashville.
- **Red Grooms** was born and raised in Nashville. Grooms is a prominent modern American artist whose pop art depicts frenetic scenes of urban life.
- **Al Gore Jr.,** though born in Washington DC and raised in Carthage, Tennessee, is closely associated with Nashville. After the Vietnam War, he attended Vanderbilt University for one year and then spent five years as a reporter for the *Tennessean.* The former U.S. vice president has had a home in Nashville for many decades.
- Aussie actress **Nicole Kidman** may have moved to Nashville because of the career of her country-singing hubby, **Keith Urban,** but she has made it her own. She is frequently seen around town with her family.

children 12 and under $30) was Nashville's first professional theater and continues to put on Broadway-style plays for dinner patrons. There's nothing cutting-edge about the shows or the meal, but they are family-friendly fun.

Music

The **Nashville Symphony Orchestra** (One Symphony Pl., 615/687-6400, www.nashvillesymphony.org) is housed in the remarkable Schermerhorn Symphony Center next to the Country Music Hall of Fame, one of the downtown buildings that was renovated as a result of 2010 flood damage. Nominated for four Grammies and selling more recordings than any other American orchestra, the symphony is a source of pride for Music City. Costa Rican conductor Giancarlo Guerrero is the symphony's seventh music director.

The symphony puts on more than 200 performances each year, including classical, pops, and children's concerts. Its season spans September-May. Buying tickets online is a breeze, especially since you can easily choose where you want to sit. There is discounted parking for symphonygoers in the Pinnacle at Symphony Place, across the street from the Schermerhorn.

During the summer, the symphony plays its **Centennial Park Concert Series.** Head to the Centennial Park band shell to hear free big-band, ballroom, and classical concerts with other parkgoers. It is a classic Nashville experience.

The **Blair School of Music** (2400 Blakemore Ave., 615/322-7651) presents student, faculty, and visiting artist recitals frequently during the school year. Vanderbilt University's music school, Blair addresses music through academic, pedagogical, and performing activities.

Opera

Middle Tennessee's only opera association, the **Nashville Opera Association** (www.nashvilleopera.org) puts on an average of four main-stage performances per season (October-April) and does a six-week tour to area schools. They perform at the Tennessee Performing Arts Center at 505 Deaderick Street.

Ballet

Founded in 1981 as a civic dance company, the **Nashville Ballet** (505 Deaderick St., www.nashvilleballet.com) became a professional dance company in 1986. Entertaining more than 40,000 patrons each year, the ballet performs both classical and contemporary pieces at the Tennessee Performing Arts Center.

Cinemas

Once the home of the Grand Ole Opry (as is true of so many buildings in Nashville), the **Belcourt Theatre** (2102 Belcourt Ave., 615/383-9140, www.belcourt.org) is the city's best venue for independent films. Built in 1925 as a silent movie house, the Belcourt now screens a refreshing variety of independent and unusual films, plus hosts live music concerts. In the summer the Belcourt screens some films outdoors. Parking in the theater's Hillsboro Village lot is free for moviegoers. Ask for a code when you buy your ticket. In 2016 the 90-year-old building began a $4.5 million renovation project.

More mainstream arty flicks are shown at the **Regal Cinemas Green Hills** (3815 Green Hills Village, 615/269-5910). Mainstream multiplex cinemas can be found near Opryland, 100 Oaks, Rivergate, and other neighborhoods.

FESTIVALS AND EVENTS

January

There's only one day all year that **The Hermitage, the Home of Andrew Jackson** (4580 Rachel's Ln., 615/889-2941, www.thehermitage.com) is free to the public, and that's to celebrate the former president's victory at the Battle of New Orleans. The free day is typically on a weekend closest to January 8.

More than 150 dealers set up in the Nashville Convention Center for the upscale **Antiques and Garden Show of Nashville** (1200 Forrest Park Dr., 615/352-1282, www.antiquesandgardenshow.com, $20) in February. One of the largest such shows that combines both indoor furniture and outdoor, garden antiques, the event includes workshops, demonstrations, and vintage finds to meet most budgets and tastes. Proceeds from the show benefit the Cheekwood Botanical Garden and Museum of Art.

February

The second week of February is **Antiques Week** (www.nashvilleantiquesweek.com) in Nashville. During this period, four separate antiques events top the bill. At the Tailgate Antique Show at the Fiddler's Inn Hotel in Music Valley, antiques dealers set up their shops in hotel rooms and parking spaces. A similar setup exists at the Radisson Hotel Opryland for the Music Valley Antiques Market. The biggest sale is at the Gaylord Opryland Resort and Convention Center. The final event for Antiques Week is the upscale Antiques and Garden Show of Nashville, which features antiques dealers, exhibition gardens, and lectures at the Nashville Convention Center.

March

Many Nashville music events celebrate the performers. But the **Tin Pan South Songwriters Festival** (www.tinpansouth.com) honors the people who come up with the lyrics for all those great tunes. Typically held the last week of March, Tin Pan South, organized by the Nashville Songwriters Association International, schedules performances at venues across the city.

April

The **Country Music Television Music Awards** (www.cmt.com) was country music's first fan-voted awards show. Founded in 2002, the show lets fans participate in both the first and final rounds of voting. The show is broadcast live on television from Nashville, usually from the Curb Event Center at Belmont University.

Film lovers throughout the country look forward to the **Nashville Film Festival** (www.nashvillefilmfestival.org), held every April at the Green Hills Cinema 16. The film festival was founded in 1969 as the Sinking Creek Film Celebration. These days, upwards of 20,000 people attend the weeklong event, which includes film screenings, industry panels, and lots of parties.

Part of the Rock 'n' Roll Marathon circuit, the **Country Music Marathon** (www.cmmarathon.com) takes place every April. More than 15,000 professional and amateur runners take part, and tens of thousands more come out for the live music and cheer squads that line the racecourse. The postrace concert usually boasts nationally known country music artists.

May

Held in Centennial Park, the **Tennessee Crafts Fair** (www.tennesseecrafts.org) showcases the work of more than 180 different fine craftspeople. More than 45,000 people come to the three-day event every year, which also includes craft demonstrations, a food fair, and entertainment. The fair repeats in September.

For something a little different, plan to attend the **Running of the Iroquois Steeplechase** (www.iroquoissteeplechase.org) at Percy Warner Park. Taking place on the second Saturday of May, the race is the nation's oldest continuously run weight-for-age steeplechase in the country. Fans in sundresses or suspenders and hats enjoy watching some of the top horses in the country navigate the race course. You can pay for general admission to sit on the hillside overlooking the stadium. Pack a blanket, food, and drinks (and mud boots if it has rained recently), and you'll have an excellent day. Various tailgating tickets are available and are priced according to how good the view is from the parking spot. If you want to tailgate, you need to buy tickets well in advance.

Taking place every weekend in May, the **Tennessee Renaissance Festival** (www.tnrenfest.com) celebrates all things medieval. Come to watch jousting matches, hear 16th-century comedy, or buy capes and swords. The festival takes place off Highway 96 between Franklin and Murfreesboro, about a 25-minute drive south from Nashville.

June

What was once called Fan Fair, and is now hosted by the Country Music Association and called the **CMA Music Festival** (www.cmafest.com), is a four-day mega-music show in downtown Nashville. The stage at Riverfront Park along the Cumberland River is occupied by day with some of the top names in country music. At night the hordes move to Nissan Stadium to hear a different show every night. Four-day passes, which cost $135-355 per person, also give you access to the exhibit hall, where you can get autographs and meet up-and-coming country music artists. This is one of Nashville's biggest events of the year, and you are wise to buy your tickets and book your hotel early. Get a room downtown so you don't need a car; parking and traffic can be a nightmare during the festival. Locals tend to steer clear of downtown during CMA Fest.

Early June sees Nashville's gay, lesbian, bisexual, and transgender community show its colors at the **Nashville Pride Festival** (www.nashvillepride.org), a three-day event at Riverfront Park.

July

Independence Day (www.visitmusiccity.com) is celebrated in a big way with fireworks

Fans Meet the Stars at CMA Fest

Like country music itself, the annual event once known as Fan Fair has evolved from a down-home meet-and-greet to a large-scale musical theater.

The **CMA Music Festival,** called CMA Fest for short and hosted by the Country Music Association, began in 1972 as a convention for music fans. Each year, the event grew as more and more people wanted to meet their country idols in person. Fans bought tickets months in advance, camped out at the state fairgrounds, and yearned to see, touch, and speak with the stars. It delivered on the name it had back then: Fan Fair. Stars endured marathon autograph sessions—Garth Brooks famously spent 23 hours signing autographs without a bathroom break—and they performed to crowds of their most dedicated fans.

But country music's remarkable boom of the 1990s was the end of that kind of Fan Fair—the music simply outgrew the event. Country music was no longer the stepchild of the recording industry; it was corporate, and it was big business. Fans, politicians, and industry representatives tangled over the future of Fan Fair. One plan to move Fan Fair to the Nashville Superspeedway in Lebanon was nixed because it would take the event out of Nashville.

In the end, CMA Fest replaced Fan Fair in 2000. With venues at Riverfront Park and Nissan Stadium, it still has plenty of music. Stars perform day and night. The autograph sessions continue in the Nashville Convention Center, but the artists you'll find here are the unknowns and up-and-comings. You need an invitation to meet and greet the big stars.

The rebirth of Fan Fair as the CMA Fest still attracts criticism, especially from those who remember the glory days of the old Fan Fair. But today's fans delight in the modern event, and even some of the critics are coming around, as it continues to bring tourists to Music City and fans to the genre.

and a riverfront concert that's broadcast live on television. The event is free and attracts upwards of 100,000 people every year.

The **Music City Brewer's Festival** (www.musiccitybrewersfest.com) is a one-day event at the Music City Walk of Fame downtown. Come to taste local brews, learn about making your own beer, and enjoy good food and live music. Tickets are required, and the event usually sells out.

The temperature is almost always hot at the **Music City Hot Chicken Festival,** but so is the chicken. This east side event (www.mchcf.blogspot.com) is a feast of Nashville's signature spicy pan-fried dish.

August

The **East Nashville Tomato Art Festival** (www.tomatoartfest.com) is a tongue-in-cheek celebration of tomatoes and the hip, artsy vibe of East Nashville. Events include a parade of tomatoes, the "Most Beautiful Tomato Pageant," biggest and smallest tomato contests, tomato toss, and Bloody Mary taste-off. The festival usually takes place on the second Saturday of August.

September

The **Belle Meade Plantation** (www.bellemeadeplantation.org) hosts its biggest fundraising event of the year, **Fall Fest,** every September. The two-day festival features antiques, arts and crafts, live music, and children's activities.

Nashville's annual **Greek Festival** (615/333-1047) is hosted by the Holy Trinity Greek Orthodox Church. Nashville residents flock here for homemade Greek food and entertainment, which includes dancing and tours of the historic cathedral.

The **John Merritt Classic** (www.merrittclassic.com), held over Labor Day, starts with fashion shows and concerts, and culminates with a football contest between the Tennessee State University Tigers and another historically black collegiate football team. The annual showdown is named for legendary former TSU football coach John Ayers Merritt.

The **Cumberland River Compact Dragon Boat Festival** (www.nashvilledragonboat.com) is a one-day race that takes place at Riverfront Park. More than 40 boats with big dragon heads and 20 costumed paddlers each race each other on the water. There are river-themed activities for spectators.

A multi-venue conference/music showcase, the **Americana Music Festival** (americanamusic.org) has become one of the city's most popular events. Professionals (musicians, songwriters, producers, and more) come for the connections and the workshops during the day. Locals join them at night for concerts—more than 165 at nine different venues—that show off the genre. There's an awards show and an end of week big budget concert at Ascend Amphitheatre.

October

The **Southern Festival of Books** is held during the second full weekend of October on Legislative Plaza in downtown Nashville. Featuring book readings, autograph sessions, and discussions, the festival is a must for book lovers. It has activities for children, too. The festival is organized by Humanities Tennessee (www.humanitiestennessee.org).

Oktoberfest (www.nashvilleoktoberfest.com) is a Nashville tradition. Held in historic Germantown north of the Bicentennial Mall, this weekend festival is enhanced by its setting in what was once Nashville's German enclave. The events include a walk-run, church services, and a street fair with German music, food, and other entertainment. Oktoberfest usually takes place in mid-October.

The Metro Parks department took over the **Celebrate Nashville Cultural Festival** (www.celebrationofcultures.org) from the Scarritt-Bennett Center. But this international festival in Centennial Park still features food and music from around the world.

November

Beginning in November and continuing until New Year's Eve, several Nashville institutions put up special holiday decorations. Belmont University, Travellers Rest Plantation, and Belle Meade all celebrate the holiday season with special decorative flair.

December

The **Music City Bowl** (www.musiccitybowl.com) pits a Southeastern Conference team against a Big Ten rival. This nationally televised football game is held at Nissan Stadium and typically includes a night-before free concert downtown.

New Year's Eve in downtown Nashville includes—what else?—a music note drop along the river. This is a huge celebration with big crowds and lots of free outdoor fun. It has been part of the national program *Dick Clark's New Year's Rockin' Eve*. Bands like Kings of Leon play free concerts while the Music City Bowl game attracts football fans.

Shopping

You'll find many good reasons to shop in Nashville. Who can pass up Western wear in Music City? Fine boutiques cater to the well-heeled in tony West End. Malls in the suburbs offer upscale department stores or outlet bargains. And downtown you'll find unique art and gifts.

Critics have bemoaned that historic buildings have been demolished for new construction, and this is true. But upscale clothing stores, used books, and trendy housewares are just a few of the things you'll find in this neighborhood that's best explored on foot. East Nashville is a mecca for those who crave handmade goods.

It may sound cliché, but don't pass up the opportunity to buy Western wear in Music City. Seriously, don't go home without a pair of boots.

MUSIC

The Texas Troubadour, Ernest Tubb, founded his famous record store on Broadway in 1947. The **Ernest Tubb Record Shop** (417 Broadway, 615/255-7503, www.etrecordshop.com, 10am-8pm Mon.-Thurs., 10am-11pm Fri.-Sat., noon-7pm Sun.) remains an excellent source of classic and modern country music recordings, as well as DVDs, books, clothing, and souvenirs. At the back of the shop you can see the stage where Ernest Tubb's *Midnite Jamboree* was recorded and aired after the Grand Ole Opry on Saturday nights. The *Jamboree* still airs, but it's recorded at the Texas Troubadour Theatre in Music Valley.

For new and used CDs, DVDs, and vinyl, go to **Grimey's New and Preloved Music** (1604 8th Ave. S., 615/254-4801, www.grimeys.com, 11am-8pm Mon.-Fri., 10am-8pm Sat., 1pm-6pm Sun.). Here you'll find a wide selection of not just country, but rock, folk, blues, R&B, and other genres. The staff is knowledgeable and friendly.

If you want to make your own music, head to **Gruhn Guitars** (2120 8th Ave. S., 615/256-2033, www.gruhn.com, 9:30am-6pm Mon.-Sat., closed Sun.), a guitar shop with one of the best reputations in the music world. Founded by guitar expert George Gruhn, the shop is considered by some to be the best vintage guitar shop in the world. Shiny guitars, banjos, mandolins, and fiddles look like candy hung up on the walls of the Broadway storefront, which serves both up-and-coming and established Nashville musicians.

Third Man (623 7th Ave. S., 615/891-4393, www.thirdmanrecords.com, 10am-6pm Mon.-Sat., 1pm-4pm Sun.) is a record label, recording studio, and record store all in one fairly small building. The idea behind the label is simple: All the music in the building has Jack White's stamp on it in some way. It's not a bad thing. Blue Series records are recorded by bands traveling through town, recording one or two songs, and are available on 7-inch vinyl. Green Series are nonmusical recordings, such as spoken word, poetry, or instructional discussions.

WESTERN WEAR

No city is better endowed with places to buy Western-style wear than Nashville. The best selection is in shops along Broadway in downtown Nashville, where you'll find hats, boots, shirts, belts, jeans, and everything else you'll need to look the part. Opry Mills, the mall next to the Grand Ole Opry, also has a good selection of Western wear.

Boot Country (304 Broadway, 615/259-1691, 10am-10:30pm Mon.-Thurs., 10am-11pm Fri., 11am-7:30pm Sun.) specializes in all styles and sizes of cowboy boots and often has a buy two pair, get the third free deal. The name says it all at **Manuel Exclusive Clothier** (1922 Broadway, 615/321-5444, 10am-6pm Mon.-Fri., closed Sat-Sun.), a clothing shop where the cowboy shirts start at $750 and jackets at more than $2,000. This is where to go when you want a custom outfit for your big stage debut.

A boot is not just a boot—at least not in Nashville, where boots are a status symbol as much as footwear. And in a town that loves boots, people really love **Lucchese Boot Co.** (pronounced "LU-kay-see.") (12th Ave. S., 615/242-1161, www.lucchese.com, 10am-7pm Mon.-Sat., noon-6pm Sun.). This brand has been around since 1883, but only since 2012 has it had its own retail shop in the Gulch. The boots (and belts and clothes) are made in the United States, and custom orders are taken.

CLOTHING

Jamie (4317 Harding Pk., 615/292-4188, 10am-5:30pm Mon.-Fri., 10am-5pm Sat., closed Sun.) has long been the height of couture for Nashville women who want something without rhinestones. Go there for attentive service and killer shoes, but be prepared to pay for it.

Celebrities like Gwyneth Paltrow love 12 South's **Imogene + Willie** (2601 12th Ave. S., 615/292-5005, www.imogeneandwillie.com, 10am-6pm Mon.-Fri., 11am-6pm Sat., 1pm-5pm Sun.). The shop carries clothes for men and women, but its specialty is custom-fit blue jeans at a price tag of $200 and up.

Downtown at 305 Church Street, **Fire Finch** (615/942-5271, 10am-6pm Mon.-Sat., noon-5pm Sun.) is known for trendy jewelry and accessories. Its downtown location has a few home decor items as well.

One of a number of sleek Germantown boutiques, **ABEDNEGO** (1210 4th Ave. N., 615/712-6028, 11am-7pm Tues.-Sat., noon-5pm Sun., closed Mon.) carries local- and American-made clothes and accessories. Owned by a local musician, ABEDNEGO stocks goods for men and women in a minimalist loft-like environment. Phillip Nappi, owner of **Peter Nappi** (1308 Adams St., 615/248-3310, www.peternappi.com/studio, 11am-6pm Mon.-Sat., closed Sun.) has made boot- and shoe-making an art. The shop's studio is in Italy, where artisans create footwear in the old-world style in limited runs, with the highest quality vegetable-tanned leathers. But the retail location in Germantown is totally Music City.

Bargain-hunting fashionistas cannot skip **UAL** (2918 West End Ave., 615/340-9999, www.shopual.com, 9am-8pm Mon.-Fri., 10am-8pm Sat.-Sun.). Designer samples of clothes, handbags, shoes, and jewelry are shoved onto crowded racks in this shop near the Vanderbilt campus. UAL stocks both men's and women's clothing, but the women's selection is significantly larger.

ART

While not exactly a gallery, **Hatch Show Print** (224 5th Ave. S, 615/256-2805, www.countrymusichalloffame.org/our-work, 9:30am-6pm Mon.-Wed., 9:30am-8pm Thurs.-Sat., 9:30am-6pm Sun.) is one of Nashville's best-known places to buy and see art. Hatch has been making colorful posters for more than a century, and its iconic letterpress style is now one of the trendiest looks in modern design. It continues to design and print handouts, posters, and T-shirts for local and national customers. Visitors to the shop can gaze at the cavernous warehouse operation and buy small or large samples of its work, including reproductions of classic country music concert posters. This is a great place to find a special souvenir of your trip to Nashville or just see another part of Music City's history. Hatch posters are up all over town, including in the airport.

Transplanted New Yorkers Theo Antoniadis and Veta Cicolello opened **Ovvio Arte** (425 S. Chestnut St., 615/838-5699, www.ovvioarte.com, hours vary by performance) in 2008. This art gallery and performance space

Historic Hatch Show Print creates Nashville's signature posters.

is a venue for the unexpected. It offers regular theater, dramatic readings, and art shows.

One of downtown's most accessible and eclectic galleries, **The Arts Company** (215 5th Ave. of the Arts, 615/254-2040, www.theartscompany.com, 11am-5pm Tues.-Sat., closed Sun.-Mon.) offers outsider art, the works of local artists, and other contemporary works ranging from the avant-garde to the everyday.

Perhaps the most cosmopolitan of all Nashville's galleries, **The Rymer Gallery** (233 5th Ave. of the Arts, 615/752-6030, www.therymergallery.com, 11am-5pm Tues.-Sat., closed Sun.-Mon.) installs thought-provoking exhibits with works from artists of national renown. The Rymer is also home to Nashville's Herb Williams (www.herbwilliamsart.com), a gifted artist who creates sculpture from crayons. Williams's work has been on display in the White House and other prestigious addresses.

The upper level of **The Arcade,** between 4th and 5th Avenues, houses several artist studios that open as galleries during downtown's monthly Art Crawl, which takes place 6pm-9pm the first Saturday of each month.

The **Art + Invention Gallery** (1106 Woodland St., 615/226-2070, www.artandinvention.com, 11am-6pm Mon.-Thurs., 10am-7pm Fri.-Sat., noon-5pm Sun.) is an East Nashville institution. Proprietors Meg and Bret MacFayden put on 5-6 shows each year, including their signature Tomato Art Show, part of the annual Tomato Art Festival, and are well loved for their support of other Music City creative types.

HOME DECOR

Find fine crystal, tableware, jewelry, and other upscale housewares at **AshBlue** (2170 Bandywood Dr., 615/383-4882, www.ashblue.com, 10am-6pm Mon.-Sat., noon-5pm Sun.). This sophisticated shop is perfect for bridal registries, housewarming gifts, or that special touch for your home or office.

Owned by Grammy-award-wining songwriter Liz Rose and her daughter, **Castilleja** (1200 Villa Place, Suite 403, 615/730-5367, castillejanashville.com, 10am-6pm Mon.-Sat., noon-4pm Sun.) brings a little taste of Texas to Tennessee. Expect to find home décor with a Lone Star twist, including blankets, leather goods, pillows, and lots of items made with turquoise and silver. The shop is nestled in the Edgehill Village complex.

New York transplants Ivy and Josh (she was a Rockette and he was a member of Blue Man Group) brought their interior design eyes to the south. The duo opened a Germantown atelier called **Wilder** (1212 4th Ave. N, 615/679-0008, www.wilderlife.com, noon-5pm daily) to show off the kinds of wares with which they can transform a home. Come browse the furnishing, textiles, lightning, mirrors, and more, all with a modern sensibility and many not found elsewhere in the area.

Nashville native Reese Witherspoon put the flagship of her **Draper James** (2608 12th Ave. S., www.draperjames.com, 10am-6pm Mon.-Sat., noon-5pm Sun.) lifestyle brand in her hometown. Find pillows, cocktail napkins, and more with a southern drawl.

BOOKS

Like many cities, Nashville has lost several of its chain bookstores, but it still has other options for the book lover. **Bookman Bookwoman Used Books** (1713 21st Ave. S., 615/383-6555, 10am-6pm Mon.-Tues., 10am-8pm Wed.-Fri., 9am-8pm Sat., 10am-5pm Sun.), in the trendy Hillsboro neighborhood, is chockablock with used books, including cheap paperbacks and rare must-haves.

A famous owner (novelist Ann Patchett) and her willingness to open a new independent bookstore in the "books-are-dead" year of 2011 allowed **Parnassus Books** (3900 Hillsboro Pk., 615/953-2243, www.parnassusbooks.net, 10am-8pm Mon.-Sat., noon-5pm Sun.) to make national headlines. Located in a strip mall across from the Mall at Green Hills, Parnassus specializes in a well-edited selection, personal service, and literary events for both kids and adults.

McKay's (636 Old Hickory Blvd., 615/353-2595, www.mckaybooks.com, 9am-9pm Mon.-Thurs., 9am-10pm Fri.-Sat., 11am-7pm Sun.) both buys and sells used books, CDs, and DVDs, which contribute to its always bustling energy. A Knoxville institution for years, the Nashville location of McKay's encourages readers to return books for store credit after they've read them.

ANTIQUES

Near the old 100 Oaks Mall in South Nashville you'll find Nashville's largest and most popular antiques mall. **Gaslamp Antique and Decorating Mall** (100 Powell Ave., 615/297-2224, www.gaslampantiques.com, 10am-6pm Mon.-Sat., noon-6pm Sun.) is squeezed behind a Staples and next to a Home Depot. It has more than 150 vendors and a great selection of all types of antiques.

For something closer to town, head to **Eighth Avenue Antiques Mall** (2015 8th Ave. S., 615/279-9922, 10am-6pm Mon.-Sat., noon-5pm Sun.) or **Wonders on Woodland** (1110 Woodland St., 615/226-5300) in East Nashville, which has a particularly strong collection of midcentury-modern finds.

SHOPPING MALLS

The finest shopping mall in Nashville is the **Mall at Green Hills** (10am-9pm Mon.-Sat., noon-6pm Sun.), an indoor mall located about 15 minutes' drive south from downtown Nashville along Hillsboro Road. Stores include Macy's, Brooks Brothers, Tiffany & Co., and Nordstrom. The mall has spawned additional shopping opportunities nearby, including the upscale Hill Center (www.hillcentergreenhills.com), so this is a good place to head if you're in need of just about anything. Call the mall concierge (615/298-5478, ext. 22) to find out if your favorite store is there. The parking lot can get packed on weekends, but the mall offers free valet service, which makes it tolerable.

Farther south of Nashville, at the Moore's Lane exit off I-65, is the large **Cool Springs Galleria** (1800 Galleria Blvd., 615/771-2128, www.coolspringsgalleria.com, 10am-9pm Mon.-Sat., noon-6pm Sun.). Four major department stores anchor the mall, which includes 100 specialty shops. The mall is surrounded by acres more of drive-up shopping centers and restaurants.

shopping mall Opry Mills

OUTLET SHOPPING

Shuttered for almost two years after the 2010 flood, the **Opry Mills** (433 Opry Mills Dr., 615/514-1000, 10am-9pm, Mon.-Sat., 11am-7pm Sun.) discount mall in Music Valley is the city's most-maligned favorite destination. Indeed, if upscale shopping is your thing, don't come here. But if good deals on name-brand merchandise appeal to you, or you are looking to kill time before a show at the Opry, Opry Mills is the mall for you. Brands include Old Navy, Disney, LEGO, Coach, Ann Taylor, and Off Fifth. There is also a 20-screen movie theater, IMAX, and Bass Pro Shop with all sorts of outdoor equipment.

FLEA MARKETS

Nashville's largest flea market takes place on the fourth weekend of every month at the Tennessee State Fairgrounds. The **Tennessee State Fairgrounds Flea Market** (615/862-5016, www.tennesseestatefair.org) is a bargain lover's dream, with thousands of sellers peddling clothes, crafts, and all sorts of vintage and used housewares, often at lower prices than you'd find in bigger cities. The fairgrounds are located on 4th Avenue, south of downtown. Admission is free, but parking is $5.

The **Nashville Farmers Market** (nashvillefarmersmarket.org) next to the Bicentennial Mall downtown, has a small weekend flea market, with crafts and vintage items, plus tube socks and T-shirts.

Sports and Recreation

Nashville has good parks, numerous sports teams, and nice weather to enjoy both.

PARKS

Centennial Park

Nashville's best city park, **Centennial Park** is best known as home of the Parthenon. It is also a pleasant place to relax. A small lake provides a habitat for ducks and other water creatures; paved trails are popular for walking during nice weather. The park hosts numerous events during the year, including Shakespeare in the Park each August and September.

Greenways

Nashville has a remarkable network of connected green spaces, thanks to its **Greenways** (www.nashville.gov/greenways). The master plan is for this system to eventually connect the entire city. Today there are more than 46 miles of paved pathways and 20 miles of primitive trails used by bicyclists, runners, dog walkers, and more. The Greenways run through the city's prettiest natural areas and, in places, along the Cumberland River. Some Greenways include nature centers and other educational facilities. For the most part, the routes are clean and safe. Good maps are available for download from Greenways for Nashville (www.greenwaysfornashville.org).

Radnor Lake State Natural Area

Just seven miles southwest of downtown Nashville, **Radnor Lake State Natural Area** (Otter Creek Rd., 615/373-3467) provides an escape for visitors and residents of the city. Eighty-five-acre Radnor Lake was created in 1914 by the Louisville and Nashville Railroad Company, which impounded Otter Creek to do so. The lake was to provide water for the railroad's steam engines. By the 1940s, the railroad's use of the lake ended, and 20 years later the area was threatened by development. Local residents, including the Tennessee Ornithological Society, successfully rallied against development, and Radnor Lake State Natural Area was established in 1973.

There are six miles of hiking trails around the lake, and Otter Creek Road, which is closed to vehicular traffic, is open to bicycles and walkers. A nature museum at the visitors center describes some of the 240 species of birds and hundreds of species of plants and animals that live at Radnor. The visitors center is open 9am-4pm Sunday-Thursday and 8am-4pm Friday and Saturday.

Radnor is well used and well loved by Nashvillians, and for good reason. Very few American cities have such a large and pristine natural area so close to the urban center.

Edwin and Percy Warner Parks

The largest city parks in Tennessee, **Edwin and Percy Warner Parks** (7311 Hwy. 100, 615/352-6299, www.nashville.gov/parks/locations/warner, open year-round) are a 2,600-acre oasis of forest, fields, and quiet pathways located just nine miles southwest from downtown Nashville. Nashvillians come here to walk, jog, ride bikes and horses, and much more. The parks have scenic drives, picnic facilities, playgrounds, cross-country running trails, an equestrian center, bridle trails, a model-airplane field, and athletic fields. Percy Warner Park is also home to the Harpeth Hills Golf Course, and Edwin Warner Park has a nature center that provides year-round environmental education. The nature center also hands out maps and other information about the park.

Warner Parks hosts the annual Iroquois Steeplechase Horse Race in May. A 10-mile bridle path is open to horseback riding year-round. Visit the park's Equestrian Center (2500 Old Hickory Blvd.) for more information.

J. Percy Priest Lake

J. Percy Priest Lake was created in the mid-1960s when the U.S. Army Corps of Engineers (USACE) dammed Stones River east of Nashville. The lake is a favorite destination for fishing, boating, swimming, paddling, and picnicking.

J. Percy Priest Lake sprawls over 14,200 acres. Access is provided through more than a dozen different parks and access areas on all sides of the lake. Many of these areas bear the names of communities that were inundated when the lake was created.

The lake's main visitors center, operated by the USACE, is located at the site of the dam that created the lake. The visitors center is located on Bell Road at exit 219 off, I-40 heading east from downtown Nashville. There you will find a lake overlook and one of four marinas on the lake.

In addition to access areas managed by the USACE, Nashville operates **Hamilton Creek Park** (www.hamcreek.com) on the western shore of the lake. The State of Tennessee operates **Long Hunter State Park** on the eastern shore.

There are several hiking trails around the lake. The **Three Hickories Nature Trail** is an easy 1.6-mile trail found in the Cook Recreational Area. **Anderson Road Fitness Trail** is a paved one-mile trail that travels through woodlands and along the lake.

For a long hike, or for horseback riding, go to the **Twin Forks Horse Trail,** an 18-mile trail located in the East Fork Recreation Area on the southwestern shore of the lake. Within Long Hunter State Park there are three hiking trails, including a nature loop trail and the mile-long Deer Trail, leaving from the visitors center.

Boating, fishing, and water sports are among the most popular activities on J. Percy Priest Lake. Launch ramps are found in Long Hunter State Park and at several marinas around the lake. **Elm Hill Marina** (3361 Bell Rd., 615/889-5363, www.elmhillmarina.com) is the marina closest to downtown Nashville.

The USACE operates three day-use **swim areas** that have sand beaches, bathrooms, and other amenities for a day in the water. These swim areas are located at Anderson Road, Cook Campground, and Seven Points Campground. There is a $4-per-vehicle fee at Anderson and Cook. There is swimming at Long Hunter State Park's Bryant Grove as well.

GOLF

Nashville operates seven public golf courses in the city. Many of these are in parks and offer excellent golf in beautiful settings. You can find details about all city courses at www.nashville.gov/parks/golf. Most courses are open year-round; call ahead for operating hours and to reserve a tee time. Nine-hole greens fees are $18 on weekdays and $17 on weekends, with additional fees for carts and senior and member discounts.

Harpeth Hills Golf Course (2424 Old Hickory Blvd., 615/862-8493, Weekday green fee $13 for 9 holes and $26 for 18 holes, weekend green fee is $14 for 9 holes, $28 for 18 holes.) is a par 72 course built in 1965 and renovated in 1991. It is located in Percy Warner Park and is considered one of Tennessee's best public golf courses.

Percy Warner Park is also home of Percy Warner Golf Course, a nine-hole course good for beginner golfers, available on a walk-in basis only. (Green fee $9.)

Probably the most-used public golf course in Nashville, **McCabe** Golf Course (615/862-8491) is located in West Nashville near Sylvan Park. McCabe consists of a par 70 18-hole course and 9-hole course. Upgrades have introduced new green complexes and tee complexes. Weekday green fee $12 for 9 holes and $24 for 18 holes, weekend green fee is $13 for 9 holes, $26 for 18 holes.

The oldest city golf course in Nashville is **Shelby** Golf Course (615/862-8474), located in Shelby Park in East Nashville. Shelby is a short course with small mounded greens that places a premium on accuracy.

Situated on the Cumberland River in North Nashville, **Ted Rhodes** Golf Course (615/862-8463) is scenic and pleasant to walk. Built in 1953 as a nine-hole course, Ted Rhodes was expanded to 18 holes in 1992. It is par 72.

Located near Music Valley in Donelson, **Two Rivers** Golf Course (615/889-2675) offers a challenging course for golfers of all skill levels. A bonus is the view of the Nashville skyline at the eighth hole.

All of the above city-operated courses have the following hours: May 1-Labor Day, 7am-dark daily. Tues. after Labor Day-Sept. 30, 7:30am-dark Mon.-Fri., 7am-dark. Sat.-Sun., Oct. 1-First Sunday in Dec. 7:30am-dark Mon.-Fri., 7am-dark Sat.-Sun., First Monday in Dec.-Sat. of Daylight Savings Time weekend in March, 8am-dark Mon.-Fri., 7am-dark Sat.-Sun. First Sun. of Daylight Savings Time-April 1, 7:30am-dark daily, April 1-30, 7am-dark daily. During the winter, Harpeth Hills, Ted Rhodes, and Shelby are closed Mondays from first week in December to first week in March. Percy Warner, McCabe and Two Rivers are closed Tuesdays from the first week in December to the first week in March.

There are many privately owned golf courses in Nashville, some of which are open to the public. Gaylord Springs (18 Springhouse Ln., 615/458-1730), located next to the Gaylord Opryland Resort in Music Valley, is a par 72 18-hole course built in 1990. Tee times are typically between 7am-5pm. Greens fees are $50–90. Nashboro Golf Club (1101 Nashboro Blvd., 615/367-2311) offers a par 72 18-hole course with fees $27–41. Tee times are typically 7am-7pm.

BIKING

Nashville is no Portland; you won't see a bicycle rack at every storefront. But the city has a growing bike culture, and it is easy to pedal your way across the city to see its highlights.

The first step is to bring your own bike, rent one, or borrow one. City residents (with a local ID) can check out a bike from **Nashville GreenBikes** (nashvillegreenbikes.org). Once you have your two wheels it is easy to connect to more than 90 miles of greenways and 133 miles of on-road bike lanes and shared-use bike routes. B-Cycle (nashville.bcycle.com) offers 24-hour usage for just $5 or membership for more frequent peddlers.

The first destination for bikers around Nashville is the **Natchez Trace Parkway** (www.nps.gov/natr), a historic two-lane 444-mile blacktop scenic drive that originates in Nashville and journeys south through Tennessee and Mississippi countryside, eventually terminating in Natchez, Mississippi. The parkway is closed to commercial traffic, and the speed limit is strictly enforced, making it popular for biking.

Biking the Trace can be an afternoon outing or a weeklong adventure. The National Park Service maintains three campgrounds along the Trace, plus five bicyclist-only campsites with more modest amenities. The northernmost bike campsite is located at the intersection of the Trace and Highway 50, about 36 miles south of Nashville.

When biking on the Trace, ride in a single-file line and always wear reflective clothing and a helmet. Pack food and water, and carry a cell phone, ID, and emergency information.

Short paved trails good for biking can be found at Radnor Lake State Natural Area, Warner Parks, and in any of Nashville's greenways, including those at Shelby Bottoms along the Cumberland River.

Nashville's only dedicated mountain bike trail is at **Hamilton Creek Park** (www.hamcreek.com) on J. Percy Priest Lake, on the east side of the Nashville airport. This 10-mile bike trail consists of an eastern trail better for beginning bikers and a western trail for advanced bikers. The two trails meet at a tunnel that crosses Bell Road.

The **Harpeth Bike Club** (www.harpethbikeclub.com) is Nashville's largest bike club. It organizes weekend and weekday group rides April-October, plus races and social events where you can meet other bike enthusiasts.

If you're looking for the inside scoop on biking around Nashville and recommended routes in the surrounding countryside, check out **NashvilleCyclist.com** (www.nashvillecyclist.com), an online community of bikers.

Bike Shops

There are several good bike shops in Nashville. If you need bike gear, repairs, or advice, check out **Cumberland Transport** (2807 West End Ave., 615/321-4069), **Nashville Bicycle Company** (2817 West End Ave., 615/321-5510), or **Trace Bikes** (8400 Hwy. 100, 615/646-2485), located next to the Loveless Café near the Natchez Trace Parkway. East Nashville's **East Side Cycles** (103 S. 11th St., 615/469-1079) has bike tools around back if you need DIY repair during off hours.

TENNIS

The **Centennial Sportsplex** (222 25th Ave. N., 615/862-8480, www.sportsplextennis.com) has 15 lighted outdoor tennis courts and 4 indoor courts, as well as a ball machine, pro shop, and concession stand. The center is open seven days a week; specific hours vary by season. Indoor court rental fees are $18 per hour; courts may be booked up to three days in advance. Outdoor courts are available for $3 per hour per person, and they can be reserved up to six days in advance.

The Sportsplex organizes numerous tennis tournaments, leagues, and classes during the year. Call or stop by for details.

SWIMMING

The city's biggest pool is found at the **Centennial Sportsplex Aquatic Center** (222 25th Ave. N., 615/862-8480, www.centennialsportsplex.com, 5:30am-7:50pm Mon.-Thurs., 5:30am-5:50pm Fri., 9am-4:50pm Sat., adults $6, children 5-12, military, disabled, seniors, and students $5, children 4 and under free). The center, located near Centennial Park in midtown, has both a large lap pool and a small play pool. Various swim classes are offered; call for a schedule.

Take the kids to **Wave Country** (2320 Two Rivers Pkwy., 615/885-1052, 10am-6pm daily Memorial Day-Labor Day, adults $12, children 2-11 $10, children under 2 free, prices tend to increase annually). This water park has exciting slides, a wave pool, and sand volleyball courts. Wave Country is managed by the city parks commission.

A great destination for a hot summer day is **Nashville Shores** (4001 Bell Rd., Hermitage, 615/889-7050, www.nashvilleshores.com, 10am-6pm Mon-Sat., 11am-6pm Sun. Memorial Day-Labor Day, 48 inches and taller $22, under 48 inches $17, children two and under free). Here you'll find miles of sandy beaches along the shore of J. Percy Priest Lake, pools, waterslides, and water sports. Admission includes the opportunity to take a 45-minute lake cruise.

PADDLING

Nashville's easy access to multiple rivers and lakes makes it a natural gateway for kayaking, canoeing, and stand-up paddleboarding. **Nashville Paddle Co.** (2901 Bell Rd., 615/682-1787, www.nashvillepaddle.com) offers lessons and rentals for this fast-growing sport, which is like a hybrid of kayaking and surfing, and is well suited for Middle Tennessee's flat water. **Tip-a-Canoe** (800/550-5810, www.tip-a-canoe.com) is the summer go-to spot for canoe and kayak rental on the Harpeth River.

GYMS

The City of Nashville operates a fitness center in the **Centennial Sportsplex** (222 25th Ave. N., 615/862-8480, www.centennialsportsplex.com, 5:30am-8pm Mon.-Thurs., 5:30am-6pm Fri., 9am-5pm Sat., adults $6, children 5-12, military, disabled, seniors, and students $5, children 4 and under free). The fitness center has modern cardiovascular and weight-lifting machines. Fitness classes are also offered.

The Sportsplex also has two pools, tennis courts, and an ice rink. The ice rink offers public skate periods every week, with more during the winter months and holiday season.

SPECTATOR SPORTS

Football

You simply cannot miss 68,000-seat **Nissan Stadium,** home of the NFL **Tennessee Titans** (1 Titans Way, 615/565-4000, www.titans-online.com). The stadium, which was finished in 1999 and renovated after the 2010 flood, towers on the east bank of the Cumberland River, directly opposite downtown.

The Titans moved to this stadium (then called LP Field) in 1999, and initially sold out almost every home game. But a spotty win-loss record in recent years has made tickets easier to come by. If you want to see a game on short notice, your best bet is the online NFL ticket exchange, where season ticket holders can sell their seats to games they don't want to attend.

Finally, the most distinctive brand of football played in Nashville is Australian rules. The **Nashville Kangaroos** (www.nashvillekangaroos.org) were founded in 1997 and were one of the first Australian football

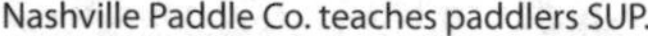

Nashville Paddle Co. teaches paddlers SUP.

teams in the United States. The "Roos" play at Elmington Park (3500 West End Ave.) and sometimes practice with Vanderbilt's own Aussie rules squad. One of the missions of the club is to promote cultural understanding and exchange, so the social calendar can be just as grueling as the sports one. The Roos also sponsor a women's netball team.

Baseball

What an appropriate name for a minor-league baseball team. **The Nashville Sounds** (401 Jackson St., 615/690-4487, www.nashvillesounds.com) are an affiliate of the Oakland Athletics, and they play about 30 home games a year June-October. In 2015 the team moved from the aging Greer Stadium, their home in south Nashville, to the new **First Tennessee Park** between downtown and Germantown. The new stadium has a guitar-shaped scoreboard as a hat-tip to the old one.

Ticket prices range from $9-$15. There's an alcohol-free section of the stadium, which often appeals to families with small kids. The Band Box serves better-than-stadium-food fare.

Ice Hockey

Nashville celebrated the 10th anniversary of its National Hockey League franchise, the **Predators** (501 Broadway, http://predators.nhl.com), in 2008. It was a sweet victory for fans who fought to keep the team in the city in the face of lackluster support from the community with a "Save the Predators" campaign. The Predators play in the 20,000-seat Bridgestone Arena, located on Broadway in the heart of downtown. Home games include live country music performances and other activities for the fans. The regular season begins in October and ends in early April. Single-game tickets start at $20 and can cost as much as $195, although there are often special discounts.

College Sports

In addition to Nashville's smorgasbord of professional and semiprofessional sports teams, the city's colleges provide lots of good spectator sports. Vanderbilt plays football, men's and women's basketball, and baseball in the Southeastern Conference. Tennessee State University and Belmont University play Division 1-A basketball, and Lipscomb University is a member of the Atlantic Sun Division. Vanderbilt football games are an unusual sporting event, as students traditionally dress in coat and tie or dresses and high heels.

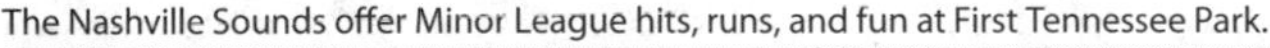
The Nashville Sounds offer Minor League hits, runs, and fun at First Tennessee Park.

Accommodations

Nashville has more than 33,000 hotel rooms. Accommodations range from historic downtown hotels to standard motels, many of which have Music City touches, from recorded wake-up calls from country stars to guitar-shaped swimming pools. One study cited in the Nashville Tennessean newspaper in September 2015 found that there were a whopping 62 Music City hotel projects in the works.

Downtown has the most appealing and convenient hotels. More budget-friendly options are found in midtown and Music Valley.

DOWNTOWN

Hotels in this neighborhood are as close as you can get to attractions including the Country Music Hall of Fame and Broadway honky-tonks.

$150-200

Located across Broadway from the Frist Center for the Visual Arts, **Holiday Inn Express Nashville-Downtown** (902 Broadway, 615/244-0150, $145-170) offers a comfortable compromise between value and location. There is an on-site fitness room, free wireless Internet, a business center, and a guest laundry. Guest rooms have desks, coffeemakers, and two telephones. Suites ($270) have refrigerators and microwave ovens. All guests enjoy free continental breakfast. On-site parking is available for $19 a day. The Holiday Inn is located about five blocks away from lower Broadway.

Over $200

One of Nashville's most notable downtown hotels is ★ **Union Station** (1001 Broadway, 615/726-1001, www.unionstationhotelnashville.com, $234-274), a 125-room hotel located in what was once the city's main train station. Distinctions include magnificent iron work and molding, and an impressive marble-floored great hall that greets guests, contributing to what makes this one of the National Trust's Historic Hotels of America. High ceilings and lofty interior balconies make this one of Nashville's great old buildings, and hotel guests get to make it their home away from home. Union Station is a fine hotel, with amenities like free turndown service, a fitness center, wireless Internet, plasma televisions, complimentary morning newspapers, and room service. Rooms have cathedral ceilings, stylish furnishings, and a subtle art deco touch. The bathrooms have soaking tubs, walk-in showers, and expansive marble vanities. You can choose from a standard room with one double bed or a premium room with a king-size bed or two double beds. Four suites are also available.

The all-suite **Hilton Nashville Downtown** (121 4th Ave. S., 615/620-1000, www.nashvillehilton.com, $279-349) is next door to the Country Music Hall of Fame, Broadway's honky-tonks, and the home of the Nashville Symphony. All of the hotel's 330 suites have two distinct rooms—a living room with sofa, cable television, microwave oven, refrigerator, and coffeemaker, and a bedroom with one or two beds. The rooms are appointed with modern, stylish furniture and amenities. An indoor pool, workout room, valet parking, and two restaurants round out the hotel's amenities.

The last of a dying breed of hotels, the ★ **Hermitage Hotel** (231 6th Ave., 615/244-3121, www.thehermitagehotel.com, $300-800) has been the first choice for travelers to downtown Nashville for more than 100 years. The 123-room hotel was commissioned by prominent Nashville citizens and opened for business in 1910, quickly becoming the favorite gathering place for the city's elite. Prominent figures including Al Capone, Gene Autry, and seven U.S. presidents have stayed at the Hermitage. In modern times, its roll call includes some of country music's biggest names.

You don't have to be famous to stay at the Hermitage, but having plenty of cash will help your cause. Rooms start at $300 a night, but check for last-minute specials on its website, when rates will dip to $200. You can chose to have $2 from your room rate contributed to the Land Trust for Tennessee. Guests enjoy top-of-the-line amenities, including 24-hour room service, pet walking, valet parking, and laundry services. Rooms are furnished in an opulent style befitting a luxury urban hotel and have CD/DVD players, refreshment centers, marble baths, and high-speed wireless Internet access. Many rooms have lovely views of the capitol and city.

Courtyard by Marriot (179 4th Ave. N., 615/256-0900, $200-250) is a 181-room renovated hotel set in a century-old downtown high-rise. It is located right next to Printer's Alley and is set midway between the downtown business district and Broadway's entertainment attractions. Guest rooms are tastefully decorated, with web TV, wired Internet access, coffeemakers, ironing boards, cable TV, voice mail, and super-comfortable beds. There are two restaurants on-site, and guests can take advantage of valet parking for $22 a day.

Located just steps from the Tennessee State Capitol and near dozens of downtown office buildings, the **Doubletree Hotel Nashville** (315 4th Ave. N., 615/244-8200, $190-250) is a popular choice for business travelers. Rooms are spacious and bright, and even basic rooms have a comfortable desk and chair, coffeemaker, free Internet access, voice mail, and ironing boards. The hotel boasts a beautiful indoor swimming pool, business center, above-average fitness center, and on-site restaurant and coffee shop. Parking at the Doubletree is valet only and costs $24 per day.

The **Sheraton Downtown Nashville** (623 Union St., 615/259-2000, $200-270) is a city landmark. The 472-room hotel stands tall above neighboring buildings, providing most guest rooms with views of the city below. Located in the middle of Nashville's bustling downtown business district, it is another good option for business travelers. The hotel is 100 percent smoke-free and has a fitness room, business center, indoor pool, and laundry and concierge services. Internet access and on-site parking are available for an additional fee.

The Omni Nashville Hotel (between 5th and 8th Aves. at Demonbreun St., 615/782-5300, www.omnihotels.com, $219-308) is

Even if you don't sleep here, stop to see the lobby at the Hermitage Hotel.

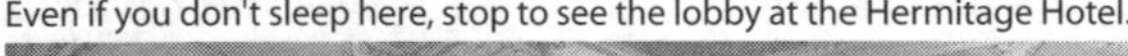

adjacent to the 1.2 million-square-foot Music City Convention Center. It has more than 80,000 square feet of meeting and event space, more than 800 guest rooms, plus easy access to the convention center, the Hall of Fame, restaurants, and other attractions south of Broadway. Don't miss the cool displays of musicians' costumes in the hallway that connects Hatch Show Print to the hotel.

MIDTOWN

Midtown hotels are near Music Row, Vanderbilt and Belmont Universities, and the entertainment, dining, and shopping attractions of Hillsboro Village.

Under $100

The **Music City Hostel** (1809 Patterson St., 615/692-1277, www.musiccityhostel.com, $25-79) is located among doctors' offices and commercial buildings in between downtown Nashville and Elliston Place. The low-slung '70s-style building looks like nothing much on the outside, but inside it is cheerful, welcoming, and a comfortable home base for budget travelers. Music City Hostel offers the usual dorm-style bunk-bed accommodations, as well as a handful of private apartments, which rent for $79 a night. You can also have a private bedroom with private bath plus shared kitchen and common room for $49 a night. Common areas include a large kitchen, dining room, reading room, cable TV room, computer with Internet access, and a coin laundry. The entire facility is smoke-free. Parking is free, and the hostel is within walking distance of restaurants, a bus stop, car rental agency, post office, and hospitals. It is a hike to get downtown on foot from here.

$100-150

Best Western Music Row (1407 Division St., 615/242-1631, $110-150) is a no-nonsense motel with an outdoor pool, free continental breakfast, Internet access, and indoor corridors. Rooms have cable TV, AM/FM alarm clocks, and coffeemakers. Pets are allowed for $10 a day, and parking is free. The 75-room hotel is located a few steps away from the Music Row traffic circle and nearby restaurants.

Located near Elliston Place and Vanderbilt University, **Guesthouse Inn and Suites** (1909 Hayes St., 615/329-1000, $109) offers a free shuttle to nearby hospitals, including Baptist Hospital, Vanderbilt Medical Center, and the Veterans Administration Hospital. All rooms have microwave ovens, refrigerators, and coffeemakers, and guests enjoy free breakfast, including made-to-order waffles. Suites ($140) include a sleeper couch. Rooms are typical motel style, with two double beds or a single king-size bed. The property is convenient to Hillsboro Village, Music Row, and Centennial Park.

$150-200

A bed-and-breakfast choice in this part of the city is **1501 Linden Manor B&B** (1501 Linden Ave., 615/298-2701, www.nashville-bed-breakfast.com, $175-275). This cheerful yellow-brick home on a corner lot has three guest rooms, each with stylish furniture and hardwood floors; one room has a private whirlpool, and another has a fireplace.

The **12 South Inn** (918 Knox Ave., 615/260-8015, www.nashvillehouse.biz, $170-185) has suites, giving you lots of extra room, with private porches, private entrances, and, in the case of the King Suite, a separate living room. Unlike some B&Bs that lack hotel-style amenities, the 12 South Inn has free wireless Internet, TV, refrigerators, and other perks, as well as the home-style digs that separate an inn from a traditional hotel. Discounted rates are available for extended stays.

Over $200

For luxurious accommodations near Vanderbilt, consider **Loews Vanderbilt Plaza** (2100 West End Ave., 615/320-1700, $260-310), a 340-room hotel on West End Avenue close to Centennial Park and Hillsboro Village. Loews boasts 24-hour room service; luxurious sheets, towels, and robes; natural soaps; and spacious bathrooms. Guests enjoy in-room tea kettles and top-of-the-line coffee, evening turndown service, and free high-speed Internet access. Many rooms have views of the Nashville skyline; premium rooms provide guests with access to the concierge lounge, with continental breakfast, and evening hors d'oeuvres and a cash bar. All guests can enjoy a fine fitness room, spa, art gallery, and gift shop.

You can't get closer to Vanderbilt University than the **Marriott Nashville Vanderbilt** (2555 West End Ave., 615/321-1300, $180-300). Set on the northern end of the university campus, the Marriott has 301 guest rooms, six suites, and meeting space. It is located across West End Avenue from Centennial Park, home of the Parthenon, and a few steps from Vanderbilt's football stadium. There is an indoor pool, full-service restaurant, concierge lounge, ATM, and business center.

Since its opening in 2009, the ★ **Hutton Hotel** (1808 West End Ave., 615/340-9333, www.huttonhotel.com, $194-512) has become Nashville's eco-friendly darling. This swanky hotel near the Vanderbilt campus also offers an easy commute to Music Row and downtown, but regular visitors stay here less for the great location and more for the ambience. The lobby and guest rooms are stocked with well-edited art collections, the bathrooms include sleek granite showers, and the entire hotel has an emphasis on sustainability, with biodegradable cleaning products and bamboo flooring. The pet-friendly property has all the expected amenities, such as flat-screen TVs and wireless Internet access. An added bonus is the likelihood of a celebrity sighting.

EAST NASHVILLE

While it has more appeal for locals than it does for visitors, there are a few good reasons to stay in East Nashville. For football fans, this part of the city is close to the Tennessee Titans' stadium. Others will enjoy bed-and-breakfasts in Edgefield, the intimate live music venues, and a cool, laid-back, and diverse residential neighborhood. Good dining and funky shopping abounds, and downtown is a short drive or walk across the Cumberland River.

Under $100

Located on the east bank of the Cumberland River, **Clarion Hotel at the Stadium** (211 N. 1st St., 615/254-1551, www.clarionhotel.com, $75-100) is near Nissan Stadium, where the Tennessee Titans play. The hotel's 180 rooms have clock radios, cable TV, and wireless Internet. Some have nice views of the Nashville skyline. Guests enjoy access to a fitness room, indoor pool, and laundry facilities, plus free breakfast. There is a bar and restaurant inside the hotel. While not within easy walking distance of downtown Nashville, the Clarion is just across the river from the city's premier attractions. Free parking is a plus.

$150-200

The Big Bungalow (618 Fatherland St., 615/256-8375, www.thebigbungalow.com, $150-225) a Craftsman-style early-1900s town house, offers three guest rooms, each with its own private bath and television. Guests have shared access to a computer (no wireless Internet), microwave, and refrigerator. Common areas are comfortable and stylish, with tasteful decor and hardwood floors. Hostess Ellen Warshaw prepares breakfast for her guests and sometimes hosts in-the-round concerts in her living room. She is also a licensed masseuse and sometimes offers discounted massage rates with room. This is a pet-free, nonsmoking facility; children over 10 are welcome. The bed-and-breakfast is located about seven blocks from the John Seigenthaler Pedestrian Bridge that takes you to the heart of downtown.

MUSIC VALLEY

There are a dozen or more chain hotels in Music Valley, all close to restaurants and a short drive from the Grand Ole Opry and Opry Mills mall. Nashville's most famous hotel, Gaylord Opryland Resort, is luxurious and a destination on its own.

These hotels tend to provide more for your

money than downtown digs, but they are a 10- to 15-minute drive to the city center.

Under $100

If you're looking for a clean, comfortable room, look no further than the **Fiddler's Inn** (2410 Music Valley Dr., 615/885-1440, www.fiddlers-inn.com, $65-85). This 202-room no-frills hotel offers a solid Tennessee welcome to its guests, who come in droves to see the Opry and enjoy other Music Valley attractions. It's right next to a Cracker Barrel restaurant, and there's plenty of parking for cars and tour buses. Guests enjoy cable TV, free coffee and pastries in the morning, an outdoor pool, and a gift shop stocked with kitschy Nashville souvenirs.

The all-suite **Best Western Suites near Opryland** (201 Music City Cir., 615/902-9940, $75-95) is a comfortable compromise between the luxury of the Opryland Hotel and the affordability of a motel. Each of the hotel's 100 suites has a couch, desk, high-speed Internet access, coffee- and tea maker, microwave, ironing board, and refrigerator. Rooms with whirlpool tubs are available for about $80 more per night. Guests enjoy an on-site fitness room, 24-hour business center, outdoor pool, free continental breakfast, and weekday newspaper. The Best Western is located along a strip of motels and restaurants about one mile from the Grand Ole Opry and other Opryland attractions.

Located about two miles from the Opryland, **Comfort Inn Opryland Area** (2516 Music Valley Dr., 615/889-0086, $75-90) offers 121 clean, comfortable guest rooms with cable TV, free HBO, wireless Internet, ironing board, hair dryer, and free daily newspaper. There is free outdoor parking, interior corridors, and an outdoor pool. Pets are permitted with an additional fee.

$100-150

Guests at the **Courtyard by Marriott Opryland** (125 Music City Cir., 615/882-9133, $129-150) enjoy refurbished rooms with soft beds, wireless Internet, coffeemakers, ironing boards, and refrigerators. The on-site restaurant serves breakfast, and business rooms come with a desk, dataport, voice mail, and speakerphone.

Over $200

Said to be the largest hotel without a casino in the United States, the **Gaylord Opryland Resort** (2800 Opryland Dr., 615/889-1000, $199-350) is more than just a hotel. Completely renovated after the 2010 flood shuttered it for six months, the 2,881-room luxury resort and convention center is built around a nine-acre indoor garden. Glass atriums invite sunlight, and miles of footpaths invite you to explore the climate-controlled gardens. Highlights include a 40-foot waterfall and flatboats that float along a river.

Set among the gardens are dozens of different restaurants and cafés, ranging from casual buffets to elegant steak houses. Hundreds of room balconies overlook the gardens, providing some guests with views of the well-kept greenery, even in winter. If you stay, choose between a traditional view looking outside the hotel, or an atrium view.

The property has a full-service salon, spa, and fitness center; multiple swimming pools (indoor and outdoor); on-site child care and "kid's resort"; and a car rental agency. You can walk to Opry Mills mall and the Grand Ole Opry from the hotel or take the free shuttle. Guest rooms are luxurious and feature coffee- and tea makers; two telephones; wireless Internet access; pay-per-view movies, games, and music; daily national newspapers; and other usual amenities. Service is impeccable. Press the "consider it done" button on the phone in your room, and any of your needs will be met. Guests can buy onetime or daily passes on the downtown shuttle for about $20 a day, and the airport shuttle costs $30 round-trip. Self-parking is $23 a day: valet is $30 per day.

While room rates at Opryland are steep, the hotel offers attractive packages that add on other Gaylord-owned attractions and properties. These often include tickets to the Grand

Ole Opry, a ride on the General Jackson Showboat, trips into Nashville to visit the Ryman Auditorium or the Wildhorse Saloon, and extras like spa visits and golf games at the hotel. Many of these packages are a good deal for travelers who want to pay one price for their whole vacation. Christmastime always brings interesting kid-friendly packages.

AIRPORT

Under $100

The **Alexis Inn and Suites Nashville Airport** (600 Ermac Dr., 615/889-4466, www.nashvillealexishotel.com, rooms $80-100, suites $95-115) is a comfortable and convenient place to stay near the airport. Rooms have all the usual amenities, plus guests get free popcorn in the lobby, a free airport shuttle 7am-9pm daily, and free continental breakfast. All rooms have refrigerators, and most have microwaves. There is a business center on-site.

$100-150

Drury Inns and Suites (555 Donelson Pk., 615/902-0400, $79-159) offers guests an appealing array of extras, including a free hot breakfast, free evening beverages and snacks, a free airport shuttle, 60 minutes of free long-distance calls, and $7 daily park-and-fly parking. There is both an indoor and outdoor pool and a fitness center. Drury Inn is about two miles north of the airport and five miles south of Music Valley.

$150-200

Hotel Preston (733 Briley Pkwy., 615/361-5900, www.hotelpreston.com, $149-260) is a boutique hotel near the airport. Youthful energy, modern decor, and up-to-date rooms set this property apart from the crowd. Rooms are stocked with Tazo tea and Starbucks coffee, and there's a 24-hour fitness center. The "You-Want-It-You-Got-It" button in each room beckons the 24-hour room service, and whimsical extras, including a lava lamp, pet fish, and an art kit, are available by request when you check in. Two restaurants, including the Pink Slip bar and nightclub, which features a sculpture by local artist Herb Williams, is known to both locals and hotel guests as a place with friendly barkeeps and good energy. Café Isabella serves a classic Italian menu and also provides room service to those staying in the hotel.

Food

Nashville has been called "Nowville" by *GQ* Magazine, among others. Nowhere is its "newness" more evident than in the culinary scene. More than a few high-profile chefs—including Chopped's Maneet Chauhan, Top Chef's Dale Levitski, and world-famous Jonathan Waxman, just to name three—have opened local kitchens, adding serious street cred to the serious eats.

You can eat in a different restaurant each day in Nashville and never get bored. Southern cooking stars at meat-and-three diners and barbecue joints, fine-dining restaurants cater to the well-heeled, and international eateries reflect the city's surprising diversity.

The Arcade

One of two downtown food destinations, the Arcade is an old outdoor shopping mall that lies between 4th and 5th Avenues. The ground floor of the Arcade is full of small, casual restaurants that cater to the downtown lunchtime crowd with quick, cheap eats. Upstairs are professional offices and a few art galleries and artists' studios.

The Greek Touch (13 Arcade, 615/259-9493) has gyro, sausage, veggie, and divine chicken sandwiches, platters, and salads, all for under $6. There are also several sandwich shops and **Manny's House of Pizza** (15 Arcade, 615/242-7144, www.mannyshouseofpizza.com), which many consider the city's best slice.

Most restaurants at the Arcade have some seating inside, or you can sit outside and watch the world go by.

Nashville Farmers Market

The **Nashville Farmers Market** (900 8th Ave. N., 615/880-2001, www.nashvillefarmersmarket.org) has undergone a resurgence in recent years and, as a result, is one of the best places to grab an interesting meal in the city. The outdoor components of the market include a farm shed with fresh produce year-round. This is a growers' market, so produce is farmed locally. When you're hungry, head to the interior for the Market House food court, with choices ranging from Southern specialties to Caribbean cuisine. **Jamaicaway** (615/255-5920, 10:30am-5pm Sun.-Fri., closed Sat., $9) serves oxtail, steamed fish, and Jamaican patties Sunday-Friday. There is also Mexican food, wood-fired pizza, barbecue, and Greek dishes, as well as enough baked goods to give you a toothache. Hours vary by merchant.

The monthly night market brings specialty food and drink, plus live music, dancing, and a magical ambience to the market.

DINERS AND COFFEE SHOPS

Downtown

Provence (601 Church St., 615/664-1150, 7am-6pm Mon.-Fri., 9am-3pm Sat.-Sun., $5-12), located inside the Nashville Public Library, serves excellent European-style pastries, breads, and salads, as well as coffee. Provence's signature sandwiches include creamy chicken salad and turkey and brie. Or you can try a sampler of the café's salads, including roasted-vegetable salad, parmesan potato salad, or creamy penne pasta. Save room for a decadent pastry, or at least a cookie, which come in varieties like raspberry hazelnut, chocolate espresso, and ginger molasses. For breakfast, nothing beats a buttery croissant spread with jam. Provence also has locations at 1600 Division Street at Roundabout Plaza; at 315 Deaderick Street, in the AmSouth Building downtown; and in Hillsboro at 1705 21st Avenue South.

For homemade salads, wraps, and sandwiches, follow the crowds of downtown office workers to the **Frist Center Café** (919 Broadway, 616/244-3340, Mon.-Wed. and Sat. 10 am -5:30pm, Thurs.-Fri. 10am-9pm, noon-5pm Sun., $5-8), located at the rear of the Frist Center for the Arts. Sandwiches are available whole or half, and you can add a soup, salad, or fries for a well-rounded lunch. The café has daily hot lunch entrées, plus a case of tempting desserts.

Midtown

There's a lot of hype surrounding Nashville's favorite breakfast restaurant, the **Pancake Pantry** (1796 21st Ave. S., 615/383-9333, 6am-3pm Mon.-Fri., 6am-4pm Sat.-Sun., $6-14). Founded in 1961 and still family owned, the Pantry serves some of the best pancakes in the city. Owner David Baldwin says that the secret is in the ingredients, which are fresh and homemade. Many of the flours come from Tennessee, and the syrup is made right at the restaurant. The Pantry proves that a pancake can be much more than plain. The menu offers no fewer than 21 varieties, and that doesn't include the waffles. Try the fluffy buckwheat cakes, savory cornmeal cakes, sweet blintzes, or the old standby buttermilk pancakes. And if you decide to order eggs instead, the good news is that most of the other breakfast platters on offer come with a short stack of pancakes, too. To its credit, the Pantry offers no-yolk omelets for the health conscious, and it's very kid friendly as well.

The Pantry also serves lunch, which is limited to sandwiches, salads, and soups. Beware that on weekend mornings, and many weekdays, the line for a seat at the Pantry goes out the door.

In today's retro-happy world, it isn't too

Follow That Food Truck!

Like every big city with a hipster population worth its salt, Nashville has scores of food trucks driving to and fro, selling gourmet delicacies from their wheel-based restaurants. These snack-masters tend to show up at places with big lunch crowds, late-night after concerts, and large public events, so you may just run into them. Centennial Park is a popular stop for many of the trucks, but they do make it to many neighborhoods at some point during the week.

The website for *Nashville Food Truck Association* (foodtrucksnash.org) lists menus and upcoming planned stops for more than 60 trucks. If you prefer your meals alfresco, check out this list.

- One of Nashville's first food trucks, **The Grilled Cheeserie** (http://thegrilledcheeserietruck.com) serves delicious grilled cheese sandwiches and tomato soup. It travels all over the city, particularly to farmers markets in the summer. Track it via Twitter (@GrilldCheeserie), or text CHEESE in a message to 88000.
- It Is hard to miss the bright pink presence that is **Barbie Burgers.** To find its tasty burgers and sweet potato fries, follow Barbie Burgers on Twitter (@BarbieBurgers).
- **Bao Down** (@baodownTN) uses local meats to fill its authentic Chinese steamed buns, for a Tennessee take on a traditional food.

hard to find an old-fashioned soda shop. But how many of them are the real thing? **Elliston Place Soda Shop** (2111 Elliston Pl., 615/327-1090, 7am-8pm Mon.-Thurs., 7am-10pm Fri.-Sat., $5-11), near Centennial Park and Vanderbilt, is one of those rare holdovers from the past, and it's proud of it. The black-and-white tile floors, lunch counter, and Purity Milk advertisements may have been here for decades, but the food is consistently fresh and good. Choose between a sandwich or a plate lunch, but be sure to save room for a classic milk shake or slice of hot pie with ice cream on top.

Nashville's original coffee shop, **Bongo Java** (2007 Belmont Blvd., 615/385-5282, 7am-11pm Mon.-Fri., 8am-11pm Sat.-Sun.) is just as popular as ever. Located near Belmont University, Bongo, as its frequent patrons call it, is regularly full of students chatting, texting, and surfing the Internet, thanks to free wireless Internet. Set in an old house with a huge front porch, Bongo feels homey and welcoming, and a bit more on the hippie side than other Nashville coffee shops. Nonetheless, expect the latest in coffee drinks, premium salads, and sandwiches. Breakfast, including Bongo French toast, is served all day. There is a bulletin board, a good place to find and seek roommates or apartments.

Bongo Java's big brother, **Fido** (1812 21st Ave. S., 615/777-3436, daily 7am-11pm) is more than a coffee shop. It is a place to get work done, see deals made, and see and be seen. Take a seat along the front plate-glass windows to watch the pretty people as they stroll by Posh, one of Nashville's most upscale clothing boutiques. In addition to coffee, sandwiches, and salads, baked goods are on the menu.

Said to have the best burger in Nashville, **Rotier's** (2413 Elliston Pl., 615/327-9892, 10:30am-9:30pm Mon.-Tues., 10:30am-10pm Wed.-Fri., 9am-10pm Sat., $6-14) is also a respected meat-and-three diner. Choose from classic sandwiches or comfort-food dinners. The Saturday breakfast will fuel you all day long. Ask about the milk shake, a city favorite that appears nowhere on the menu. Don't miss the hash brown casserole.

Dessert takes center stage at **Bobbie's Dairy Dip** (5301 Charlotte Ave., 615/292-2112, 11am-7pm Mon.-Sat., noon-5pm Sun., closed winter, $4-7), a walk-up ice cream joint. The cheeseburgers and chili dogs are the comfort food you've dreamed of, and you can finish off with soft-serve ice cream, dipped cones, sundaes, and banana splits. Bobbie's closes during the winter months and may stay open later in the summer; call ahead to confirm.

East Nashville

Not a deli in the traditional sense, **Mitchell Delicatessen** (1306 McGavock Pk., 615/262-9862, 7am-10pm Mon.-Sat., 8am-4pm Sun., $6-13) is the most creative sandwich shop in town. Order the roasted lamb and raita; a Vietnamese-style creation with pork, liver pate, and veggies; or a BLT fit for a king. Breakfast is served until 11am, and there is also a daily menu of soups and hot plate specials. Stop here for top-notch bread, cheese, and meats for your own sandwiches, too.

SOUTHERN

Downtown

Run, don't walk, to ★ **Arnold's Country Kitchen** (605 8th Ave. S., 615/256-4455, Mon.-Fri. 10:30am-2:45pm, $7-10) for some of the best Southern cooking in town. Set in a red cinder-block building on the southern edge of downtown, Arnold's is a food-lover's dream. No haute or fusion cuisine here—this is real food. It's set up cafeteria-style, so start out by grabbing a tray while you peer at the wonders before you: chocolate pie, congealed salad (that's Jell-O to those who don't know), juicy sliced tomatoes, turnip greens, mashed potatoes, squash casserole, macaroni and cheese—and that's just the "vegetables." Choose a vegetable plate, with either three or four vegetables, or a meat-and-three for just about a buck more. Common meat dishes include ham, baked chicken, fried fish, and beef tips. All meals come with your choice of pillowy yeast rolls or corn bread. The full lunch, plus a drink, will run you under $10. An expansion started in 2014 will make for more room at the tables, but there likely will always be a line out the door.

Midtown

One of Nashville's most beloved meat-and-threes is **Swett's** (2725 Clifton Ave., 615/329-4418, daily 11am-8pm, $8-12), family owned and operated since 1954. People come from all over the city to eat at this Nashville institution, which combines soul food and Southern cooking with great results (and, in 2012, they added barbecue to their offerings). The food here is homemade and authentic, down to the real mashed potatoes, the vinegary greens, and the yeast rolls. Swett's is set up cafeteria-style. Start by grabbing dessert—the pies are excellent—and then you move on to the good stuff: Country-fried steak, pork chops, meat loaf, fried catfish, and ham are a few of the usual suspects. A standard plate comes with one meat, two sides, and a serving of either yeast roll or corn bread, but you can add more sides if you like. Draw your own iced tea—sweet or unsweet—at the end, and then find a seat if you can.

North Nashville

Nashville's most sublime food experience is not to be found in a fine restaurant or even at a standard meat-and-three cafeteria. The food that you'll still be dreaming about when you get home is found at ★ **Prince's Hot Chicken Shack** (123 Ewing Dr., 615/226-9442, noon-10:30pm Tues.-Thurs., noon-1am Fri., 2pm-4am Sat., $4-7) in North Nashville. Hot chicken is pan-fried chicken that is also spicy, and you can find hot chicken outlets in Nashville, Memphis, and a few other Southern cities. But no hot chicken shop does it quite as well as Prince's, where the hot chicken comes in three varieties: mild, hot, and extra hot. Most uninitiated will find the mild variety plenty spicy, so beware. It is served with slices of white bread—perfect for soaking up that spicy chicken juice—and a pickle slice. You can add a cup of creamy potato salad, coleslaw, or baked beans if you like. When you walk into Prince's, head to the back, where you'll place your order at the window, pay, and be given a number. Then take a seat—if you can find one—while you wait for your food. You can order to go or eat in. Your food is made to order, and Prince's is very popular, so the wait often exceeds

30 minutes. Take heart, though—Prince's chicken is worth the wait.

Music Valley

Outside of the cuisine at the Gaylord Opryland Resort hotel, Music Valley isn't much known for its food. But the **Opry Backstage Grill** (2401 Music Valley Dr., 615/231-8854, and Sun. 11am-10pm Mon.-Thurs. and Sun., 11am-11pm Fri.-Sat., $8-18) tries to offer something that is at least unique to Nashville, albeit with the flair of a chain. This themed restaurant serves classic Southern dishes amid photos and art of classic Opry performers and occasionally hosts live concerts for ambience.

West of Nashville

The **Loveless Café** (8100 Hwy. 100, 615/646-9700, 7am-9pm daily, $8-16) is an institution, and some may argue it's a state of mind. But this little café-that-could is increasingly a destination, too, for visitors not just to Nashville but the entire heartland of Tennessee. The Loveless got its start in 1951, when Lon and Annie Loveless started to serve good country cooking to travelers on Highway 100. Over the years the restaurant changed hands, but Annie's biscuit recipe remained the same, and it was the biscuits that kept Nashvillians, including many famous ones, coming back for more. In 1982, then owner George McCabe started the Hams & Jams mail-order business, and in 2003 the Loveless underwent a major renovation that expanded the kitchen and dining rooms, and added additional shops in the rear. The food at the Loveless is good, no doubt about it. The biscuits are fluffy and buttery, the ham salty, and the eggs, bacon, and sausage will hit the spot. The supper and lunch menu has expanded to include Southern standards like fried catfish and chicken, pit-cooked pork barbecue, pork chops, and meat loaf, as well as a few salads. Loveless is located about 20 miles from downtown Nashville; plan on a 30-minute drive out Highway 100. Once you get out of the congestion of West End, it's a pretty trip.

BARBECUE

Downtown

If you are downtown and craving barbecue, **Jack's Bar-B-Que** (416 Broadway, 615/254-5715, 10:30am-8pm Mon.-Wed., 10:30am-9pm. Thurs., 10:30am-10pm Fri.-Sat., $6-15, hours may be extended during the summer) is your best option for a bite on Broadway. It isn't the best in the city, but the location can't be beat. Choose from barbecue pork shoulder, brisket, turkey, ribs, or sausage, and pair it with classic Southern sides like green beans, macaroni and cheese, and fried apples. Jack's serves five types of barbecue sauce, including classic Tennessee, Texas, and Kansas City. Most diners opt for a plate of one meat, two vegetables, and bread for $8-9, but if you're really hungry, go for the three-meat platter for $13. Adding to the appeal of the decent, affordable food is the fact that Jack's service is fast and friendly. There's a second location (334 W. Trinity Lane, 615/228-9888, 10:30am-8pm Mon.-Thurs., 10:30am-9pm Fri.-Sat., 11am-7pm Sun.) near East Nashville and a third location (1601 Charlotte Ave., 615/341-0517, 10:30am-8pm Mon.-Thurs., 10:30am-9pm Fri.-Sat., 11am-7pm Sun.) called Jack's Cawthon's Bar-B-Que.

Midtown

Near Centennial Park and Vanderbilt, **Hog Heaven** (115 27th Ave. N., 615/329-1234, www.hogheavenbbq.com, 10am-7pm Mon.-Sat., $5-10) is a nondescript yet well-known landmark for barbecue. Pulled-pork sandwiches and beef brisket are among the most popular at this mostly takeout eatery; locals like the white barbecue sauce.

South Nashville

Tucked on Nolensville Pike, the land of international eateries, is one of the city's favorite barbecue houses. **Martin's Bar-B-Que Joint** (7215 Nolensville Pk., 615/776-1856, www.martinsbbqjoint.com, 11am-9pm daily, $4-15) has pulled pork, barbecue spareribs, smoked wings, and beef brisket, plus all the side dishes you could want: coleslaw, green beans, potato salad, and the best corn cakes this side of town. You can also order burgers and a mean catfish po'boy. Martin's is located inside the Nolensville city limits, about 30 minutes' drive south from downtown Nashville.

STEAK HOUSES

Midtown

Jimmy Kelly's (217 Louise Ave., 615/329-4349, www.jimmykellys.com, 5pm-midnight Mon.-Sat., $18-42) is a family-run old-school steak house. Set in an old Victorian mansion a few blocks from Centennial Park and Vanderbilt, Jimmy Kelly's has been operated by the Kelly family since 1934. During its lifetime, food fads have come and gone, but Jimmy Kelly's has continued to serve excellent steaks and other grill foods. Dinner begins with irresistible corn cakes and continues with classic appetizers like crab cakes or fried calamari. Entrée choices include a half-dozen different steaks, lamb, grilled chicken, and seafood, including the best blackened catfish in the city. Jimmy Kelly's offers low lighting, wood paneling, and attentive, but not fussy, service. Tables are set throughout what were once parlors, bedrooms, and porches in the old home, giving diners a feeling of homey intimacy.

CONTEMPORARY

Downtown

The thoughtful menu, careful preparations, and green restaurant credentials at the **Mad Platter** (1239 6th Ave. N., 615/242-2563, www.themadplatterrestaurant.com, 11am-2pm Mon.-Fri., 5:30pm-10pm Wed.-Thurs., 5:30pm-11pm, Sun. 5pm-9pm Fri.-Sat., $18-35) have made it one of Nashville's favorite "nice" restaurants for years. Located among restored town houses in the tiny Germantown neighborhood, just north of the Bicentennial Mall, the Mad Platter is the work of Craig and Marcia Jervis, two chefs who met while catering the mid-1980s Michael Jackson's Victory tour. The Jervises married and opened the Mad Hatter, where they demonstrate their love for food, and each other, every day. Signature entrées include the Mad Platter rack of lamb, which is tender and juicy, and the porcini-dusted shrimp. For a special occasion, or just to enjoy one of the city's best dining deals, choose the five-course special. The chicken salad is sweet and tangy, and comes with fresh banana bread. Reservations are advisable at dinner; for lunch, come early to head off the business crowd.

Rub elbows with legislators, lobbyists, and other members of the jet set at the ★ **Capitol Grille** (23 6th Ave. N., 615/345-7116, www.thehermitagehotel.com, 6:30am-11am, 11:30am-2pm, and 5:30-10pm daily, $18-52). Located in the ground floor of the elegant Hermitage Hotel and set a stone's throw from the Tennessee State Capitol, this is the sort of restaurant where marriages are proposed and deals are done. The menu is fine dining at its best: choice cuts of meat prepared with exacting care and local ingredients. In fact, the ingredients are grown at the nearby Farm at Glen Leven, and this connection to the land has made the restaurant one of the leaders in the farm-to-fork movement. Dinner features rack of elk, sea bass, and pork chops; the provenience of each is noted on the menu. The lunch menu is more modest, including the Capitol Grille burger, a grilled pimento cheese sandwich, and meat entrées for $11-18. The business lunch offers a lunch entrée and your choice of soup or salad for $20. Breakfast ($4-16) may be the most decadent of all, with cinnamon-swirl French toast, eggs Benedict, lobster and shirred eggs, and an array of fresh pastries and fruit. The Sunday brunch (11am-2pm) features the best of the grill's lunch and breakfast menus, and is consistently popular.

Adjacent to the Capitol Grille is the old-school Oak Bar, a wood-paneled and intimate bar for pre- or postdinner drinks and conversation.

East Nashville

Named for the former coin laundry in which it was located when it first opened, **The Family Wash** (626A Main St. 615/645-9930, www.familywash.com, 7am-midnight Mon.-Sat.,

$9-15) is part live music listening room, part bar, part restaurant, part neighborhood gathering place. It captures the offbeat energy that so well defines Nashville. Come here to hear local musicians of all stripes (definitely not just country) and eat supper that is better than average bar food. Locals love the shepherd's pie. There's also a small take-out coffee area for that early-morning caffeine fix.

There's something about a place that pays attention to the details, and **Holland House Bar and Refuge** (935 W. Eastland Ave., 615/262-4190, www.hollandhousebarandrefuge.com, 5pm-10pm Mon.-Thurs., 5pm-midnight Fri.-Sat., $15-40) is one of those spots. This East Nashville hideaway is exactly as its name suggests: a refuge from louder restaurants and more frantically paced bars. The impressive cocktail and food menus change seasonally, and the bartender will craft your drink with precision, so expect to wait for that perfectly sized ginger ice cube or muddle mint (try the truffled popcorn while you wait). The food menu isn't as extensive as the cocktail menu, but everything is made with local and seasonal ingredients, ranging from duck to catfish. Locals like Monday night's happy hour and its burger special. This is not a place to bring little ones—it is a bar as much as a restaurant. Kids are welcome for Sunday brunch, however. The folks at Holland House are the minds behind **The Pharmacy Burger Parlor & Beer Garden** (731 McFerrin, 615/712-9527, www.pharmacynashville.com, 11am-10pm Sun.-Thurs., 11am-11pm Fri.-Sat.) right next door. The Pharmacy makes sodas by hand and has a killer grassy backyard beer garden.

INTERNATIONAL

Downtown

Maneet Chauhan is known for appearing on *Iron Chef America*, *The Next Iron Chef*, and *Chopped*. She opened **Chauhan Ale & Masala House** (123 12th Ave. N, 615-242-8426, chauhannashville.com, 11am-2:30pm and 5pm-10pm Mon.-Thurs., 5pm-11pm Fri.-Sat., 11am-3pm and 5pm-10pm Sun., $12-$25). The eatery brought Indian street food and a fusion of dishes and tastes to a city that wasn't known for its Indian cuisine. The vibe is fun and friendly, the cocktails go down easy, and there is even an interpretation of Nashville hot chicken dish.

Midtown

The venerable **International Market and Restaurant** (2010 Belmont Blvd., 615/297-4453, 11am-9:30pm daily, $5-10) near Belmont University and Hillsboro Village is a time-honored choice for a cheap lunch in Nashville. The cafeteria serves lots of vegetable, noodle, and rice dishes, many of them Thai in origin, at prices that seem not to have risen much since the restaurant was established in 1975. If you want to splurge, order a "from the kitchen" special of pad thai or another dish, which will be made from scratch just for you. Owner Patti Myint is the mother of *Top Chef* contestant and local restaurateur Arnold Myint.

For the best Italian food in Nashville, head west to the neighborhood of Sylvan Park, where you'll find **Caffe Nonna** (4427 Murphy Rd., 615/463-0133, www.caffenonna.com, 11am-2pm and 5pm-9pm Mon.-Thurs., 11am-2pm and 5pm-9pm Fri., 5pm-10pm Sat., $12-21). Inspired by Chef Daniel Maggipinto's own *nonna* (grandmother), the café serves rustic Italian fare. Appetizers include salads and bruschetta, and entrées include the divine Lasagne Nonna, made with butternut squash, ricotta cheese, spinach, and sage. The service at Caffe Nonna is friendly and attentive, and the atmosphere is cozy, but the space is small. Call ahead for a table.

Located just west of the Kroger grocery store, **K&S World Market** on Charlotte Avenue, the second in a chain whose original location is on Nolensville Pike, will keep any foodie happy for hours with its obscure and unusual food items. In the same shopping center you'll find Nashvillians' favorite Vietnamese restaurants, **Kien Giang**

(5825 Charlotte Ave., 615/353-1250, 11am-9pm daily, $6-12) and **Miss Saigon** (5849 Charlotte Ave., 615/354-1351, 10am-9pm Mon., Wed.-Sun., $7-12).

Drive a bit farther out to find **La Hispana Panaderia** (6208 Charlotte Pk., 615/352-3798, 6am-9pm daily), whose bread and pastries are as good as the finest European bakery but at a fraction of the cost.

One of Nashville's oldest Indian restaurants, **Shalimar** (3711 Hillsboro Rd., 615/269-8577, www.shalimarfinedining.com, 11am-2:30pm and 5pm-10pm Mon.-Sat., $15-17) offers fine food and efficient service. The Saturday lunch buffet brings in mall shoppers and ladies who lunch. At dinner, Shalimar takes on a slightly more elegant cast with vegetarian, chicken, lamb, and seafood entrées in popular preparations, including masala, biryani, tikka, saag, and korma. Shalimar is just a few blocks from the Mall at Green Hills.

South Nashville

Chosen by Nashvillians as the best Mexican restaurant in a very crowded field, **La Hacienda Taqueria** (2615 Nolensville Pk., 615/256-6142, www.lahaciendainc.com, 10am-9pm Sun.-Thurs., 10am-10pm Fri., 9am-10pm Sat., $2-14) is located within a colorful storefront on Nolensville Pike, Nashville's most ethnically diverse thoroughfare. The menu offers a dizzying array of choices—tacos, enchiladas, tamales, burritos, quesadillas, and tortas, just to name a few. Most come with your choice of chicken, chorizo, tripe, pork, or steak filling, and many have an authenticity often missing from Mexican restaurant fare. Combination platters, which offer three items plus rice and beans, are a good way to sample the options if you aren't sure what to order.

If you aren't in the mood for Mexican, just drive a bit farther along Nolensville Pike for other choices. Among them is **Dunya Kabob** (2521 Nolensville Pk., 615/242-6664, 11am-9pm daily, $5-10), which offers Kurdish specialties of chicken, lamb, beef, and seafood kabobs and gyro sandwiches (Nashville has a large Kurdish immigrant population; this is the place to try the cuisine).

Not far from Nolensville, you'll find two more international favorites in the same shopping center on Trousdale Drive. **Back to Cuba** (4683 Trousdale Dr., 615/837-6711, 11am-9pm Tues.-Sat., $8-12) serves traditional Cuban favorites: Grilled sandwiches of pork, ham, cheese, and pickle are a popular choice at lunchtime. For dinner, try the roast pork or grilled shrimp, and don't skip the lacy fried plantains and spicy black beans.

For homemade, old-school Italian fare (think red sauce), go to **Mama Mia's** (4501 Trousdale Dr., 615/331-7207, 11am-2pm Mon.-Fri., 5pm-9pm Mon.-Thurs, 5pm-10pm Fri.-Sat., $7-16), which offers lasagna, ravioli, chicken, veal, and seafood dishes. Bring your own wine.

DESSERTS

Downtown

Nashville's legendary candy company has been selling sweets for more than a century. In this flagship red, white, and blue **Goo Goo Cluster Store** (116 3rd Ave. S., 615/490-6685, http://googoo.com, 10am-8pm daily, hours may change seasonally) it serves its full array of sweets, plus some varieties only made in this open kitchen. Watch the chef create something you'll love (even if your dentist doesn't). Goo Goo-branded hats, T-shirts, Hatch Show Print posters, and other goodies are also for sale. Don't miss the historical exhibit about the Goo Goo brand.

Midtown

Need to satisfy your sweet tooth? Call **Jake's Bakes** (2422 Elliston Place, 616/645-5916, www.jakesbakesnashville.com, 10am-11:30pm Mon.-Fri., noon-11:30pm Sat.-Sun.) and within 30 minutes warm cookies will be delivered to your hotel room, conference center, meeting room, or college dorm room (of course you can add milk to your order, too).

MARKETS

For fresh fruits, vegetables, preserves, and honey, go to the **Nashville Farmers Market,** held daily in the large covered building between 8th Avenue and the Bicentennial Mall. In recent years this shifted to become an all-growers' market: Goods for sale here are grown at farms near Nashville. During the summer there are many smaller farmers markets around town, including on the Vanderbilt campus, in Franklin, and in East Nashville.

There is an abundance of traditional grocery stores around Nashville. Common chains are Kroger, Harris Teeter, and Publix. Drive out any of the main corridors into the city, and you will quickly find a grocery store. There is a Trader Joe's, which specializes in organic and specialty items, in Green Hills, just south of the Mall at Green Hills, as well as a Whole Foods.

Information and Services

VISITORS CENTERS

The main visitors center (615/259-4747, www.visitmusiccity.com/visitors, 8am-5pm Mon.-Sat., 10am-5pm Sun.) is located at the corner of 5th Avenue and Broadway, inside the Bridgestone Arena. Here you can pick up brochures, get a free map, and find answers to just about any question. It is open late when there is an event at Bridgestone.

There is another visitors center a few blocks uptown at 150 4th Ave. N. (615/259-4700, 8am-5pm Mon.-Fri.).

MAPS

Visitors centers offer a free hand-out map of downtown and an area map that shows major thoroughfares. This will be sufficient for many travelers. However, if you plan to do a lot of driving or off-the-beaten-track exploring, pick up a city map such as those published by Rand McNally or AAA. Detailed maps may be purchased from local drugstores and bookstores. Save time by buying a map before you arrive or downloading a GPS app to your smartphone. Nashville's system of changing street names can be tricky; a good map or GPS is essential.

MEDIA

Newspapers

Nashville's daily morning broadsheet is the ***Nashville Tennessean*** (www.tennessean.com). Published under various names since 1812, the *Tennessean* offers what every big-city newspaper does: local, regional, and national news, plus lots more. The paper's entertainment insert is published with the Friday newspaper.

The ***City Paper*** (www.nashvillecitypaper.com) is a free twice-weekly tabloid with a strong website that specializes in local news, sports, and events. It offers an alternative viewpoint to that of the *Tennessean* and makes a good, compact read for locals and visitors. You can pick up *City Paper* in dozens of downtown locations.

The ***Nashville Scene*** (www.nashvillescene.com) is a fat tabloid-size alternative weekly that balances its coverage of the local arts, music, and social scene with some political and local news coverage. This is a good go-to choice to understand what's going on in the city.

In addition, the ***Nashville Business Journal*** (615/248-2222, www.bizjournals.com/nashville) is a weekly business publication covering industry, commerce, and finance. It is distributed on Monday. ***Nashville Pride*** (615/292-9150) covers news for a mainly African American readership.

Also published by the *Tennessean*, ***Nashville Lifestyles*** is a monthly glossy magazine with local celebrity profiles, home and garden tips, event information, and advertising. You can pick it up at newsstands throughout the city.

American Songwriter Magazine (1303 16th Ave. S., 615/321-6069, www.americansongwriter.com) is a bimonthly magazine devoted to the art of songwriting. It has been published in Nashville since 1984.

Radio

The Nashville dial is chockablock with the usual commercial radio prospects (what else would you expect in Music City?). There are a few radio stations worth mentioning, however. **WSM 650 AM** is the legendary radio station that started it all when it put a fiddler on the air in 1925. Still airing the Grand Ole Opry after all these years, WSM plays country music at other times.

Nashville Public Radio has two stations, **WPLN 90.3 FM** and **91.1 FM.** The first plays National Public Radio news and talk, the second is all classical music. **WPLN 1430 AM** is a companion station with all-day news and talk, including BBC broadcasts. Nashville's only community radio station is **Radio Free Nashville** (107.1 FM, www.radiofreenashville.org). While its signal only reaches a small part of the city now, Radio Free Nashville is looking to expand its reach as soon as it raises the necessary funds.

WKDA 900 AM is Nashville's Spanish-language radio station. **WAMB 1160 AM** plays big-band music, and **WNAH 1360 AM** plays old-fashioned Southern gospel.

Several Nashville universities liven up the radio dial. Fisk's **WFSK 88.1 FM** plays jazz. Middle Tennessee State University has **WMTS 88.3 FM,** the student-run station, and **WMOT 89.5 FM,** a jazz station.

Television

Nashville's network affiliates offer local news morning and night. These include **WKRN** (Channel 2 ABC), **WSMV** (Channel 4 NBC), **WTVF** (Channel 5 CBS), and **WZTV** (Channel 17 FOX).

The local public-television station is **WNPT** (Channel 8 PBS).

Remember that since Nashville is in the Central time zone, most nationally televised programs air one hour earlier than they do on the East Coast.

INTERNET ACCESS

You can go online free at the **Nashville Public Library** (615 Church St., 615/862-5800). There is free wireless access at the visitors center located at 5th and Broadway.

POSTAL SERVICE

Mail a letter or buy stamps from the downtown post offices at 901 Broadway (in the basement of the Frist Center for the Visual Arts) and 1718 Church Street. Both are open 8:30am-5pm Monday-Friday. There is also a post office in the downtown Arcade.

EMERGENCY SERVICES

Dial 911 for police, fire, or ambulance in an emergency. For help with a traffic accident, call the **Tennessee Highway Patrol** (615/741-3181).

Because health care is such a big industry in Nashville, there are a lot of hospitals. The **Monroe Carell Jr. Children's Hospital at Vanderbilt** (2200 Children's Way, 615/936-1000, www.childrenshospital.vanderbilt.org) is among the best in the country. **Baptist Hospital** (2000 Church St., 615/284-5555, www.baptisthospital.com) is another major player.

Rite Aid, CVS, Walgreens, and the major grocery store chains have drugstores all over Nashville. Try the **CVS** at 426 21st Avenue South (615/321-2590, www.cvs.com).

LIBRARIES

Nashville's downtown library is the crown jewel of its library system. The **Nashville Public Library** (615 Church St., 615/862-5800, www.library.nashville.org, 9am-6pm Mon.-Fri., 9am-5pm Sat., 2pm-5pm Sun.) opened in 2001, replacing an older library that had served the city since 1965. The library is dynamic and busy serving its community. There are story hours, children's

The *Nashville* of the Small Screen

It is perhaps the most meta of Music City's attractions: Since 2012 Nashville has been the subject of ABC's TV show called ***Nashville.*** The hour-long nighttime drama is filmed on location and many of the show's actors, who are also songwriters and singers, have relocated to Music City to launch their music careers.

As the show has become more popular, the lines between the real Nashville and the one on TV have blurred. Many of the actors have now appeared on the stage of the Grand Ole Opry both in character and as themselves. There are CDs and concert tours from the cast. The homes and sets of the characters have been featured on HGTV. Eric Close, who played the mayor on TV, has led the city's annual Christmas parade several times, instead of the city's actual mayor!

Part of the reason that the show is popular is that, for all its soap opera-ness, part of it feels authentic. Episodes are named using Hank Williams song titles, a hat tip to the man who made country music what it is. Backup musicians on the show are actual full-time, professional musicians who live and work in Nashville.

For fans, it is easy to take a tour of the sites of the show as part of a tour of Nashville. The most comprehensive is from Gray Line: a 3.5-hour tour showing off characters' homes and venues that pop up in the show (graylinetn.com/abcs-nashville, $49). Grand Avenue offers a custom *Nashville* tour (www.grandavenueworldwide.com/tours/nashville-tour.html, $75). Many of the city's popular attractions, including The Bluebird Café and Ryman Auditorium, now have sections of their tours devoted to the TV show. Art imitates life.

programs, art exhibits, a local history collection, and meeting rooms. Visitors to the city will find the public Internet access and wireless Internet network most useful. There is a nice courtyard inside the library where people eat lunch, relax, and enjoy occasional concerts. One Saturday a month the Nashville Shakespeare Festival gathers here for the free **Shakespeare Allowed!,** an afternoon where attendees read, not perform, one of the Bard's plays aloud.

If you are visiting the library, you can park in the Nashville Public Library Parking Garage. Enter on 6th or 7th Avenue between Church and Commerce Streets. The first 90 minutes of library parking is free, and the daily maximum is $8. Be sure to validate your ticket at the security desk as you enter the library.

Getting There and Around

GETTING THERE

Air

Nashville International Airport (BNA, 615/275-1675, www.nashintl.com) is located eight miles east of the city center. To get downtown from the airport, head west on I-40; it's a short 15-minute drive. The flat one-way taxi fare from the airport to downtown or Music Valley is $25. The airport has been renovated Music City style. It has outposts of local restaurants and musicians playing live music (and selling CDs).

AIRPORT SHUTTLE

Many of the major hotels offer shuttles from the airport; there's a kiosk on the lower level of the terminal to help you find the right one.

Gray Line Transportation (615/883-5555, www.graylinenashville.com) offers regular shuttle service from the airport to downtown, West End, and Music Valley hotels. The shuttle departs from the airport every 15-20 minutes 4am-11pm; reservations are not required. Call ahead to book your hotel pickup. Fare is $14 one-way and $25 round-trip.

BNA was the first airport in the United States to include transportation network companies such as Lyft and Uber (download the smartphone apps to utilize these services) in their plans. There is a designated ride-sharing area on the ground floor where the hotel shuttles wait.

Car

Driving is the most popular way to get to Nashville. The city is 250 miles from Atlanta, 330 miles from St. Louis, 400 miles from Charlotte, 550 miles from New Orleans, and 670 miles from Washington DC.

No fewer than three major interstate highways converge in Nashville. I-40 runs east-west, connecting Nashville with Knoxville and Memphis. I-65 runs north-south, connecting the city with Louisville, Kentucky, and Birmingham, Alabama. I-24 travels at a southeastern angle down to the city, connecting it with the cities of Clarkesville and St. Louis in the north, and Chattanooga and Atlanta in the south.

Bus

Greyhound (800/231-2222, www.greyhound.com) serves Nashville, with bus service to the city from Memphis, Jackson, Chattanooga, and Knoxville, Tennessee, as well as Paducah and Bowling Green, Kentucky. The **Greyhound station** (1022 Charlotte Ave., 615/255-3556) is well marked and well staffed, with ample parking, and is several blocks west of downtown. Expect to pay about $50 for a one-way ticket from Memphis to Nashville.

GETTING AROUND

Driving

The easiest way to get around Nashville is by car. Although visitors staying downtown will be able to find plenty to do and places to eat within walking distance, many of the best attractions are located outside of the city center. So unless your stay is but a few days, it is best to bring or rent a car to get around.

If you don't bring your own, a dozen different major rental agencies have a fleet of cars, trucks, and SUVs at the airport. Agencies include **Alamo** (615/361-7467, www.alamo.com), **Avis** (615/361-1212, www.avis.com), and **Hertz** (615/361-3131, www.hertz.com). For the best rates, use an online travel search tool, such as Expedia (www.expedia.com) or Travelocity (www.travelocity.com), and book the car early, along with your airline tickets.

NAVIGATING NASHVILLE

Even locals are perplexed by Nashville's city planning, with street names that repeat and change, and few straight roads. The interstates are a little easier to navigate than side streets. I-65 and I-24 create a tight inner beltway that encircles the heart of the city. I-440 is an outer beltway that circles the southern half of the city, while I-40 runs horizontally from east to west. Briley Parkway, shown on some maps as Highway TN-155, is a highway that circles the north and east perimeters of the city.

City residents use the interstates not just for long journeys, but also for short cross-town jaunts. Most businesses give directions according to the closest interstate exit.

Non-interstate thoroughfares emanate out from Nashville like spokes of a wheel. Many are named for the communities that they eventually run into. Murfreesboro Pike runs southeast from the city; Hillsboro Pike (Route 431) starts out as 21st Avenue South and takes you to Hillsboro Village and Green Hills. Broadway becomes West End Avenue and takes you directly to Belle Meade and, eventually, the Loveless Café. It does not take long to realize that roads in Nashville have a bad habit of changing names all of a sudden, so be prepared and check the map to avoid getting too confused.

For real-time traffic advisories and road construction closures, dial 511 from any touch-tone phone, or go to www.tn511.com.

PARKING

There is metered parking on most downtown streets, but some have prohibited-parking signs effective during morning and afternoon rush hours. Always read the fine print carefully.

There is plenty of off-street parking in lots and garages. Expect to pay about $22 a day for garage parking. **Park It! Downtown** (www.parkitdowntown.com) is a great resource for finding downtown parking deals, plus information about the shuttle that transports parkers to Nissan Stadium during downtown events.

Public Transportation

Nashville's **Metropolitan Transit Authority** (MTA) operates city buses. Pick up a map and schedule from either of the two downtown visitors centers, or online at www.nashvillemta.org.

Improvements to the city's public transport system have made it easier to use, but few tourists ride the buses because they can be difficult to understand if you're new to the city. One favorite is the Music City Circuit, a free bus that runs between downtown and the Gulch. These Blue and Green Circuit buses stop at 75 different spots on three different routes. One route that is helpful, however, is the Opry Mills Express that travels from downtown Nashville to Music Valley, home of the Grand Ole Opry, Opryland Hotel, and Opry Mills, the shopping mall. The Opry Mills Express departs the Bridgestone Arena 13 times a day on weekdays. Fare is $1.70 one-way; $0.85 for senior citizens. You can pick up a detailed route timetable from either of the two downtown visitors centers or online.

COMMUTER RAIL

In 2006, Nashville debuted the **Music City Star Rail** (501 Union St., 615/862-8833, www.musiccitystar.org), a commuter rail system designed to ease congestion around the city. With service Monday-Friday, several times a day, trains connect Donelson, Hermitage, Mount Juliet, and Lebanon to downtown Nashville. There is often additional service during special events, such as the Fourth of July celebration downtown. More routes are planned for the future.

One-way tickets can be purchased for $5.25 each from vending machines at any of the stations. You can prepurchase single-trip tickets, 10-trip packs, and monthly passes at a discount online. For a complete list of ticket outlets, contact the railway.

Taxis

Licensed taxicabs will have an orange driver permit, usually displayed on the visor or dashboard.

Several reliable cab companies are **Allied Cab Company** (615/244-7433 or 625/320-9083, www.nashvillecab.com), **Checker Cab** (615/256-7000), **Music City Taxi Inc.** (615/865-4100, www.musiccitytaxi.com), and **United Cab** (615/228-6969). Taxi rates are $2.10 per mile.

If cruising around in a stretch limo is more your style, call **Basic Black Limo** (615/430-8157, www.basicblacklimo.net). The rate is $125 per hour on Saturday nights; the limo seats up to 14 passengers.

Ride-hailing companies, including **Lyft** and **Uber**, are popular in Nashville. Download their apps to find a local to drive you to your destination. **Joyride Nashville** (615/285-9835, http://joyridellc.com) offers licensed rides around downtown in a golf cart for a pay-what-you-wish model. Many of the drivers are happy to provide recommendations and tours as well as transportation.

Middle Tennessee

Perhaps no region of Tennessee is as diverse—geographically and demographically—as Middle Tennessee, the state's heartland.

From Clarksville on the Cumberland River to Cowan at the foot of the Cumberland Plateau, Middle Tennessee satisfies visitors with its surprising collection of campuses, kitsch, and countryside.

Much of this region is familiar. Its scenes are winding country roads cutting through horse pasture, perfectly fried chicken, and charming old railroad towns where the trains still run.

But there are other attractions that just might surprise you: Amish buggies traveling the back roads, a celebration dedicated to the lowly mule, and some of the best shopping in all of the Volunteer State. Middle Tennessee is a landscape of quiet beauty and some outstanding stories that will captivate its visitors.

There's the tale of Sam Davis, boy hero of the Confederacy, who went to his grave without divulging the name of his Union informant. There's the story of the sanctuary for retired circus and zoo elephants, tucked in the lush Tennessee countryside near Hohenwald. And there's the legend of the Natchez Trace, the old Indian road that cuts from Nashville through the countryside bound for the Mississippi port town of Natchez.

In the end, there are dozens of good reasons to travel through Middle Tennessee. But the best one is a wish to slow things down a bit and enjoy the simple pleasure of natural beauty, notable history, and the company of friendly people.

PLANNING YOUR TIME

The rural byways of Middle Tennessee are best explored at a slow pace. The beauty of the region is best enjoyed on small back roads, where the friendliness of its people can be appreciated over a leisurely conversation.

Explore Middle Tennessee gradually if you can. The region can be dipped into over a series of weekend drives or weeklong expeditions. If you have only a few days, choose one of the subregions to explore. If shopping and dining are your preferences, Franklin is a natural choice. For a quaint small-town feel, go to Bell Buckle and Wartrace, crown jewels

Previous: Falls Mill; George Dickel Distillery. **Above:** Carnton Plantation.

Look for ★ to find recommended sights, activities, dining, and lodging.

Highlights

★ **RiverWalk:** There's no better way to see Clarksville's gems than to stroll around this 15-acre park along the banks of the Cumberland (page 205).

★ **The Hermitage:** The home of America's seventh president is also one of Tennessee's finest historic homes and gardens, preserving not only the story of Andrew Jackson, but also that of his family, paid staff, and slaves (page 211).

★ **Franklin Theatre:** This 1937 movie theater underwent an extensive restoration that brought it back to its original glory (page 221).

★ **Carnton Plantation:** This mansion served as a Confederate field hospital during the Battle of Franklin and is the setting of the novel *The Widow of the South* (page 223).

★ **Tennessee Walking Horse National Celebration:** Watch the world's greatest show horses compete in the heart of horse country (page 247).

★ **George Dickel Distillery:** Tennessee whiskey is world-famous, but you can beat the crowds at this lesser-known distillery in beautiful Cascade Hollow (page 261).

★ **Old Stone Fort State Archaeological Park:** This ancient earthen structure has confounded scientists for decades (page 263).

Middle Tennessee

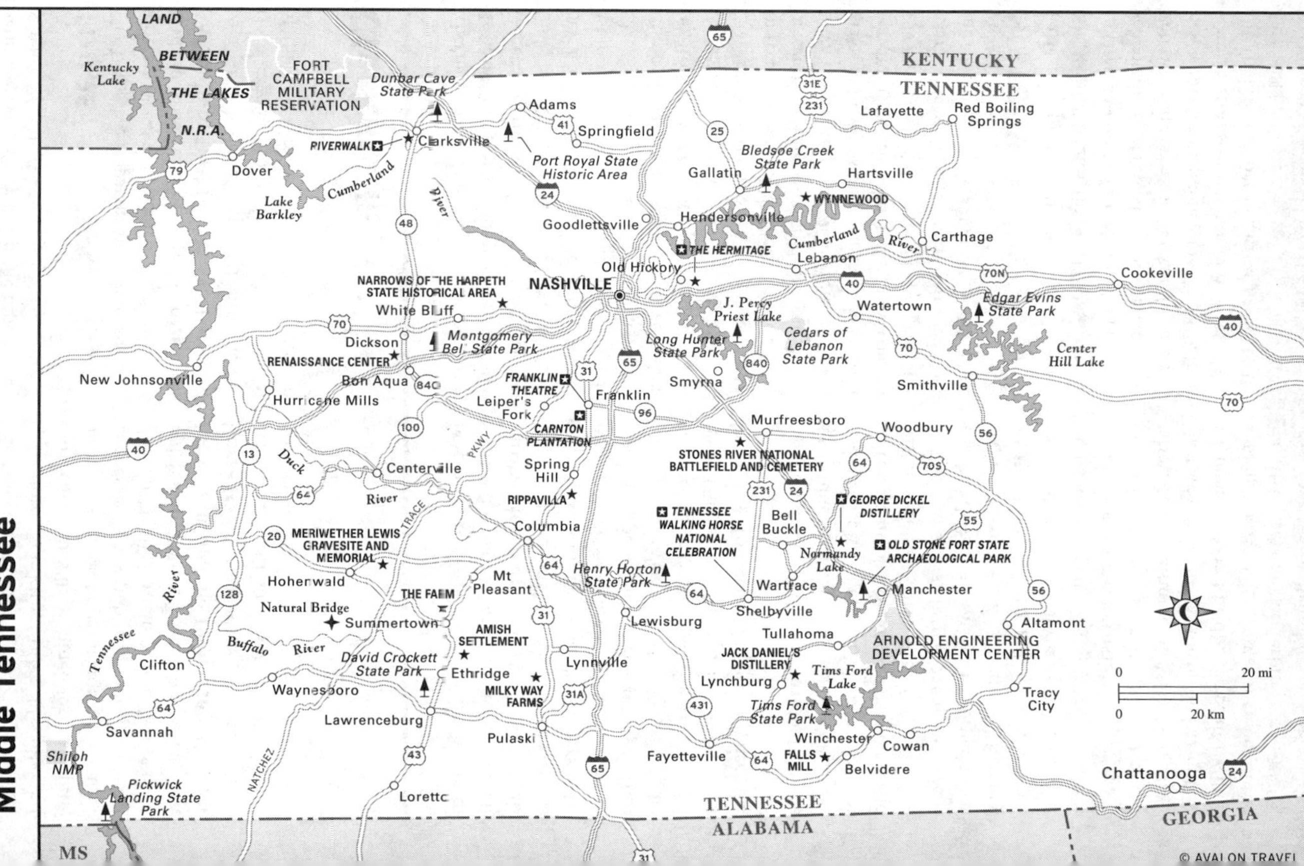

in Tennessee Walking Horse Country. For a natural escape, drive down the remarkable Natchez Trace Parkway.

TOURS

The Tennessee Department of Tourism promotes several self-guided tours through Middle Tennessee. The **Tennessee Antebellum Trail** (www.antebellumtrail.com) is a 90-mile loop beginning at the Hermitage in Nashville. It stops at several of the best-known antebellum homes in the region, including Belle Meade and the Carnton Plantation.

Bedford, Franklin, Coffee, Lincoln, and Moore Counties have joined forces to promote back-roads tourism in south-central Tennessee. They publish guides to several themed "trails," including a **Tennessee Spirits and Wine Trail,** a **You Pick 'Em Farm Trail,** and the **Tennessee Walking Horse Trail.** You can request free guides from Tennessee's Trails and Byways (www.tntrailsandbyways.com).

Clarksville

Alternately known as the town of spires (for its beautiful historic church spires) and the Queen City (for the Cumberland River that flows by), **Clarksville** is an old city with a new lease on life. By some accounts the oldest incorporated city in Tennessee (in 1785), Clarksville owed its early prosperity to the Cumberland River and the tobacco industry. Today, the Fort Campbell military base is the city's biggest economic engine, and Clarksville is Tennessee's fifth-largest city. In recent years, Clarksville has done a lot to preserve its waterfront and historic downtown. Its centerpiece waterfront park is a major draw, and so is its historic downtown, which was largely rebuilt after a destructive 1999 tornado. Many riverside properties in Clarksville were also severely damaged when the Cumberland River flooded in May 2010.

HISTORY

Early attempts to settle the area that is now Clarksville began in the 1760s, and the town was founded in 1785. In 1806, the first school, the Rural Academy, was established, and two years later the *Clarksville Chronicle* newspaper began publication. By 1819, there were 22 stores in town, and one year later the first steamboat began to navigate the Cumberland River.

During the second half of the 19th century, no crop or industry was more important to Clarksville than tobacco. In 1855, a special variety of tobacco grown in the fields and valleys of north-central Tennessee was known as the strongest in the world. This "Clarksville dark" tobacco was used primarily to make cigar wrappers and snuff—not cigarettes. During these years, Clarksville grew to be the second-largest tobacco market in the United States, and in 1880 sales moved to a brand-new Tobacco Exchange built near the public square.

The tobacco industry declined by the 1930s, due to changing agricultural practices and the Great Depression, although you can still see small tobacco farms in the valleys and pastures around Clarksville.

The most disruptive event of recent Clarksville history was an F3 tornado that struck downtown at 4:15am on January 22, 1999. The twister left a 4.3-mile-long, 880-yard-wide path. It destroyed 124 buildings and damaged 562 more, many of them in the historic downtown district.

Clarksville has seen its share of celebrities. It is the home of Miss USA 2007, Rachel Smith, and was the birthplace of U.S. Olympic track-and-field gold medalist Wilma Rudolph. Poet Allen Tate, a member of the Fugitive poets at Vanderbilt in the 1920s, was from nearby Benfolly, and Robert Penn

Clarksville

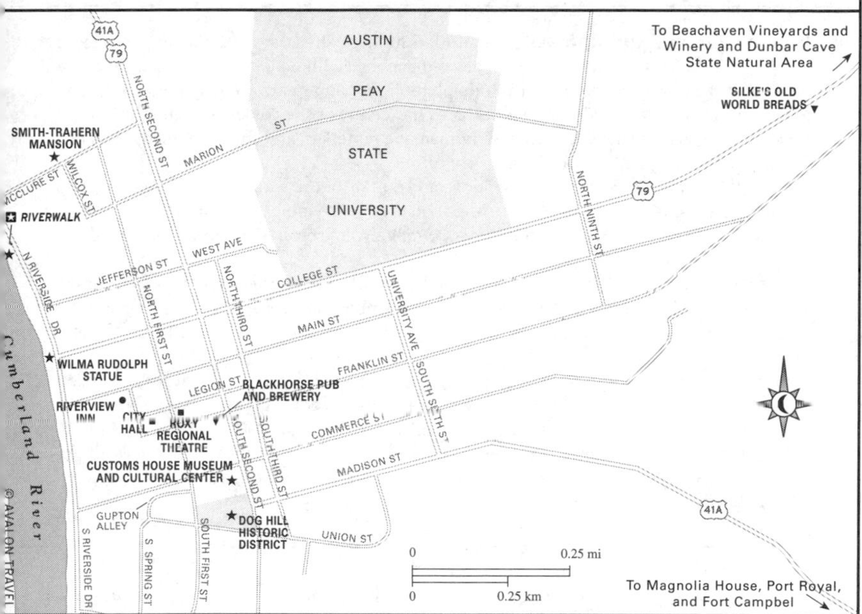

Warren attended Clarksville High School. Jimi Hendrix lived in Clarksville while he was stationed with the 101st Airborne Division at Fort Campbell in 1962.

SIGHTS

★ RiverWalk

Opened in 1987, **RiverWalk** (602 N. Riverside Dr., 931/645-7476, 7am-midnight daily, free) is Clarksville's crown jewel. The 15-acre park stretches along the Cumberland River, and paved walkways make it easy to enjoy a stroll along the banks of the river. There are also playgrounds, a boat ramp, picnic tables, and an amphitheater where the city hosts events like summer's RiverFest and Christmas on the Cumberland. The Rotary Clubs of Clarksville have also built an avenue of flags designed to reflect the diversity of the city.

If you want to learn more about the river, visit the **Cumberland River Center** (931/645-7476) near the center of the park, where a permanent exhibit chronicles the history of the river and of Clarksville. Among other things, the exhibit describes the river's significance in the Civil War and also its role in the city's lucrative tobacco industry. The center is located near the main parking lot for RiverWalk and is open daily.

At the southern end of RiverWalk you will find a bronze statue of Clarksville native and U.S. Olympic gold medalist **Wilma Rudolph.** The statue sits at the base of the pedestrian overpass at College Street and Riverside Drive.

Historic Clarksville

Pick up a copy of "Walk Clarksville" from the visitors center, RiverWalk, or at the Customs House (or download it from www.clarksvillepartnership.com). This 2.2-mile walking tour allows you to slow down and appreciate the city's fine architecture and its interesting history. The tour begins at the Customs House Museum on South 2nd Street and includes the downtown historic district, the public square, the Smith-Trahern Mansion, and Austin Peay

Wilma Rudolph: A True Olympian

Wilma Glodean Rudolph was born on June 20, 1940, the 20th of 22 children born to Ed and Blanche Rudolph, in Clarksville. Wilma was diagnosed with polio as a young child and as a result used leg braces to walk. Blanche Rudolph took her daughter to Meharry Medical College in Nashville, a hospital for African Americans, as frequently as she could. When they could not travel, Blanche treated her daughter with homemade remedies, and she spent many evenings massaging her daughter's stricken legs.

When Wilma was 12, she overcame her polio and quickly became a standout athlete. She was a high school basketball star and earned a spot on the U.S. Olympic track-and-field team when she was just 16 years old. At the 1956 Summer Olympics Wilma brought home a bronze medal in the 4 by 100 meter relay.

Four years later, Wilma Rudolph made Olympic history when she became the **first American woman** to win **three gold medals** in a single Olympic games. Her medals came in the 100 meters, 200 meters, and the 4 by 100 meter relay. Rudolph was heralded as the "fastest woman in history."

Wilma returned home to Tennessee and retired from athletics in 1962. A year later, she enrolled at Tennessee State University, where she earned a degree in education. She later married and had four children. Rudolph wrote her autobiography, *Wilma: The Story of Wilma Rudolph*, in 1977. She died at her home in Brentwood in 1994 of brain and throat cancer; she was just 54 years old.

A bronze statue depicting the young Wilma Rudolph stands on the waterfront in her hometown of **Clarksville.**

State University. Along Franklin Street you will see a large outdoor mural, *Bursting with Pride,* that depicts several of the city's most historic buildings. The walking tour includes a number of historic downtown churches, including Mount Olive Baptist Church, where Wilma Rudolph worshipped as a child, and the First Presbyterian Church, founded in 1822. Don't skip the walk through the Dog Hill Historic District, a clutch of 1890s wood-framed cottages, named Dog Hill because neighborhood dogs would howl at the whistles of passing trains and steamboats. Plan on 2-2.5 hours for the walking tour.

Customs House Museum and Cultural Center

Clarksville's old post office houses its largest museum, which has a wide-ranging collection that includes regional art and historical artifacts. The **Customs House Museum and Cultural Center** (200 S. 2nd St., 931/648-5780, www.customshousemuseum.org, 10am-5pm Tues.-Sat., 1pm-5pm Sun., adults $7, seniors $5, students $3-5; second Sat. of the month free) gets points for variety, if nothing else. Its permanent exhibits include Lucy Dunwody Boehm porcelains and a *Memory Lane* exhibit with clothes, forms of transportation, and firearms from the 18th and 19th centuries. The Explorers' Gallery has exhibits and activities for children, including bubbles, a grocery store, and optical illusions. A wonderfully intricate model train set is on display, and volunteer engineers run trains on Sunday afternoons.

There is also a small exhibit about the remarkable building itself, which was built in 1898 as a post office and customs house for the collection of tobacco taxes. The unique architecture consists of Italianate ornamentation, a Far East-inspired slate roof, Romanesque arches, and Gothic copper eagles perched at four corners. In addition to the permanent exhibit, the Customs House hosts traveling exhibits year-round.

Smith-Trahern Mansion

Built around 1858 by tobacconist Christopher Smith, this Greek Revival-Italianate mansion sits high above the banks of the Cumberland River. The **Smith-Trahern Mansion** (311 N. Spring St., 931/648-9998, 9:30am-2:30pm Mon.-Fri., evenings and weekends by appointment, $2) contains a unique curved staircase and a widow's walk looking out at the Cumberland River. It is now the setting for an education outreach program provided by the University of Tennessee's extension office. Tours are also available to visitors, and the home is used frequently for weddings and other private functions.

Dunbar Cave

The **Dunbar Cave** has been a site of importance to successive waves of people living around present-day Clarksville. Prehistoric Native Americans took shelter inside the cave as early as 10,000 years ago. Mississippian Indians also used the cave, leaving as evidence cave art on the cavern's walls.

In the 1930s, it became a mineral bath resort, and people traveled for miles to take the baths and enjoy big-band and swing music played on the stage at the mouth of the cave. Artie Shaw and Benny Goodman were among the artists who performed at Dunbar Cave, and there are still jazz concerts here in the summer. In 1948, country music star Roy Acuff bought the property and broadcast a live country music show from the location.

Dunbar Cave was purchased by the state in 1973. It is located just four miles from downtown Clarksville, making it a popular retreat for the city's residents. There are three miles of hiking trails, including one-mile and two-mile loops and a short 0.7-mile paved walk to the mouth of the cave. Guided hikes inside the cave were offered on weekends year-round and on certain weekdays in summer, but, as is the case with many publicly owned caves all across the eastern United States, Dunbar Cave's underground tours are closed indefinitely in an effort to curb white-nose syndrome in bats. This fungus (which looks white on a bat's noses, hence the name) causes low body fat and death. It is transmitted from one bat to another, and by closing caves, the hope is that it will not spread from one cave to another. Despite the cave's closure, you can still enjoy the aboveground hikes and visit the **nature museum** (401 Old Dunbar Cave Rd., 931/648-5526, 8am-4:30pm daily, staff permitting) at the park office.

There are plans for an interpretive center to be added to the park, which would describe how the cave was used by Native Americans, early European settlers, and the early-20th-century vacationers who came to Dunbar to get well.

Beachaven Vineyards and Winery

You can take a free vineyard tour and sample local wines at **Beachaven Vineyards and Winery** (1100 Dunlop Ln., 931/645-8867, www.beachavenwinery.com, 9am-5pm Mon.-Sat., noon-5pm Sun.).

ENTERTAINMENT AND EVENTS

Theater

You can see professional company shows and black-box theater at the **Roxy Regional Theatre** (100 Franklin St., 931/645-7699, www.roxyregionaltheatre.org) in downtown Clarksville. First opened as a movie house in 1912, the Roxy (then called the Lillian Theater) was a first-run theater until 1980. In 1983, it reopened as a regional theater. The Roxy puts on 10 shows per year, including musicals and classic American and European drama. The Other Space is a black-box theater also located at the Roxy that puts on innovative and cutting-edge productions.

Festivals and Events

Clarksville's biggest party is **Riverfest** (www.clarksvilleriverfest.com, free), a September extravaganza held at the Cumberland RiverWalk. It includes live music, food vendors, children's activities, and fireworks.

Other annual events include **Oktoberfest** (931/647-0243, www.edelweissclarksville.org), held at the Fairgrounds Park in October, and **Jazz on the Lawn** (1100 Dunlop Ln.,

931/645-8867, www.beachavenwinery.com), monthly free concerts held during the summer at Beachaven Vineyards and Winery.

SPORTS AND RECREATION

There are three golf courses around Clarksville: **Mason Rudolph Golf Course** (1514 Golf Club Ln., 931/645-7479), which offers inexpensive rates for 9- and 18-hole play; **Swan Lake** (581 Dunbar Cave Rd., 931/648-0479), right next to Dunbar Lake State Natural Area; and **Eastland Green** (550 Clubhouse Ln., 931/358-9051).

There are eight outdoor lighted tennis courts at **Swan Lake Tennis Complex** (2002 Sanders Rd.), which you can use for $4 per hour during warm-weather months. Call the city's parks department at 931/647-6511 for details.

ACCOMMODATIONS

The best hotel in Clarksville has the best location. The **Riverview Inn** (50 College St., 931/552-3331, www.theriverviewinn.com, $98-106) is located just steps from the Cumberland River and Clarksville's historic downtown. Probably even more in its favor is that it's located miles from the noisy, congested, and unappealing strip of highway that is home to a seemingly endless array of chain-hotel choices. The Riverview offers suites, king-size rooms with a desk and couch, and traditional double rooms. All guests can enjoy breakfast, a fitness room, business center, free wireless Internet, free daily newspaper, and laundry. You can even get your hair done at the on-site salon. And while the exterior of the hotel is about as charming as a concrete box, the inside is cheery and the staff pleasant. A real winner for road warriors.

If you prefer more homey accommodations, call Russ and Almeida Welker at **Magnolia House** (1231 Madison St., 931/552-4545, www.magnoliabb.com, $119-129), a well-run and welcoming bed-and-breakfast in Clarksville's historic district. Margaret has two guest suites, each with a private bathroom, desk, wireless Internet access, fine linens, and a refrigerator. One of the rooms also has a kitchenette and can sleep up to three people.

FOOD

Every town deserves a restaurant like **Silke's Old World Breads** (1214A College St., 931/552-4422, www.silkesoldworldbreads.com, 7:30am-6pm Mon.-Sat., $6-9). Silke's is a bakery that makes European pastries and breads in a stone-hearth oven. There is sourdough, whole wheat, rye, and lots more. On the sweet side, Silke's offers traditional coffee-shop favorites like cheesecake and tiramisu, plus European-style fruit cobblers, turnovers, and genuine pretzels. If you're dining in, you can get sandwiches, salads, or pizzas. The salmon burger is a delicious alternative to a beef burger, and the pizzas are crisp and chewy. Or try one of the German sausage sandwiches, which feature long, skinny sausages served on a little round bun. The menu offers a variety of choices for vegetarians and decidedly different breakfast specialties: Try the cheese plate of fresh-baked bread, sliced cheese, herb/cheese spread, and fruit. And don't forget your coffee; you can choose from varieties that include Silke's Old World Blend, designed to taste German! To ease the conscience while you eat, know that Silke goes out of her way to use organic and local ingredients and that she donates leftovers to charity. Silke's is located just north of town inside an old tobacco warehouse.

Clarksville's favorite brewpub, the **Blackhorse Pub and Brewery** (132 Franklin St., 931/552-3726, www.theblackhorsepub.net, 11am-midnight daily, $7-19) has good beer, of course. But locals swear by the pizza, steak sandwiches, and other pub fare. The restaurant is nestled in the historic downtown area.

INFORMATION AND SERVICES

Clarksville and Montgomery County operate a tourist information center near exit 4 off I-24 north of Clarksville. The center is open 8am-5pm daily during the summer and 8am-4pm in winter. Call it at 931/553-8467. You can also pick up brochures and maps of Clarksville at the Customs House Museum and at RiverWalk.

The **Clarksville–Montgomery County Public Library** (Montogmery County Veterans Plaza, 350 Pageant Ln., 931/648-8826, 9am-8pm Mon.-Thurs., 9am-6pm Fri.-Sat., 1pm-5pm Sun.) has free public Internet access.

Clarksville's ***Leaf-Chronicle,*** one of the oldest newspapers in Tennessee, is published daily. Its name reflects the prominence of tobacco during Clarksville's earlier years.

AROUND CLARKSVILLE

Cross Plains

Tiny **Cross Plains** (pop. 1,714) might just look like a blip on the map en route to Nashville. But it is worth taking a detour I-65 at exit 112 for at least one reason: **Thomas Drugs** (7802 state highway 25, 615-654-3877, thomasdrugs.net, Mon.-Fri. 10am -2 pm). Inside this traditional drugstore is an old-fashioned 1930's soda fountain. The grill is open on weekdays and is packed with locals enjoying classic sandwiches and salads. The real attraction is a salty lemonade which is the best $1.59 you'll spend, regardless of the season. The town has several antique shops if you want a post-lemonade stroll.

Port Royal State Historic Park

One of the earliest settlements in West Tennessee was at **Port Royal** (3300 Old Clarksville Hwy., Adams, 931/358-9696, www.tn.gov/environment/parks/PortRoyal, 8am-sunset daily), along the Red River, about 15 miles west of Clarksville. The town was settled in 1782 and incorporated in 1797. Set along an old Native American trail that later became a major stagecoach route, Port Royal was a waypoint for travelers of all kinds.

In the 1830s, hundreds of Cherokee who were forcibly removed from their lands in Tennessee, North Carolina, and Georgia traveled through Port Royal on their way to Oklahoma. Diaries of soldiers who traveled with the displaced Cherokee say that some groups remained camped at Port Royal for a day or two to grind corn and rest before they left Tennessee.

Port Royal became a state historic park in 1977 and was later designated one of five sites in Tennessee along the National Trail of Tears Historic Trail.

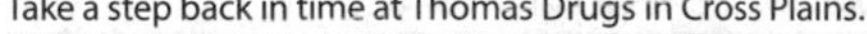

Take a step back in time at Thomas Drugs in Cross Plains.

Sadly, there is nothing on display regarding the Cherokee displacement, except for what they can conjure up in their imaginations while strolling along the banks of the Red River. There are a few picnic tables and a parking area. The park closes at sundown.

Adams

A picturesque rural town, Adams is located about 30 miles west of Clarksville, along the Red River. The town isn't famous for much, but it is known as the home of the Bell Witch, a spooky specter that captivated the imaginations of Tennesseans in this neck of the woods around the turn of the 19th century. According to lore, the witch haunted the Bell family after they moved to Adams from North Carolina. The Bell Witch was never visible, but it's believed to have thrown objects, spoken, pulled hair, yelled, and generally behaved very badly. Hearing stories of the witch, Andrew Jackson and some friends came up from Nashville to combat the terror, only to give up after suffering a night of the witch's inhospitable treatment.

You can revel in tales of the Bell Witch at the **Bell Witch Cave** (430 Keysburg Rd., 615/696-3055, www.bellwitchcave.com, 10am-5pm Wed.-Mon. June-Aug., weekends only May, Sept., and Oct., $12, with a 2-person minimum per tour). Here you can tour a cave that was on the Bell property, as well as tour a replica of the Bell log home. The cave is closed November-April.

Historic Collinsville

Proprietors JoAnn and Glen Weakley have re-created the old settlement of Collinsville about 15 miles south of Clarksville in lovely rural countryside. **Historic Collinsville** (4711 Weakley Rd., 931/648-9141, www.historiccollinsville.com, 1pm-5pm Thurs.-Sun. May 15-Nov. 15, $5, children under five free) includes a restored schoolhouse, log cabin, dogtrot house, and other buildings that would have been seen in the period 1830-1870. There is also a "wildlife center," with a number of stuffed wild animals, including wildcats, owls, and deer.

Fort Campbell

In February 1942, during World War II, construction began on Camp Campbell, which came to be a training ground for the 12th, 14th, and 20th Armored Divisions, and headquarters of the IV Armored Corps and the 26th Infantry Division. In 1950, the camp was redesignated Fort Campbell and became a permanent base.

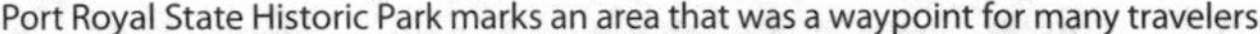
Port Royal State Historic Park marks an area that was a waypoint for many travelers.

Over the years, Fort Campbell soldiers have been deployed to many parts of the world and in every war since World War II. The fort is home to more than 30,000 soldiers and 10,500 military family members; 4,300 civilian employees work there. An additional 46,000 military family members live off the base, in the Clarksville area. The presence of the military base has a major economic and social impact on Clarksville and the surrounding area. For example, the median age of Clarksville is 32 to the statewide average of 36.

Visit the **Don F. Pratt Memorial Museum** (Bldg. 5702, Tennessee Ave., 270/798-3215, 9:30am-4:30pm, Mon.-Sat., free), which traces the history of the Screaming Eagles from World War II to Operation Iraqi Freedom. The museum also includes the history of Fort Campbell, from its initial survey as Camp Campbell in 1941 to the present day. The museum displays more than 50 uniformed figures and nine historical aircrafts, plus military vehicles and artillery pieces.

Along the Cumberland

Northeast of Nashville, the **Cumberland River** winds emphatically like holiday wrapping ribbon. It is a calm river, though, and in places impoundment has created "lakes": Old Hickory Lake close to Nashville, Cordell Hull Lake in Jackson County, and Dale Hollow Lake along the Kentucky border.

The Nashville suburbs absorb a little more of this quiet countryside every year. Towns like Hendersonville and Gallatin are within the city commuters' range. Out in the countryside, historic homes and the charm of an almost-forgotten resort town are the main attractions.

This part of Tennessee was hit by powerful tornadoes in February 2008. Macon and Sumner Counties were the most badly affected, with more than two dozen fatalities and widespread damage.

OLD HICKORY

Old Hickory was once a village distinct from Nashville, but now this enclave east of the city is part of the city. Old Hickory is named for Andrew Jackson, whose home, the Hermitage, is located nearby. The town has an interesting history. It was founded in 1918 by DuPont as a company town for a smokeless gunpowder plant being built nearby. Hundreds of "temporary homes" were constructed for workers using materials made with asbestos. The "permanent village" consisted of more substantial buildings for managers.

The gunpowder plant was short-lived. By 1919 it had closed, and workers moved away. In 1923, however, DuPont returned and retooled the factory into one that would make rayon. The asbestos-riddled houses were torn down, but the permanent village, called Rayon City, was restored and once again became homes for people employed at the factory. In 1946, DuPont sold the village, and Rayon City ceased operating as a company town. Many of the old-style company homes are still standing, however. There are a few small restaurants and bars, including biker bar **Dilligaf's Bar** (333 Swinging Bridge Rd.).

★ The Hermitage

Andrew Jackson's plantation and home, 16 miles east of Nashville, is the area's best historical tourist attraction. The **Hermitage** (4580 Rachel's Ln., 615/889-2941, www.thehermitage.com, 9am-5pm daily, adults $20, seniors $17, students 13-18 $15, children 9-12 $10, active military and children 5 and under free) is where Jackson retired following his two terms as president of the United States, and it is where he and his beloved wife, Rachel, are buried.

Jackson bought the property in 1809; he and Rachel initially lived in a rustic log cabin, which has since been restored. Jackson first named the home and property Rural Retreat, and later he chose the more poetic name the Hermitage. Jackson ran a successful cotton plantation on the property, owning as many as 150 slaves. In 1819, he and Rachel started construction of what is now the mansion. They moved in in 1821.

In 1831, two years after he became the nation's seventh president, Jackson expanded the mansion so it was more suitable for presidential entertaining. While Jackson was in Washington, his adopted son, Andrew Jackson Jr., managed the property, and when a chimney fire damaged the house in 1834, Jackson Jr. and his wife, Sarah, saw to its restoration. At the end of Jackson's second term in office in 1837, he retired to the Hermitage and lived here happily until his death in 1845.

Following President Jackson's death, the Hermitage remained in family hands until 1853, when it was sold to the State of Tennessee to pay off the family's debts. It opened as a museum in 1889 and was restored largely due to the persistence of the Ladies Hermitage Association. Because the property never left family hands before it was sold to the state, many of the furnishings are original, and even the wallpaper in several rooms dates back to the years when Andrew Jackson called it home.

One major strength of the present-day Hermitage tour and museum is that it focuses not only on Jackson and the construction and decoration of the mansion, but also the African American slaves who worked at the Hermitage plantation, and makes no effort to gloss over some of Jackson's less-favorable legacies. Curators and archaeologists have studied the Hermitage to learn about the hundreds of men and women who made the Hermitage profitable and successful for so many years. The tour of the grounds takes visitors to Alfred's Cabin, a slave cabin occupied until 1901 by former Hermitage slave Alfred Jackson. You also learn about the agriculture that took place on the Hermitage and can see cotton being cultivated during the summer months. To learn even more about the Hermitage's slaves, take an add-on wagon tour, offered April-October ($10).

Visitors to the Hermitage begin with a video about Andrew Jackson and the Hermitage, and can continue on to a museum. Even if you are not typically an audio-tour-type person, consider the one of the grounds, which includes a kids' version narrated by Jackson's pet parrot. Guided tours are offered of the mansion. You wind up in the gift shop and café. Plan on spending at least three hours here to make the most of your visit. Try to come when the weather is good.

Old Hickory Lake

The Old Hickory Dam was built in 1952 and became operational in 1957. At normal water levels, the lake is 22,500 acres.

Old Hickory is well within Nashville's sprawl zone, and private development along the lakeshore is extensive. The Army Corps of Engineers manages the lake, including its public recreation areas.

There are nearly a dozen different day-use facilities along Old Hickory Lake. The following have covered picnic facilities, swimming beaches, and restrooms: Rockland and Lock 3 in Hendersonville, Cedar Creek in Mount Juliet, Old Hickory Beach in Old Hickory, and Laguardo in Laguardo. Old Hickory is popular with kayakers, stand-up paddlers, boaters, and other water lovers.

Located on the shore of **Old Hickory Lake, Bledsoe Creek State Park** (400 Zieglers Fort Rd., Gallatin, 615/452-3706, www.tn.gov/environment/parks/BledsoeCreek) has six miles of hiking trails, 57 campsites, a boat ramp, and day-use facilities. Bledsoe Creek is located just east of the city of Gallatin.

HENDERSONVILLE

A speck of a town that has become an upscale suburb of Nashville, **Hendersonville** has a few things going for it: It is home to some of country music's most famous names, it is near Old Hickory Lake, and it is the locale of

Trinity Music City U.S.A., a major religious broadcasting attraction.

Trinity Music City U.S.A. (1 Music Village Blvd., 615/822-0093, trinitymusiccity.com, 10am-5pm Tues.-Sat., free) owes its existence to Conway Twitty, a rock and country musician who opened his house in Hendersonville to fans and called it Twitty City. After Twitty died in 1993, the property sold to Trinity Broadcasting Network (TBN), which retooled the idea and came out with its own "City" destination.

Nationally televised programs are produced at the Hendersonville TBN campus, and visitors can sit in on weekly church services on Friday nights and Sunday afternoons, or a live taping on Monday 7pm-9pm. Special religious films are screened throughout the day, and there are exhibits about TBN and Trinity City. Special events are held year-round, and visitors are welcome at other times to tour the grounds and browse the gift shop.

Another star long associated with Hendersonville is Johnny Cash, and his second wife, June Carter Cash. The couple's home on Old Hickory Lake in Hendersonville was where they lived for 35 years. The Cashes both died in 2003, and in 2006, former Bee Gee Barry Gibb bought the property for $2.3 million. The home was destroyed by fire in 2007. A small cabin used by June and Johnny, and later restored by their son, John Carter Cash, survived, but it is not open to the public. A new Johnny Cash museum, with some of their artifacts, is in the works for Nashville.

CASTALIAN SPRINGS

This small town a few miles east of Gallatin was one of the towns devastated by tornadoes in 2008. Twisters destroyed entire houses and tossed mobile homes around like they were toys. The town made headlines when rescuers found alive an 11-month-old boy who had been tossed some 150 yards.

Previously, what put **Castalian Springs** on the map were its mineral springs and two nearby historic homes. The Castalian Springs Archaeological Project is researching the extent of a prehistoric Native American town on this location dating to AD 1000-1400.

Cragfont

General James Winchester was one of those men who seems to have been just about everywhere. He fought in the American Revolution and the War of 1812, was a Middle Tennessee pioneer, and was one of the founders of Memphis. Winchester's home, Historic **Cragfont Mansion** (200 Cragfont Rd., 615/542-7070, historiccragfont.org, 10am-5pm Tues.-Sat., 1pm-5pm Sun. Apr. 15-Nov. 1, and by appointment, adults $5, seniors $4, children 6-12 $3) is now a Tennessee Historic Site.

Construction on Cragfont started in 1798 and finished four years later. It was the finest mansion of the Tennessee frontier—appropriate for a man of Winchester's stature. Cragfont was so named because it stood on a rocky bluff with a spring at its base. The home was built in the late Georgian style. Today it is furnished with Federal-period antiques.

Following his involvement in the War of 1812, Winchester moved to Cragfont full-time, where he farmed and speculated in land. Winchester died in 1826, but his wife, Susan Black Winchester, lived here until 1862. The property was purchased by the Tennessee Historical Commission in 1958.

CARTHAGE

Carthage, the seat of Smith County, is a river town. The first steamship traveled here from Nashville in 1829, and the trade persisted even into the 20th century, when the first good paved roads were constructed through the rugged countryside.

Landmarks in this quiet town include the **Cordell Hull Bridge,** built in 1936 and noteworthy for its intricate steel grid work, and the **Smith County Courthouse,** a Second Empire-style structure built in 1875. About five miles outside of town is the **Cordell Hull Lock and Dam.**

The **Smith County Heritage Museum** (3rd Ave. N., 615/735-1104, 10am-2pm Wed.,

Old Hickory

Andrew Jackson, the seventh president of the United States, was one of the most important American political figures of the first half of the 19th century. His impact was so great that we now refer to his era as the Age of Jackson and his ideology as Jacksonian Democracy.

Jackson was born in 1767 on the American frontier in South Carolina. His father, an immigrant from Northern Ireland, died before Jackson was born. Jackson's two brothers, Hugh and Robert, died during the Revolutionary War. His mother, Elizabeth, died of smallpox in 1781. Jackson was 14 years old and alone in the world.

Remarkably, Jackson not only survived; he flourished. In 1784, he moved to Salisbury, North Carolina, where he studied law. In 1787 he became a licensed lawyer and moved west to Tennessee. In 1788, he was appointed the district attorney for the Mero District, now Middle Tennessee.

In Nashville, Jackson met Rachel Donelson, the daughter of John Donelson, one of the founding fathers of Nashville. Jackson fell in love with Rachel, and in 1791 they were married. Later, when they learned that Rachel's previous, unhappy marriage to Lewis Robards of Kentucky was not legally dissolved, Andrew Jackson remarried Rachel in 1794. The Jacksons set about to establish a home and livelihood. Jackson practiced law, speculated in land, and dabbled in politics. The couple bought farmland in Davidson County, where they built the Hermitage, which would be the Jacksons' home for the rest of their lives. The couple adopted a nephew, who was known as Andrew Jackson Jr., and reared several Indian orphans.

By 1798, Jackson was a circuit-riding judge on the Tennessee Superior Court, but he also developed a reputation for resolving his own conflicts through violence. He brawled with a set of brothers, killed a man in a duel, caned another, and ran a sword through a third. In 1803, he quarreled publicly with governor John Sevier and nearly dueled him as well.

In 1802, Jackson was elected major general of the Tennessee militia, and with the outbreak of war in 1812, his leadership was required. Jackson earned the nickname "Old Hickory" in 1812 when he disobeyed orders and refused to dismiss his Tennessee soldiers in Natchez, Mississippi, marching them back to Tennessee under great hardship instead. He earned national fame three years later when he marched his men from Florida to New Orleans, where he resoundingly defeated

Fri.-Sat., free) houses historical exhibits, including Civil War, steamboat, and farm memorabilia.

Carthage is best known in some circles as the hometown of former U.S. vice president Al Gore. While it may seem dated, **Markham's Department Store** (222 Main St. N., 615/735-0184) has a special "Gore-Lieberman Store," where campaign memorabilia from the historic 2000 presidential election is on sale. You can even buy a coffee cup that celebrates a Gore victory in 2000 (this is the area where the Gores lived for decades, after all). The Gore family farm is located a few miles outside Carthage along U.S. 70. It's closed to the public.

CORDELL HULL LAKE

The 72 miles of the Cumberland River impounded by the Cordell Hull Dam are popular areas for recreation. Operated by the U.S. Army Corps of Engineers, Cordell Hull Lake's recreation areas consist of two large campgrounds and numerous day-use areas with swimming beaches, picnic facilities, and boat ramps.

Cordell Hull Lock and Dam

The lock and dam that impounds the river was built between 1963 and 1973. You can see the dam from the Tater Knob overlook, located about four miles outside of Carthage, off State Route 263. It is an impressive vista.

You can learn more about the science of hydroelectric power and the natural history of the Cumberland River at the **Cordell Hull Lake Visitors Center** (71 Corps Ln., 615/735-1034, www.lrn.usace.army.mil/op/COR/rec, 9am-3pm Mon.-Fri. in the British. The American public was so pleased with their new war hero that they did not mind when they learned the British had actually surrendered two weeks earlier. Neither did they mind some of his tactics: military executions, imposition of martial law, suspension of habeas corpus, and defiance of a federal court order.

In the succeeding years, Jackson fought battles with Native American tribes and negotiated land treaties with them. By 1821, he quit his post as major general and came home to the Hermitage for a short retirement.

In 1822, the Tennessee state legislature nominated Jackson for U.S. president, and his nomination was seconded by other states. In the 1824 contest, Jackson received more votes than any other contender in the crowded field. But when the U.S. House of Representatives gave the presidency to John Quincy Adams, Jackson called the decision a "corrupt bargain" that violated the will of the voters. His 1828 presidential campaign had begun.

The 1828 campaign was spirited and dirty, and later historians would point to this as a turning point in American elections. Opponents found seemingly countless stories of Jackson's indiscretions. Specifically, they brought up his marriage to Rachel before her previous marriage was dissolved. When Rachel Jackson died on December 22nd, 1828, Jackson accused his opponents of hastening her death by slander. He never remarried and is buried next to his wife at The Hermitage.

During his two terms as president, Jackson enraged his opponents and delighted supporters. He took unprecedented actions in the name of reform, including several controversial banking decisions. He believed in a strong federal government and stood in the way of state nullification of federal laws. By the end of his eight years in the White House, Jackson was known by his opponents as "King Andrew," while his supporters still saw him as a spokesman of the common man.

Jackson, who never remarried, spent the remaining years of his life at the Hermitage, where he entertained guests, helped to manage the farm, and dispensed advice to politicians. His health declined, though, and in 1845, at age 78, he died and was buried in the Hermitage garden next to his beloved Rachel.

warm-weather months, free), located adjacent to the dam off State Route 263 east of Carthage.

The half-mile **Turkey Creek Nature Trail** departs from the visitors center.

Defeated Creek Park attracts day-trippers and campers alike. Defeated Creek was named by early settler John Peyton after his party was defeated by a Native American attack when Peyton's party had camped along the creek. (The nearby town, **Difficult,** was named by the same party after they made the difficult trek back home after the attack.)

Chief among the attractions is a lovely six-mile hiking trail from the Tater Knob overlook to the Defeated Creek Campground and recreation area.

Another hike, the **Bearwaller Gap Trail** follows the lakeshore and is named after bear "wallers," cool depressions where black bears once came to wallow. Today, there are no black bears in these hills. There's also a marina with full facilities for boaters (160 Marina Dr., 615/774-3131, www.defeatedcreekmarina.com) and a sandy beach and the **Bear Wheels Mountain Bike Trail** trailhead.

The marina at Defeated Creek offers powerboat rentals for $175-225 per day, with a $100 deposit. Paddleboats are also available for $15 for two hours.

Want to stay longer than just for a hike, bike ride, or boat ride? The 155-site Defeated Creek Campground (615/774-3141, $3 per car of campers, open Mar.-Oct.) can accommodate tents and RVs; it has bathhouses with showers, a playground, and laundry. There is a backcountry campsite for hikers about halfway, at the Two Prong camping area.

Cordell Hull's second campground, **Salt Lick,** is a 150-site campground. It also has a swim beach, playground, water and electrical hookups, dump stations, laundry, and a shower house.

Two more day-use areas have picnic facilities and public swimming beaches. **Wartrace Creek** is located near the town of Gladdice, and **Roaring River** is located near Gainesboro.

RED BOILING SPRINGS

This onetime resort town is still welcoming visitors. **Red Boiling Springs** had as many as eight different hotels during its heyday from 1890 to 1930, when thousands of people traveled by train and horse-drawn wagon to "take the waters" at the town's mineral springs.

The atmosphere in the holiday town was relaxed but also a tad refined. Tourists spent their days enjoying the cool air, playing croquet on the lawn, taking walks, and soaking in mineral baths. There was live music and good conversation, and mealtimes were a celebration.

Times have changed in Red Boiling Springs, but not as much as in some Tennessee towns. The Salt Lick Creek flows through the city park and is a lovely place to stroll or even wade. Three hotels keep up the town's tradition, and each offers a bona fide welcome to its guests.

If old-time atmosphere is not your thing, perhaps **Cyclemo's Motorcycle Museum** (319 E. Main St., 615/699-5049, www.cyclemos.com, 10am-4pm Sat.-Sun., $5) is. Here you can see restored antique motorcycles and bike memorabilia, and buy biker clothing and other goods. There are plans in the works for a full restoration center that would specialize in fixing up old bikes. The business hopes to attract bikers who come to the area for the winding country roads so good for motorcycles. The museum has extended hours in the summertime.

About two miles west of Red Boiling Springs along Highway 52 is the turnoff for **Long Hungry Creek Farm** (Long Hungry Rd., 615/699-2493, www.barefootfarmer.com), one of Tennessee's largest and most established organic and biodynamic farms. Farmer Jeff Poppen has also written and taught extensively on the subject of farming. Visitors are welcome but ought to call in advance. The farm hosts special events and workshops during the year.

SHOPPING

You can order custom-made wooden chairs from **Newberry and Sons Chairs** (1593 Jennings Creek Rd., 615/699-3755, www.newberryandsonschairs.com). Located in the countryside along State Route 56 south of Red Boiling Springs, the Newberry workshop is a testament to doing things the old-fashioned way. Footstools, rocking chairs, corner chairs, and traditional ladder-back dining chairs are among the iconic styles available. Call in advance if you would like to visit the workshop.

ACCOMMODATIONS

The **Donoho Hotel** (500 Main St., 615/699-3141, www.thedonoho.com, $89-120, with breakfast) first opened in 1914 and was renovated in 2001. Guest rooms open onto a generous wraparound porch, where rocking chairs invite you to sit a spell and relax. Rooms have an antique feel but modern amenities, including central air and heating, and new bathrooms. Guests can relax in the parlor or lobby, where there are board games and memorabilia from the hotel's early days. Or walk to the nearby Salt Lick Creek. As part of the 2001 renovations, the owners built an entertainment hall that can be used for meetings, performances, or conferences.

Located on the outskirts of town atop a quiet hill, **The Thomas House** (520 E. Main St., 615/699-3006, www.thomashousehotel.com, $110-140, includes breakfast) is a brick-and-lumber structure dating to the 1890s. Its guest rooms are furnished with antiques, and each is decorated with its own individual flair. There is also a swimming pool. The Thomas House stages frequent dinner theater. Meal plans are available for about $13.50 per person per meal. The hotel offers spooky ghost hunts on weekends in October.

Armour's Red Boiling Springs Hotel (321 E. Main St., 615/699-2180, www.armourshotel.com, $85-129) is the only hotel with a working mineral bath on the property. Guests (and nonguests) can enjoy a massage, a stint in the steam room, and a soak in the town's long-revered mineral waters. Built in 1924, Armour's has 16 rooms, including two suites. It was the first brick hotel in Red Boiling Springs, and so it was known for several years as Smith's Brick Hotel, after John Smith, the first owner. Later the hotel was called the Counts Hotel. All rooms have private baths, and each is decorated just a little bit differently. Breakfast is included in the room rate; dinner is available family-style for $14 per person, with reservations. Perhaps the greatest attraction is the wide, open porch that looks out on the hotel's lush green lawn. It is a scene that beckons you to stop and relax.

FOOD

Red Boiling Springs' three hotels serve breakfast and dinner daily; reservations are recommended. You can also drive about seven miles east along Highway 52 to the **Hermitage Hill Restaurant** (16150 Hwy. 52, 615/699-3919, daily 6am-8pm daily, $5-15). This is a traditional country-cooking restaurant, with full breakfast offerings, steak, burgers, grilled sandwiches, and country ham. The lunch buffet is served daily, plus a dinner buffet on Friday and Saturday nights.

Big Ed's BBQ (111 Whitley Hollow Rd., 615/699-3288, 8am-8pm Wed.-Sat., $3-6) serves plates of pork and beef barbecue, as well as sandwiches, burgers, and classic sides such as coleslaw and baked beans.

INFORMATION

You can get information about Red Boiling Springs and other towns in Macon County from the **Macon County Chamber of Commerce** (208 Church St., Lafayette, 615/666-5885, www.maconcountytn.com).

West of Nashville

The countryside that lies south of Clarksville, west of Nashville, and north of Columbia is the most rural and sparsely populated in Middle Tennessee. It is ideal for back-roads driving. There are excellent state parks and a few notable pit stops, such as Montgomery Bell State Park and an old-fashioned tearoom at Bon Aqua.

The Duck River, the longest river totally contained in Tennessee, flows from the east toward Hickman and Perry Counties, eventually emptying into the Tennessee River near Johnsonville. The Buffalo River, a tributary of the Duck and the largest unimpounded river in Middle Tennessee, flows westward through Wayne and Lawrence Counties before turning northward through Perry County. Both rivers contribute natural beauty and recreational opportunities to the area.

HARPETH RIVER STATE PARK

Harpeth River State Park (615/952-2009) follows the Harpeth River as it winds through parts of Dickson County near the towns of Bell Town, Kingston Springs, and Pegram. This is a do-it-yourself state park. Bring a map (available at tnstateparks.com) with you, since there are few signs and even fewer people to assist you should you need it.

The **Narrows of the Harpeth,** located north of Highway 70, is where the river nearly bends back onto itself. Here iron magnate Montgomery Bell built the Pattison Forge, which harnessed the power of the river to manufacture a wide range of iron implements. Slaves built the forge between 1818 and 1820, and it remains a marvel of engineering and labor. The tunnel that brought water power to

Minnie Pearl's Hometown

Centerville, in Hickman County, is best known as the hometown of Minnie Pearl. What's less well known is that the first lady of country comedy was not a real person, but rather a character created and portrayed by actress and comedian **Sarah Ophelia Colley** (1912-1996).

Colley, born in 1912 and raised in Centerville, attended Nashville's prestigious Ward-Belmont College, then a finishing school for women, where she majored in expression. In 1934, Colley joined a theater group for women that traveled throughout the South to organize local dramatic productions. It was in the course of these journeys that Colley experienced the Southern culture that she would later portray through her alter ego, Minnie Pearl. Minnie Pearl, to the extent that she was real at all, was a kind country woman from Sand Mountain, Alabama, who housed Colley when she was stuck in town with no lodging. This lady's comic stories, impeccable timing, and outlook on life left an impression on young Colley, who began performing as Minnie Pearl soon after.

Colley's big break came in 1939 when a Centerville banker invited Colley to perform at a Lions Club event. WSM radio program director Harry Stone spotted her, and the rest is history. "Minnie Pearl" performed on the Grand Ole Opry for more than 50 years. Generations of Americans have heard her greeting, "Howdee! I'm just so proud to be here," and witnessed her frilly dresses and outlandish hats (with the price tag hanging over the brim).

Offstage, Colley married Air Army Corps pilot Capt. Henry Cannon and worked for a number of charities. Colley had a foot in both of Nashville's worlds: its hillbilly opry and the Athens of the South. She was uniquely able to shuttle between these two very different universes.

Minnie Pearl's legacy is on display at the **Grinder's Switch Center** (405 W. Public Sq., Centerville, 931/729-5774). Operated by the local chamber of commerce, the center houses Minnie Pearl memorabilia and recordings of the famous lady of country comedy.

the forge was 300 feet long, 15 feet wide, and 6 feet high. When the river is low, visitors can wade into the tunnel and look at it.

Recreation

Canoeing, kayaking, stand-up paddleboarding, and fishing are popular along the river. Canoe accesses are found at the U.S. 100 bridge southwest of Nashville, the 1862 Newsom's Mill ruins, and at the McCrory Lane Bridge at Hidden Lake. Downstream, the Narrows of the Harpeth provides upstream and downstream access, the Bell's Bend five-mile float, and a unique 0.25-mile portage. Swimming is also permitted, but there are no lifeguards.

Three different trails originate at a common trailhead at the Narrows. The trails include a two-mile bluff overlook trail, a 0.5-mile trail leading to the site of Pattison Forge, and a 0.5-mile spur that connects the canoe launch to the canoe take-out.

At Gossett Tract, a few miles downriver from the narrows, there are two hiking trails. A one-mile trail circles a meadow, and another one-mile trail winds along the river, providing a glimpse of Mound Bottom Archaeological Site. There are also picnic tables and grills here.

At Hidden Lake, near the town of Pegram, a one-mile trail meanders around and through a wildflower meadow. Another trail offers a 0.25-mile hike through the forest and along majestic bluffs to a small lake with a one-mile spur trail ascending to the top of a ridge where the remains of an old marble dance floor are all that are left of a 1940s resort.

MONTGOMERY BELL STATE PARK

One of Tennessee's resort parks, **Montgomery Bell State Park** (1020 Jackson Hill Rd., 615/797-9052, tnstateparks.com/parks/about/montgomery-bell) has a great deal to offer visitors. Named for iron magnate Montgomery Bell, who established the iron ore industry in this part of Tennessee, the 3,842-acre park is set amid rolling hills. It was one of three parks built in Tennessee by the federal government in the 1930s. Young men in the Civilian Conservation Corps built the original structures at Montgomery Bell, including the stone dams that impound Lakes Woodhaven and Acorn. In more recent years, the park inn and golf course were built as Montgomery Bell became one of the state's resort parks.

The hardwood forest that was cut to clear farmland and to produce charcoal for the iron furnaces has given way to second-growth forest and a habitat for fox, squirrel, raccoon, opossum, deer, and a wide variety of birds and wildflowers.

The park's proximity to Nashville makes it quite popular for weekend retreats, conferences, and family getaways.

Golf

Montgomery Bell's **Frank G. Clement Golf Course** (615/797-2578) is a par 72 18-hole course. Built in 1973 and redesigned by Gary Roger Baird in 1988, the course is considered one of the top public courses in the state. The entire course is heavily wooded, and you will often see wildlife, including deer and wild turkey.

Tee times are required; greens fees are $9-24. There is a pro shop with club and cart rentals.

Other Recreation

There are some 20 miles of dirt **mountain bike trails,** ranging from easy to difficult. No motorized vehicles are allowed, and bikers must not use hiking trails (and vice versa).

There are 19 miles of **hiking trails** in the park. The longest is 12 miles, and the shortest is less than a mile. There are three overnight shelters for backpackers. You can pick up detailed maps from the park office or at the inn. A short nature trail that departs from the park office is ideal for those with less grand ambitions.

You can rent paddle- and johnboats Memorial Day-Labor Day Monday-Saturday at **Lake Acorn,** a 17-acre lake in the park. Private boats are allowed on Lake Acorn September-April, or on Lake Woodhaven year-round. Outboard attached motors are not allowed; trolling motors are permitted. There is no boating permitted on Creech Hollow Lake, the third lake at Montgomery Bell.

Fishing is allowed in all three lakes. Bluegill, catfish, bass, and creel are some of the species that you will find. A valid Tennessee fishing permit is required; you must also adhere to seasonal limits.

There is a **swimming** beach on Lake Acorn, open Memorial Day-Labor Day. No lifeguards are on duty. There is also a swimming pool for inn and cabin guests.

Other recreational facilities include horseshoe pits, softball fields, basketball courts, playgrounds, and tennis courts.

Accommodations

Montgomery Bell has a 120-room, five-suite park inn, **The Inn at Montgomery Bell State Park** (120 Jackson Hill Rd., Burns, 615/797-3101 or 800/250-8613, rooms $74-98, suites $145-195). Rooms are equipped with two beds, telephones, television, and views of Acorn Lake. There are also conference and meeting facilities.

Camping

There are eight two-bedroom vacation cabins with kitchens, bathrooms, and modern amenities. They rent for $75 per night.

There are 40 tent sites ($11) and 75 RV campsites ($25) at the Montgomery Bell campground, which is set in a woodland along a creek.

One of the most distinctive features of Montgomery Bell State Park are the 47 1930s-era stone rustic cabins built by the Civilian Conservation Corps during the Depression. These cabins are available for group rental only. The beautiful buildings overlook Lake Woodhaven and are considered a historic site. Central bathroom and cooking facilities are provided.

Food

The restaurant at the **Park Inn and Conference Center** (1000 Hotel Ave., Burns, 615/797-3101, 7am-10am, 11am-2pm, and 5pm-8pm daily, $8) serves all three meals, with a seafood buffet Friday night and a steak buffet Saturday night.

DICKSON

Tennessee governor Frank Clemet was born in the old Halbrook Hotel in Dickson, the largest city, but not the county seat, of Dickson County. This old railroad town has a pleasant downtown district.

The **Renaissance Center** (855 Hwy. 46 S., 615/740-5600, www.fhu.edu/rcenter, 8am-9pm Mon.-Fri., 9am-9pm Sat.) is a unique multimedia, technological, and arts center. Designed to encourage interest in all types of artistic expression, the center has visual art exhibits, a theater, a planetarium, computer courses, and dance classes. The center is located a few miles south of downtown Dickson, heading toward the interstate.

House Blend (124 N. Main St., 615/446-3311, 6am-9pm Mon.-Thurs., 6am-10pm Fri., 9am-6pm Sat., www.houseblendonline.com, $4-6) has above-average sandwiches, salads, and a whole array of coffee drinks and fruit smoothies. The grown-up grilled cheese is perked up with some parmesan and feta cheeses, and the Mighty Mississippi is a delicate barbecue delight. You get to choose between tortilla chips and orange mini muffins to accompany your sandwich. The chefs will gladly prepare a half-salad, half-sandwich plate; just ask.

WHITE BLUFF

This small hamlet along Highway 70 is home to one of the region's most celebrated barbecue joints. **Carl's Perfect Pig** (4991 Hwy. 70 E., 615/797-4020, carlsperfectpig.com, 10:30am-6pm Wed.-Thurs., 10:30am-7pm Fri.-Sat., 10:30am-2:30pm Sun., $9) lives up to its name with tender and tangy pulled-pork shoulder and ribs. Chef Carl Teitloff also serves popular lunch specials and grilled foods, including fried catfish and burgers.

BON AQUA

Named for the healing waters that once drew people to this area, Bon Aqua is now little more than a huddle of homes and a small business district with some lovely hiking trails. Today, its chief attraction is the **Beacon Light Tea Room** (6343 Hwy. 100, 931/670-3880, www.beaconlighttearoom.com, 4pm-9pm Tues.-Fri., 8am-10pm Sat., 8am-9pm Sun., $7-17), a glorious stop for country ham, skillet-fried chicken, and Biblical wisdom reproduced on the walls, tables, and decor of this unique country eatery. The menu encourages you to "please give your order by number," and you'll be good enough to comply. The No. 4, half a skillet of fried chicken, two vegetables, biscuits, preserves, and gravy, will have you whistling all day long. Breakfast is available on weekends.

The 35-acre **John Noel Natural Area at Bon Aqua** (www.tn.gov/environment/na/natareas/johnnoel) includes the site of the old Bon Aqua Springs Hotel and Resort. There's room for three cars to park off Old Highway 46, where you can access a pretty, easy one-mile loop hiking trail. From here you can see the remains of the old springs pool, as well as some of Middle Tennessee's picturesque landscape.

Franklin

For much of its life, Franklin was just another small town in Tennessee. The bloody Battle of Franklin that took place in the fields surrounding the town on November 30, 1864, was probably the single most important event to take place in the town. Like other towns in the region, it took many years for Franklin to fully recover from the impact of the Civil War.

Starting in the 1960s, Franklin underwent a metamorphosis. Construction of I-65 near the town spurred economic development. Today, Franklin is a well-heeled bedroom community for Nashville professionals and music industry bigwigs. The city, whose population runs around 69,000, is the 10th largest in Tennessee and one of the wealthiest in the state. What sets Franklin apart from other small towns in the state is the efforts it has made to preserve and protect the historic downtown. Its location, only 20 miles from Nashville, is also a major plus.

Franklin's attractions are all within a few miles of the city center, except for Cool Springs Galleria, a mega mall located several miles out of town along the interstate.

SIGHTS

Historic Downtown

Franklin is one of the most picturesque small towns in Tennessee. Contained within four square blocks, downtown Franklin consists of leafy residential streets with old and carefully restored homes. The center of town is a traffic circle crowned by a simple white Confederate monument. The circle is fronted by banks, more offices, and the 1859 Williamson County courthouse.

The best way to explore downtown Franklin is on foot. Free parking is available along the streets or in two public garages, one on 2nd Avenue and one on 4th Avenue. Pick up a printed walking-tour guide from the visitors center on East Main Street, or download the free mobile app.

The walking tour takes you past 39 different buildings, including the **Hiram Masonic Lodge,** the oldest Masonic lodge in Tennessee, and also the building where Andrew Jackson in 1830 signed the treaty that led to the forced removal of thousands of Native Americans from Tennessee, Georgia, and other Southern states. You will also see the old city cemetery and the old **Franklin Post Office,** as well as lots of beautiful old houses and churches, all of which remain in use today. The walking tour is a good way to become familiar with the town and to appreciate the different types of architecture. It takes 1-2 hours to complete.

Guided walking tours of Franklin are offered by **Franklin on Foot** (615/400-3808, www.franklinonfoot.com). The Classic Franklin tour provides an overview of the history of the town and its buildings. The *Widow of the South* tour is combined with admission to the Carnton Plantation and is a must for lovers of that popular novel. Other tours include a children's tour and Haunted Franklin tour. Tours cost $5-18 per person. Private tours start at $140.

★ Franklin Theatre

The newest gem in historic downtown Franklin is the **Franklin Theatre** (419 Main St., 615/538-2076, www.franklintheatre.com, box office noon-5pm Mon., 11am-6pm Tues.-Sat.), a 1937 movie theater that had seen better days until it finally closed in 2007. In 2011, it reopened after an $8 million restoration, funded primarily by donations from locals through the efforts of the Heritage Foundation. The renovation is spot on, bringing the theater, including its striking outdoor marquee, back to its former glory. Lush carpeting, detailed wallpaper, comfortable seats—everything about the theater evokes moviegoing in a different era.

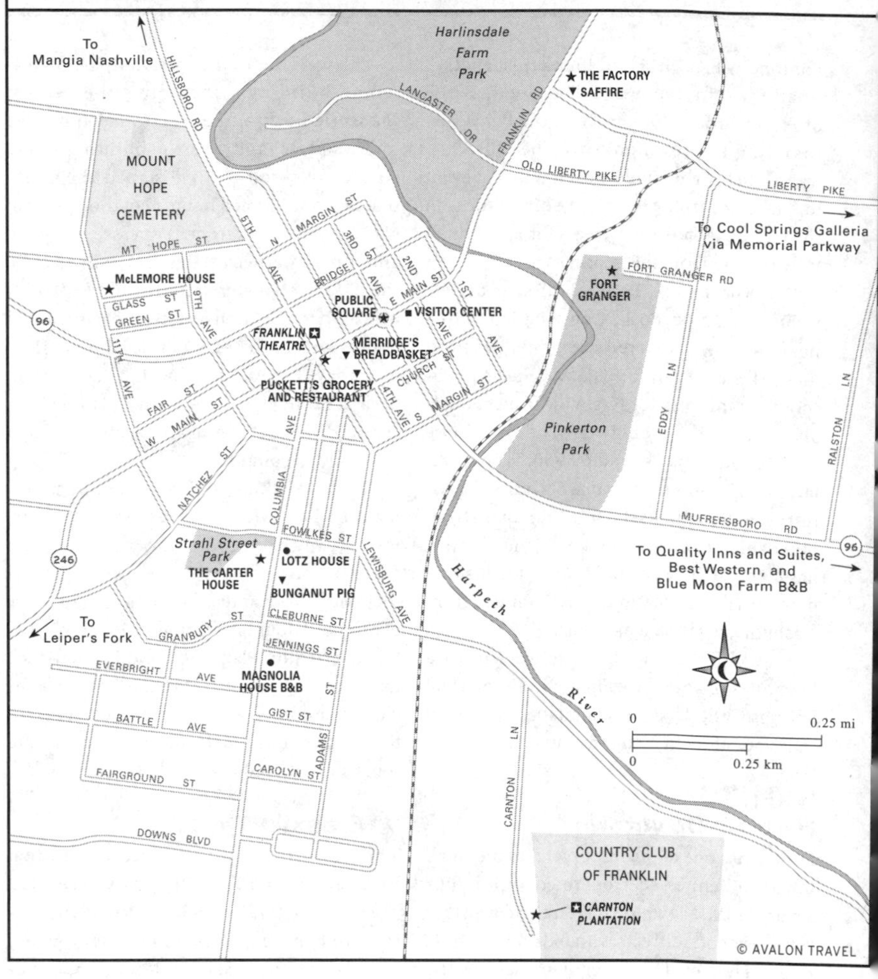

But the Franklin Theatre isn't stuck in the past. It has many modern amenities that make it a great place to have a night out, complete with a concession stand that serves beer, wine, and spirits, with a menu that delineates Jack Daniel's from bourbon and whiskey (you've gotta love a place that knows its audience). The Franklin Theatre hosts live concerts as well as films, ranging from black-and-white classics to recent releases.

McLemore House

Five generations of the McLemore family lived in the white clapboard home at the corner of Glass Street and 11th Avenue in downtown Franklin. **McLemore House** was built in 1880 by Harvey McLemore, a former slave and farmer. Inside, a small museum has been created that documents the story of African Americans in Williamson County.

McLemore House is open by appointment

only. Contact Mary Mills at 615/794-2270 or the convention and visitors bureau (615/591-8514) to arrange a tour; cost is $5.

★ Carnton Plantation

When Robert Hicks's novel *The Widow of the South* became a best seller in 2005, the staff at the Carnton Plantation (1345 Carnton Ln., 615/794-0903, www.carnton.org, 9am-5pm Mon.-Sat., noon-5pm Sun., adults $15, seniors $12, children 6-12 $8, children under 5 free) noticed an uptick in the number of visitors. The novel is a fictionalized account of Carrie McGavock and how her home, the Carnton Plantation, became a Confederate hospital during the Battle of Franklin in the Civil War (how fictionalized the account is is subject for discussion on the tours here).

The Carnton mansion was built in 1826 by Randal McGavock, a former Nashville mayor and prominent lawyer and businessman. Randal had died by the time of the Civil War, and it was his son, John, and John's wife, Carrie, who witnessed the bloody Battle of Franklin on November 30, 1864. Located behind the Confederate line, the Carnton Plantation became a hospital for hundreds of injured and dying Confederate soldiers. As late as six months after the battle, the McGavock home remained a refuge for recovering veterans.

In the years that followed the battle, the McGavocks raised money, donating much of it themselves, to construct a cemetery for the Confederate dead and donated two acres of land to the cause.

A new visitors center opened at Carnton in 2008, providing much-needed space for the museum and gift shop. Visitors to the Carnton Plantation can pay full price for a guided tour of the mansion and self-guided tour of the grounds, which include a smokehouse, slave house, and garden. You can also pay $5 for the self-guided tour of the grounds. There is no admission charged to visit the cemetery.

Packages include discounts if you want admission to nearby **Lotz House** (www.lotzhouse.com), the Carter House, and Carnton Plantation. It's a good choice for hard-core history buffs but perhaps too much Civil War lore for one day for the average visitor.

Fort Granger

An unsung attraction, Fort Granger is a lovely and interesting place to spend an hour or so. Built between 1862 and 1863 by Union forces, the earthen fort is set on a bluff overlooking

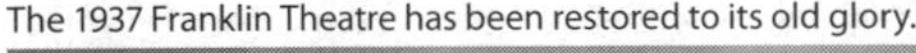
The 1937 Franklin Theatre has been restored to its old glory.

the Harpeth River just south of downtown Franklin. The fort was the largest fortification in the area built by Capt. W. E. Merrill during the Federal occupation of Franklin. It saw action twice in 1863 and also in 1864 during the Battle of Franklin.

Many features of the fort remain intact for today's visitors. You can walk around portions of the breastworks. The interior of the fort is now a grassy field, perfect for a summer picnic or game of catch. An overlook at one end of the fort provides an unmatched view of the surrounding countryside.

You can reach Fort Granger two ways. One is along a short but steep trail departing Pinkerton Park on Murfreesboro Road, east of town. Or you can drive straight to the fort by heading out of town on East Main Street. Turn right onto Liberty Pike, right onto Eddy Lane, and, finally, right again onto Fort Granger Drive.

The fort, which is maintained by the City of Franklin, is open during daylight hours only. While there is no office or visitors center at the fort, you may contact Franklin's parks department (615/794-2103) for more information.

The Carter House

Some of the fiercest fighting in the Battle of Franklin took place around the farm and house belonging to the Carter family on the outskirts of town. The family took refuge in the basement while Union and Confederate soldiers fought hand to hand right above them. Today, the **Carter House** (1140 Columbia Ave., 615/791-1861, www.battleoffranklintrust.org, 9am-5pm Mon.-Sat., noon-5pm Sun., $15) is the best place to come for a detailed examination of the battle and the profound human toll that it exacted on both sides.

You will see hundreds of bullet holes, which help to illustrate the ferocity of the fight. Guides describe some of the worst moments of the battle and bring to life a few of the people who fought it. The house also holds a museum of Civil War uniforms and memorabilia, including photographs and short biographies of many of the men who were killed in Franklin. There is also a video about the battle, which shows scenes from a reenactment.

If you can't get enough Civil War history, consider one of the packages that offer discounts on joint admission to nearby **Lotz House** (www.lotzhouse.com), the Carter House, and Carnton Plantation.

ENTERTAINMENT AND EVENTS

Live Music

Venues that sometimes offer live music include restaurants **Saffire** (The Factory, 230 Franklin Rd., Bldg. 11, 615/599-4995), **Puckett's Grocery and Restaurant** (120 4th Ave. S., 625/794-5527), and **The Bunganut Pig** (1143 Columbia Ave., 615/794-4777). The **Franklin Theatre** (419 Main St., 615/538-2076, www.franklintheatre.com) has an impressive concert schedule, typically with affordable ticket prices.

As great as the Grand Ole Opry is (and it *is* great), sometimes the music seems a little, well, dated. On Wednesday nights you can experience an Opry-style live radio show, but with more cutting-edge country, Americana, and bluegrass acts during **Music City Roots** (www.musiccityroots.com). This two-plus-hour multiple-act show includes live interview segments with the artists, on-the-air commercials, and an audience that often gets up and dances. Stay till the very end for the Loveless Jam, when all the night's performers cram on stage for one last song. The show takes place at the Factory in Franklin; tickets are just $10.

Theater

Franklin's community theater is **Pull-Tight Players** (112 2nd Ave. S., 615/791-5007 or 615/790-6782, www.pull-tight.com, tickets are $18 adults, $16 seniors, $12 children). Performing in an intimate theater in downtown Franklin, Pull-Tight Players put on about six productions each season, which runs

September-June. Productions include many classic stage favorites.

Cinemas

The restored **Franklin Theatre** (419 Main St., 615/538-2076, www.franklintheatre.com) shows classic black-and-white films as well as recent releases (although not first-run movies). Movie ticket prices are typically $5, and there are many kid-friendly flicks shown on the weekends.

Head to Cool Springs to find **Carmike Thoroughbred 20** (633 Frazier Dr., 615/778-0775), a 20-screen multiplex showing first-run movies.

Festivals and Events

SPRING

The city's biggest festival of the year is the **Main Street Festival** (615/591-8500, www.historicfranklin.com) during the last full weekend of April. Local arts and crafts are the major draw of this showcase, which also includes food, music, theater, and children's activities.

The town's Rotary Club organizes the annual **Franklin Rodeo** (www.franklinrodeo.com), a weeklong event in May that includes a Rodeo Parade, Miss Tennessee Rodeo pageant, and a Professional Rodeo Cowboys Association (PRCA)-sanctioned rodeo with steer wrestling and bronco and bull riding. It takes place at the Williamson County Ag Expo Park, and proceeds go to local service projects.

SUMMER

During the first full weekend of June you can join the Heritage Foundation on a **Town and Country Tour of Homes** (www.historicfranklin.com). Tours go to private and historic homes that are closed to the public during the rest of the year.

Franklin celebrates Independence Day with **Franklin on the Fourth** (www.tneventinfo.com/fr_4thofjuly.cfm), a patriotic family concert on the public square. The fireworks finale takes place near Mack Hatcher/Hillsboro Road.

During the last weekend in July the city celebrates **Bluegrass Along the Harpeth** (615/390-3588, www.bluegrassalongtheharpeth.com, free), a music festival featuring bluegrass, old-time string bands, and buck dancing.

The **Williamson County Fair** (www.williamsoncountyfair.org) starts on the first Friday in August and features agricultural exhibits, a midway, live entertainment, and competitions. It is bigger than the Tennessee State Fair that takes place in Nashville in September.

FALL

Re-enactors descend on Franklin for **Blue and Gray Days** (www.boft.org), two days of living history, including a Civil War soldiers' camp.

WINTER

The Carter House organizes a **holiday tour of homes** during the first full weekend of December. During the second full weekend of the month, the city of Franklin is transformed into a bustling English Victorian town at **Dickens of a Christmas.** There are costumed characters, carolers, artisans, strolling minstrels, and unique foods.

The **Middle Tennessee Civil War Show** has become a favorite destination of history buffs each December.

SHOPPING

In many respects, shopping is Franklin's greatest attraction. Trendy downtown shops, the unique environment of The Factory, and proximity to a major mall make this a destination for shoppers. It is also one of Tennessee's most popular antiques shopping destinations.

Antiques

Franklin declares itself "the new antiques capital of Tennessee." Indeed, antiquing is one of the most popular pursuits of Franklin's visitors, and at least two dozen antiques shops serve to quench the thirst for something old. The town's antiques district is huddled around the corner of Margin Street and 2nd Avenue. Here you'll find no fewer than six major antiques stores. Other shops are found along Main Street in the downtown shopping district.

The best place to start antiquing is the **Franklin Antique Mall** (251 2nd Ave. S., 615/790-8593, www.franklinantiquemall.com), located in the town's old icehouse. The mall is a maze of rooms, each with different goods on offer. Possibilities include books, dishware, quilts, furniture, knick-knacks, and housewares. You can also follow 5th Avenue about two blocks south of downtown to find **Country Charm Antique Mall** (301 Lewisburg Ave., 615/790-8998, countrycharmmall.com), whose three buildings house a vast array of furniture, quilts, glassware, china, and home decor.

Just outside the Franklin Antique Mall are at least five other antiques shops to roam through, including **J. J. Ashley's** (125 S. Margin St., 615/791-0011), which specializes in French and English country accessories, as well as European furniture. **Scarlett Scales Antiques** (212 S. Margin St., 615/791-4097, scarlettscales.com), located in a 1900s shotgun house, has American country furnishings, accessories, and architectural elements arriving daily.

Downtown

Retail is alive and well in Franklin's downtown. West Main Street is the epicenter of the shopping district, although you will find stores scattered around other parts of downtown as well. Home decor, classy antiques, trendy clothes, and specialty items like candles, tea, and gardening supplies are just a few of the things you'll find in downtown Franklin.

Most shops in downtown Franklin are open by 10am, and many stay open until the evening to catch late-afternoon visitors. You can easily navigate the downtown shopping district on foot, although you may need to stow your parcels in the car now and then.

Bink's Outfitters (421 Main St., 615/599-8777, www.binksoutfitters.com, 10am-9pm Mon.-Sat., 11am-7pm Sun.,) sells outdoor clothing and equipment. Go to **ENJOUE** (400 Main St., 615/599-8177) for funky fashions and trendy styles.

The city's best bookstore is **Landmark Booksellers** (114 E. Main St., 615/791-6400, 10am-5pm daily), found on the other side of the town square. It has a wide selection of used and new books, including many regional titles. It is friendly and welcoming, with fresh coffee for sale in the mornings.

Toys old and new are on sale at **Main Street Toy Co.** (412 Main St., 615/790-4869, 10am-6pm Mon.-Thurs., 10am-7pm Fri.-Sat., noon-5pm Sun.). For the best in paper, gift wrap, and stationery, go to **Rock Paper Scissors** (317 Main St., 615/791-0150, www.rockpaperscissor.com, 10am-6pm Mon.-Fri., 10am-5pm Sat.). **Heart and Hands** (418 Main St., 615/794-2537, www.heartandhandsonline.com, 10am-5pm Mon.-Sat., noon-5pm Sun.) is one of several area shops specializing in crafts and home decor.

The Factory

Franklin's most distinctive retail center is **The Factory** (230 Franklin Rd., 615/791-1777, www.factoryatfranklin.com). A 250,000-square-foot complex of 11 different old industrial buildings, The Factory once housed stove factories and a textile mill. In the mid-1990s, Calvin Lehew bought the dilapidated eyesore and began the lengthy process of restoring the buildings and converting them to a space for galleries, retail shops, restaurants, and other businesses.

Today, The Factory is a vibrant commercial center for the city of Franklin. It houses a refreshing array of local independent retailers, including galleries, salons, candy shops, and a pet boutique. **The Little Cottage** (615/794-1405) sells children's fashions.

There are also several studios and learning centers, including **South Gate Studio & Fine Art** (615/559-3660), which offers art classes. There are also talent agencies, a publishing company, and a tae kwon do academy.

In addition to retail and learning centers, The Factory has four restaurants, a fish market, and is home to the weekly **Music City Roots** (musiccityroots.com) Americana show.

Cool Springs Galleria

Cool Springs Galleria (1800 Galleria Blvd., Cool Springs, 615/771-2128, www.coolspringsgalleria.com) is a mall with 165 specialty stores, 5 major department stores, 20 restaurants, and a 500-seat food court. It is located a few miles north of Franklin, convenient to I-65. Shops include Zales, Wild Oats, Talbots, Pier 1, Pottery Barn, Macy's, JCPenney, and Eddie Bauer. The mall is found at exits 68B and 69 on I-65.

SPORTS AND RECREATION

Pinkerton Park (405 Murfreesboro Rd.), just southeast of town off Murfreesboro Road, is a pleasant city park. Walking trails, playgrounds, and picnic tables draw dozens of town residents, who come to exercise or simply relax. A short hiking trail takes you to Fort Granger, overlooking the city. You can also take the Sue Douglas Berry Memorial pedestrian bridge over the Harpeth River and walk the six blocks to the town square.

Jim Warren Park (705 Boyd Mill Ave., 615/794-2103) is a large public park with baseball and softball fields, tennis courts, covered picnic areas, and 2.5 miles of walking trails.

Harlinsdale Farm

One of the most famous Tennessee Walking Horse breeding farms became a public park in 2007. **Harlinsdale Farm** (239 Franklin Rd., 615/794-2103) was a famed Franklin landmark for many years, thanks to a very famous horse. Midnight Sun, a stallion, was a world champion Walking Horse in 1945 and 1946, and all subsequent champions can trace their ancestry to him.

In 2004, Franklin bought the 200-acre farm for $8 million, and three years later the first 60 acres opened as a public park. It is a pleasant place to walk or picnic. There are plans for a visitors center, an overlook, and extensive walking trails. For now, you can park, picnic, and look at the horses and the landscape.

Golf

Located a few miles southeast of Franklin, **Forrest Crossing Golf Course** (750 Riverview Dr., 615/794-9400, www.forrestcrossing.com) is an 18-hole par 72 golf course designed by Gary Roger Baird. Just shy of 7,000 yards, the course rating is 77.8, and the slope is 135.

There are more golf courses in Cool Springs, a few miles north of Franklin. **Vanderbilt Legends Club** (1500 Legends Club Ln., 615/791-8100, www.legendsclub.com) is a top-of-the-line golf club. There are two 18-hole courses at the club, as well as a complete array of club services, including a putting green and chipping green. Greens fees are $75-85 and include a cart. Lower rates are available after 3pm No blue jeans, T-shirts, or athletic shorts are allowed.

The **Fairways on Spencer Creek** (285 Spencer Creek Rd., 615/794-8223, www.fairwaysonspencercreek.net) is a nine-hole alternative. The course rating is 64.6, and the slope is 105. Greens fees are $16.

ACCOMMODATIONS

Franklin has two types of accommodations: cozy bed-and-breakfast inns and chain motels. The bed-and-breakfasts are located in downtown Franklin and the surrounding countryside. The chain motels are located around exit 65 off I-65, about two miles from the city center. The bed-and-breakfast accommodations are far more congruous with Franklin's charm than the interstate motels.

Under $100

Several chain motels surround the interstate near Franklin. Closest to town are the 89-room **Quality Inns and Suites** (1307 Murfreesboro Rd., 615/794-7591, $65-110) and the 142-room **Best Western Franklin Inn** (1308 Murfreesboro Rd., 615/790-0570,

$55-70). Both offer wireless Internet, free continental breakfast, and an outdoor pool. The Quality Inn is pet friendly with a mere $10 fee.

$100-150

The **Magnolia House Bed and Breakfast** (1317 Columbia Ave., 615/794-8178, www.bbonline.com/tn/magnolia, $140-155) is less than a mile from downtown Franklin, near the Carter House. A large magnolia tree shades the early-20th-century Craftsman home. There are four carpeted guest rooms, each with a private bath. Three house queen-size beds; the fourth has two twin beds. Common areas include a polished sitting room, cozy den, and sunroom that looks out on the quiet residential neighborhood. Hosts Jimmy and Robbie Smithson welcome guests and prepare homemade breakfast according to your preferences.

Over $200

Designed for couples, **Blue Moon Farm Bed and Breakfast** (4441 N. Chapel Rd., 800/493-4518, www.bluemoonfarmbb.com, $350-475) is a three-room cottage complete with kitchen, spa-style bathroom, and master bedroom. The art deco decor is unique among country bed-and-breakfasts, as is the sophistication of the welcome. Touches like spa robes, an ultra-luxurious tub, and a decadently dressed king-size bed make this a real getaway. The kitchen is stocked with drinks, snacks, and the ingredients for light meals. A "grocery bag breakfast" is left in the refrigerator for you and your companion to enjoy when you want, and in privacy. During waking hours, you can stroll the grounds or take advantage of wireless Internet access. Hosts Susan and Bob Eidam will also be happy to recommend and arrange activities for your stay in the Franklin area. Children older than one year are welcome at a cost of $20 extra per night.

A more hip, urban-feeling hotel option is **Aloft/Cool Springs** (7109 South Springs Dr., 615/435-8700, www.aloftnashvillecoolsprings.com, $124-149). The hotel boasts a saltwater pool, a better-than-average hotel bar, and a good location for business or recreation in Franklin.

FOOD

Downtown

The best choice for baked goods, coffee, and light fare, including soups, salads, and sandwiches, is **Merridee's Breadbasket** (110 4th Ave., 615/790-3755, www.merridees.com, 7am-5pm Mon.-Wed., 7am-9pm Thurs.-Sat., $3-11). Merridee grew up in Minnesota and learned baking from her mother, a Swede. When Merridee married Tom McCray and moved to Middle Tennessee in 1973, she kept up the baking traditions she had learned as a child. In 1984, she opened Merridee's Breadbasket in Franklin. Merridee McCray died in 1994, but her restaurant remains one of Franklin's most popular. Come in for omelets, scrambled eggs, or sweet bread and fruit in the morning. At lunch choose from the daily soup, casserole, or quiche, or order a cold or grilled sandwich. Merridee's also bakes fresh bread daily; take home a loaf of the always-popular Viking bread. Merridee's attracts a variety of people—students, businesspeople, and families out on the town. The creaky wood floors and comfortable seating make it a pleasant and relaxing place to refuel.

Puckett's Grocery and Restaurant (120 4th Ave. S., 625/794-5527, 7am-3pm Mon., 7am-9pm Tues.-Sat., 7am-7pm Sun., $7-10), the Leiper's Fork institution, has a second location in Franklin (and a third in Nashville). The Franklin shop offers traditional breakfasts with eggs, bacon, country ham, and biscuits, and plate lunches during the day. In the evening, order up a handmade burger (the locals swear that they're the best in town), a Southern dinner of fried catfish, or a traditional steak, chicken, or fish entrée. For vegetarians, they offer a veggie burger or a vegetable plate, as well as salads. Do not skip the fried green beans. The food is well prepared and the service friendly, and there's almost always a crowd, regardless of whether or not there's live music on tap.

The Cool Café coffee shop is transformed into **Mangia Nashville** (1110 Hillsboro Rd., 615/538-7456, 8pm Fri. and 6pm Sat., $45), a New York-style Italian bistro, only on Friday and Saturday nights. You'll get an old-school five-course Italian dinner. There's a $5 corkage fee if you BYOB.

Always popular, award-winning ★ **Saffire** (The Factory, 230 Franklin Rd., Bldg. 11, 615/599-4995, 11am-3pm and 5pm-9pm Tues.-Thurs. and Sun., 5pm-10pm Fri.-Sat., $14-35) uses primarily organic and biodynamic ingredients. The menu sparkles with unique dishes such as the tender and flavorful Cuban roasted-pork appetizer plate or a simple salad of heirloom tomatoes. Entrées include upscale dishes like prime rib and ahi tuna. The fried chicken is dusted with panko, topped with country ham gravy, and served with luscious macaroni and cheese. Saffire has an extensive wine and cocktail list, including organic choices. Take $4 off signature cocktails during happy hour (5pm-6pm), and on Tuesday nights most bottles of wine go for half price. The lunch menu is casual, featuring sandwiches, salads, and lunch-size entrées. Or choose the "green plate" daily special, featuring local and organic ingredients. There is also a midday kid's menu with favorites like grilled cheese and chicken bites. Set within an old warehouse, Saffire's dining room is spacious, with exposed brick and beams. The kitchen opens out onto the dining room, so you can watch the cooks work. With live music many nights, Saffire is a solid choice for excellent food in a pleasant and exciting environment.

Franklin Farmers Market

The **Franklin Farmers Market** (230 Franklin Rd., www.franklinfarmersmarket.com, 8am-noon Sat.) takes place at the rear of The Factory. This is one of the finest small-town farmers markets in the state, featuring a wide variety of fruit and vegetable growers; cheese, milk, and meat sellers; as well as craftspeople and live music.

INFORMATION AND SERVICES

The **Williamson County Convention and Visitors Bureau** (615/791-7554 or 866/253-9207, www.visitwilliamson.com) publishes guides and maintains a website about Franklin and the surrounding area. It also operates the **Williamson County Visitor Center** (209 E. Main St., 615/591-8514, 9am-4pm Mon.-Fri., 10am-3pm Sat., noon-3pm Sun.).

The **Williamson Medical Center** (Hwy. 96 E., 615/435-5000) is a 185-bed full-service medical facility with a 24-hour emergency room.

King Neptune (1533 Columbia Ave., 615/790-7682) is a clean and comfortable laundry open 24 hours a day. A single wash costs $1.50.

GETTING AROUND

Traffic can be heavy in and around Franklin. As a bedroom community for commuters working in Nashville, the morning and afternoon rush hours are to be avoided. The City of Franklin offers a trolley bus service around the town and to outlying areas, including Cool Springs Galleria, Williamson Medical Center, Watson Glen Shopping Center, and Independence Square. The trolleys run three different routes 6am-6pm.

You can pick up a full schedule and route map from the visitors center or download it from www.tmagroup.org. Fares for the Cool Springs Galleria bus are $3 for a one-way trip and $5 for a round-trip.

If you need a taxi, call Brentwood Taxi at 615/373-4950.

The Natchez Trace

The Natchez Trace Parkway cuts a diagonal path through the Middle Tennessee area south of Nashville. The two-lane limited-access highway passes through mostly undeveloped countryside.

Towns and sites in this region are a short drive off the Trace, and these villages and county seats embody small-town Tennessee.

LEIPER'S FORK

Part bucolic small town, part yuppified enclave, Leiper's Fork is a pleasant place to spend a few hours. It is located about a 15 minutes' drive from Franklin and near milepost 420 on the Natchez Trace Parkway. The town runs for several miles along **Leiper's Fork**, a tributary of the West Harpeth River. Beautiful old farmhouses line Old Hillsboro Road, which serves as the main thoroughfare through town.

One of the earliest settlers of the area was the Benton family, including Thomas Hart Benton, who would go on to become a U.S. senator from Missouri. For many years, Leiper's Fork was called Hillsboro after Hillsborough, North Carolina, where many of its early settlers came from. There is another Hillsboro in Coffee County, Tennessee, however, so when this Hillsboro petitioned for a post office in 1818, the U.S. Postal Service insisted that it change its name. Leiper's Fork was born.

Acclaimed furniture maker Dick Poyner was from the Leiper's Fork area. Poyner, a former slave, was famous for his sturdy ladder-back wooden chairs, one of which is on display at the Tennessee State Museum in Nashville.

Leiper's Fork is a pleasant community, with a die-hard group of locals who are proud of their town. Art galleries and antiques shops line the short main drag. Unusually good food can be found at local restaurants, and a laid-back let's-laugh-at-ourselves attitude prevails. Many music powerhouses live here; if you see a celebrity, don't make a fuss. That's why they choose to live in Leiper's Fork.

Bed-and-breakfast inns in the area make it a viable destination or a pleasant pit stop during a tour of the region.

Entertainment

Friday night is songwriter night at **Puckett's Grocery** (4142 Old Hillsboro Rd., 615/794-1308, www.puckettsgrocery.com). For $30 you enjoy dressed-up dinner—fresh seafood, poultry, and steak are usually among the options—at 7pm and an in-the-round performance from Nashville singer-songwriters starting at 8:30pm. If you prefer, pay $12 for the concert only. Reservations are essential for either, so call ahead. Check the website to find out who is performing.

Jailhouse Industries operates the Leiper's Fork **Lawn Chair Theatre** behind Leiper's Creek Gallery from May to September. Bring your lawn chair or blanket and enjoy classic movies and kids' favorites on Friday and Saturday nights, plus concerts. Call 615/477-6799 for more information, or just ask around.

Shopping

Leiper's Fork retailers are open Wednesday-Saturday 10am-5pm and Sunday 1pm-5pm.

The **Leiper's Creek Gallery** (4144 Old Hillsboro Rd., 615/599-5102, www.leiperscreekgallery.com) is the finest gallery in town. It shows a wide selection of paintings by local and regional artists, and hosts a variety of arts events year-round.

Neena's Primitive Antiques (4158 Old Hillsboro Rd., 615/790-0345) specializes in primitive antiques, linens, home decor items, and leather goods.

The 3,000-square-foot **Serenite Maison** (4149 Old Hillsboro Pk., 615/599-2071, www.serenitemaison.com) houses a well-edited inventory thanks to the smart design sense of Alexandra Cirimelli. A California transplant, Cirimelli has appeared on an episode of *American Pickers* and is known for finding her well-heeled clients (including Holly Williams and several actors and actresses from ABC's *Nashville*) the perfect farm table or pie safe for their kitchen. Don't overlook the pickin' corner, where locals stop in to play the antique guitars, banjos, and mandolins that hang on the walls.

Recreation

The Leiper's Fork District of the Natchez Trace National Scenic Trail runs for 24 miles, starting near milepost 427 and ending at milepost 408, where State Highway 50 crosses the parkway. The trail follows the old Natchez Trace through rural countryside. The best access point is from Garrison Creek Road, where there is parking, restrooms, and picnic facilities. You can also access the trail from Davis Hollow Road.

Food

★ **Puckett's Grocery** (4142 Old Hillsboro Rd., 615/794-1308, www.puckettsgrocery.com, 6am-7pm Mon.-Thurs., 6am-10:30pm Fri.-Sat., 6am-6pm Sun. summer, reduced hours Dec.-Feb., $6-25) is the heartbeat of Leiper's Fork. An old-time grocery with a small dining room attached, Puckett's serves breakfast, lunch, and dinner to the town faithful and visitors alike. The original country store opened about 1950. In 1998, Andy Marshall bought the store and expanded the restaurant offerings. Solid country breakfasts are the order of the day in the mornings, followed by plate lunches. The pulled pork is a favorite, as is the Puckett Burger. Dinner specials include catfish nights, family nights, and a Saturday-night seafood buffet. Friday night the grocery turns upscale with a supper club and live music. Reservations are essential for Friday night. Puckett's hours vary by the season, so it is best to call ahead, especially for dinner arrangements. A second Puckett's Grocery location in Franklin offers a more varied menu.

Information

The **Leiper's Fork Merchant's Association** (615/972-2708, www.leipersfork.net) promotes the town, maintains a listing of local businesses, and publishes an annual calendar of events.

ARRINGTON

The sleepy town of Arrington wasn't much more than a dot on a map for tourists (or locals, for that matter) until 2005. That's when country megastar Kix Brooks and his business partners picked these rolling hills as the place they were going to start a winery and set out to change the perception of Tennessee wines.

While no one (yet) is confusing these vintages for those grown in Napa, and, in fact, some of the grapes used are brought into the state at this point, **Arrington Vineyards** (6211 Patton Rd., 615/395-0102, www.arringtonvineyards.com, 11am-8pm Mon.-Thurs., 11am-9pm Fri.-Sat., noon-6pm Sun.) has impressed even the skeptics.

You don't have to be an oenophile to appreciate a day at Arrington, however. There's a popular free Music in the Vines concert series in the summer, and almost any pleasant day of the year you'll see others with picnics who came to enjoy the scenery and the great outdoors. There's not a restaurant on the premises, but you can buy boxed meals, cheeses, and chocolates. The place is kid friendly, and there are board games to borrow while you stretch out on the lawn. Because of Tennessee's quirky liquor laws, you can't buy a glass of wine here, but you can buy a bottle that you can then go open on your picnic blanket.

Initiatives have converted some of Arrington's building to solar power, and the vineyard is becoming a green leader in the area.

SPRING HILL

A small town midway between Franklin and Columbia, Spring Hill is best known by many as the site of a large General Motors automobile factory. To students of the Civil War, the town is the site of one of the South's greatest

The Natchez Trace Parkway

The first people to travel what is now considered the Natchez Trace were probably Choctaw and Chickasaw, who made the first footpaths through the region. French and Spanish traders used the 500 miles of intertwining Indian trails that linked the Mississippi port of Natchez to the Cumberland River.

Early white settlers quickly identified the importance of a land route from Natchez to Nashville. In 1801, the Natchez Trace opened as an official post road between the two cities. Boatmen who piloted flatboats from Nashville and other northern cities to Natchez and New Orleans returned along the Trace by foot or horse, often carrying large sums of money. One historian characterized the diverse array of people who used the Trace as "robbers, rugged pioneers, fashionable ladies, shysters, politicians, soldiers, scientists, and men of destiny, such as Aaron Burr, Andrew Jackson, and Meriwether Lewis."

The Trace developed a reputation for robberies, and few people traveled its miles alone. Many thieves disguised themselves as Indians, fanning the flames of racial distrust that existed during this period of history. By 1820, more than 20 inns, referred to as "stands," were open. Many were modest—providing food and shelter only.

In 1812, the first steamship arrived at Natchez, Mississippi, marking the beginning of the end of the Trace's prominence. As steamboat travel became more widespread and affordable, more and more people turned away from the long, laborious, and dangerous overland route along the Trace.

The road's historical importance is evident in the fact that it was not easily forgotten. While it faded from use, the Natchez Trace was remembered. In 1909, the Daughters of the American Revolution in Mississippi started a project to mark the route of the Trace in each county through which it passed. The marker project continued for the next 24 years and eventually caught the attention of Rep. Thomas J. Busby of Mississippi, who introduced the first bills in Congress to survey and construct a paved road along the route of the old Natchez Trace.

During the Great Depression, work on the Natchez Trace Parkway began under the Public Works Administration, the Works Project Administration, and the Civilian Conservation Corps. Following the New Deal, construction slowed dramatically, and it was not until 1996 that the final leg of the parkway was completed.

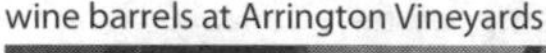

wine barrels at Arrington Vineyards

The 445-mile parkway follows the general path of the old Natchez Trace; in a few places, they fall in step with each other. More than 100 miles of the parkway lie within Tennessee. It runs along the Western Highland Rim through Davidson, Williamson, Hickman, Maury, Lewis, and Wayne Counties.

The parkway passes scenic overlooks, historic sites, and quiet pastures. In many places along the route you have the opportunity to walk along the original Trace.

ACCOMMODATIONS AND FOOD

There are no hotels on the parkway. Look for accommodations in nearby cities, including Franklin, Columbia, and Lawrenceburg. The Hampshire-based **Natchez Trace Reservation Service** (800/377-2770, www.bbonline.com/natcheztrace) books bed-and-breakfast inns along the parkway, from Nashville all the way to Natchez. This service is worth considering, especially since many of these inns are located closer to the parkway than motels are.

The closest accommodations to the parkway are three **campgrounds,** one of which lies in Tennessee. The Meriwether Lewis Campground at milepost 385 has 32 sites and a bathhouse. The next campground is Jeff Busby, at milepost 193 in Mississippi.

There are no restaurants or food concessions along the parkway. Picnic facilities abound, however, so wise travelers will pack a few sandwiches and avoid traveling off the parkway to eat.

INFORMATION AND SERVICES

The **National Park Service** (800/305-7417, www.nps.gov/natr) publishes a fold-out map and guide to the parkway. The official visitors center for the parkway is in Tupelo, Mississippi. For detailed hiking information, visit the website about the Natchez Trace National Scenic Trail at www.nps.gov/natt.

The only gas station along the parkway is at Jeff Busby, milepost 193 in Mississippi. Fill up your tank before you take off to explore.

missed opportunities of the war. While it is doubtful that a different outcome at Spring Hill would have changed the course of war, it would very likely have saved the many thousands of lives lost at the Battle of Franklin.

Spring Hill is located along U.S. 31. Downtown consists of a few blocks between Beechcroft and Kendron Roads. The town's main street was destroyed by fire and tornado in 1963, leaving only a few remnants of Spring Hill's former charm. To see these remainders, drive up and down the town's side streets, including Murray Hill, Depot, and McLemore Streets. Spring Hill's main attractions are along Highway 31, less than a mile outside of town.

The **Spring Hill Battlefield** (931/486-9037) is a 118-acre park with a one-mile trail that climbs to the top of a hill overlooking the battlefield. Interpretive markers tell the story of Spring Hill. The park is open during daylight hours. To find it, turn east onto Kendron Road and look for the park on the right-hand side of the road, just before the road passes I-65.

Rippavilla

You can tour an 1850s-era mansion at **Rippavilla Plantation** (5700 Main St./Hwy. 31, 931/486-9037, www.rippavilla.org, 10am-4pm Tues.-Sat., adults $10, seniors $8, children 6-12 $5, children under 6 free), just south of downtown Spring Hill on Highway 31. Rippavilla, originally called Rip-o-villa, was built in 1851 by wealthy plantation owner Nathaniel Cheairs and his wife, Susan. The story is told that there was a tradition in the Cheairs family for the men to marry women

The South's Last Stand

In the waning days of the Confederacy, Confederate president Jefferson Davis met with his commanders to plan strategy. It was September 1864, and the Federals were pushing southward in Virginia and Georgia.

The plan that Davis and his commanders agreed upon was a daring march northward through Middle Tennessee. It was hoped that General Hood's Army of the Tennessee would draw Federal forces away from the battles elsewhere and that they would eventually be repelled from the South entirely.

The last-ditch plan failed and cost the Confederacy some 13,500 lives. The battles of Spring Hill, Franklin, and Nashville were major blows to the Southern cause and its last losing stratagem.

SPRING HILL

On November 29, 1864, Gen. John M. Schofield and his Federal troops were stationed in Columbia. Moving northward, Hood went around Columbia and headed toward Spring Hill. From here, Hood could either have marched to Nashville ahead of the Federals or returned to Columbia and attacked them from the rear. It was a promising position.

But the opportunity was squandered when the Confederates camped just short of a critical road northward. Schofield, who suspected Hood's strategy, moved his men in the dead of night and marched them safely northward.

Explanations for Hood's mistake suggest that he was not himself on that day. He was probably in tremendous physical pain from earlier war injuries (Hood had already lost the use of his left arm and had his right leg amputated below the hip) and was probably taking opium. He may also have been drunk.

Whatever the cause, on the morning of November 30, when Hood realized what had happened, he resolved to battle the Federals in Franklin. Fueled by shame and desperation, Hood ordered the charge at the Battle of Franklin, one of the South's bloodiest defeats of the war.

named Sarah, so when Nathaniel told his father that he intended to ask Susan McKissak to marry him, his father offered to pay the young man $5,000 in gold not to. Susan McKissak's father, one of the richest men in the area, heard of this, and in reply he offered Cheairs all the bricks and slave labor he needed to build his home.

In the end, Cheairs married Susan and received both the gifts from his father-in-law and the $5,000 from his father—not a bad way to start out in life.

Rippavilla was sold out of the family in the 1920s, and the new owner modernized many of the finishes and also connected what was once a detached smokehouse and kitchen to the main building. Guided tours of the mansion last about 45 minutes, and guests may also walk around the property, which includes an 1870s freedman's school that was moved from another part of the county when it was threatened to be destroyed.

Tennessee Museum of Early Farm Life

For an educational trip back in time, stop at the **Tennessee Museum of Early Farm Life** (5700 Main St./Hwy. 31, 931/381-3686, Apr.-Oct. 9am-3:30pm Fri.-Sat. and by appointment, adults $3, children and seniors $2), which displays farm, kitchen, and other useful implements used at Tennessee farms and homes in days gone by. Operated by a group of enthusiastic and knowledgeable retired farmers, the museum lovingly preserves plows, cultivators, seeders, wagons, and many other pieces of machinery that helped make a hard life just a bit easier for farmers and their

FRANKLIN

By the time Hood and his army reached Franklin on November 30, 1864, the general was frustrated and the men exhausted. The missed opportunity at Spring Hill stung, but worse was yet to come.

Ignoring the advice of his commanders, Hood ordered a full frontal attack on the Federal line around Franklin. Unlike many other battles of the Civil War, the troops at Franklin had a full view of each other. There were some 23,000 Federal soldiers on one side and 20,000 Confederates on the other. That evening, 18 brigades of Confederate soldiers, many of them from Tennessee, marched toward the Federal line. With the rebel yell that made them famous, the attack had begun.

It was a bloody and fierce battle. Even those commanders and soldiers on the Confederate side who had doubts about the battle strategy fought bravely and often to the death. The hand-to-hand combat around the Carter House near downtown Franklin was some of the fiercest of the battle. One Federal soldier said that the fighting was in such close quarters that "even the poorest marksman could not fail to hit a human target."

The Confederate assault failed. The fighting ended around 9pm, and overnight Federal general Schofield and all his soldiers who could walk marched to Nashville. They left their dead on the battlefield. Two weeks later, they defeated Hood's army again during the Battle of Nashville.

The death toll at Franklin was staggering. Some 7,000 Confederates were killed, wounded, or captured in just five hours of battle. The Federals lost 2,500 men. Many injured warriors died on the battlefield overnight, when temperatures dropped below freezing.

The townspeople of Franklin were left to tend to the wounded on both sides of the battle. Nearly every home in the city became a makeshift hospital. The most famous of these was the Carnton Plantation, where visitors today can still see bloodstains on the floor left by injured and dying soldiers.

In 1866, John and Carrie McGavock established a Confederate cemetery on the grounds of Carnton. It holds 1,500 graves, making it the largest private military cemetery in the nation, and it's still a solemn place. Carrie kept a careful record of the men who were buried there, and her cemetery book was used by thousands of people who came to Franklin to mourn loved ones who died there.

families. You can see machinery and equipment used to make brooms, to make molasses, to sow seeds, to bale hay, and to cure pork. Through the descriptions provided by your tour guide, you begin to understand the ingenuity and inventiveness of these pioneers, as well as the hard work that went into fulfilling their basic needs.

The museum is located a few hundred yards behind the Rippavilla Plantation and was once called the Mule Museum, the name that is still reflected on the road sign at Rippavilla.

Accommodations

There is a **Best Western Spring Hill Inn and Suites** (102 Kedron Pkwy., 931/486-1234, $95-130) in town with an outdoor pool, laundry facility, free full breakfast, fitness room, and business services.

COLUMBIA

Columbia is the seat of Maury County. Founded in 1809 and named for Christopher Columbus, Columbia was the commercial hub for Middle Tennessee's rich plantations. In 1850 it became the third-largest city in Tennessee, behind Nashville and Memphis. A decade later Maury County was the wealthiest county in the whole state. The city's prominence did not survive, however. The economic trauma of the Civil War was largely to blame.

No city in all of Tennessee is more closely associated with mules than Columbia. During the 19th and early 20th centuries, Columbia's mule market opened on the first Monday of April, and people flocked here to buy and sell mules. Other towns, including Lynchburg and Paris, were known for large "First Monday" sales, but Columbia's was the largest.

Younger travelers may be interested to know that the Hannah Montana movie was filmed here in 2008.

Ancestral Home of James Knox Polk

The 11th president of the United States, James Knox Polk, was born in North Carolina but moved to Middle Tennessee with his family when he was 11 years old. Before moving to town, Polk's family lived for several years on a farm north of Columbia, from where Polk's father ran successful plantations, speculated in land, and was involved in local politics.

The home where Polk lived as a teenager and young man in Columbia is the only house remaining, besides the White House, where Polk ever lived. It is now known as the **Ancestral Home of James Knox Polk** (301-305 W. 7th St., 931/388-2354, www.jameskpolk.com, 9am-5pm Mon.-Sat., 1pm-5pm Sun., Apr.-Oct., 9am-4pm Mon.-Sat., 1pm-5pm Sun. Nov.-Mar., adults $10, seniors $8, youths 6-18 $5-7, children under 6 free) and home to a museum about Polk's life and presidency.

The home has a number of furnishings that belonged to President Polk and his wife, Sarah, while they lived at the White House. Other pieces come from Polk Place, the home that the couple planned and built in Nashville following the end of Polk's presidency in 1849. Sadly, Polk died of cholera just five months after leaving office and so had little opportunity to enjoy the home; Sarah Polk lived for another 42 years following her husband's death, and she spent them all at Polk Place.

The Polk home in Columbia was comfortable, but not luxurious, for its time. It was while living here that Polk began his career as a Tennessee lawyer and eventually won his first seat in the U.S. House of Representatives. He would go on to serve 14 years in the House, four of them as Speaker. He was governor of Tennessee from 1839 to 1841 and defeated Henry Clay, a Whig, to become president in 1845. Polk's presidency was defined by his drive to expand the Union westward, and it was during his term in office that the United States added California, Texas, and Oregon to the territory of the United States.

ancestral home of President James Knox Polk

The Polk home provides a good introduction to this little-known, but nonetheless important, U.S. president.

The Athenaeum Rectory

Once part of a famous finishing school for girls, The **Athenaeum Rectory** (808 Athenaeum St., 931/381-4822, 10am-4pm Tues.-Sat., closed in Jan., adults $6, seniors $5, children $1-4) is also an unusual architectural gem. Designed and built by Maury County master builder Nathan Vaught, the Rectory was the home of Rev. Franklin Gillette Smith and his family. Smith came to Columbia from Vermont in 1837 to run the Columbia Female Institute, an Episcopal girls' finishing school.

In 1851, Smith decided to open his own school for girls. He built the Columbia Athenaeum School next to the Rectory, which remained his family home. Its name refers to

Athena, the goddess of wisdom, and has come to mean "seat of learning."

For 52 years the Athenaeum educated young women in art, music, history, science, and business. The library housed more than 16,000 volumes, and the school sat on 22 wooded acres of land. Ladies took part in gymnastics, bowling, croquet, and tennis. At its peak, the Athenaeum boarded 125 students, plus day students from the surrounding area.

The Athenaeum remained open until 1904; after the deaths of Reverend Smith and his wife, it was operated by their son. From 1904 to 1914, the Athenaeum served as the community's high school, and in 1915 the school was torn down and the Columbia High School built in its place. The Athenaeum Rectory was preserved, however, and visitors can tour the Moorish-Gothic structure that housed the parlor and reception area for the school.

The rectory is operated by the Association for the Preservation of Tennessee Antiquities (www.theapta.org). For a week every summer it offers the 1861 Athenaeum Girls' School, when girls 14-18 years old dress up in period clothing and study topics like etiquette, penmanship, and archery. Every May, they offer a weekend course for women 19 and older.

Mule Day

Columbia's **Mule Day** (931/381-9557, www.muleday.com) takes place over four days in mid-April and is perhaps the thing for which Columbia is best known. The festival's roots are in the First Monday mule market that took place in Columbia during the period when work animals were indispensable to Tennessee farmers. In many cases, mules were a farmer's most valuable asset—a good pair of mules could make a poor farmer rich.

Mules were more expensive than horses or oxen because they were more highly prized. They were said to be stronger, smarter, and more surefooted than other work animals. Their temperament can be stubborn, but some mules are easy and willing to work. For this reason, mule breeders were important, influential, and, often, quite wealthy.

Today's Mule Day is more festival than mule market, although the event still does includes mule sales, mule and donkey seminars, and mule shows and competitions. The highlight is Saturday morning's Mule Day Parade, when thousands of people crowd to see school bands, mules, and colorful troops parade down the road. There is also live music, storytelling, dancing, gospel singing, and the crowning of the Mule Day Queen. Activities take place at various locations in Columbia, but the heart of Mule Day is the Maury County Park on Lion Parkway.

Accommodations

Columbia has more choices of chain hotels than any other city in Maury County. A host of motels are found around exit 46 on I-65, about 10 miles east of Columbia. They include **Comfort Inn** (1544 Bear Creek Pk., 931/388-2500, $75-100) and **Holiday Inn Express** (1558 Bear Creek Pk., 931/380-1227, $75-120).

Locally owned, the **Richland Inn** (2405 Pulaski Hwy., 931/381-4500, www.richlandinncolumbia.com, $85-115) is a 107-room inn with singles, doubles, and suites. There is a continental breakfast and a family restaurant next door.

Food

Located on the courthouse square, **Square Market and Café** (35 Public Sq., 931/840-3636, www.squaremarketcafe.com, 9am-4pm Mon.-Thurs., 9am-9pm Fri., 10:30am-9pm Sat., $6-19) serves breakfast and lunch throughout the week, and dinner on Friday and Saturday nights. The weekday menu features salads, sandwiches, and soups. The signature Polk's Roasted Pear Salad of greens, blue cheese, walnuts, and roasted-pear vinaigrette is a favorite for lunch. Heartier appetites can choose hot steamed sandwiches or the Tennessee Hot Brown, a hot open-faced turkey sandwich topped with white sauce, cheddar cheese, and bacon. The café brews good coffee, and the desserts are homemade.

Weekend dinner includes entrées like baked salmon with dill caper sauce, spinach-and-garlic ravioli, and Eastern Shore crab cakes. There is live music, too.

For country cooking, hearty breakfasts, and plate-lunch specials, head to **Bucky's Family Restaurant** (1102 Carmack Blvd., 931/381-2834, 5am-2pm daily, $4-12).

Information

The **Maury County Visitors Bureau** (8 Public Sq., 888/852-1860, www.antebellum.com) operates a **visitors center** (931/840-8324, 9am-4pm Mon.-Sat.) across the street from the James K. Polk house. There's also a free mobile app with more details on what to see in Columbia.

MOUNT PLEASANT

A few miles down Highway 43 from Columbia is the small town of Mount Pleasant. Once known as the Phosphate Capital of the World, Mount Pleasant is now a quiet town with an unusually large number of beautiful antebellum homes. Many of them were built with money earned from the phosphate industry. During the early boom years of the 1890s, the promise of quick money attracted hundreds of men to work in the mines. Law and order was haphazard until a Texas Ranger named Captain Russell arrived.

Sights

HISTORIC BUILDINGS IN TOWN

You can learn about the phosphate industry at the **Mount Pleasant/Maury County Phosphate Museum** (Public Sq., 931/379-9511, 9:30am-4:30pm Mon.-Sat., free, donations accepted). In addition to information about phosphate, the museum houses artifacts of local history, Civil War memorabilia, and local crafts.

Mount Pleasant has a nice variety of historic homes, but most are closed to the public. The **Breckenridge Hatter's Shop** (205 N. Main St.), believed to be the oldest building still standing in town, is an original log cabin covered with weatherboarding in the 1920s. It is on the National Register of Historic Places. The **Price-Jackson House** (209 N. Main St.) was built in 1849 and served as an insurance office for many years.

A few blocks away from the town square, Pleasant Street is home to at least three elegant old homes. **Manor Hall** (300 Pleasant St.) once sat on a property of more than 1,200 acres. Martin Luther Stockard had it built in 1859 for his second wife, using money he inherited from his first wife and her brother. The **John Ruhm-Graham Home** (106 Pleasant St.) was built in 1910 for Mr. John Ruhm, one of the "captains of the phosphate industry." It has the only elevator in Mount Pleasant. The **Jenkins-Bradburn House** (104 Pleasant St.) is a three-story log house built in 1917.

Drive northward on Main Street (Highway 243) to find more stately homes. **Walnut Grove** (510 N. Main St.) was built in 1858 and includes a detached kitchen believed to be the oldest brick building in Mount Pleasant. Inside, ash floors are laid at random widths.

RATTLE AND SNAP

Considered by some to be the finest antebellum home in Tennessee, **Rattle and Snap** (1522 N. Main St./Hwy. 243, 931/379-1700, www.rattleandsnapplantation.com, adults $20, children 7-12 $8 for groups with a 4-person minimum, adults $15, children 7-12 $8 for groups of 4-14, adults $13, children 7-12 $8 for groups of 5 or more, children under 7 free; call if you have fewer than 4 people in your party, open by appointment only, please call three days in advance to make a tour reservation) was built by George Washington Polk in 1845. Its extravagance was unmatched by any other home of the period: The 10 Corinthian columns that stand at the front of the mansion were made in Cincinnati, shipped by steamboat to Nashville, and brought over land by oxcart to Maury County. The marble mantels came from Italy, the gardens were designed by a German landscape architect, and a glorious

Waterford chandelier hangs over the dining room table. The fine craftsmanship throughout the home is attributed to slaves who labored on the construction.

The story goes that Rattle and Snap was named after an eponymous popular game of the period involving dried beans that were rattled and rolled with a snap of the fingers. Polk claimed that he won the land on which the mansion sits in a rattle and snap game with the governor of North Carolina.

The house was spared during the Civil War, reportedly after the Union commander and field captain noticed that Polk was wearing a Masonic ring in his portrait. Polk's wealth did not survive the war, however, and in 1867 he sold the property to J. J. Granberry, who occupied the home for 50 years and renamed it Oakwood Hall. In 1919, it changed hands again, and for many years tenant farmers lived in the deteriorating mansion. Rattle and Snap owes its restoration to Amon Carter Evans, former publisher of the *Nashville Tennessean.*

Today, Rattle and Snap is open year-round for group tours of two people or more. Tours must be booked and paid for in advance. Overnight guests are also welcome at its Carriage House, and special events are hosted here. Even without a tour, you can admire the property from the highway.

Accommodations

Sleep in the Carriage House at **Rattle and Snap Plantation** (1522 N. Main St./Hwy. 243, 931/379-1700, www.rattleandsnapplantation.com, $250 for up to two guests, $25 for each additional person), and you will enjoy your own private tour of one of the state's most famous antebellum homes. The Carriage House is a three-bedroom guesthouse located at the rear of the mansion. It includes two queen-size bedrooms and a sleeping loft with two twin beds. There is also a kitchen, sitting room, and patio where guests can relax and prepare meals. No children are allowed, and smoking is not permitted. There is a two-night minimum stay.

HOHENWALD

The unassuming county seat of Lewis County, Hohenwald developed in the 1890s when a railroad was built through the rural county. Starting in 1895, immigrants from Switzerland moved to the area as part of a settlement scheme advanced by a Swiss American developer, J. G. Probst. The immigrants laid out and built New Switzerland immediately adjacent to the older town of Hohenwald. The two communities are now united.

For many years, the Alpine character of Hohenwald was evident. A Swiss Singing Society was formed, and Swiss and German Reformed Churches held services in German. The European heritage survived until World War II, when anti-German sentiment caused many to abandon their cultural heritage. Today, traces of Hohenwald's Alpine heritage are faint, having been supplanted by those of Middle Tennessee.

Meriwether Lewis Gravesite and Memorial

Lewis County is named for Meriwether Lewis, the U.S. army captain and private secretary to President Thomas Jefferson, who is best known as the leader, along with William Clark, of the Lewis and Clark expedition to the Pacific Ocean from 1805 to 1806. His gravesite and a memorial sit along the Natchez Trace Parkway about seven miles east of Hohenwald. This is where Lewis died, under mysterious circumstances, while traveling the Trace bound for Washington DC in 1809.

According to accounts, Lewis, who was appointed governor of the Louisiana Territory following his successful expedition, was upset by accusation of financial mismanagement. He was traveling to Washington to clear his name, and on the night of October 11, 1809, he stayed at Grinder's Stand, a homestead whose owners boarded travelers along the Trace. In the morning, Lewis was found shot to death in his bed. His death was called a suicide, although a few months later a friend came to investigate the circumstances and pronounced

The Elephant Sanctuary

Tucked into the rural landscape of central Tennessee near the small town of Hohenwald, more than 20 African and Asian elephants retired from circuses and zoos have found refuge.

The Elephant Sanctuary at Hohenwald is a licensed and enlightened nonprofit program that provides a place where retired elephants can live peacefully and as naturally as possible.

The sanctuary was established in 1995 and has grown with support from donors and grants. Today it is a 2,700-acre park with a heated barn (this is the South, but it can get cold in January) and a spring-fed lake. There are presently more than 20 elephants living at the sanctuary. They spend their days walking around, interacting with each other, eating, and being bathed or cared for in other ways.

In 2006, elephant caregiver Joanna Burke was killed in a tragic accident when Winkie, one of the sanctuary elephants, knocked her over and stepped on her. The elephant was apparently afraid that Joanna would touch her right eye, which had been stung and was swollen and painful. Elephant experts say that Winkie's behavior was consistent with posttraumatic stress disorder, which has been diagnosed in other retired zoo and circus elephants.

Burke's death was a sad event for the sanctuary, but in keeping with the wishes of Burke and her family, Winkie was not put to sleep, although new protocols were established for animals with a history of aggression. Burke is buried at the elephant sanctuary.

Visitors are not allowed at the elephant sanctuary (unless you are a major donor), but you can watch live elephant cams on its website at www.elephants.com. The sanctuary is planning to build a visitors center once it raises the necessary funds.

that Lewis was murdered. Lewis was just 35 years old when he died.

While the circumstances of Lewis's death remain a mystery, his legacy remains alive. Several monuments to him have been erected at and around his gravesite, and a modest museum tells the story of his life.

The **Meriwether Lewis Gravesite and Memorial** is located at the intersection of the Natchez Trace Parkway and U.S. 20. There is a campground, picnic area, and restroom nearby.

Natural Bridge

Hidden away at the privately owned and operated **Tennessee Fitness Spa and Retreat** (299 Natural Bridge Rd., 931/722-5589, www.tfspa.com) is one of this area's most remarkable natural attractions, a double-span natural bridge.

Here a tributary of the Buffalo River has etched away at the bedrock for thousands of years, eventually creating a natural bridge formation that is marvelous to look at.

The bridge invites exploration. You can walk along the side of the trickling stream and climb up to view the bridge from above. The sight of layer upon layer of rock, which has been carved out over many thousands of years, is remarkable.

A few hundred yards from the natural bridge is a small cave, also open to visitors. Lights have been placed inside to make it easy to explore.

Natural Bridge is located along State Route 99, between Hohenwald and Waynesboro. Tennessee Fitness allows the public to visit Natural Bridge and the cave on Sunday only. Come between 9am and 5pm and check in at the office first. Admission is free.

Accommodations

Located about 15 minutes from Mount Pleasant in Hampshire, **Ridgetop Bed and Breakfast** (Hwy. 412, 931/285-2777, $85-105) is a rural getaway with a standard guest room and two private cottages. The cottages are unique: The Swiss Cottage is a postage-stamp-size Swiss chalet with a queen-size bed downstairs and sleeping loft with two additional beds upstairs. The log cabin evokes frontier life, but with modern amenities, including air-conditioning and a private bathroom. All meals are served in the main dining room.

THE FARM

In 1970, hippie spiritual leader Stephen Gaskin and 320 others established a commune in the rural countryside near Summertown, Tennessee. Initially governed by beliefs that forbade alcohol and birth control and promoted nonviolence and respect for the environment, **The Farm** has evolved over the years. While it has loosened some rules, it remains committed to peace, justice, and environmental sustainability.

The Farm (Summertown, 931/964-3574, www.thefarmcommunity.com) has established a number of successful businesses, and it has contributed to its mission for a more peaceful and healthy world. Its businesses include a book publishing company, a soy dairy that manufactures tofu and soy milk, and a yoga studio. Farm books include *The Farm Vegetarian Cookbook* and Ina May Gaskin's works on natural childbirth. Nonprofits on The Farm include Plenty International, an international aid organization, and The Farm School, which provides alternative education for primary through secondary grades.

The Farm is glad to receive visitors. The Ecovillage Training Center puts on workshops and conferences throughout the year, many of them dealing with organic gardening, permaculture, construction, and other sustainable technologies. The Farm also operates a midwifery training center and birthing houses where women can come to give birth.

About 200 people live at The Farm today. A few have been there since the beginning, but there are also recent transplants. Some work at Farm enterprises, but others have jobs "off The Farm." Farm members become shareholders in the company that owns The Farm land and other assets.

Visiting The Farm

The Farm is a welcoming and friendly place where people wave at each other and you can strike up a conversation with just about anybody. The **Welcome Center** (100 Farm Rd., 1pm-4pm Mon.-Fri., reduced hours Nov.-Mar.) has a museum about the community and sells The Farm books, T-shirts, and other products. It is a good idea to call ahead to confirm hours. You can arrange for a tour with a member of The Farm by calling the welcome center. There are also twice-yearly Farm Experience weekends for people who want to see what Farm living is about.

The Farm Store (931/964-4356, 9am-7pm daily) sells organic and natural groceries, household items, vegetarian sandwiches, and drinks.

Accommodations

You can sleep the night at The Farm. The **Inn at The Farm Eco Hostel** (184 Schoolhouse Rd., Summertown, www.thefarm.org, 931/964-4474, $12) is part of the Ecovillage Training Center, and it offers dormitory-style accommodations. Reservations are required, and the inn is sometimes full when there are workshops or conferences under way.

A half-dozen Farm residents rent out rooms to visitors, usually for about $40-80 a night. Meals may be available for an additional fee. There is also a campground, where you can pitch your own tent for about $14. For more information about staying at The Farm, call the welcome center or go online.

Getting There

The Farm is located off Drake's Lane Road, a few miles west of Summertown along Route 20. Detailed directions and a map are available on The Farm website.

ETHRIDGE

In 1944, three Amish families moved to the countryside near Ethridge, in rural Lawrence County. According to some accounts, they came seeking a place where they would not be required to send their children to large, consolidated secondary schools. They also were in search of land where they could farm and make a home.

Over the years the Amish population in Lawrence County has waxed and waned, with estimates of 100-200 families now. The Amish are known for their conservative dress; rejection of modern technology, including electricity; and their preference to keep to themselves. They are also excellent farmers, craftsmen, and cooks; devout Christians; and peace lovers. Most of the Amish in this part of Tennessee speak English and Pennsylvania Dutch, and some also know German.

As you drive through the back roads that crisscross the Amish area, you will be able to identify the Amish homes because they are old-fashioned farmhouses without electrical wires, cars, or mechanized farm equipment. You will also notice their fields of corn, peanuts, wheat, tobacco, hay, and oats, and you may see a black horse-drawn buggy—their primary form of transportation.

Many Amish sell goods, ranging from handmade furniture to molasses. As you drive, you will see signs advertising various products for sale. You are welcome to stop by and buy something. Remember that due to their religious beliefs, the Amish do not allow their pictures to be taken. Please respect this fact when you visit them.

If you prefer, you can explore Amish country with a guide on a wagon tour. Such tours are offered by local Lawrence County residents who are not Amish. Each tour lasts about 90 minutes and will take you to several farms where you can meet the Amish and buy products from them. Tours are provided twice daily Monday-Saturday at 10am and 3:30pm by the **Amish Country Store** (4011 Hwy. 43 N., 931/829-1621). The rate is $10 for adults.

If you want to drive through on your own, start in Ethridge and explore the narrow back roads bounded by Highway 43 on the east, State Route 242 on the west, Highway 20 on the north, and U.S. 64 on the south. You can pick up a free detailed map of Amish country, with specific farms identified, from the **Lawrence Chamber of Commerce** (1609 Locust Ave./Hwy. 43, 931/762-4911, www.selectlawrence.com).

A half-dozen stores along Highway 43 just north of Ethridge sell Amish-made goods for those who don't have time to venture into Amish territory themselves. One of the best is **Dutch Country Bakery** (3939 Hwy. 43 N., 931/829-2147, 7am-5pm Mon.-Sat.), which sells Amish baked goods, cheeses, and bulk goods. It also serves breakfast and lunch daily.

The Amish work Monday-Saturday. Sunday is their Sabbath, the day that they worship and spend time with family. You won't find Amish farm stands or homes open for business on Sunday.

LAWRENCEBURG

Lawrenceburg is the seat of Lawrence County, named for a U.S. naval hero of the War of 1812. Built along the Jackson Military Road, Lawrenceburg has long been a center of trade and commerce for the surrounding countryside.

Sights

You can see a replica of Davy Crockett's office at the **Davy Crockett Cabin Museum,** located one block south of the public square. It is free and open daily during daylight hours.

The man who popularized Southern gospel music called Lawrenceburg home, and the town has remembered him with a museum. The **James D. Vaughan Museum** (SunTrust Bank Bldg., Public Sq., 931/762-8991, http://vaughanmuseum.tripod.com, 9:30am-11:30am and 1pm-2:30pm Mon.-Fri., weekends by appointment, free) tells the story of its namesake, who sponsored and recorded the first professional gospel quartets and established the first Southern gospel magazine and radio station. He also established the Vaughn School of Music, where he taught students to sing, and published millions of shape-note songbooks. Vaughn has been called the father of Southern gospel music, and Lawrenceburg has been declared its birthplace.

Festivals and Events

Taking place in early June and again over Labor Day weekend, the **Summertown Bluegrass Reunion** (64 Monument Rd., Summertown, 931/964-2100, www.summertownbluegrassreunion.com, Fri. $8, Sat. $10) is an authentic showcase of homegrown bluegrass music. Bring your lawn chair and take a seat under the canopy of trees to enjoy a seemingly limitless smorgasbord of bluegrass music. During the late afternoons, the main stage closes for an hour for a shade-tree band contest, a real case of dueling banjos. The audience picks the winner. Dance for fun, or in one of the afternoon buck dancing contests.

The bluegrass reunions take place at a private campground in Summertown, located about 13 miles north of Lawrenceburg. Most festival attendees camp in RVs on the grounds; tents are also allowed.

Accommodations

Choose from a handful of standard-issue motels in Lawrenceburg. The **Best Western Villa Inn** (2126 N. Locust Ave./Hwy. 43, 931/762-4448, $65-80) has been refurbished, is pet friendly, and has free wireless Internet. The **Richland Inn** (2125 N. Locust Ave./Hwy. 43, 931/762-0061, $60-75) has rooms with double- and king-size beds, plus executive suites. Rooms have cable TV, in-room dataports, and irons. There is a free continental breakfast, a business center, and plenty of RV and truck parking.

Food

Square Forty Restaurant (40 Public Sq., 931/762-2868, 7am-2pm Sun.-Fri., noon-2pm Sat., $5-15) serves traditional Southern food and a popular Sunday-morning buffet, and a view of a statue of Davy Crockett.

Information

The **Lawrence County Chamber of Commerce** (1609 Locust Ave./Hwy 43, 931/762-4911, www.selectlawrence.com) publishes brochures and has information about local businesses and attractions.

DAVID CROCKETT STATE PARK

One of Lawrenceburg's earliest residents was also one of its most famous. David Crockett, the larger-than-life frontiersman who seems to have been everywhere in Tennessee, was one of Lawrenceburg's first commissioners and justices of the peace. He and his family operated a gristmill, powder mill, and distillery on the Shoal River a few miles west of town starting in 1817. In 1821, after a flood swept away their home and businesses, the Crocketts moved to northwest Tennessee, where Crockett was elected to Congress. Crockett died in 1836 at the Alamo Mission. The place where he lived in Lawrence County is now the **David Crockett State Park** (1400 W. Gaines, Lawrenceburg, www.tn.gov/environment/parks/DavidCrockettSP, 931/762-9408, 7am-dark daily).

Recreation

David Crockett is a pleasant park with a lot of amenities, including picnic tables, tennis courts, a restaurant, and an Olympic-size swimming pool. Crockett Falls is a pleasant place for a picnic.

You can rent paddleboats or fishing boats to explore 40-acre Lindsey Lake (no private boats are allowed). Fishing is permitted from the lake banks or from a boat; people older than 13 need a valid Tennessee fishing license, and everyone must follow state regulations. There is a paved 2.3-mile bike trail and three different hiking trails.

Festivals and Events

Davy Crockett and the pioneer spirit that he symbolizes is celebrated during **Davy Crockett Days** (931/762-9408), a two-day festival that takes place in early October at David Crockett State Park. Festival enthusiasts spend the weekend dressed in period costumes and do things that Crockett and his contemporaries would have. Activities include shooting, games, music, food, and reenactments of Old West trading posts where travelers bartered for goods.

Camping

There are 107 campsites, each with a picnic table, fire pit, and electrical and water hookups for RVs. Bathhouses have hot showers and commodes. As is the case with all Tennessee State campgrounds, sites are allocated on a first-come, first-served basis only.

WATERTOWN

Quaint **Watertown** (615/237-0270, www.watertowntn.com) has a charming downtown filled with shops and restaurants, fueled by **Historic Watertown, Inc.** (615/237-9999), an organization that works hard to keep it that way. Some days Watertown can come off as sleepy, but not when the **Tennessee Central Railway** (www.tcry.org) drops off a trainload of passengers for lunch, shopping, and a good old-fashioned shoot-out. The Fourth of July festivities include a squirt gun parade. Nashvillians make this 40-minute drive to go to a real drive-in movie.

Entertainment

The **Stardust Drive-In Theatre** (310 Purple Tiger Dr., 615/237-0077, www.stardustdrivein.com, adults $7.50, children $5) is just like you remember. Or, just like you remember hearing about drive-ins. The Stardust plays first-run flicks after dark; prices include a double feature. There's no sneaking in folks in the trunk; price is per person, not carload. And no sneaking outside food, either. You must buy from the concession stand or pay a $6 outside food permit. Fortunately, the concession stand has decent choices, including Philly cheesesteak and pizza. Once you get past the rules, this is good, clean old-fashioned fun. If you are using a GPS, enter "201 Tennessee Boulevard"; the Purple Tiger address often does not come up.

Shopping

Watertown's Public Square, at the intersection of Main and Depot Streets, is surrounded by antiques stores, jewelers, artisans, and others who set up in storefronts. These vendors change often, and many don't have predictable hours, but they are certain to be open during Watertown events, such as when the train rolls in. Standouts include Susan Thornton's **Thornton Metals Studio** (100 Public Sq., www.thorntonmetals.com) and **Jim's Antiques** (312 Public Sq., 615/237-1777).

Food

The oft-crowded **Depot Junction Café** (108 Depot Ave., 615/237-3976, 5am-8pm Mon.-Sat., $3-12) is known for its cheese sticks,

Watertown

burgers, and milk shakes. When there is a special event in Watertown, expect a wait, as this is one of the places visitors stop first.

Nona Lisa Pizzeria (208 E. Main St., 615/237-0102, 4pm-9pm Wed.-Thurs., 11am-9pm Fri.-Sun., $10-22) caters to families, vegetarians, and others looking for something other than Southern classics. Locals love the plum chicken, made with locally grown plums.

Walking Horse Country

The countryside surrounding Shelbyville is the capital of the Tennessee Walking Horse. The beloved high-stepping creatures known for their smooth gait are bred and shown at farms that dot the rolling hills of south-central Tennessee. The annual Walking Horse National Celebration is one of the largest horse shows in the world. Small towns Wartrace and Bell Buckle are two of the most charming in the whole of Middle Tennessee.

The Tennessee Walking Horse Parkway

Highway 31A from Pulaski to Lewisburg, and Highway 64 from Lewisburg to Wartrace, via Shelbyville, has been designated the **Tennessee Walking Horse Parkway**, and it is the best scenic route through this beautiful terrain. You will pass dozens of horse farms—some large and some small—and you will see some of the handsome horses out grazing in the field.

LEWISBURG

Lewisburg is best known for two very different animals: the Tennessee Walking Horse and the fainting goats of Marshall County. Lewisburg is the home of the business end of the famous horse breed: It is here that the Tennessee Walking Horse Breeders' and Exhibitors' Association is located. As for the goats, the story goes that in the 1880s, a mysterious man named Tinsley moved to Marshall County with four goats and a cow. He stayed for only one growing season, and when he left, he sold his "bulgy-eyed" goats to a local doctor. The goats displayed a strange habit of becoming rigid to the point of losing their balance when startled. Over the years, the fainting goats reproduced. It is now known that their condition is a neurological abnormality called mytonia, which doesn't harm the animals.

Downtown Lewisburg is set around the 1920s-era courthouse. On the north side of the square you'll find one of the most unusual buildings in all of Tennessee. The **Ladies' Rest Room** on 3rd Avenue was built in 1924 to accommodate rural women who traveled to town to shop or sell goods. The building included a reception room, toilets, a bedroom, and a kitchen. In his excellent guide to the area, Judge Robert Brant quotes an unsigned letter received at the county court not long after the restroom was built: "In behalf of the ladies of the county, I desire to thank the gentlemen of the County Court for the beautiful restroom they have given us. . . . We praise this beautiful gift, not merely for its beauty and many conveniences but because it shows that the women of the county are held in love and honored by our men."

Today, the restroom is no longer open to the public and is in disrepair, although efforts are being made to preserve it.

Entertainment and Events

The **Marshall County Community Theater** operates in the historic Dixie Theater (www.dixietheatre.org), on the east side of the town square. Check local listings or contact the chamber of commerce to find out about upcoming performances.

There is an authentic 1940s-era drive-in movie theater less than two miles out of town. The **Hi-way 50 Drive In** (1584 Fayetteville

Vannoy Streeter's Wire Horses

Self-taught folk artist Vannoy "Wireman" Streeter (1919-1998) drew inspiration for his life's work from the elegant stride and unique step of the Tennessee Walking Horse. Born in Wartrace in 1919 and raised on a horse farm, Streeter first displayed his remarkable talent as a child. His family could not afford to buy toy airplanes and cars, so he made them—bending them out of bailing wire.

Streeter was in Wartrace for the first Walking Horse Celebration, and in later years he returned to the event after it moved to Shelbyville. Streeter was proud of the fact that African Americans trained Strolling Jim and many other world-champion Walking Horses. He created hundreds, if not thousands, of sculpted horses, each with the distinctive high-stepping front leg and each with an African American rider on the back. Other favorite subjects were performers—he sculpted Tina Turner and Elvis Presley, in particular—and vehicles, including big-rig trucks, locomotives, and airplanes.

Streeter made most of his sculptures out of coat-hanger wire; he bought hangers by the hundreds. He did detail work with fine-gauge wire and large-scale work with bracing wire. He worked with regular pliers, wire cutters, and needle-nose pliers.

Streeter worked on the railroads and as a lumberyard hand, janitor, and hospital orderly. In 1960, he met and married his wife, Marie, and became a father to her six children. He continued to make his wire sculptures, eventually gaining national attention. In 1990, he was a demonstrating artist at the National Black Arts Festival in Atlanta. Shelbyville proclaimed April 25, 1992, Vannoy Streeter Day. His work has been displayed in the White House and at the Tennessee State Museum in Nashville.

Streeter continued to work until his death in 1998, although his productivity declined after his wife's death. His work is sold in folk art galleries in Nashville and other cities, and has been included in African American and folk art exhibits in Tennessee and elsewhere.

Hwy., 931/270-1591) screens first-run movies Friday, Saturday, and Sunday evenings. For just $7 for adults and kids 12 and up and $5 for children 6-11 (5 and under free), guests get to see back-to-back movies at this vintage drive-in theater. The sound system is modern, however (it's tuned to your car radio). There is a concession stand that sells burgers, fries, pizza, and popcorn, but patrons are also welcome to bring their own food. This is a popular weekend treat for local residents.

To celebrate Marshall County's fainting goats, the city of Lewisburg hosts the **Goats, Music, and More Festival** (931/359-1544, www.goatsmusicandmore.com) in October. The free two-day fair features goat shows, arts and crafts displays, live music, and a barbecue cook-off. In the evening major country music and rock acts perform at the town's Rock Creek Park.

Information

For information about Lewisburg, contact the **Marshall County Chamber of Commerce** (227 2nd Ave. N., 931/359-3863, www.marshallchamber.org).

HENRY HORTON STATE PARK

A few miles north of Lewisburg, near the small town of Chapel Hill, is **Henry Horton State Park** (4358 Nashville Hwy., 931/364-2222, tnstateparks.com). The park is known for its 18-hole championship golf course, skeet range, and inn and conference facilities.

Park amenities include an on-site restaurant that serves country-style meals and buffets, an Olympic-size swimming pool (inn and cabin guests swim free), hiking trails, and a gift shop.

The park's 18-hole **Buford Ellington golf course** (931/364-2319, 7:30am-dusk daily, first tee time at 9am) is a popular destination for golfers in the region. It has a pro shop, dressing rooms, rental clubs, gasoline and pull carts, a driving range, and a practice

The Tennessee Walking Horse National Celebration is one of the country's largest.

green. Greens fees are $14-24, depending on the season and day of the week.

Day-trippers can also enjoy the skeet range, fishing on the Duck River, picnics, horseshoes, tennis courts, volleyball, basketball, and table tennis.

Accommodations

Accommodations include the park inn, with motel-style rooms; a campground with both tent and RV sites; and seven cabins ideal for families or small groups. Rooms at the park inn rent for $70-86, depending on the season and day of the week. Rooms are air-conditioned and come with a television and telephone. Cabins, which are fully equipped for cooking and housekeeping, rent for $95-150 a night. Campsites are available for $8-25, depending on the season.

SHELBYVILLE

If any single Tennessee city is home to the Tennessee Walking Horse, it is Shelbyville. Considered the world's greatest pleasure, trail, and show horse, the Tennessee Walking Horse is the first breed of horse to bear the name of a state. Tennessee Walkers existed for many years before the breed was identified and named; early settlers needed horses that could travel easily and comfortably over rocky and uneven terrain. These early Walkers were not trained to show—they were purely utilitarian.

Tennessee Walkers are known for their docile temperament and kind manner. They are also known for their unique running walk—in which each of the horse's hooves hits the ground separately at regular intervals. In this gait, the animal's front legs rise in an exaggerated step, and the horse's head nods in time with the rhythm of its legs.

Sights

For information on farms that welcome visitors, or opportunities to ride a Tennessee Walking Horse, contact the **Walking Horse Owners' Association** in Murfreesboro at 615/494-8822.

★ Tennessee Walking Horse National Celebration

The premier event in Shelbyville is the annual **Tennessee Walking Horse National Celebration** (931/684-5915, www.twhnc.com), which takes place in late summer for 11 days, ending on the Saturday before Labor Day. This is the event that determines the best of the high-stepping Walking Horses, and it is an exciting time to be a horse fan.

The national celebration routinely attracts 30,000 people per night and more than 5,000 entries. The event takes place at the Celebration Grounds, a few blocks from the courthouse square in Shelbyville.

The Celebration was founded in 1939 as a way to promote Tennessee Walkers. It is an economic experiment that worked. Prize money now tops the half-million-dollar mark, and organizers boast that more than a quarter million tickets are sold over the 11-day event. Winning a show at the Celebration makes a horse more valuable and cements its reputation in the industry.

For horse lovers, the Celebration is exciting and beautiful. For breeders and horse farmers, it is their chance to make it in this competitive and high-stakes business. For the city of Shelbyville and the whole region, it is an economic powerhouse, pumping more than $20 million into the local economy every year.

The Celebration Grounds are used for other horse shows, plus sporting and musical events, year-round. The Nashville Symphony has played here, and shows featuring alpaca, miniature horses, and ponies take place.

Tickets for reserved seats at the Celebration range from $7-20 per night, and a pass for the whole event is $100. Box seats are more expensive, while general admission tickets to the South Grandstand are cheaper. Tickets for the best seats must be reserved in advance, but you can almost always get a seat at the Celebration, even if you show up on the day of the event.

Accommodations

Located within walking distance of the Celebration Grounds in Shelbyville, **Cinnamon Ridge Bed and Breakfast** (799 Whithorne St., 931/685-9200, $65-75) is a five-bedroom guesthouse. Each room has a private bath and television; provisions may be made for a private telephone, daily newspaper, and other services that appeal to business travelers. Full breakfast is served in your choice of the formal dining room or the sunny garden room. There is also a family room, patio, and backyard deck where you can unwind.

Also within walking distance of the Celebration Grounds, the **Bedford Inn** (727 Madison St., 931/684-7858, www.bedfordinnmotel.com, $40) is a stalwart motel with clean and comfortable rooms. Amenities include televisions, telephones, microwaves and refrigerators, and plenty of parking.

You will enjoy privacy in a rural setting at the **Tennessee Horse Country Bed and Breakfast** (311 Robinson Rd., 931/684-1863, www.tennesseehorsecountry.com, $75-135), located on a horse farm about eight miles south of Shelbyville along Highway 231. The property has a guesthouse that sleeps up to four people, with a whirlpool tub, full kitchen, living room, and porch, as well as a smaller cottage with a queen-size bed, full bath, and kitchenette. Both accommodations are entirely private. Your kitchen will be stocked with breakfast foods at your request.

Immerse yourself in the world of the Tennessee Walking Horse at the ★ **Clearview Horse Farm** (2291 Hwy. 231 S., 931/684-8822, www.clearviewhorsefarm.com, $75-135). This working horse farm has an indoor area for horse shows, a comfortable and modern barn, and horse trainers. There are three guest rooms at the farm, each with a private bath. The rooms are modern and neat, with ranch-like touches. The Tennessee Walking Horse Room can sleep up to four and would be ideal for families. Guests can enjoy a pool on the property, as well as a fishing lake. There is a continental breakfast. Many guests here are horse owners themselves, although "nonhorseys" are welcome, too.

Food

For coffee and other pick-me-ups, try **The Coffee Break** (121 South Side Sq., 931/680-2552, 7am-3pm Mon.-Fri., 8am-3pm Sat., $4-7).

WARTRACE

This tiny railroad town about 10 miles east of Shelbyville is the birthplace of the Tennessee Walking Horse. It was on the grounds of the town's Walking Horse Hotel, across the railroad tracks from the town square, that Albert Dement trained a $350 plow horse into **Strolling Jim,** the first world grand champion Walking Horse. Strolling Jim died in 1957 and is buried in the pasture behind the hotel.

The annual Walking Horse celebration that now draws a quarter million people to Shelbyville every year started in Wartrace, but it got too big for the small town and moved to Shelbyville in 1935.

Today, Wartrace is a sleepy yet pleasing town. The old residential district lies along a few quiet side streets that climb gently along a hillside. The howl of frequent freight trains—20-25 pass through daily—harkens to an earlier era.

Shopping

In certain circles, the name J. W. Gallagher is well known. Gallagher was born near Wartrace in 1915 and opened a woodworking shop in 1939. Skilled at furniture and cabinet making, Gallagher's guitars are what made him famous. From 1969 onwards Gallagher only made guitars. In 1976, Gallagher's son, Don, took over the business. There are not many Gallagher guitars out there—between 1965 and 1990, just over 2,000 were made—because each heirloom instrument is handcrafted from beginning to end.

Gallagher's Guitar Shop (5 Main St., 931/389-6455, www.gallagherguitar.com, 8am-5pm Mon.-Fri.) is an otherwise nondescript storefront with the word *Gallagher's* on the front.

Accommodations

The ★ **Walking Horse Hotel** (101 Spring St., 931/389-7030, www.walkinghorsehotel.com, $100) is the best place to stay not only in Wartrace, but for a good distance in any direction. When Joe Peters bought the hotel in 2007, he was intent on paying tribute to his late wife, Chais, who loved the old 1917 hotel. Peters and his family have brought new life to the old hotel by refurbishing the rooms, recruiting beloved chef Bill Hall to run the Strolling Jim Restaurant, and opening the Chais Music Hall, a state-of-the-art venue for all types of music. Rooms are a fusion of old and new. Classic touches from the hotel's early days have been preserved, but guests can expect the best modern amenities, including flat-screen televisions, free wireless Internet, super-comfortable beds, and good linens. The hotel, which may or may not be haunted, is not pet friendly, but it does offer pet boarding.

Food

The **Iron Gait** (106 Fairfield Rd., 931/389-6001, 7am-2pm Mon.-Fri., 7am-7pm Sat., 1pm-4pm Sun., $3-8) serves breakfast, burgers, and meat-and-three dinners. The monster burger is a favorite, as are the plate lunches. Find the Iron Gait just around the corner from Main Street, on the road to Bell Buckle.

In spring and summer, head to **Valley Home Farm** (310 Potts Rd., 931/389-6470, www.valleyhomefarm.com) to pick your own tasty strawberries.

For other dining choices, look in Bell Buckle, Normandy, and Shelbyville.

Information

The **Wartrace Chamber of Commerce** (931/389-9999, www.wartracechamber.org) promotes the town.

BELL BUCKLE

A tiny town nestled in the northern reaches of the Walking Horse region, Bell Buckle is a charming place to visit. Founded in 1852 and once a railroad town, **Bell Buckle** has successfully become a destination for antiques shopping, arts and crafts, small-town hospitality, and country cooking. The town's single commercial street faces the old railroad tracks; handsome old homes—some of them bed-and-breakfast inns—spread out along quiet residential streets.

What makes Bell Buckle so appealing is the sense of humor that permeates with just about everything that happens here. T-shirts for sale on the main street proclaim "Tokyo, Paris, New York, Bell Buckle," and the town's quirky residents feel free to be themselves. Tennessee's poet laureate, Margaret "Maggi" Britton Vaughn, who operates the Bell Buckle Press and had an office on Main Street for many years, once told an interviewer that William Faulkner "would have killed" for a community with the ambience, and characters, of Bell Buckle.

Bell Buckle's name is derived from the Bell Buckle Creek, named thus because a cow's bell was found hanging in a tree by the creek, attached by a buckle.

The town's annual RC and MoonPie Festival in June attracts thousands to the small town, and the well-respected Webb School Arts and Crafts Festival in October is one of the finest regional arts shows in the state. This is also home to the annual Tennessee Shakespeare Festival each summer.

Sights

Bell Buckle is noted as the home of the elite and well-regarded **Webb School** (319 Webb Rd. E., www.thewebbschool.com, 888/733-9322). Founded in 1870 and led by William Robert Webb until his death in 1926, Webb School has graduated 10 Rhodes scholars, several governors, attorneys general, and numerous successful academics. The school now has about 300 students in grades 8-12 from around the country and the world. While it was all male for many years of its life, Webb School now admits both male and female students. Its athletic mascot is the "Webb Feet."

The Webb campus is about three blocks north of downtown Bell Buckle. You can visit the main administrative office during regular business hours, where there are photographs and school memorabilia on display. Pay attention as you drive by; the speed limit in this school zone is considerably lower than that on all the nearby country roads.

Festivals and Events

Bell Buckle's biggest annual event is the **RC and MoonPie Festival** (931/389-9663) in mid-June, a nod to one of the South's favorite culinary combos, RC Cola and MoonPies, which are a Southern obsession: marshmallow fluff, sandwiched between graham crackers covered in chocolate, vanilla peanut butter, or other flavors. This hilarious weekend event includes country and bluegrass music, MoonPie games (such as the MoonPie toss), arts and crafts booths, the crowning of a MoonPie King and Queen, and a 10-mile run. You can also witness the cutting of the world's largest MoonPie (and if you are willing to join the mob, you can taste it, too). In case you're wondering why Bell Buckle has rights to the MoonPie festival, it's because it asked for the rights.

It is held in June in Tennessee, so it is almost always oppressively hot at the MoonPie Festival, which is a good excuse to drink another RC.

The **Webb School Arts and Crafts Festival** (931/389-9663, www.bellbuckle-chamber.com) in October brings hundreds of artisans to town. It is one of the finest arts and crafts shows in the region, attracting fine and folk artists from Tennessee and beyond.

Shopping

The single most popular pursuit in Bell Buckle is shopping. Antiques are the main attraction, but arts and crafts are a close second. Several Nashville interior designers and antiques dealers have booths in shops in Bell Buckle because of the goods found here. You can spend an entire day rummaging through these shelves, although it is generally too crowded to do so the day of the MoonPie Festival.

The **Painted Clay Studio** (26 Railroad Sq., 615/220-8888, 10am-8pm, Mon.-Sat., noon-6pm Sun. www.paintedclaystudio.com) sells a wide selection of artwork, from pottery and sculpture to paintings. Most pieces here have a fresh, modern appeal.

The **Froggie Went a Shoppin'** (6 Railroad Sq., 931/813-3034) and **Doodle Bug Too** (Railroad Sq., 931/389-9009) are sister shops that sell jewelry, housewares, gifts, and folk art.

For antiques try the **Bell Buckle Antique Mall** (112 Main St., 931/389-6174, 10am-4pm Mon.-Sat., noon-4pm Sun.).

Accommodations

Host and hostess James and Ina Mingle run the **Mingle House Bed and Breakfast** (116 Main St., 931/389-9453, www.themin-glehouse.blogspot.com, $80-85) in a restored 1898 Victorian home. Rooms are furnished with antiques, and guests can fuel up with a country-style breakfast of eggs, sausage, bacon, and more in the morning.

Food

There's no debate about where to eat in Bell

The Bell Buckle Café is a local institution.

Buckle. The ★ **Bell Buckle Café** (Railroad Sq., 931/389-9693, 10:30am-2pm Mon., 10:30am-8pm Tues.-Thurs., 10:30am-9pm Fri.-Sat., 11am-5pm Sun., $5-15) is not only a Bell Buckle institution, but it is also one of the only games in town. The menu is Southern, with a few refined touches (like ostrich burgers and spinach-strawberry salad) you won't find at most small-town cafés. The menu is also mighty diverse, with seafood, pasta, and sandwiches in addition to the usual plate lunches and dinner entrées. The large dining room fills up quickly, especially for lunch, so there's no shame in coming a bit early. The Bell Buckle Café takes care of your entertainment needs, too. There's always live music on Thursday, Friday, and Saturday nights, usually bluegrass or country. Local radio station WLIJ broadcasts a musical variety show from the café on Saturday 1pm-3pm, which is a great reason to come to the café for lunch.

If you managed to pass up homemade dessert at the Bell Buckle Café, then head to **Bluebird Antiques and Ice Cream Parlor** (15 Webb Rd., 931/389-6549, 8am-5pm Mon.-Sat., 11am-5pm Sun.). Here you'll find a turn-of-the-20th-century soda fountain with hand-dipped ice cream and homemade waffle cones. Come in the morning to see (and smell) the staff making the cones. Not to be missed.

Information

The **Bell Buckle Chamber of Commerce** (931/389-9663, www.bellbucklechamber.com) publishes brochures, promotes the town, and operates as a clearinghouse for information.

The Southern Heartland

The region of Tennessee south of Walking Horse Country and east of the Natchez Trace is a fertile area known for farming, the railroad, and a very famous brand of sipping whiskey. The Jack Daniel's Distillery in Lynchburg is the greatest single draw in this region, but there are many other reasons to come.

Tims Ford Lake near Winchester and Tullahoma is ideal for boating and fishing. The Elk River that runs near Fayetteville is perfect for canoeing, and the tiny railroad town of Cowan is a down-home gem waiting to be discovered. The biggest music festival in all of Tennessee, Bonnaroo, takes place every June near Manchester. Perhaps the best-kept secret in the whole area is the George Dickel Distillery in lovely Normandy.

PULASKI

The city of **Pulaski** has two significant claims to fame. The first is that it was here that a 21-year-old Confederate soldier, Sam Davis, was executed by the Union army for spying. Davis was captured in Giles County on November 20, 1863, carrying sensitive

Union papers. When he refused to say where he got them, Davis was sentenced to death. The young soldier's final words, written in a letter to his mother, immortalized his sacrifice: "If I had a thousand lives, I would give them all before I would betray a friend or the confidence of my informer."

Pulaski's second, and better-known, claim to fame (or claim to infamy, rather) is that it was here that the Ku Klux Klan was established, in the spring of 1866.

Sights

If you see only one county courthouse in this part of Tennessee, let it be the **Giles County Courthouse** (1 Square, Pulaski, 931/424-4044), an elegant neoclassical courthouse that has been called the most beautiful in Tennessee. Built of brick and marble, its finest feature is a three-story rotunda capped by a dome and skylight. In the cupola, the 1858 bell strikes the hours. A ladies' restroom in the basement was a place where women and children who had come to town to shop could rest a spell before making the long journey back into the countryside. The restroom was furnished with several beds and a cradle.

The courthouse is the county's fifth. The first was a rough log cabin, and it was abandoned as the county grew. The second and third courthouses were destroyed by fire, and the fourth courthouse, completed in 1859, survived the Civil War only because Thomas Martin, a prominent citizen and the founder of Martin College, paid a $3,000 bribe to the Federals. The fourth courthouse did not survive to the present, however; it too was destroyed by fire, this time in 1907. The current courthouse was completed in 1909 at a cost of $132,000 and was made fireproof.

The courthouse is surrounded by a bustling courthouse square, fronted by businesses, including antiques shops and restaurants.

Pulaski has two monuments to the boy hero of the Confederacy. A statue of Sam Davis stands at the south side of the courthouse. The statue was erected in 1909 by the United Daughters of the Confederacy.

The second monument is on Sam Davis Avenue, where Davis was executed. A small museum is located here, but it does not have regular hours. Call the Giles County Tourism Foundation at 931/363-3789 during business hours (8am-5pm Mon.-Thurs., 8am-4:30pm Fri.) to arrange for someone to open it for you.

Pulaski is a lovely town, with a number of beautiful old homes. Two of the most noteworthy are the **Brown-Daly-Horne Home** (307 W. Madison St.), which was the home of onetime Tennessee governor John C. Brown. Brown served as the chairman of the convention that rewrote the Tennessee constitution in 1870. He did so well that Tennesseans elected him their 19th governor in 1870. The home is an excellent example of the Queen Anne style and is on the National Register of Historic Places.

The second prominent home is the **Thomas Martin House** (302 S. 2nd St.), built in 1842 by Thomas Martin, who founded Martin College. It was a hotel in the early 20th century and is now a bank.

Two different groups of Cherokee passed through Pulaski during the 1838-1839 removal, now called the Trail of Tears. The Pulaski Trail of Tears Interpretive Center (Stadium Street, 931/424-4044, www.nativehistoryassociation.org, by appointment only) tells the story of this terrible period in America's history through maps and educational materials. Even if you can't get inside there are sculptures and other educational monuments to this dark past in Pulaski that are worth a visit.

Entertainment

The **Martin Movie Theater** (S. 5th St., 931/424-7373, www.moviesatmartin.com) shows movies on Friday and Saturday nights and Saturday and Sunday afternoons.

Accommodations

Located on a quiet residential street in town, **Miss Butler's Bed and Breakfast** (429 W. Jefferson St., 931/424-0014, www.missbutlers.

The Origins of the Ku Klux Klan

The Ku Klux Klan (KKK) was established in the spring of 1866 in Pulaski by six ex-Confederate soldiers who saw it as a secret society for fun and entertainment. They adopted some of the trappings of a college fraternity and performed initiation rituals and pranks. During the second half of 1866, new "dens" of the Ku Klux Klan were formed in nearby counties, but there was no evidence of the vigilantism and violence that has come to be associated with the KKK.

Between 1867 and 1868, the political nature of the KKK emerged. Ex-Confederate soldiers home from the war were unhappy with Reconstruction policies that promoted voting rights for African Americans and gave preferences to former Union soldiers and sympathizers. The KKK was seen as a way to resist these policies. Members met for a convention in Nashville in 1867, and a year later Nathan Bedford Forrest was elected to be the grand wizard of the Klan.

During this period, the Klan was strongest in Giles, Humphreys, Lincoln, Marshall, and Maury Counties in Middle Tennessee and Dyer, Fayette, Gibson, Hademan, and Obion Counties in West Tennessee. Klansmen intimidated African Americans with attacks, whippings, and murder. They were particularly active during the 1868 election, when many African Americans were allowed to vote for the first time.

Tennessee governor William Brownlow was a staunch Unionist and was resolved to putting an end to the Klan's activities. In 1868, he announced new, harsh penalties for being associated with the Klan. He hired a private detective from Cincinnati to infiltrate the Klan and give names of people who were involved. After the detective turned up dead in February 1869, Brownlow declared martial law in six Middle Tennessee counties.

Brownlow's tenure as governor was just about up, however. A week later he resigned to take a seat in the U.S. Senate. His successor, Dewitt Senter, was less strident in his views and less controversial in his actions. Later that year, Forrest called for the end of the Klan, saying that it had served its purpose.

For about 50 years, the KKK was dormant. But in Georgia in 1915 it was resurrected, and it remained active in the Deep South, including Tennessee, for the next three decades. Members intimidated and terrorized blacks, Jews, and other minorities; they murdered and maimed men and women; and they attacked whites who were seen to sympathize with minorities. The Klan's political influence helped to elect Tennessee governor Austin Peay in 1923 and U.S. senator Lawrence D. Tyson in 1924, among others.

Since the Klan was officially disbanded in 1944, its name has been adopted by various extremist organizations, some of which have tried to stage events in Pulaski, the birthplace of the KKK. Town residents have fought these events, wishing to leave behind their historic association with the Ku Klux Klan.

com, $95-125) is an 1888 Georgian-style town house that has five separate guest rooms. Each room is named for a historical figure with ties to Giles County: Among them are Sam Davis, Frank Mars, and Tennessee governor John C. Brown. The house is named after Miss Margaret Butler, an educator and historian of the area. Each room has a private bath and telephone. Guests have access to a fax machine, and there is wireless Internet throughout the home. Guests also enjoy privileges at the local Hillcrest Country Club, where you can play golf or tennis or swim.

For standard hotel accommodations, choose from the **Richland Inn** (1020 W. College St., 931/363-0006, $80-85) and the **Comfort Inn of Pulaski** (1140 W. College St., 931/424-1600, $130).

Food

There are several casual restaurants downtown, perfect for lunch. **Reeves Drugs** (125 N. 1st St., 931/363-2561, 8am-5:45pm Mon.-Sat., $3-5) is an old-fashioned drugstore lunch counter and soda fountain serving sandwiches and ice cream. Skip the after-school rush if you are in a hurry. **The Coffee Corner** (102 S. 2nd St., 931/363-1911, 7am-6pm Mon.-Fri.,

10am-4pm Sat., $2-5) serves sandwiches, wraps, salads, pastries, and coffee.

The Pulaski **farmers market** takes place on Saturday mornings during the growing season on the south side of the courthouse.

Information

The **Giles County Tourism Foundation** (110 N. 2nd St., 931/363-3789, ext. 22, gilescountychamber.com) publishes brochures and keeps information about attractions, events, and accommodations. Stop in at their office in Pulaski to ask questions or pick up brochures.

CORNERSVILLE

If you've ever fantasized about staying in a log cabin, here's your chance. ★ **Lairdland Farm Bed and Breakfast** (3174 Blackburn Hollow Rd., 931/363-9090, www.bbonline.com/tn/lairdland, $145) consists of two genuine log cabins set on a large 19th-century horse farm. Both the Clock Creek Cabin and the Springhouse Cabin can sleep up to six people. And while they are log cabins, modern amenities abound. Each has a kitchen, bathroom, television, and heating and air-conditioning. The downstairs living rooms are centered on a working fireplace.

The kitchens come stocked with the makings for a country breakfast—ham, coffee, biscuits, pastries, and more—and you can prepare other meals in the kitchen or on the grill. Since Lairdland is a working horse farm, there are also opportunities for recreation. Horse owners can bring their own animals and board them for $15 per night. Miles of wooded trails on the farm are ideal for horseback riding, hiking, or mountain biking.

Lairdland Farm is located about 15 minutes' drive northeast of Pulaski, off Highway 31A.

LYNNVILLE

About 15 miles north of Pulaski is the quaint town of Lynnville. Almost 60 different buildings in this small town of just about 400 people are listed on the National Register of Historic Places.

Sights

The **Lynnville Depot Museum and Train Station** (162 Mill St., 931/527-3158, www.lynnville.org/railroadmuseum.htm, 8:30am-3:30pm Mon., Wed., and Fri., free) is the town's main attraction. Built around a 1928 locomotive, the museum invites you to climb aboard an old passenger train.

The museum also includes an exhibit

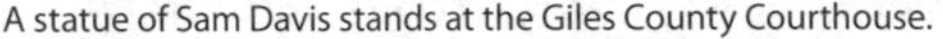

A statue of Sam Davis stands at the Giles County Courthouse.

about the nearby **Milky Way Farm** (931-808-2281, milkywayfarm.org), where candy bar giant Frank Mars lived. The farm was built between 1930 and 1934 with money Mars earned from the sale of Milky Way candy bars. He had invented the Milky Way in 1923, and by 1930 it was the number-one selling candy bar in the world. The Milky Way farm included several dozen buildings, cottages, and miles of fences. The crown jewel was a 25,000-square-foot 21-bedroom English Tudor-style manor house. Frank Mars died in 1934, and the property continued to operate as a horse farm for many years. More recently, it fell into disrepair, and parts of the 2,000-plus-acre estate were sold. In 2005, the property was purchased by a real estate development company that is working on preserving the manor. Some of the preservation work has already been completed and portions of the manor and grounds are open for tours (10am-3pm Mon.-Wed and select Fri-Sat, $5-$30, depending on the tour and whether or not you choose lunch, tea, and dessert with your tour). Horseback trail rides are available Memorial Day-Labor Day.

Food

In Lynnville, you must stop at **Soda Pop Junction** (111 Mill St., 931/527-0001, 7 a.m.-2 p.m. Mon.-Thurs., 7am-9pm Fri.-Sat., 7am-5pm Sun. $3-13), a classic old soda fountain. Besides the fountain drinks, malts, and other treats, Soda Pop Junction serves breakfast, grilled sandwiches, and dinner plates. The burger is one-third pound, juicy, and costs less than $3. The grilled bologna sandwich is a favorite, and dinners include steak, pork chops, and fried catfish. Friday night is the fish fry, and on Sunday a country buffet is on offer for just $7 per person. The Soda Pop Junction is a great place to fuel up. There's live music on weekend nights.

Information

The **Giles County Tourism Foundation** (110 N. 2nd St., 931/363-3789, ext. 22, gilescountychamber.com) publishes brochures and keeps information about attractions, events, and accommodations. Stop in at the office in Pulaski to ask questions or pick up brochures.

FAYETTEVILLE

The county seat of Lincoln County, Fayetteville is a bustling little city. Its proximity to Huntsville, Alabama, helps keep it lively, and its old homes and classic courtyard square make it attractive.

Sights

From 1861 until 1969, Fayetteville's most famous structure was a stone bridge that spanned the Elk River. It included six elliptical arches spanning 450 feet and was very rare. Legend has it that after marching his troops over it in 1863, Union general William Tecumseh Sherman ordered it destroyed, but the man chosen to carry out the mission could not bear to destroy such a beautiful bridge.

In 1969, the bridge collapsed into the Elk River, but the town has built a replica at **Stone Bridge Memorial Park,** located at the corner of Highway 431/231 and Thornton Taylor Parkway.

Located in the old Borden Milk factory, the **Fayetteville Lincoln County Museum and Civic Center** (521 Main Ave. S., 931/438-0339, www.flcmuseum.com, 12:30pm-4:30pm Thurs. and Sat. May-Nov., free) preserves the history and heritage of Fayetteville and Lincoln County. The museum houses military, medical, and agricultural exhibits, including an outstanding arrowhead collection. The building also houses a community center. To visit at times other than the listed hours, call the Fayetteville-Lincoln County Chamber of Commerce at 931/433-1234 to make arrangements.

Fayetteville's town square and the adjoining residential streets are dotted with beautiful and historic buildings. Ask at the Fayetteville-Lincoln County Chamber of Commerce for a printed guide to historic structures, and spend an hour or so strolling the streets of this lovely town.

Festivals and Events

The **Lincoln County Bluegrass and Crafts Festival** (931/433-1234) in September attracts regional musicians who compete in bluegrass, band, and dance contests. It takes place at the Lincoln County Fairgrounds.

Fayetteville gets a head start on the holiday season with **Host of Christmas Past** (931/433-1234, www.hostofchristmaspast.com) over the second weekend of November. The festival includes high tea, trolley rides, strolling musicians, and a candlelight walking tour of the city. It is held in downtown Fayetteville, on Main Avenue and College Street.

Shopping

Fayetteville may be the only city in Tennessee whose most celebrated retail establishment is a fabric store. **Sir's Fabric Store** (110 N. Elk Ave., 931/433-2487, www.sirsfabric.com, 9am-5pm Mon.-Sat.) has been in business since the 1940s and is still operated by the Sir family. It receives new fabric shipments every week and sells them at outlet prices.

Accommodations

There are a number of standard hotel chains in Fayetteville. **Cate's Corner** (37 Deer Trace Rd., 931/438-2447, www.catescornerevents.com, $100) has four guest rooms, plus a piano room and other amenities tucked away on an old dairy farm. Don't miss the Christmas decorations.

Food

The old Fayetteville jail is now **Cahoots Restaurant** (114 W. Market St., 931/433-1173, 10:30am-8pm Tues.-Thurs., 10:30am-9pm Fri.-Sat., $13-20). This is a popular choice for just about any meal; the menu is diverse, with burgers, chicken, and Mexican cuisine on offer. Locals like the homemade chips and salsa.

Information

The **Fayetteville-Lincoln County Chamber of Commerce** (208 S. Elk Ave., 931/433-1234, www.fayettevillelincolncountychamber.com) operates a welcome center and publishes visitor information, including a guide to historic homes and buildings in the city.

KELSO

Located about 10 miles east of Fayetteville, along the Elk River, is **Kelso**. Here you will find the award-winning **Prichard's Distillery** (11 Kelso Smithland Rd., 931/433-5454, www.prichardsdistillery.com, 9am-4:30pm Mon.-Sat., free), which uses water and premium molasses to create rum, which it then ages in handmade charred white-oak barrels. Visitors can see the copper pot stills and the barrel warehouse. The distillery, which also makes bourbon and country lightning, is open for tours, but Kelso asks that you call before visiting to arrange a tour time.

Recreation

The Elk River winds up from Alabama and empties into Tims Ford Lake. The river, tamed by damming, is an ideal river to float in a canoe. Its current is strong yet calm, and it winds through beautiful countryside. **Elk River Canoe Rental** (190 Smithland Rd., 931/937-6886, www.elkrivercanoes.com) is a rental outfit located nine miles east of Fayetteville, along Highway 64. It rents top-quality canoes ($17-66 per person), along with lifejackets and paddles. It also provides transportation to and from put-in and take-out points, and will arrange for multiple-day journeys if you like. The facility is open April-October. Call ahead to reserve your canoe.

LYNCHBURG

Lynchburg has been transformed by the popularity of Jack Daniel's Tennessee Whiskey, which is made a few blocks from the town square. No other small town in Tennessee sees as many visitors, from as many different places, as this one.

Critics may object to the tour buses and crowds, but for now, the town has managed to survive its success with relative grace. It has maintained its small-town feel, and it offers its guests a hospitable and heartfelt welcome.

Lynchburg is centered around the Moore County courthouse, a modest redbrick building. Souvenir shops, restaurants, and a few local businesses line the square. Outside of this, Lynchburg is quiet and residential. The Jack Daniel's Distillery is about three blocks away from the town square; a pleasant footpath connects the two.

Jack Daniel's Distillery

As you drive into Lynchburg, or walk around the town, you might notice some odd-looking gray warehouses peeking out above the treetops. These are barrel houses, where Jack Daniel's Distillery ages its whiskey. Around Moore County there are 74 of these warehouses, and each one holds about one million barrels of whiskey.

Thousands of whiskey drinkers make the pilgrimage every year to **Jack Daniel's Distillery** (280 Lynchburg Hwy./Hwy. 55, 931/759-4221, www.jackdaniels.com, 9am-4:30pm daily, free) to see how Jack Daniel's is made. And what they find is that, aside from the use of electricity, computers, and the sheer scale of the operation, things have not changed too much since 1866, when Jack Daniel registered his whiskey still at the mouth of Cave Spring near Lynchburg.

Jack Daniel was an interesting man. He stood just five feet, two inches tall and liked to wear three-piece suits. He was introduced to the whiskey business by a Lutheran lay preacher named Dan Call, who sold the distillery to Daniel shortly after the Civil War. In 1866, Daniel had the foresight to register his distillery with the federal government, making his the oldest registered distillery in the United States. He never married and had no known children.

Daniel died of gangrene in 1911. He got it from kicking a metal safe in frustration after he couldn't get it open and breaking his toe. After Daniel died, the distillery passed to his nephew, Lem Motlow. The distillery remained in the Motlow family until it was sold in 1957 to the Brown-Forman Corporation of Louisville, Kentucky.

Jack Daniel's offers two tours: The free tour takes a little more than an hour; there is a fee for the "sampling tour" that takes less than two hours and you must be over 21. All tours are offered first come, first served and they sell out, so get there early. The one-hour tour of the distillery begins with a video about the master distillers—Jack Daniel's has

Jack Daniel's Distillery in Lynchburg

had seven in its lifetime—who are the final authority on all facets of the product. You then board a bus that takes you up to the far side of the distillery, and from here you'll walk back to the visitors center, stopping frequently to be told about the key steps in the process. The highlight of the tour for some is seeing Cave Spring, where the distillery gets its iron-free spring water. Others enjoy taking a potent whiff of the sour mash and the mellowing whiskey.

The tour ends back at the visitors center, where you are served free lemonade and coffee. Moore County, where Lynchburg is located, is a dry county, and for 86 years the irony was that Jack Daniel's could not sell any of its whiskey at the distillery. In 1995, however, the county approved a special exemption for the distillery.

Other Sights

Drive by the stately two-story brick building on the southwest corner of the square that is the **Old Jail Museum** (231 Main St., 931/993-1791, www.lynchburgtn.com, 11am-3pm Tues.-Sat. mid-Mar.-Dec., adults $1 donation), which served as the sheriff's residence and the county jail until 1990. The building is now a museum and is operated by the local historical society. You can see law-enforcement memorabilia, old newspaper clippings, and vintage clothes. Go upstairs to see the prisoners' cells.

Just down Main Street is the **Tennessee Walking Horse Museum** (27 Main St., 931/759-5747, http://tennesseewalkinghorsenationalmuseum.org, 9am-5pm Tues.-Sat., winter: 10am-4pm Fri.-Sat., $5). The museum was originally located in Shelbyville, heart of Walking Horse country, but moved to Lynchburg in the early 2000s to take advantage of the bustling tourist trade here.

The Walking Horse Museum displays photographs, trophies, and other memorabilia from walking horse champions. You can admire both show and posed photographs of top horses and watch a video that explains what makes the Walking Horse so special. The films include show footage of the breed's distinctive flat walk, fast walk, and canter.

Festivals and Events

Spring in the Hollow is an arts, crafts, and music festival that takes place in early May. At the end of May, the **Spotted Saddle Horse Show,** an annual horse show, takes place.

Frontier Days in mid- to late June is a weekend celebration of early settlers. Costumed performers and traders evoke bygone days. July sees the **Tennessee Walking Horse Show** and August the second Spotted Saddle Horse Show.

The biggest event of the year in Lynchburg is the **Jack Daniel's World Championship Invitational Barbecue,** which takes place the last weekend of October. Teams must qualify to take part—they must have won another large barbecue tournament—and even then teams must be invited. Despite serious competition, the event is a whole lot of fun. Spectators compete in bung tossing and butt bowling (basic games to pass the time where you throw corks and other objects into a hole in the top of a barrel). There is clogging and bluegrass music, and lots of county-fair-type food is sold. The barbecue competition takes place at Wiseman Park on the outskirts of the town square. An arts and crafts festival takes place at the town square.

Christmas in Lynchburg livens up an otherwise quiet time in town, with seasonal performances and decorations.

For information about any events, contact the Metropolitan Lynchburg/Moore County Chamber of Commerce (931/759-4111, www.lynchburgtn.com).

Accommodations

The **Tolley House** (1253 Main St., 931/759-7263, www.tolleyhouse.com, $149, $179 with breakfast) is located about a mile from the town square and is a pleasant country retreat. A handsome antebellum farmhouse once owned by Jack Daniel's master distiller Lem Motlow, the Tolley House provides touches of luxury. Rooms have private baths, television, and wireless Internet access, and are furnished tastefully with antiques. Hosts Frank and Karen Fletcher provide your choice of a full country or light continental breakfast. Discounts are available for stays of two or more nights.

The **Belle Fleur Cottage** (Mulberry Creek, 931/580-0671, www.cottagebellefleur.com, $115-125) is a quick walk from town square and the Jack Daniel's Distillery. The three rooms in the B&B are set up for you to relax back to an earlier time, but still have some modern-day comforts. Families can enjoy board games or lounge on private patios and porches.

There are chain hotels and motels in Shelbyville, Tullahoma, and Manchester.

Food

The most popular place to eat in Lynchburg is **Miss Mary Bobo's Boarding House** (295 Main St., 931/759-7394, 11am and 1pm, Mon.-Sat., with a 3pm service in high season, $19). Miss Mary Bobo's started life as the home of Thomas Roundtree, the founder of Lynchburg. It later became the home of Dr. E. Y. Salmon, a Confederate captain who maintained an office there and rented out rooms to boarders. In 1908, Lacy Jackson Bobo and his wife, Mary Evans Bobo, bought the house and continued to operate it as a boardinghouse until the 1980s. Over the years, word of Mary Bobo's legendary home-cooked meals spread, and this boardinghouse became one of the region's best-known eating houses. Today, Miss Mary Bobo's is no longer a boardinghouse, and the restaurant is operated by Miss Lynne Tolley, who has worked hard to keep up the traditions established by Miss Mary. The restaurant is owned by the Jack Daniel's Distillery, and servers are hired from the local community college. A meal at Miss Mary's will easily be the most distinctive of your trip.

Guests should arrive at least 15 minutes early to check in, pay, and be assigned to a dining room. When the dinner bell rings, you will be taken to your dining room by a hostess who stays with you throughout the meal. Everyone sits family-style around a big table. The meal served at Miss Mary Bobo's is a traditional Southern dinner with no fewer than six side dishes and two meats, plus iced tea (unsweetened), dessert, coffee, and bread. Almost every meal features fried chicken. Side dishes may include green beans, mashed potatoes, fried okra, carrot slaw, and corn bread. Your hostess will make sure that everyone has enough to eat, will answer questions about the food, and will tell you some stories about the restaurant—if you ask. Be sure to call well ahead to make your reservations. Meals are fully booked weeks and even months in advance, especially during the busy summer months and on Saturdays.

For a more low-key meal, go to the **Bar-B-Que Caboose Café** (217 Main St., 931/759-5180, www.bbqcaboose.com, year-round 11am-5pm daily, 6:30pm-8pm Fri. Apr.-Oct., $7-12). The menu offers pulled-pork barbecue sandwiches, jambalaya, red beans and rice, and hot dogs. You can also order pizzas. On Friday night you can enjoy a barbecue plate dinner ($9) while you listen to live music. On Saturday, 10am-11am, a live country music radio show is broadcast from the Caboose Café.

There are a handful of other restaurants in Lynchburg, all on the town square. **Elk River Coffee** (12 Short St., 931/759-5552, 7am-5:30pm Mon.-Wed., 7am-8pm Thurs.-Sat., $6-12) sells lighter fare, including wraps and salads.

Information

The **Lynchburg Welcome Center** (182 Lynchburg Hwy./Hwy. 55, 931/759-6357, www.lynchburgtenn.com, open daily), at the intersection of Majors Boulevard and Mechanic Street, has public restrooms and information about local businesses and attractions.

TULLAHOMA

A quintessential railroad town, Tullahoma straddles what was once the Nashville and Chattanooga Railroad. Atlantic Street, actually two streets, runs on both sides of the tracks. The Depot Historic District on the east side of the railroad has a fine collection of old Victorian-era homes.

Sights

Arnold Engineering Development Center (Arnold Air Force Base, 931/454-5655, www.arnold.af.mil) is the nation's premier aerospace ground flight testing facility. Founded in 1951 by President Truman and named for Gen. Henry H. Arnold, a World War II commander, the center is also a major economic engine for the Tullahoma and Manchester area. The base has more than 50 different test facilities, ranging from large wind tunnels to space chambers. It has played a key role in developing all of the military's high-performance jet aircraft, missiles, and space systems.

Free tours for groups of 12 or more are available by reservation only. They last about three hours and require a good deal of walking; wear comfortable shoes. While individual tours are not provided, you can ask to be scheduled with a larger group, usually on Fridays.

Immediately adjacent to the Tullahoma Regional Airport is the **Beechcraft Heritage Museum** (570 Old Shelbyville Hwy., 931/455-1974, www.beechcraftheritagemuseum.org, 8:30am-4:30pm Tues.-Sat., by appointment in winter, adults $10, students $5, children under 12 free). The museum tells the story of Beech Aircraft Company, founded by aviation pioneer and Pulaski native Walter H. Beech. The museum features dozens of antique airplanes, including the very first Beechcraft ever made. Built out of love of aviation and Beechcraft planes, the museum is a must if you share either of these passions. Children will also enjoy seeing old-fashioned planes that look like modern-day cartoon characters.

The **Tullahoma Fine Arts Center** (401 S. Jackson St., 931/455-1231, tullahomafinearts.wordpress.com, 9am-3pm Tues., Thurs., and Fri., and by appointment, free) offers art classes, hosts the annual Tullahoma Fine Arts and Crafts Festival every May, and operates an art museum with regional art exhibits displayed on a changing basis. The center is usually open during its listed hours, but it is a good idea to call ahead. Look for the bronze sculpture of a female dancer, called *Summer Song*, in the front yard of the center.

The arts center is located in a historic Italianate home built by the Baillet family after they migrated from New York to rural Tennessee in 1868. The three Baillet sisters, Jane, Emma, and Affa, were noted milliners, poets, and artists, and it was their memory and legacy that inspired local residents to restore the home and open the arts center in the 1960s and 1970s.

Located in the South Jackson Civic Center, the **Mitchell Museum** (404 S. Jackson St., 931/455-5321, www.southjackson.org, during Center events and by appointment, free) displays items collected over a lifetime by former Tullahoma postmaster Floyd Mitchell and his wife, Margaret Noland Mitchell. Other citizens have donated artifacts to the collection over the years. The Center is happy to have a volunteer open the museum for visitors; just call ahead.

Accommodations

Designed for business travelers, small-scale conferences, and those seeking upscale accommodations, ★ **The Grand Lux Inn** (212 E. Lincoln St., 931/461-9995, www.thegrandluxinn.com, $115-125) is a stunning old Victorian home now converted into a thoroughly modern inn. Six guest rooms are available, each with a private entrance, bath, and amenities, including cable television, writing desks, hair dryers, and wireless Internet. The styling is modern. A continental breakfast of hot and cold cereals, fruit, pastries, coffee, and juice is served in the Breakfast Room, but this is not a traditional bed-and-breakfast. An added bonus is that Emil's Bistro & Marketplace is right next door.

The **Lodge at Gunter Hollow** (149 Gunter Hollow Rd., 931/433-5214 or 931/438-1665, www.lodgeatgunterhollow.com, $95-150, including breakfast) is a Christian conference center and bed-and-breakfast inn. Its seven guest rooms are new, neat, and comfortable. Each has its own private entrance, a spacious private bath, and a covered deck outside. Breakfast is served in the conference center dining room. There is also a parlor where you can watch television or relax with a book. There are also 400-square-foot sleeping cabins with bunk beds available.

Food

Once a fine-dining destination **Emil's Bistro** (210 E. Lincoln St., 931/461-7070, www.emilstullahoma.com, 11am-2pm Tues.-Fri., 5pm-9:30pm Thurs.-Sat., lunch $7.50-14, dinner $16-30) is now a casual, family-friendly spot but with a chef's influence. Chef Georges Martin is the brain behind the menu, which combines genteel Southern fare and fine French cuisine. You'll find everything from burgers to the boneless fried chicken with milk gravy to mussels in white wine and garlic broth. It is a good idea to reserve your table in advance and to call ahead to check the hours, which vary by season.

Information

The **Tullahoma Chamber of Commerce** (135 W. Lincoln St., 931/455-5497, www.tullahoma.org) publishes a directory of local businesses and hands out brochures and other information to stoppers-by.

NORMANDY

Normandy is a tiny one-street town notable for its position on the railroad and its location amid some of the most beautiful countryside in this part of Tennessee. The rural routes surrounding Normandy are well worth exploring.

★ George Dickel Distillery

About seven miles south of Wartrace, just outside of the old railroad town of Normandy, is one of the best-kept secrets in this part of Tennessee. The **George Dickel Distillery** (Cascade Hollow, 931/857-3124, 9am-4:30pm Mon.-Sat., $10 with tasting, otherwise free) makes thousands of gallons of Tennessee sipping whisky every year, and all of it comes from the Dickel distillery up Cascade Hollow on the Highland Rim of the Cumberland Plateau. (In deference to its connection to scotch, Dickel uses the Scottish spelling of "whisky," without the *e*.)

It's no secret that the best-known name in whiskey is distilled a few miles down the road in Lynchburg, but the folks at George Dickel don't seem to mind. The Dickel distillery is a smaller operation, and visitors are given a more personalized and detailed look at the operations of the plant. And the setting in the Cascade Hollow is one of the most charming in this part of the state.

George Dickel, a German immigrant, distilled his first bottle of whisky at Cascade Hollow in 1870. Dickel created a unique cold mellowing process, which made his product smoother than others. The distillery still uses Dickel's cold mellowing process, as well as his signature proportions of corn, malt, and rye. The Dickel distillery closed down during Prohibition, only to reopen in the 1950s. The distillery has changed hands several times over the past 50 years, and it is now owned by Diageo, one of the largest beer, wine, and spirits manufacturers in the world.

Visitors are welcome to take a free one-hour tour of the distillery, which takes you through every step in the process. The last tour departs at 3:30pm.

To find George Dickel, take Route 269 to Normandy, where you will see signs pointing you to Cascade Hollow Road.

Accommodations

For a high-class country escape, head to the **Parish Patch Farm and Inn** (1100 Cortner

Rd., 931/857-3017, www.parishpatch.com, $99-258), an inn, conference center, and restaurant set in the rural countryside near Normandy. The more than 21 guest rooms are scattered in six buildings on this working farm. They include spacious suites, private cottages, standard-size bedrooms, and rustic rooms in an old gristmill. The two least-expensive rooms share a bath; all other rooms have private bathrooms, televisions, and telephones. Rollaway beds are available. All guests can enjoy the full country breakfast served daily in the inn dining room. Other amenities include a swimming pool, walking trails, a book and video library, hammocks, and lots of countryside to explore. Parish Patch is a working farm, so you can also watch (or join in on) farm chores, pick your own blackberries (in season, of course), or just watch the animals. The Duck River flows through the property, providing opportunities for fishing and canoeing.

Food

The **Cortner Mill Restaurant** (1100 Cortner Rd., 931/857-3018, www.parishpatch.com, 5:30pm-9pm Tues.-Sat., 11:30am-1:30pm Sun., $16-44) is an upscale country restaurant that serves dinner five nights a week and is often booked for special events. Specialties include Memphis-style dry-rub barbecue ribs, grilled rack of lamb, baked rainbow trout, and frog legs. There is an extensive wine list, and desserts include a flaming bananas Foster made tableside. The restaurant hosts special buffets on Easter, Thanksgiving, Christmas, and New Year's Day, and the Champagne Sunday Brunch is a popular treat for locals and visitors.

The restaurant is located in a restored 1825 gristmill, and the dining room overlooks the river. It is an elegant choice for a special dinner.

NORMANDY LAKE

The largest non-power-generating lake created by the Tennessee Valley Authority, Normandy Lake is a 3,200-acre reservoir located between Tullahoma, Shelbyville, and Manchester. It is named for the tiny railroad town of Normandy nearby.

The lake was created in 1976 by a 2,800-foot-long dam across the Duck River. The river was dammed to control flooding and create recreational opportunities.

On the southern shore of the lake is the **Barton Creek Recreation Area** (158 Barton Springs Rd., 931/857-9222). Here you will find a campground with 67 sites, including 40 with electricity and water, a swimming beach, boat dock, picnic tables, and playground. Campsites cost $16-20 per night. The facility is managed by the Tennessee Valley Authority.

A 420-acre protected area near Normandy Lake north of Tullahoma, **Short Springs Natural Area** is a delightful corner of the world. Gorges and slopes carved by water, waterfalls, and abundant wildflowers characterize the area. It also captures two of Tennessee's defining geologic regions, the Highland Rim and the Central Basin. Because of the difficult terrain, parts of the natural area were never farmed and remain undisturbed to this day.

Access to the area is provided across from a parking area and water tower on Short Springs Road. To find the access point from Tullahoma, drive northward on Jackson Street (Highway 41A). Turn right onto Hogan Street after four blocks, and then left onto Country Club Drive after five blocks. Country Club Drive becomes Short Springs Road.

From the parking area, hiking trails head to Upper and Lower Busby Falls as well as the 60-foot Machine Falls. The Machine Falls loop is 1.4 miles, and the Busby Falls Loop is just under one mile. The 1.4-mile Laurel Bluff Loop circles the top of Laurel Bluff, providing lovely views of the area.

Short Springs is managed by the Tennessee State Natural Area Program and the City of Tullahoma. Camping, biking, horseback riding, rock climbing, motorized vehicles, and collecting plants are all prohibited.

You can download a color map from the State of Tennessee website (www.state.tn.us/

environment) or call 615/532-0431 for more information.

Long a favorite destination for area residents, **Rutledge Falls** is a natural beauty. Located near Short Springs Natural Area and sharing many of its characteristics, Rutledge Falls is on private property (the property owners allow visitors). Look for the Rutledge Falls Baptist Church on Short Spring Road. There is a parking lot just beyond the church, in front of an old brick farmhouse. Follow the short path to the falls.

MANCHESTER

Opened in 2003, **Beans Creek Winery** (426 Ragsdale Rd., 931/723-2294, www.beanscreek.com, 10am-6pm Mon.-Thurs., 10am-7pm Fri.-Sat., 1pm-5pm Sun.) is a pleasant diversion. Using grapes and fruits grown themselves or on farms in the region, Beans Creek makes a wide variety of wines, ranging from dry to sweet to sparkling. Their tasting bar and store is welcoming and spacious, and they sell other Tennessee wines as well. "Walk-throughs" around the property and plant are also offered.

People come from around the world to visit **Northside Clocks** (2032 McArthur Dr., 931/728-4307, www.northsideclock.com, 9am-5pm Mon.-Fri., 9am-1pm Sat., closed Sun.) in Manchester. This family-owned shop sells and repairs clocks. Its inventory includes new and antique pieces, including beautiful grandfather clocks, mantel clocks, and cuckoo clocks. It also sells exquisite Lefton lighthouses and Fenton Glass porcelain.

★ Old Stone Fort State Archaeological Park

Located a few miles' drive north of Manchester, on Highway 41, is one of the most mysterious historic sites in Tennessee. The **Old Stone Fort State Archaeological Park** (732 Stone Fort Dr., 931/723-5073) is home to a Native American construction some 2,000 years old.

Sometime around the birth of Christ, early Woodland Indians started to build a massive stone and dirt embankment encompassing 52 acres of woodland between two branches of the Duck River. The embankment was not constructed for military purposes, and there is no evidence that it was the site of a settlement. Archaeologists don't know why the Native Americans undertook such a mammoth job—without pack animals or wheels—but they suspect that the site was of spiritual, political, or community significance for a

Old Stone Fort State Archaeological Park

Bonnaroo Music and Arts Festival

Bonnaroo Music and Arts Festival (www.bonnaroo.com) started out in 2002 as a jam band music festival, but diversification has made this summertime mega event a destination for all types of music fans. The Bonnaroo takes place over four days in June on a rural farm in Manchester. Between 75,000 and 90,000 people come each year.

Bonnaroo has a hippie heart with a slightly hard edge. Place-names are Seussian—the music tents are called, from largest to smallest, What Stage, Which Stage, This Tent, That Tent, and The Other Tent. Activities run the gamut from a Mardi Gras parade to children's art activities. Of course, it's the music that really draws the crowds: reggae, rock, Americana, jam bands, world, hip-hop, jazz, electronic, folk, gospel, and country. The event is truly a feast for the ears.

In 2007, the Police were reunited at Bonnaroo. In 2008, headliners included Kanye West, Willie Nelson, and Pearl Jam. But quality permeates every echelon of the stage. Unknowns and barely-knowns routinely wow audiences, including names like The Civil Wars, Moon Taxi, and Feist. There is an emphasis on world artists and folk music. A jazz tent provides nightclub ambience, and there's even a comedy tent.

A few things to know about Bonnaroo: First, it's huge. The event takes place on a 700-acre farm, and the list of offerings is seemingly endless: four stages of music, whole villages dedicated to the arts, a 24-hour movie tent, yoga studio, salon, music-industry showcase, food vendors, and a whole lot more.

Second, Bonnaroo has above-average logistics. Organizers seem to consider everything, including the basics: drinking water, medical care, parking, traffic control, and a general store where you can buy necessities. Food vendors sell Tennessee barbecue, veggie burgers, and just about everything in between. A shuttle service between the Nashville airport and the Bonnaroo helps minimize traffic. Rules about camping, RVs, reentry, and security are commonsense and easy to follow.

All that said, you can't turn up with the clothes on your back and expect to have much fun. It's important to pack well: A good camping tent, folding chairs, and water bottles are necessities. It is June in the South, so it will be unspeakably hot. If it rains, it will be muddy. If it doesn't rain, it will be dusty. Even if you plan to buy most of your food at the festival, at least pack some snacks. There are ATMs at the Bonnaroo, but lines can be very long, so bringing plenty of cash is also a

great number of Woodland Indians. Studies have shown that the site was built and used for 13 generations.

After Indians left the area, white settlers used the site for industry. They built mills on the river and called the enclosure a "stone fort" since that is what it looked like to them.

Sights

Since the 1970s, the site has been owned by the State of Tennessee, and it is now a state park. The **museum** (8:30am-4:30pm, free) explains what is known about the so-called fort, including the people who built it. You can watch a 15-minute video about the site and learn about the paper and gristmills that 19th-century settlers built on the site.

The museum's gift shop carries a wide selection of works about Native Americans.

Festivals and Events

Flintknapping is the art of creating spears and arrowheads from stone, and twice a year the Old Stone Fort plays host to an eponymous event celebrating the ancient art form. Held over the first weekend of May and the last weekend of September, Flintknapping includes demonstrations, competitions, and material sales.

Recreation

About two miles of trails circle the fort and are a delightful and easy hike. The paths take you along the Duck River, past three waterfalls,

More than 70,000 head to Middle Tennessee for the annual Bonnaroo Music and Arts Festival.

good idea (but not so much that you attract trouble). Also bring garbage bags, sunscreen, and hot-weather, comfortable clothes.

Plenty of Bonnaroo fans take the opportunity to do a lot of drinking and drugs, partly because they're somewhere they don't have to drive for four days. There are police at the festival, but they don't seem to crack down on every recreational drug user at the fest (although they do comb the streets on the way in). Beer—including good microbrews—are sold and consumed generously.

Most people buy a four-day pass to the festival, but day-pass tickets are available, too. Four-day passes cost $200 and up; a limited number of reduced-price early-bird tickets go on sale in January each year. Regular tickets go on sale in the spring after the lineup has been announced, typically in February. VIP packages are pricier but offer amenities that are priceless, such as VIP restroom and shower facilities.

and along the interior of the site, now a serene and beautiful prairie. The sound of rushing water mingles with the symphony of prairie insects and birds.

Parts of the trail take you along and over the embankments constructed so painstakingly by Native Americans more than 2,000 years ago.

The Old Stone Fort park also has a picnic area with grills, a restroom, and picnic shelters.

About two miles down the highway from the park is the **Old Stone Fort Golf Course** (931/723-5075), a nine-hole golf course built along the Duck River. It is open year-round; carts and clubs are available for rent from the pro shop.

Camping

There are 51 campsites with water and electrical hookups, grills, picnic tables, and hard-surface pads. A dump station is available during the summer. One of two restroom facilities includes showers. Campsites are available on a first-come basis; the maximum stay is two weeks.

WINCHESTER

The seat of Franklin County is named for Gen. James Winchester, whose influence during the first 50 years of Tennessee state history went far beyond the military (www.winchester-tn.com). Among other things, Winchester was Tennessee's first speaker of the Senate and voted in the North Carolina convention that ratified the U.S. Constitution in 1788. He fought in both the Revolutionary War and the War of 1812. When Franklin County was created in 1807, it was decided to name its main city in honor of Winchester.

The town's most famous daughter is Dinah Shore, born Francis "Fannie" Rose Shore. Although she moved away at age seven, Dinah Shore is remembered fondly in her hometown. So fondly, in fact, that the main drag is named Dinah Shore Drive. Shore became famous singing for World War II troops and is best known for her television shows, including *The Dinah Shore Chevy Show.* She wrote cookbooks, was an avid golfer, and won nine Emmy awards. Shore died of cancer in 1994. There is a Dinah Shore exhibit at Winchester's Jail House Museum.

Sights

Franklin County's old jail was retired from use as a detention center in 1972, but instead of tearing it down, city officials decided to turn it into a museum. **The Jail House Museum** (400 Dinah Shore Dr., 931/967-0524, 10am-4pm Tues.-Sat. mid-Mar.-mid-Nov. 10, adults $1, children $0.50) now houses exhibits on local history, the Civil War, and Dinah Shore, among other things. The highlight for many is seeing an old jail cell, leg irons, and handcuffs.

One of Winchester's most notable structures is the **Hundred Oaks Castle** (Hundred Oaks Dr., 931/967-8583, open for guided tours by appointment). Originally built as a two-story plantation home in the 1830s, the property was purchased in the 1860s by Albert Marks, the 21st governor of Tennessee. Marks's son, Arthur Handley Marks, was inspired by the castles and estate homes of Europe. Starting around 1880, Arthur Marks and his wife, Mary Hunt, a wealthy native of Nashville, turned Hundred Oaks into a castle. When the work was completed, Hundred Oaks was a 12-bedroom building with a 40-foot-high great hall, a wine cellar, and many features of medieval architecture. The stones were quarried at Sewanee and the bricks baked locally. Unfortunately for Arthur Marks, he did not get to enjoy the fruits of his investment. Marks died of typhoid fever in 1882, at age 28. Mary Hunt remarried, and the estate was the subject of a long-running legal battle. From 1900 until 1990, the property went through a number of different incarnations, from a Roman Catholic Church and school to a dairy creamery and a private restaurant and club. In 1981, it was leased to the Franklin County Adult Activity Center, which used it as an adult training center for many years. The castle was badly damaged by fire in 1990. In 1997, it was purchased by the Kent Bramlett Foundation, a charitable organization. Special events take place here. Guided tours are available only to groups of at least 20 at a cost of $15 per person.

Entertainment

Winchester's downtown movie theater is **The Oldham** (115 1st Ave. NE, 931/967-2516).

Estill Springs

North of Winchester on the road to Tullahoma, **Estill Springs** is home to the **Montana Drive-In** (10251 Tullahoma Hwy., 931/694-3454, www.montanadrivein.com), one of only a few drive-in movie theaters left in the state. The double feature begins at 7pm nightly. Admission is per person, not per car, so no hiding in the trunk.

Franklin State Forest

A 7,291-acre forest managed by Tennessee's Forestry Division, **Franklin State Forest** (310 Firetower Rd., Sewanee, 931/598-0830) was acquired in 1936 from the Cross Creek Coal Company. Trails were constructed by the Civilian Conservation Corps during the Great Depression. Many of these trails remain today. Hunting and hiking are the two most popular activities here.

Belvidere

Named for Belvidere, Illinois, this community, set amid beautiful and productive countryside west of Winchester, was settled by Midwesterners after the Civil War.

A few miles west of **Belvidere** on Highway 64 there is a historical marker for Polly Finlay, Davy Crockett's first wife. The Crocketts settled on the banks of Beans Creek in Franklin County in 1812. The couple had two sons, and they named their Franklin County home "Kentuck." In 1815, Polly died. A year later, Davy Crockett married Elizabeth Patton, a widow with several small children of her own. The new family moved to Lawrence County in 1817.

The pretty **Falls Mill** (134 Falls Mill Rd., 931/469-7161, www.fallsmill.com, 9am-4pm Mon.-Tues. and Thurs.-Sat., 12:30pm-4pm Sun., adults $4, seniors $3, children $2) makes a perfect pit stop. The large three-story mill is a lovingly restored 1873 cotton factory. The water-powered mill now grinds flour and cornmeal, and the Falls Mill country store sells whole wheat flour, grits, cornmeal, and pancake mix. Visitors can also pay the modest admission fee to hear a presentation about the old mill and take a self-guided tour of the picturesque grounds.

In addition to a grain mill and country store, Falls Mill also has a two-story log cabin **bed-and-breakfast cottage** (134 Falls Mill Rd., 931/469-7161, www.fallsmill.com, $110). The cozy cabin includes a full kitchen, sitting room, and bedroom with queen-size bed. There is a television, heat and air-conditioning, and a working fireplace. The kitchen is stocked with the makings for breakfast, and guests can sample the home-milled pancake mix and grits. The cabin can sleep up to five people.

To find Falls Mill, travel to the Old Salem community along Highway 64. Turn north off the highway onto Salem-Lexie Road. Drive 1.3 miles, and turn left onto Falls Mill Road.

TIMS FORD STATE PARK

Tims Ford State Park (931/962-1183) is a 431-acre park built on the shores of Tims Ford Lake, between Winchester and Tullahoma. Tims Ford Lake was created in 1970, when the Tennessee Valley Authority dammed the Elk River; eight years later the park opened. The park is named for an early river crossing.

Recreation

Fishing and boating on the lake are the two most popular activities at the park. There are seven public boat ramps in the park and two marinas: **Lakeview Marina** (931/967-6711) has pontoon and johnboat rentals, fishing bait, camp supplies, and marine gas; **Holiday Landing Resort and Marina** (931/455-3151) is a full-service marina, with slip rentals, gas, and pontoon boat rentals.

The lake is known for smallmouth and striped bass, but you may also catch largemouth bass, crappie, catfish, and bluegill. Bait and cleaning stations are available at the Lakeview Marina.

There are eight miles of trails. They include the **Marble Plains Trail,** a 1.1-mile wheelchair-accessible paved path that winds through trees and fields past the Old Marble Plains Church and ends at an overlook of the Tims Ford Lake. From the overlook you can press on along the **Shoreline Trail,** a 3.1-mile path that follows the shoreline of the lake. The **Bicycle Trail** is a 4.4-mile paved bike path that winds through wooded coves on the Weaver's Point peninsula. Walking is also allowed.

There is an Olympic-size swimming pool, open Memorial Day-mid-August.

Bear Chase at Tims Ford is an award-winning 18-hole Jack Nicklaus signature golf course. It is located on a peninsula and offers beautiful views of the lake. Call 931/968-0995 for tee times. Greens fees are $40-50, but there are reduced rates for senior citizens and juniors.

Camping

There are two campgrounds associated with the park. The **Tims Ford Campground** has 52 RV and tent sites set in a wooded area in the main park. It is open year-round and has bathhouses with hot and cold showers. The **Fairview Campground** is located eight miles away on Highway 50, toward Winchester. Its 88 RV and tent sites are located on the lake. Fairview Campground is open April-October. Campsites at both campgrounds are $17.50 per night, or $20.50 with a sewer connection.

Cabins

The park has 20 large cabins overlooking the lake. Each cabin can sleep up to eight people in two bedrooms. There is a full kitchen with modern appliances, a full bath with shower, a living area with a gas log fireplace, and a deck off each room overlooking the lake. Cabins rent for $90-125 a night, depending on the season and day of the week. There is a two-night minimum stay, and the cabins are open year-round. For reservations, call 800/471-5295.

Food

There is a full-service restaurant, **The Blue Gill Grill** (912 Old Awalt Rd., Tullahoma, 931/455-3151, 7am-8pm Sun.-Thurs., 7am-9pm Fri.-Sat., $5-13) at the Holiday Landing Resort and Marina inside the park.

COWAN

The town of **Cowan**, a few miles east of Winchester, is proving itself to be the little engine that could. A town of and for the railroad, Cowan is reinventing itself as a lovely tourist destination. Located just off the Cumberland Plateau, its attractions include historical railroad-inspired landmarks and the lovely scenery of the surrounding countryside.

The railroad was important in Cowan's history and development. The Nashville & Chattanooga line, chartered in 1848, made its first complete journey between the two cities in 1854. Engines based in Cowan helped trains make it up the steep, winding track to Tracy City. This portion of the rail rose 1,200 feet in seven miles and was referred to as the "Mountain Goat" because of the steepness of the climb. The Cowan station that still exists was built in 1904.

The last passenger train stopped in Cowan in 1965. Eleven years later a group of citizens with foresight purchased the old railroad depot with the hopes of turning it into a museum. They succeeded, and it is now the most charming railroad museum in the state. And while passenger trains no longer pass through Cowan, it remains a stop on the CSX freight train system.

Sights

Cowan's old railroad station is now the **Cowan Railroad Museum** (108 Front St., 931/967-7365, www.cowanrailroadmuseum.org, 10am-4pm Thurs.-Sat., 1pm-4pm Sun., May-Oct., free). The museum displays an antique locomotive and train memorabilia and equipment. Photographs, period costumes, old railroad timetables, and machinery combine to evoke the heyday of railroad travel and transportation. There are also model trains and a pleasant park with picnic tables and other facilities outside. Call in advance if you would like to see the museum outside its usual open hours.

Accommodations

Cowan's heyday as a railroad depot is remembered at the **Franklin Pearson House Bed and Breakfast** (108 E. Cumberland St., 931/962-3223, www.franklinpearson.com, $75-99). Originally a modest railroad boardinghouse, it enjoyed a period of success from 1906 until World War II as the elegant and sophisticated Franklin House, and, later, the Parker House. Today this historic downtown property is a nine-room bed-and-breakfast.

The end of passenger rail service and a major fire in 1965 threatened to destroy Cowan's downtown hotel. After almost 40 years of various uses, the property was restored and reopened in 2003 as a bed-and-breakfast. The handsome white brick facade and elegant reception era evoke a bygone era, but one that is alive in spirit.

Each of the nine rooms has its own look and feel. Antique furniture, some of it original to the property, adds to the ambience. Rooms include several with a king- or queen-size bed, one room with twin-bed accommodations, and two suites. All rooms have a private bathroom, cable television, and a telephone. Breakfast is served in the lobby each morning and includes cereal, fruit, and hot specialties including eggs. In addition to the lobby, guests can relax in an upstairs library and sitting room.

Food

For a town of its size, Cowan offers a pleasant variety of dining. The **Corner House** (401 E. Cumberland St., 931/967-3910, 11am-2pm Mon.-Sat., $7-9) is a traditional Southern teahouse located in a Victorian-style home. Dine in homey sophistication on seasonal sandwiches, salads, and casserole entrées. The luncheon plate includes a muffin, entrée, and salad. Be sure to save room for dessert.

If Italian cooking is more your style, then head to **Sernicola's** (108 S. Tennessee Ave., 931/962-3380, www.sernicolas.com, 11am-2pm and 5pm-8:30pm Tues.-Sat., $9-15). Sernicola's has taken the unusual path of combining Italian specialties with good Southern cooking. The result is bound to please just about anyone. The weekday lunch buffet ($6-8) is always popular, as are the pizzas and the Pusher Burger, named for Cowan's pusher railroad engines.

Information

Cowan welcomes its visitors at the **Monterey Café and Welcome Center** (101 E. Cumberland, 931/968-9877, www.visitcowan.com, 9:30am-5pm daily), in the Texaco Station. Stop here for a refreshment and to pick up brochures and maps.

Murfreesboro

A city of more than 80,000 people, Murfreesboro is, quite literally, the heart of Tennessee. The geographic middle of the state lies just northeast of the city's courthouse square and is commemorated with a stone marker.

The presence of **Middle Tennessee State University** (MTSU) enlivens Murfreesboro. The public university with more than 26,000 students was founded in 1911 as a teacher's college and became a university in 1965. Student life revolves around the campus, located just east of downtown.

SIGHTS

Murfreesboro's downtown is centered around its 1857 **courthouse,** the oldest in the state. It is one of only six pre-Civil War courthouses remaining in Tennessee.

Stones River National Battlefield

The second most deadly Civil War battle in Tennessee is remembered at the **Stones River National Battlefield** (3501 Old Nashville Hwy., 615/893-9501, www.nps.gov/stri). Only a fraction of the actual battlefield is included in the national park, but enough remains to give you a sense of the battle that took place here from December 31, 1862, to January 2, 1863.

Start your visit to Stones River at the **Visitors Center** (8am-5pm daily, free). Here is one of the best interpretive Civil War museums in all of Tennessee. It is modern and dynamic, and portrays much more than the tactical events of the battle. It depicts the lives and privations experienced by Civil War soldiers, the effect of the battle on Murfreesboro, and the propaganda war that took place after the battle to determine which side was considered the "winner." Plan on spending at least one hour at the museum; the visitors center also has a gift shop and bookstore, restrooms, and staff who can answer your questions.

There are self-guided walking and driving tours to other Stones River landmarks. These include the **Stones River National**

Cemetery, where some 6,100 Union dead were buried. Confederates killed at Stones River were taken to their hometowns or buried in a mass grave south of town. Later, these soldiers were reinterred in a mass grave at Evergreen Cemetery in Murfreesboro.

Following the Battle of Stones River, General Rosecrans ordered the construction of the depot and fortification at Murfreesboro. He wanted to press on along the railroad to Chattanooga, but he needed a place from which to launch the attack. From January to June 1863, soldiers and African American laborers built **Fortress Rosecrans,** the largest enclosed earthen fortification built during the Civil War. Part of the fort remains standing today.

Historic Sites

The elegant Italianate mansion at **Oaklands** (900 N. Maney Ave., 615/893-0022, www.oaklandsmuseum.org, 10am-4pm Tues.-Sat., 1pm-4pm Sun., adults $15, students and children $6) was one of Murfreesboro's finest. It started as a modest two-room brick house in 1818 on the property of Dr. James Maney and his wife, Sallie Hardy Murfree. Additions in 1820, 1830, and 1857 left an elaborate and elegant mansion, now restored to its former glory. The tour of the home lasts about 45 minutes. You will see evidence of the various additions and hear stories about some of the notable people who visited at Oaklands, including Confederate president Jefferson Davis. Oaklands was badly deteriorated, vandalized, and quite nearly razed during the 1950s. Local residents fought for its preservation, and in 1958 it was purchased by the City of Murfreesboro. It was later deeded to Oaklands Association, which restored the home and opened it as a museum in the early 1960s. Today, Oaklands offers a range of special events and educational programs for local schools.

The city took over the old schoolhouse, which houses the **Bradley Academy Museum and Cultural Center** (415 S. Academy St.). Bradley Academy was established in 1806 as the only school for Rutherford County. Students paid $24 a session and were required to bring firewood. Courses included Latin, Greek, mathematics, logic, writing, and literature. James K. Polk, who would go on to become president of the United States, was one of the school's early students.

Bradley Academy closed in the 1850s after it was absorbed into the newer Union University. During the Civil War the building served as a hospital for the wounded. In 1884, it was repaired and opened as a school for African Americans. In 1918, the old building was torn down and a new one built in its place.

Bradley Academy remained a school, cultural center, and gathering place for the African American community until it closed in 1955. The non-profit Bradley Academy Historical Association took over the building, creating the Bradley Academy Museum (415 S. Academy St., 615/867-2633) but ran into financial difficulties. At this writing, the city of Murfreesboro proposed a plan to take over the museum, which includes exhibits about Rutherford County, community center, a restored 1917 classroom, and changing local art exhibits.

Murfreesboro pays tribute to its pioneer past at **Cannonsburgh Village** (312 S. Front St., 615/890-0355, 9am-4pm Tues.-Sat. May-Dec., adults $2.50, children $1.50). Reconstructed log cabins, a one-room schoolhouse, general store, and working blacksmith's shop evoke the town's early settlement. Cannonsburgh was the original name for Murfreesboro. The village grounds are open year-round, and admission is free if you simply want to look around. Fees are charged for a guided tour.

ENTERTAINMENT AND EVENTS

Nightlife

Liquid Smoke (Public Sq., 615/217-7822, liquidsmoke.biz, 2pm-late night Mon.-Sat.) is a pub that sells cigars and specialty and imported beer.

The Battle of Stones River

After Union forces took Nashville in early 1862, the Federals looked southward toward Chattanooga and Atlanta. It was their objective to drive a wedge through the southland, using the railroad as their path.

Following the Battle of Perryville in October 1862, two large armies were gathering for a battle. Maj. Gen. William S. Rosecrans's 43,000-strong Army of the Cumberland was camped in Nashville, and Gen. Braxton Bragg's 38,000 Confederates were camped 33 miles southeast in Murfreesboro. On the day after Christmas 1862, Rosecrans marched his men to Murfreesboro to prepare for the fight that was to come.

In a strange prelude to battle, on the still night of December 30, 1862, military bands from both sides played long into the night. It began as a musical duel between armies, with songs like "The Bonnie Blue Flag" and "Hail Columbia." But after one army began playing "Home Sweet Home," the other joined in. It was a poignant and unusual moment before one of the war's bloodiest battles.

The Battle of Stones River took place on December 31, 1862, and January 2, 1863. The first day's fighting was fierce and deadly. When dawn broke on New Year's Day, both sides tended to wounded men and gathered the dead from the battlefield. Fighting resumed on January 2 in a cold and driving rain. In what would eventually become the definitive moment of the battle, a brutal Confederate drive to push the Federals back failed in the late afternoon on January 2. Overnight, after he heard that Rosecrans was getting reinforcements, Bragg ordered a retreat. The low-spirited Southerners, who up until the retreat felt they had won the battle, marched 30 miles south toward Tullahoma in cold, wet weather. They were forced to leave their fallen brothers on the battlefield.

Tactically speaking, the battle was a draw, but Bragg's withdrawal allowed Rosecrans to declare it a Union victory. His claim was quickly accepted by the North, which was in bad need of a win. President Abraham Lincoln wrote to General Rosecrans these words: "I can never forget, whilst I remember anything, that about the end of last year and at the beginning of this, you gave us a hard-earned victory, which, had there been defeat instead, the nation could scarcely have lived over."

Stones River was the second-bloodiest Civil War battle in Tennessee, behind Shiloh. Nearly 24,000 men were killed or injured at the battle—13,249 Federal and 10,266 Confederate.

For live music, head to **Wall Street Restaurant and Bar** (121 N. Maple St., 615/867-9090). In addition to serving breakfast and lunch daily, it has happy hour 5pm-10pm and live music on the weekends. Locals love microbrewery **Mayday Brewery** (521 Old Salem Rd. 615/479-9722, www.maydaybrewery.com, 4pm-8pm Wed.-Fri., 1pm-8pm Sat.). No reservations are required for the $10 tours.

The Arts

Local and regional artists are shown at the **Murfreesboro/Rutherford County Center for the Arts** (110 W. College St., 615/904-2787, www.boroarts.org, 10am-4pm Tues.-Sat., free). The center is located in a restored 1909 Italian Renaissance building that served as the customs house and later a post office. Since 1995 it has been an arts center with gallery space. Theater performances take place on weekends in a charming 168-seat theater. Tickets are usually $12 for adults, with discounts for students and seniors.

Horse and Livestock Shows

Check the calendar at the **Tennessee Miller Coliseum** (340-B W. Thompson Ln., 615/494-8961, www.mtsu.edu), a 220,000-square-foot air-conditioned coliseum specially designed for horse and other livestock shows. In October, Miller Coliseum also hosts the **Cynosport World Games**, (cynosport.com), which are dog agility competitions, complete with dock diving.

Festivals and Events

In May, the Main Street Association and MTSU's McLean School of Music present the two-day **Main Street JazzFest** (www.jazzfestmainstreet.com) in downtown Murfreesboro.

Oaklands presents **Oaklands Victorian Fair** (www.oaklandsmuseum.org) in early June. This daylong event features tours, craft and game demonstrations, storytelling, Victorian music, and an old-fashioned cake walk.

In mid-July, Murfreesboro celebrates **Uncle Dave Macon Days Festival** (615/890-0355 uncledavemacondays.com) in Cannonsburgh Village. Old-time music is the main draw at this free festival, which features banjo music, buck dancing, and clogging. There is also a gospel showcase.

Oaklands was once Murfreesboro's finest Italianate mansion.

RECREATION

Murfreesboro has 5 miles of paved riverside **greenways** for walking, biking, and in-line skating. There are **canoe access points** and four **fishing piers.** There are 11 trailheads, including those at Thompson Lane, Broad Street, Redoubt Brannan, Manson Pike, and Cannonsburgh Village. Download a map from www.murfreesborotn.gov. A master plan calls for 24 new trailheads, 14 blueways (water trails), and 67 miles of off-road trails in the next 25 years.

ACCOMMODATIONS

The **Carriage Lane Inn** (337 E. Burton St., 615/890-3630, www.carriagelaneinn.com, $109-375) is unique among bed-and-breakfasts, quite simply for its size. The property comprises three individual buildings located next to each other in a quiet residential neighborhood. All three are historic homes, and each has been carefully restored to preserve the antique feel of the homes but to also provide guests with modern comforts and amenities. The Main Inn, the Cottage, and the Yellow House can each be rented as a whole or by the room. Individual room rentals include a hearty breakfast. The property hosts frequent family reunions, weddings, and special events.

The interstate exits surrounding Murfreesboro are host to dozens of different chain motels, including **Fairfield Inn and Suites** (175 Chaffin Pl., 615/849-1150, $90-120), **Wingate Inn** (165 Chaffin Pl., 615/849-9000, $80-100), and **Super 8** (127 Chaffin Pl., 615/867-5000, $60-90).

FOOD

For something elegant, go to **B. McNeel's** (215 N. Church St., 615/896-1002, 11am-2pm Mon-Fri., $10-30). Exposed brick walls, high ceilings, and a charming outdoor patio put this downtown lunch spot high on the ambience list. Choose from designer salads and sandwiches or midday versions of entrées usually seen only on dinner menus, including steak, chicken, and seafood. The fried oysters are a favorite.

Another favorite downtown eatery is **Marina's Italian Restaurant** (125 N. Maple St., 615/849-8881, 11am-9pm Tues.-Sat., $5-18). Choices include pizzas, calzones, pasta, and the gargantuan stuffed pizza, a real crowd pleaser. The lunchtime menu features full- and half-size plates, all under $8. For dinner, you can choose from the standards, as well as upscale dishes like shrimp pasta and baked salmon.

Maple Street Grill (109 N. Maple St., 615/890-0122, www.maplestreetgrill.com, 11am-9pm Mon.-Thurs., 4pm-10pm Fri., 4pm-9pm Sat., $8-19) is a reliable, popular better-than-bar food option that attracts a cross-section of diners to a vibrant downtown eatery.

INFORMATION

The **Rutherford County Chamber of Commerce and Visitors Center** (501 Memorial Blvd., 615/893-6565, www.rutherfordchamber.org, 8am.-4:30pm Mon.-Fri.) publishes visitor information and operates a visitors center. If you arrive on the weekend or after hours, there is an outdoor information kiosk available.

AROUND MURFREESBORO

Smyrna

Boy hero of the Confederacy, Sam Davis grew up in Smyrna, once a hamlet, now a stop on the interstate highway. Davis's legacy brings travelers here today to see his boyhood home. The city of more than 33,000 people is also home to Nissan's North American headquarters, which attracts workers and a few visitors interested in seeing how cars are made.

Sam Davis Home and Museum (1399 Sam Davis Rd., 615/495-2341, www.samdavishome.org, 10am-4pm Mon.-Sat., 1pm-4pm Sun., closed in Jan., adults $12, seniors $10, children $6) is the childhood home of Confederate hero Sam Davis. Born in Smyrna and raised in an upper-middle-class family, Davis was enrolled at the Western Military Academy in Nashville when the Civil War broke out.

Davis volunteered for the Confederate cause, and in 1863 he was a member of Coleman's Scouts, soldiers who worked behind enemy lines to disrupt communications. He was detained by Union troops in November 1863 on his way to Chattanooga. Davis had in his possession papers that could only have been given to him by a high-level Union official.

Thinking that Davis would betray the name of his informant, Gen. Grenville Dodge arrested Davis and charged him with spying. Sentenced to hang, Davis still refused to reveal the name of his source, and he went to the gallows with the secret. His sacrifice made him a legend and a hero among Confederates.

His childhood home and museum keep this legend alive. Visitors see a short video about Davis and his sacrifice and are then taken on a guided tour of the boyhood home. The house, which has been a museum since the 1930s, includes hundreds of original Davis family items.

Nissan North America (983 Nissan Dr., 601/855-8687, tours at 10am Tues.-Thurs., free) is Rutherford County's largest single employer, with some 6,700 workers. The plant sprawls over 884 acres and cost $2.1 billion to build. Some half-million vehicles roll off the assembly line yearly, including Maxima and Altima sedans, and the new all-electric LEAF. Advance reservations for the tours are required; no children under 10 are allowed, and cameras, including camera phones, are not permitted.

LONG HUNTER STATE PARK

Long hunters were traders and hunters who ventured into the yet-unsettled Western frontier to trap wild animals and trade with Native Americans. They existed in Middle Tennessee during the 18th century, sometimes establishing rough farmsteads, called stations. One such long hunter was Uriah Stone, and the river that runs southeast of Nashville still bears his name.

Stones River was impounded in the mid-1960s to form J. Percy Priest Lake. Located on the lake's eastern shore is **Long Hunter State Park** (2910 Hobson Pk., 615/885-2422). Consisting of some 2,600 acres, the park comprises four units: Couchville, Baker's Grove, Sellar's Farm, and Bryant Grove, each named for farming communities that were inundated when the lake was made. Notably, Bryant Grove was named for Sherrod Bryant, who in the 1850s was one of the state's wealthiest African American landowners. In addition to the park's natural attractions, hikers may see stone remnants of early homesteads, standing witness to the area's past.

Recreation

J. Percy Priest Lake is the main attraction at Long Hunter State Park. There are two boat ramps that provide access to the 14,000-acre lake. Pleasure boating, fishing, and waterskiing are popular pursuits. Catches include large- and smallmouth bass, rockfish, striper, crappie, bream, and catfish. Rental boats are available at the Couchville unit.

For hiking, choose from the short Lake Trail, Nature Loop Trail, or Inland Trail. Deer Trail is a mile-long path through woodland beginning at the park office. The Bryant Grove Trail connects Bryant Grove and Couchville.

Longer hikes include the Day Loop and Volunteer Trail. Overnight camping shelters are available on these longer hikes.

In addition, there is a small swimming beach, volleyball courts, playground, and picnic facilities.

Camping

There is no campground at Long Hunter State Park. A group camp facility can be reserved by youth groups and other organized groups with advance reservations.

Cumberland Plateau

Look for ★ to find recommended sights, activities, dining, and lodging.

Highlights

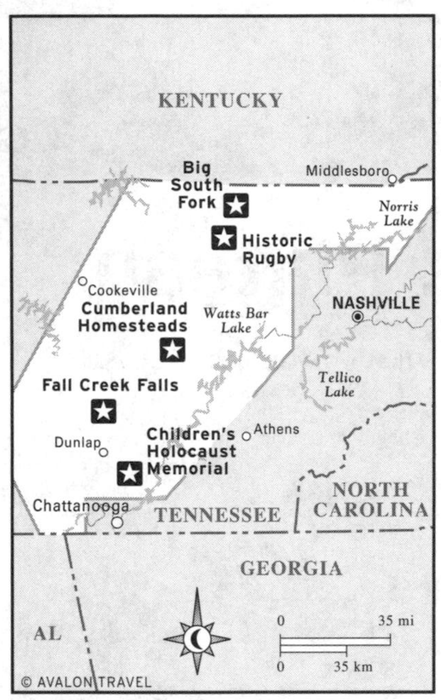

★ **Historic Rugby:** In the 1880s, English settlers founded a utopian colony on the Cumberland Plateau. This site remains a beautiful, spellbinding, and now educational place (page 281).

★ **Big South Fork:** The river gorge carved by the Big South Fork over millions of years is a lush playground for hikers, bikers, riders, and paddlers (page 283).

★ **Cumberland Homesteads:** Remnants of a New Deal project to bring homesteaders to the plateau are still apparent in this town near Crossville (page 296).

★ **Fall Creek Falls:** The tallest falls east of the Rocky Mountains as well as three others dot this expansive and popular outdoor destination (page 305).

★ **Children's Holocaust Memorial:** What started as a project to teach middle school students about tolerance is now a breathtaking public monument to peace and activism (page 314).

The Cumberland Plateau stretches across the entire state of Tennessee from north to south. A flat-topped ridge that stands 1,000 feet higher than its surroundings, the plateau covers 4,300 acres, or about 10 percent of the state.

In the northeastern corner of the plateau are the Cumberland Mountains, a rugged and rural region with Tennessee's largest deposits of coal. At the southern end of the plateau is the Sequatchie Valley, a pleasant, agriculturally rich valley that lies in the middle of the plateau.

The Cumberland Plateau takes in swaths of wilderness, including Fall Creek Falls, one of the state's best (and most popular) parks and home of the eponymous Fall Creek Falls, the highest waterfall east of the Rockies. In the northern plateau is the Big South Fork National River and Recreation Area, where the Big South Fork River cuts a dramatic gorge into the plateau. Hiking, horseback riding, and rafting are at their best here. In the southern plateau, Savage Gulf is a natural area with dramatic rock formations and steep gorges.

Cookville and Crossville are the largest cities of the plateau—mostly it is a rural, sparsely populated area. The New Deal-era project at Cumberland Homesteads is a remarkable story of idealism and perseverance. Historic Rugby, an English-style village founded by British author Thomas Hughes, is enchanting even today. The story of the Children's Holocaust Memorial at Whitwell Middle School on the lower plateau is a modern-day miracle that inspired a major studio film in 2004.

PLANNING YOUR TIME

The Cumberland Plateau is a region best explored leisurely. You should get off the interstate and take secondary routes to small towns like Jamestown, Oneida, Grassy Cove, Dayton, and Sewanee. Many of the parks and recreation areas are relatively rugged and undeveloped, so you will want to get out of the car and hike a little.

It is usually a few degrees cooler on the plateau than it is in the surrounding countryside,

Previous: Burgess Falls; Cookeville. **Above:** Motorcyclists enjoy the Cumberland Plateau.

Cumberland Plateau

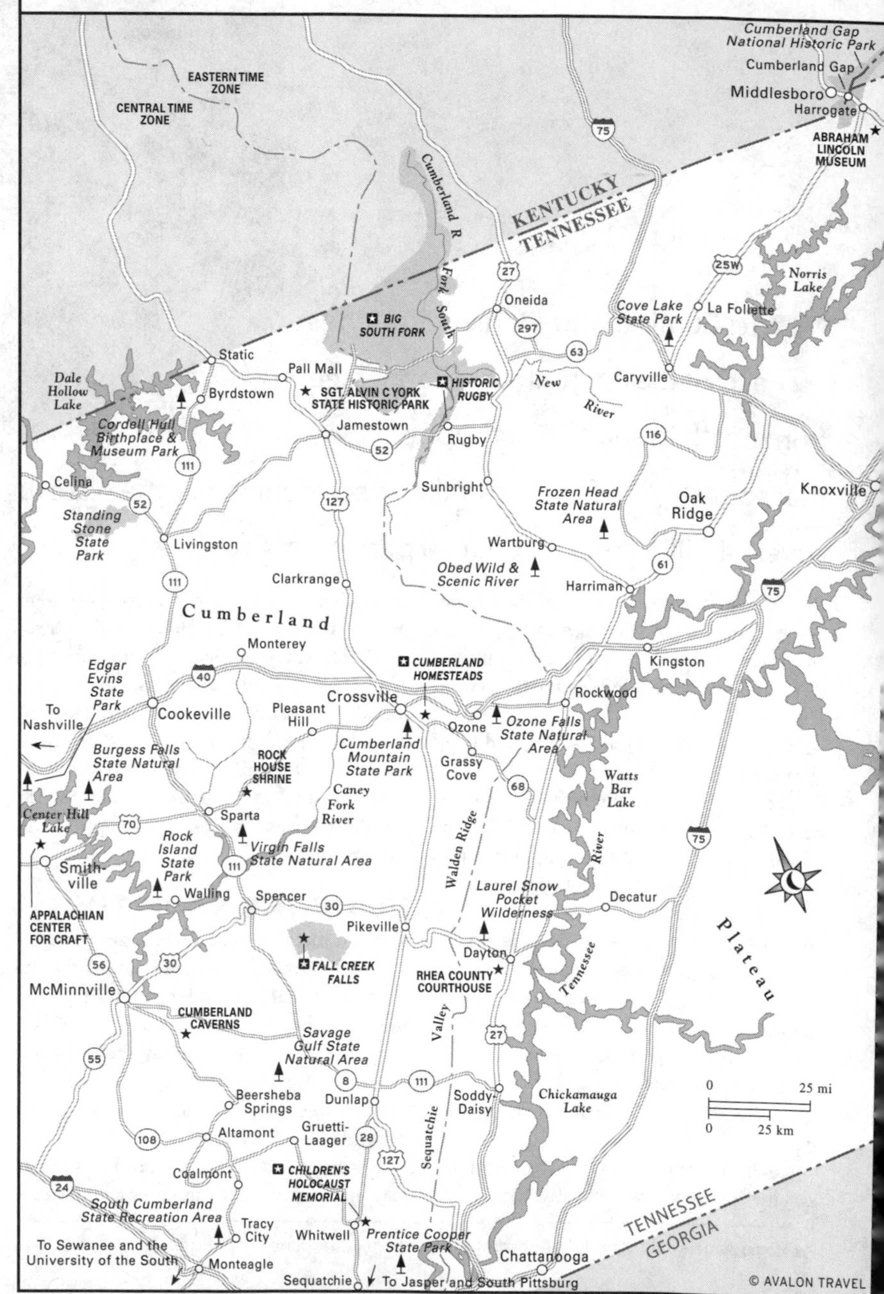

a plus during the hot, humid Tennessee summer. Also remember that the boundary between **Eastern time** and **Central time** cuts right through the plateau, so you need to be mindful when making plans in this part of Tennessee.

The Upper Plateau

The northern reaches of the Cumberland Plateau contain some of the most rural and isolated countryside in the state of Tennessee. Here the flat expanse of the plateau gives way to the rugged terrain of the ancient Cumberland Mountains, creating a landscape that is as beautiful as it is difficult to penetrate.

Case in point: When Tennessee officials were looking for a remote and desolate place to put a state prison back in 1893, they chose Brushy Mountain in Morgan County, where the prisoners could conveniently work in nearby coal mines, too. The isolation of this region makes it a lovely place to visit, as long as you are happy to slow down to the pace of winding two-lane roads.

Today, visitors who make the journey to the northern plateau are rewarded with beautiful landscape—mostly rural with small towns here and there. Prosperity is only modest in these parts; these counties are among the poorest in the state of Tennessee. Coal mining has been and continues to be a mainstay of the economy here, along with logging and manufacturing.

THE CUMBERLAND GAP

Once the gateway to the western frontier, Cumberland Gap is now a national park with great natural beauty and historical significance. An estimated 30,000 people walked, rode, or were carried through the Cumberland Gap over the Appalachian Mountains between 1760 and 1850.

Located where Tennessee, Virginia, and Kentucky come together, the Cumberland Gap has remained an important transportation link. The first tunnel through the gap was constructed in 1888, and soon after a macadamized road was built. In 1996, new twin tunnels were built through the mountain and the aboveground highway was removed in an effort to return the gap to its 1750 appearance.

Cumberland Gap National Historical Park

Most of Cumberland Gap National Historical Park lies in Kentucky and Virginia; only the southernmost reaches are in Tennessee. The **Cumberland Gap Visitor Center** (U.S. 25E, Middlesboro, Kentucky, 606/248-2817, 8am-5pm daily, free) is located just over the Tennessee-Kentucky state line; it offers exhibits about the Cumberland Gap, information about recreation opportunities, and tours of Gap Cave and the historic Hensley Settlement.

Take a drive to the **Pinnacle Overlook,** located at the end of a windy four-mile road that climbs more than 1,000 feet. From the pinnacle you can see the Great Smoky Mountains 80 miles away, and the gap itself, some 900 feet below. While there is no guarantee, when park staff is available, $5 shuttles to the Pinnacle Overlook can be arranged.

Cumberland Gap

You'll find the small, quiet town of Cumberland Gap nestled in the curve where Highway 58 meets Tennessee State Highway 32, just north of the Cumberland Gap Tunnel. The town sits on the southern side of the gap, surrounded on all sides by hills. Set as it is in the bottom of a geological bowl, the town of Cumberland Gap has been protected from the ravage of development. Historic homes line the streets, and there is a circa-1899 railroad depot and a railroad tunnel that was carved by hand in the late 1890s. Modern-day improvements include a network of greenways and hike-bike trails that connect the town with the Wilderness Road Trail, which in turn makes its way to the saddle of the Cumberland Gap.

One of the most unusual attractions in town is **Little Congress Bicycle Museum** (Llewellyn St., 423/869-9993, www.bicyclemuseum.net, 8am-8pm daily, free). Here you can see antique bicycles from the 19th and 20th centuries, including a 1934 Quadricycle and an 1895 Penny Farthing. Curator and owner Ralph McClanahan II, a district judge in Kentucky, is a bicycle enthusiast who grew up in Cumberland Gap.

Accommodations

Located in a charming historic mill, the **Olde Mill Bed and Breakfast Inn** (603 Pennlyn Ave., 423/869-9839, www.oldemillinnbnb.com, $109-159 and up to $193 for holiday weekends) offers unique accommodations in a lovely setting. The six rooms and one suite range from rustic comfort to modern luxury. There is a private log cabin, cozy upstairs "pinnacle" room, and a honeymoon suite with whirlpool tub and a beautiful four-poster bed. All rooms have private bathrooms and comforts like air-conditioning, microwave, refrigerator, and wireless access. A hearty home-style breakfast is served buffet-style in the morning.

HARROGATE

This small town a few miles south of the Cumberland Gap, where Highway 58 meets Tennessee State Highway 32, is home to Lincoln Memorial University (LMU), an independent four-year university with more than 3,200 students. The LMU mascot is the Railsplitters. To the visitor, LMU offers the **Abraham Lincoln Museum** (U.S. 25E, 423/869-6235, www.lmunet.edu/museum, 10am-5pm Mon.-Fri., noon-5pm Sat., 1pm-5pm Sun., adults $5, seniors $3.50, children 6-12 $3, children under 6 free), dedicated to the life of this celebrated president. This somewhat dated museum follows Lincoln from his boyhood in Kentucky to his leadership during the Civil War. A highlight is a wall that contains more than 100 different photographs of Lincoln, from the iconic to lesser-known images, which gives the viewer a greater sense of what Lincoln actually looked like. Among the museum's collection are the bed in which Lincoln slept on the night of his 52nd birthday and a rare photograph of his father, Thomas Lincoln.

ONEIDA

Oneida is the largest town in Scott County and one of the principal gateways to the Big South Fork National River and Recreation Area. Incorporated in 1913, it was a way station for the Cincinnati Southern Railroad. After Highway 27 opened in the late 1920s, Oneida continued to serve as a transportation hub for the logging and mining industries of this remote and largely rural county.

Today, Oneida is a workingman's town. The railroad still passes through town, and local industries include manufacturing, health care, and education.

It is a 70-mile drive west along Highway 63 from the Cumberland Gap, just east of the three-way intersection of highways 297, 27, and 456.

Accommodations

For accommodations, check into the **Grand Vista Hotel** (11597 Scott Hwy. 888/854-6300, www.grandvistahotels.com, $95), located at the intersection of Highways 27 and 63, near Huntsville. This full-service hotel offers free hot (biscuits and gravy) breakfast, refrigerators and microwaves, a heated pool, a business center, Internet access, and a fitness room. There are picnic areas if you want to enjoy the great outdoors before hitting the road.

Food

Phillip's Drive In (18499 Alberta St., 423/569-4002, 8am-10pm Mon.-Sat., $5-14) is home to the juicy Jerryburger, plus milk shakes, hotdogs, chicken tenders, taco salad, BLTs, and other diner food. Phillip's is a

Christ Church Episcopal has been active in Rugby since 1880.

longtime fixture in Oneida, and locals say the food is as good as it has always been.

RUGBY

North of Wartburg, the terrain of the plateau becomes more rugged and the towns less frequent. Settlements like Deer Lodge, Sunbright, and Burrville appear to be past their prime. If the countryside seems remote now, imagine how it must have felt to hundreds of young English gentry and American settlers who came to the Tennessee wilderness in the 1880s to develop a new type of colony.

You'll find Rugby nestled along the banks of the Clear Fork, a tributary of the Big South Fork of the Cumberland River. Rugby is approximately seven miles west on Highway 52 from Highway 27.

★ Historic Rugby

The story of these unlikely settlers, and what remains of their community, is well preserved in Historic Rugby (1331 Rugby Hwy./Hwy. 52, 423-628-2441, 888/214-3400, www.historicrugby.org), located in the northernmost corner of Morgan County (and also the westernmost edge of the Eastern time zone).

Rugby was the creation of British author and social reformer Thomas Hughes, who imagined a place where the second sons of English gentlemen, who would not inherit their fathers' wealth, could come to make their way in the world. Rugby was founded on principles of community, hard work, education, and the arts. Rugby opened in 1880, and "colonists" from America and Europe settled here. The experiment attracted considerable attention from the media, which both praised and ridiculed Rugby's unusual ambitions.

There were triumphs and tragedies: Typhoid outbreaks felled dozens of settlers, and economic pursuits failed due to harsh weather, poor soil, and the seeming lack of interest in hard manual labor among many colonists. For a time, tourism was a mainstay of the enterprise, since people were attracted to this odd English village in the Cumberland Mountains where residents stopped to drink tea in the afternoon. One of the oldest libraries in the state of Tennessee was founded in Rugby in 1882, and other pursuits such as a letterpress and restaurant were successful.

But Rugby could not overcome its challenges. A bad drought in 1887 was the final blow. When Thomas Hughes died in 1896, after investing a considerable portion of his own personal fortune in the colony, Rugby was considered to be a failure and an embarrassment. While most settlers moved away by the turn of the 20th century, a handful stayed on and passed the old Victorian-era homes built by colonists down to their children and grandchildren.

In the 1960s, a young man from Deer Lodge name Brian Stagg became fascinated by the enchanting ghost town of Rugby, and he organized Historic Rugby, the private nonprofit corporation that now runs the town.

Begin your visit to Historic Rugby at the **visitors center** (1331 Hwy. 52, no phone, 10am-6pm Thurs.-Sat., noon-6pm Sun., tours $7, $6 seniors, $4 students), where, after paying your tour fee, you'll watch a video about Rugby and view a small museum. A guided walking tour of the grounds covers just about one city block but much information, including **Christ Church Episcopal,** a one-room wooden chapel with original hanging lamps, stained glass, and an 1849 rosewood organ. The church was built in 1887 and remains in use today. The public is welcome at Sunday service at 11am. The **Hughes Public Library** looks almost exactly as it did when it opened in 1882, down to the original paint colors. Its simple unadorned walls are covered floor to ceiling with one of the best collections of Victorian literature in the country (about 7,000 volumes donated by American publishers). The tour also stops at **Kingstone Lisle,** the modest home that Hughes built for his mother, who lived out the end of her years, happily by all accounts, at Rugby. There's also a stop at a one-room schoolhouse that was used for all grades until 1951, and a number of smaller specialty tours (www.historicrugby.org/other-tours), such as a lantern tour and one of the old print shop. Private tours of groups of 10 or more are offered by appointment Monday-Wednesday.

Rugby's old commissary has been restored and converted into a **gift shop** (5569 Rugby Hwy., 423/628-5166, 10am-6pm Mon.-Sat., noon-6pm Sun.), which stocks an above-average selection of handicrafts, plus English- and Victorian-inspired specialty items. You can also pick up a copy of *Tom Brown's School Days,* the novel that made Thomas Hughes famous and rich enough to bankroll Rugby in the first place.

Rugby today is a marriage of old and new. The new visitors center was opened in 2006, and house lots are being sold according to the original Rugby development plan. But the presence of original Rugby buildings like the Hughes Public Library anchors the newness to its past.

In Rugby you cannot help but be enchanted by the atmosphere of natural beauty, unhurried life, and Victorian-era buildings. Coming here is a journey, not necessarily back in time, but certainly away from it.

Festivals and Events

Rugby puts on dozens of workshops and special events year-round, from heirloom plant sales to yarn spinning to other craft workshops, so you can pick the time of year that fits with your interests. Naturalists, artists, craftspeople, and historians lead these courses, which take place many, if not most, weekends during the year. Download a calendar from the Historic Rugby website.

Rugby's premier event is the **Festival of British and Appalachian Culture** (www.historicrubgy.org) in mid-May. Entertainers usually include well-known bluegrass and folk musicians, and there are traditional arts-and-crafts demonstrations. The British bit comes in with a maypole, bagpipe players, and food of the British Isles.

Accommodations

Fall completely under Rugby's spell by staying the night at ★ **Historic Rugby Lodging** (423/628-2441, $57-135). Historic Rugby offers overnight accommodations in the Newbury House, Pioneer Cottage, and Percy Cottage, all of which are on the National Register of Historic Places. In Newbury House, restored in 1985, there are five guest rooms and one suite. Two of the guest rooms share a bath; others have private facilities. All guests can relax in the downstairs parlor or on the sunporch, and there are coffee, tea, and cookies in the kitchen. Percy Cottage offers free wireless Internet. Rates at Newbury include breakfast. The three- and five-bedroom cottages rent for $80-135 per room, and guests have the use of a kitchen.

All Rugby accommodations are comfortable and unique among Tennessee lodging. Not quite your typical bed-and-breakfast and certainly not your average hotel, these accommodations are rustic yet entirely comfortable, with DVD players, wireless, and other modern amenities, depending on the

Beautiful Big South Fork is one of the state's lesser-known outdoor gems.

property. They are a favorite escape for many travelers in the region.

Grey Gables (Hwy. 52, 423/628-5252, www.rugbytn.com, $145 ($90 single) is a bed-and-breakfast unaffiliated with Historic Rugby but influenced by it nonetheless. The farmhouse-style inn has ten bedrooms, each furnished with antique furniture and colorful draperies and linens. The overnight rate includes breakfast and dinner prepared by hostess Linda Brooks Jones, a celebrated local chef. She also hosts a number of themed special events during the year.

Food

The ★ **Harrow Road Café** (5517 Hwy. 52, 423/628-2350, 11am-4pm Thurs., 8:30am-9pm Fri.-Sat., 8:30am-4pm Sun., $5-12) rounds out Rugby's attractions. Serving breakfast and lunch, and offering dinner by lamplight on weekends, the café is the heartbeat of Rugby. Tourists, residents, and the legions who drive Highway 52 daily meet here in the name of good eats. The menu reflects the hybrid nature of Rugby's appeal: There is Welsh rarebit and shepherd's pie next to fried catfish and turnip greens. All the food is good, though, and there is an effort to stay true to some of the English traditions. You can order hot tea without fear of being laughed out of the room. They may even offer milk. If you get hooked on a particular dish, check the website; recipes are often posted.

The Harrow Road Café closes at 3pm on weeknights in winter.

★ BIG SOUTH FORK

Big South Fork National River and Recreation Area (4564 Leatherwood Rd., Oneida, 423/286-7275, www.nps.gov/biso) was established in 1974 to preserve this northern-flowing large tributary of the Cumberland River and approximately 119,000 surrounding acres. Threatened with coal-mine damage and what would have been the highest dam in the eastern United States, local conservationists, with the help of then U.S. senator Howard Baker from nearby Huntsville, Tennessee, succeeded in saving this outstanding gorge and rim terrain in one of the most remote areas of Tennessee and Kentucky. About three-fourths of the park is in Tennessee. It is a land bejeweled with a wild river surrounded by natural forms such as steep sandstone bluffs and high arches, including famous side-by-side arches, arguably the largest in the eastern United States. It isn't as well known as the nearby Smokies, but it is some of the loveliest scenery in the state, and often substantially less crowded than the Smokies. This is the place to get out and commune with nature.

Orientation

State Highway 297 cuts through the Tennessee portion of the Big South Fork. It is a pleasant, scenic drive that takes you down to the bottom of the river gorge and back up again. The closest towns are Oneida (about 10 miles to the east) and Jamestown (about 22 miles to the west).

Sights

Soon after you enter the park from the east, you pass the park headquarters and a turnoff to the East Rim Overlook, a picturesque spot where you can peer out over the gorge. From the overlook it is a quick, steep descent to the bottom of the gorge at Leatherwood Ford, where you'll find picnic tables, an information kiosk, and trailheads.

Past the gorge is Bandy Creek, a focus of activity and recreation on the Tennessee side of the park. The complex, which sits on the site of an abandoned homestead of earlier days, includes a campground, horse stables, visitors center, and trails. The visitors center (423/286-7275, 9am-5pm Sept.-May, 8am-6pm May-Aug.) offers free information and detailed maps, guidebooks, and ice for sale. For those preferring a pool to the many swimming holes along the river, there is Bandy Creek Pool.

Hikers in the Big South Fork love the Twin Arches, a remarkable double natural bridge formation. This is one of their favorite destinations.

In the Kentucky portion of the park there are attractions that commemorate the historic coal-mining communities and railroads of the region. From 1937 to 1962, people lived in Blue Heron, a remote coal-mining town operated by the Stearns Coal and Lumber Company. Today, **Blue Heron Mining Community** (Kentucky Hwy. 742, 606/376-3787, year-round during daylight hours, free) is an outdoor museum where visitors can hear the stories of onetime residents, told through audio recordings and displays about daily life in this remote and beautiful place. From April to October, rangers are on hand to answer questions. At other times, you may explore on your own. From mid-April through November you can ride the **Big South Fork Scenic Railroad** (800/462-5664, www.bsfsry.com, Wed.-Sun., adults $25.25, seniors $23.75, children 3-12 $15.50) from Stearns, Kentucky, to Blue Heron.

In addition, the park hosts two festivals each year, usually in late April and late September, which celebrate the cultural heritage of the area. While Blue Heron is the largest cultural heritage site in the park, the Big South Fork is sprinkled with the remains of many more old settlers' cabins and farmsteads. Hikers, bikers, and horseback riders are asked not to disturb or dig around ruins that may be encountered.

River Recreation

The Big South Fork is a center for white-water sports, including canoeing, kayaking, stand-up paddleboarding, and rafting. Floating through the Big South Fork gives you entry to a remote and beautiful countryside where you can still see evidence of previous agricultural, mining, and logging use. The rivers and streams in the park offer placid floats and dangerous white water. The character of the rivers can change with heavy rains; check conditions before setting out.

For those without their own craft, there is only one permitted outfitter. **Sheltowee Trace Outfitter** (Whitley City, Kentucky, 800/541-7238, www.ky-rafting.com) leads beginner and intermediate white-water rafting trips down the Big South Fork mid-May-mid-September. Participants in these trips meet near Oneida. Sheltowee also rents canoes, kayaks, and tubes. They offer shuttle service to put-in points and provide maps and itineraries to help plan your river outing.

For those needing only a guide, **Against the Flow** (Byrdstown, 931/510-6939) offers professional guide services for the park's waters and others in the area. The river can be hazardous, and floaters need to be sure of their skills and equipment and know the area they are floating.

Horseback Riding

On land, there are 300-plus miles of trails marked by self-evident icons for specific uses. The remoteness of this park calls for horseback travel, and there are 130 miles of back-country horse trails. The *Trails Illustrated* map of the Big South Fork is the best resource for trail navigation in the park.

Southeast Pack Trips (299 Dewey Burke

Rd., Jamestown, 931/879-2260, www.southeastpacktrips.com) and **Saddle Valley Campground** (350 Dewey Burke Rd., Jamestown, 931/879-6262, www.saddlevalleycampground.com) are permitted horse outfitters for the Big South Fork. They offer overnight horseback excursions or half-day journeys. Expect to pay about $20 per hour to rent a horse or $100 per day for a guide if you have your own horses. Short as well as longer rides may be arranged directly at the **Bandy Creek Stable** (1845 Old Sunbright Rd., Jamestown, 423/286-7433,) in the park, which is also a place to board horses while you camp in the nearby Bandy Creek Campground.

Other Recreation

Big South Fork allocates trails for all manner of uses. Hikers may use all of the trails in the park. Mountain bikers may use specified bike trails or any horse trail. Wagon trails are open for all nonmotorized traffic, and multiuse trails include motor vehicles, such as ATVs. Users should check for specific ATV regulations before setting out.

Fishing and hunting in season and with appropriate licenses are allowed and popular. Big South Fork also has many locations open for rock climbing and rappelling, though arches and other fragile landforms are closed to these activities. There are no outfitters for these activities.

Accommodations

For an experience unique in the Big South Fork, reserve a bed at the ★ **Charit Creek Lodge** (865/429-5704, www.ccl-bsf.com). This is a privately operated concession offering rustic overnight stays at an old farmstead, plus supper and breakfast. It is especially good for groups since each cabin or lodge room can sleep up to 12 people.

The complex consists of three cabins (two for visitors), a barn, and a communal dining/gathering hall. There is no electricity or telephones. Pack light because the lodge is accessible only on horseback, foot, or bike. Full accommodations cost $100 per night per adult ($60 for children under 12) and includes dinner and breakfast. Hostel accommodations cost $40 per night and include access to showers, restrooms, and modest kitchen privileges. All guests enjoy wood-burning fireplaces, heated (in season) showers, and access to outdoor games, including volleyball and horseshoes. Meals are hearty and served family style. Tent campers are welcome at $10 per guest per day.

Charit Creek Lodge is situated about a mile down the trail from the Fork Ridge Road, at the confluence of the Charit Creek and the Stations Camp Creek. You can also reach it via the Twin Arches Trail.

Charit Creek is operated by the same company that operates LeConte Lodge in the Great Smoky Mountains National Park, and the reservation office is at 250 Apple Valley Road, Sevierville.

Camping

Bandy Creek Campground ($19-22) is the only campground in the Tennessee section of the Big South Fork, and it is easily accessible from Leatherwood Road (Highway 297), the only paved road through the heart of the park. There are 181 sites, 96 with water and electrical hookups, and 49 for tents only, and two group-camping loops with 19 sites in one and 17 sites in the other. The facility is open year-round, with reservations (877/444-6777, www.nps.gov/biso) accepted April-October. Bandy Creek is popular with families in part because it is that rare campground with a swimming pool ($3). Campgrounds located in Kentucky include Blue Heron ($17) and Alum Ford ($5). Nearby **Station Camp Horse Camp and Bear Creek Horse Camp** (931/319-6893, the state line in Kentucky) allows you to camp with your horses).

Backcountry camping is allowed in some areas with a permit, available at the park and from many area businesses.

As is the case at all area campgrounds, you are asked not to bring firewood in from outside the park to help in efforts to decrease the spread of the emerald ash borer.

PICKETT STATE PARK

Pickett CCC Memorial State Park (4605 Pickett Park Hwy., 931/879-5821, tnstateparks.com/parks/about/pickett) and the surrounding Pickett State Forest comprise 11,000 acres of land obtained by the state from the Sterns Coal & Lumber Company in the midst of the Great Depression of the 1930s. The park is named after the small and isolated county in which it is located, which in turn was named after Howell L. Pickett, an otherwise unnoted Tennessee state representative involved in the county's formation in 1879. The Civilian Conservation Corps (CCC), a New Deal program to assist the unemployed, built the basic infrastructure of the park in its early days. The original administrative buildings, various roadside and trailside improvements, several rustic stone cabins (still comfortably in use), and the Thompson Creek Dam that creates the park's 15-acre recreation lake, were constructed by the local workers who joined the CCC.

Picket State Park is just five miles south of the Kentucky/Tennessee border, about 14 miles northeast of Jamestown.

Recreation

Seasonal uses of the lake include a free swimming area with a fine-sand beach, changing facilities, and rental canoes and fishing boats. No private boats are allowed, but limited recreation equipment such as horseshoes and tennis rackets can be borrowed.

The jewels of Pickett, however, are the natural features and forms that the slow forces of deep geological time have wrought. The soft sandstone under harder caprock and above less-permeable layers eroded to form numerous rock overhangs called variously caves or rock houses, or more spectacularly, the famous natural bridges of the park. In the case of natural bridges, the forces of erosion have worked on both sides of a narrow ridge to form a passage all the way through the sandstone. Several of these forms, such as **Hazard Cave, Indian Rock House,** and a natural bridge, can be reached by short and clearly marked walks from State Highway 154, the road to and through the park.

There are 58 miles of hiking trails in Pickett. A network of one- to two-mile loops highlights the park's features. Those seeking backcountry hiking can set out on either the **Hidden Passage Trail** or the **Rock Creek Trail.** The former follows Thompson Creek into the adjacent Big South Fork National River and Recreation Area, where it becomes the Shiltowee Trace Trail and can take the hiker some 40 miles into the Daniel Boone National Forest in Kentucky. The Rock Creek Trail follows this creek into the Big South Fork, where it becomes the John Muir Trail and extends a further 40 miles. The two Pickett trails intersect and form a pair of double loops each about 8-10 miles long, just right for a pleasant day of hiking.

Backcountry camping in Pickett can be arranged at the park office (931/879-5821), and Big South Fork allows it with a permit as well. Pets are allowed on a leash on trails. Hunting is allowed in backcountry areas during specific fall and winter hunting seasons.

Accommodations and Camping

Pickett's overnight facilities include 32 tent and trailer camping sites available year-round on a first-come, first-served basis ($16 per night); a large group facility with dorm space for 144 people and an indoor dining and cooking facility ($3 per person per night, minimum charge $200 per night); and four types of cabins: rustic (sleeps four), chalet (sleeps two), deluxe (sleeps six), and villa (sleeps eight). Only one cabin (the deluxe unit) is pet friendly, and there is a $15 pet fee. Cabins cost $85-120 per night, with a $20-per-night discount during the off-season, November-March. Reservations can be made up to a year in advance. There is no restaurant, but there is a large picnic area with a few rentable covered sites.

For more information, call the park office

at 931/879-5821. Cabin reservations can be made by calling 877/260-0010.

JAMESTOWN

Jamestown is the second gateway city to the Big South Fork. Located on the western side of the wilderness, Jamestown is the seat of Fentress County and features a lovely stone courthouse. The town's claim to fame is that Samuel Clemens, better known as Mark Twain, was conceived here. Twain was born in Missouri seven months after his family left Jamestown. It is said that Obedstown in Twain's book *The Gilded Age* approximates Jamestown. The folk of Jamestown created **Mark Twain Spring Park,** across from the post office, to celebrate their connection with this literary genius. (For those who want to take the story even further, note that you may see the Tennessee home where the Clemenses lived on display at the Museum of Appalachia, in Norris.)

Jamestown's main attraction is the **Ye Olde Jail Museum** (114 Central Ave. W., 931/879-9948, 8am-4:30pm Mon.-Fri., free). The old jail housed prisoners from 1900 to 1979 and now houses the Fentress County Chamber of Commerce. You may tour the old cells, which now include exhibits about local history.

Tennessee's oldest licensed winery is the **Highland Manor Winery** (2965 S. York Hwy., 931/879-9519, www.highlandmanorwinery.net, 9am-5pm Mon.-Sat., 11am-5pm Sun., free), located about four miles south of Jamestown. This Tudor-style winery makes grape, such as muscadine wines, as well as other fruit wines for sale and tasting. The winery hosts two large annual events, Wine and Swine Day in May and Upper Cumberland Cajun Day in July.

It is easy to get to Jamestown from I-40; it is about 40 miles north on Highway 127. Note in the era of GPS and Google: There is also a Jamestown, Kentucky, also on Highway 127 (about 56 miles to the north). It is a lovely town and popular for those who like to shop on the World's Longest Yard Sale. But it isn't in Tennessee. Pay attention to which one you enter in your device.

Practicalities

Visitors to Jamestown will find plenty of grocery stores, gas stations, and camp supplies with which to stock a trip to the Big South Fork or Pickett State Park, or for thrifting on the World's Longest Yard Sale. Highways 154 and 297 leading out of town toward the parks are littered with enterprises geared to outfitting hunters and hostlers.

ALVIN C. YORK STATE HISTORIC AREA

Alvin C. York State Historic Area, established in 1968, is located approximately 8.5 miles north of Jamestown on U.S. 127. Situated on the edge of the beautiful valley of the Wolf River, not far from Kentucky, it is a remembrance of the most decorated American military hero of World War I. The small town of Pall Mall includes the York home and farm, which he received as a gift from grateful Tennesseans when he returned here. There is also his store and gristmill. Nearby are York's grave and the church where he served as Sunday school teacher, elder, and occasional preacher.

Alvin York was a poor, ill-educated farm boy when he left America to fight in World War I. He returned an international hero, after his courage and marksmanship led him and seven surviving members of his squad to kill 25 German soldiers and capture 132 prisoners in a single engagement on October 18, 1918. York was feted by the Allied countries and their leaders, and offered wealth and fame when he returned to the United States. He chose instead to return to rural Tennessee, marry his childhood sweetheart, and live his life there, while seeking to improve the future for his remote community. York used his celebrity to obtain better roads and educational improvements for the Upper Cumberland Plateau. The Alvin York Institute was founded in 1929 and provided generations of mountain children with education and vocational opportunities. When York died in 1964, 7,000 people attended his funeral.

The bucolic Alvin York State Historic Area

The World's Longest Yard Sale

You'll find unique items at the World's Longest Yard Sale.

In a place where "yard saleing" is a bona fide pastime as well as a spectator sport, it should be no surprise that the world's biggest, baddest, and longest yard sale makes its way through the Cumberland Plateau. Officially headquartered in Jamestown, the **Highway 127 World's Longest Yard Sale** (800/327-3945, www.127sale.com) wends its way through 690 miles from Michigan to Alabama, although the Tennessee and Kentucky sections are generally the busiest and best for bargain hunters.

It works like this: On the first weekend of August, thousands of people set up booths and tents to sell their unwanted goods along Highway 127. Some of these folks are antiques dealers who come from all over to get in front of a high concentration of shoppers. Others are folks who happen to live on Highway 127, which the other 51 weeks of the year may be a sleepy stretch of road, and drag the stuff from the attic to their front yard. Along with goods for sale there's plenty of food and drink and homespun entertainment. Many people make driving this sale an annual trip with friends.

There is no telling what you'll find for sale, but expect things like quilts, antiques, household items, books, clothing, crafts, and toys. There are a few things, however, that are certain:

- It will be hot. It is summer in the South. Pack water bottles and stop often to hydrate.
- It will be crowded. People drive along the road and pull over when something catches their eye, so drive slowly and pay attention.
- Hotels will be booked up. In some areas, like Jamestown and Crossville, hotel rooms are booked well in advance. If you can't get enough of *American Pickers*-style adventures, make your reservations now.
- You'll find a treasure you didn't know you needed but now can't live without.

(Pall Mall, 931/879-6456, free, tnstateparks.com/parks/about/sgt-alvin-c-york) is a fitting tribute to this most remarkable American war hero. The park includes the old York home, which is full of photographs and memorabilia reflecting on the famous soldier and his community. The old York gristmill is picturesque, and a picnic ground provides an excuse to linger.

DALE HOLLOW LAKE

Dale Hollow Lake (www.dalehollow.com) is a 27,700-acre man-made lake located in parts of Pickett, Clay, Fentress, and Overton Counties, plus Clinton and Cumberland Counties in Kentucky, west of Highway 111, about a 40-minute drive from Byrdstown. Created in 1943, the Dale Hollow Dam impounds the Obey River about seven miles above its junction with the Cumberland. Byrdstown on the east and Celina on the west are the main gateways to the lake and its recreational opportunities. You're likely to see bald eagles flying above in the fall and winter.

The **Dale Hollow National Fish Hatchery** (50 Fish Hatchery Rd., Celina, 931/243-2443, www.fws.gov/dalehollow, 7:30am-3:30pm daily, free) produces rainbow, brown, and lake trout for restocking rivers and lakes in Tennessee and neighboring states. The hatchery yields more than 300,000 pounds of trout each year for stocking programs. There is a visitors center where you can learn about trout and the hatchery process. You can also tour the facility.

Recreation

Fishing, paddleboarding, and boating are popular pastimes on Dale Hollow Lake. There are 14 commercial marinas on the lake, including **East Port** (5652 East Port Rd., 931/879-7511, www.eastport.info), near Alpine, and **Star Point** (4490 Star Point Rd., 931/864-3335, www.starpointresort.com) and **Sunset Marina** (Hwy. 111, 931/864-3115, www.sunsetmarina.com), both near Byrdstown. Because of its above-average water quality, the lake is sometimes used by freshwater scuba divers. The only commercial dive shop is located at **Willow Grove Resort and Marina** (9990 Willow Grove Hwy., 931/823-6616, www.willowgrove.com), near Allons.

Camping

The U.S. Army Corps of Engineers provides six campgrounds around the lake. They include the **Obey River Campground** (931/864-6388, $15-24), which has 131 RV and tent sites, dump stations, electrical hookups, bathhouses, and a developed swimming area on the lake. Obey River Campground is located near Byrdstown, sitting picturesquely on the lakeshore. Reserve campsites by calling 877/444-6777 or by visiting www.recreation.gov.

CORDELL HULL BIRTHPLACE STATE HISTORIC AREA

Congressman, U.S. secretary of state, and Nobel laureate, Cordell Hull was born in 1871 and raised in upper Pickett County. Hull's family was poor; he was educated in part at home and then in free schools until his parents were able to afford a private education.

Education was not wasted on Cordell Hull, who possessed a quick and astute mind. In 1891, he received a law degree after just one year of course work at Cumberland University in Lebanon. Hull went on to work as a lawyer and judge before entering into a political career that would eventually take him to the highest reaches of the U.S. government.

Hull was a member of the U.S. House of Representatives from 1906 to 1931, when he was elected to the U.S. Senate. In 1933, Hull was chosen as secretary of state under President Franklin D. Roosevelt, a position he would hold for 11 years. Hull received the Nobel Peace Prize in 1945 for his role in helping to establish the United Nations. He was also an ardent supporter of free trade, believing that world peace and progress depended on nations having free access to the raw materials and markets of the world.

Hull left public service in 1944 and lived out the remainder of his years in Washington DC. He did not return to the rural Tennessee countryside from whence he came.

The **Cordell Hull Birthplace State Historic Area** (Hwy. 325, Byrdstown, 931/864-3247) consists of a visitors center, a replica of Hull's childhood home, a one-mile nature trail, and a day-use picnic area. Special events are scheduled all year long. A **museum** (9am-5pm. daily, closes at 4pm Nov.-Mar., free) contains artifacts belonging to Hull, including his Nobel Peace Prize, plus original papers and photographs. The cabin portrays the lifestyle that Hull would have experienced while he lived here from 1871 to 1874.

T. B. Sutton General Store, on the lake in nearby Granville, has antiques, ice cream, and live bluegrass every Saturday.

The area is located just west of Highway 111, about five miles from Byrdstown. Take state highway 325 to Cove Branch Road.

STANDING STONE STATE PARK

Covering almost 11,000 acres of hills and valleys on the Upper Cumberland Plateau, Standing Stone State Park (1674 Standing Stone Hwy., Hilham, 931/823-6347, tnstateparks.com/parks/about/standing-stone) is a place for relaxing recreation. The park is named for Standing Stone, a 12-foot-tall rock that was said to serve as a boundary line between two Native American nations. It once stood along the Avery Trace, an early road that is now Highway 70. The stone is no longer in its original location; a portion of it is on display in Monterey.

The park is located 11 miles northwest of Highway 111, about 30 miles from Byrdstown. Take state highway 52 from Highway 111 to state highway 136.

Recreation

The 70-acre **Standing Stone Lake** offers fishing and boating. **Paddleboats** may be rented from the park office year-round, and you can bring your own electric trolling motor and battery if you wish. No private boats are allowed. Fishers often catch largemouth bass, bluegill, crappie, lake trout, and catfish.

There are eight miles of day-use **hiking trails,** including several that climb to points where you can enjoy views of the surrounding area.

The park **swimming pool** is open Memorial Day-Labor Day.

Camping

A pleasant campground has 36 trailer and tent sites ($20), each equipped with a table, charcoal grill, and water and electrical hookups. The campground is open year-round, but the bathhouses close December-March. Sites are available on a first-come, first-served basis.

Cabins

Standing Stone has 14 rustic cabins ($65-75) that can accommodate 2-8 people and are open April-October. Three timber lodges and four modern cabins ($115-130) have central heat and air-conditioning and are open year-round. They sleep up to 10 people. There also are a group lodge and a meeting room.

All cabins are equipped for housekeeping; however, there are no televisions, microwaves, or telephones.

CLARKRANGE

Located on Highway 127 south of Jamestown is **Clarkrange** and the **Cumberland Mountain General Store** (Hwy. 127, 931/863-3880, cumberlandmountaingeneralstore.net, 10am-5pm daily), an old-time general store that dates back to 1923. Inside, it is stocked with old-fashioned household items, antiques, and local crafts. A 1950s-style diner serves burgers, fries, and milk shakes. Hours are erratic, particularly in the off-season. Call before you make a special trip.

COOKEVILLE

Cookeville is the seat of Putnam County and the largest city on the Upper Cumberland Plateau. **Cookeville** is closely associated with

I-40, which passes just south of town, just 80 miles due east of Nashville. For road-weary travelers, Cookeville is a pit stop or a mile mark to show one's progress.

Off the interstate, Cookeville's greatest source of energy and vitality is **Tennessee Tech University** (1 William Jones Dr. 931/372-3101, www.tntech.edu), a public university with an enrollment of more than 10,000. Tennessee Tech was founded in 1909 as Dixie College and was affiliated with the Church of Christ. Since 1965 it has been part of the state's higher-education system. The campus is located on the northwest side of town, near 12th Street and Peachtree Avenue, and includes historic Henderson and Derryberry Halls. The Bryan Fine Arts Building hosts concerts and the campus **art gallery.**

Sights

Visitors to Cookeville should find their way to the **West Side District,** located along West Broad Street, North Cedar and Church Avenues, and 1st Street. This is the best area for shopping and dining. It is also where you will find the **Cookeville Depot Museum** (116 W. Broad St., 931/528-8570, 10am-4pm Tues.-Sat., free, www.cookevilledepot.com). Located in the town's old train depot, the museum houses railway artifacts, memorabilia, and photographs of the railroad in Putnam County over the years. The depot was built in 1909.

The **Cookeville History Museum** (40 E. Broad St., 931/520-5455, www.cookevillehistorymuseum.com, 10am-4pm Wed.-Sat., free) houses an extensive collection of artifacts, photographs, and other items of interest from Cookeville's history.

Families love the **Kiwanis Cookeville Children's Museum** (36 W. 2nd St., 931/979-7529, www.kiwaniscookevillechildrens-museum.org, 10am-4pm Mon., Wed. and Fri.-Sat., noon-6pm Tues. and Thurs., adults $4, children two years and up $4). Opened in 2007, the children's museum houses interactive and educational exhibits for children 2-12. They include music making, arts exploration, and outdoor games.

Also in Cookeville is one of the state's newest parks. **Cummins Falls State Park** (1081 Cummins Mills Rd., 931/261-3471) is a day-use only park. It has quickly become a favorite destination for locals thanks to its 75-foot high waterfalls. There is an ADA compliant overlook for those who don't want to make the trek down to the bottom.

Cookeville Depot Museum demonstrates how important the railroad was to the area.

Entertainment

Tennessee Tech University lends sophistication to Cookeville's arts scene. The university's Bryan Fine Arts Building is home of the Bryan Symphony Orchestra, which performs six times per year. The **Joan Derryberry Gallery** (Roaden University Center, 931/372-3123, Mon.-Fri. 10am-4:30pm, free) exhibits student and faculty work, plus special exhibits from the university's collection.

The **Cookeville Drama Center** (10 E. Broad St., 931/528-1313, www.cookeville-tn.org/cpac) is a performing-arts venue where local and touring productions are staged. The Cookeville Mastersingers also perform here. The Drama Center also organizes summer shows at the **Dogwood Park and Performance Pavilion,** including Shakespeare in the Park, Symphony in the Park and After Dark Movies in the Park.

The **Cumberland Art Society Backdoor Gallery** (186A S. Walnut St., 931/526-2424) showcases fine art and photography, plus an annual juried membership show. Visitors may see an artist at work in the open studio space. The gallery offers special workshops and demonstrations throughout the year.

Accommodations

For something different try **Blackberry Bramble Cottage**, (1580 Blackburn Fork Rd., 931/520-6420, www.blackberrybramblecottage.com, $100-155). This 1920s cottage used to be part of a working farm. Now it is a renovated three-bedroom retreat with fireplaces, wireless internet, TV, and modern amenities.

Food

For a fine Italian meal, make reservations at **Mauricio's Ristorante Italiano** (232 N. Peachtree Ave., 931/528-2456, www.mauricioscookeville.com, 11am-2pm Thurs.-Fri., 4pm-9pm Mon.-Sat., $15-32), a perfect place for a special night out or a business meal. The richly painted walls and rustic decor are easy yet elegant, and the service is careful but not fussy. The menu offers authentic and well-executed Italian dishes.

Dipsy Doodle Drive Inn (2331 W. Broad St., 931/372-2663, 5:30am-8pm. Mon.-Thurs. and Sat., 5:30am-9pm Fri., 7am-2pm Sun., $5-12) offers Southern-style cooking in a classic diner setting, and **Bobby Q's BBQ** (1070 N. Washington Ave., 931/526-1024, www.bobbyqsrestaurant.org, 11am-8:45pm Tues.-Thurs., 11am-9:45pm Fri., 4pm-9:45pm Sat., 11am-3pm Sun., $5-12) is one of Cookeville's oldest, and most favorite, barbecue restaurants.

MONTEREY

The city park in downtown Monterey is home to part of the stone that once stood in Standing Stone State Park, north of town.

The countryside north of Monterey is home to the Muddy Pond Mennonite Community. This is good countryside to explore if you are looking for handicrafts or home-baked bread and other specialty items. It is also a beautiful area to drive through.

To find Muddy Pond, drive north from Monterey on Highway 164 until you reach Muddy Pond Road. Turn right onto Muddy Pond, and travel a couple miles. You have arrived. The **Muddy Pond General Store** (3608 Muddy Pond Rd., 931/445-7829) sells handicrafts, quilts, pottery, bulk foods, and clothing. The **Country Porch** (3130 Muddy Pond Rd., 931/445-7370) also has gift items, as well as light lunch fare, including soups and sandwiches.

One of the community's best attractions is the **Guenther's Sorghum Mill** (4064 Muddy Pond Rd., 931/445-3509, www.muddypondsorghum.com). On Tuesday, Thursday, and Saturday in September and October you can watch as the sorghum mill makes its molasses. If you come at this time, you may see a horse-powered mill squeezing cane juice from the sorghum stalks. The juice is boiled in the evaporator pan until it turns into the thick, golden-hued syrup.

At other times of the year, come by the mill to purchase sorghum and other specialty items in their variety store.

Cumberland Trail State Park

In 1998, Tennessee established its 53rd state park, the **Justin P. Wilson Cumberland Trail State Park** (423/566-2229, tnstateparks.com/parks/about/cumberland-trail). When it is completed, the park will be a 300-mile linear trail that runs from Cumberland Gap National Park, on Tennessee's northern border, all the way to Chickamauga and Chattanooga National Military Park and Prentice Cooper Wildlife Management Area in the south.

More than 185 miles of the Cumberland Trail are open, and others are being developed. The nonprofit **Cumberland Trail Conference** (www.cumberlandtrail.org) is spearheading trail projects and is the best source of information on current conditions, campsites, and other useful hiking information.

The trail traverses the ancient Cumberland Mountains. Passing through 11 counties, the trail and associated parklands encompass gorges, valleys, mountain peaks, waterfalls, and geological formations.

Portions of the trail include:

- **Cumberland Mountain,** which begins in Cumberland Gap National Park and travels to Cove Lake State Park;
- **Smoky Mountain,** a 25-mile segment beginning at Cove Lake and crossing through the heart of the Cumberland Mountains to Frozen Head State Park;
- **Frozen Head,** which begins at Frozen Head State Park and ends at the Obed Wild and Scenic River, traversing from the ridgeline to a watershed gorge;
- **Obed River,** a 17-mile pass through the Obed Wild and Scenic River and the Catoosa Wildlife Management Area;
- **Grassy Cove,** which traverses Brady and Black Mountains surrounding Grassy Cove;
- **Stinging Fork,** a 15-mile segment using an already-established trail system through the Bowater Pocket Wilderness;
- **Piney River,** a 22-mile segment that includes 10 miles of the Piney River Pocket Wilderness Trailhead, and then leaving the escarpment above Spring City;
- **Laurel-Snow,** a 32-mile segment passing through the existing Laurel-Snow Bowater Pocket Wilderness Trail;
- **North Chickamauga,** a 20-mile segment located almost exclusively within the North Chickamauga Creek Gorge; and
- **Tennessee River Gorge,** the final leg of the trail, located in Prentice Cooper State Forest.

The trail terminates at Signal Mountain.

Monterey is easy to find; just 15 miles east of Cookeville along I-40.

Accommodations

For lodging, check out the chain hotels along the interstate, or call for a room at **The Garden Inn Bed and Breakfast** (1400 Bee Rock Rd., 931/839-1400 or 888/293-1444, www.thegardeninnbb.com, $145-155). This 11-room inn offers private bathrooms, full breakfast, and a lovely, rural location on the plateau. The grounds include the Bee Rock overlook, from which you can see Calfkiller Valley and Stamps Hollow below.

OBED WILD AND SCENIC RIVER

The **Obed Wild and Scenic River**, added to the National Park system in 1976, is—like its nearby and better-known neighbor, the Big

South Fork National River and Recreation Area—based around a prized white-water recreation stream. The Obed park, managed jointed by the U.S. Department of the Interior and the Tennessee State Wildlife Management Agency, encompasses 56 miles of the rugged Obed and Emory River system, with adjacent riparian areas. The park offers Class II-IV white water and excellent rock-climbing opportunities. For hikers there is a 14.2-mile section of the Cumberland Trail State Park along the Obed and its Daddy's Creek tributary, though portions of this trail are closed during certain hunting seasons.

From Kingston, drive north 33 miles on Highway 27. Turn onto state highway 62 (Kingston Street), look for the brown Obed road signs for the visitors center on North Maiden Street.

Camping

The **Rock Creek Campground,** a no-reservation, 12-site facility, with pit toilets and no water or electrical hookups, provides a place to sleep. Backcountry camping is also allowed. There is a $7 fee per campsite.

Information

The park's **visitors center** (208 N. Maiden St., Wartburg, 423/346-6294, www.nps.gov/obed, 9am-5pm daily, free) has a small museum and information about recreation in the park.

FROZEN HEAD STATE NATURAL AREA

Frozen Head State Natural Area (964 Flat Fork Rd., Wartburg, 423/346-3318, tnstateparks.com/parks/about/frozen-head) is famous for its beautiful spring wildflowers. The park takes its name from Frozen Head Mountain, a 3,324-foot peak often covered by ice and snow in winter.

On a clear day, the views from the top of Frozen Head extend to the Smoky Mountains in the east, the Cumberland Mountains to the north, and the Cumberland Plateau to the west. Cross Mountain (3,534 feet), the tallest peak in the Tennessee portion of the plateau, is within view.

You can reach the summit of Frozen Head Mountain on the South Old Mac Trail (2.4 miles) or the North Old Mac Trail (3.3 miles).

The land here was not always a park. Much of Frozen Head State Natural Area was part of Brushy Mountain State Prison, and convict labor was used to mine coal from the hills.

Frozen Head State Natural Area

During the early 20th century, the forest was heavily logged, and in 1952 it was burnt by a forest fire. Over the past decades, a new forest has grown up, including an exceptional array of spring wildflowers.

To see the blooms, hike along any of the lower trails, especially those that hug the Flat Fork Creek that flows through the park. Panthers Branch Trail (2.1 miles) is a favorite walk for flowers. It also passes the DeBord Falls. Want to learn more about what you're seeing? Download the park's wildflower brochure from the website.

There are 20 primitive campsites for backpackers in Frozen Head. As many as 75 people can be accommodated at the group camp. There are picnic tables, pavilions, an amphitheater, and a visitors center, plus a 6.9-mile bike/horse trail. All the rest of the 50 miles of trail are for hiking only.

The Flat Fork Creek is stocked with rainbow trout in the spring, and it is a favorite place for fishing.

To get to Frozen Head from Harriman, take Highway 27 North to Wartburg and turn right (east) on Highway 62. After two miles turn left on Flat Fork Road, then continue four miles to the park entrance.

The Middle Plateau

The center swath of the plateau is the most populated—it is close to I-40 and the population centers of Crossville and Cookeville. Universities in the area lend greater sophistication and wealth to some parts of the middle plateau. Highway 70, once called the Broadway of America, runs east-west through this part of the plateau, providing a much more pleasant experience than the nearby interstate.

KINGSTON

Kingston, the seat of Roane County, sits on the banks of Watts Bar Lake. The lake was formed in 1942 when the Clinch, Emory, and Tennessee Rivers were dammed by the Tennessee Valley Authority's Watts Bar Dam.

Kingston is an old city. It was founded in 1799 around an army garrison on the Clinch River. You can see a replica of this installation at **Fort Southwest Point** (1226 Hwy. 58, 865/376-3641, www.southwestpoint.com, 10am-4pm Tues.-Sat., free). The fort was built in 1797 as settlers moved westward and came into conflict with Native Americans whose lands were being encroached upon. The fort and its soldiers were supposed to protect the Cherokee land from white settlement. At its peak, Fort Southwest Point housed 600 soldiers.

Fort Southwest Point was abandoned by the army in 1811. Beginning in 1974, archaeologists began to study the ruins. Today, parts of the original fort have been re-created, including a barracks, blockhouse, and more than 250 feet of palisade walls. The museum also has artifacts found on the site.

In the heart of downtown Kingston is the **Roane County Courthouse,** one of only seven remaining pre Civil War courthouses in Tennessee. Inside is the **Roane County Museum of History** (119 Court St., 865/376-9211, www.roanetnheritage.com, Mon.-Fri. 8:30am-4:30pm, closed noon-1pm for lunch, free), which is part of the Roane County Archives.

Route 40 runs right through the middle of Kingston, located on the east bank of the Clinch River, about 36 miles west of Knoxville.

Recreation

Watts Bar Lake is located just a few blocks from downtown Kingston. There is a walking trail along the riverbank. Popular activities include fishing and boating.

Accommodations

Nestled on Watts Bar Lake is **Whitestone** (1200 Paint Rock Rd., 865/376-0113, www.whitestoneinn.com, $165-335). Just 15 minutes' drive south of Kingston, this B&B offers 21 rooms in serious luxury. You'll find spa showers and fireplaces in the rooms, and kayaks, canoes, and hiking trails outside. Whitestone is popular for weddings in this bucolic setting.

HARRIMAN

Harriman, a town of fewer than 10,000, has an interesting history. It was founded in 1890 by a Methodist minister who wanted to form a town on the foundation of social temperance and industry, where no alcohol would be permitted. His idea struck a chord with people from all over the country, and when he held a one-day land sale in 1890, more than 570 lots were sold and more than $600,000 made.

The town's **Cornstalk Heights** historic district between Roane and Cumberland Streets comprises 135 historic Victorian houses, many built by these early investors. The **Harriman Heritage Museum** (330 Roane St., 865/882-3122, free) is open by appointment and tells the story of the city's founding. A guide to the town's historic homes has been published by the Cornstalk Heights Community Organization and is available from the **Roane County Visitors Bureau** (1209 N. Kentucky St., 423/376-4201), located in the courthouse.

Harriman is about 40 miles west of Knoxville on Highway 40.

OZONE FALLS STATE NATURAL AREA

Ozone Falls State Natural Area is located a few steps from Highway 70, near the town of Ozone, located between Harriman and Crossville. This dramatic waterfall is also a short drive from I-40 (you can get there from either exit 329 or 338), so it's a popular stop for road-weary travelers who want to breathe some fresh air and stretch their legs. Be wary, however, because the path that goes to the top of the falls dead-ends at a 110-foot drop. There is no guardrail or fence to keep you from falling, so exercise caution. Families with small children may want to skip this trail altogether.

For a safer and better look at the falls, take the 0.5-mile path to the bottom of the falls. It passes through a lovely gorge with interesting rock formations and old-growth forest.

Ozone Falls is a unit of the Cumberland Mountain State Park (931/484-6138). There is an information board at the parking area, but no rangers are on duty.

GRASSY COVE

On Highway 68, just a few miles outside the town of Homestead, is the lovely rural community of **Grassy Cove**. Surrounded by Brady and Black Mountains, the cove is more than 10,000 acres. In 1974, it was declared a National Natural Landmark because it is one of the largest limestone sinkholes in North America. Remarkably, the cove is drained by a cave, and after the water flows into the cave, it emerges later at the mouth of the Sequatchie River, on the other side of the mountain.

For casual visitors, however, Grassy Cove's appeal is not geologic; it is the countryside. Drive along any of the secondary roads and soak in the landscape of lightly rolling hills, largely used for livestock farming, surrounded by steep wooded hillsides. Take Kemmer Road off Highway 70 to find the **Grassy Cove Methodist Church and Cemetery,** built in 1803, and the picturesque **Grassy Cove Community House,** built in 1894 and used as part of the Presbyterian Grassy Cove Academy from 1880 to 1906.

On Highway 68, check out the classic mercantile **J. C. Kemmer & Sons General Store** (931/484-4075). It offers old-fashioned cookware, overalls and other workingman's attire, and an array of other odds and ends, some of which you may actually need.

★ CUMBERLAND HOMESTEADS

The town of Homestead, southeast of Crossville, is named for **Cumberland**

Homesteads, the New Deal project that saw the construction of more than 250 homesteads for poor families during the Great Depression. Organized by the government's Division of Subsistence Housing (later called the Resettlement Administration), the project was designed to give poor Tennessee families an opportunity to work for the basics of life, plus learn new skills and acquire a permanent home.

The countryside around Homestead—U.S. 127 and 70, and Highway 68—is dotted with old Homestead houses, distinctive for their cottage features and the use of golden-hued Crab Orchard stone. These gems are just six miles southeast from Crossville.

To learn more about the Homestead experiment, visit one of two (or both) museums in the area. The **Homesteads House Museum** (2611 Pigeon Ridge Rd./U.S. 127, 931/456-9663, www.cumberlandhomesteads.org, 10am-5pm Mon.-Sat., 1pm-5pm Sun. Apr.-Oct., adults $2, youths $1, children under six free)) is one of the original Homestead homes restored to 1930s condition.

The **Homesteads Tower Museum** is about two miles away, at the junction of Highways 127S and 68 (www.cumberlandhomesteads.org, 10am-5pm Mon.-Sat., 1pm-5pm Sun., adults $4, youths $1, children under six free). This octagonal stone tower has a 50,000-gallon water tank, with a winding stairway to the top and exhibits on the ground floor. Located in the distinctive Homesteads tower and administration building, the museum tells the story of the project, depicts what life was like for homesteaders, and includes a gallery about the original homestead families. The building itself is remarkable; the ground floor consists of four "wings," each of which now contains exhibits. The tower, which housed a water tank for the homesteaders, reaches up above the trees and offers views of the surrounding countryside. No one can really explain why the planners chose to build such an unusual building, but one theory is that it was to expose the workmen to advanced building techniques.

The folks at the Homesteads museums are remarkably friendly, and the gift shop has locally made crafts, books and pamphlets about the project, and a hefty cookbook of recipes collected from homesteaders.

CUMBERLAND MOUNTAIN STATE PARK

Cumberland Mountain State Park (U.S. 127 S., 931/484-6138) was developed as a

The Homesteads Tower Museum was originally a project of FDR's new deal.

A New Start at the Cumberland Homesteads

President Franklin Roosevelt's New Deal made anything seem possible. On several thousand remote acres of land atop the Cumberland Plateau, that thing was Cumberland Homesteads, a radical project to give hundreds of out-of-work laborers a second chance.

Under the plan, poor families would agree to work and contribute to collective projects, including the construction of their own homes. In return, workers were paid for a portion of their labor. The rest was turned into credits in order to pay off their own homestead, which consisted of a family home, chicken pen, smokehouse, privy, two-story barn, and lands where families were expected to raise their own food.

Between 1934 and 1938, 262 homesteads were built, and thousands of people, many of them from other parts of Tennessee, moved to the Cumberland Plateau to make a new life. It was, by all accounts, a hard life, but also a happier and more promising one than many people left behind. In addition to the homesteads themselves, the community built a school where children could be educated. There were also opportunities to learn new skills—from canning to masonry—which would help families after the Depression, and the New Deal, ended.

There were a handful of similar homestead projects around the country, including one for African Americans in Virginia. To reformers and planners, the project meant an opportunity to demonstrate that a planned, cooperative community could work.

Cumberland Homesteads did work for several years. A labor dispute in which Homesteaders complained they were being shortchanged on work credits created animosity between the project architects and those who lived there. But despite the difficulties, many Homestead families remained, even after the formal project wrapped up around 1940.

The legacy of Cumberland Homesteads is strong. A handful of Homestead family members are still alive, and their descendants live all over the plateau. Some still live in the Homestead houses, distinctive for their common Tudor-style cottage design and the Crab Orchard stone with which they were built. An association of Homestead descendants and other supporters runs the Cumberland Homesteads Museums (www.cumberlandhomesteads.org).

recreation area for the Cumberland homesteaders and built between 1938 and 1940 by the Civilian Conservation Corps (CCC). Its focal point is a seven-arch dam and bridge made from Crab Orchard stone, which impounds Byrd Creek to make pleasant 50-acre Byrd Lake. The 70-year-old dam, which got a face-lift in 2008, is a monument to the labors of the young men of the CCC. World War I hero Sgt. Alvin York briefly served as a foreman on the project until he was called away in 1940 for the filming of his life story.

Recreation

There are six **hiking** trails, ranging from easy paths around the lake to an overnight loop. During the summer months, you can rent boats for use on Byrd Lake, and fishing is popular. There is a swimming pool and tennis courts.

Accommodations

There are 37 cabins ($95-135), which range from modern to rustic, and a group lodge. The recently upgraded campground ($22.50-27.50) has 145 sites with electric and water hookups.

Food

The **park restaurant** (931/484-6138, 11am-2:30pm and 4pm-8pm daily summer, 11am-2:30pm Tues.-Sat., 4pm-8pm Fri.-Sat. Jan.-Apr., $6-15) overlooks the lake and serves three meals daily. Friday evening is catfish night.

CROSSVILLE

Named because it was here that the old Nashville-Knoxville road crossed the Chattanooga-Kentucky road, **Crossville** is now a pleasant town and the unofficial capital of the Cumberland Plateau. Smaller than nearby Cookeville and more appealing, Crossville is a pleasant place to spend a few hours. This is one of the most popular places to jump on the Highway 127 World's Longest Yard Sale, which takes place the first weekend in August. Crossville is also one of the state's premier golfing destinations.

One of the first things you should look for in Crossville is Crab Orchard stone, a distinctive tan-colored sandstone that is quarried in the area and derived its name from the community of Crab Orchard just down the road. Crab Orchard stone was used by local builders for years, but in 1925 it grew in popularity after a Nashville architect used it at Scarritt College. It has been used all over the country.

Crab Orchard stone was used to build Crossville's first courthouse and the Palace Theatre on Main Street, among many other buildings around town.

Sights

The **Cumberland County Courthouse,** designed by W. Chamberlin and Company and built in 1905, sits in the center of town. Its yard has been used over the years for public art displays and memorials, the most recent being a memorial to U.S. soldiers killed in Iraq and Afghanistan. Across Main Street from the present-day courthouse is the older one, built in 1886. It houses the homegrown **Upper Cumberland Military Museum** (20 S. Main St., 931/456-5520, 9am-4pm Mon.-Fri., free), with memorabilia from the Civil War through to the war in Iraq. There is an interesting display about the prisoner of war camp built in Crossville during World War II.

About a block away from the courthouse is the **Palace Theatre** (72 S. Main St., 931/484-6133, www.palacetheatre-crossville.com). Built in 1938 out of Crab Orchard stone with art deco flourishes, the Palace was a first-run movie theater for 40 years. In 1993, it was listed on the National Register of Historic Places, and after being abandoned and derelict for many years, the community decided to preserve the Palace. A restored and expanded Palace Theatre opened in 2001.

The 302-seat facility hosts events ranging from high school band concerts to regional musical events. It also shows movies. Pop in while you're in town, and someone is bound to offer to show you around, as long as it is not in use.

At the corner of North and Main Streets is the old **Crossville Depot** (931/456-2586). The depot was built in 1900 and served as the town's train station until 1960, when the trains stopped running through Crossville. In the 1980s, the old tracks were removed. In 1996, three local Rotary Clubs spearheaded a project to restore the old depot. Today, it houses a gift shop/art gallery/tearoom. Inside there are a few photographs and displays about the old railroad.

For more than 25 years, flea market types have flocked to the **Highway 127 World's Longest Yard Sale** (first weekend of Aug., 800/327-3945, www.127sale.com). It spans 690 miles, and Jamestown is officially considered the epicenter, but the area near Crossville is a great spot for newcomers to try it out. Crossville is near the I-40 intersection and is often filled with antiques dealers, who set up booths, rather than just locals who drag the contents of their basements to their yards (not that there's anything wrong with that). Plan ahead if you want to stay here during the sale; small inns and hotels can get all booked up a year in advance.

Entertainment

The Cumberland Plateau's foremost arts facility is the **Cumberland County Playhouse** (221 Tennessee Ave., 931/484-5000, www.ccplayhouse.com), located a few miles west of downtown Crossville, near the Crossville airport. Founded in 1965 and nurtured by successive generations of committed Cumberland residents, the playhouse presents mainstream theatrical works like *Hello, Dolly!* and *Oklahoma!*, plus regional and local works. They also organize acting, dance, and music classes for all ages.

Recreation

Crossville calls itself the Golf Capital of Tennessee because there are 10 different golf courses in the area. **The Bear Chase at Cumberland Mountain** (407 Wild Plum Ln., 931/707-1640, www.tngolftrail.net) is one of the public golf courses operated in partnership with the state park system. It was designed by Jack Nicklaus. The 6,900-yard, par 72 layout features a design that capitalizes on elevation changes as well as natural features, such as flowing brooks and clustered, mature pines. The club also offers a driving range, practice green, pro shop, rental clubs, and golf lessons.

Lake Tanasi Village (2479 Dunbar Rd., 931/788-3301, www.laketansipoa.com) is a top-rated golf course that places a premium on accuracy off the tee. The fairways of this 6,701-yard course are gently rolling, with tiered greens, water hazards, bunkers, and thick rough. There is also a driving range, practice green, pro shop, rental clubs, golf lessons, and on-site lodging.

For a detailed rundown of each golf course in the Crossville area, and special packages and discounts, contact the Crossville Chamber of Commerce's special golf desk (877/465-3861, www.golfcapitaltenn.com).

Accommodations

A number of chain hotels are located near Crossville's three interstate exits. The **Quality Inn** (exit 317, 4035 Hwy. 127 N., 931/484-1551, $67-129) is a sprawling hotel with indoor corridors, queen- and king-size rooms, and a hot breakfast. There is also an indoor heated pool, fitness room, and business center. Children 12 and under stay free. Discounts are available for 7-, 14-, and 30-day nonrefundable advance reservations.

The **Cumberland Mountain Lodge** (1130 Clint Lowe Rd., 931/493-2615, www.cumberlandmountainlodge.com, $200) is a rural bed-and-breakfast located on a working livestock farm. The farmhouse was fully restored in 2005, and the three guest rooms are comfortably and elegantly furnished in Mission style. Hardwood paneling and Crab Orchard stone feature prominently in the construction. Amenities include a continental breakfast, high-speed Internet, wood-burning fireplaces, a stocked fishing pond, and miles of hiking trails. Guests may also relax in the common areas, including the great room and a large, homey dining area.

Rates at Cumberland Mountain Lodge are $200 per night per couple, and $50 for each additional adult in your party, with a minimum two-night stay. The lodge can sleep up to six adults.

The farm is located on a permanent conservation easement, and it is a relaxing and quiet place. It is located about 15 miles from Crossville, south of Cumberland Mountain State Park.

The **McCoy Place Bed and Breakfast** (525 McCoy Rd., 931/484-1243, $100 double, $90 single) has three rooms and traditional B&B ambience.

Food

Folks in Crossville like to eat lunch at **Boston's** (42 North St., 931/456-1925, 10:30am-2pm Mon.-Sun., closed Sat., $4-12). It offers daily hot lunch specials, plus sandwiches, salads, and soups.

The **Stagecoach Place Café** (4355 Hwy. 127, 931/456-9631, 11:30am-2pm and 4:30pm-9pm Wed.-Sun., $12-18) is inside the Stagecoach Place inn and offers Indian, Italian, and French-inspired lunches and dinners.

Information

The **Cumberland County Chamber of Commerce** (34 S. Main St., 931/484-8444, www.crossville-chamber.com, 9am-5pm Mon.-Fri.) has an information center, or you can order a package of brochures before you arrive. The **Palace Theatre** (72 S. Main St., 931/484-6133, www.palacetheatre-crossville.com) also has an information center with brochures, and the staff there is friendly and helpful.

PLEASANT HILL

About 10 miles west of Crossville on Highway 70 is the small town of **Pleasant Hill**. The **Pioneer Hall Museum** (Main St., 931/277-3872, pioneerhallmuseum.net, 10am-4pm Wed., 2pm-5pm Sun. May-Oct., free,) is a local history museum. Pioneer Hall was a dormitory for the Pleasant Hill Academy, established in 1884 and closed in 1947.

SPARTA

There is just something special about downtown **Sparta**, but it's hard to put your finger on the one thing that makes it so. Taken individually, each component seems insignificant, but together they make a pleasant whole and a nice place to stop to stretch your legs or grab a meal.

Storefronts along Liberty Square and Bookman Way are colorful, with art deco touches. The old Oldham movie theater facade was rebuilt, and there are plans to fix up the inside and make it into a functioning performing-arts center. The town amphitheater is used frequently for concerts and civic events, plus a monthly bluegrass concert. Down by the Calfkiller River, the river park has covered picnic tables, a playground, and walking paths.

Bluegrass star Lester Flatt was raised in Sparta, and he maintained a home here throughout this life. There is a historical marker on the east side of town and a monument in his honor in front of the courthouse.

Sparta, the seat of White County, was founded in 1809. Over the years the town grew along with coal, lumber, and other industries on the plateau. Sparta's newspaper is the *Expositor,* and it has been in print for more than a century.

Drive south in a straight line on Highway 70 from I-40 in Cookeville to Sparta. This is a 19-mile drive.

Shopping

Sparta has several antiques stores. **Finders Keepers** (222 W. Bockman Way, 931/837-3463) has furniture, glass, quilts, porcelain, and Barbies, just for starters. Across the river, but still within walking distance, is **J&J Antiques** (16 Bockman Way, 931/836-8123), three buildings of antiques, primitives, and collectibles.

Wheel-thrown pottery, soaps, and candles are the specialties at **The Fragrant Mushroom Pottery Gallery & Studio** (15 Rhea St., 931/836-8190, www.fragrantmushroom.com).

Perhaps Sparta's most distinctive store is **Simply Southern Quilts & Gifts** (12 Liberty Sq., 931/836-3271, www.simplysouthernquilts.com). Opened in 2007, Cheryl Hackett's shop sells all the equipment you need to make a quilt. But what makes her store special are the sewing and quilting classes that she offers upstairs and her open-door policy for area quilters. Anyone is welcome to come in and sew in her spacious third-floor classroom (provided there's not a class in session, of course). There is a "men's lounge" on the mezzanine, with a television, comfortable couch, and snacks. Crafters of all kinds will feel as if they have come home when they arrive at Simply Southern.

Food

Brenda Pope serves homemade soups, fresh salads, and light sandwiches at **Miss Marenda's Tea Room** (5 E. Maple, 931/836-2542, tea room: 11am-2pm Tues.-Sat., gift shop: 10am-5pm Tues.-Sat., $5-8). The modest **Yanni's Grille** (19 S. Spring St. 931/836-3838, 11am-9pm Tues.-Thurs., Sun., 11am-10pm Fri.-Sat., $5-12) is a favorite of locals who like the pizza and Greek entrees. The local lunch spot is **Caribbean Café** (20 W. Bockman Way, 931/836-1550, www.caribbean-cafe-sparta.com, Mon.-Fri., Sun. 10am-3pm, Sat. 10am-2pm, $6-13). Don't miss the Caribbean shrimp with rice.

Information

Stop at the **Sparta-White County Chamber**

of Commerce (16 W. Bockman Way, 931/836-3552, spartatnchamber.com) for information, maps, and brochures.

AROUND SPARTA

Rock House Shrine

About four miles east of Sparta off Highway 70 is **Rock House Shrine** (931/739-7625, 10am-3pm Wed., Fri., Sat. Apr.-Oct., or by appointment, free), a 175-year-old sandstone house that once served as a stagecoach stop on the Wilderness Road. The likes of Andrew Jackson and Sam Houston slept here, along with hundreds of less-famous men and women. The Daughters of the American Revolution has maintained and protected the building over the years. It is usually open for tours during the published hours, but call to confirm.

You can get to the Rock House from Sparta two ways. Follow the new Highway 70 if you like, but a more pleasant drive departs Gains Street downtown and becomes Country Club Lane. This is the old Highway 70 and takes you directly there.

Virgin Falls State Natural Area

One of the best all-day hikes in the Sparta area is to the **Virgin Falls,** a mysterious 110-foot waterfall. No surface water leads to the falls or away from it; the falls appear from an underground stream and disappear at the bottom into another cave.

The eight-mile round-trip hike to Virgin Falls is through the state-owned 1,157-acre **Virgin Falls State Natural Area**. The natural area has at least three additional waterfalls and several caves and sinkholes. From the Caney Fork Overlook you enjoy a dramatic view of Scott's Gulf and the Caney Fork River 900 feet below.

The parking lot for the natural area is located on Scotts Gulf Road southeast of Sparta. To find it, drive 11 miles east of Sparta along Highway 70. Turn onto Eastland Road (also called Mourberry Road) and drive six miles until you reach Scotts Gulf Road. The parking lot and trailheads are two miles up the road, on the right side.

For information contact the State's Division of Natural Areas in Nashville at 615/532-0436.

Mennonite Community

There is a **Mennonite community** just outside of Sparta. Follow Young Street south out of town about three miles and look for Pleasant Hill Road. Take a right, and in less than 100 yards is the **Country Store and Bakery,** operated by Mennonites. The store carries salvage groceries, a handful of Amish- and Mennonite-made goods, and some practical goods specific to Mennonite people, such as dark-blue cloth. You can also buy bulk cheese and Amish and Mennonite cookbooks. The store is next door to a Mennonite school and church. It is open Monday-Saturday and does not allow patrons wearing shorts, sleeveless shirts, or tank tops inside.

Walling

Real Cajun food is on the menu at the **Foglight Foodhouse** (275 Powerhouse Rd., 931/657-2364, foglight-foodhouse.com, 5pm-8pm Tues.-Thurs., 5pm-9pm Fri.-Sat., $15-38) in **Walling**. The first thing you will notice here is a view of the Caney Fork River. In nice weather, you can eat in the fresh air on a deck overlooking the river. Cajun specialties include pecan fried catfish, smoked rib-eye steak, and grilled entrées.

CENTER HILL LAKE

Formed when the Army Corps of Engineers dammed the Caney Fork River, **Center Hill Lake** sprawls between Smithville and Sparta. There are seven recreation areas around the lake, where you can picnic, swim, and enjoy being near the water. Eight commercial marinas cater to boaters. **Edgar Evins State Park** (Silver Point, 931/858-2115) sits on the northern banks of the lake, near I-40. Boating and other forms of water recreation are the focus at this 6,000-acre park. The **Edgar Evins Marina** (931/858-5695) is the center of activity for boating and fishing.

Burgess Falls

There are also 11 miles of hiking trails, including the 9-mile Jack Clayborn Millennium Trail and a short nature walk departing from the park visitors center. A **campground** ($8-25) and cabins with **economy suites** ($60-80) are also available.

Rock Island State Park (931/686-2471), at the south end of the lake, is located near the town of Walling, southwest of Sparta. The Tennessee Electric Power Company built a dam and hydroelectric plant here in 1917, creating the Great Falls Reservoir. Later, the Tennessee Valley Authority took over the facility, and in 1971, the state leased the first 350 acres from TVA to form the park.

Rock Island has a sandy beach for swimming, public boat ramps, picnic tables, playgrounds, and facilities for basketball, volleyball, tennis, and more. Fishing is popular on the lake, especially during spring.

You can stay in one of 10 **cabins** ($135-150) or at the **60-site campground** ($16-27.50), which is unusual in that it has wooden platforms, some with great views, for the campsites.

BURGESS FALLS STATE NATURAL AREA

The Falling Water River is the focal point of **Burgess Falls State Natural Area** (931/432-5312, http://tnstateparks.com/parks/about/burgess-falls), located northwest of Sparta near the town of Bakers Crossroads. A three-quarter-mile hike brings you to the breathtaking 130-foot Burgess Falls, named for the 18th-century Revolutionary War veteran who received this land as payment for his service to the young country. There is also a picnic area and fishing piers.

This stretch of river has long been acknowledged as a source of energy. The Burgess family operated a gristmill here for many years, which used the power of the water to grind flour and cornmeal. During the early 1920s, the City of Cookeville built a dam and power plant along the river to provide electricity for the city. The dam broke during a 1928 flood, but a new one was built in its place. The new dam operated until 1944, when it became obsolete due to the Tennessee Valley Authority's hydroelectric projects.

Get to Burgess Falls along Highway 135 or 136. The park is located between Sparta and Smithville, north of Highway 70.

SMITHVILLE

Smithville, the seat of DeKalb County, is known as the venue for the **Smithville Fiddler's Jamboree** (615/587-8500, smithvillejamboree.com), held over Fourth of July weekend. Arts and crafts sellers line the street, and a stage is built in front of the courthouse for two days of Appalachian music and dance.

Smithville is also associated with the Evins family, prominent businesspeople and politicians. Joe L. Evins was a U.S. congressman representing Smithville and its neighbors from 1947 to 1977. Joe's father, Edgar, was one of the chief developers of Smithville. The nearby state park is named in his honor.

Quilters, sewers, and other craftspeople might like to stop at **Becky's Fabrics and More** (105 W. Main St., 615/597-8521, www.sewcleverfabric.com, 9am-5pm Mon.-Fri., 9am-2pm Sat.), which has more than 2,000 bolts of fabric in stock, plus fat quarters by the thousands. It also stocks specialty equipment for hand and machine quilting.

Smithville is 20 miles west of Sparta on Highway 70.

Food

On the other side of the courthouse you'll find ★ **Sundance** (107 E. Main St., 615/597-1910, 11am-2:30pm Tues.-Thurs., 11am-8:30pm Fri., 5pm-8:30pm Sat., $7-20), a popular choice for its daily home-cooked lunch specials, specialty salads, fresh-brewed fruit teas, and hot-from-the-oven desserts. The menu is not extensive, but it changes daily, and you can be assured that everything is made from scratch. Sundance serves dinner on weekends, when diners will also enjoy live acoustic guitar music while they eat.

AROUND SMITHVILLE

Appalachian Center for Craft

A fine-arts education center affiliated with Tennessee Tech University in Cookeville, the **Appalachian Center for Craft** (1560 Craft Center Dr., 615/597-6801, www.tntech.edu/craftcenter, 10am-6pm daily, closed holidays, free) is located on the banks of Center Hill Lake, about six miles north of Smithville.

The name is a bit misleading: The center is not located in the Appalachian Mountains (it's on the Cumberland Plateau), and it is not focused on traditional crafts. Instead, the center teaches students the latest techniques in clay, fibers, glass, metal, and woods. The results are pieces that are more a reflection of trends in contemporary art making than of the mountain heritage of the area. But it is remarkable and housed in a breathtaking setting.

Visitors can tour three exhibits areas, which feature the works of artists in residence, students, and others. The gallery has a variety of artwork for sale, ranging from jewelry to candles to sculptures, all of which make great one-of-a-kind gifts. The pieces are serious works of art. The shop also sells some art-making supplies, should you be hit with creative inspiration while here (a likely scenario, given the true peaceful atmosphere here). The center offers more than 50 day- and weeklong workshops during the year.

The Lower Plateau

As you head south, the Cumberland Plateau narrows, eventually reaching a width of about 38 miles near Chattanooga. The Sequatchie River flows down the southern half of the plateau, creating the Sequatchie Valley, a wide, fertile valley that extends all the way to Chattanooga. West of the Sequatchie Valley is the Cumberland Plateau, and to the east the ridge is called Walden's, or Walling, Ridge.

FALL CREEK FALLS STATE PARK

Tennessee's largest state park, **Fall Creek Falls State Park** (2009 Village Camp Rd., Pikeville, 423/881-5298, tnstateparks.com/parks/about/fall-creek-falls) is a prime area for outdoor recreation on the Cumberland Plateau. The 25,000-acre park derives its name from its largest waterfall and chief attraction, but there are three other falls within the bounds of the park. In addition, Fall Creek Lake offers fishing and boating, and the Cane Creek Gorge offers dramatic vistas and bluffs. An oak and hickory forest that covers most of the park gives way to tulip poplar and hemlock in the gorges.

Fall Creek Falls got its start as a public park in the 1930s, when the National Park Service

Fall Creek Falls

established a Recreation Demonstration Area here around the falls. During the New Deal, some park infrastructure was built. In 1944, the park was deeded to the State of Tennessee. Construction of the dam began in 1966, and in 1970 other major park facilities, including the inn, were built. In the 1990s, an 18-hole golf course was added.

The park is 42 miles south of Cookeville on Highway 70.

PLANNING YOUR TIME

If you have only a few minutes, go to the Fall Creek Falls overlook and then drive to the nature center, where you can see two more waterfalls and walk across a swinging bridge. If you have a few hours, travel to the nature center, view the Cane Creek Falls, and then hike the two-mile loop that takes you along the Cane Creek Gorge and Fall Creek Falls.

Over a few days you could hike to all the falls and add the recreational activity of your choice: swimming, boating, bicycling, fishing, or even shuffleboard.

Fall Creek Falls is located within a few hours' drive of three of Tennessee's biggest cities, but it is far from any real towns. The park is about a 45-minute drive along two-lane blacktop roads to the nearest towns of McMinnville, Sparta, Crossville, and Dayton. On the outside bounds of the park are convenience stores that sell canned goods and a few basic necessities. Pikeville, a small town with a few restaurants and a grocery, is located about 20 minutes' drive away.

Fall Creek Falls is beautiful year-round—there are those who think the falls are even lovelier in winter (and certainly less crowded)—but the summer and fall are the most popular times to visit. The fall foliage show here is spectacular; book your cabin or other accommodations early to avoid being disappointed.

★ Fall Creek Falls

At 256 feet, Fall Creek Falls is the tallest waterfall east of the Rocky Mountains. Here water plunges past millennia of rock layers and into a pool of water that is deep and mysterious. Talking is difficult at the overlook, because you have to shout to speak over the sound of falling water.

Visitors to Fall Creek Falls can take an easy stroll from the parking lot to the overlook. The hike down to the bottom of the falls is a strenuous 0.5-mile trip, but it's worth the effort for the sure-footed. You can also hike a two-mile loop from the nature center to Fall Creek Falls.

There are other waterfalls at the state park. **Cane Creek Falls** and **Cane Creek Cascade** are immediately behind the park's nature center. In the summer you'll see families playing in the water at the bottom of these falls. Though not as tall as Fall Creek Falls, these are just as splendid. **Piney Falls,** accessible from an overlook on the western side of the park, is considered by some to be the park's most beautiful falls.

For impressive views of the Cane Creek Gorge, go to **Millikan's Overlook** and **Buzzard's Roost.** At Millikan's you are looking out at the point where the Cane Creek Gorge joins the Piney Creek Gorge. A five-minute walk from the parking lot brings you to Buzzard's Roost, where you are eye level with the hawks and turkey vultures that soar along the bluffs.

For information about the flora, fauna, and geologic history of the Cumberland Plateau, visit the **nature center** (423/881-5708, 9am-4:30pm daily, free). Here you can see a three-dimensional map of the park and learn about the plants and animals that make it home. There is also a movie about the park.

Recreation

Fall Creek Lake is fun to explore by **boat.** Paddleboats, canoes, and fishing boats without motors are available for rent for $6-9 a day; hourly rates are available. A fishing permit costs an extra $2, and you'll need to make sure you have a Tennessee fishing license, too. You can also fish from the lakeshore.

There is an 18-hole **golf** course at the park. Greens fees are $23-28 depending on the day. You can rent carts and clubs, and there is a driving range and practice green. Call the pro shop at 423/881-5706 for details.

There is a **swimming** pool at the inn, which nonguests can use for $4. Swimming is not permitted in the lake.

There are three paved **bicycle** paths, for a total distance of just over three miles. Bikes are also permitted on the park roads. Chinquapin Ridge and Piney Creek are mountain bike trails. Both are about seven miles long and are appropriate for intermediate or advanced mountain bikers. For details on the trails, including current conditions, call the nature center (423/881-5708).

During the summer, the Fall Creek Falls Stables, a private concession, offers guided **horseback riding** tours of the park for $20 per person. Contact them directly at 423/881-5952 for reservations.

There more than a dozen **hiking** trails in the park, many of which leave from the nature center. The **Woodland Trail** is a 0.9-mile path that passes through forest to Fall Creek Falls. The **Gorge Overlook Trail** is 1.2 miles and passes three overlooks on its way to Fall Creek Falls. The three-mile **Paw Paw Trail** crosses Rockhouse Creek. Experienced hikers may want to try the **Cable Trail,** a steep path that runs from the Paw Paw Trail to the base of the Cane Creek Falls. It's so steep that the park has erected a cable to help you, and you should consult with park staff about the trail's condition before setting out.

Leaving from the rear of the inn parking lot is a paved 1.35-mile trail that follows the lakeshore.

Several of the trails can be combined to make for longer hikes, and there is one overnight campsite for backpackers.

Accommodations

Fall Creek Falls has an inn, campground, and cabins for its visitors. The lovely blue ★ **fisherman's cabins** sit picturesquely on the lakefront. The landside cabins are tucked into the woods, with partial views of the water. All cabins sleep up to 8 or 10 people and rent for $145-160 per night; between Memorial Day and Labor Day you must rent them by the week.

The inn is a concrete fortress on the lake, with about as much charm as a worn-out college dormitory. The view of the lake out your window may not be enough consolation for the institutional feel, although as of this writing the rooms were in the process of being renovated and that may change. Nonetheless, the beds are comfortable, and it does beat an interstate motel—but just barely. Rooms rent for $74-220.

Campsites are set in a pleasant forest near the nature center. Rates are $11-25, but you'll pay $5 extra for a site with sewer hookup.

For inn and cabin reservations, call 423/881-5241 or 800/250-8610. For camping information, call 800/250-8611.

Food

The **Gaul's Gallery Restaurant** (6:30am-10am, 11am-3pm, 4pm-8pm Sun.-Thurs., 6:30am-10am, 11am-3pm, 4pm-9pm Fri-Sat.,

$5-18) is located at the inn and serves breakfast, lunch, and dinner. Billing itself as country cooking at affordable rates, the menu features burgers, sandwiches, fried fish, and a buffet. The buffet ($10 at supper, 4pm-8pm Sun.-Thurs., 4pm-9pm Fri., less at other times) includes a salad bar, about five side dishes, and three main-dish meats, plus dessert and soup. The quality of the food is decent, albeit not innovative, and vegetarians may struggle to cobble together a satisfying meal.

Around the Park

A few commercial enterprises have popped up around Fall Creek Falls. Four miles from the south gate of the park is **The Way Inn Grill** (Hwy. 284, 931/946-2800, 7am-5pm Mon.-Sat., 10am-5pm Sun., $2-5, www.thewayinntn.com), which serves food off the grill. Its lunch special is popular and home cooked. It also stocks groceries and select camping supplies. Rooms start at $60.

On the north side of the park, **The Fire House Grill** (12959 Park Rd., Pikeville, 423/881-5118) sells pizza, barbecue, and groceries. This is a downhome kind of place: Meat goes on the barbecue; when it is gone, the grill closes up for the day. Call ahead if you have a craving.

For those who like a little more excitement with their outdoor exploration, **ZIPStream Zip Line Aerial Adventure Park** (615/499-5779, www.zipstreamfallcreekfalls.com, $49.95) offers more than 2.5 hours of speeding through treetops.

DAYTON

This town of 7,000 is the seat of Rhea County and the site of one of Tennessee's (if not the country's) most famous legal events: the trial in July 1925 of teacher John Scopes on the charge that he taught evolution at the local high school.

Sights

Visitors should head directly to the **Rhea County Courthouse,** where the trial took place. In the basement there is a **museum** (9am-5pm Mon.-Fri., free) that gives an overview of the trial, including panels about its two principal characters: defense attorney Clarence Darrow and lawyer for the prosecution Williams Jennings Bryan. Thanks to the widespread media coverage of the trial, there are photographs and contemporary accounts of the events.

If court is not in session, you can head upstairs and see the courtroom, a broad, high-ceilinged, and elegant room. The original hard-backed chairs fill the gallery, and it is easy to imagine the heat and emotions that were stirred up here in 1925. It was so hot, in fact, that on at least one occasion court adjourned to a stage set up on the lawn outside.

Bryan, who won the case for the prosecution, died during an afternoon nap five days after the trial, while he was still in Dayton. A college was founded in his honor five years later, and today **Bryan College,** on the outskirts of town, is a Christian college with an extensive collection relating to Bryan and the Scopes trial. The college celebrates Bryan's position that the Bible is the literal truth.

Festivals and Events

Every July since 1988, the Dayton Chamber of Commerce and Bryan College have organized a four-day performance of ***The Scopes Trial,*** a documentary drama of the court case, based closely on the actual transcripts. Tickets are about $15 per person, and onlookers are expected to dress as their counterparts in the mid-1920s would have. That means no blue jeans or T-shirts, and no pants for the ladies.

During the Scopes festival, there are arts and crafts booths open on the courthouse lawn, while the reenactment takes place upstairs in the courthouse. For information and tickets, call the chamber of commerce at 423/775-0361.

Accommodations

Rooms at the **Holiday Inn Express** (2650 Rhea County Hwy., 423/570-0080, $95-115) come with cable TV, microwaves, refrigerators, coffeemakers, hair dryers, and

The Scopes Monkey Trial

For a few weeks in the heat of July 1925, Dayton, Tennessee, was the site of much national attention. If it had been 2016, it would have been flooded with 24-hour news crews. High school football coach and biology teacher John Scopes was on trial for violating a new and controversial Tennessee law, passed just four months earlier, which made it illegal to teach "any theory that denies the story of Divine Creation of man as taught in the Bible, and to teach instead that man has descended from a lower order of animal."

F. E. Robinson, owner of a local drugstore, is often credited with proposing and championing the cause that Dayton be the first city to test Tennessee's new antievolution law. He recruited Scopes, who agreed to be the test case. Scopes's alleged crime took place the previous April when he taught biology out of a state-sanctioned textbook.

Dayton's interest in testing the law had little to do with the issue of evolution (although most town residents took the Fundamentalist view of Divine Creation). Instead, it was an economic decision, since many in town knew that a trial like this would fill up all the hotels and put Dayton on the map like never before. But Robinson and other organizers probably never imagined that more than 80 years after the fact people would still be coming to Dayton on account of the trial.

One reason for the continued interest in the Scopes trial is the charismatic cast of characters who took part. Clarence Darrow was one of three volunteer lawyers who made up Scopes's defense team. "Great Commoner" William Jennings Bryan was a special prosecutor. The climax of the trial took place on July 20, when Darrow called Bryan to the stand as an expert witness on the Bible.

The courtroom duel between these two lawyers was captured in the 1955 play *Inherit the Wind,* which was performed on Broadway and was made into a Hollywood film in 1960 starring Gene Kelly, Spencer Tracy, and Fredric March. The story has been the subject of at least three subsequent television remakes.

The narrow legal question of whether Scopes taught evolution to Dayton high school students was not at issue during the trial, and on July 21 the jury took 10 minutes to return a guilty verdict. The judge fined Scopes $100. Later, the Tennessee Supreme Court overturned the conviction on a technicality. Dayton prosecutors decided not to retry John Scopes, who by then was at the University of Chicago studying geology.

The legacy of the Scopes trial, and the publicity it stirred, was a wave of similar state laws banning the teaching of evolution. Tennessee's own antievolution statute remained on the books until 1967, although there were no other prosecutions.

speakerphones, among other things. There is a free hot breakfast in the morning, a business center, and a fitness room.

Food

Travel by boat or car for dinner at **Jacob Myers Restaurant** (185 Chickamauga Dr., 423/570-0023, www.jacobmyersrestaurant.com, 11am-9pm Tues.-Thurs., 11am-10pm Fri.-Sat., 11am-6pm Sun., $6) for a waterfront view with your catfish dinner. Coffee and pastries are available at **Harmony House Coffee** (378 First Ave., 423/570-7656, harmonyhousecoffee.com, 7am-5pm Mon.-Fri., 9am-noon Sat.).

MCMINNVILLE

The roads leading to **McMinnville** are scattered with dozens of tree and plant nurseries. Several are retail operations, but most are wholesalers, selling only to garden and home stores around Tennessee and the Southeast. As a result, McMinnville and Warren County are known as the Nursery Capital. The nurseries are attracted by the good soil, temperate climate, and availability of supplies and specialist services.

The greatest tourist attraction in this part of the plateau is **Cumberland Caverns** (1437 Cumberland Caverns Rd., 931/668-4396, www.cumberlandcaverns.com, 9am-5pm daily, adults $19.50, children $12.50 for daytime walking tour; other tours, including overnight stays, are available.). Best known for its underground ballroom, equipped with seating and a quarter-ton crystal chandelier, Cumberland Caverns also has cave formations, underground waterfalls and pools, and a historic 1812 saltpeter mine. The underground tour is 1.5 miles long and includes the sound and light show *God of the Mountain*. Kids will also enjoy the Cumberland Caverns gem mine, where they can search for semiprecious stones. It is a constant 56 degrees down in the cave.

One Saturday a month music lovers from Nashville and elsewhere descend on McMinnville for ★ **Bluegrass Underground**, a monthly concert series held inside Cumberland Caverns, thanks to the excellent acoustics. Ticket prices vary based on the act, but they typically start around $30, with packages for making a weekend of the event (adding on cave tours and overnight accommodations). The Christmas show is typically less bluegrass-y than most, and very popular. Doors open around noon for 1pm shows. Seeing and hearing a concert 333 feet underground is something everyone should experience at least once. Because the concerts are held in the caverns' famous Volcano Room, please note that the space is not wheelchair accessible.

Cumberland Caverns is located six miles southeast of McMinnville, off Highway 8. It is about an hour-and-half drive from Nashville.

SAVAGE GULF STATE NATURAL AREA

Carved over millions of years by Big Creek, Collins River, and Savage Creek, **Savage Gulf State Natural Area** is a network of gorges resembling a giant chicken's foot. It is also one of the Cumberland's most lovely natural areas, but you have to get out of your car to enjoy it. Fast-moving streams, steep bluffs, and the divergent habitats of the gorge and the plateau make it a fascinating place to explore.

Savage Gulf comprises 14,500 acres, 500 of which are virgin forest. There are 55 miles of trails. We owe its existence to several local residents who raised money and support for the area to be preserved. Several of the most prominent champions of the park were descended from the Swiss immigrants who settled this area in the 19th century.

ORIENTATION

There are two ways to access Savage Gulf. The Stone Door Ranger Station (931/692-3887) is located off Highway 56 near Beersheba Springs. The Savage Ranger Station (931/779-3532) is located off Route 399 between Palmer and Cagle. It is a half-hour drive from one ranger station to the other.

The park offers programs and guided hikes year-round. Contact South Cumberland State Park (931/924-2956) for an upcoming calendar.

Recreation

There are 16 hiking trails throughout the natural area. Some are easy and flat; others are strenuous, taking you up, down, and around the deep gorges. Some 10 primitive campsites scattered throughout the park make it easy to plan an overnight hiking trip. A camping permit is required; contact the ranger stations for details.

The single greatest sight at Savage Gulf is the **Stone Door,** a rock formation that looks like a giant door that has been left ajar. Native Americans used it to travel from the plateau to the gorges. It is an 0.8-mile hike from the Stone Door Ranger Station along the plateau to the Stone Door. Also leaving from the Stone Door Ranger Station is the **Laurel Falls Loop,** a short 0.3-mile walk to a waterfall.

The **Savage Day Loop** is a 4.2-mile hike that begins and ends at the Savage Ranger Station. Along the way you walk across a suspension bridge, stop at Rattlesnake Point Overlook, and follow an old logging road.

For a detailed map of the hiking trails and campsites at Savage Gulf, stop by or call one of the ranger stations and ask for the trails map.

DUNLAP

Dunlap, Tracy City, Coalmont, and other small towns in this part of the plateau owe their existence to coal. From the 1860s until the 1920s, coal was mined in this area. During the 20th century, much of the coal was turned to coke—a refined coal product used in iron and steel foundries. Coke ovens were built all over the countryside.

Dunlap has preserved the history of these coke ovens at the **Dunlap Coke Oven Park** (423/949-3493, www.cokeovens.com, dawn to dusk daily, free), a 62-acre park where some 268 old coke ovens have been preserved. The Coke Oven Museum at the park is open by appointment. To find the park, drive south on Highway 127 through Dunlap and turn right on Cherry Street at the stoplight. Cross the railroad tracks and follow the signs to the park.

For more information about the park and the coke ovens, contact the Sequatchie Valley Historical Association at 423/949-2156.

Take state highway 111 northwest from Chattanooga and turn left on US-27, which turns into Rankin Avenue. Turn off Rankin to Mountain View Circle.

TRACY CITY

Tracy City is a quiet town today. From 1858 until the 1920s, it was a busy coal mining town and the site of bitter labor disputes between miners and the owners of the mines.

Sights

Several historic buildings have links to the city's mining history. **Miner's Hall** on Jasper Road was the headquarters of the local United Mine Workers Union. You can see homes built by coal capitalists next door to each other along Depot Street.

Grundy Lakes State Park (Hwy. 41, 931/924-2980) is a lovely little park and the best place in the area to see old coke ovens. A one-way road skirts a small lake, built by the Civilian Conservation Corps during the New Deal of the 1930s. You can see old ovens across the lake from the swimming beach, and also along the road just past the beach entrance. As you become better at spotting the ovens, you will notice that they are scattered all over the forest throughout the park.

In addition to the coke ovens, Grundy Lakes has a playground, picnic tables, and walking trails. The 1.3-mile **Lone Rock Trail** skirts the lake. The 12.5-mile **Fiery Gizzard Trail** starts at Grundy Lakes and traces the Fiery Gizzard Gorge. It is a beautiful and challenging hike through a diverse and rugged landscape. This hike includes incredible views of several waterfalls along the way. But there are boulders to climb along the way and no way other than to walk back out if you slip. Wear hiking boots and be prepared before you do this lovely hike.

In 2015 owners of private property that hikers crossed to reach Fiery Gizzard Trail made that land no longer open to the public. The Tennessee State Parks and the Land Trust of Tennessee and many volunteers started working on rerouting a small section of the trail as a result. Construction then began on bridges, staircases, and a 1.5-mile new connector at the Raven's Point section of the trail. Check on its status before you head out.

There are two backcountry campsites along the way, and the trail ends up at the parking area for **Foster Falls,** a 60-foot waterfall. You can also drive to Foster Falls by heading east along Highway 41 from Tracy City. The access point is located shortly after you pass into Marion County.

Shopping

Stop at **The Marugg Company** (88 Depot, 931/592-5042, www.themaruggcompany.com), manufacturers of hand-hewn rakes and other implements. It also operates an antiques shop next door. Hours are limited in the winter.

Food

The Swiss heritage of this part of Tennessee is evident at ★ **Dutch Maid Bakery** (109 Main St., 931/592-3171, www.thedutchmaid.com, 7am-5pm Mon.-Sat., 10am-3pm Sun.). The bakery was founded in 1902 by six brothers of the Baggenstoss family, and it remained in the family until 1992. In 2005, it was purchased by Cynthia Day, who continues to use the old Baggenstoss recipes, plus some of her own. You will find loaves of breakfast bread and whole wheat, potato, and salt-rising bread, along with pastries and fruitcakes.

A café (7am-2:30pm Mon.-Sat., 11am-2:30pm Sun., $5-9) next door serves breakfast and lunch Monday-Saturday and a buffet lunch on Sunday. There are traditional breakfast options, all served with toasted bread made at the bakery. At lunch you can get sandwiches or choose the daily lunch special, such as pork chops, chicken and dumplings, or meat loaf.

SOUTH CUMBERLAND STATE PARK

To newcomers, **South Cumberland State Park** (Hwy. 41, 931/924-2980) is confusing because it seems to be in so many places at the same time. The reality is that South Cumberland is an umbrella park for 10 different "units" that are scattered around the southern plateau. Units will be presented in this book where they fit in geographically.

The headquarters of the park is located along Highway 41 about halfway between Monteagle and Tracy City. There is a visitors center, museum, and gift shop, and recreation facilities including a ball field and picnic tables. The museum eloquently describes the natural and human history of the area through hand-stitched narrative panels. It is a good starting place for an overview of the area.

MONTEAGLE

Few communities in Tennessee are as surprising as **Monteagle**. A speck on the map and a rest stop on the interstate, Monteagle is also home to a 125-plus-year-old summer retreat that continues to this day. The **Monteagle Assembly** (1 Assembly Ave., 931/924-2286, www.monteaglesundayschoolassembly.org) was founded in 1882 as the Chautauqua of the South. Created out of enthusiasm for Christian living, temperance, and intellectual and artistic development, the Monteagle Sunday School Assembly was initially meant as an ecumenical training center for Sunday school teachers. Over the years, the assembly became more secular in its focus; the annual summer program taught literature, physics, drawing, music, and education. For a time, Nashville's Peabody College held its summer school here.

The Monteagle Assembly

What is most remarkable about the Monteagle Assembly is that it persists. Of the hundreds of similar assemblies patterned after the Chautauqua Institution in New York, fewer than 10 remain active. Monteagle is one of them. After a period of decline in the mid-20th century, Monteagle came back, and the 100th-anniversary celebrations in 1982 were a major success.

Every summer, from early June until August, families return to Monteagle to live and take part in workshops, church activities, lectures, and community events. If you are having a hard time understanding what happens, imagine it as a wholesome summer camp for the whole family.

Even if you're not a member of the Assembly, you can attend workshops and other events by buying a daily gate ticket ($16). Temporary passes are also available if the workshop lasts only a few hours. Workshops range from art classes to bridge instruction. Lecture topics are equally diverse. Many have a religious perspective, but others focus on local history, health and fitness, or nature and the environment. There are also musical performances.

Part of Monteagle's appeal comes from its physical setting. The Assembly is located in a wooded, hilly area, and the 161 cottages are charming examples of 19th- and early-20th-century architecture, including Carpenter Gothic, Queen Anne, and Craftsman. All are well maintained, and walking or driving through the community makes you feel as if you have stepped back in time.

If you visit during the summer, you will have to pay the gate fee, which is $16 for adults per day. Outside of the summer season, visitors may drive or walk through the Assembly on their own. Stop in at the office, located to the right of the gate, for a map and other information. If you come during the summer, respect the quiet hours, which are 1pm-2:30pm daily.

Accommodations

The ★ **Edgeworth Inn** (19 Wilkins Ave., 931/924-4000, www.edgeworthinn.com, $150-225) is a six-room bed-and-breakfast located inside Monteagle Assembly. Built in 1896, this handsome Victorian offers atmosphere unmatched by other area bed-and-breakfasts. Each room has a private bath, and three suites are available. The generously proportioned porch is a focal point for visitors, as is the lovely garden. The same owners also have a suite available on the University of the South campus in beautiful Sewanee.

Just outside the gates of the Assembly is the ★ **Monteagle Inn** (204 W. Main St., 931/924-3869, www.monteagleinn.com, $165-275), a 14-suite boutique bed-and-breakfast. Guest rooms are neatly appointed with plush linens, four-poster beds, newly refurbished bathrooms, and color schemes reminiscent of Italy. Common rooms include a comfortable sitting room, gardens, and a front porch.

You can also rent a room inside the Assembly from one of the more than 150 Assembly members. Ask at the office for a listing of properties and contact information. Rates, policies, availability, and amenities vary considerably among properties, and many book up for the season well in advance.

Food

Thanks to the presence of the Assembly, Monteagle supports more than the average number of upscale restaurants. **The High Point** (224 E. Main St., 931/924-4600, www.highpointrestaurant.net, 5pm-9pm Sun.-Thurs., 5pm-10pm Fri.-Sat, $24-46) is Monteagle's original fine-dining restaurant. Built in 1929 by Al Capone, the High Point is famous for its hidden escape hatches and secret storage areas where Capone hid liquor and other contraband. Today, the High Point is hardly criminal. Its upscale ambience emanates from a sturdy stone facade, hardwood floors, and beautiful dark-wood window casings. During the summer, you may dine on the stone terrace. The menu features an array of fresh seafood—grouper, mahimahi, lobster, and shrimp—plus prime steaks, pork chops, and lamb. The wine and spirits bar is superb.

Located on the road to Sewanee, ★ **Pearl's Foggy Mountain Café** (15344 Sewanee Hwy., 615/598-5770, pearlsfoggymountaincafe.com, 5pm-9pm Tues.-Wed., 5pm-10pm Thurs.-Sat., noon-3pm Sun. for special occasions, $17-35) is your best choice for an innovative yet comforting meal in these parts. Proprietors Jim and Susan Wofford escaped the rat race of Atlanta to open a high-quality restaurant in the wilds of the Cumberland Plateau. A favorite among Sewanee and Monteagle residents and visitors, the Foggy Mountain serves a modern version of Southern-style cuisine for dinner and Sunday brunch. Home-smoked trout, stuffed pork chops, and lots of fresh salads are just some of the dishes you can expect.

For something more everyday, go to **Papa Ron's Pizza and Pasta Grill** (402 W. Main St., 931/924-3355, www.paparons.net, 11am-9pm Mon.-Thurs. and Sun., 11am-10pm Fri.-Sat., $6-18), which serves lunch and dinner daily. The menu offers a variety of creamy and tomato-based pasta dishes, personal and large pizzas, soup, and sandwiches. The service is efficient.

SEWANEE

The town of Sewanee is synonymous with the **University of the South** (735 University Ave., 931/598-1000, www.sewanee.edu), the private liberal arts college that has educated 24 Rhodes scholars and earned a reputation as one of the South's finest universities.

It was 1857 when the Episcopal Church announced it was planning to establish an educational center in the region. The plans were grand: The center would include 30 schools and colleges offering classical education as well as practical subjects like agriculture and forestry. The citizens of Franklin County and the Sewanee Mining Company offered 10,000 acres of land on the Cumberland Plateau for the school, and in 1860 the cornerstone was laid.

The Civil War nearly dashed all hopes for this educational paradise. By the end of the war, all the original leaders were dead, and the cornerstone had been blown apart. Promised funds for the school had evaporated.

Despite the challenges, bishops Charles T. Quintard and William M. Green persisted with the dream. They raised 2,500 British pounds, built a clapboard chapel, donned ecclesiastical robes, and led a procession to establish the University of the South on September 18, 1868. During its first year, nine students were enrolled.

Over the years, Sewanee's fortunes have improved. Today, it has one of the largest per-student endowments in the country. Its academic reputation is strong, and the *Sewanee Review* is the oldest literary quarterly in the United States. The university is still owned by the Episcopal Church, and in addition to its undergraduate liberal arts college, it is home to the Episcopal School of Theology.

Sewanee enrolls about 1,500 students. The original "domain" of 10,000 acres that was donated to establish the school remains, making it the largest college campus in America. The campus, with its Gothic-style architecture and classical feel, is a pleasant place for a walk. Stop at the admissions office for a campus map.

Sewanee's architecture is grand. Even the newer buildings are carefully constructed to fit in on the campus, which feels like it would be just as at home in old England as on the Cumberland Plateau of Tennessee.

For a dramatic view over the western edge of the plateau, drive to an overlook located at the end of Tennessee Street, past the School of Theology.

Of note is the **University Bookstore** (735 University Ave., 931/598-1153), which is the best bookstore between Chattanooga and Nashville. The shelves include an extensive selection of religious works, Sewanee merchandise, and a wide selection of modern and classic works. The *Sewanee Review* is on sale for $8 a copy.

Accommodations

Accommodations in Sewanee itself are limited. **Cabin 111** (289 University Ave.,

National Cornbread Festival

If there is one thing Southerners know, it is corn bread. They have strong opinions on what makes for a good corn bread and how to prepare it, and they descend on South Pittsburg at the end of April each year to share these thoughts at the National Cornbread Festival (www.nationalcornbread.com).

A $5 admission gets you inside the festival, which features Cornbread Alley (locals showing off their favorite recipes), corn bread cook-offs, buttermilk-chugging and ice-cream-eating contests, arts and crafts shows, a quilt exhibit, and tours of the local Lodge Foundry Plant, where cast-iron skillets (essential for corn bread making) are manufactured. Winning recipes tend to shy away from straight-up corn bread—past finalists have included a sweet corn bread shrimp cakes with mango salsa and a corn bread/bacon cobbler—but there is plenty of unadulterated corn bread around, too.

931/598-5311, www.cabin111.com, $95) is a cozy one-bedroom cottage located 0.5 mile from the university campus. The simple yet comfortable accommodations include a queen-size bed and kitchenette. The cabin is nonsmoking, and pets are not permitted.

The owners of the **Edgeworth Inn** in Monteagle have two **Sewanee Suites** (931/924-4000, www.edgeworthinn.com, $225) available for rent on campus.

If you are in some way affiliated with the university, you may reserve a room at **The Sewanee Inn** (1235 University Ave., 931/598-1686). For other choices, look in nearby Monteagle.

Food

Sewanee's commercial district is located along Highway 41, a few blocks south of the university. **The Blue Chair** (41 University Ave., 931/598-5434, www.thebluechair.com, opens 7am Mon.-Fri., 7:30am Sat., $7-14) should be your first stop for coffee, sandwiches, breakfast, and take-away dinners and boxed lunches. Call ahead for hours; closing time varies with the season and the university's schedule.

Around Sewanee

The **Sewanee Natural Bridge** is about four miles outside of town. Part of South Cumberland State Park, the rock formation is 25 feet tall, with a 50-foot span. Visitors reach it at the end of a short footpath from a parking area. Take care as you walk over and around the natural wonder.

To find the natural bridge, drive west out of town along Highway 41. Turn left onto Highway 56 and follow the signs.

WHITWELL

A small town on the southern end of the Sequatchie Valley, Whitwell is the type of place you might just pass right through. Don't. This rural community that huddles along Highway 28 northeast of Chattanooga is home to one of the most moving sights in this part of Tennessee, the Children's Holocaust Memorial.

★ Children's Holocaust Memorial

The story started in 1998, when the principal of Whitwell Middle School wanted to start a project about tolerance. She sent an eighth-grade teacher, David Smith, to a workshop on the subject. Mr. Smith returned with an idea to offer an after-school class about the Holocaust. Another teacher, Sandra Roberts, led the first session in the fall of 1998. As Roberts told the students about the six million Jews killed by the Nazis, she realized that six million was a number that her students just could not grasp.

It was a student who first suggested the paper clips. The idea was for students to collect 6 million paper clips as a way of demonstrating the horrific scale of the Holocaust. The idea caught on. Over the years that followed, Whitwell Middle School received paper clips from all 50 states and more than 50 countries. Along with them have come letters and documents, over 30,000 of them. The school still receives paper clips.

The tale of the Children's Holocaust Memorial goes even further. After the paper clips began to pour in and interest in the project grew, the school recognized the need for a memorial. Things came together when two correspondents for a German newspaper bought a 1917 German rail car that had been used to transport Jews during the Holocaust and donated it to the school. Local businesses pitched in to build the memorial, where visitors can come to see the millions of paper clips that the students collected. The message of the memorial is one of rebirth and a call to action: The students ask you as you leave to reflect on what you can do to eliminate hatred and bigotry from the world.

Visitors can see the **Children's Holocaust Memorial** (1130 Main St., 423/658-5631, www.whitwellmiddleschool.org) at any time. During school hours, stop at the front door of the school, where you can pick up an audio tour. On Friday when school is in session there are student-led tours at 9:15am. Reservations are required. After hours you can pick up a key from Smith Bros. Grocery, 13835 Hwy 28, 9am-7pm.

In 2004, Miramax Pictures released a documentary by Joe Fab about the project, titled *Paper Clips*.

SOUTH PITTSBURG

Established in the 1870s and named in the hope it would become an industrial center of the New South, South Pittsburg is a small town that has seen better days. It is located just a few miles north of the Alabama state line.

Thousands of people head to South Pittsburg for the **National Cornbread Festival** (www.nationalcornbread.com), which takes place during the last weekend of April and includes cook-offs, live music, church services, and lots of corn bread.

It is almost impossible to fight the lines at the **Lodge Factory Store** (503 S. Cedar Ave., 423/837-5919) during the corn bread festival. (Everyone needs cast iron for their new corn

the Children's Holocaust Memorial

bread recipes.) But the rest of the year it is a less hectic place to stock up on this beloved brand.

South Pittsburg is near I-24, just 30 miles west of Chattanooga, and so there are several mainstream hotels nearby. **Comfort Inn** (exit 152, 205 Kimball Crossing Dr., 423/837-2479, $75-110) and **Holiday Inn Express** (exit 152, 300 Battlecreek Rd., 423/837-1500, $82-115) are two choices.

Chattanooga and the Overhill Country

Look for ★ to find recommended sights, activities, dining, and lodging.

Highlights

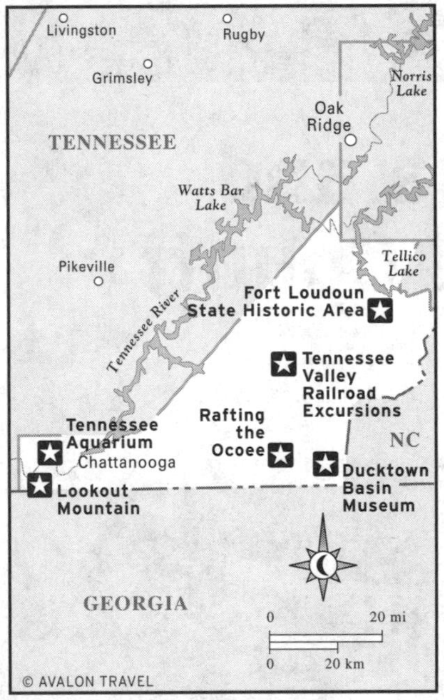

★ **Tennessee Aquarium:** See freshwater and ocean creatures up close at one of the best aquariums in the country (page 324).

★ **Lookout Mountain:** This narrow finger of the Cumberland Plateau offers great views as well as Rock City, Ruby Falls, and the setting of a Civil War battle (page 327).

★ **Rafting the Ocoee:** High-velocity rapids keep even the most experienced paddlers at the edge of their rafts on a journey down the Ocoee River (page 345).

★ **Ducktown Basin Museum:** Learn about the legacy of copper mining at this top-notch yet down-home museum (page 349).

★ **Tennessee Valley Railroad Excursions:** All aboard! See old mining towns and beautiful mountain passes on a scenic railroad ride (page 354).

★ **Fort Loudoun State Historic Area:** The complex dynamics of the Tennessee frontier come to life at this re-created 18th-century British fort (page 358).

Nicknamed the Scenic City, Chattanooga, the smallest of Tennessee's four main cities, is also regarded as its most livable.

In 2011 *Outside* magazine's readers named it their "ultimate dream city," and the years since have solidified the city's outdoors cred. Perched on the banks of the Tennessee River, surrounded by mountains, Chattanooga was once an industrial powerhouse. After some hardscrabble years, now it is a model for urban eco-friendly redevelopment. City parks, a pedestrian bridge, free downtown (electric, zero-emission) buses, and an abundance of nearby recreation have brought people back downtown. Its arts district is anchored by a museum with one of the best collections of American art in the South. The University of Tennessee has a downtown Chattanooga campus, which lends an additional youthful energy to the city.

In addition, Chattanooga is one of the best destinations for families in Tennessee. The Tennessee Aquarium is its flagship attraction, but there is also a downtown IMAX theater, the Creative Discovery Museum, the Chattanooga Zoo, and railroad excursions. On Lookout Mountain, families will enjoy riding the Incline Railroad, going beneath the earth to see the hard-to-describe Ruby Falls, and exploring the fairyland-style rock gardens at Rock City. On top of this are downtown parks, the local AA baseball team, nearby Lake Winnepesauka, and an amusement park, not to mention lots of hiking, paddling, and other outdoor activities.

The nearby Overhill region in southeastern Tennessee is a region of natural beauty and rich heritage. Five rivers wend down the mountains and through the valleys here, with names—Hiwassee, Ocoee, Tellico, Conasauga, and Tennessee—that trace back to the Overhill Cherokee people. The Ocoee's white-water rapids attract rafters and kayakers; the calms of the Hiwassee are a refuge for Sandhill crane and other waterfowl.

The foothill country here is dotted with towns and landmarks named in

Previous: Point Park is part of the Chickamauga and Chattanooga National Military Park; the Chattanooga Choo Choo. **Above:** the underground Ruby Falls.

Chattanooga and the Overhill Country

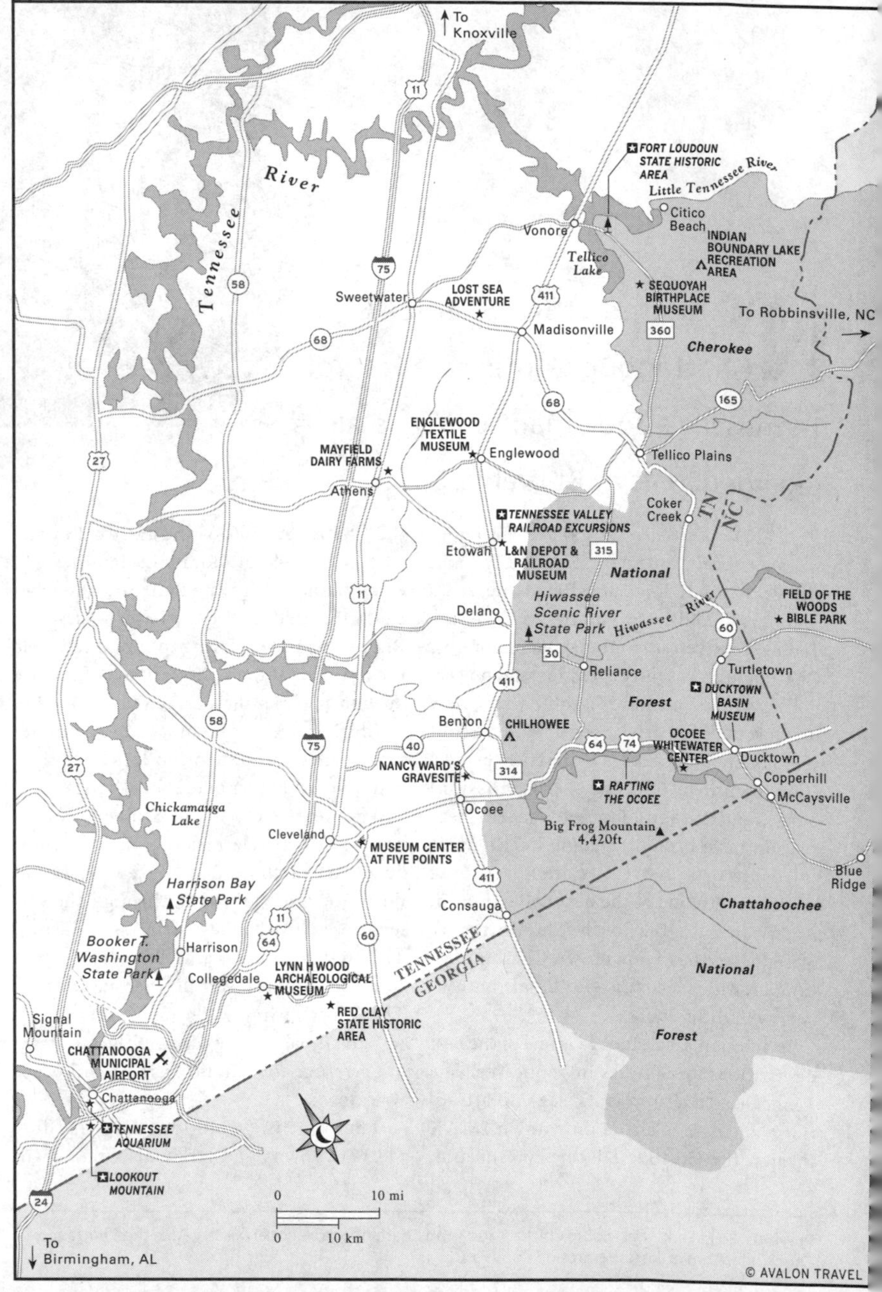

the Cherokee language, and others—like Reliance, Copperhill, and Cleveland—that are linked to lives and industries of more modern settlers. Museums in Ducktown, Etowah, and Englewood preserve the stories of Tennesseans who earned their livelihoods in the mines, on the railroads, and in the textile factories of East Tennessee.

It is the natural beauty of the region that is its greatest calling card, however. The Cherokee National Forest contains hiking trails, bike paths, lakes, and rivers. The landscape invites you to slow down and enjoy the seasons and the gentle passage of time. For more to do near Chattanooga, Monteagle and Sewanee are good places to visit.

PLANNING YOUR TIME

This region of the state is perfect for a two-in-one vacation: Start with three days in Chattanooga and follow it with three days in the Overhill region. It's a plan that offers a nice balance of urban sophistication and outdoor exploration, and can be an ideal family vacation. If you have more time, add a day in Monteagle and Sewanee (in the Cumberland Plateau).

If you have only a long weekend and pine for the outdoors, cut your time in Chattanooga to two days and spend your third day at the Ocoee River.

Remember that many attractions in Chattanooga—such as the aquarium—may be very crowded during summer weekends.

Chattanooga

Cradled in a tight bend of the Tennessee River, Chattanooga is a city that has risen from the ashes. Chattanooga's first boom was after the Civil War, when industry and transportation flourished. Expansive warehouses and railway yards bustled with activity, and the city that grew up around them was lively and sophisticated.

Chattanooga's prosperity was not to last, however. By the 1970s and 1980s, the Scenic City was dirty, dilapidated, and nearly deserted by all but the most loyal residents.

Chattanooga's turnaround is one of the great stories of the success of urban planning and downtown redevelopment. Starting with the flagship Tennessee Aquarium in the early 1990s, Chattanooga has flourished with the addition of new attractions. Planners have also emphasized quality of life for residents; Chattanooga is pedestrian friendly, easy to navigate, and boasts several lovely downtown parks.

HISTORY

Chattanooga's location in the bend of the Tennessee River made it secure, temperate, and fertile. The Cherokee called the area *Chado-na-ugsa,* rock that comes to a point, referring to nearby Lookout Mountain.

After the forced removal of the Cherokee, settlers established Ross's Landing, a trading post on the river. In 1839, the town of Chattanooga was incorporated. Eleven years later, the first rail line, the Western and Atlantic, arrived in the city.

Chattanooga was of great strategic importance during the Civil War. Confederates moved in to defend her in 1861, and for the first two years of the war Chattanooga was an important supply depot for the Southern states. In the fall of 1863, after the bloody battles of Chickamauga and Chattanooga, the city was in Federal hands. William Tecumseh Sherman used Chattanooga as a staging point for his march through Georgia and South Carolina, and Union troops built warehouses, stockyards, and hospitals to support the army. Many of these sights are historic draws to the area today.

After the Civil War, northern industrialists sought to capitalize on Chattanooga's location, infrastructure, and proximity to natural resources. These industrialists relied heavily on the political support of newly enfranchised

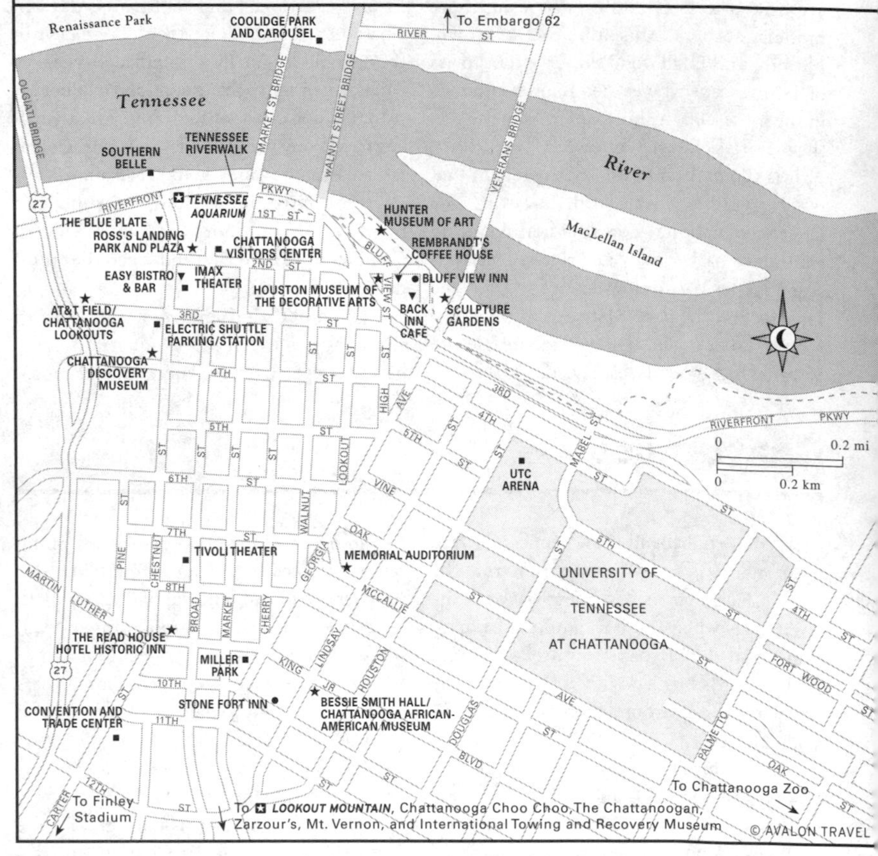

African Americans. During this period, African Americans were elected to local office, established businesses, and pursued education. Jim Crow arrived in Chattanooga and would remain until the civil rights movement of the 1950s and 1960s.

In 1899 the city secured exclusive bottling rights to Coca-Cola, and the Chattanooga Coca-Cola bottling plant grew into one of the city's largest and most successful businesses. (Coke still rules the beverage counters in town today. You might also find an RC, but likely not a Pepsi.) After the Tennessee Valley Authority (TVA) built dams, increased electricity supply, and eased flooding during the 1930s and 1940s, Chattanooga experienced another boom, further bolstered by World War II. Unfortunately, by the late 1960s, Chattanooga was one of the most polluted cities in America. But over the past two decades, Chattanooga has experienced an exciting period of rebirth.

ORIENTATION

Chattanooga is defined and confined by its geography. The city sits in the bend of the Tennessee River and is hemmed in by mountains on three sides. Missionary Ridge, which runs along the fourth side, was a barrier for earlier residents, but now tunnels pass through it.

The best place to get an understanding of Chattanooga's setting is from atop Lookout Mountain, where you can see the Cumberland Plateau, the Tennessee River, and Missionary Ridge.

Downtown

Market Street and **Broad Street** are the two major north-south thoroughfares downtown. Market Street continues across the river via the Market Street Bridge; Broad Street dead-ends in front of the aquarium. Cross streets 1st-9th make navigation simple.

South and east of the aquarium district is the city's business and government center. Here you will find large office buildings; city, state, and federal offices; the University of Tennessee; the city's African American museum; and Warner Park, home of the Chattanooga Zoo.

Farther south is the world-famous Choo Choo and Chattanooga's old commercial district, centered along **Main Street.** Explore around the Choo Choo, and you will see lots of old brick buildings that once housed warehouses, hotels, and manufacturers that needed to be near the railroad. Many of these buildings have been restored and now house new businesses; some still sit empty.

Bluff View is a smattering of elegant old homes located about three blocks east of the aquarium, along the river, with, as its name suggests, a view from the bluff over the river. The city's art museum is here, along with a collection of outstanding restaurants. You can get to Bluff View on foot either by walking about four blocks along 3rd Street from downtown, along the Riverwalk boardwalk that follows the river, or across the remarkable Holmberg pedestrian bridge, a 250-foot lighted glass bridge that connects the south end of Walnut Street to Bluff View.

Across the river from downtown is the **Northside.** Accessible by car via the Market Street Bridge or by foot along the Walnut Street pedestrian bridge, Northside is a dining, shopping, and entertainment center with a fresher, more youthful feel than downtown. Coolidge Park along the waterfront is another attraction on this side of the river.

Lookout Mountain

Many of Chattanooga's most famous attractions are on **Lookout Mountain**, located south of downtown. The best way to get to Lookout Mountain from the city is by driving

Market Street Bridge

south on Broad Street. After about two miles, Broad splits into the Ochs Highway (Route 58) and the Cummings Highway (Highways 42, 72, 11, and 64). Follow Ochs to get to the base of the Incline Railroad or Rock City; follow Cummings to get to Point Park and Ruby Falls. Both roads take you to Lookout Mountain.

You can also get to Lookout Mountain by parking at the bottom and riding the Incline Railroad. When you reach the top, you can walk to Point Park. Other attractions are beyond walking distance, however.

Whenever you are driving on Lookout Mountain, do it with caution. The roads are narrow, windy, heavily trafficked, and—in some places—precarious. Drive slowly and carefully (seriously, no texting!).

SIGHTS

★ Tennessee Aquarium

The **Tennessee Aquarium** (1 Broad St., 800/262-0695, www.tnaqua.org, 10am-6pm daily, adults $26.95, children 3-12 $16.95) is Chattanooga's landmark attraction. Two huge buildings with angular glass roofs house Ocean Journey and River Journey, salt- and freshwater aquariums with more than 12,000 animals in all. It has a more educational bent than facilities like Atlanta's Georgia Aquarium, which is more entertainment focused. Built in 1992, the aquarium was the first act in Chattanooga's remarkable comeback as a city.

Ocean Journey showcases saltwater creatures, including sharks, rays, and colorful coral reef fish. River Journey follows the watershed from an Appalachian cove forest to a humid delta swamp and includes exhibits on the major rivers of the world, including the Tennessee, which is literally right out front. Standout exhibits include the playful river otters, the boneless beauties—jellyfish, octopus, and cuttlefish—and the American alligator. In between these, there are literally hundreds of captivating and high-quality exhibits of all types of water creatures. The music you hear is designed to reflect the music you'd hear in the region of the world where you'd find the fish you see. On some days you may even experience live music, such as a bluegrass fiddler in the delta exhibit.

Outside the aquarium there are fountains and a wading pool. Or you can walk over the riverfront and look out at the mighty Tennessee.

In addition to the aquarium itself, there is an IMAX 3-D theater, which shows

Learn about both fresh water and ocean creatures at the Tennessee Aquarium.

nature-related films daily. Tickets may be purchased separately (adults $9.95, children $8.50) or as part of a discounted admission package with the aquarium.

The aquarium can get crowded on weekends, as well as on weekdays in summer. Start out early to avoid the worst crowds, and remember that your admission ticket is good all day, so you can take a midday break for lunch and return.

Other Downtown Sights

Chattanooga's African American history is preserved at the **Bessie Smith Hall and Chattanooga African American Museum** (200 E. Martin Luther King Blvd., 423/266-8658, www.bessiesmithcc.org, 10am-5pm Mon.-Fri., noon-4pm Sat., adults $7, seniors and students $5, children 6-12 $3). The museum is located at the site of the Martin Hotel, once a popular African American hotel and restaurant. There are hundreds of photographs of black Chattanoogans, with panels that describe the African American community's contributions in sports, the arts, business, government, and culture. There are pictures of famous black Chattanoogans, including Bessie Smith, Samuel L. Jackson, Valaida Smith, and Roland Hayes. The exhibits include information about African culture, accomplishments, and art.

Just down the hall, in the lobby of the Bessie Smith Hall, is an exhibit dedicated to the legendary blues singer. Smith grew up poor in Chattanooga, having been orphaned at age nine. She developed her singing talent performing for pennies on the streets of Chattanooga. Smith was discovered by Ma Rainey and, later, Columbia Records, and for a period in the 1920s she was the highest-paid American black woman in the entertainment world.

Smith's success did not last. After a bad marriage and personal problems, including alcohol abuse, Smith was in the early stages of a comeback when she died in a car accident in northern Mississippi in 1937. She was buried in an unmarked grave in Philadelphia. In 1970, rock singer Janis Joplin found out about the grave and bought a headstone, which reads "The greatest blues singer in the world will never stop singing."

Inside the hall you will see photographs of Smith, old concert posters, and a dress she wore in the early days of her singing career.

The **International Towing and Recovery Hall of Fame and Museum** (3315 Broad St., 423/267-3132, www.internationaltowingmuseum.org, 9am-5pm Mon.-Sat. Mar.-Oct., 10am-4:30pm Mon.-Sat. Nov.-Feb., 11am-5pm Sun. year-round, adults $10, seniors $9 children 6-18 $6) showcases antique and modern tow trucks and other recovery vehicles. The museum is located in Chattanooga because the first tow truck was fabricated nearby at the Ernest Holmes Company. The museum's hall of fame memorializes people who have made significant contributions to the towing and recovery industry. The Wall of the Fallen remembers operators who lost their lives on the job.

The **Creative Discovery Museum** (321 Chestnut St., 423/756-2738, www.cdmfun.org, 10am-5pm Mon.-Sat., noon-5pm Sun., extended summer hours 9:30am-5:30pm daily, closed on Wed. Sept.-Feb., $12.95, $2 discounts with your aquarium ticket stub) is a hands-on museum specifically designed for children under 12. Activities include an archaeological dig area; RiverPlay, where kids can pilot a riverboat; and a regularly rotating collection of temporary exhibitions. There is a special play area for toddlers, too.

The **Chattanooga History Center** (2 W. Aquarium Way., 423/265-3247, www.chattanoogahistory.org, 9am-5pm Mon.-Fri.) closed its location at 400 Chestnut Street in 2007. The museum is developing its new facility, and has run into some budget issues as it has done so. Even in progress, the center is worth a visit, as its architecture is something to behold. The center also leads themed tours around the city, including several Civil War tours. Fees vary based on tour. Custom tours can also be arranged.

The **Chattanooga Zoo** (Warner Park,

1254 E. 3rd St., 423/697-1322, www.chattzoo.org, 9am-5pm daily, adults $8.95, seniors $6.95, children 3-12 $5.95, children 2 and under free) is a modest yet fun animal park. The six-acre facility located inside Warner Park houses chimpanzees, red pandas, snow leopards, spider moneys, and jaguars, among others. There is also a petting zoo. A $4.2 million front entrance to the zoo from Holtzclaw Avenue (Warner Park) was constructed in 2008; this makes it easier to see and find the zoo, not that the zoo is not within walking distance of the main downtown attractions.

Recent upgrades include the Deserts and Forests of the World exhibit; a giraffe habitat is in the works. The zoo celebrated its 75th anniversary in 2012.

Bluff View

The bluff overlooking the Tennessee River and downtown Chattanooga is the city's arts center. The foremost attraction here is the **Hunter Museum of American Art** (10 Bluff View, 423/267-0968, www.huntermuseum.org, 10am-5pm Mon.-Tues., noon-5pm Fri.-Sat., Wed. and Sun., 10am-8pm Thurs., adults $9.95, children 3-17 $4.95, children under 3 free, free first Sunday of the month). Housed in the former home of Coca-Cola magnate and philanthropist George Thomas Hunter, the Hunter Museum has one of the most important collections of American art in the Southeast. The permanent collection includes works from the Hudson River School, American Impressionism, Ashcan School, Regionalist, Early Modern, and Contemporary movements. Major touring exhibits are also on display, and visitors enjoy dramatic views of the river below.

On a pleasant day, stroll through the **Bluff View Art District Sculpture Garden,** affiliated with the Hunter Museum but open to the public at no charge.

The **Houston Museum of the Decorative Arts** (201 High St., 423/267-7176, www.thehoustonmuseum.org, noon-4pm Wed-Sat., first Sunday of each month or by appointment, adults $9, children 4-17 $3.50) houses the decorative arts collection of Anna Safley Houston. Houston was a colorful character who died in relative poverty in 1951, having refused to sell any part of her valuable collection of porcelain and glassware.

Inside the museum you will find parts of Houston's remarkable collection, including antique money banks, steins, face mugs, miniature lamps, and glass baskets, as well as early American furniture and coverlets.

the Hunter Museum of American Art

Main Street

South of downtown, at the corner of Main and Market Streets, is the legendary **Chattanooga Choo Choo** (1400 Market St., 423/266-5000, www.choochoo.com), a railroad car. The Choo Choo is located inside the city's old Terminal Station, which is now a hotel. The terminal was built in 1909 to accommodate the increasing number of passengers who arrived in the city aboard trains including the Chattanooga Choo Choo, which ran from Cincinnati, Ohio, to Chattanooga starting in 1880. The train was made famous in a song by Harry Warren and Mack Gordon, performed in the late 1940s by the Glenn Miller Orchestra. The tune starts with the lines: "Pardon me, boy, is that the Chattanooga Choo Choo?" It is impossible to stand here and not have that refrain pass through your head.

The main sight here is an old wood-burning engine, which is similar to what would have powered the famous Choo Choo. The engine you see actually came from the Smoky Mountain Railroad, which ran between Knoxville and the Smokies in the 1940s.

There are shops, restaurants, and a small garden around the old railroad engine. Children will enjoy the **Model Railroad Museum** (1400 Market St., 423/266-5000, 3pm-7pm Mon.-Thurs., 10am-7pm Fri.-Sun., adults $4, children 3-17 $2), a miniature world with 3,000 feet of model railroad track, 120 locomotives, and 80 passenger cars.

Better than the Choo Choo, however, is Chattanooga's real, working railroad. The **Tennessee Valley Railroad** (4119 Cromwell Rd., 423/894-8028, www.tvrail.com, adults $17, children $11) offers railroad excursions departing from Grand Junction Station on the other side of Chickamauga Creek and Missionary Ridge. The hour-long ride covers six miles, travels through the Missionary Ridge railroad tunnel, and includes a stop at the East Chattanooga repair shop and turntable. The Missionary Ridge Local, as the excursion is named, leaves several times per day, depending on the time of year.

The railroad also offers occasional trips to other destinations in Tennessee and north Georgia.

★ Lookout Mountain

Lookout Mountain is part of the Cumberland Plateau. It extends 83 miles through Tennessee, Alabama, and Georgia, but the northernmost tip, which overlooks Chattanooga, is its most famous part. No journey to the city is complete without taking a drive up the mountain to enjoy exceptional views and some of the most iconic of Tennessee attractions.

Point Park (1110 E. Brow Rd., adults $5, children 15 and under free) offers the best views off Lookout Mountain. This park is maintained by the National Park Service as part of the Chickamauga and Chattanooga National Military Park, and there is a **visitors center** (423/821-7786, 8:30am-5pm daily) at the gates of the park. The best thing about the park, however, are the views of the Cumberland Plateau, Chattanooga, and the Cherokee National Forest in the eastward distance. The Tennessee River winds languidly through the landscape. On a clear day, it is stunning.

Students of the Civil War should visit the **Battles for Chattanooga Electric Map and Museum** (1110 E. Brow Rd., 423/821-2812, www.battlesforchattanooga.com, 10am-5pm daily, 9am-6pm daily summer, adults $8, children 3-12 $6), a private museum that chronicles several Civil War battles, including the Battle Above the Clouds on Lookout Mountain, that took place in the area. An electric map, which shows 5,000 miniature soldiers and hundreds of lights, is a showpiece of the museum. Don't miss the gift shop if you are a collector of things relating to Civil War history. The museum is located next door to Point Park.

Chattanooga's most famous attraction may well be **Rock City** (1400 Patten Rd., 800/854-0675, www.seerockcity.com, Opens at 8:30am year round, but closes at different times depending on the season; check

Lookout Mountain

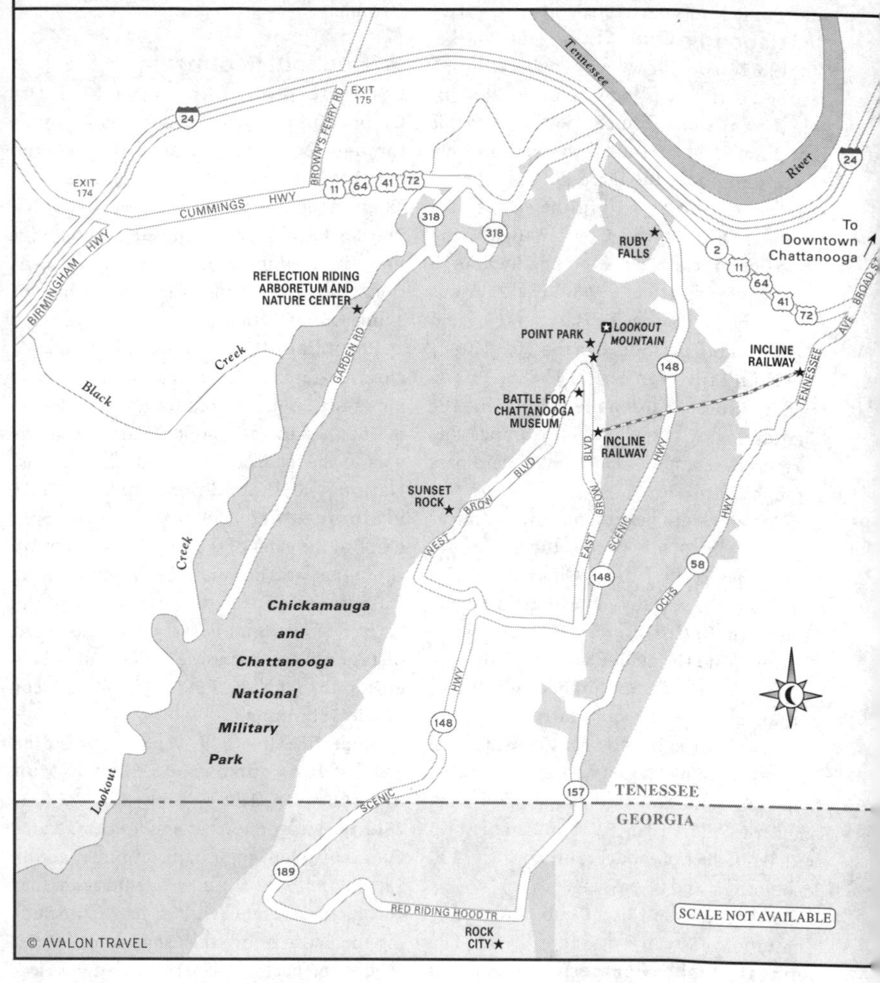

website for current calendar, adults $19.95, children 3-12 $11.95, package discounts available if you buy the tickets in combination with Lookout Mountain attractions). A remarkable yet hokey rock garden with exceptional views, including one that encompasses seven states, Rock City was one of the first tourist attractions in the area, opening in 1932. The See Rock City billboards painted on barns throughout the South were legendary and iconic; today the gift shop at Rock City overflows with related mementos, including birdhouses with the message painted on them.

Visitors to Rock City travel a 4,100-foot "Enchanted Trail" that winds through ancient rock formations, including a 90-foot waterfall, narrow walkways, and a 1,000-ton balancing rock. Lover's Leap is the viewpoint from which you can see, on a clear day, Georgia, Alabama, North Carolina, South Carolina, Virginia, Kentucky, and, of course, Tennessee. Fairyland Caverns and Mother Goose Village are underground collections of quirky folk art (illuminated by black light). The 180-foot swinging bridge over the open air is memorable, as are the gardens of perennials and native plants. Unlike most botanic gardens, Rock City welcomes dogs. More than half a million people check out Rock City every year, but the parking lots and trails are well designed to handle crowds.

Ruby Falls (1720 S. Scenic Hwy., 423/821-2544, www.rubyfalls.com, 8am-8pm daily, adults $18.95, children 3-12 $10.95, although there are package discounts if you buy the tickets in combination with other Lookout Mountain attractions) is an underground waterfall located deep within Lookout Mountain (in fact, it claims to be the tallest underground waterfall in the country). The traditional entrance to Lookout Mountain Cave was closed in 1905, when the Southern Railway Company sealed it during the construction of a railroad along the side of the mountain. Chemist and entrepreneur Leo Lambert had explored the cave before and believed it would be a lucrative tourist attraction. So in 1928, he started to bore an elevator shaft down into the mountain to the cave. Lambert's unusual plan worked, and by 1930, visitors were touring the cave and the 145-foot waterfall, which Lambert named not for a color, but for his wife, Ruby.

The entrance to Ruby Falls is in a massive limestone building modeled after an Irish castle. It was built out of stone brought up while Lambert was drilling the elevator shaft through the mountain; the top floor was added in 1976.

The tour of Ruby Falls takes about 1.5 hours in total and involves walking a bit less than a mile on paved underground paths. Your tour guide will tell the standard kitschy jokes, and the lighting on many of the rock formations feels forced. But when you get to the spot where Ruby Falls' waters thunder 145 feet to the pool beneath, it is hard not to be impressed. The tour guide will turn off the lights and then turn on the ruby-tinted bulbs, and you'll get the chance to hear and see the falls close up, if you choose.

Much of the power that now illuminates the Ruby Falls complex is generated by green energy options.

The steepest passenger train in the world is the **Incline Railway** (3917 St. Elmo Ave. and 827 E. Brow Rd., 423/821-4224, www.ridetheincline.com, 9am-6pm Mon.-Fri., 9am-7pm Sat.-Sun., adults $15, children 3-12 $7, although there are package discounts if you

the Incline Railway at Lookout Mountain

buy the tickets in combination with other Lookout Mountain attractions), which climbs from Chattanooga to the top of **Lookout Mountain**. The railway was built in 1895 and has been ferrying visitors up the mountain ever since.

It takes about 10 minutes to make the journey from the bottom of the mountain to the top, where there are gift shops and restaurants. **Point Park** is a short walk away, but other Lookout Mountain attractions require a car. Parking is $2 at the bottom of the mountain, with parking meters at the top.

On the western edge of Lookout Mountain, in the midst of the upscale residential neighborhood, is **Sunset Rock.** A natural landmark admired for generations, this sheer bluff looks westward, and the view at sunset is indeed spectacular. It draws rock climbers who rappel down the sheer face of the bluff. The short hike (0.2 mile) down to the rock is steep and rough; wear comfortable shoes and take your time. There is no wall or fence blocking the sheer drop down the face of the rock (which makes for much better pictures).

Nestled on Lookout Mountain are 317 acres of the **Reflection Riding Arboretum and Nature Center** (400 Garden Rd., 423/821-1160, reflectionriding.org, 9am-5pm Mon.-Sat., 1pm-5pm Sun. summer only, adults $10, seniors and children 4-11 $7). This is a park, nature preserve, and environmental education facility. Visitors have the opportunity to see 30 different native animal species, including red wolves, bald eagles, bobcats, and raccoons, in the Wildlife Wanderland. There is also a 1,400-foot boardwalk that meanders through a seasonal wetland and lowland forest, and takes you to the George S. Bryan Tree House. Gardens include a fragrance garden and organic community garden, and there is a bird and butterfly café. Come on a pleasant day and plan on spending several hours exploring the nature center. As is the case at many nature centers, dogs are not permitted.

Signal Mountain

Signal Mountain perches on the top of Walden's Ridge about 15 minutes' drive north of Chattanooga. Named because it is believed the Cherokee used it for signal fires, Signal Mountain later evolved into an upscale residential community. The Signal Mountain Inn once was a popular tourist destination; today it is a retirement home.

Visitors should make the challenging uphill

Point Park is part of the Chickamauga and Chattanooga National Military Park.

drive to visit **Signal Point** (Signal Point Rd., 423/821-7786), a park that offers a dramatic view of the Tennessee River below. The site, managed by the National Park Service, is part of the **Chickamauga and Chattanooga National Military Park** (www.nps.gov, 6am-sunset daily) and was an important vantage point during the Civil War. It is the southern terminus of the 300-plus-mile Cumberland Trail.

To get to Signal Mountain from Chattanooga, take Highway 127 north about 8 miles to Mountain Creek Road. The scenic road winds through the mountainside.

ENTERTAINMENT AND EVENTS

The Arts

Chattanooga has made significant investment in its arts offerings during the last decade, and it shows. Programs like CreateHere helped develop loans for individual artists to encourage them to buy property in the Main Street/Southside District). The programs had the intended effect: More artists of all stripes both came to and stayed in the city.

ArtsBuild (406 Frazier Ave., 423/756-2787, www.artsbuild.com, 8:30am-5pm Mon.-Fri.) is an umbrella organization that promotes the arts. Contact it for an arts guide to the city or for information about upcoming events.

Chattanooga's **Southern Lit Alliance** (3069 Broad St., 423/267-1218, southernlitalliance.org) organizes a variety of programs, including film festivals and literary conferences.

VENUES

The jewel of Chattanooga's arts venues is the **Tivoli Theater** (709 Broad St., 423/757-5050, chattanoogaonstage.com), a beaux arts-style performance hall that has been restored and equipped with modern amenities. Built in 1921, the Tivoli played films and live dramas to sold-out Chattanooga audiences through the 1950s. But with the advent of television, shopping malls, and the automobile, the downtown theater declined and narrowly escaped demolition in 1961.

After years of consideration and fundraising, the Tivoli was totally restored in the late 1980s and reopened to adoring crowds in 1989. Its domed ceiling, crystal chandeliers, and ornate finishes make this a lovely venue. There's typically free parking for ticket holders at the BlueCross/BlueShield of Tennessee garage.

Chattanooga's Soldiers and Sailors **Memorial Auditorium** (399 McCallie Ave., 423/642-8497, chattanoogaonstage.com) is another popular venue for concerts, performances, and special events. Built in 1924 as a memorial to the soldiers and sailors of World War I, it was then the largest space in Chattanooga for concerts and other events. It housed boxing matches, roller derbies, tennis matches, banquets, and religious revivals. It is now the home of the **Robert Kirk Walker Community Theatre** and hosts large concerts.

VISUAL ARTS

Once a forgotten part of the city, the **Southside** neighborhood, which largely is made up of Main Street, is a collection of former industrial buildings that have been repurposed as artist studios, galleries, boutiques, and more. On the last Friday of every month, 5pm-8pm is the art stroll here, when galleries are open late and artists are on hand to talk about their new works, but any day is a good day to walk by and gaze at the creativity on display in these windows.

The work of local and regional artists is featured at the **Association for Visual Artists Gallery** (30 Frazier Ave., 423/265-4282, www.avarts.org, 11am-5pm Tues.-Sat.), located on Chattanooga's North Shore.

The **River Gallery** (400 E. 2nd St., 423/265-5033, www.river-gallery.com, 10am-5pm Mon.-Sat., 1pm-5pm Sun.) is located in a turn-of-the-20th-century home in the Bluff View Arts District. It exhibits fine arts and crafts from local, regional, and international artists.

MUSIC AND DANCE

The **Chattanooga Symphony & Opera** (701 Broad St., 423/267-8583, www.chattanoogasymphony.org) performs classical, opera, pops, and family concerts every year at the Tivoli Theater.

Ballet Tennessee (3202 Kelly's Ferry Rd., 423/821-2055, www.ballettennessee.org) is Chattanooga's foremost ballet company and school. It performs at the Tivoli Theater and Memorial Auditorium.

Track29 (1400 Market St., 423/521-2929, track29.co), named for its location at the historic Chattanooga Choo Choo, is the city's hippest concert venue. Shows are booked by the same folks who pull together Bonnaroo, so they get access to a diverse cross section of acts.

THEATER

The **Chattanooga Theatre Centre** (400 River Rd., 423/267-8534, www.theatrecentre.com) is a community theater that produces musicals, comedies, and dramas.

FESTIVALS AND EVENTS

Spring

Billed as a writer's conference for readers, the **Celebration of Southern Literature** (southernlitalliance.org) brings heavyweights in Southern literature to Chattanooga for three days of lectures, discussions, and readings in April. On off years, the Arts and Education Council hosts the **Chattanooga Festival of Writers,** a celebration of the craft of writing.

In April, the **4 Bridges Arts Festival** (www.4bridgesartsfestival.org) brings 150 artists (chosen from more than 700 applicants) to the First Tennessee Pavilion downtown for two days of exhibits, children's activities, and acoustic music. It is a good opportunity to purchase original artwork in a wide variety of formats or just people-watch. There is typically a modest admission fee.

In May, the Chattanooga Bicycle Club and Outdoor Chattanooga host **3 States, 3 Mountains** (www.chattbike.com), a 100-mile bicycle race that originates and ends at Finley Stadium in downtown Chattanooga. There are also options for 88-, 62- and 25-mile courses.

Summer

One of Chattanooga's largest annual events is the **Riverbend Festival** (www.riverbendfestival.com). Taking place in mid-June, the festival runs for eight days and stretches for one mile along the city's waterfront and features multiple stages with jazz, blues, rock, pop, country, folk, and classical performers. The festival also includes the Bessie Smith Strut, a street festival along Martin Luther King Boulevard. You'll get a discount on the entrance fee if you buy tickets online in advance.

On Fridays May-August, **Rhythm and Noon** provides free midday concerts at Miller Plaza downtown. Performers play classical, folk, rock, jazz, swing, choral music, and blues. The concerts are a warm-up for **Nightfall** (nightfallchattanooga.com), free Friday-evening concerts held at Miller Plaza May 1-Labor Day in September. Each concert starts out with a local act and concludes with a headliner. The schedule includes a wide range of genres, from world music to bluegrass.

Fall

On the Friday night of Labor Day weekend, kick off your shoes at **SwingFest** (www.downtownchattanooga.org), an open-air concert featuring local and regional big-band performers.

Bluegrass music comes to the waterfront with the **Three Sisters Festival** (www.3sistersbluegrass.com), a two-day festival held in early October at Ross's Landing. Three Sisters is held in conjunction with **RiverRocks Chattanooga** (www.riverrockschattanooga.com), a month-long celebration of all things outdoor. There are more than 90 events at RiverRocks, including stand-up paddling races, hot-air balloon rides, cycling, biking, and running events, plus live music, kids' activities, and funky demonstrations.

Winter

Each November brings the **Head of the Hooch Regatta** (www.headofthehooch.org), the second-largest regatta in the country, to Chattanooga.

SHOPPING

Local Market

The Chattanooga Market (summer: Sun. and Wed. First Tennessee Pavilion, Sat. Aquarium Plaza, chattanoogamarket.com) is more than just a producer-only farmers market; it welcomes local artists of all types. These are folks who make and grow their goods. An expansion of this public market, which is considered one of the best in the country, is in the works.

Malls

Hamilton Place (2100 Hamilton Place Blvd., 423/894-7177, www.hamiltonplace.com) is Chattanooga's foremost place for shopping. Located at exit 4A off I-75 northeast of downtown, Hamilton Place has more than 150 stores, including JCPenney, Sears, Dillard's, and Belk.

Books

Chattanooga's best downtown bookstore is **Winder Binder** (40 Frazier Ave., 423/413-8999, www.winderbinder.com), which is also an art gallery and hipster hangout. While you're in the area, don't miss **Mayfield's All Killer No Filler** (199 River St., 423/486-1379, www.mayfieldsallkiller.com) music and vintage store next door. Hours are generally on a whim, so call ahead or wander by.

RECREATION

Parks

In many ways, Chattanooga, with countless ways to get out and enjoy nature, is like one big park. It seems like there are as many boat access spots along the banks of the river as there are parking lots.

Two of the best city parks are located on the banks of the Tennessee River. **Ross's Landing Park and Plaza,** adjacent to the Tennessee Aquarium at the end of Broad Street, is a sculpted park that uses concrete, glass, stone, and grass to depict the timeline of Chattanooga's history. It is a nice place to stroll, people-watch, or enjoy a picnic.

On the other side of the river, **Coolidge Park** is even nicer. This grassy park has paths for walking, benches for sitting, and a glass-enclosed carousel to entertain children and adults. A ride on the old-style merry-go-round

Musicians play at the eight-day-long Riverbend Festival.

is just $1. Come here for lovely views of Chattanooga's downtown.

Outside of town, **Booker T. Washington State Park** (5801 Champion Rd., 423/894-4955) is a day-use park located off Highway 58, on the northeast side of town, whose primary attraction is Lake Chickamauga. There are several boat-launching ramps. Waterskiing, fishing, stand-up paddling, kayaking, and pleasure cruising are popular activities. There are also picnic facilities and an Olympic-size swimming pool.

Farther outside of town, **Harrison Bay State Park** (8411 Harrison Bay Rd., Harrison, 423/344-6214) is also located on Lake Chickamauga. It is named for the part of the lake, Harrison Bay, that covers what was once the last Cherokee settlement in this area. The land was inundated in 1940 with the construction and closure of the Chickamauga Dam by the Tennessee Valley Authority.

There are public boat ramps, and all types of boats are allowed. In addition, there are picnic facilities, an Olympic-size pool, and a campground with RV and tent sites. There are also six miles of hiking trails and a bike path.

Biking

Bicycling is a required mode of transport for Chattanoogans. With bike-to-work programs and an innovative 300-bike fleet initiative, Chattanooga is well ahead of the curve when it comes to promoting alternative ways of getting around town.

There are bike lanes on many downtown streets, as well as bike-friendly trails along the Chattanooga waterfront, at the Chickamauga Dam, and at the TVA's Raccoon Mountain Reservoir, making the area accessible on two wheels for both visitors and locals.

Bike Chattanooga (www.activelivingtn.org) provides safety courses for bikers, promotes bike riding, and publishes information about recreational bike riding in the area, as well as details on the public bike-sharing program. The **Chattanooga Bicycle Club** (www.chattbike.com) is another good option for local biking info.

For rentals and other bike-gear needs, try **Trek Bicycle Store of Chattanooga** (307 Manufacturers Rd., 423/648-2100, http://trekstorechattanooga.com), **River City Bicycles** (5864 Brainerd Rd., 423/265-7176, http://rivercitybikes.net), or **Suck Creek Cycle** (321 Cherokee Blvd., 423/266-8883, http://suckcreek.com).

River Cruises

When visiting a city built on the river, you might as well take advantage and get *on* the river. **Blue Moon Cruises** (888/993-2583, $40) offers seasonal cruises down the Tennessee River aboard a 70-foot SkipperLiner cruise boat. Blue Moon's cruise down the Tennessee River Gorge lasts about 3.5 hours and departs morning and afternoon from the Chattanooga Pier, off Ross's Landing waterfront park. The naturalist-led eco cruise emphasizes the animals and plants you see on the riverbanks, as well as the cultural and historical significance of the river over the years. There are also seasonal fall color cruises and other specialty tours.

Spectator Sports

The **Chattanooga Lookouts** (201 Power Alley, 423/267-2208, box office 423/267-4849, www.lookouts.com, general admission adults $5, children $3, box seats $6-9), a farm team for the Cincinnati Reds, play at AT&T Field downtown. The baseball season runs April-September.

Amusement Parks

Just over the state line in Georgia is **Lake Winnepesaukah** (1730 Lakeview Dr., Rossville GA, 706/866-5681, www.lakewinnie.com, 10am-8pm Wed.-Thurs., 10am-10pm Fri.-Sat., noon-8pm Sun. May.-Sept., unlimited rides pass adults $27, seniors and children $12), a family-oriented amusement park operating since 1925. The Cannon Ball is a wooden roller coaster, and the Boat Chute is the oldest mill chute ride in the United States. There are also modern rides, including the Oh-Zone and Wild Lightning. In addition to rides, Lake

Winnepesaukah has a midway and food vendors. Along with the unlimited pass, individual ride tickets can be purchased.

To find Lake Winnepesaukah, drive south on I-75 to the Route 41 exit. Drive on Ringold Road for two miles to McBrien Road. Turn left, and the park is two miles ahead on Lakeview Drive.

Hang Gliding

The mountains around Chattanooga are ideal for hang gliding. The **Lookout Mountain Flight Park** (7201 Scenic Hwy., Rising Fawn GA, 706/398-3541, www.hanglide.com, 9am-6pm Sun., Mon, Thurs.-Sat.) offers tandem glides with a certified instructor and lessons appropriate for all levels. The flight school is the largest hang gliding school in America. A single tandem flight, which lasts about 15 minutes, is $199. A daylong package that includes a tandem flight plus five "bunny hill" low-altitude flights is $249.

Paddling

Whether it is in a kayak, a canoe, or on a stand-up paddleboard, Chattanoogans love to get on the local waters, both flat water and whitewater. Rent boards from Chattanooga Paddleboards (111 Frazier Ave., 423/702-1442, www.chattanoogapaddleboards.com, $20/hour) or **L2 Outside** (First and Market Sts., 423/531-7873, www.l2outside.com, $30/hour). For canoes, try **Chattanooga Nature Center** (400 Garden Rd., 423/821-1160, reflectionriding.org, $10 for non-member day pass).

ACCOMMODATIONS

Under $100

Interstate motels offer good value in the Chattanooga area. In this category, the **Econo Lodge Lookout Mountain** (150 Browns Ferry Rd., 423/821-9000, $59-125) is a good choice for its location convenient to downtown and Lookout Mountain, and for its clean rooms and amenities, including in-room microwaves, refrigerators, free wireless, and coffeemakers. Guests also enjoy a free continental breakfast. There's an outdoor pool open in the summer.

$100-150

★ **Bluff View Inn** (Bluff View Art District, 800/725-8338, ext. 2, www.bluffviewartdistrict.com, $105-240) consists of 16 rooms in three different historic properties located in the peaceful Bluff View Art District. Guest rooms in the Maclellan House, Martin House, and Thompson House range from modest-size quarters with a shower-tub combination to luxurious suites with river views, private balconies, and sitting rooms. A full sit-down breakfast is included in room rates and is served at the Back Inn Café.

If you thought it was a new idea to turn an outmoded train station into a hotel, think again. The Chattanooga Station stopped operating as a train station in 1970, and just three years later it reopened as a tourist attraction. Nineteen years later it was retooled again, this time into the hotel that you see today. The **Chattanooga Choo Choo Holiday Inn** (1400 Market St., 800/872-2529, www.choochoo.com, $138-145, discounts for reservations in advance and packages with other attractions available) consists of three buildings of hotel rooms, plus distinctive train-car accommodations. The hotel rooms are clean and generous in size, although not particularly modern or charming; they feature amenities such as wireless Internet, in-room coffeemakers, and king-size beds.

But what makes the Choo Choo special is its railcar accommodations. These old sleeper cars have been converted into hotel-style rooms with four-poster beds, desks, and private bathrooms. Each room has a queen-size bed, and some feature pull-out trundle beds ideal for family accommodations, although all are very small (because they used to be sleeper cars). The lobby is the most interesting feature of the hotel.

In addition to hotel rooms, the Choo Choo has three different restaurants, an ice-cream shop, retail shops, and a railway museum. The lobby and upscale restaurant located in the atrium of the old train station lobby are dramatic and beautiful.

The Chattanoogan (1201 S. Broad St., 423/756-3400, www.chattanooganhotel.com, $134-189) is an upscale hotel and conference center located just south of downtown. The hotel offers 199 guest rooms and suites, many of them with views of Lookout Mountain, and all appointed with modern furnishings, fabrics, and amenities. A dramatic see-through glass fireplace in the lobby is a talking point and attraction in its own right. An on-site spa, conference center, and three restaurants round out the resort's amenities. The Chattanoogan opened in 2001 and underwent extensive renovation in 2007 to keep the decor current and comfortable.

$150-200

Mayor's Mansion Inn (801 Vine St., 423/265-5000, www.mayorsmansioninn.com, $139-279) is a luxury bed-and-breakfast located in an 1889 Victorian mansion built for the mayor of Chattanooga. Mayor's Mansion has 11 guest rooms and is located in the Fort Wood District near the University of Tennessee, less than one mile from downtown Chattanooga. Each guest room is unique, with distinctive fabrics, wallpaper, and antique furniture. Guests may feel like they are bedding down in a home that could just as easily be open for tours. Common areas include a stone terrace, verandahs, and a library. Elegant indulgences include nightly turndown service, a three-course breakfast, and soft cotton robes. Guests may also take advantage of concierge service, Internet access, and other amenities like ironing boards and a video library.

The **StoneFort Inn** (120 E. 10th St., 423/267-7866, www.stonefortinn.com, $163-192) is an old-fashioned city hotel with a modern, chic feel. Located about 10 blocks from the aquarium and close to federal and state office buildings, the StoneFort Inn has 20 guest rooms of varying sizes. All rooms have high-speed Internet connections, oversized whirlpool tubs, luxury bath soaps, claw-foot soaking tubs, TV/DVD players, and cheerful decor. Polished terrazzo floors, marble fireplaces, well-stocked bookshelves, an 1885 grand piano, and a 1920s slate pool table all conjure an atmosphere of cozy elegance in this circa-1909 hotel building. On weekdays there is a continental breakfast and on weekends a gourmet sit-down morning meal. The dining area becomes a public café and restaurant on Wednesday and Thursday evenings, with

the lobby of the Chattanooga Choo Choo Holiday Inn

inviting selections from the bar, live acoustic music, and a menu of inventive small plates. Children under 12 are not permitted at the Stone Fort Inn, unless you rent the whole hotel for a special event.

Another longtime favorite downtown hotel is **The Read House Hotel Historic Inn** (827 Broad St., 423/266-4121, $109-209, except for the presidential suite, which is more than $500, www.thereadhousehotel.com). Located in a historic redbrick Georgian-style building near the theater district, and about 10 blocks from the aquarium, the Sheraton offers its guests luxury and comfort. Its 219 guest rooms and suites include high-speed Internet, Drexel Heritage furniture, and luxurious beds. There is an indoor zero-edge pool with a waterfall, top notch workout room, on-site steak house, and Starbucks coffee shop. It is a short walk to the riverfront attractions.

Camping

Harrison Bay State Park (8411 Harrison Bay Rd., Harrison, 423/344-6214, tnstateparks.itinio.com), located about a 20-minute drive from downtown, has 134 RV sites and 28 tent-only sites in its lakefront campground. Rates are $11-27.50. Use the Tennessee State Park reservation system to book ahead; the sites sell out well in advance.

FOOD

Downtown

For good food, casual-yet-polished service, and a convivial atmosphere, go where many Chattanoogans go for a meal out. **212 Market** (212 Market St., 423/265-1212, www.212market.com, 11am-3pm daily, 5pm-9:30pm Mon.-Thurs., 5pm-10pm Fri.-Sat., 5pm-9pm Sun., lunch $7-14, dinner $15-30) serves upscale daily lunch and dinner specials like ginger-glazed salmon, wild mushroom ravioli, and Carolina mountain trout. The 212 Pecan Chicken Club is a delectable lunchtime favorite. This was one of the first downtown restaurants to open following the area's rebirth in the early 1990s, and it is still a first choice for dining in the city.

When you give an old-fashioned diner a makeover, the result is **The Blue Plate** (191 Chestnut St., Unit B, 423/648-6767, www.theblueplate.info, 7:30am-9pm Tues.-Fri., 8am-9pm Sat. - Sun., $6-18), a downtown eatery with sleek lines, fresh food, and a home-style heart. You can order breakfast, such as eggs and pancakes, all day, or choose a plump, juicy burger. The chef salad is piled high with pulled chicken, diced eggs, and mixed cheeses, and the entrées include fried-to-order chicken and not your mother's baked meat loaf. Don't skip the green beans. Or the MoonPie cheesecake. To prove that this is not your everyday lunch counter, you can also order from a full bar, although the spot is perfectly kid friendly.

Chattanooga's history is tied to Coca-Cola bottling, so dining in a former Coke bottling plant is about as Scenic City as you can get. **Easy Bistro & Bar** (203 Broad St. 423/266-1121, easybistro.com, 5pm-10pm Mon.-Fri., 11am-10pm Sat., 11am-9pm Sun. $20-34) uses the décor to show off its cocktail menu and French-meets-Southern menu.

You might be surprised how good England tastes in Chattanooga. The **English Rose Tearoom** (1401 Market St., 423/265-5900, www.englishrosetearoom.net, 11am-5pm Tues.-Sat., $5-20) serves authentic British Isles fare, including finger sandwiches, ploughman's lunch, and cottage pie. Come into this welcoming spot for an afternoon tea with scones and sandwiches, or for a meal of steak pies, Dover sole, flounder, or Cornish pasties. The atmosphere is on the refined side, but it's not uptight. The English Rose offers a nice change of pace.

Upscale Southern comfort food is the draw at **Mt. Vernon Restaurant** (3535 Broad St., 423/266-6591, www.mymtvernon.com, 11am-9pm Mon.-Thurs., 11am-9:30pm Fri., 4pm-9:30pm Sat., $9-16). Located near the base of Lookout Mountain, Mt. Vernon is a favorite among Chattanoogans, who come for its familiar food, generous portions, and hometown feel. Specialties include Southern fried chicken ($13) and Maryland crab cakes ($17). The fried green tomatoes appetizer is always a favorite. At lunchtime you can also order from the under-$10 sandwich menu, with choices like BLT, grouper sandwich, and the Mt. Vernon Club.

Chattanooga's best meat-and-three diner is **Zarzour's Café** (1627 Rossville Ave., 423/266-0424, 11am-3:30pm Mon.-Fri., $5-8), a hole-in-the-wall tucked away in the wrong part of town. Zarzour's was founded by Lebanese immigrant Charles Zarzour in 1913, and the eatery has persisted through good times and bad for the past nine-plus decades under the family's ownership. But it is not Middle Eastern specialties that bring in the regulars; it is some of the best home-cooked Southern food in the city. Flavorful turnip greens, creamy potatoes, comforting baked spaghetti, and hot-from-the-skillet corn bread are among the dishes on the menu. Each day you can choose from one of three main-dish entrées, accompanied by your choice of two side dishes. Or order a hand-patted burger from the grill. This is a cash-only joint. Daily specials are posted on Facebook.

Bluff View

As ubiquitous as the coffee-sandwich-dessert bar is these days, it is still refreshing when someone does it well. **Rembrandt's Coffee House** (204 High St., 423/265-5003, 7am-10pm Mon.-Thurs., 7am-11:30pm Fri., 8am-11:30pm Sat., 8am-10pm Sun., $5-7) is one such place. Located catty-corner from the Hunter Museum of American Art, Rembrandt's serves excellent hot and cold sandwiches on superb locally baked bread. The menu also offers salads, including a delicious spinach salad with bacon, hard-boiled eggs, and walnuts. The ingredients are fresh and flavorful. For breakfast choose from French toast panini filled with fruit compote and mascarpone cheese, hot breakfast sandwiches, or lighter options such as bagels, yogurt and fruit, or banana bread. The coffee here is excellent, and you can finish off your meal with a wide array of sweets. Rembrandt's is not without a sense of humor. Step outside, and you will see a plate-glass window with a sign reading Working Artist. He or she will be making hand-dipped chocolate treats you can buy inside. There's a second location inside Memorial Hospital.

The setting at ★ **Back Inn Café** (412 E. 2nd St., 423/265-5033, 5pm-9pm Tues.-Thurs., 5pm-10pm Fri.-Sat., $17-28) is romantic and relaxing. Located in a stately old home, the Back Inn offers diners the choice of dining in the library, sunroom, or on the terrace overlooking the river. Polished wood floors, elegant old-world finishes, and a lovely view make you feel distinctly at home in this restaurant. The menu features global cuisine with a good wine list.

At dinner, choose from entrées such as Thai curry chicken, seafood gratin, and the house specialty Martin House steak tenderloin, with a few gluten-free entrée options. Reservations are recommended.

Southside

Main Street, near the famous Choo Choo, has become one of the city's favorite dining districts. The sleek, modern **Alleia** (25 E. Main St., 423/305-6990, http://alleiarestaurant.com, 5pm-10pm Mon.-Thurs., 5pm-11pm Fri.-Sat., $12-27) is cozy enough for date night, but not so romantic that it doesn't work for a business dinner. The wine list is impressive.

For morning meals, join the locals at ★ **Bluegrass Grill** (55 E. Main St., 423/752-4020, http://bluegrassgrillchattanooga.com, 6:30am-2pm Tues.-Fri., 6:30am-1pm Sat., $2-9). Breakfast is served whenever this homey joint is open; don't miss the homemade breads and potatoes. Look for the sign with the banjo on it.

The owners of boutique hostel The Crash Pad also own funky bar and restaurant **The Flying Squirrel** (55 Johnson St. 423/602-5980, flyingsquirrelbar.com, 5pm-2am Tues.-Thurs., 5pm-3am Fri.-Sat., 10:30am–3pm Sun., $13-23) next door. Expect outdoor seating, eclectic snacks and entrees, and a drink menu packed with craft cocktails and local brews. Travelers with kids please note: The Flying Squirrel is for those 21-plus except for Sunday brunch.

North Shore

In recent years, the streets across the river from downtown Chattanooga have become popular locations for restaurants.

Terra Nostra Restaurant and Wine Bar (105 Frazier Ave., 423/634-0238, www.terranostratapas.com, 4:30pm-10pm Tues.-Thurs., 4:30pm-11pm Fri.-Sat., 4:30pm-9pm Sun., $7-18) is a tapas restaurant with vegetarian, seafood, and meat plates. Come for an afternoon glass of wine to be enjoyed with a plate of cheese and bread. Or come for a more filling dinner; try the handcrafted spinach ravioli, fresh seafood plates, or osso buco. The restaurant's bold colors and metal sculptures give it a rustic-hip feel. In the tapas tradition, each plate is a small portion, about appetizer size, and you should order several as part of your multicourse meal. In addition to tapas, Terra Nostra has 80 different wines available by the glass and 90 available by the bottle.

Locals love **Embargo 62** (301 Cherokee Blvd., 423/551-4786, embargo62bar.com, 11am-midnight Sun.-Thurs., 11am-1:30am Fri.-Sat., $8.50-13.50). Don't let the exterior fool you. This is not just a bodega, but a hip Cuban-inspired cantina serving traditional eats such as pressed Cuban sandwiches and ropa vieja. The drink menu features plenty of rum-spiked concoctions to match.

For sushi, many Chattanoogans head to **Sushi Nabe** (110 River St., 423/634-0171, www.sushinabechattanooga.com, 11:30am-2:30pm and 5pm-9:30pm Tues.-Fri., noon-10pm Sat., noon-9pm Sun., sushi $4-7 per roll, combination plates $15-18). Located adjacent to Coolidge Park, this chic eatery offers seating at the sushi bar or at tables. In addition to sushi, you can order stir-fries and other Japanese specialties. There are also convenient dinner combination plates.

INFORMATION AND SERVICES

Visitor Information

The **Chattanooga Area Convention and Visitors Bureau** (215 Broad St., 423/756-8687 or 800/322-3344, www.chattanoogafun.com, 10am-5pm daily,) provides information online, over the telephone, and in person at its visitors center, located right next door to the Tennessee Aquarium.

Media

The ***Chattanooga Times Free Press*** (www.timesfreepress.com) is the city's daily newspaper. *The Pulse* (www.chattanoogapulse.com) is a free alternative weekly paper with a focus on arts, entertainment, and culture.

Libraries

The **Chattanooga-Hamilton County Bicentennial Library** (1001 Broad St., 423/757-5310, chattlibrary.org, 9am-8pm Mon.-Thurs., 9am-6pm Fri.-Sat.) is the city's main downtown library. The entire library is a wireless Internet hot spot, and there is also free Internet access on library terminals.

Laundry

Gordon's Cleaners (315 N. Market St. 423/266-3252 and 3546 Broad St., 423/265-5875, gordonscleaners.com) has dry cleaning and laundry service downtown.

GETTING THERE

Chattanooga is located along three major interstate highways. I-75 travels north-south from Knoxville in the north to Atlanta in the south. I-24 runs from Nashville to Chattanooga, and I-59 runs from Birmingham to Chattanooga.

Chattanooga is about 115 miles from Knoxville, 130 miles from Nashville, 120 miles from Atlanta, and 150 miles from Birmingham.

The **Chattanooga Metropolitan Airport** (CHA, 423/855-2200, www.chattairport.com) is served by a half-dozen airlines providing nonstop service to nine different U.S. cities, although many people fly to either Atlanta or Nashville and take shuttles to Chattanooga.

The Chattanooga airport is located about 14 miles east of the city center. To get downtown from the airport, take Highway 153 south to I-75 and follow the signs to downtown Chattanooga.

GETTING AROUND

Chattanooga is an exceedingly pedestrian-friendly city. There is plenty of downtown parking, and it is easy to get around on foot or by the free public trolleys. You can walk from downtown to Bluff View and even to the North Shore via the Walnut Street pedestrian bridge.

You'll need a car to get to Lookout Mountain attractions.

Public Transportation

Chattanooga's public transit service operates an electric (zero-emissions) shuttle bus service around downtown. The **CARTA Electric Shuttle** (www.carta-bus.org, runs every five minutes 6:30am-11pm Mon.-Fri., 9:30am-11pm Sat., 9:30am-8:30pm Sun., free) runs from the Chattanooga Choo Choo building on the south side of town to the Tennessee Aquarium along the waterfront. There are stops about every block; if you need to get to a specific place, just ask your driver. Maps are posted around the city, and free guides are available at the north parking lot.

The route is convenient to all downtown hotels. There are large parking garages at both ends of the shuttle route. It costs $3 to park by the Choo Choo and $7 to park by the aquarium. Since there is no such thing as free parking anywhere around downtown Chattanooga, parking and riding the shuttle is a very good idea.

Parking

All parking around downtown Chattanooga is paid. If you find a metered space along the road, grab it, because these are the cheapest, at least for short-term parking. There are large lots located across from the Tennessee Aquarium. All-day parking will run you about $7, and evening parking will cost $5. There is a large public lot next to the Choo Choo, where all-day parking is just $3. Rates are higher during special events.

The Ocoee

The lands east of Chattanooga are speckled by towns that still bear names bestowed by some of their first settlers. Citico, Chota, Hiwassee, and Tellico were named by Overhill Cherokee who made the journey over the mountains and into southeastern Tennessee during the 17th century. Red Clay State Historic Park was the site of the last council meeting of the Cherokee before their forced removal in 1838. Today, these lands are part of the southern portion of the Cherokee National Forest, an expanse of 300,000 acres of federal lands that contain rivers, mountains, and rural farmland.

The southern part of the Cherokee National Forest is defined by the powerful Ocoee River, which attracts thrill-seeking rafters and kayakers. Sightseers enjoy scenic drives up Chilhowee Mountain and along the river, past recreation areas and opportunities for hiking and swimming.

Several towns in the southeastern corner of this region have strong mining histories. Ducktown, Copperhill, and Coker Creek are among the quiet towns that now preserve their unique history with museums and historic tours.

The Hiwassee River cuts through the national forest north of the Ocoee, passing the historic town of Reliance and posing opportunities for laid-back canoe and raft outings.

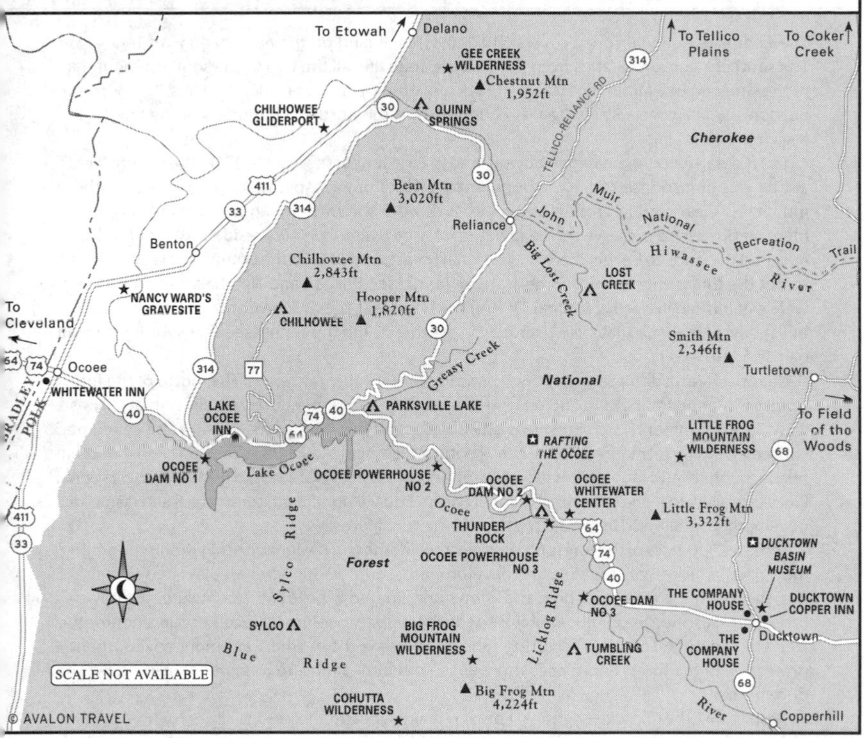

CLEVELAND

Cleveland is one gateway to the Cherokee National Forest. The seat of Bradley County, Cleveland is home to Lee University, a four-year Christian college operated by the Church of God, as well as the Church of God Theological Seminary, a graduate school for Christian ministry. To get to Cleveland from Chattanooga, drive 33 miles east on Highway 74.

Sights

Find your way to Johnston Park downtown to see the ***Cherokee Chieftain,*** a large sculpture carved by Peter "Wolf" Toth. The sculpture was presented to the city of Cleveland in 1974 and represents the close association this region has with the Cherokee people.

The **Museum Center at Five Points** (200 Inman St., 423/339-5745, www.museumcenter.org, 10am-5pm Tues.-Fri., 10am-3pm Sat., adults $5, children $4) is a history museum dedicated to telling the story of the different groups of people who have lived along the Ocoee River. The museum is located at the end of the Old Copper Trail, the road by which copper traveled from the Copper Basin, through the mountains, and to the railroad at Cleveland.

Accommodations

The **Whitewater Lodge** (2500 Pointe South Rd., 423/479-7811, $40 or $139/week plus a $25 deposit) is a bit far from the action of the Ocoee River, but the price can't be beat. Rooms have a kitchenette with coffeemaker,

The Cherokee National Forest

The Cherokee National Forest covers 640,000 acres of land on the eastern edge of Tennessee. The southern portion extends from the Georgia state line all the way to the southern boundary of the Great Smoky Mountains National Park, encompassing some 300,000 acres. The northern portion—which covers 327,000 acres—ranges from the northern boundary of the Smokies to the Virginia state line.

The federal government began buying land in East Tennessee around 1912. The government's action was in response to the environmental effects of widespread logging in the southern mountains. Clear-cutting, erosion, and wildfires ravaged the environment, and the federal government stepped in to preserve the headwaters of area rivers. In 1920, President Woodrow Wilson declared the lands to be the Cherokee National Forest, and in 1936 the boundaries were redrawn to put the forest entirely within the state of Tennessee (Pisgah and Natahala National Forests were established in North Carolina). During the New Deal, the Civilian Conservation Corps (CCC) built many of the trails that still exist today in the forest, and the Tennessee Valley Authority built dams and reservoirs.

National forests differ from national parks in several important ways. The motto of the forest service is "Caring for the land and serving the people," a statement that reveals its dual purpose. So while environmental stewardship is one objective of park managers, they are also concerned with encouraging recreation and the use of natural resources. Activities such as off-road mountain biking, hunting, and logging—which are not permitted in the Great Smoky Mountains National Park—are allowed in the Cherokee National Forest. Equally significant, commercial and residential development is allowed in certain parts of the national forest.

Some 66,000 acres of the forest is classified as wilderness, a designation that prohibits logging, motorized vehicles, construction, and development. Some 20,000 acres are classified as scenic, a designation that prohibits logging and allows only limited vehicle use. Meanwhile, 46,000 acres have been classified as primitive, which opens them up to low-impact recreation in a nonmotorized environment. There is a recurring tension between those who want more environmental protection in the forest and those who want to open the lands up to more intensive uses and development.

Despite this, the Cherokee National Forest remains a beautiful, ecologically rich, and—in some parts—wild area. The forest is home to some 120 bird species, including wild turkey, golden eagle, and peregrine falcon; 47 mammal species, including the black bear, red wolf, wild boar, and coyote; and 30 species of reptile, including rattlesnake, copperhead, and salamander. It is home to many endangered species, including the northern flying squirrel and two varieties of river mussels.

Hiking, camping, horseback riding, swimming, boating, white-water sports, and biking are just a few of the activities that draw people to the Cherokee National Forest. Annual passes are $20 if purchased before May 1 and $30 if purchased on or after May 1. Day-use permits are $3 per vehicle.

The supervisor's office for the entire forest—north and south—is at 2800 North Ocoee Street in Cleveland. Call it at 423/476-9700. The southern forest has two ranger districts and corresponding ranger stations. The **Ocoee/Hiwassee District** (3171 Hwy. 64, 423/338-3300) is located along the Ocoee River near Benton. The **Tellico Ranger Station** (250 Ranger Station Rd., 423/253-8400) is located along the Cherohala Skyway near Tellico Plains.

The northern forest has two ranger stations. The **Nolichucky/Unaka District Ranger Station** (4900 Asheville Hwy./State Rte. 70, 423/638-4109) is located near Greeneville. The **Watauga District Ranger Station** (4400 Unicoi Dr., Unicoi, 423/735-1500) is in Unicoi.

Ranger stations are generally open daily 8:30am-4:30pm, and they are the best places to buy maps and get other information about recreation in the national forest. You can also visit the online store maintained by the Cradle of Forestry (www.cradleofforestry.com).

sink, and stovetop, adding to the bargain. Weekly rates are also available.

COLLEGEDALE

More than 200 ancient artifacts from the Near East are on exhibit at the **Lynn H. Wood Archaeological Museum** (Industrial Dr., Southern Adventist University, 423/236-2030, http://archaeology.southern.edu, 9am-noon and 1pm-5pm Mon.-Thurs., 9am-noon Fri., 2pm-5pm Sat.-Sun., free. Closed during the summer and school breaks). Museum curators strive to depict life in the Biblical world with artifacts from Egypt, Babylonia, Persia, Syria-Palestine, Greece, Cyprus, and Anatolia. Highlights include a complete series of lamps from the Chalcolithic to early Arabic periods and handwritten cuneiform tablets from Ur. **Collegedale** is a 30-minute drive east from Chattanooga, along I-24.

RED CLAY STATE HISTORIC PARK

Red Clay State Historic Park (1140 Red Clay Park Rd., 423/478-0339, daily 8 a.m.-sunset, $3 per vehicle) was the site of the Cherokee capital from 1832 to 1838. In the years leading up to 1832, the State of Georgia outlawed Cherokee councils, so in 1832 the Cherokee moved their capital from New Echota, Georgia, to Red Clay, Tennessee, just over the state line. As many as 5,000 people attended the 11 council meetings held here until 1838, the year of the Cherokee's forced removal via the Trail of Tears. It was here at Red Clay that many Cherokee first learned of the planned removal.

The park consists of a **visitors center** (8am-4:30pm Mon.-Sat., 1pm-4:30pm Sun.), re-created Cherokee settlement and council house, and a permanent exhibit on the Cherokee culture. The most prominent natural landmark is the spring, which rises from beneath a limestone ledge to form a deep pool that flows into Mill Creek, a tributary of the Conasauga and Coosa River system. The spring is about 15 feet deep and produces more than 500,000 gallons of water each day.

The park is an official interpretive center on the National Historic Trail of Tears. Cherokee Days of Recognition is held on the first weekend of August each year. It includes authentic Cherokee crafts, food, storytelling, and music.

Red Clay State Historic Park sits on the border of Tennessee and Georgia. It is just 45 minutes from Chattanooga, east along I-24.

OCOEE

The town of Ocoee is a smattering of businesses and homes located on Highways 64 and 411.

A few miles north of the intersection, along Highway 411, is the **Gravesite of Nancy Ward,** located atop a small hill. There is a parking area and pathway to the summit. Nancy Ward was born in 1738 at the Cherokee town of Chota, and she was named Nanye-hi. Nanye-hi had a queenly appearance and commanding bearing, and she fought alongside her husband and other men in a raid on the Creek during the 1755 Battle of Taliwa. Ward was chosen as *Agi-gau-u-e* (Beloved Woman) of the Cherokee. As such, she sat on the Council of Chiefs, had complete power over prisoners, and led the Women's Council.

In the late 1750s, an English trader named Bryant Ward moved in to the area and married Nancy, as she was called by the white settlers, although he already had a wife and family in South Carolina. They had a daughter, Betsy, who joined Five Killer and Catherine, children of Ward's first marriage, as her offspring.

Ward was influential in her tribe and with the white settlers. She advocated peace between Indians and settlers, and more than once she warned settlers of an impending Indian attack. She spoke at the negotiations held on the Long Island of the Holston and at the Treaty of Hopewell.

With the Hiwassee Purchase of 1819, Ward, along with all Cherokee, was forced to abandon Chota, the capital city of Tennessee Overhill. She moved south and settled near where her gravesite lies today. Ward died in 1822.

The oldest monument at Ward's gravesite was erected in 1923 by the Nancy Ward Chapter of the Daughters of the American Revolution. Newer exhibits by the Tennessee Overhill Association detail her life.

Accommodations

The **Whitewater Inn** (120 Whitewater Dr., 423/338-1201, www.ocoeewhitewaterinn.com, $70-90) is a standard-issue motel that still has a good deal of polish left. Designed to feel a bit like a mountain lodge, this inn offers comfortable rooms with two queen-size beds, satellite TV, and telephones. There is free continental breakfast, wireless Internet, and fax and copy service. Rates are higher in season. One apartment with a full kitchen ($155) is also available.

ALONG THE OCOEE

Just past Ocoee on Highway 64, you enter the Cherokee National Forest. The next 26 miles are a winding two-lane blacktop road that follows the Ocoee River.

Chilhowee Mountain

For breathtaking views of Parksville Lake, the Ocoee River, and the Great Eastern Valley of Tennessee, take a seven-mile detour up Forest Service Road 77 to the summit of **Chilhowee Mountain**. There are no fewer than five overlooks on the drive, which terminates at the Cumberland Recreation Area, a day-use facility and campground. There is also a historical marker that recalls the Confederate soldiers who camped in these hills and waged guerilla war on Unionists during the Civil War.

Once at the Cumberland Recreation Area, you can hike 1.5 miles to **Benton Falls** or take any of the seven other trails in the area. There is also a swimming beach, bathhouses, and picnic tables.

Parksville Lake

This nearly 2,000-acre lake formed by the Ocoee River is operated as a Forest Service recreation area. There is a swimming beach, campground, picnic area, and boat launches. The lake is popular for fishing, waterskiing, and riding personal watercraft.

Ocoee River Dams

The Tennessee Valley Authority operates three powerhouses along the Ocoee River, which together produce some 70,000 kilowatts of electricity. Ocoee 1, the westernmost facility, predates TVA and forms the Parksville Lake (also called the Ocoee Lake). There is a marker and overlook next to the dam, which was built in 1910.

Ocoee 2 was built in 1913 and consists of a diversion dam, wooden flume, and powerhouse. When the powerhouse is on, the river water is diverted into the flume, which carries it five miles downstream to the Ocoee 2 powerhouse, where it is dropped from a height of 250 feet, creating far more power than it would otherwise. The flume, which is visible as you drive along the river, is on the National Register of Historic Places. Ocoee 3, built in 1942, follows a similar pattern. It has a diversion dam, a tunnel, and a powerhouse.

When the river water is being used to generate electricity, the Ocoee River is just a trickle down a dry riverbed. But TVA releases water for recreation on certain days of the year, according to a published schedule. A one-mile section below Ocoee 3 is the Olympic white-water section, and it passes in front of the Ocoee Whitewater Center. A four-mile segment below Ocoee 2 is used by commercial outfitters and water-sports enthusiasts for rafting and kayaking trips.

The Ocoee River was not always recognized as a site for white-water sports. In fact, it was only due to the deterioration of the Ocoee 2 water flume that the river's recreational potential was discovered. It was around 1976 that years of weathering caused TVA to shut down the flume for repairs, causing river water to flow unimpeded down the Ocoee for the first time in decades.

It did not take long for the first daredevils to discover the thrill of the rapids; the first river riders rode Navy surplus rafts. The first

Hiking in the Southern Cherokee

If you plan to do much hiking in the southern Cherokee National Forest, you should invest in good boots, a water bottle, a GPS, and a good trail map. The best is National Geographic's Trails Illustrated No. 781 *Tellico and Ocoee River Cherokee National Forest.*

There are dozens of hiking trails in the southern Cherokee National Forest. The following are some of the best.

The **Old Copper Trail** begins at the Ocoee Whitewater Center and is a 2.3-mile (one-way) hike along an old mining road. The Old Copper Trail is the last remaining portion of a road that was built around 1851 to connect the copper-mining towns of Ducktown and Copperhill with Cleveland. It took miners two days to haul the copper by mule the 33 miles to Cleveland. When Highway 64 was built in the 1930s, it followed the old Copper Road route, and subsequent upgrades widened and improved the current highway.

The present-day hiking trail follows the edge of the river, passing apple trees and stone foundations left by farm families, some of whom were Cherokee, in the early 19th century. You'll also pass a beaver pond and cross four footbridges, including three timber stringer plank bridges and one heavy timber bridge.

Other hikes that start at the Whitewater Center include **Bear Paw Loop** (1.7 miles) and the **Chestnut Mountain Loop** (6 miles).

One of the most famous trails in the forest is the **Benton MacKaye Trail** (www.bmta.org), a 150 mile trail named for the creator of the Appalachian Trail (AT). When the AT was getting congested, a group of dedicated hikers set out to create a new long-haul hike through the southern mountains. The Benton MacKaye Trail begins at Spring Mountain, Georgia, as does the AT. It follows a different path, however, and ends at Davenport Gap, North Carolina, in the Great Smoky Mountains National Park. The trail enters the Cherokee National Forest at Big Frog Mountain. Access points are at Forest Service Road 221, Forest Service Road 45, Thunder Rock Campground, and Highway 64 across from Ocoee Powerhouse No. 3.

Benton Falls Trail is an easy 1.5-mile (one-way) trail that leaves from Chilhowee Campground and follows Rock Creek to 65-foot Benton Falls.

The **John Muir Trail** covers 18.8 miles along the Hiwassee River from Childers Creek near Reliance to Highway 68 at Farmer. The trail follows a route described by naturalist and writer John Muir in his book *A Thousand-Mile Walk to the Gulf.*

The **Oswald Dome Trail** climbs 3.9 miles up Bean Mountain from the Quinn Springs Campground on Highway 30 near Reliance. The trail ends at an elevation of 3,500 feet near the Oswald Dome fire tower.

Lastly, the **Unicoi Turnpike Trail** is a 2.5-mile portion of the historic Unicoi Turnpike, an old road that settlers, hunters, and Native Americans used to get over the mountains. The trail connects Doc Rogers Fields near Coker Creek with the Unicoi Gap. Along the way you will see a marker for a murdered tollgate keeper and the remnants of Rolling Stone Civilian Conservation Corps (CCC) Camp.

two outfitters, Ocoee Outdoors and Sunburst Expeditions, opened their doors in 1977.

But meanwhile TVA was repairing the flume, and in 1984 it was ready to again divert the river water away from the riverbed. By this time, however, the rafting industry had blossomed. So in 1984 the Outfitters Association and TVA reached a 35-year agreement where rafting companies would get a minimum of 116 days of rafting water each year and would pay $2 per customer to compensate TVA for the loss of power generation. It is an agreement that has allowed TVA to continue operation and the rafting industry to flourish.

★ Rafting the Ocoee

Whitewater rafting is the most popular activity of the southern Cherokee Forest between June and September. The four miles between the Ocoee 2 diversion dam and the Ocoee 2

Biking in the Southern Cherokee

Mountain biking is permitted on dozens of trails within the Cherokee National Forest, making this a popular destination for off-road bicyclists. The **Chilhowee Mountain Bike Trail System** is centered in the Chilhowee Mountain recreation area, near the town of Ocoee. It includes nine different trails ranging from easy to advanced. The two-mile Azalea Trail is a favorite; the 5.4-mile Clear Creek Trail is challenging, with wrenching uphill and screaming downhill segments.

The **Tanasi Mountain Bike Trail System** is located near the Ocoee Whitewater Center and has five trails, including the 11.5-mile advanced Chestnut Mountain-West Fork Loop. The Thunder Rock Express is a 1.5-mile stretch of trail with exciting downhill segments and lots of jumps. The Tanasi system is so revered by mountain bikers that a top-of-the-line titanium-frame mountain bike is named after it.

Elite road bikers head to the **Cherohala Skyway** for endurance rides. The road climbs for 21 miles on the Tennessee side before beginning a 15-mile descent in North Carolina. Steep switchbacks and high elevation make this a challenging ride for even the most experienced bikers. The Skyway is the location of the 100-mile **Cherohala Challenge** every June.

The **Tellico Ranger District Trail System,** north of the Cherohala Skyway, includes the 11-mile Citico Creek and Tellico River Trail, a challenging ride along a gravel road, and the Indian Boundary Loop, a 3.2-mile level track that circles Indian Boundary Lake.

Bike rentals and gear are available from **Trailhead Bicycle Company** (225 1st St. NE, Cleveland, 423/472-9899, www.trailheadbicycle.com), which offers superior gear and repair services.

Copperhill's **Ocoee Adventure Center** (4651 Hwy. 64, 888/723-8622, www.ocoeeadventurecenter.com) offers guided mountain bike trips and personalized instruction. Rates are $45 per person for a half day, and $89 per person for a whole day.

powerhouse are where the fun happens, over 20 different rapids with names like Grumpy, Broken Nose, Double Suck, Slingshot, and Hell's Hole.

The Ocoee River is for experienced or adventurous outdoorspeople (this is where whitewater events were held during the 1996 Summer Olympics in Atlanta). With Class III-IV rapids, the river can be frightening or dangerous if you're not experienced or confident enough. No one under 12 is permitted to raft anywhere on the Ocoee. Beginners or families with young children should raft down the Hiwassee instead. If you are uncertain, talk to an experienced outfitter about which rafting trip would be best for your group.

Watching as other people make their way down the river is also an enjoyable pastime. Places where you can pull over and parking areas along the rafting portion of the river are often full of onlookers on summer afternoons and other busy periods.

The Ocoee rafting and floating season runs March-September. During the spring and fall, outfitters will offer trips on weekends or holidays only. During the summer, there are trips every day. Rafting on the river is dependent on TVA's schedule of water releases. You can pick up a schedule from the Ocoee Whitewater Center (4400 Hwy. 64 W., Copperhill, 423/496-0100).

When you go rafting, do plan to get wet. Don't carry anything with you, like a camera, that can't be submerged. In summer, wear your bathing suit, shorts, a T-shirt, and tennis shoes. During the cooler months, suit up in a wet suit or wear a windbreaker or wool sweater to keep warm. Wool socks and tennis shoes are also nice. Regardless of the season, avoid cotton clothing and bring a change of clothes to put on after your trip. Most rafting companies offer somewhere to store your belongings until after the trip.

There are more than 20 companies offering rafting trips down the Ocoee. Some of the best are **Ocoee Rafting** (Ducktown, 423/496-3388, www.ocoeerafting.com), **Nantahala Outdoor Center (NOC)** (13077

U.S. 19, Bryson City NC, 828/785-5082, www.noc.com), **Ocoee Inn Rafting** (2496 Hwy. 64, 423/338-2064, www.ocoeeinn.com), and **Ocoee Adventure Center (OAC)** (4651 Hwy. 64, 888/723-8622, www.ocoeeadventurecenter.com).

If you want to make a more significant commitment to the sport of kayaking or paddleboarding, sign up for a clinic at OAC or NOC.

OCOEE WHITEWATER CENTER

Built for the 1996 Atlanta Summer Olympics, the **Ocoee Whitewater Center** (4400 Hwy. 64 W., 423/496-0100, www.fs.usda.gov/cherokee, 9am-5pm daily Apr.-Nov., 9am-5pm Fri.-Sun. Thanksgiving-Mar., free) is a central source of information about the Ocoee River, has restrooms and other amenities, and is a starting point for several hikes.

The riverbed in front of the center is pockmarked and rugged; the natural contours of the river were "improved" in preparation for the Olympics. When the water is low, children and adults will enjoy walking around the pools and streams on the riverbed or sunning on the rocks. When the water is high, marvel at the power and sound of fast-running water while you watch rafters and kayakers maneuvering down the rapids.

There are rocking chairs and plenty of benches around for relaxing. The Olympic Legacy Bridge spans the river, providing nice views of the water below. During spring and summer, plan to walk through the gardens, which showcase native plants. You can find a guide to the gardens at the visitors center, which has great additional information about the area.

Visitors to the center can park for 30 minutes in the lot right next to the center. Long-term users must park below and pay a fee of $3 per vehicle.

Food

Burgers, breakfast, and free food on your birthday are just some of the reasons active folks stop at the **Ocoee Dam Deli & Diner** (1223 Highway 64, 423/338-8184, www.ocoeedamdeli.com, $8, 11am-9pm Sun.-Tues and Thurs, 11am-10pm Fri.-Sat. summer, hours may be limited in the off-season.). This is the place to indulge on sweet potato fries and a gooey dessert before or after a run down the river. Breakfast is served until 11am on weekends. The eatery is located on Lake Parksville. Live bluegrass music plays on Saturday nights (no cover charge).

Accommodations

The ★ **Lake Ocoee Inn** (2496 Hwy. 64, 423/338-2064, www.ocoeeinn.com, $75-105) is located about 15 miles west of the Ocoee Whitewater Center and sits on the shore of placid Lake Ocoee (Parksville Lake). This motel opened in 1936 and has nondescript motel rooms, plus five fully equipped cabins. There is also a marina. Generally speaking, Lake Ocoee attracts an outdoorsy crowd. It is also family friendly.

Practicalities

Gas, food, and lodging are somewhat limited along the Ocoee River. There are **gas stations** at Ocoee, Ducktown, and at Greasy Creek, about five miles up Highway 30. There are restaurants in Ocoee, Ducktown, and Copper Hill, plus one restaurant along the river. The best way to handle food during a trip to the river is to pack a picnic lunch and enjoy it at one of the many picnic areas in the forest. There are modest groceries in Greasy Creek, Reliance, and Ocoee. In Ducktown, there's a **Piggly Wiggly** (125 Five Points Dr.).

DUCKTOWN

Ducktown, and its sister city Copperhill, are the heart of the Copper Basin of Tennessee. Here, copper was mined from the 1850s until the 1980s.

In order to fuel the copper smelters, timber was harvested all around. By 1876, all the trees in the area were gone, and logs had to be floated in from Fannin County, Georgia. Between 1865 and 1878, 24 million pounds of copper were removed from the earth and 50 square miles of the basin had been stripped of its trees.

Camping in the Southern Cherokee

There are more than a dozen developed campgrounds in the southern region of the Cherokee National Forest. Campgrounds vary from developed areas with electrical hookups for RVs and hot showers to rustic grounds with chemical toilets and no shower facilities at all. Most Forest Service campgrounds are open mid-March-December, although some are available year-round, and most are open on a first-come, first-served basis. Where reservations are available, they must be made through the government's centralized reservation service at www.reserveusa.com or by calling 877/444-6777.

Camping rates range $10-20 depending on the type of site you choose and the popularity of the campground. The following are some of the most popular campgrounds; for a complete list, contact the nearest ranger station.

OCOEE/HIWASSEE DISTRICT

The largest campground is **Chilhowee Recreation Area,** located along Forest Service Road 77. There are 86 campsites, warm showers, and flush toilets. You are next door to the McKamy Lake beach and have easy access to 25 miles of hike/bike trails.

Thunder Rock is located near Ocoee Powerhouse No. 3 and is convenient to the Whitewater Center. There are 39 sites, warm showers, and flush toilets. This is a popular campsite for rafters and other water-sports enthusiasts.

Parksville Lake, open April 1-October 31, is located along Rock Creek and has 17 campsites, warm showers, and flush toilets. It is convenient to the white-water section of the Ocoee River and to swimming, boating, and fishing on Parksville Lake.

Lost Creek, located off Highway 30 near Reliance, has 15 sites and is set in a mature hardwood forest next to Big Lost Creek. It is a peaceful and wild area, but the flush toilets and hot showers provide basic creature comforts. RVs are welcome.

TELLICO DISTRICT

Big Oak Cove is an 11-site campground located on the banks of the Tellico River. A retreat for tent campers, the grounds are open mid-March-December. Hiking, fishing, and wading are available nearby. The fee is $10 per night. There are chemical toilets and cold showers.

Located off the Cherohala Skyway at an elevation of 1,800 feet, **Holly Flats** is an 18-site tent-friendly campsite with limited facilities. There are chemical toilets and cold showers, but little in the way of other comforts. The setting is peaceful and typically uncrowded.

One of the most popular campgrounds in this part of the forest is **Indian Boundary,** an 88-site campground located on Indian Boundary Lake along the Cherohala Skyway. Four loops offer various levels of comfort, from full RV hookups to rustic tent sites. Recreation includes hiking or biking around the lake, boating, fishing, and swimming. Reservations are accepted.

The area's mines declined between 1878 and 1890, until a new railroad spur arrived in the area. In 1899 the Tennessee Copper Company opened the Burra Burra Mine in Ducktown and built a new smelter. During this period, mining companies used an open roasting process to remove copper from the raw ore. This open roasting required lots of timber for fuel, and it let off sulfuric acid, which killed vegetation and left the landscape eerily empty. Acid rain fell, polluting the Ocoee River and other nearby bodies of water.

The environmental abuse of more than a century left its mark on Tennessee's Copper Basin. For years, this area was distinctive for its barren orange-red hills and craters, the legacy of many years of deforestation and the open release of sulfuric acid. Residents had mixed feelings about the landscape—it was strangely beautiful, but at the same time it was a constant reminder of environmental damage. There were also concerns about health effects. Early efforts to reforest the old mines date back to the early 20th century, but it was not until the 1970s that scientists figured out a way to successfully introduce trees back into the denuded landscape. Since then, pine trees have grown to cover virtually all of the hills that were once barren.

Copper was mined here until 1987, and the plant at Copperhill still processes sulfur, although the raw materials are trucked in—not mined.

Ducktown was a company town, a fact that is evident as you take a short drive around. Main Street is little more than two blocks with a handful of elegant homes built by mine owners and bosses. The main residential neighborhood is a collection of modest homes in a slight hollow. The newer parts of town, including gas stations, motels, and a school, are found near the intersection of Highways 64 and 68.

★ Ducktown Basin Museum

The **Ducktown Basin Museum** (212 Burra Burra St., 423/496-5778, www.ducktownbasinmuseum.com, 10am-pm Mon.-Sat., hours may be extended 30 minutes in summer and closed Mondays in winter, adults $5, seniors $4, teens $2, children $1) captures the unique history and culture of Tennessee's Copper Basin. Located in the offices of the old Burra Burra Mine, the museum has displays about the historical development of the mines, the culture that developed in the company towns, and the mining business itself. Special topics include mine safety, the railroad, and the history of strikes at the mine. The visit includes a 15-minute video that tells the story of the entire region and describes the three periods during which the hills here were mined for copper and other minerals.

At the rear of the museum is one of the only "copper craters" that was not reforested. Although volunteer pine trees are beginning to take root in the red soil, you can still imagine how distinctive the landscape once looked.

Accommodations

Ducktown is close enough to the Ocoee and several outdoor outfitters to make it a popular place for outdoor thrill seekers. But the additional draw of the mining museum is another reason to make this your home base in the Overhill region.

For a bed-and-breakfast option in Ducktown, try **The Company House** (318 Main St., 423/496-5634, www.bbonline.com/tn/companyhouse, $89-99). It has seven guest rooms, each named for a mine in the area. All rooms have private baths and in-room telephones.

The Ducktown Basin Museum is located near the old Burra Burra Mine.

If motel lodging is more your thing, then there are two options. The **Ducktown Copper Inn** (U.S. 64 and Hwy. 68, 423/496-5541, $59) is an aging motel with no-frills accommodations. Rooms have microwaves, refrigerators, and televisions. The **Ocoee Inn** (5082 Hwy. 64, 877/546-2633, www.ocoeeinn.com, $60-80) is a newer outfit, with many of the same amenities (but less grunge) than its nearby neighbor. In addition to the motel, there are several cabins (including a dog-friendly option) available.

COPPERHILL

Copperhill sits on the state line and on the banks of the Ocoee River. On the Georgia side, the town is called McCaysville and the river is called the Toccoa.

There is more going on in Copperhill than Ducktown, due largely to the scenic train excursions that stop here for midday layovers. A pleasant main street district with restaurants and shops makes this a nice place to spend an hour or so. Walk up the hillside that faces Ocoee Street for views of the town and the Ocoee/Toccoa River.

Food

For solid Mexican fare in a clean environment with good service, stop at **Habaneros Fresh Tex Mex** (120 Ocoee St., 423/548-2111, Sun. 12pm-9:30pm, 11am-9:30pm Mon.-Tues. and Thurs., 11am-10pm Fri.-Sat., $8-10). Burgers, sandwiches, Panini, fried pickles, and more are on the menu at **The Copperhill Grill** (109 Ocoee St., 423/548-1530, 11am-4pm Sun.-Thurs., 11am-9pm Fri.-Sat., $6-13). Both restaurants experience a rush when the train rolls into town.

An old-school, roadside fast-food joint, **Roger and Carol's Quick Burger** (205 Ocoee St., 423/496-3714, noon-4pm Sun., 6am-7pm Mon.-Fri., 7am-7pm Sat., $4-10) has been in business for more than 30 years. Treat yourself to a thick shake after a day on the river.

Rail Excursions

In addition to the rail excursions offered by the Tennessee Valley Railroad, the **Blue Ridge Scenic Railway** (241 Depot St., Blue Ridge, GA, 706/632-9833, www.brscenic.com, adults $40, children $25) offers railroad excursions that come to Copperhill. The trip leaves from Blue Ridge, Georgia, and makes a one-hour journey north through the mountains to Copperhill, where you have two hours to eat and shop.

TURTLETOWN

Drive north from Ducktown on Highway 68 to find more quiet towns and rural countryside.

Just beyond the small community of **Turtletown**, Highway 294 splits off Highway 68, headed toward North Carolina. About four miles down this road, and about two miles past the state line, there is a remarkable monument to the Christian faith. **Fields of the Wood Bible Park** (10000 Hwy. 294, Murphy NC, 828/494-7855, www.fieldsofthewoodbiblepark.com, sunrise-sunset daily, free) is a project of the Church of God of Prophecy that contains, among other things, the world's largest cross and the largest representation of the Ten Commandments. The latter is located just inside the park's gates and is laid out on a hillside. Each letter spelling out the commandments is five feet high and four feet wide. This is just the beginning of what Fields of the Wood has to offer. You will also find replicas of Joseph's tomb, where Christ was buried and rose from the dead, and Golgotha, where Jesus offered himself as a sacrifice. There is also a gift shop and the Burger Mountain Café, which are open Monday-Saturday 9am-5pm.

The Hiwassee

Named from the Cherokee word *ayuwasi* (savannah or meadow), the Hiwassee River drains fertile agricultural lands and passes through the heartland of the southern Cherokee National Forest.

RELIANCE

The **Reliance** historic district is located along the Hiwassee River, near where Highways 30 and 315 intersect. The **Hiwassee Union Church** is a two-story board structure built jointly by the local Masonic lodge and the Union Church in 1899. On the north side of the river is the **Higdon Hotel,** also built around 1899.

Your pit stop in Reliance should be the **Webb Brothers Texaco** (3708 Hwy. 30, 423/338-2373, www.webbbros.com), a gas station, post office, general store, river outfitter, and community hub. Inside the shop you'll find a placard with historical information about Reliance. Lodging is available at the historic Watchman's house, which has four different rooms.

Reliance is located about 10 miles north of the Ocoee River, along Highway 30. The drive south follows Greasy Creek, a pretty, clear stream that defies its name. You will pass old wood-frame houses and farms that have been in this valley for generations.

HIWASSEE SCENIC RIVER STATE PARK

A 23-mile section of the Hiwassee River has been designated a Tennessee Scenic River. From Highway 411 to the North Carolina state line, the Hiwassee River offers prime opportunities for canoeing, rafting, fishing, hiking, and wildlife viewing.

Hiwassee Scenic River State Park (404 Spring Creek Rd., Delano, 423/263-0050, tnstateparks.com/parks/about/hiwassee-ocoee) and the neighboring **Gee Creek Campground** (Spring Creek Rd., Delano, 423/263-0050) are good places to come to explore the river. There are picnic grounds, restrooms, and boat-launch areas. The Gee Creek Campground has 47 particularly tent-friendly campsites, some of which are right next to the river. As is the case with most Tennessee state parks, campsites can be booked online (tnstateparks.itinio.com).

Fishing is popular along the river; anglers frequently catch rainbow and brown trout, largemouth bass, yellow perch, and catfish.

Unlike the Ocoee River, the Hiwassee is a calm river, with Class I-II (rather than III-IV) rapids. Children six and up are allowed on the Hiwassee.

Because the Hiwassee is calmer, many people rent the necessary equipment and make the journey downriver without a guide. Expect to pay $40 and up per day for a six-person raft or $24 per day for a one-person Duckie. Inner tubes and other equipment are also available. Hiwassee outfitters include **Hiwassee Scenic Outfitters, Inc.** (155 Ellis Creek Rd., Reliance, 423/338-8115, www.hiwasseeoutfitters.com) and **Webb Brothers Float Service** (Reliance, 423/338-2373, www.webbbros.com).

DELANO

Located on the edge of the national forest, between Etowah and Benton, the town of Delano is known for **Delano Daylilies** (153 County Rd. 854, 423/263-9323, www.delanodaylilies.com, 10am-5pm Tues.-Sat. late May-early July, free), a noteworthy seasonal attraction and nursery. This nursery raises some 1,300 varieties of colorful daylilies, and from late May to early July every year their garden is busy with area growers shopping for blooms. Casual visitors are also welcome to come and enjoy a stroll throughout the patches of daylilies, but you'll be hard-pressed not to wind up with at least one plant in your possession by the end of your visit. A covered pavilion is a

Sandhill Cranes

Located along the Hiwassee River between Dayton and Birchwood, the **Blythe Ferry Unit of the Hiwassee Refuge** (423/614-3018) is an important stop for bird-watching. Because it is near the confluence of the Tennessee and Hiwassee Rivers, it is home to more than 20 different kinds of seasonal shorebirds, waders, and common waterfowl such as wintering ducks and geese. But the real reason migrating humans stop is because Blythe Ferry Unit has become a winter stopover for migrating sandhill and whooping cranes.

The concentration has grown from just a few birds to more than 7,000 at times, making this one of Tennessee's premier wildlife spectacles November-March. It is the only major resting stop for these amazing birds between Florida and their northern starting points. During the open season you can walk along paths. The refuge trails are closed to the public during the winter except for a Sandhill Crane Festival in January, but viewing is possible along the roads and from an observation deck. No matter what time of year you stop, remember to view birds at a distance. Submit reports about the birds you see to ebird.org.

To get to the refuge, find the junction between Highways 58 and 60 near Georgetown. Drive 7.8 miles west on Highway 60 and turn right at the wildlife sign.

lovely place to sit and relax while your traveling companion chooses lilies. There are also benches throughout the gardens.

An 1861 barn provides the centerpiece for the 11,000 acres of vineyard at **Savannah Oaks Winery** (1817 Delano Rd., 423/263-2762, 10am-6pm Mon.-Thurs., 10am-7pm Fri.-Sat., 1pm-6pm Sun., free). Tours and wine-and-cheese tastings are available by appointment, and in the summer the winery hosts a number of events with live music. Visitors appreciate the mountain views as much as the wines.

Gliding

Gliding is flying without an engine, and you can experience this sublime form of travel at **Chilhowee Gliderport** (Hwy. 411, 423/388-2000, www.chilhowee.com), near Benton. A half-hour ride costs $219 and takes you high above the scenic Cherokee National Forest and the Hiwassee and Ocoee Rivers. Chilhowee Gliderport also offers lessons and rentals for gliding enthusiasts.

COKER CREEK

Before copper was mined in the Copper Basin, this area was famous for its gold. The Cherokee had known about the gold for years, but whites discovered it around 1825. It didn't take long for a full-fledged gold rush to begin. Trouble was that the gold was on Cherokee land. When the Cherokee complained to the federal government in 1826, the U.S. Army established a garrison here supposedly to enforce the Cherokee's land rights. Even the presence of soldiers did little to keep settlers from tapping into the Cherokee's resources, and the pressure from people such as these was probably one thing that sealed the Cherokee's later fate.

Sights

For the best views of this part of the Cherokee Forest, drive to **Buck Bald,** the site of an old fire tower. The tower was removed in the 1970s, but the site remains a place to enjoy 360-degree views of the surrounding landscape. To get there, drive seven miles south of Coker Creek along Highway 68, then turn left onto Buck Bald Road. It is 2.5 miles to the top.

A designated scenic area with four waterfalls and several miles of hiking trails, **Coker Creek Scenic Area and Falls** is a wonderful place for a picnic. The four waterfalls—Upper Coker Creek Falls, Coker Creek Falls, Hiding Place Falls, and Lower Coker Creek Falls—are all located within a quarter mile of the parking area. There are picnic tables, but no toilets or potable water.

To find the falls, drive south of Coker Creek 3.1 miles along Highway 68. Turn right onto County Road 628 (Ironsburg Road) and travel 0.8 mile. Veer left at the Ironsburg Cemetery onto County Road 626 (Duckett Ridge Road) and travel for three miles. The road will become gravel. Turn left onto Forest Service Road 2138 and travel one mile to the parking area.

Festivals and Events

Since 1968, Coker Creek's **Autumn Gold Festival** (www.cokercreek.org) has been the community's largest event of the year. Taking place during the second full weekend of October—while the autumn leaves are on full display—the festival includes a crafts fair, gold panning, and the crowning of the Autumn Gold Queen.

Shopping

Coker Creek is home to several art galleries. **Coker Creek Gallery** (206 Hot Water Rd., 423/261-2157, cokercreekgallery.com), located just a few hundred yards from Highway 68, has wind chimes, pottery, glass and metal sculptures, jewelry, and more. The **Coker Creek Heritage Group Gift Shop** (mile marker 34, Highway 68, 423/261-2286, Cokercreek.org) exhibits the works of local artists; proceeds support the local post office.

Panning for Gold

Although the gold industry petered out at Coker Creek after the Civil War, hobby mining and panning continues. You can buy panning supplies at the **Coker Creek Welcome Center** (Hwy. 68, 423/261-2286, www.cokercreek.org).

It's unlikely that anyone will tell you the best places to pan for gold, but the most popular are easy to find. You can pan at Coker Creek, just 0.3 mile from the welcome center, near Doc Rogers Field. Coker Creek Falls, eight miles south of the welcome center, is also a nice place to pan, although you may soon grow weary of the work and choose to enjoy the falls and swimming hole instead.

ETOWAH

Etowah didn't much exist until 1902, when the Louisville and Nashville (L&N) Railroad chose the settlement for its new headquarters and rail center. The railroad was planning a new, more direct route between Cincinnati and Atlanta, and it needed a place for crew changes and engine servicing. The passenger station was built first, in 1906. A veritable railroad complex followed: roundhouse, sand house, cinder pits, coal bins, oil house, machine shop, blacksmith shop, boiler shop, planing mill, cabinet shop, powerhouse, car repair shop, water tanks, a store, offices, freight depot, and nearly 20 tracks.

The L&N also built houses for its workers, and Etowah was truly a company town, where everyone lived, breathed, and worked the railroad. At its peak, more than 2,000 men were employed by the L&N here.

Etowah and its railroad industry flourished until 1928, when the L&N started to replace its wooden railroad carts with steel ones. Two hundred shop men were laid off. In the same year, the L&N closed its headquarters in Etowah, moving them to Knoxville. By 1931, the workforce at Etowah had shrunk to just 80.

Over the succeeding decades, Etowah diversified, and people found other work. Passenger trains continued to run until 1968. CSX, the freight train company, still operates a terminal in Etowah.

There isn't much in the way of accommodations in Etowah, so look at nearby Athens for a comfortable bed-and-breakfast.

Sights

Etowah's downtown district faces Highway 411 and the railroad. The historic **Gem Theater** (700 S. Tennessee Ave./U.S. 441, www.gemplayers.com), built in 1927, has been renovated and is the home of the Gem Theater Players. For information about upcoming shows, contact the Etowah Arts Commission at 423/263-7608. They typically produce about five shows annually.

You can relive Etowah's railroad history at the **L&N Depot and Railroad Museum** (Tennessee Ave./Hwy. 411, 423/263-7840, 10am-4pm Mon.-Sat., free). The old passenger station is elegant, with high ceilings and delicate wood finishes. It comes alive through old photographs and recollections by area residents who talk about the hardships and pleasures of a railroad life. The exhibit, called "Growing Up with the L&N: Life and Times of a Railroad Town," is more about the social history of Etowah than the railroad itself, although the two are interlinked.

Ask to go upstairs, where you can see more general exhibits about Etowah's history. Sometimes there are local art exhibits on display.

After touring the museum, go outside to see a railroad caboose. There is also a picnic area and a walking trail that follows the railroad tracks.

★ Tennessee Valley Railroad Excursions

The **Tennessee Valley Railroad** (423/894-8028, www.tvrail.com), based in Chattanooga, organizes sightseeing tours of the Cherokee National Forest during the summer and fall. The **Hiwassee River Rail Adventure** (adults $40, children $30) is a 3.5-hour, 50-mile journey that follows the path of the Hiwassee River and includes the breathtaking corkscrew loop around Bald Mountain. The **Copperhill Special** (adults $60, children $40) follows the same route as the Hiwassee journey but adds an additional 40-mile trip and lunchtime layover in Copperhill.

Passengers on either journey meet at the L&N Depot and Railroad Museum in Etowah and are bused to nearby Gee Creek State Park, where they board the train. Train cars are comfortable, with big windows and air-conditioning.

The scenic train excursions are made possible by the combined efforts of the Tennessee Overhill Association and the Tennessee Valley Railroad Museum.

Food

Directly across Tennessee Avenue (also known as Highway 411) from the L&N Depot is **Tony's Italian Restaurant** (718 Tennessee Ave., 423/263-1940, 11am-10pm daily, $5-14), which serves pasta, pizza, calzones, and Italian-style subs and what they call the Heart Attack Bacon Cheese Burger, which is served on a 10-inch bun. There is a buffet at lunch and dinner that includes lasagna, pizza, salad, and other house specialties.

Information

Contact the **Etowah Area Chamber of Commerce** (727 Tennessee Ave., 423/263-2228, etowahchamber.com), located in the L&N building next to the museum, for visitor information. The **Tennessee Overhill Heritage Association** (423/263-7232, www.tennesseeoverhill.com) is a regional tourism agency based in Etowah, with offices in the railroad depot.

The Tellico

The headwaters of the **Tellico River** are high atop the peaks of the Cherokee Forest. The stream, noted for fishing, flows down the mountain and along the scenic Cherohala Skyway to Tellico Plains, where it flows northward to its confluence with the Little Tennessee. The Tellico Dam impounds the rivers and forms Tellico Lake. Here, near the town of Vonore, are two of the most significant historic attractions in the region: Fort Loudoun State Historic Area and the Sequoyah Birthplace Museum. Both have important ties to Cherokee history.

Towns including Athens, Englewood, and Madisonville are located in the foothills of the mountains, in the Great Valley of East

Tennessee. These centers of industry, education, and commerce are still the heartbeat of the Overhill region.

TELLICO PLAINS

Located where the Tellico River emerges from the national forest, **Tellico Plains** was once a logging and industrial town. It is now a gateway to the Cherokee National Forest and the official beginning point of the Cherohala Skyway, a scenic parkway that extends into North Carolina.

The **Cherohala Skyway Visitor Center** (225 Cherohala Skyway/Hwy. 165, 423/253-8010, www.cherohala.org/visitor-center.html, 9am-5pm daily), near the official start of the skyway, has maps as well as staff to answer questions. There is also a large gift shop and bathrooms. Right next door is the **Charles Hall Museum** (229 Cherohala Skyway, 423/253-8000, www.charleshallmuseum.com, 10am-5pm daily, free), a local history museum packed with antiques, 98 percent of which came from the collection of Tellico-area resident Charles Hall. There are more than 200 guns, an extensive telephone collection, and an impressive coin collection, among others. It is a small museum, brings in more than 30,000 people annually.

Tellico Plains consists of an older "down town" located on the south side of Highway 165, and several miles of sprawl along Highway 68. The downtown area is home to several real estate offices, building supply companies, local businesses, restaurants, and shops. **The Bookshelf** (108 Scott St., 423/253-3183, www.tellicobookshelf.com) is a used-book store with a knowledgeable staff that also repairs books. Galleries including **The Tellico Arts Center** (113 Scott St., 423/253-2253) cater to visitors looking for local arts and crafts.

For food, head first to **Tellico Grains Bakery** (105 Depot St., 423/253-6911, www.tellico-grains-bakery.com, 8am-4pm Tues.-Sat., $4-8), a bakery and café with its own wood-fired oven. The menu of bread, sandwiches, and pizza are as clever as the bakery's name.

For plate lunches, burgers, and other grilled sandwiches, go to **Town Square Café and Bakery** (Public Sq., 423/253-2200, 8am-2:45pm daily, $3-8), a cozy eating house where everyone seems to know each other. The daily lunch special comes with your choice of two sides and bread. It also sells pizza, but it is the homemade gravy on the breakfast dishes that brings in the locals.

Cherohala Skyway

Completed in 1996, this is a two-lane highway that passes through the highest peaks of the southern Unaka Mountains. The 54-mile road, which begins in Tellico Plains, climbs to more than 5,300 feet at its highest level and provides stunning scenic views. It follows the Tellico River for several miles at the beginning before starting its serious ascent. The road terminates in Robbinsville, North Carolina; about one-third of the road is in Tennessee.

The **Cherohala Skyway** was originally called the Cheoah Parkway and the Overhill Skyway; the states of Tennessee and North Carolina eventually agreed on the existing name, which combines the words *Cherokee* and *Nantahala*. The highway, which took 34 years and some $100 million to build, replaced narrow, unpaved Forest Service roads that had for many years been the only means of travel over the peaks in this part of the forest. Despite predictions to the contrary, the skyway remains relatively uncrowded, providing a pleasant alternative to congested highways through the Great Smoky Mountains National Park.

It will take you about 1.5 hours to drive nonstop from one end of the skyway to the other. Although the road is well maintained and easy to drive, plan to take it slow. It is windy, and you will want to stop frequently to admire the view. Beware of snow and ice during winter.

Sights and stops along the way include **Tellico Ranger Station** (250 Ranger Station Rd., 423/253-8400), a source of information about the forest, the area, and the drive. The station is located in a New Deal-era CCC building. **Bald River Falls,** a 100-foot waterfall, is located off the skyway along Forest Service Road 210.

After you pass the ranger station, the road begins to climb. Overlooks on the Tennessee side include **Turkey Creek, Lake View,** and **Brushy Ridge.** There are picnic tables at Turkey Creek and Brushy Ridge. All overlooks are wheelchair accessible.

The skyway is popular with motorcyclists and serious bicyclists who enjoy the scenic curves and fresh mountain air.

Indian Boundary

One of the most popular destinations in the southern Cherokee Forest, **Indian Boundary** (Forest Service Rd. 345, Apr.-Sept.) is a Forest Service campground and recreation area. Located high atop the mountains off the Cherohala Skyway, Indian Boundary is cool in the summer and an ideal place for a camping vacation. Cool off with a swim at the Indian Boundary beach, hike or bike along the three-mile loop that circles the 100-acre Indian Boundary Lake, or go for a boat cruise on the lake. No gasoline engines are allowed in the lake.

The **campground** (877-444-6777, $20, open mid April-early November) has 87 sites, hot showers, and potable water available from spigots around the campground. All sites have electricity. There is also a camp store (no phone) and picnic area. Despite Indian Boundary's isolation, it is quite popular, particularly during the summer. For information on recreation, contact the Tellico Ranger Station at 423/253-8400.

ENGLEWOOD

A small town located in the foothills of the Appalachian mountains, Englewood is home to the **Englewood Textile Museum** (101 S. Niota St., 423/887-5455, 10am-5pm Mon.-Sat., free), which is a collection of adjacent buildings. The museum remembers the hundreds of area working-class women who toiled at textile mills in Englewood. A hand-painted mural on the outside of the museum depicts a pastoral company town. Inside, you can see some of the clothing that was manufactured here for nearly 100 years. There is an adjacent antiques store. Sometimes the museum closes early on Saturdays, so call ahead.

Food

The ★ **Tellico Junction Café** (17 E. Main St., 423/887-7770, 6am-3pm Mon.-Fri., 7am-2pm Sat.-Sun., $5-12) is a large, open restaurant facing the railroad tracks in downtown Englewood. Dozens of polished wood tables and a wide lunch counter invite you to stop and linger over cups of coffee or plates of grilled sandwiches, plate-lunch specials, or homemade dessert. Locals head here after church on Sunday or for fish fry on Friday. No matter when you come, don't miss the chance to check out the decor in the men's restroom.

ATHENS

The seat of McMinn County, **Athens** is home to **Tennessee Wesleyan University** (204 E. College St., 423/745-7504, www.twcnet.edu), a Methodist-affiliated four-year university. Chartered in 1857, it is the home of the Old College Harp Singers, a shape-note singing group.

The **McMinn Living Heritage Museum** (522 W. Madison Ave., 423/745-0329, livingheritagemuseum.com, 10am-5pm Tues.-Fri., 10am-4pm Sat., adults $5, seniors $3, students $1) is home to 30 different exhibit rooms, including an extensive collection of antique quilts.

One of the Southeast's most distinctive food brands is Mayfield, a maker of milk, dairy, and juice products. Mayfield's largest bottling and processing plant is located just outside of Athens, near where Thomas B. Mayfield Sr., a local dairy farmer, first opened his creamery in 1923. Visitors are welcome at **Mayfield Dairy Farms** (4 Mayfield Ln., 423/649-2653, www.mayfielddairy.com,

9am-5pm Mon., Tues, Thurs, Fri., 9am-2pm Sat., $4.50 adult, $3.50 over 3). The 40-minute tour includes a short video and visits to viewing areas where you can see Mayfield's distinctive yellow milk jugs being made, jugs and other containers being filled, and ice cream being packaged. You also walk by giant vats of milk being pasteurized, and others that are being made into buttermilk. Milk is not made on Wednesday, and ice cream is not made on Saturday.

Don't expect to see any cows, though, except for the bronze cow sculpture outside the welcome center. Mayfield buys its raw milk from area dairy farmers; it arrives in giant trucks that enter the dairy gates by the dozens every day.

Be aware that it is awfully hard to pass up the ice-cream shop at the end, particularly on a hot summer day. It's almost as if the dairy planned it that way.

Accommodations

There are a number of standard chain hotels within walking distance of the location attractions, including the **Hampton Inn Athens** (1821 Holiday Dr., 423/745-2345, $114) and the **Holiday Inn Express** (1819 Holiday Dr., 423/649-0003, $103).

MADISONVILLE

Epicureans should make a beeline to **Benton's Country Hams** (2603 Hwy. 411, 423/442-5003, bentonscountryhams2.com), a family-run ham house that depends on brown sugar, salt, and a lot of time to cure its hams. Housed in a low-slung, inconspicuous cinderblock building on the side of busy Highway 411, Benton's has been a destination for cooks and eaters for generations. Its smoked and unsmoked country hams sell like hotcakes. You can also buy prosciutto, bacon, and luncheon meats that will have you dreaming pig. You know this is the real thing because the scent of hickory smoke clings to your clothes and hair after you depart.

SWEETWATER

The Lost Sea Adventure (140 Lost Sea Rd., 423/337-6616, www.thelostsea.com, 9 a.m.-5 p.m. daily Nov.-Feb., 9am-6pm daily Mar.-Apr. and Sept.-Oct., 9am-7pm daily May-June, and 9am-8pm daily Aug., July, adults $18.95, children $9.95) is a cave noted for its four-acre underground lake. That's right, you'll take 0.75-mile guided tour of the caverns, as well as a ride aboard a glass-bottomed boat on the lake. You can even sign up to camp out down in the cave in one of the Lost Sea's so-called

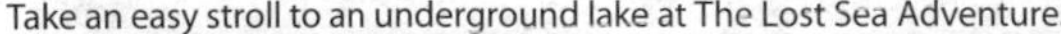

Take an easy stroll to an underground lake at The Lost Sea Adventure.

wild tours. This is a memorable experience. The Lost Sea is located at exit 60 off I-75.

While in Sweetwater, satisfy your sweet tooth at **Hunter's Bakery and Café** (101 E. Morris St., 423/351-1098, www.hunterscafesweetwatertn.com, 11am-4pm Mon.-Thurs., 11am-8pm Fri., 11am-5pm Sat., $7-22). This cozy downtown hot spot has a fox-hunting theme and solidly good food that keeps people coming back again and again. Salads, pasta, and entrées including steak, pork, chicken, and shrimp are offered at lunch and dinner. At the midday meal, you can also pick from signature sandwiches like the tuna melt or the Reuben.

No matter how full you are after your meal, grab one of the café's home-baked big cookies or other confectionaries for the road.

VONORE

Two side-by-side historical attractions located on Tellico Lake focus on the state's Native American history, but from distinctly different eras and perspectives. Fort Loudoun State Historic Area marks the early era of contact between colonists and the Cherokee, while the Sequoyah Birthplace Museum looks in greater detail at the tribe's later interactions with white settlers, including its tragic removal via the Trail of Tears in 1838.

★ Fort Loudoun State Historic Area

The **Fort Loudoun State Historic Area** (338 Fort Loudoun Rd., 423/884-6217, fortloudoun.com, 8am-4:30pm daily, free) recalls the British fort that was built in this spot in 1756 to woo the Cherokee during the French and Indian War. The war between the British and the French, and their respective Indian allies, was fought to decide which European power would control the new American colonies. The British built Fort Loudoun in an effort to cement its alliance with the Cherokee, and therefore strengthen their position to win the war against the French.

Fort Loudoun was located along the Little Tennessee River, and it was the very edge of the American frontier. At first, the British managed to maintain good relations with their Cherokee neighbors. But the uncertain alliance ultimately failed, and violence broke out, with each side blaming the other for the problems. After a five-month siege of Fort Loudoun in 1760, the British surrendered. The British negotiated the terms of their surrender with the Cherokee, who agreed to let the 180 men together with 60 women and children retreat to Charleston, South Carolina.

When the British party stopped to camp their first night, their Cherokee guides slipped into the forest, and by the next day some 29 of the Fort Loudoun party had been killed, including three women. While the basic facts of the ambush are clear, the motivation of the Cherokee is not. Their actions may have been in retribution for the earlier deaths of some 30 Cherokee at the hands of the British. Or they may have been angry that the British had buried the cannons and destroyed the gunpowder at the fort, contrary to the terms of the surrender.

Whatever the cause, it was a bloody and somber end to the Cherokee-British alliance in the Overhill Tennessee region.

Today, Fort Loudoun sits on the bank of Tellico Lake. The last and most controversial of TVA's dam projects, Tellico Dam was finally closed in 1979 after nearly a decade of debate over its impact on the environment and the loss of historic Cherokee sites.

Don't miss the **Living History Garrison and Museum**, a reconstructed collection of exhibits that were re-opened in 2015. The museum is all about living history presentations and recreations, including an 18th century infirmary, the soldiers' barracks, and a Cherokee encampment. The film, *Fort Loudoun: Forsaken by God and Man*, covers the area's history.

The park visitors center houses a good museum about the fort, and the film here is one of the best at a Tennessee state park. About 200 yards behind the visitors center is a replica of Fort Loudoun, built according to the archaeological evidence and contemporary accounts from the fort. The simple wooden buildings and the fort walls have been faithfully reconstructed. It is a pleasant place that conjures up the remoteness that would have existed in the 18th century, when the original fort was built.

Every September the **18th Century Trade Faire** depicts a colonial-era marketplace with merchants, artisans, and entertainers. At Christmas, there are candlelight tours of the fort. In addition, every month there are special programs that include costumed British soldiers and Cherokee.

Fort Loudoun State Historic Area also has a picnic area, five miles of hiking trails, and fishing from a 50-foot pier that projects over Tellico Lake.

Sequoyah Birthplace Museum

Sequoyah was a Cherokee born in about 1776 to Nathaniel Gist, a Virginia fur trader, and Wurteh, the daughter of a Cherokee chief. A silversmith by trade, Sequoyah is most famous for creating a written syllabary for the Cherokee language.

It was 1809 when Sequoyah first started to experiment with a written language for the Cherokee. During this period there was extensive interaction between white settlers and the Cherokee, and Sequoyah saw that a written language would allow his people to record their history, write letters, and communicate news.

Sequoyah developed the language independently, and his first student was his young daughter, Ayoka. Together, in 1821, Ayoka and Sequoyah introduced the language to Cherokee elders, and within a few months thousands of Cherokee were using the system of 85 symbols. By 1825 much of the Bible and numerous hymns had been translated, and in 1828 the *Cherokee Phoenix* became the first national bilingual newspaper in the country.

The story of Sequoyah's accomplishment and the broader legacy of the Cherokee people is preserved at the **Sequoyah Birthplace Museum** (576 Hwy. 360, 423/884-6246, www.sequoyahmuseum.org, 9am-5pm Mon.-Sat., noon-5pm Sun., adults $3, seniors $2.50, children 6-12 $1.50), a museum that is managed by the Eastern Band of the Cherokee.

Though dated, the museum provides a thorough and detailed rendering of the Cherokee way of life, the history of the tribe, and the story of Sequoyah himself. At the rear of the museum, at the end of a 100-yard gravel walkway, there is a mound where the remains of 221 Cherokee people are buried. The graves were moved here during the excavation that took place before Tellico Lake was formed.

Every September, the Sequoyah Birthplace Museum hosts a **Fall Festival,** featuring a Cherokee living-history camp, music, storytelling, Cherokee games, and dance.

Chota and Tanasi Memorials

The towns of Tanasi and Chota were the mother towns of the Overhill Cherokee. It is from the word *Tanasi* that the name Tennessee is derived. The Cherokee were forced to leave Tanasi, Chota, and other settlements as white settlers moved west into Tennessee, taking more and more Cherokee land.

When Tellico Lake was created in 1979, the sites of these historic Cherokee settlements were flooded. Before the inundation, University of Tennessee archaeologists explored the sites and found the remains of a great town house and the grave of the Cherokee warrior and chief Oconostota, who died in 1783.

After the lake was formed, the Tennessee Historical Commission erected a stone memorial that overlooks the actual site of Tanasi. The pavement in front of the marker is an octagonal slab representing a town house, and in the center of this is a granite marker engraved with a seven-pointed star, which represents the seven clans of the Cherokee.

One mile north of the Tanasi monument is the parking area for the Chota memorial. It is a 0.25-mile walk from the parking area to the memorial, which consists of a full-scale replica of a Cherokee town house. The memorial, which stands on a raised surface built above the level of the lake, was erected by the Eastern Band of the Cherokee.

The **Tanasi and Chota memorials** are located off Bacon Ferry Road. To get there, take Highway 360 to Monroe County Road 455. After about six miles on Route 455, you will see the turnoff for Bacon Ferry Road and signs to the memorials. Both sites are also popular places for bird-watching.

Knoxville

Look for ★ to find recommended sights, activities, dining, and lodging.

Highlights

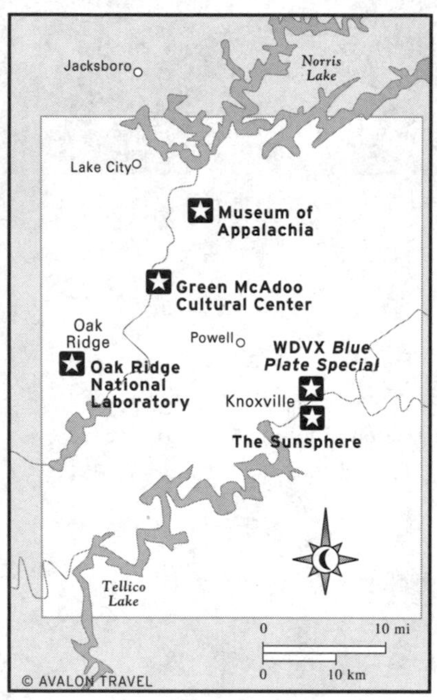

★ **The Sunsphere:** The gold-plated globe of the Sunsphere defines the Knoxville skyline. Ride to the top for views of Knoxville and the surrounding area (page 370).

★ **WDVX *Blue Plate Special*:** Community radio station WDVX is Knoxville's musical icon. It provides a live lunchtime concert every weekday at the Knoxville Visitors Center (page 379).

★ **Green McAdoo Cultural Center:** The story of the desegregation of Clinton's high school is movingly presented at this multimedia museum (page 391).

★ **Museum of Appalachia:** This museum pays tribute to the ingenuity, creativity, and tenacity of the mountain folk (page 393).

★ **Oak Ridge National Laboratory:** Get the behind-the-scenes look at what makes the Secret City tick when you tour this essential stop in atomic history (page 397).

Perhaps the state's most underappreciated city, Knoxville sits on the banks of the Tennessee River, in the foothills of the Appalachian Mountains.

Knoxville lacks the immediate identity of other major Tennessee cities—it is not the birthplace of the blues, Music City USA, or the home of the Choo Choo. (Unless, of course, you are a college sports fan, then you're already an expert on the Marble City.) But that's OK with locals. Knoxville's viewpoint is ultimately an insular one—this is a city that does not strive to be. It just is.

And what is Knoxville? It is the gateway to the Smokies and the home of the orange-clad University of Tennessee (UT) Volunteers. It is an old industrial city with a long, rich history.

Whatever name you choose to put on Knoxville, dedicate some time to exploring it. The city skyline is dominated by the iconic gold-plated Sunsphere, built during the 1982 World's Fair. Along Gay Street and in the Old City downtown you will find a vibrant city scene with restaurants, bars, and concert halls that are putting Knoxville on the musical map. The University of Tennessee campus is a hotbed of athletic and cultural events. In old suburbs scattered around the city you will find jewels in the rough, including the Knoxville Zoo, Beck Cultural Center, and Ijam's Nature Center.

Knoxville is a city without pretensions. It is a place that gets better the more you get to know it.

Within a half-hour drive from Knoxville are several must-see communities with their own history and attractions. Oak Ridge is one of three places in the United States that built the components of the atomic bombs used at Hiroshima and Nagasaki, and it continues to be home to a nuclear facility. The glimpse of the United States you'll find here is unlike anything anywhere else in the nation. Sleepy Norris houses a remarkable museum about the Appalachian way of life, and Clinton is the site of a significant, but oft-overlooked, scene in the U.S. civil rights movement.

HISTORY

Knoxville's first settler was James White, who in 1786 built a fort where First Creek flows into the Tennessee River and named it after

Previous: Knoxville's Gay Street Bridge spans the Tennessee River; The Sunsphere was built for the 1982 World's Fair and is a Knoxville icon. **Above:** Giraffes can be seen at the Knoxville Zoo.

Knoxville

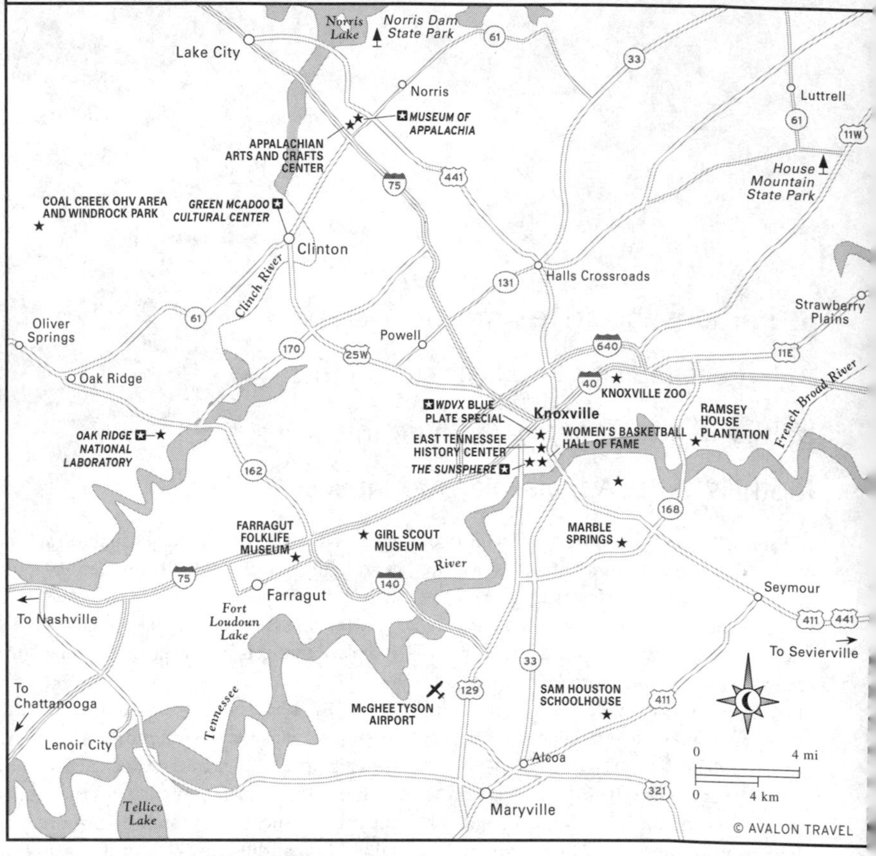

himself. In 1791, the fort was chosen as capital of the Territory South of the River Ohio and renamed after secretary of war Henry Knox. Knoxville was incorporated in 1815.

During its first 50 years, Knoxville was primarily a way station for travelers making their way along the Tennessee River or overland on stage roads.

A majority of Knoxvillians voted to secede from the Union in the June 1861 referendum. But some city residents, and most East Tennesseans who lived in the rural countryside surrounding Knoxville, supported the Union. Initially Knoxville was occupied by the Confederate Army, but remained under Union control for much of the war. Union supporters returned to the city and retaliated against the Confederate sympathizers who had had the upper hand during the early period of the war.

After the Civil War, Knoxville experienced an industrial expansion. Thanks to the railroad, the city was a major distribution center; in 1896, Knoxville was the third-largest wholesale center in the South, behind Atlanta and New Orleans.

Like any city, Knoxville was not without problems. Pollution from factories made the city air and water unhealthy. Race relations were strained, and African Americans were stripped of power by political gerrymandering and economic discrimination. As urban problems grew, the city's elite moved into suburbs farther and farther from the city center.

During the mid-20th century the trend of outward expansion continued in Knoxville. From the 1950s to the 1980s, Knoxville's downtown deteriorated as retail shops closed and people moved to the suburbs. Central Knoxville became a no-man's-land, where only downtown office workers dared to venture. In the early 1980s, Knoxville was famously dubbed "a scruffy little city."

Some people trace the present downtown renaissance to the 1982 World's Fair, when the Sunsphere and the World's Fair Park were built and 11 million people came to visit the internationally themed festival event. *Time* magazine uncharitably dubbed the event "Barn Burner in a Backwater," and the *Philadelphia Inquirer* said the grounds were built along a wasted gully of Second Creek, a place that was "like a hole in your sock."

Despite the fears that the World's Fair was overly ambitious, it did break even financially and left Knoxville with a park that the city—some 20 years later—finally decided to use to its full advantage. Over the succeeding years, downtown Knoxville has staged a comeback, with the addition of a downtown art museum, the birth of an entertainment district in the Old City, and the rebirth of Gay Street and Market Square as centers for business, commerce, and residences.

PLANNING YOUR TIME

Knoxville is an ideal destination for a long weekend: Spend a day exploring downtown attractions around Gay Street and the World's Fair Park, and then choose two destinations outside of town—such as the Museum of Appalachia, Oak Ridge, or Clinton—for your second and third days. For the best atmosphere, find a hotel within walking distance of Gay Street and the Old City so you can walk to restaurants and music venues.

Whatever you do, don't plan your trip to coincide with a University of Tennessee home football game, unless that's your purpose for coming to town. Traffic will be at its height and hotel rooms largely unavailable.

ORIENTATION

Knoxville lies on the shore of the Tennessee River, also called Fort Loudoun Lake. The original city and today's downtown center sit atop a bluff overlooking the river. The main thoroughfares through downtown are **Gay Street,** with its delightful historic storefronts, and **Henley Street,** which becomes Chapman Highway to the south and Broadway to the north. The Henley Street and Gay Street bridges are the primary routes over the Tennessee River.

Immediately west of downtown is the **World's Fair Park,** identifiable by the gold-plated Sunsphere. The **University of Tennessee** and one of the city's first suburbs, **Fort Sanders,** lie just west of the World's Fair Park. Cumberland Avenue, also known as "The Strip," is the university's main drag, and it divides UT from Fort Sanders. In recent years, many beautiful old historic homes in Fort Sanders have been torn down for the construction of condominiums.

Cumberland Avenue turns into Kingston Pike, which heads westward from UT, passing suburbs of progressive vintage, beginning with **Sequoyah Hills** and **Bearden.** This land of shopping malls, traffic jams, and sprawl is now called **West Knoxville.**

There are several pleasant historic neighborhoods north and east of the city center. **Fourth and Gill** lies north of town near Emory Place, once a commercial center at the northern end of Gay Street. **Mechanicsville,** north of Western Avenue, developed as housing near Knoxville's old industrial center and is now anchored by Knoxville College. Magnolia Avenue was the primary thoroughfare headed eastward, to neighborhoods including **Park City** and **Holston Hills.**

Sights

DOWNTOWN

Downtown Knoxville lies east of Henley Street and includes the oldest areas of the city, plus its modern-day commercial and government center.

East Tennessee History Center

There is an excellent museum about the history of East Tennessee at the **East Tennessee History Center** (601 S. Gay St., 865/215-8830, www.easttnhistory.org, 9am-4pm Mon.-Fri., 10am-4pm Sat., 1pm-5pm Sun., Mon-Sat., adults $5. seniors $4, children 16 & under free, Sun., free). The permanent exhibit, titled *Voices of the Land: The People of East Tennessee*, offers a sweeping survey of East Tennessee history, from its early Native American inhabitants to the beginnings of the modern-day tourist trade in the Great Smoky Mountains. In between, you learn about the region's groundbreaking abolitionists, its writers and musicians, and the everyday lives of residents during tumultuous periods, like the Civil War and the civil rights movement. The voices of more than 350 people are used to bring the tale to life, as are artifacts such as Davy Crockett's rifle, a ring once belonging to Cherokee "Beloved Woman" Nancy Ward, and the painting *Hauling of Marble* by Lloyd Branson. The underlying message is that East Tennessee's story cannot be lumped into that of the entire state; the region is unique.

The exhibit includes several audio and video presentations, and hundreds of panels to read and examine. Plan on spending at least two hours here.

The history center is located in the city's old customs house, a handsome white-marble structure built in 1874. For most of its life, the building housed federal offices and a U.S. post office. Later, it was a headquarters for the Tennessee Valley Authority.

The *East Tennessee Streetscape* exhibit is also on permanent view.

James White Fort

The oldest home in Knoxville is found at **James White Fort** (205 E. Hill Ave., 865/525-6514, www.jameswhitesfort.org, 9:30am-5pm

the East Tennessee History Center

Downtown Knoxville

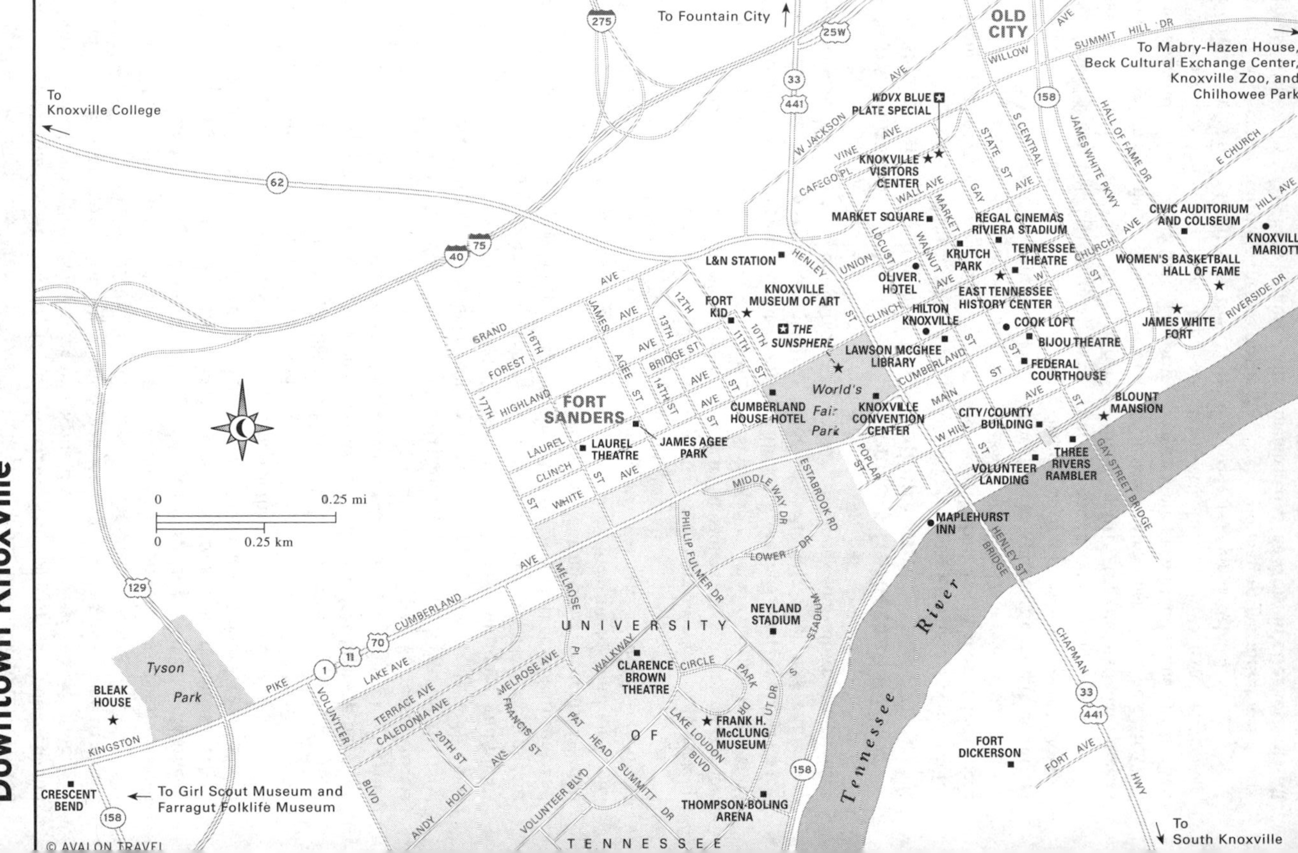

Mon.-Sat. Apr.-Nov., closed during UT home football games, 10am-4pm Mon.-Fri. Dec.-Mar., adults $7, children 5-17 $3). Gen. James White acquired more than 1,000 acres of land in 1783 under the so-called Land Grab Act passed by the North Carolina legislature. White and his wife, Mary Lawson, moved to the frontier in 1785 and constructed a log cabin near the junction of the French Broad and Holston Rivers, to the west of First Creek. Soon, White built additional log structures and protected them with a stockade; he called the place James White's Fort. Later, William Blount chose the location as the first capital of the Southwest Territory and renamed the fort Knoxville.

White hired Charles McClung to survey his 1,000 acres, and in 1791, he sold lots in the new city of Knoxville for $8 each. White donated lots for a town common, church, and cemetery, and he sold lots for Blount College for a nominal amount.

As Knoxville grew, White's rough-hewn log cabin was threatened by development. In 1906, a local citizen, Isaiah Ford, bought the fort and carefully moved the structures to a site on Woodland Avenue. In 1960, the fort was moved again to its present location on Hill Avenue. Visitors will learn about White, the establishment of Knoxville, and the rugged way of life on the Tennessee frontier.

Blount Mansion

The **Blount Mansion** (200 W. Hill Ave., 865/525-2375, www.blountmansion.org, 9:30am-5pm Tues.-Sat. summer, 9:30am-5pm Tues.-Fri., 10am-2pm Sat. Oct.-May, adults $7, seniors $6, children 6-17 and students $5) is Knoxville's best historic attraction. First built between 1792 and 1796 by territorial governor William Blount, the "mansion" underwent no fewer than six periods of construction and alteration during its lifetime. The original structure was the first frame home in Knoxville and one of the first in the whole state. The Cherokee called Blount's home the House with Many Glass Eyes because of its large glass windows.

Significant events in Tennessee history took place at Blount Mansion. It is believed that it was here that governor William Blount wrote the first Tennessee constitution. The mansion also served as the second territorial capitol of the soon-to-be state.

Blount Mansion consists today of restored living quarters, office, kitchen, and gardens, as well as a visitors center that houses exhibits about Blount and his home. Guided tours depart at the top of every hour.

Market Square

Knoxville's old **Market Square** has been given new life, thanks to downtown redevelopment over the past 20 years. Once a dirty and depressing corner of the city, Market Square is alive again with commerce. Restaurants, boutiques, and nightclubs populate the square. It is the venue for the city's farmers market on Saturday and Wednesday during the summer and fall, and it is a popular location for outdoor events and concerts as well as movie screenings during the fall.

Come here to people-watch or to soak up some of Knoxville's youthful downtown vibe.

Find Market Square near the intersection of Market Street and Union Avenue, just a few blocks behind Gay Street. It is within easy walking distance of downtown attractions.

Women's Basketball Hall of Fame

In 1892, one year after James Naismith invented basketball, a woman coach introduced the sport at Smith College in Massachusetts. The female sport underwent countless changes during its 100-plus-year history. A few of them: In 1918, bounce passes were legalized; in 1926, the first national women's collegiate championship was held; in 1962, players were permitted to "snatch" the ball from each other, and in 1976 women's basketball made its Olympic debut.

These and many other milestones are remembered at the **Women's Basketball Hall of Fame** (700 Hall of Fame Dr., 865/633-9000, www.wbhof.com, 10am-5pm Mon.-Sat. summer, 11am-5pm Tues.-Fri., 10am-5pm Sat. Sept.-Apr., adults $7.95, seniors and children 6-15 $5.95), a museum dedicated to celebrating women's achievement on the basketball court and to fostering future talent.

The Hall of Fame consists of interactive exhibits that recall the history and development of women's basketball. Visitors will hear women's basketball "inventor" Senda Berenson Abbott share her thoughts on the early days of the game. They will sit in a modern-day locker room and hear half-time talks by some of the best coaches in the modern sport. This is not just a spectator museum. Downstairs are basketball courts where you can test your skill against the sport's best, shoot into baskets from different eras in history, and try on old and new uniforms. In addition, there are exhibits about international women's basketball, the Women'omen her thoughts on the early days WNBA), and top women's basketball college programs. Finally, visitors can pay tribute to the sport's best at the 127-member hall of fame.

The Women's Basketball Hall of Fame is located in an eye-catching building near the eastern end of Knoxville's waterfront. It is home to the world's largest basketball—30 tons heavy—which protrudes from the roof.

The Hall of Fame opened in Knoxville in 1999, and there was really no better city for it. The UT Tennessee Lady Vols is one of the most successful women's basketball teams in the country. Former coach, Pat Summitt, was renowned for style and success. Current coach Holly Warlick worked with the legendary Summitt, first as a player, then as an assistant and associate head coach. Summitt is the all-time winningest coach in men's or women's collegiate basketball, and Warlick was there for 922 of the 1,071 wins collected by her mentor.

Volunteer Landing

Volunteer Landing, a one-mile city park, sits along the banks of the Tennessee River, providing a nice place to walk or bring the family.

At the eastern end of the park there is a playground and a statue symbolizing the Treaty of the Holston, which took the land on which Knoxville sits away from the Cherokee. This is where Tennessee riverboats depart.

Farther west is another playground and a series of fountains, perfect for romping around in on a hot summer day.

the Women's Basketball Hall of Fame

The Cradle of Country Music

Knoxville's place in country music history is not as well-known as that of Memphis or Nashville, but the roots of several seminal country artists are buried deep in Knoxville history. Several Knoxville institutions are also closely linked with the emergence of country music on the national stage.

The Andrew Johnson Hotel (912 S. Gay St.) is now a government office building, but for many years it was Knoxville's landmark hotel. WNOX broadcast the live Midday Merry-Go-Round from the hotel, and in 1952, Hank Williams checked in on what would be the final day of his life. It is still a matter of discussion whether Williams was alive when his teenage chauffeur put him in the backseat of a Cadillac and drove north for a gig in Canton, Ohio. During a pit stop in Oak Hill, West Virginia, the driver discovered that Williams was dead; he was just 29 years old.

In 1932, the **Tennessee Theatre** (604 S. Gay St.) hosted the first public performance by Union County native Roy Acuff, who performed in a talent contest with his band, Three Rolling Stones.

Knoxville has memorialized its musical history at the **Knoxville Music Monument** (Gay St. and Summit Hill Dr.), which features likenesses of Chet Atkins, an East Tennessee native later known as Mr. Guitar; Archie Campbell, a country music comedian and radio host from nearby Bulls Gap; and Unknown Musicians, representative of jazz, blues, country, and rock 'n' roll artists whose contributions have gone largely unwritten.

It was from a storefront on Market Square that Sam Morrison of Bell Sales Company promoted Elvis Presley's "That's All Right (Mama)" by playing it on a loudspeaker outside. Morrison sold hundreds of copies of the single, including two to an RCA talent scout. Several months later, RCA bought Presley's recording contract from Sun Studio in Memphis.

For a detailed tour of Knoxville music history, follow the Cradle of Country Music Walking Tour. A printed guide is available from the **Knoxville Visitors Center** (301 S. Gay St., 865/523-7263, www.visitknoxville.com).

There are several commercial marinas and restaurants along the park. The best way to get here is to take the pedestrian bridge over Neyland Drive, which departs from the southwestern corner of the Knoxville City/County Building along Walnut Street.

WORLD'S FAIR PARK

Lying between the University of Tennessee and downtown is the grassy, pleasant grounds of the **World's Fair Park**. There are several reasons for visitors to head to this area.

★ The Sunsphere

Knoxville's foremost landmark is the **Sunsphere** (World's Fair Park, www.worldsfairpark.org, 9am-10pm daily Apr.-Oct., 11am-6pm daily Nov.-Mar., free). Built for the 1982 World's Fair, the Sunsphere has been both a source of pride and consternation for Knoxvillians in years since. The Sunsphere, symbolic of the World's Fair theme "Energy Turns the World," is 266 feet tall. It consists of a five-story golden sphere—which the *New York Times* described as similar to a gold golf ball—perched atop a steel shaft.

After the World's Fair ended, Knoxville couldn't decide what to do with the odd monument. Ideas came and wentrestaurants.s in years since. The Sunvisitors centers center's Fair ended, Knoxville couldn't decide what to do wll together. Around the 20th anniversary of the World's Fair, the city began to think again about what it could do with this iconic landmark, and five years and $280,000 later, in time for the 25th anniversary of the fair, the city reopened the observation deck to visitors.

The observation deck is located on the fourth floor of the Sunsphere. After a long and clanky elevator ride up, you are deposited in a narrow circular room with a 360-degree view of Knoxville. It is a pretty neat view, and it puts the city in perspective. The Tennessee River sweeps southward, the University of

Tennessee sits on the river bluff, and the interstate highways slice this way and that. You look right down onto World's Fair Park, and it's like seeing the world in miniature.

Panels around the observation deck tell about some of Knoxville's attractions and history, and there is a running video with footage from the 1982 World's Fair.

During the World's Fair, it housed two restaurants; today, you'll find lounge and restaurant **Icon** (865/249-7321, knoxvilleicon.com, 4pm-midnight Tues.-Thurs., 4pm-2am Fri.-Sat., $14-26) on the fifth floor. Locals like the modern take on bar food and sandwiches, but, of course, the view steals the show here.

Other floors in the Sunsphere are rented by local businesses.

Knoxville Museum of Art

Located in a building faced dramatically with white marble and designed by New York architect Edward Larabee Barnes, the **Knoxville Museum of Art** (1050 World's Fair Park Dr., 865/525-6101, www.knoxart.org, 10am-5pm Tues.-Sat., 1pm-5pm Sun., free) is Knoxville's distinguished visual arts institution. Originally called the Dulin Gallery of Art and located in an early-20th-century mansion, the Knoxville Museum of Art moved to the World's Fair Park after the 1982 World's Fair. The current structure opened in 1990.

The museum has five galleries, an outdoor sculpture garden, gift shop, and an interactive exploratory gallery for children. From the rear of the great hall, visitors can step outside onto the museum balcony for views of the World's Fair Park and downtown Knoxville. The museum's growing permanent collection is bolstered by numerous visiting exhibitions. On Friday evenings, the museum hosts Alive After Five, with jazz performances.

UNIVERSITY OF TENNESSEE

The preeminent public university in Tennessee, the **University of Tennessee** was founded in 1784 as Blount College. Originally centered at "the hill" on the eastern end of Cumberland Avenue, UT has spread out along the entire length of Cumberland. Its colors—orange and white—were inspired by the orange and white daisies that grow outside on the hill. UT has a student enrollment of more than 27,000.

At UT, it is athletics that are truly center stage, or at least so it seems. Take, for example, the fact that in recent years UT has renamed

World's Fair Park

two major roads on campus not after prize-winning scientists or writers, but after Peyton Manning, the UT quarterback who went on to take the Indianapolis Colts to the Super Bowl (and then played for the Denver Broncos), and Phillip Fulmer, UT football's former head coach.

Frank H. McClung Museum

The best all-around museum in Knoxville, the **Frank H. McClung Museum** (1327 Circle Park Dr., 865/974-2144, http://mcclungmuseum.utk.edu, 9am-5pm Mon.-Sat., 1pm-5pm Sun., free) houses a wide variety of historical, cultural, and natural-history exhibits. Longstanding exhibits explore ancient Egypt, the native peoples of Tennessee, and the Civil War in Knoxville. Other exhibits look at Tennessee's freshwater mussels and decorative arts in the state. The museum also hosts special temporary exhibits.

Ewing Gallery

UT's art museum is the **Ewing Gallery** (1715 Volunteer Blvd., 865/974-3200, www.ewinggallery.utk.edu, 10am-5:30pm Mon., 10am-5pm Tues., Wed., Fri., 10am-7:30pm Thurs., 1pm-4pm Sun. during the school year, free). Located on the first floor of the university's Art and Architecture Building, the Ewing Gallery is named for the founder of UT's art program. Student and faculty art share the 3,000-square-foot exhibition space with visiting shows from other museums.

Fort Sanders

Knoxville's original suburb, **Fort Sanders** is a quickly disappearing historic neighborhood that lies between World's Fair Park and UT. The site of an earthen fort named for Gen. William Sanders, who died in the Battle of Knoxville in 1863, Fort Sanders was developed into a residential area beginning in the 1880s. This was home to Knoxville's upper-class merchants, mayors, university professors, and other persons of note. Author James Agee was raised in Fort Sanders.

Because of its vintage and the relative affluence of its residents, Fort Sanders's homes are lovely examples of American Victorian and early-20th-century architecture. Towers, broad porches, colorful shutters, and intricate details set Fort Sanders homes apart.

As the university grew, Fort Sanders was encroached. By the 1970s, many owners stopped occupying their homes and instead rented them to students. Homes deteriorated. During the 1990s and early years of this century, development has taken a great toll on Fort Sanders. In 1999 alone, 15 historic homes were razed to make room for condominium developments. The destruction caused an outcry, and some of Fort Sanders's historic homes are now protected from development.

You can see what is left of Fort Sanders along Highland, Laurel, Forest, and Grand Avenues, between 11th and 17th Streets. In 2009, the City of Knoxville and the Metropolitan Planning Commission began work on developing a long-range plan for sustainable development. A historical district was created, so steps are being taken to save this neighborhood and enhance its beauty. **James Agee Park,** at the corner of James Agee Street and Laurel Avenue, is located near the site of Agee's childhood home, where parts of Agee's Pulitzer Prize-winning work *A Death in the Family* are set.

WEST KNOXVILLE

Kingston Pike is the thoroughfare that connects downtown Knoxville with its western suburbs. Immediately past the University of Tennessee, Kingston Pike passes several historic homes. Farther west, you reach the communities of Bearden, West Hills, and Farragut.

Crescent Bend

The Armstrong-Lockett House, also called the romantic-sounding **Crescent Bend** (2728 Kingston Pk., 865/637-3163, www.crescentbend.com, 10am-4pm Wed.-Fri., 10am-2pm Sat., adults $7, students $5, children 12 and under free), was built in 1834 by Drury Paine Armstrong, a local merchant and public official. The brick farmhouse was once the centerpiece of a 600-acre farm. Now it consists of the elegant home and formal Italian gardens facing the Tennessee River.

Visitors who take the guided tour will see a fine collection of china, silver, and other antiques, including wallpaper originally meant for the Hermitage, President Andrew Jackson's home near Nashville.

During March and April, Crescent Bend celebrates spring with Tuliptime. This is a delightful time to visit, when more than 20,000 tulips are in bloom. During Tuliptime, the home schedules candlelight dinners, high teas, and other special events.

Bleak House

Knoxville's Confederate Memorial Hall, better known as **Bleak House** (3148 Kingston Pk., 865/522-2371, www.visitknoxville.com, 1pm-4pm Wed.-Fri., adults $5, seniors $4, discount for students and children, call first as hours are subject to change), was Gen. James Longstreet's headquarters during the Battle of Fort Sanders and other Civil War battles that took place November-December 1863. Built in 1858 for Robert Houston and Louisa Armstrong, the Italian villa-style home was named after the popular Charles Dickens novel of the day.

Visitors may be given a tour, which includes the tower where, legend has it, Confederate sharpshooters were stationed during the Civil War. There is a museum that includes Confederate artifacts.

Girl Scout Museum

Whether you have a sash of badges in the basement or just like the cookies, you'll want to make a stop here. East Tennessee's Girl Scout Council operates the **Girl Scout Museum** at Daisy's Place (1567 Downtown West Blvd., 800/474-1912, www.girlscoutcsa.org/about/museums-2, 8:30am-7pm Mon., 8:30am-4:30pm Tues.-Fri., free). The museum, one of six such Girl Scout museums in the United States, features exhibits about the history of Girl Scouting, Girl Scout cookies, and scouting in East Tennessee. You can see handbooks, songbooks, vintage uniforms, and scrapbooks dating back to 1912. There are lots of hands-on exhibits to experience. Bring a pin or trinket from your troop to swap for another.

Farragut Folklife Museum

The first U.S. admiral, David Glasgow Farragut, was born west of Knoxville in an area called Stoney Point. The family moved to New Orleans when Farragut was just five years old. When his mother died of yellow fever, Farragut was adopted by David Porter and moved to Chester, Pennsylvania. Farragut, who was born James Glasgow Farragut, changed his name to David in honor of his patron and entered the U.S. Navy. His naval career was long and proud; Farragut's military service during the Civil War led to his promotion in 1866 to the rank of admiral. It was during an August 1864 battle aboard the USS *Hartford* when Farragut reportedly said, "Damn the torpedoes, full speed ahead," a phrase that lives on today.

The town that now exists near Admiral Farragut's birthplace took his name, and now the Farragut City Hall houses a museum dedicated to this mostly unknown Tennessean. The **Farragut Folklife Museum** (11408 Municipal Center Dr., Farragut, 865/966-7057, www.townoffarragut.org, 10am-4:30pm Mon.-Fri., free) also houses exhibits about the local marble industry, the Battle of Campbell's Station, and arts, crafts, and other memorabilia from the communities of Farragut and Concord.

Farragut is located near the intersection of Kingston Pike and Campbell Station Road, off I-40 exit 373.

EAST KNOXVILLE

Magnolia Avenue (U.S. 25 West) and Martin Luther King Boulevard are two thoroughfares that head east from downtown Knoxville. Originally a series of quiet residential neighborhoods, **East Knoxville** has gradually evolved into a mixture of low-rise office buildings, modest sprawl, and historic homes.

Mabry-Hazen House Museum

The **Mabry-Hazen House Museum** (1711 Dandridge Ave., 865/522-8661, www.mabry-hazen.com, 11am-5pm Mon.-Fri., 10am-3pm Sat. Mar.-Dec., adults $10, children under 12 free) is located on a pleasant rise in East Knoxville. This handsome home, with green shutters and a wide porch, housed three generations of the same family from 1858 to 1987 and served as headquarters for both Confederate and Union troops during the Civil War. Since 1992, it has been open to the public for tours. The Mabry name comes from Joseph Alexander Mabry Jr., a businessman who donated the land for Market Square and owned the *Knoxville Whig* from 1869 to 1870. The murders of Mabry and his son on Gay Street in 1882 were documented in Mark Twain's *Life on the Mississippi*. Mabry's daughter, Alice Mabry, married Rush Strong Hazen, a wealthy businessman. The third generation to live in the house was Evelyn Montgomery Hazen, who helped author the *Harbrace College Handbook*, a reference guide used by generations of English students.

Because staff at the home is limited, the house sometimes closes for appointments or tours of the nearby **Bethel Civil War Cemetery Museum** (1917 Bethel Avenue, 10am-3pm Sat., or by appointment.) Call the museum director at 865/951-6614 if you arrive and find no tour guide. Your wait until one arrives may be just a few minutes.

Beck Cultural Exchange Center

Knoxville's foremost African American historical and cultural center is the **Beck Cultural Exchange Center** (1927 Dandridge Ave., 865/524-8461, www.beckcenter.net, 10am-6pm Tues.-Sat., free). Founded in 1975, Beck is a museum, education center, archive, and community gathering place. In addition to putting on a variety of programs throughout the year, Beck also welcomes visitors who want to learn more about Knoxville's African American history.

Among Beck's permanent exhibits is the *William H. Hastie Room*, dedicated to preserving the memory of the Knoxville native who became the first black governor of the U.S. Virgin Islands in 1946 and the first African American federal judge in the United States four years later. Beck also features a gallery with photographs and biographies of prominent African Americans from Knoxville.

The center also preserves the history of the struggle to desegregate Knoxville's public schools, the University of Tennessee, and Maryville College. There is also information about the historic desegregation of schools in Clinton, Tennessee, and the legacy of Austin High School, Knoxville's onetime all-black secondary school.

Alex Haley Square

Pulitzer Prize-winning author Alex Haley has roots in both East and West Tennessee. He grew up in Henning, a sawmill town along the Mississippi River, but he spent a great deal of his adult life in East Tennessee, giving both regions a claim to his legacy.

Haley's preeminence—but also his disarming and loving nature—is evident in a larger-than-life statue of the writer at **Alex Haley Square** (1600 Dandridge Ave.) in East Knoxville. In the figure, Haley is reading a book, seeming to invite the viewer to gather round and listen to a story. The statue, park, and playground opened in 1998, six years after Haley's death.

Knoxville Zoo

Children and adults alike love the **Knoxville Zoo** (3500 Knoxville Zoo Dr., 865/637-5331, www.knoxville-zoo.org, 9:30am-6pm daily summer, 10am-4:30pm daily winter, adults $19.95, seniors 65-plus and children 2-12 $16.95). More than 800 species of animals live at the zoo, in habitats including Grassland Africa, the Red Panda Village, and penguin pool. Giraffes, elephants, camels, giant tortoise, and gorillas are just a few of the iconic animals you will see at the zoo.

Attractions include a petting zoo, camel rides ($5), a colorful carousel ($2), and a Komodo dragon named Khaleesi.

Surrounding the zoo is Chilhowee Park, with picnic tables, walking paths, and a lake. Parking at the zoo costs $5 per vehicle.

East Tennessee Science Discovery Center

Also located at Chilhowee Park is the **East Tennessee Science Discovery Center** (Chilhowee Park, 865/594-1494, www.etdiscovery.org, 9am-12pm Mon., 9am-5pm Tues.-Fri., 10am-5pm Sat., 1pm-5pm Sun., adults $5, seniors and children 2 and older $4, children 3-4 $2), an interactive children's museum. Exhibits include aquariums, whisper dishes, a replica space shuttle, and a liquid-crystal wall. There is also a planetarium; shows are offered every hour, half of which are recommended for children over 4.

SOUTH KNOXVILLE

Chapman Highway (U.S. 441) begins south of the Henley Street Bridge and brings you to **South Knoxville**.

Ijams Nature Center

Knoxville's best outdoor attraction is **Ijams Nature Center** (2915 Island Home Ave., 865/577-4717, www.ijams.org, visitors center 9am-5pm Mon.-Sat., 11am-5pm Sun., grounds 8am-dusk daily, free). The visitors center is a modern earth-friendly construction that houses exhibits about lost animal species and the Ijams family. There is also an enclosure with a red-tailed hawk and a turkey vulture, plus native plant and animal species.

The real attraction at Ijams is the 160 acres of protected woodlands and meadows. Come here for a walk through the woods or a stroll along the Tennessee River boardwalk. The grounds also include the Ijams family historic homesite and Mead's Quarry. In total, there are seven miles of walking trails.

Ijams offers a regular schedule of special events: workshops, talks, guided walks, and fairs. Check the website for details.

Fort Dickerson Park

A Civil War-era earthen fort and three replica cannons are the historical attractions at the Knoxville city park on the south side of the Tennessee River. Panels explain the fort's significance during the battles of Knoxville that took place in the fall of 1863.

Visitors will also enjoy the view (particularly during the fall and winter, when the trees have shed their leaves) of the Knoxville skyline and the view of an old quarry.

Fort Dickerson Park is located 0.75 mile south of the Henley Street Bridge on Chapman Highway (U.S. 441). Look for the signs on your right.

Ramsey House Plantation

The home called "the most costly and most admired building in Tennessee" by the 1800 census taker is open for public tours in the 21st century. **Ramsey House Plantation** (2614 Thorngrove Pk., 865/546-0745, www.ramseyhouse.org, 10am-4pm Wed.-Sat., adults $7, children 6-12 $5) was built between 1795 and 1797 by master carpenter and cabinetmaker Thomas Hope for Col. Francis Alexander Ramsey. Built in the late Georgian style out of pink marble, Ramsey House features intricately carved consoles and other distinctive decorative features. It was said to be the first stone house in Tennessee, as well as the first home in the state with an attached kitchen.

The site of the house is near the fork of the Holston and French Broad Rivers. It was close to a site called Swan Pond, a beaver dam pond well-known by hunters and travelers. Col. Ramsey drained the pond to create pasture and farmland.

Ramsey House was the home of Colonel Ramsey's son, James G. M. Ramsey, a doctor, businessman, and author of an authoritative early history of Tennessee, *The Annals of Tennessee to the End of the Eighteenth Century.* James Ramsey and his wife, Margaret

Crozier, raised 11 children at the home (then called Mecklenburg). During the Civil War, Ramsey supported the Confederate cause and Mecklenburg was burned by Union troops, destroying a valuable library and collection of early Tennessee antiquities. During the war years and until the early 1870s, Ramsey and his family lived in Atlanta, Savannah, and parts of North Carolina. He returned to East Tennessee in the 1870s and remained here until his death in 1884.

Ramsey House was purchased in 1952 by the Association for the Preservation of Tennessee Antiquities. It has been fully restored and is open for tours, which include all rooms of the house, the kitchen, and the grounds. Ramsey House has a nice garden where heirloom vegetables and other plants are grown.

Ramsey House is located off Gov. John Sevier Highway southeast of downtown. The easiest way to get there from downtown is to take Chapman Highway (U.S. 441) south out of town. Turn left onto John Sevier Highway (Highway 168). After crossing the Tennessee River, look for Thorngrove Pike on your right and signs to Ramsey House.

Marble Springs

The early home of Tennessee's first governor, John Sevier, is preserved at **Marble Springs** (1220 W. Governor John Sevier Hwy., 865/573-5508, www.marblesprings.net, 10am-5pm Wed.-Sat., noon-5pm Sun., tours adults $5, seniors, military, and children 5-17 $4), five miles south of downtown Knoxville. Sevier received 640 acres at the foot of Bays Mountain for his service in the Revolutionary War, and he named the property Marble Springs because there were marble deposits and a large spring. By 1792, Sevier established a farm residence at Marble Springs, although he and his family lived here only periodically. They also had a home in Knoxville.

After Sevier died in 1815, the property changed hands several times until the State of Tennessee bought it in 1941. It remains state owned and is operated by the Gov. John Sevier Memorial Association. Over the years, the log home has been restored, and several historically accurate outbuildings have been added. Workshops and living-history days are offered year-round.

NORTH KNOXVILLE

Broadway (U.S. 441) travels from downtown Knoxville to Fountain City, an early suburb of the city.

Old Gray Cemetery

Just past Knoxville's scruffy Mission District—past the old 5th Avenue Hotel, a flophouse turned affordable housing project—is the **Old Gray Cemetery** (543 N. Broadway, 865/522-1424, www.oldgraycemetery.com). This 13-acre cemetery was established in 1850 and is the final resting place of hundreds of prominent and not-so-prominent city residents. It is a pleasant, wooded, parklike place—nice for a quiet stroll.

Among the buried are William "Parson" Brownlow, minister, journalist, governor, and one of Tennessee's most colorful historical characters; feminist Lizzie Crozier French; and C. C. Williams, the father of playwright Tennessee Williams.

Knoxville College

Presbyterian missionaries established a school for freedmen in Knoxville in 1875, and two years later this educational institution was designated as a college. **Knoxville College** (901 Knoxville College Dr., www.knoxvillecollege.edu, 865/524-6525) has been educating African Americans ever since. The campus is an architectural mixed bag—elegant historic structures share space with low-slung modern buildings. Budget challenges have dogged Knoxville College over its modern history, but it has persisted nonetheless in its mission to educate the next generation of black leaders.

Knoxville College is located in Mechanicsville, an old neighborhood found at the intersection of Western Avenue and Middlebrook Pike.

Entertainment and Events

Knoxville boasts a lively local music scene, plus venues that attract big-name artists. The arts scene also includes professional theater, dance, and music companies.

NIGHTLIFE

Downtown Knoxville offers plenty of options for entertainment after the sun sets.

The Old City

Near the intersection of Jackson and Depot Streets, a few blocks northeast of Gay Street, is the Old City. Knoxville's former warehouse district, near the train tracks, is now its chief entertainment district.

One favorite is **Barley's Taproom and Pizzeria** (200 E. Jackson St., 865/521-0092, cover varies), a large taproom with lots of space for mingling and a stage where folk, rock, and country performers can be found just about every night of the week. The first-floor bar offers 40 different beers on tap, a full-service restaurant, and a stage. Upstairs are pool tables and dartboards. Outside is a patio where you can witness Knoxville's skyline as you meet and mingle.

The name **Hanna's Café** (1836 Cumberland Ave. hannascafe.com, no cover) may be slightly misleading. Sure, there's a food menu packed with snacks and burgers, but the drink specials, patio, and dance floor come sundown are the primary draw for UT students.

Downtown

Downtown nightlife centers on Market Square. Here you can catch up with friends at **Preservation Pub** (28 Market Sq., 865/524-2224, cover varies). In the shadow of its exposed-brick walls decorated with funky art, you just can't help but feel cool. Fabulous drink specials; a hip, youthful attitude; and a steady stream of local rock, folk, and country acts make Preservation Pub a popular destination. It is also a restaurant.

Located in the Fourth and Gill neighborhood, a few blocks north of downtown, is the cozy and intimate **Sassy Ann's House of Blues** (820 N. 4th Ave., 865/525-5839, cover varies). As the name suggests, Sassy Ann's specializes in the blues—visiting musicians, homegrown talent, and open-mic-style performers—but they also book rock and folk artists. Housed in a 100-plus-year-old town house with two bars and lots of intimate pockets for seating, Sassy Ann's is a bit like going to a grown-up house party, with live music to boot. Generally speaking, Sassy Ann's has DJ music on Sunday and Thursday nights, with bands on Wednesdays, Fridays, and Saturdays.

The International (formerly Valarium) (940 Blackstock Ave., 865/522-2820, cover varies) is a 1,000-person standing-room-only entertainment venue located under the Western Avenue Viaduct, in a seeming wasteland of highway interchanges. Once a venue for cutting-edge bands, then a gay dance hall, this cavernous hall now books performing artists of all types. The bar is outside, allowing the owners to make this an all-ages club.

THE ARTS

Venues

Knoxville's historic theaters are something special. In 1928, the **Tennessee Theatre** (604 S. Gay St., 865/684-1200, www.tennesseetheatre.com) opened its doors on Gay Street. The theater operated nearly uninterrupted for 50 years as a movie house and concert hall. After being shuttered for a few years, the theater operated during the 1980s and 1990s, although the venue was showing its age. Thankfully, in 2001, plans were announced for a full-fledged restoration that would bring the Tennessee back to its former glory.

Since 2005, when the Tennessee Theatre reopened to praises from concertgoers and performers alike, it has become Knoxville's favorite venue for music, theater, and film. Its interior is awash with ornate detail, including plush fabric, intricate woodwork, gold-painted trim, and glistening chandeliersing the 1980sent of the Roaring Twenties, when the theater was built. The theater's 1928 original Mighty Wurlitzer pipe organ is also a showstopper.

Check the theater's website for upcoming performances for an opportunity to experience entertainment at its finest. You can also call to request a tour of the theater, if no show is in the offing.

Knoxville's best-sounding concert hall is also located on Gay Street. The **Bijou Theater** (803 S. Gay St., 865/522-0832, www.knoxbijou.com) opened in 1909 as part of the Lamar Hotel. Since then, it has been a venue for concerts and other performances. With a capacity of 700, it is more intimate than the Tennessee Theatre; it is also far less ornate and upscale. The Bijou underwent restoration in 2005, which resulted in a brand-new sound and stage system, better seats, and a new heating and air-conditioning system.

Other Knoxville concert and theater venues include the **Knoxville Civic Auditorium and Coliseum** (500 E. Church Ave., 865/215-8999, www.knoxvillecoliseum.com), which seats 2,500, and the **Thompson-Boling Arena** (1600 Phillip Fulmer Way, 865/974-0953, www.tbarena.com), with a capacity of almost 25,000.

Dance and Opera

The **Appalachian Ballet Company** (865/982-8463, www.appalachianballet.com) is a regional dance group chartered in 1972. The company puts on three performances each year, including a holiday production of *The Nutcracker.*

Circle Modern Dance (865/309-5309, www.circlemoderndance.com) is a grassroots dance group founded in 1990 to provide an alternative to mainstream dance performances. It offers classes as well as the occasional show.

The **Knoxville Opera** (865/524-0795, www.knoxvilleopera.com) offers four performances annually at the Tennessee Theatre in downtown Knoxville. The opera also organizes

The 1920s-era Tennessee Theatre hosts music, theater, and film.

the Rossini Festival and International Street Fair, an Italian street fair, every April.

Theater

The University of Tennessee's **Clarence Brown Theatre Company** (865/974-5161, www.clarencebrowntheatre.com) presents a wide repertoire of plays featuring nationally and internationally recognized guest artists. The company performs in the 570-seat Clarence Brown Theatre (1714 Andy Holt Blvd.) on the UT campus, named for UT alumnus and distinguished film director Clarence Brown. UT is also home to the 350-seat Ula Love Doughty Carousel Theater and a 100-seat black-box theater, which are used for campus productions.

Knoxville's **Carpetbag Theatre** (865/544-0447, www.carpetbagtheatre.org) is a community-based nonprofit professional theater company founded in 1970. It is one of the few tenured African American professional theater companies in the South. The company produces plays, festivals, youth-theater workshops, and other events throughout the year. Its performances often bring to the fore the stories and experiences of people who are otherwise overlooked by history.

The **Tennessee Stage Company** (865/546-4280, www.tennesseestagecompany.com) produces *Shakespeare in the Square*, a free summertime production of Shakespeare's work at Market Square Mall, and the New Play Festival, which brings to life unpublished theatrical works.

Music

★ WDVX *BLUE PLATE SPECIAL*

Back in the 1930s and 1940s, Knoxville radio station WNOX hosted a lunchtime musical variety show called the *Midday Merry-Go-Round*. Hosted by Lowell Blanchard, the show attracted hundreds of patrons and thousands more who tuned in to listen to the show live on the radio. It was a stepping stone to the Grand Ole Opry, and legendary performers like Roy Acuff, Chet Atkins, Kitty Wells, and Bill and Charlie Monroe were among the entertainers.

So when Knoxville radio station WDVX started its own lunchtime live-music program back in the 1990s, it was following in hallowed footsteps. But it also felt like something quite new and exciting for downtown Knoxville.

Today, the **WDVX *Blue Plate Special*** takes place Monday-Friday noon-1pm at the Knoxville Visitors Center at 301 South Gay Street (the building also houses the WDVX studios). The performers vary from bluegrass to Americana to rock. It is a wonderful way to pass an hour since you get to listen to live music and watch a radio show being made at the same time. The atmosphere is intimate, casual, and—at times—electric. A coffee bar serves sandwiches and drinks, but you are welcome to bring your own bag lunch as well.

KNOXVILLE SYMPHONY ORCHESTRA

Established in 1935, the **Knoxville Symphony Orchestra**, or KSO, (865/291-3310, www.knoxvillesymphony.com) is one of the oldest orchestras in the southeast. The KSO, a professional orchestra since 1973, performs its season September-May in Knoxville venues including the Civic Auditorium, the Tennessee Theatre, and the Bijou. Special guest conductors and soloists are frequent additions, and seasonal shows include the annual holiday concert.

UNIVERSITY OF TENNESSEE SCHOOL OF MUSIC

The University of Tennessee School of Music (www.music.utk.edu) puts on a full schedule of recitals and concerts during the academic year. All events are free and open to the public. They take place in one of three performance halls in the **Alumni Memorial Building** (1408 Middle Dr.).

JUBILEE COMMUNITY ARTS

One of Knoxville's finest musical institutions is **Jubilee Community Arts**, which promotes traditional Appalachian music and other folk traditions. Jubilee offers a full schedule of concerts and other special events at the **Laurel Theater** (1538 Laurel Ave., 865/522-5851, www.jubileearts.org), a 19th-century church in the Fort Sanders neighborhood that has been converted into a performance hall. The space is intimate, with excellent acoustics and a homey atmosphere. The concert schedule is heavy on regional bluegrass, folk, Americana, and country performers. It also includes Celtic, zydeco, and world music artists. Concerts are scheduled most weeks. The Jubilee Festival in March is a three-day weekend event with a smorgasbord of performances.

When the Laurel Theater is not being used for concerts, various community groups use the space for meetings and other purposes. Several community dance groups have weekly sessions here, as does the Knoxville Writer's Guild. In addition to its live performance schedule, Jubilee Community Arts works with local radio stations to produce programming for the airwaves, including the long-running *Live at Laurel* program, which features recordings of Laurel Theater concerts and is broadcast on WDVX (89.9 FM and 102.9 FM) at 7pm on Sunday.

Cinemas

First-run movies came back to downtown Knoxville with the opening of **Regal Cinemas Riviera Stadium** (510 S. Gay St., 865/522-5160), an eight-screen theater in the heart of downtown.

Knoxville's best art-house movie theater is at **Downtown West** (1640 Downtown West Blvd., 865/693-6327), in the West Hills area near West Town Mall.

FESTIVALS AND EVENTS

Spring

Knoxville's stalwart arts festival celebrated its 50th anniversary in 2010. The **Dogwood Arts Festival** (www.dogwoodarts.com) takes place in April to coincide with the springtime blooming of dogwood trees. The core of the festival is the opening of 70 miles of dogwood trails that pass through historic and architecturally significant neighborhoods and by thousands of blooming dogwood trees.

The Dogwood Arts Festival also includes a variety of art shows and other eventsoming of dogwood trees. The core of the d at promoting the arts in the community and in area schools.

In April, the Knoxville Opera organizes the **Rossini Festival** (http://www.knoxvilleopera.com/rossini/), an Italian street fair that takes place on Gay Street and at Market Square Mall in downtown Knoxville. Special wine tastings, opera performances, and European music combine with a vibrant street fair with a pronounced Mediterranean theme.

Summer

The **Kuumba Festival** is an African-inspired street festival that takes place in late June at Market Square downtown and in Chilhowee Park in East Knoxville. The event features parades, music, arts demonstrations, and vendors, all with an African theme.

The end of summer is marked annually with **Boomsday,** one of the largest fireworks displays in the nation, over the Tennessee River on Labor Day.

Shopping

DOWNTOWN

Some of Knoxville's most distinctive stores are found on Gay Street. The first **Mast General Store** (402 S. Gay St., 865/546-1336, 10am-6pm Mon.-Wed., 10am-9pm Thurs.-Sat.) opened in Valle Crucis, North Carolina, in 1883, and it sold everything that folks needed, "from cradles to caskets," as it is said. Mast is now a chain with locations in several Southern mountain cities, including Asheville, North Carolina, and Greenville, South Carolina. Like the others, Knoxville's Mast General Store sells an amazing variety of sturdy clothing and footwear, classic cookware like cast-iron skillets, old-fashioned candy, and games.

Also on Gay Street, the **East Tennessee Historical Society Gift Shop** (601 S. Gay St., 865/215-8824, 10am-4pm Mon.-Sat., 1pm-5pm Sun.) has a good collection of books about Tennessee, local arts and crafts, and T-shirts from the 1982 World's Fair.

Nearby Market Square is dotted with fun boutiques, as well as the open-air **Market Square Farmers Market** (marketsquarefarmersmarket.org, 11am-2pm Wed., 9am-2pm Sat. May-Nov.). **Bliss** and **Bliss Home** (24 and 29 Market Sq., 865/329-8868, www.shopinbliss.com, 10am-9pm Mon.-Thurs., 10am-9pm Fri.-Sat., 11am-8pm Sun.) stock shelves of crave-worthy things for yourself and for gifts.

GALLERIES

Gay Street is major contributor to Knoxville's vibrant gallery scene. Knoxville's Arts & Culture Alliance manages an art gallery in an old furniture store at the **Emporium Center for Arts & Culture** (100 S. Gay St., 865/523-7543, www.theemporiumcenter.com, 9am-5pm Mon.-Fri., 11am-3pm Sat., free). Home to two art galleries, the Emporium puts on 12 different shows annually that showcase local and regional arts.

The Emporium also provides studio space for area artists and office space for arts organizations. The galleries are open until 9pm on the first Friday of each month.

Located next door to the Emporium galleries is a downtown satellite of UT's Ewing Gallery. The **University of Tennessee Downtown Gallery** (106 S. Gay St., 865/673-0802, 11am-6pm Wed.-Fri., 10am-3pm Sat., free) has a modern, fresh feel. Student and faculty artwork are exhibited alongside shows of regional and national artists.

The Art Market (422 S. Gay St., 865/525-5265, artmarketgallery.net, 11am-6pm, Fri. 11am-9pm Tues.-Thurs. and Sat., 1pm-5pm Sun.) is a stalwart artists' co-operative that traces its roots to the 1982 World's Fair. More than 60 area painters, sculptors, jewelers, weavers, and printmakers display their work at this attractive and welcoming space.

BOOKSTORES

Mid Mod Collective (formerly Central Street Books) (1617 N. Central St., 865/573-9959, 11am-6pm Sun.-Sat.) is an above-average used-book store with a notable collection of local books and collector's editions.

Another option for used books is **McKay's** (230 Papermill Place Way, 865/588-0331, 9am-9pm Mon.-Thurs., 9am-10pm Fri.-Sat., 11am-7pm Sun.), a warehouse-size bookstore that is well organized and well loved by readers of all stripes. McKay's also has a location in Nashville.

The closest new-book store to downtown Knoxville is **Barnes and Noble** (8029 Kingston Pk., 865/670-0773, 9am-9pm Mon.-Thurs., 9am-11pm Fri.-Sat., 11am-8pm Sun.), located next to West Town Mall.

Sports and Recreation

Sports may be Knoxville's single biggest draw. The University of Tennessee Vols play football at Neyland Stadium, on the banks of the Tennessee River. The Lady Vols basketball team is the most successful sports team at UT. There are sporting events and sports museums and, of course, plenty of sports fans.

But Knoxville is more than just UT sports. There are nice parks, too.

PARKS

Knoxville has more than two dozen city parks. For a complete list of parks and facilities, visit the city website (www.cityofknoxville.org/parks/). For information on bicycling through them, or finding a bicycle-sharing program, contact the **Knoxville Regional Bicycle Program** (cycleushare.utk.edu).

One good way to get out and explore is to stop at the **Outdoor Knoxville Adventure Center**. The **Billy Lush Board Shop** (900 Volunteer Landing, 865/332-5874, billylushboards.com) rents paddleboards for use on the Tennessee River, bikes, and other outdoor toys from this location when the weather cooperates. Billy Lush also has a location in Sevierville (1590 Dyke Rd.). **Paddleboard Knoxville** (865/771-4787, paddleboardknoxville.com) offers lessons and rentals for those with prior paddleboard experience.

World's Fair Park

Knoxville's best city park is the 10-acre **World's Fair Park**, which connects downtown with UT and brings new life to the site of the 1982 World's Fair. The park consists of walking paths, fountains, a man-made lake, grassy spaces, and a statue of Russian musician and composer Sergei Rachmaninoff, whose last public performance was at UT on February 17, 1943. The fountains are a popular attraction on hot summer days, when families come to romp in the water.

North of the fountains and adjacent to the East Tennessee Veterans Memorial is a 4,150-square-foot playground that features a climbing wall, neutron spinner, several slides, several playground rides to test balance and agility, and more. Features included were chosen by local elementary school students for their fun factor.

Tyson Park

Located at the western edge of the UT campus along Alcoa Highway, (2351 Kingston Pike), **Tyson Park** is a venerable city park with playgrounds, picnic tables, walking paths, tennis courts, and a skate park.

Sequoyah Park

Located in West Knoxville on the banks of the Tennessee River, 87-acre **Sequoyah Park** is a good place for walking, biking, or relaxing outdoors. There are playgrounds, baseball/softball fields, and lots of open space ideal for a picnic or game of Frisbee.

Sequoyah is located at 1400 Cherokee Boulevard. Get there by driving west on Kingston Pike and turning left onto Cherokee Boulevard.

Chilhowee Park

Chilhowee Park (3301 Magnolia Ave., 865/215-1450, www.chilhoweepark.org), located off Magnolia Avenue in East Knoxville, was the city's first major park. The first streetcar line in the city connected downtown with Chilhowee, and on weekends, holidays, and hot summer days, throngs would come here to picnic, splash in the lake, or watch baseball games, horse races, or concerts.

Today the reasons to head here are spectator driven rather than recreational, such as tractor pulls and gun expos. The Knoxville Zoo, Knox County Fairgrounds, and East Tennessee Science Discovery Center all abut Chilhowee Park for a nearby recreation bonanza.

Greenways

Knoxville has an expanding array of greenways that connect parks and make it possible to get around the city on foot or by bike. Those of special note include the **James White Greenway** that originates at the South Knoxville bridge and follows the Tennessee River to Volunteer Landing downtown. On the other end of Volunteer Landing, you can follow the **Neyland Greenway** to Tyson Park and onward to the **Third Creek Greenway,** which connects with both the **Bearden Greenway** and the **Sequoyah Greenway.**

On the south side of the river, the **Will Skelton Greenway** begins at Island Home Park, passes through Ijams Nature Center, and follows the shore of the Tennessee to the Forks of the River.

For information about Knoxville greenways, go to www.cityofknoxville.org/greenways or call 865/215-4311 for the Parks and Recreation Department.

Knoxville Botanical Garden and Arboretum

The **Knoxville Botanical Garden and Arboretum** (2743 Wimpole St., 865/862-8717, www.knoxarboretum.org, sunrise-sunset daily, free) is a dream that is slowly taking shape. Located on grounds once occupied by a plant nursery, the gardens are an effort by volunteers and family members of the former landowners.

The grounds are leafy and pleasant, though not very manicured. It is a pleasant place to come for a walk. Staff members are generally present on weekdays 9am-5pm; at other times the garden is unattended.

SPECTATOR SPORTS

Watching sports in Knoxville means one thing: the University of Tennessee Volunteers. Knoxville is the epicenter of Big Orange country, and this is a city that is serious about sports. UT is a member of the competitive Southeastern Conference.

Football

UT's biggest spectator sport is football. Neyland Stadium, home of the **Tennessee Volunteers football** team, is awash with bright orange on game days. Named for Gen. Robert Neyland, head coach of the UT football team from 1926 to 1952, Neyland Stadium has a capacity of just over 100,000. Most home games sell out.

The regular college football season runs September-November. Single tickets go on sale in late July or early August for the upcoming fall season and cost $45-90. You can buy tickets from the **UT box office** (1600 Phillip Fulmer Way, 865/656-1200, www.utsports.com). On game days, tickets are sold at Gate 21 at Neyland Stadium beginning four hours before kickoff.

A word to the wise: If you are not coming into town to watch the football game, avoid downtown Knoxville on a game day. The entire city becomes a knot of congestion and Big Orange mania on these days, and if you don't want to be part of it, you'll hate the experience. Longtime residents who don't particularly fancy college football say that game days are good times to go to the mall, visit the Great Smoky Mountains National Park, or just stay home. Whatever you do, plan ahead.

Basketball

In Knoxville, UT's **Volunteers** men's basketball team plays second fiddle to the legendary **Lady Vols**, eight-time national champions who have been leaders of the women's college basketball pack for a generation. The Lady Vols, under the leadership of coach Holly Warlick, play home games at Thompson-Boling Arena November-March.

Single-game tickets go on sale in October and cost $45-80 depending on your seat and the opponent. Buy tickets from the **UT box office** (1600 Phillip Fulmer Way, 865/565-1200, www.utsports.com).

Other UT Sports

UT plays a full schedule of sports: track and field, baseball, softball, tennis, soccer, rowing, tennis, swimming, golf, and volleyball. The UT women's softball team has performed well in recent years and is developing a reputation as a Southeastern Conference leader. UT tennis and track have good records, and in 2010 the university built a new golf center to bolster its program in that sport. For a full rundown of UT sports events, contact the athletics box office (1600 Phillip Fulmer Way, 865/656-1200, www.utsports.com).

Ice Hockey

The **Knoxville Ice Bears** (www.knoxvilleicebears.com) play at the Knoxville Civic Coliseum. The Ice Bears are a member of the Southern Professional Hockey League and play October-April.

TOURS

The **Three Rivers Rambler** (Volunteer Landing, 865/524-9411, www.threeriversrambler.com, adults $26.50, seniors $25.50, children 3-12 $15.50, toddlers 1-2 $7.50) is an 11-mile scenic railroad excursion that departs from downtown Knoxville. The ride travels along the Tennessee River past Island Home airport to the confluence of the Holston and French Broad Rivers. The journey lasts 90 minutes and takes you past farmland and old quarries. The open-air car is a real treat in pleasant weather.

Excursions take place on holiday weekends such as Father's Day, Independence Day, and Halloween. Call ahead for a current schedule. You can reserve tickets online or up to 30 minutes before departure at the ticket counter.

To get to the Three Rivers Rambler, take Neyland Drive (Highway 158) along the Tennessee River. Look for parking lot C-18 on the shore side of the road, where Rambler guests may park for free.

The **Tennessee Riverboat Company** (300 Neyland Dr., 865/525-7827, www.tnriverboat.com) offers dinner cruises and daytime sightseeing cruises down the Tennessee River on an old-fashioned paddleboat.

Accommodations

On the up side, Knoxville's downtown hotel rooms run a bit cheaper than those in other major Tennessee cities. On the down side, the city has one of the highest combined sales- and room-tax rates in the state: 17.25 percent. Be sure to figure this in when planning your budget.

DOWNTOWN

There is a pleasant array of boutique and chain hotels in downtown Knoxville, many of which are convenient to Gay Street, Market Square, and the riverfront.

$100-150

Knoxville's most distinctive hotel is a bit hard to find. The renovated and renamed ★ **Oliver Hotel** (407 Union Ave., 865/521-0050, www.theoliverhotel.com, $135-278) is located just around the corner from Market Square, but the 1876 town house easily blends into its surroundings. Built by German baker Peter Kern in the 19th century, the former St. Oliver was converted into a hotel for the 1982 World's Fair. It is not well advertised, but patrons find it nonetheless. Far from the cookie-cutter hotel, the Oliver offers a superior location and genuinely friendly service. Its 24 guest rooms have elegant beds, refrigerators, wet bars, and coffee service. Perhaps the best perk is the downstairs library, with soft couches and inviting reading nooks that beg you to come in and sit a spell. Parched? Stop in **Peter Kern Library** (8am-close daily), which serves coffee and espresso by day and later transitions into a speakeasy-style cocktail lounge by night.

Offering an ideal location and intimate, personalized service, the ★ **Maplehurst Inn** (800 W. Hill Ave., 865/254-5240, www.maplehurstinn.com, $79-145) is worth considering. Each of the 11 guest rooms has a private bath and personalized touches to make you feel like you're at home. Breakfast is served in a cozy dining room overlooking the Tennessee River. Maplehurst dates from the early 20th century, when the town house was built for a wealthy merchant. It was converted to a bed-and-breakfast for the 1982 World's Fair and remains one of the only bed-and-breakfasts in downtown Knoxville.

Located at the north end of downtown, near the Old City and Gay Street, is the **Crowne Plaza Knoxville** (401 W. Summit Hill Dr., 865/522-2600, $134-174). This 197-room high-rise hotel has full business services, an indoor pool and fitness center, 24-hour lounge, and updated guest rooms.

$150-200

Located in a pyramid-shaped building on the Knoxville waterfront, the ★ **Knoxville Marriott** (501 East Hill Ave. 865/637-1234, $119-199) is one of the city's most distinctive landmarks. The unusual design creates a lofty lobby and gives many of the guest rooms impressive river views. In addition to novelty, the Marriott also offers its guests a slew of thoughtful amenities especially designed for business travelers. There is an outdoor swimming pool, fitness center, and full-service salon on-site. There are also two restaurants, a gift shop, and lots of meeting space. The Knoxville Marriott is located next door to the Women's Basketball Hall of Fame and is within walking distance of downtown attractions like Blount Mansion and James White Fort.

The **Hilton Knoxville** (501 W. Church Ave., 865/523-2300, $99-199) is a high-rise hotel located in the midst of downtown office buildings. It is a few blocks from Gay Street and Market Square Mall. The Hilton offers guest rooms, suites, and executive guest rooms with upgraded amenities and the best views of the city. There is a business center, fitness room, pool, cribs and high chairs for children, an on-site ATM, car rental, and café.

Over $200

Feel like part of Knoxville's downtown renaissance at **Cook Loft** (722 S. Gay St., 865/310-2216, www.cookloft.com, $495), an urban guesthouse and event venue. Skylights, hardwood floors, high ceilings, exposed-brick walls, large windows, and sleek lines bring the loft concept to life. Two bedrooms and a spacious living room invite you to relax and spread out. The kitchen is well furnished with restaurant-grade appliances, but you probably won't be doing much cooking with all the great restaurants in your backyard. Weekly rates ($2,275) are also available.

UNIVERSITY OF TENNESSEE

$100-150

Located near the World's Fair Park on the edge of Fort Sanders, the **Cumberland House Hotel** (1109 White Ave., 865/971-4663, $110-175) is a Sheraton. The 130 guest rooms have flat-screen televisions, coffeemakers, hair dryers, and CD players. Suites with kitchenettes and couches are available. The hotel, built in 2005, boasts an on-site restaurant as well as a fitness center. Cumberland House is convenient to UT and to Neyland Stadium.

WEST KNOXVILLE

$100-150

There's no shortage of chain hotels and chain restaurants in the development near Turkey Creek Medical Center. But that means you get reliably clean, safe, albeit not necessarily interesting, places to sleep. Top among them is the **Homewood Suites** (10935 Turkey Dr., 865/777-0375, $109-209). A friendly staff, easy parking, and free access to a nearby gym make it an good place to stay.

Food

Knoxville dining is impossible to pigeonhole. Downtown eateries cater to the business lunch crowd, college students, and downtown's new young professional residents. Older neighborhoods outside of the city center are home to hole-in-the-wall eateries that defy expectation.

Whatever you do, don't head straight for the familiar chain restaurant. Explore a bit; you'll be richly rewarded.

DOWNTOWN

Gay Street, the Old City, and Market Square have a large concentration of restaurants that cater to all tastes and budgets.

Casual

For coffee, baked treats, and sandwiches, grab a table at **Old City Java** (109 S. Central St., 865/523-9817, 7am-10pm Sun.-Sat., $4-9). Hardwood floors, plenty of cozy tables, and wireless Internet make this a popular place to while away a few hours.

Market Square's most celebrated restaurant is ★ **The Tomato Head** (12 Market Sq., 865/637-4067, www.thetomatohead.com, 11am-10pm Mon.-Thurs., 11am-11pm Fri., 9am-11pm Sat., 9am-9pm Sun., $4-9), which opened its doors downtown long before it was cool. Originally a pizza joint, The Tomato Head now serves soup, sandwiches, salads, burritos, and pizza made with only the best organic and otherwise pure-at-heart ingredients. The results are way above average. Vegetarians and meat eaters can rejoice, for options range from a vegetarian sandwich made with flavorful tofu to a roast beef sandwich heaped with meat. The pizza is still mighty popular, and for good reason. The restaurant offers 14 official varieties, but you can build your own pie from a list of 45 different toppings (homemade lamb sausage, anyone?). The Tomato Head is generally crowded and noisy. You step to the counter, order, and pay, and then one of the low-key staff members will bring your order to the table. It's a good meeting place and also a great place for a quick solo lunch. The owners opened another location at the Gallery Shopping Center in West Knoxville (7240 Kingston Pike #172, 865/584-1075). They also own the popular Flour Head bakery.

The **Downtown Grill & Brewery** (424 S. Gay St., 865/633-8111, 11am-midnight Sun.-Thurs., 11am-1am Fri.-Sat., $9-18) is as popular for its selection of handcrafted brews as it is for its easy bar-style menu. Mesquite-grilled steak, jumbo pasta plates, pizza, and fajitas all come with a recommendation from the chef for the right beer accompaniment. With outdoor sidewalk seating and a prime location on Gay Street, this is a popular restaurant to meet and mingle.

Pete's Coffee Shop (540 Union Ave., 865/523-2860, 6:30am-2:30pm Mon.-Fri., 7am-2pm Sat., $4-10) is the best downtown destination for diner-style breakfasts and plate lunches. Located in a storefront a few blocks from Market Square, Pete's attracts a loyal following among downtown office workers and new residents. It is the type of place that offers you a bottomless cup of joe and no-nonsense food like club sandwiches, fried chicken, and omelets.

Contemporary

The conceit of **Five Bar** (430 S. Gay St. 865/219-1676, five-bar.com, 5pm-10pm Sun.-Thurs., 5pm-midnight Fri.-Sat., 10am-3pm Sun., $14-29) is that there are only five entrées (and five appetizers) on the menu every day, along with five red wines and five white wines. That might sound limiting, but everything is carefully chosen so that there is plenty to tempt you. The restaurant, which is inside the old Tailor Loft building, has a focus on Gulf seafood. There are also

The menu at Five Bar features tasty eats and drinks.

locations in Chattanooga, as well as in Florida and Alabama. Look up: The décor includes more chandeliers than you've likely seen in one place.

Modern twists on Southern classics preside at **Knox Mason** (131 S. Gay St. 865/544-2004, knoxmason.com, 4pm-close Tues.-Thurs., 4pm-midnight Fri., 10am-2pm and 4pm-midnight Sat., 10am-2pm Sun., $17-24). Wash down dishes made with locally sourced ingredients with modern riffs on classic cocktails. The menu changes seasonally, but expect certain staples, like dishes made with Jack Daniel's and local produce, to stick around.

Japanese

Handcrafted sushi along with cuisine that fuses Japanese, Korean, and Spanish ingredients and styles, that is what **Nama** (506 S. Gay St., 865/633-8539, www.namasushibar.com, 11am-midnight Mon.-Thur., 11am-1am Fri.-Sat., noon-10pm Sun., $8-25), a trendy sushi house on Gay Street, offers. The enlightened business set dines here at lunchtime; at night it attracts a youthful, well-heeled crowd. The half-price maki happy hour 3pm-6pm is a good deal for the budget diner.

Sandwiches

Hefty sandwiches on home-baked bread keep the patrons coming to venerable **Steamboat Sandwiches** (2423 North Central Ave., 865/546-3333, 10am-6pm Mon.-Sat., $5-8). The Steamboat is an oversized sandwich packed with ham, Genoa salami, and Swiss cheese, finished with a mild hot sauce, mayonnaise, mustard, and pickle. Thankfully for those with smaller appetites, you can also order a half size.

OLD CITY

Breakfast

For more than a morning muffin, try **OliBea** (119 S. Central St. 865/200-5450, olibea.net, 7am-1pm, Mon.-Fri., 8am-2pm Sat.-Sun., $7-12), a cute-as-can-be café in Old City. Order specials such as breakfast tacos or huevos rancheros or compose your own plate from the a la carte offerings of biscuits, potatoes, breakfast meats, and eggs. There are plenty of vegetarian options, such as tofu chorizo and tempeh bacon.

English

Who knew that English cuisine would have its day? ★ **The Crown & Goose** (123 S. Central St., 865/524-2100, 11am-10pm Mon.-Wed., 11am-11pm Thurs.-Sat., 11am-3pm Sun., $8-28) in the Old City is proving that Welsh rarebit, fish-and-chips, and bangers and mash are indeed good food. But to be fair, The Crown & Goose is far more than British Isle pub food. It has adopted the best of the Continent, as well, and put it on display in dishes like spring vegetable and wild mushroom risotto, San Marzano tomato and Stilton bisque, and the Frenchman's Lunch, a European cheese board served with bread. Best of all, the Crown & Goose has a stylish but unpretentious atmosphere. This is a nice choice for an unexpectedly good dinner.

UNIVERSITY OF TENNESSEE

Fusion

Knoxville's best restaurant for vegetarians is the **Sunspot** (2200 Cumberland Ave., 865/637-4663, 11am-10pm Mon., Tues. & Thurs., 11am-11pm Wed., Fri. and Sat., 10am-10pm Sun., limited late-night menu, $8-17), an institution on the UT strip that features eclectic cuisine with strong Southwestern and Latin American influences. For vegetarians there is the baked enchilada, the Tofu Tier (a stack of baked tofu and fried eggplant in a savory miso sauce), and an awesome veggie burger. Carnivores have options like pan-seared tilapia served over cheese grits, and Pasta Rustica, chorizo sausage and red peppers served in a spicy tomato sauce. There are dozens of beers on tap and in the bottle.

WEST KNOXVILLE

Fine Dining

For a taste of Knoxville's most elegant food, make reservations at **The Orangery** (5412 Kingston Pk., 865/588-2964, 11:30am-2pm and 5:30pm-10pm Mon.-Thurs., 11:30am-2pm and 5:30pm-11pm Fri., 5:30pm-11pm Sat., 11am-2pm Sun., lunch $9-14, dinner $23-44). A French-inspired menu, impeccable wine list, and refined atmosphere make for a luxurious dining experience. Come for lunch for salad Niçoise, roasted-vegetable ravioli, and sautéed shrimp. Dinner specialties include veal porterhouse, prime New York strip, buffalo with caramelized shallots, and elk chop with vegetable puree. Bet you can't get that at home. Also consider the $35 prix fixe menu, which begins with an amuse-bouche and ends four courses later with desserts such as raspberry tiramisu or an amaretto brownie served with whipped cream and caramel pecan sauce.

Italian

The best New York-style pizzas, handcrafted calzones, and other authentic Italian favorites are offered at **Savelli's** (3055 Sutherland Ave., 865/521-9085, 11am-2pm and 4pm-9pm Mon.-Fri., 4pm-9pm Sat., $9-19). This homey restaurant is small and often crowded, for good reason: Savelli's serves made-from-scratch Italian food at good prices. Beer is served, but bring your own wine.

SOUTH KNOXVILLE

Steak

Beef lovers rule at **Ye Olde Steak House** (6838 Chapman Hwy., 865/577-9328, 4:30pm-9pm Sun.-Thurs., 4:30pm-9:30pm Fri.-Sat., $12-35), where the menu features nearly a dozen different cuts of beef, including a generous hand-patted burger. Seafood and chicken are also served. Ye Olde Steak House is a family-owned steak house set in a Tudor-style home (hence the name). It is a funky, family-friendly destination for diners with big appetites.

Beer is served at Ye Olde Steak House, but liquor and wine are not. You may bring your own.

Middle Eastern

For a dining experience like no other, head directly to ★ **King Tut Grill** (4132 Martin Mill Pk., 865/573-6021, 11:30am-9pm Sun.-Thurs., 11:30am-10pm Fri.-Sat., $11-30), a family-owned restaurant in otherwise unremarkable Vestal, a few miles south of the Henley Street Bridge. King Tut's has established a loyal following thanks largely to the charisma of its owner, Mo, who serves drinks in flower vases, provides suggestions for what to order, and is famous for sending out extra food to his favored customers. Mo and his family offer traditional diner-style meals—hamburgers, meat loaf, baked chicken, and the like—to appease the locals, but the reason to come here is to eat home-style Egyptian fare. The daily menu offers a handful of such favorites, like falafel sandwiches, an Egyptian platter, and the best Greek salad in Knoxville. But it is on Mo's Middle Eastern night that he and his family go all out with stuffed grape leaves, homemade *basboosa,* and the works. Believe what they tell you: This is a restaurant not to be missed.

EAST KNOXVILLE

Dessert

Buttermilk Sky Pie Shop (buttermilk-skypie.com), a husband-and-wife venture paying homage to the pie recipes of their respective grandmothers, has locations in Turkey Creek (11525 Parkside Drive, 865/966-5900, 10am-7:30pm Sun.-Thurs., 10am-9pm Fri.-Sat.) and **Bearden** (5400 Kingston Pike, 865/330-3694, 8:30am-7pm Sun.-Thurs., 8:30am-10pm Fri.-Sat.). Fruit varieties as well as chocolate meringue, coconut cream and pecan come in standard-size pies as well as 4-inch diameter Cuties Pies.

Southern

Arguably Knoxville's best meat-and-three Southern-food house, **Chandlers** (3101 E. Magnolia Ave., 865/595-0212, 11am-3pm Mon., 11am-7:30pm Tues.-Thurs., 11am-8:30pm Fri., noon-8:30pm Sat., noon-6pm Sun., $4-10) is a cafeteria-style restaurant where workingmen and businesspeople rub elbows when the dinner bell rings. The fried chicken is always reliable and comes with sides like hot rolls, collard greens, fried okra, and stewed apples.

NORTH KNOXVILLE

Diners

★ **Litton's** (2803 Essary Dr., 865/688-0429, 10:30am-8:30pm Mon.-Thurs., 10:30am-9:30pm Fri.-Sat., $7-17) is a North Knoxville institution where Knoxvillians go for the city's best burgers, blue-plate lunches, and homemade dessert. Hand-cut fries, jumbo onion rings, red velvet cake, and baked sweet potatoes are some of the things that keep people coming back to Litton's again and again. A family restaurant that began as a humble grocery in 1946, Litton's is worth the drive. To get there, drive north on Broadway (U.S. 441), passing the I-640 overpass. Litton's is located across the street from the Fountain City Park.

Information and Services

VISITOR INFORMATION

For information about Knoxville, contact the **Knoxville Tourism & Sports Corporation** (865/523-7263 or 800/727-8045, www.knoxville.org).

Downtown Knoxville (17 Market Sq., 865/637-4550, www.downtownknoxville.org) promotes the city center by publishing maps and guides, and maintaining a website.

The **Knoxville Visitors Center** (301 S. Gay St., 865/523-7263, 8:30am-5pm Mon.-Fri., 9am-5pm Sat., noon-4pm Sun.) is at the corner of Gay Street and Summit Hill Drive. This is the place to pick up information and maps, but it is also a Knoxville gift shop and bookstore, wireless Internet hot spot, and the venue of the weekday WDVX *Blue Plate Special*, a midday concert and live radio broadcast. The coffee bar serves hot beverages, basic sandwiches, and sweets.

NEWSPAPERS

Knoxville's daily paper is the ***Knoxville News Sentinel*** (www.knoxnews.com). Its alternative weekly, ***Metropulse*** (www.metropulse.com), is a better read. Smart commentary, up-to-date entertainment listings, and columns like "Secret History" make it great. Pick yours up free on Wednesday at local groceries, coffee shops, and restaurants.

RADIO

The Knoxville radio dial is crowded with the usual suspects, but a few frequencies are worth seeking out. Chief among them is **WDVX** (89.9 FM and 102.9 FM), a community-supported grassroots radio station that plays a mix of early country, contemporary Americana, and other roots music.

WUOT (91.9 FM) is the university's public radio station. It airs NPR news programs and classical music.

LIBRARIES

Knoxville's main public library is the **Lawson McGhee Library** (500 W. Church Ave., 865/215-8750, 9am-8pm Mon.-Thurs., 9am-5:30pm Fri., 10am-5pm Sat., 1pm-5pm Sun.). It has public Internet access.

GAY AND LESBIAN RESOURCES

In 2012, standard-bearer *The Advocate* named Knoxville the eighth most gay-friendly city in the United States, citing the university's LGBT groups, the Tennessee Valley Unitarian Universalist Church (www.tvuuc.org), and the gay softball league as some of the evidence of the welcoming community.

One place to network with LGBT people is at the **Metropolitan Community Church** (7820 Redeemer Ln., 865/531-2539, www.mccknoxville.org) in West Knoxville.

Getting There and Around

GETTING THERE

Air

The **McGhee Tyson Airport** (TYS, www.tys.org) is the Knoxville area's airport. It is located 12 miles south of the city in Blount County.

A half dozen airlines serve McGhee Tyson with direct flights from 20 U.S. cities, including Orlando, Dallas, Houston, Denver, Memphis, Chicago, Cleveland, St. Paul, New York, Philadelphia, and Washington DC. Airlines with service to Knoxville include American Airlines, United, Delta, American, Continental, Northwest, and Allegiant Air.

Taxis and car rentals are available at the airport. To get to downtown Knoxville from McGhee Tyson, take Alcoa Highway (U.S. 129) north to the city.

Car

Two major interstate highways cross in Knoxville. I-75 is a north-south highway that connects with Lexington, Kentucky, in the north and Chattanooga to the south. I-40 is an east-west thoroughfare. About 35 miles east of Knoxville I-40 peels off and heads into North Carolina, while I-81 heads to the Tri-Cities and points northeast. I-40 west heads to Nashville and Memphis.

Bus

Greyhound (www.greyhound.com) serves Knoxville with bus service to Nashville, Chattanooga, Asheville, Atlanta, and many other cities. The **Greyhound station** (100 East Magnolia Ave., 865/525-9483) is on Magnolia Avenue.

GETTING AROUND

Driving

Knoxville is a city where everyone drives to get where they're going. Sprawling suburbs, shopping malls, and the interstate are evidence of this.

I-640 is a bypass interstate that makes a circle on the northern fringe of Knoxville and allows I-40 through traffic to avoid downtown. Part of I-640 is also I-275.

While the interstate is efficient, there are good reasons to get off the highway. Thoroughfares like Cumberland/Kingston Pike, Chapman Highway/Henley Street/Broadway, and Central, Magnolia, and Western Avenues will give you a better sense of the character and geography of Knoxville. And with the possible exception of Kingston Pike, there's likely to be less traffic, too.

PARKING

Drive around downtown searching for a meter, or park in one of the many paid parking lots downtown. No matter what you do, all-day parking in Knoxville will rarely cost you more than $6 per day (and free parking is still very much a possibility, unlike many big cities). ParkDowntownKnoxville.com is a good resource for finding garages and lots.

Public Transportation

The **Knoxville Trolley Line** (865/637-3000, www.katbus.com) offers free air-conditioned easy transit throughout downtown Knoxville most weekdays. The **Vol Line** (7am-6pm Mon.-Thurs., 7am-10pm Fri., 9am-10pm Sat.) connects UT and the World's Fair Park with downtown, including Gay Street. The **Downtown Loop** (6am-6pm Mon.-Fri.) connects Hall of Fame Drive and the Civic Coliseum with Henley Street and downtown. The **Gay Line** runs on Gay Street to Hill (7am-6pm Mon.-Thurs, 7am-10pm Fri., 9am-10pm Sat.).

Most Knoxville Trolleys are red, although sometimes orange Knoxville Transit Authority vans fill in. They stop at locations designated by a trolley sign.

Around Knoxville

CLINTON

★ Green McAdoo Cultural Center

In 1955, Green McAdoo School was the segregated primary school for Clinton, a mill town of 4,000 people located about 20 miles northwest of Knoxville. Under the "separate but equal" policy of the segregationist South, graduates of the black primary school were bused to Knoxville's all-black Austin High School for their secondary education.

Fifty years later, the school building became the **Green McAdoo Cultural Center** (101 School St., 865/463-6500, www.greenmcadoo.org, 10am-5pm Tues.-Sat., free), which records and celebrates the remarkable story of the integration of Clinton's high school back in 1956. Don't speed, or you'll miss it'll miss itebrates the remarkable story of the integration

Tales of school desegregation in the South typically begin with Little Rock, Arkansas. But they really ought to begin with Clinton. That's because even before the Little Rock Six entered Little Rock Central High School in the fall of 1958, there were black and white students attending Clinton High School together in rural Tennessee.

In 1951, five black high school students petitioned the Anderson County Board of Education for the right to attend all-white Clinton High School. At this time, black students in Clinton were bused a long 18 miles into Knoxville to attend the all-black Austin High School.

At first, the students lost their suit. U.S. District Judge Robert Taylor declared that the bussing arrangement met the requirements of separate but equal. However, when the U.S. Supreme Court decided the landmark *Brown vs. Board of Education* in the spring of 1954, Judge Taylor reversed his earlier ruling and ordered that Clinton High School be integrated at the beginning of the school term in September.

What followed is a remarkable story, recounted at the cultural center through newspaper clippings, video remembrances by the participants, and evocative photographs of the events. Integration went smoothly at first, but as the eyes of the world focused on this trendsetting Tennessee town, tensions began to run high. The National Guard was called in, and the school building was bombed. But the school principal, student body president, local Baptist minister, and other leaders in Clinton took a strong stand in favor of the rule of law—and, therefore, for integration.

One of the most moving displays in the museum is a glass case with letters that were received by Rev. Paul Turner, the white Baptist minister who helped to escort the black students to school and preached against the segregationists. There are anonymous and

Grainger County Agritourism

Grainger County lies northeast of Knoxville. One of the state's most rural counties, Grainger has a rugged landscape, defined by steep ridges and long valleys. The area is perhaps best known for its tomatoes—during the summer it is not uncommon to see farm stands set up around Knoxville with signs touting Grainger County Tomatoes.

You can get to the source of the abundance by visiting farms in Grainger County yourself. **Ritter Farms** (2999 Hwy. 11-W S., 865/767-2575, www.ritterfarms.com) is one of the largest family-owned farms in the area. It has a commercial kitchen, where jams, jellies, salsas, and other farm-fresh provisions are prepared for retail sale. The farm market is open Monday-Saturday year-round; in the spring, summer, and fall you can buy seasonal fresh produce, and in winter Ritter Farms specialize in handicrafts, preserves, and baked goods. Call ahead to confirm hours. The farm is located between Bean Station and Rutledge.

Tennessee Homegrown Tomatoes (220 Chahokia Dr., 865/828-8316), located near Cherokee Lake on Route 375, about 3.5 miles east of Highway 92, grows all sorts of vegetables—not just tomatoes. It offers farm tours and hosts events throughout the growing season.

The crowning event for Grainger County farmers is the Grainger County Tomato Festival (www.graingercountytomatofestival.com), which takes place in Rutledge in late July every year.

hateful postcards and letters that decry Reverend Turner, as well as letters of support from unknowns to celebrities, including Rev. Billy Graham and journalist Edward R. Murrow.

Eventually, the world stopped paying a lot of attention to Clinton. New civil rights struggles were taking place all over the South, and the outsider segregationists who fomented the worst of the violence and unrest were gone. Photographers traveled to Clinton to take pictures when Bobby Cain became the first black male to graduate from a desegregated public school in May of 1957, but when Gail Epps followed in his footsteps the following year, no one paid any attention.

The events that took place in Clinton were recounted in an hour-long 1957 *See It Now* television program, and its 1960 sequel from CBS Reports, both of which may be seen at the museum. In 2006, the Green McAdoo Cultural Center produced an award-winning documentary about the events titled *Clinton 12,* which was narrated by James Earl Jones.

Outside the museum is a life-size statue of the Clinton 12, the 12 African American young people who enrolled at Clinton High School in the fall of 1956. When the museum was opened in 2006, 9 of the 12 were on hand to see the statue being unveiled.

The Green McAdoo Cultural Center was funded in part by federal, state, and local funds, as well as through private donations. In 2007, legislation was introduced in Congress that would designate the Green McAdoo Cultural Center as part of the National Park Service.

The old Clinton High School building now houses Clinton Middle School, just a few blocks from the Green McAdoo center.

Get to Clinton by taking Clinton Highway (Highway 25 West) about 15 miles out of Knoxville. Once in Clinton, there are signs directing you to the center.

Appalachian Arts Craft Center

Locals love the **Appalachian Arts Craft Center** (2716 Andersonville Hwy., Norris, 865/494-9854, www.appalachianarts.net, 10am-6pm Mon.-Sat., 1pm-5pm Sun., closed Sun.-Mon. Jan.-Feb.) because they get to meet the artists and learn to make works of art in ongoing workshops. But this small nonprofit gallery is a must-see for visitors, too, particularly if you want that one-of-kind souvenir to take home. Specialties include pottery, weaving, and quilting.

★ Museum of Appalachia

There is one place that every visitor to this region should visit if they are the least bit interested in the lifestyles and folk traditions of Appalachia. **Museum of Appalachia** (2819 Andersonville Hwy., 865/494-7680, www.museumofappalachia.org, 10am-5pm daily Jan.-Feb., 9am-5pm daily Mar. and Nov.-Dec, 9am-5pm weekdays, 9am-6pm weekends Apr., 9am-6pm daily May-Oct., adults $18, seniors $15, teens 13-18 $10, children 5-12 $6) is one of a kind. Its 65 acres contain more of the history of this region than any other place in Tennessee. The collection includes more than 250,000 artifacts, and more than 100,000 people visit annually. This is all the more remarkable given that the museum, which is now a Smithsonian Institution affiliate, started as a collection from one man's garage.

The museum is a story told in several chapters. Its indoor exhibits include the *Appalachian Hall of Fame*, a remarkable collection of items that were made, used, and treasured by the people who came and created a life in the rugged land of the southern Appalachians. There are dolls that were whittled by rugged mountain men, banjos created from food tins, and the remains of a supposed perpetual-motion machine. The exhibits are the work of John Rice Irwin, as is the whole museum. Irwin, a mountain man himself, has spent his life motivated by his admiration and love for the people who settled the mountains. He believes that the items of everyday life are important, and that through them, we can understand the people who made them and made the region what it is. It certainly seems like he's right. Take the time to read the detailed and loving descriptions of each item in the hall of fame (most handwritten), and soon you will feel admiration and marvel for the people who made them, in the midst of what we would now consider hard times.

Music fans should not overlook the museum. Its collection of handmade fiddles, guitars, banjos, and mouth harps is unrivaled, and its displays about musicians tell not only who, what, and when, but also why and how. It's not to be missed.

Outside the hall of fame, the museum has a collection of mountain buildings. There is a log church, schoolhouse, pioneer homestead, and the log home where Mark Twain's parents lived in Possum Trot, Tennessee. As you explore these old buildings—all of which have been carefully moved from original locations throughout the region—look for members of

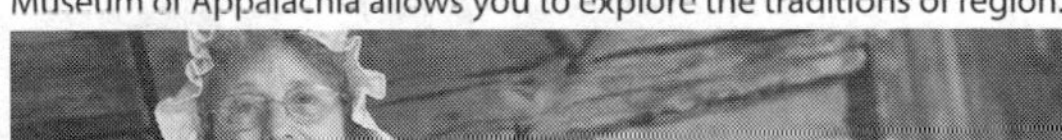
Museum of Appalachia allows you to explore the traditions of region.

the museum's menagerie: peacocks, horses, fainting goats, and sheep.

The Museum of Appalachia hosts several events during the year, but none is better known and as well loved than its annual **Homecoming** in October. The best musicians, writers, and artists come for the weekend, which offers the most authentic celebration of mountain arts in the region. Perhaps better loved by locals is the Fourth of July Anvil Shoot (yes, an actual anvil is shot into the air), which also includes music and crafts of the region.

In 2008, Irwin announced that he could no longer afford to keep the museum afloat with regular, large personal contributions, and locals, museumgoers, and historians alike were concerned that the museum would have to cut hours or otherwise look for cost-cutting measures. But his daughter, Elaine Irwin Meyer, took the reins, forged the relationship with the Smithsonian, and took steps to preserve her father's legacy, and that of his forefathers, for the future.

Wear comfortable shoes, charge the camera battery, and prepare to stay for a good part of the day to see everything this site has to offer. Don't skip the gift shop or the on-site restaurant.

NORRIS DAM STATE PARK

TVA's first hydroelectric project was to construct a dam on the Clinch River, in Anderson County, north of Knoxville. Construction of the 1,860-foot-long, 265-foot-tall dam started in 1933 and was completed in 1936. It was named for senator George Norris of Nebraska, who conceived of and championed the idea of a public power company in the Tennessee Valley. This was one of a number of projects that displaced mountain families in this region.

Hungarian-born architect Roland Wank designed Norris Dam. Wank cared not only about the function of the dam, but its appearance as well. He considered the placement of overlooks on either side of the dam and designed a visitors center. The dam was proportional; carefully placed window openings and the placement of the formwork boards created texture and pattern.

Today, Norris Dam is part of Norris Dam State Park (125 Village Green Circle, Lake City, 865/426-7461 or 800/543-9335, 10am-6pm Wed.-Sun.). Visitors may see the incredibly picturesque dam from overlooks on both sides of the lake; U.S. 441s on boam State Phfare in the park—tracks along the top of the damn. It is an impressive sight. The visitors center, on the east on the east side of the dam, has public restrooms and displays about construction of the dam.

Norris Dam is also home to the quirky **Lenoir Museum** (865/494-9688, 9am-5pm Wed.-Sun., free), named for Will G. Lenoir, a local resident who amassed a mind-boggling collection of mountain artifacts during his lifetime. Lenoir traveled the back roads of East Tennessee to purchase housewares, old farm implements, mementos, and other remnants of everyday life of the early 20th century. When Lenoir died, he donated his collection to the State of Tennessee, and eventually the Lenoir Museum was built at Norris Dam State Park.

In addition to Lenoir's collection, the museum houses displays about Native Americans and the construction of Norris Dam.

Next to the Lenoir Museum are two authentic structures that were moved to the park during construction of TVA dams and lakes. The **Caleb Crosby Threshing Barn** once sat on the Holston River where the David A. Green Bridge now spans Cherokee Lake on Highway 25 East. Before the lake flooded the farm site, the barn was carefully dismantled and put in storage, where it was kept for 34 years until 1978, when it was reconstructed at Norris Dam.

Next to the threshing barn is the **18th Century Rice Gristmill,** originally constructed in 1798 by James Rice along Lost Creek in Union County. Four generations of the Rice family operated the mill from 1798 until 1935, when TVA bought the land on which it sat in preparation for flooding of Norris Lake. The Civilian Conservation Corps labeled all the components of the mill, disassembled it, and reassembled it on its present land. During the summer, park staff still operate the mill and have gift items for sale.

Recreation

Despite its rich history, most people come to Norris Dam State Park to relax and enjoy the outdoors. Boating and fishing are popular on the Clinch River and on Norris Lake, in part because the water is so deep and cool, and the fish so plentiful. There are several licensed commercial marinas (865/426-7461) on the lake, including ones where you can rent houseboats for your stay. There are 15 miles of hiking trails and another 15 miles of multi-use dirt and gravel paths ideal for biking. An Olympic-size swimming pool is open during the summer 10am-6pm Wednesday-Sunday.

Cabins and Camping

Norris has 19 rustic cabins (865/426-7461, $60-85) and 10 three-bedroom deluxe cabins ($70-120). All cabins are located in a wooded setting and have kitchens, bathrooms, fireplaces, linens, and outdoor picnic tables and grills. The Norris campground has 75 sites ($20) with electrical and water hookups. Houseboat rates vary by season, size of boat, and availability.

OLIVER SPRINGS

The town of **Oliver Springs** is just a blip on the map, but it's worth stopping to see the general store, the library (housed in the old train depot), a few quaint antique stores, and the town hall. It is just a 30-mile drive northwest along State Highway TN 62 from Knoxville, just past Oak Ridge.

The real reason people head to Oliver Springs, though, is to get to the **Coal Creek OHV Area and Windrock Park** (865/435-1251, www.coalcreekohv.com). This park, once a coal mining area, has been repurposed into a center with more than 72,000 acres of wide-open spaces, including more than 300 miles of trails, camping, cabins, and fantastic scenery. This is essentially a playground for grownups who like to go off road. The park is the largest privately held park of its kind in the country.

OAK RIDGE

America created the atomic bomb—or parts of it, at least—at the Y-12, X-10, and K-25 plants in this city, northwest of Knoxville.

Off-road vehicles have more than 72,000 acres of wide-open spaces at Windrock Park.

Oak Ridge

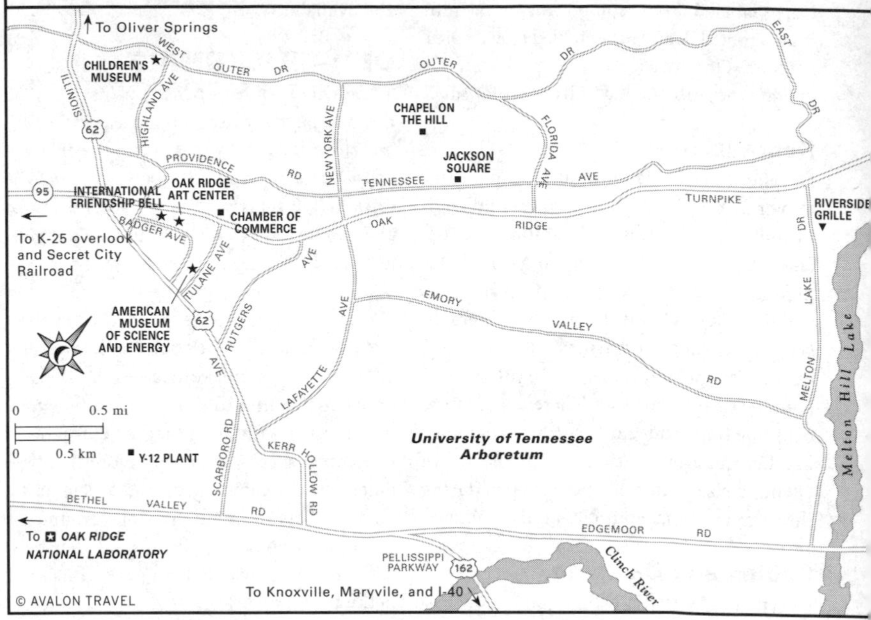

Talk about top secret! Even those involved didn't really know what was happening, and The Secret City moniker remains one people use. Today, **Oak Ridge** and its plants are still an important component in the national defense industry. Oak Ridge's heritage is part of everything in the city. You can sense how smart everyone in town is (the government recruited the best and brightest to work here, and many of their offspring have stayed): This is a little brain trust in the mountains. You can't walk away from here without a different perspective on the country.

It is easy to get to Oak Ridge; just drive 23 miles northwest along State Highway TN 62 from Knoxville.

History

Oak Ridge did not exist before 1942. When nuclear fission was discovered in the late 1930s, American scientists warned that this technology could be used to create a weapon more powerful than any known to man. As World War II escalated, and the United States joined the conflict in 1941, the U.S. military decided to exploit this technology. Sites in New Mexico, Washington state, and East Tennessee were chosen for the work. The isolated hills in Tennessee were chosen because they were close to roads and rail lines, they had ample supply of electricity, and they would be hard for spies and the curious to discover. Before the land was taken over by the government, about 3,000 people lived in homes that were scattered around the hills and valleys. Each homeowner received a letter stating that their land and home were being taken, and how much money they would receive in exchange.

Oak Ridge was built seemingly overnight. Between the spring of 1943 and the fall of 1944, the 59,000-acre tract of land bought for the project was developed into 10,000 homes and apartments, 13,000 dormitory spaces, 5,000 trailers, and more than 16,000 barracks. One of the facilities, K-25, where they processed uranium, was at the time the largest building in the world under one roof. Workers rode bicycles to get from one side of the massive structure to the other.

Social societies, schools, churches, theaters, barbershops, and much more were developed to entertain and meet the needs of the new residents.

When the United States dropped atomic bombs on Hiroshima and Nagasaki on August 6 and September 2, 1945, many workers at Oak Ridge learned for the first time what they had been doing at the facility. Many believed and were proud that they had helped to end World War II.

The end of the war did not mean the end of Oak Ridge. Y-12 continues to research, develop, and produce weapons for the U.S. military. In 1948, X-10 became the Oak Ridge National Laboratory, a center for science and research managed successively by the University of Chicago, Monsanto Chemical, Union Carbide, and Lockheed Martin corporations. It is now managed by the University of Tennessee and Battelle, and remains a center for scientific research in a wide range of fields.

American Museum of Science and Energy

Oak Ridge's premier attraction is the **American Museum of Science and Energy** (300 S. Tulane Ave., 865/576-3200, www.amse.org, 9am-5pm Mon.-Sat., 1pm-5pm Sun., adults $5, seniors $4, children 6-17 $3). The museum serves double duty: It houses an exhibit about the development of Oak Ridge, and it is a science museum for young people. The historical exhibit relies on newspaper clippings, original documents, and audiovisuals to describe Oak Ridge during World War II. The science museum has features dedicated to types of energy, including nuclear.

★ Oak Ridge National Laboratory

Before September 11, 2001, visitors were allowed walk-in tours of Y-12/**Oak Ridge National Laboratory** (865/576-7658, www.ornl.gov). But in today's security-anxious world, casual visitors are not allowed on the campus of the nuclear plant without an advance reservation. Call to arrange a tour, or get on one of the public bus and train tours offered in collaboration with the **American Museum of Science and Energy** (AMSE). These tours run daily June-September. To get on board the bus tour, you must sign up in person at the AMSE before 9am on the day of the tour. The bus leaves at noon and returns at about 3pm. The bus tour is free with paid admission to the museum.

If you're short on time or don't want to get tangled up at the AMSE, then head for the **K-25 overlook** (Highway 58), a mini-museum and viewing station located about 10 miles south of Oak Ridge. You'll drive through the city's industrial park before arriving at the overlook. Inside a small enclosed building is a short version of Oak Ridge's history. Outside you can see the K-25 plant as well as other Oak Ridge infrastructure. It is not scenic, but it's still a view.

Across from the K-25 Technology Park is the **Wheat African Burial Ground,** which houses 90 unmarked graves believed to be those of slaves from the Wheat Plantation. The cemetery dates back to 1850.

Other Sights

While most of "old Oak Ridge" has been razed and rebuilt in the ubiquitous modern American style of strip malls and parking lots, parts of the city date back to the 1940s. **Jackson Square** remains largely unchanged since it was built as Oak Ridge's original town center. The low-slung horseshoe-shaped shopping center is home to professional offices, a few cafés, and the Oak Ridge Playhouse. Across Kentucky Street from the square are the remains of the **Alexander Motor Inn,** Oak Ridge's original and only hotel during the war. Above the inn is the **Chapel on the Hill,** a church that served as the place of worship for numerous denominations during the war.

Other don't-miss attractions in Oak Ridge

include the **International Friendship Bell,** located downtown, which is a monument to peace. The **Secret City Commemorative Walk,** also downtown, is a memorial to the 75,000 men and women who built Oak Ridge during the 1940s.

The **Children's Museum of Oak Ridge** (461 W. Outer Dr., 865/482-1074, www.childrensmuseumofoakridge.org, 9am-5pm Tues.-Fri., 10am-4pm Sat., 1pm-4pm Sun., adults $8, seniors $7, children 3-18 $6) building was the Highland View Elementary School during the Manhattan Project era. Founded as a Girl Scout project in 1973, this is probably Tennessee's best children's museum, and it does a remarkable job explaining the area's complex history to even the youngest of visitors. In addition to the Secret City history, there's a child-size dollhouse, a rain forest, a bird room, a water flume, and a spectacular model railroad. Model-train buffs from Knoxville make the trek to keep this exhibit running.

When you've had enough Manhattan Project-era tourism in Oak Park, head to the **University of Tennessee Arboretum** (901 S. Illinois Ave., 865/483-3571, 8am-sunset daily). Here you can stroll through 250 acres of trees, with remarkable vistas any time of year. There are a number of easy, self-guided walking trails, each well marked should you want to learn about the flora of the region. If you just want some time to commune with nature, that works too.

Tours

The **Secret City Scenic Excursion Train** (865/241-2140, www.techscribes.com/sarm/srm_scs.htm, first and third Sat. Apr.-Sept., selected weekends Oct.-Nov., 11am, 1pm, and 3pm Sat., 1pm and 3pm Sun., adults $19 children 2-12 $15, call ahead) combines pretty scenery with the history of Oak Ridge. The train departs from Wheat Union Station, near the K-25 overlook on Highway 58. The journey travels a 12-mile route through the Manhattan Project site. The guides cram in a lot of information on these rides; the train will likely be of more interest to little ones than the lecture.

The annual Secret City Festival features World War II reenactments.

Entertainment and Events

The Oak Ridge Art Center (201 Badger Rd., 865/482-1441, www.oakridgeartcenter.org, 9am-5pm Tues.-Fri., 1pm-4pm Sat.-Mon., free) displays local and regional artwork. Exhibits change regularly and are fairly small. Getting a glimpse of the working studio is the appeal of this attraction.

Each June Oak Ridge tells its story during the **Secret City Festival** (www.secretcityfestival.com). There are World War II reenactments, live music, a juried art show, tennis tournaments, and plenty of activities for kids.

Food

For a meal in Oak Ridge, head to Jackson Square, where you can join the crowds at **Big Ed's Pizza** (101 Broadway, 865/482-4885, 11am-9:30pm Mon.-Thurs., 11am-10:30pm Fri-Sat., $8-15), the city's most famous restaurant and a well-loved pizza parlor. Also

Sam Houston: The Raven

The word *colorful* does not do justice to Sam Houston, onetime Tennessee governor and one of the state's most complex and controversial citizens during the first half of the 19th century.

Born in Lexington, Virginia, in 1793, Houston was just 13 when his father died. His mother, Elizabeth, brought Sam and his eight siblings to Blount County, where he went to school for the first time and promptly memorized Pope's translation of Homer's *Iliad*. When his teacher refused to teach Houston Greek and Latin, the teenager disappeared from his family home. Houston traveled the rural mountainsides of East Tennessee and spent long periods in a Cherokee village. Oo-Loo-Te-Ka, a Cherokee chief, became a surrogate father to Houston and named him the Raven. Houston learned the language and ways of the Cherokee.

Some years later Houston needed to pay off debts, and in 1811, he opened a school in Blount County where he charged the then-astronomical fee of $8 per student per year. After about a year, when he was 20 years old and had paid his debts, Houston joined the army and quickly rose to an officer rank. Andrew Jackson noticed Houston's bravery and intelligence at the Battle of Horseshoe Bend during the Creek Wars of 1814. The future president stationed Houston to his regional headquarters in Nashville, and the young East Tennessean became part of Jackson's so-called Tennessee Junto, his political machine.

In 1819, Houston quit the army to study law and shortly after was appointed attorney general for Davidson County. Houston ran successfully for a seat in the U.S. House of Representatives, where he served two terms. In 1827, he was elected governor of Tennessee.

Houston's station at the top of Tennessee politics was not to last. He had a tumultuous private life, fueled by bouts of drinking and depression. While campaigning for his second term as Tennessee governor, Houston married Eliza Allen, the daughter of a prominent Middle Tennessee family. She left him after just 80 days of marriage, and Houston resigned the governorship and fled to the Cherokee, now living in Oklahoma.

So began the next chapter for Houston, who went on to marry a Cherokee woman, lead the Texas army against Mexico, and be elected president of the Republic of Texas. Later, in 1840, he married again, this time to Margaret Lea of Alabama, with whom he would have eight children. He worked tirelessly to achieve Texas annexation to the United States, which occurred in 1845. While Houston served as a senator from Texas from 1846 until 1858, he promoted the transcontinental railroad, criticized the army, and supported the Union. In 1859, Houston was elected governor of Texas, where he opposed the state's secession. He died in 1863.

Tennessee historian and writer Wilma Dykeman described Houston this way: "A strange, interesting combination of scout and scholar, woodsman and humanitarian, Sam Houston balanced Homer with humor and represented a sense of the total community of man."

on Jackson Square is **The Soup Kitchen** (47 E. Tennessee Ave., 865/482-3525, 11am-7pm Mon.-Fri., 11am-2pm Sat., $5-12), which serves excellent sandwiches, salads, and soups. Don't skip the Chilios (a combination of Fritos, chili, and cheese). End the meal with ice cream at **Razzleberry's Ice Cream Lab and Kitchen** (201 Jackson Sq., 865/481-0300, 11am-9pm Mon.-Fri., 8am-7pm Sat.).

With menu items including the Y-12 and K-25 breakfast specials, you know you are in Oak Ridge when you are at the **Jefferson Soda Fountain** (22 N. Jefferson Cir., 865/482-1141, 7am-3pm Mon.-Fri., 6:30am-2pm Sat., $6-10). Try the Myrtle Burger and stay long enough to hear longtime Oak Ridgers tell their tales.

Take in the scenery at the **Riverside Grille** (100 Melton Lake Peninsula, 865/862-8646, www.riversidegrilletn.com, 11am-9pm Mon.-Thurs., 11am-10pm Fri.-Sat., 11am-3pm, $4-18). Here you will enjoy steaks, salads, and a view of Melton Hill Lake.

Information

The **Oak Ridge Welcome Center** (102C Robertsville Rd., 865/482-7821, www.oakridgevisitor.com, year-round 9am-5pm Mon.-Fri.

June-Oct., also open. 9am-1pm Sat.) hands out maps and brochures, and helps travelers plan their visit to the city.

MARYVILLE

One of the oldest cities in East Tennessee, Maryville was named for Mary Grainger Blount, the wife of territorial governor William Blount. It is the home of Maryville College, a four-year college founded in 1819. Maryville College was among the first Southern schools to admit Native Americans, African Americans, and women.

On the northern outskirts of Maryville is the city of Alcoa, established as a company town for the Aluminum Corporation of America (ALCOA) in 1914. ALCOA remains an important economic engine for Blount County.

Maryville is about halfway between Great Smoky Mountain National Park and Knoxville, taking the winding scenic route out of the park and then along Highway 441. Directly from Knoxville it is a straight 17-mile shot south on Highway 129.

Sights

The **Sam Houston Schoolhouse** (3650 Sam Houston Schoolhouse Rd., 865/983-1550, www.samhoustonhistoricschoolhouse.org, 10am-5pm Tues.-Sat., 1pm-5pm Sun., ages 10 and older $3) is the one-room schoolhouse where Sam Houston taught for about a year beginning in 1812. Houston, one of early Tennessee's most remarkable citizens, was mostly self-educated. Raised in part by the Cherokee, who named him Raven, Houston went on to be governor of Tennessee, president of the Republic of Texas, and senator and governor of the state of Texas.

The Sam Houston Schoolhouse was built around 1794 by area settlers who wanted a place for their children to be educated. Several different teachers held class in this little one-room schoolhouse until Houston's arrival in 1812. Houston, who took up teaching in order to pay off his debts, stayed for only a year. But his name has remained tied with the institution up to the present day.

Today, the Sam Houston Schoolhouse re-creates early schools on the Tennessee frontier. Reenactments can be arranged for groups.

Shopping

Southland Books (1519 E. Broadway, 865/984-4847, 10am-7pm Mon.-Sat., noon-5pm Sun.) is an excellent used-book store, popular meeting place, art gallery, and coffee shop. Stop in at any time for a pick-me-up pastry and coffee drink. Owner Lisa Misosky serves a special homemade lunch special every weekday.

Accommodations

Located at McGhee Tyson Airport is the **Hilton Knoxville Airport** (2001 Alcoa Hwy., Alcoa, 865/970-4300, www.hiltonknoxvilleairport.com, $150-190). Its 326 guest rooms offer work desks, high-end bedding, coffeemakers, and MP3-player plug-ins.

Food

Local chains include Knoxville-based **Aubrey's** (909 W. Lamar Alexander Pkwy., 865/379-8800, 11am-10pm Sun.-Thurs., 11am-11pm Fri.-Sat., $12), which serves pasta and steaks; there's also **Lemon Grass Thai Cuisine and Sushi Bar** (912 W. Lamar Alexander Pkwy., 865/681 8785, www.mylemongrass.com, 11am-3pm and 5pm-10pm Mon.-Thurs., 11am-3pm and 5pm-11pm Fri.-Sat, noon-10pm Sun., $11).

Great Smoky Mountains

Look for ★ to find recommended sights, activities, dining, and lodging.

Highlights

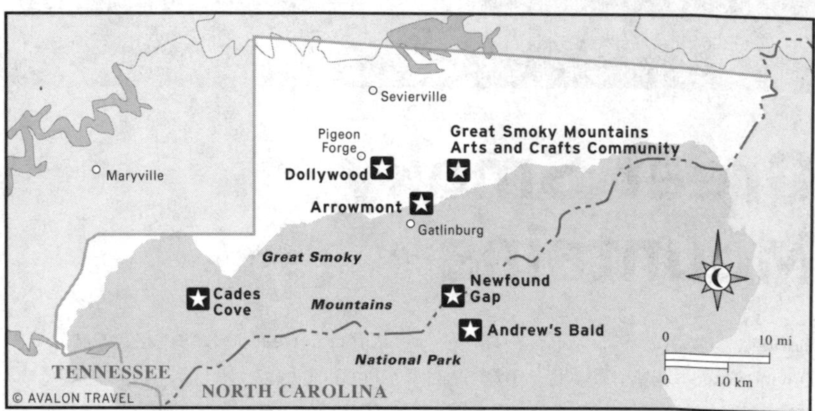

★ **Newfound Gap:** The most prominent mountain pass in the Smokies offers breathtaking vistas, cool mountain air, and a chance to hike along the famed Appalachian Trail (page 411).

★ **Cades Cove:** Historic cabins, churches, and farms dot this popular pastoral mountain cove, ideal for walking, biking, or auto touring (page 413).

★ **Andrew's Bald:** Accessible only on foot, this landscape of wild grasses, rhododendron, and clear air is the perfect destination for a day hike (page 420).

★ **Arrowmont:** It's part arts school, part gallery, with a focus on Appalachian decorative arts (page 428).

★ **Great Smoky Mountains Arts and Crafts Community:** Drive the back roads near Gatlinburg to meet artisans who keep the creativity and ingenuity of mountain crafts alive (page 428).

★ **Dollywood:** Don't turn up your nose at Dolly Parton's Pigeon Forge theme park. With roller coasters, live music, artisans, and lots more diversions, this place is the definition of good, clean fun, with spectacular views (page 433).

The Great Smoky Mountains National Park is the single most popular national park in the United States, and it is no wonder why.

The park's iconic vistas of blue-green mountains topped by the namesake smoky mists are awesome, yet somehow comforting. These are ancient mountains whose hills and valleys have secrets to keep.

The scenery in the Smokies is unrivaled. Mountaintops such as Clingmans Dome and Mount LeConte offer panoramic vistas of soft-edged mountains. Balds—clearings high up in the mountains—are enchanted places where wild blueberries and rhododendron grow, and where the sunshine is pure and warm.

Valleys such as Cades Cove are ideal for wildlife viewing—here you'll see lovely creatures, like elk and deer. Mountain streams and rivers offer a kaleidoscope of sights, both under the cold, rushing water and around the water's edge. Within the 800 square miles of parkland, scientists have documented some 10,000 species of plants, animals, and invertebrates, but they believe that as many as 90,000 more live in this remarkably diverse natural wilderness.

No matter what interests you, you won't be bored in the Smokies. There are 800 miles of hiking trails within the park, and traveling them brings you face-to-face with wildlife, waterfalls, and breathtaking viewpoints. Once you start hiking the trails of the Smokies, you might never want to stop. Cool mountain streams are ideal for wading and offer some of the best mountain fishing in the country. Visitors also enjoy picnicking and driving along the park's winding, quiet roads. The Smokies are also more car accessible than other national parks, meaning even those who can't or don't want to hike, walk, or bike can enjoy the sights.

More than 9.4 million people visit Great Smoky Mountains every year, and they need places to stay and to eat. The gateway communities in Tennessee—Cosby, Gatlinburg, Pigeon Forge, and Townsend—offer the necessities of life and so much more. If the Smokies soothe the spirit and revive your mind, then Gatlinburg and Pigeon Forge, with theme parks, mini golf, dinner theaters, and any type of retail store you can imagine,

Previous: The Great Smoky Mountains are excellent for hiking; Dollywood's Splash Country.
Above: dogwoods.

Great Smoky Mountains

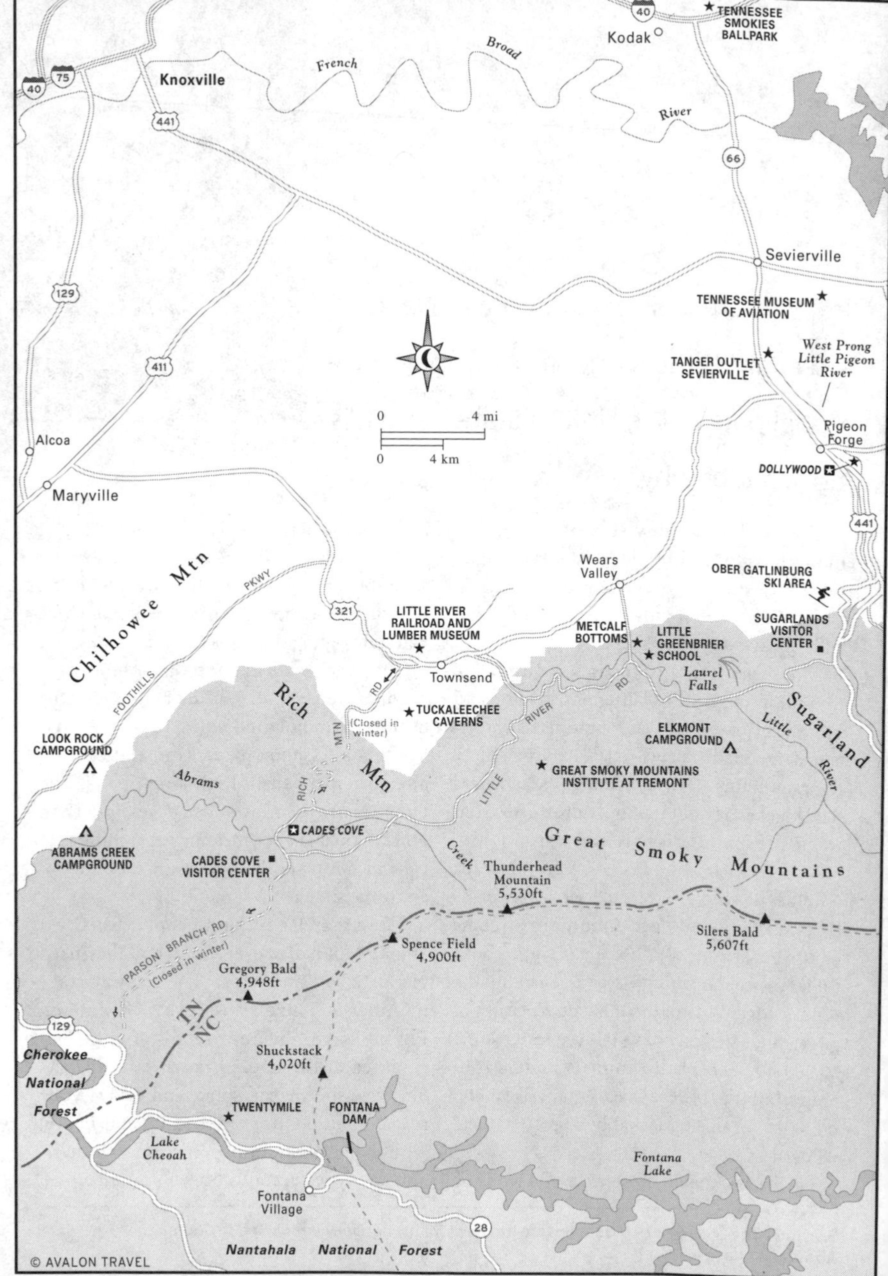

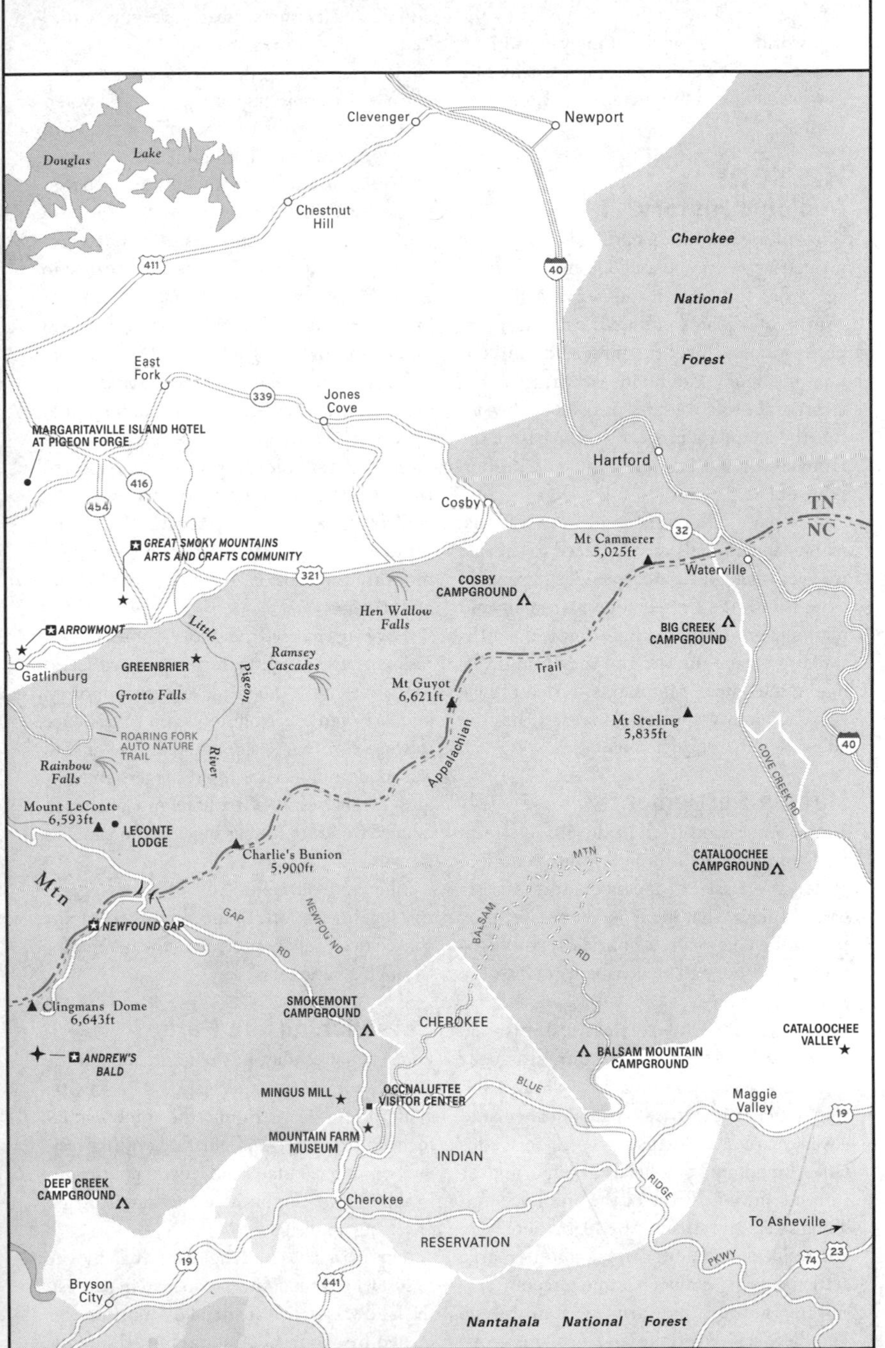

Clevenger
Newport
Douglas Lake
Chestnut Hill
411
40
Cherokee National Forest
East Fork
339
Jones Cove
MARGARITAVILLE ISLAND HOTEL AT PIGEON FORGE
Hartford
416
454
Cosby
TN
NC
32
GREAT SMOKY MOUNTAINS ARTS AND CRAFTS COMMUNITY
Mt Cammerer 5,025ft
321
Waterville
COSBY CAMPGROUND
Hen Wallow Falls
ARROWMONT
Little Pigeon River
BIG CREEK CAMPGROUND
Ramsey Cascades
GREENBRIER
Trail
Gatlinburg
Grotto Falls
Mt Guyot 6,621ft
Mt Sterling 5,835ft
ROARING FORK AUTO NATURE TRAIL
Appalachian
COVE CREEK RD
Rainbow Falls
Mount LeConte 6,593ft
LECONTE LODGE
Charlie's Bunion 5,900ft
CATALOOCHEE CAMPGROUND
MTN
Mtn
NEWFOUND GAP
GAP RD
NEWFOUND
BALSAM RD
Clingmans Dome 6,643ft
SMOKEMONT CAMPGROUND
CHEROKEE
CATALOOCHEE VALLEY
ANDREW'S BALD
BALSAM MOUNTAIN CAMPGROUND
BLUE
MINGUS MILL
OCONALUFTEE VISITOR CENTER
Maggie Valley
19
MOUNTAIN FARM MUSEUM
INDIAN
RIDGE
DEEP CREEK CAMPGROUND
Cherokee
To Asheville
RESERVATION
PKWY
74
23
19
441
Bryson City
Nantahala National Forest

send you crashing right back down to the real world. It's the yin and the yang of East Tennessee. The quieter sides of Cosby and Townsend offer a middle road for those who want it.

HISTORY

Geologic History

The Smoky Mountains are old. They were formed between 200 and 300 million years ago, when the African and North American continental plates collided, causing great peaks to form. Over the succeeding millennia, the Smoky Mountains weathered away, creating the soft, rounded peaks that now define the mountain range. By comparison, the Himalayas are nearly newborn at 50 million years old.

The park's diverse array of ecosystems, plants, and animals can be traced to the last ice age, when glaciers covered large parts of what is now the United States. Animals and plants from northern climes moved southward to escape the ice, and they found refuge in the Smoky Mountains. When the ice receded, many species remained, having adapted to their new home.

Human Settlement

Native Americans lived in the Smokies and their foothills beginning around 7000 BC. When the first European explorers traveled through what today is Tennessee, they found the Cherokee, a politically and economically sophisticated tribe linked to the Iroquois nation.

The first white settlers established homesteads in the Smoky Mountains near Cherokee, North Carolina, in 1795. In 1814, the first families settled in Cataloochee, and seven years later settlers arrived in Cades Cove. Mountain homesteads began to appear in other lowland areas of the Smokies, and along rivers and streams. By 1850, there were 451 residents in Cades Cove, and other large settlements in Cataloochee and Greenbrier.

Life in the mountains was not easy. Families survived off the land, growing crops and raising livestock. Nearly everything they had—tools, clothing, household goods, and games—came from the forests around them. Corn was the most important crop, and water-powered gristmills were used to grind corn into cornmeal—a staple of life.

The landscape of the Smokies changed dramatically during the first 30 years of the 20th century. Logging companies, which had previously passed by the mountains because to their difficult terrain, looked again, inspired by the possibility of expansion and the arrival of railroads in the region. Little River Lumber Company was the first logging company to arrive in the Smokies, in 1903, and the last to leave, in 1939, after the creation of the national park. Loggers felled millions of old-growth trees—by the time the last axe struck, just 20 percent of the virgin forest remained. Logging led to forest fires, which sometimes raged for months, and erosion, which polluted rivers and streams.

Logging changed the lifestyle of mountain residents, too. Logging towns appeared seemingly overnight. Logging jobs paid money, and so began the evolution from subsistence to wage earning. Residents were also able to sell goods and services to the loggers and logging executives; the first hotel in Gatlinburg opened to house timber buyers who came to the area.

The environmental toll of such aggressive logging was one of the reasons that folks started to talk about protecting the mountains through a national park.

Establishing the Park

Looking back today, it is remarkable that the Great Smoky Mountains National Park exists at all. It took 17 years, and the combined efforts of Tennessee and North Carolina residents, plus local, state, and federal politicians, to achieve the complicated and daunting job of setting up the park.

The primary challenge was that by the 1920s, when talk of the park began in earnest, the land was in private hands. A portion was owned by about 4,000 mountain residents,

Logging in the Smokies

You wouldn't know it from looking at the lush treetops today, but at the time the Great Smoky Mountains National Park was dedicated in 1940, it had been largely denuded by logging. Beginning around 1903, timber companies logged the mountains, felling trees to satisfy the growing demand for lumber. It is estimated that two billion board feet of lumber came out of the Smokies during this period.

Logging companies built railroads, roads, and towns, the names of which—Elkmont, Tremont, Smokemont, and Proctor—remain as place-names in the park today. The environmental effects of logging were devastating. Fires burnt logged areas, leaving the mountainside bare. Streams and rivers swelled with muddy water, caused by erosion and landslides.

Lumber companies fought against the creation of a park. They took the government to court—one case reached the U.S. Supreme Court. The last timber was extracted from the Smokies in 1939 by Little River Lumber Company in the Tremont area. By 1940, only 20 percent of the park's lands were covered by old-growth forests.

but the greatest expanses belonged to lumber companies, which had been harvesting the mountainsides for timber since the turn of the 20th century.

Early park boosters were businesspeople and politicians from East Tennessee and western North Carolina who argued that a park would be an economic boon for the region. They foresaw a future when visitors would come in droves to see the park, spending money in the gateway communities on their way. Boosters launched an all-out public relations campaign to promote a park, and in 1926 alone residents pledged $1 million toward the purchase of lands.

The popularity of the park idea among residents drew the attention of state and federal politicians. In 1926, President Calvin Coolidge signed a bill committing the federal government to begin development of a national park in the Great Smokies, as soon as 423,000 acres of land were provided by the states of North Carolina and Tennessee. The states then offered $1 million each for land purchases, and the final $5 million was given by philanthropist John D. Rockefeller Jr. in memory of his mother, Laura Spellman Rockefeller.

Money in hand, states-appointed commissions who had the difficult task of purchasing land. The timber companies resisted. First they tried to derail the project itself, and later they sought to get the highest possible price for their land—much of which had now been stripped bare of trees. The states took five of the companies to court, a process that depleted funds meant for land purchase and allowed the timber companies time to continue logging in the Smokies.

In part because of the devastating effects of continued logging, support for a park grew even stronger. In 1933, President Franklin D. Roosevelt reversed a previous federal position and earmarked federal money for the purchase of land. By 1940, when the park was dedicated, the U.S. government had contributed more than $2 million.

Perhaps the biggest losers from the park project were the 4,000 people who lived within park boundaries. Without deep pockets like those of the timber companies, they were often stuck taking very little in financial compensation for their homes and farms. Some older residents chose to stay in the park—they sold their property to the government and leased it back for the duration of their lives. But making a livelihood on a land where they were now forbidden to hunt, fish with bait, or cultivate crops was close to impossible. Some residents, including the five Walker sisters who lived in a cabin in Little Greenbrier until the 1950s, managed to survive. Others, however, moved to communities outside the park and began new lives.

Great Smoky Mountains National Park was dedicated on September 2, 1940. President

Roosevelt stood at Newfound Gap to dedicate the park, and among his words were these:

In this park we shall conserve the pine, the redbud, the dogwood, the azalea, the rhododendron, the trout and the thrush for the happiness of the American people. The old frontier that put the hard fiber in the American spirit and the long muscles on the American back, lives and will live in these untamed mountains to give future generations a sense of the land from which their forefathers hewed their homes.

If you watch the short introductory video at park visitors centers, you will see footage of the presidential caravan as it made its way up the mountain to Newfound Gap for the dedication ceremony. The footage of that difficult drive up to the top of the mountain is a powerful symbol of the remarkable efforts and convergence of circumstances that gave rise to this remarkable national park.

Take a moment to listen to the sounds of the streams in the Great Smoky Mountains.

VISITING THE PARK

The crest of the Smokies forms the boundary between Tennessee and North Carolina, bisecting the park from northeast to southwest in an unbroken chain that rises more than 5,000 feet for more than 36 miles. Elevations in the park range from 875 feet to 6,643 feet.

As the most-visited national park in the nation, Great Smoky Mountains can feel crowded at peak times of the year. More than nine million people visit the park each year, most of them in their own cars, which clog roadways and fill parking lots. The busiest months are June, July, and August, when more than 3.5 million people will visit. The second most popular time is during the peak of the fall foliage show, which generally happens during the last two weeks of October. More than one million people come to the Smokies each October.

There are some effective strategies for circumventing the crowds. First, avoid peak seasons. If you must come during the summer or October visit during the week instead of on weekends. Next, don't sleep in! Set out early in the day. Most park roads get busy after 10am, and the early mornings can be lovely times to see the sights.

Another good way to avoid the crowds in the Smokies is to get off the beaten track. There is a crowd mentality among most park visitors, which takes them to Sugarlands, Cades Cove, Newfound Gap, and Clingmans Dome, leaving the rest of the park to you. Plan an itinerary that allows you to enter the park through Cosby, Townsend, or another of the secondary gateways and then to explore some of the lesser-known attractions, such as Abrams Creek, Greenbrier, and Cosby.

The final, and single best, way of shedding the crowds is to get out of your car. Among the miles of hiking trails in the Smokies, only a few are highly trafficked. Even the most popular of hiking trails, such as Chimney Tops and Grotto Falls, are downright empty compared to the park's roads. It is well worth a few sore muscles and a little sweat to enjoy some of the park's majesty all alone.

Weather

Always check the weather forecast before you come to the Smokies. Temperatures in the park, and particularly at the high elevations, can be as much as 30°F colder than those in the surrounding area. In summer this is welcome, but in the winter it can be deadly. Rainfall in the park ranges from 55 inches per year in the valleys to 85 inches per year on the peaks, more than is received anywhere else in the United States except the Pacific Northwest.

Seasons

Spring in the Smokies is the season of variable weather; it can be sunny and warm one day and snowy the next. Spring rainfall can cause rivers and streams to swell without warning. Summer is generally hot, with lots of haze and humidity. Afternoon thunderstorms are not uncommon.

Autumn is the park's greatest season. The fall foliage draws thousands of people, and for good reason. The weather is generally cool and crisp, with snow beginning at the high elevations in November. Winter snow is deep in the high elevations; Newfound Gap experiences an average of 69 inches of snowfall per year. In lower elevations only a few inches fall. Many secondary roads are closed during the winter due to frequent snow and ice.

ENTRANCES

Most people arrive in the park through Gatlinburg, a touristy yet picturesque hamlet (and popular wedding destination) located in the middle of the northern park boundary. Everything you forgot to bring is available to you at this entrance. You may encounter some traffic jams in and out of the park here during peak seasons. To the southwest is Townsend, which has some hotels and restaurants but few of both. Cosby, at the eastern side of the Tennessee boundary, is the quietest gateway point of all.

PARK FEES AND RESERVATIONS

Yet another reason Americans love Great Smoky Mountains National Park and visit it so often (and in such great numbers) is that entrance to the park, unlike many other national parks, is free.

The no-cost admission dates back to the park's founding. The land was once privately owned. When the state of Tennessee transferred ownership of the then-new Newfound Gap Road to the federal government, it stipulated that "no toll or license fee shall ever be imposed" to travel the road. This was done in part because, at the time, the road was the major thoroughfare through the Appalachian Mountains. The Tennessee legislature would have to vote to lift this restriction, which seems unlikely.

While entrance to the park is free, there is a charge for certain activities, such as camping ($14-23) and renting pavilions at picnic areas. Reservations are recommended for camping, staying at LeConte Lodge, and using the horse camps.

VISITORS CENTERS

There are four park visitors centers inside the park and three outside its boundaries. Each visitors center sells maps, guides, and books. There are volunteers at each center who can help you plan your visit to the park. Information about current weather conditions, road closures, and ranger-led events is also available. All visitors centers both in and outside the park are open daily year-round but close on Christmas Day.

Sugarlands Visitor Center (865/436-1291, 8am-4:30pm daily Dec.-Feb., 8am-5pm daily Mar. and Nov., 8am-6pm daily Apr.-May, 8am-6:30pm daily Sept.-Oct., 8am-7:30pm daily June-Aug.), located two miles south of Gatlinburg on Highway 441, is the busiest visitors center. In addition to the aforementioned services, the visitors center has a museum about the flora and fauna of the park and a free 20-minute video about its history and natural features.

Cades Cove Visitor Center (no phone, 9am-4:30pm daily Jan. and Dec., 9am-5:30pm daily Feb. and Nov., 9am-6:30pm daily Mar. and Sept.-Oct., 9am-7pm daily Apr. and Aug., 9am-7:30pm daily May-July) is located at the midway point of the 11-mile Cades Cove Loop Road.

On the North Carolina side of the park, the **Oconaluftee Visitor Center** (828/497-1904, 8am-4:30pm daily Jan.-Feb. and Dec., 8am-5pm daily Mar. and Nov., 8am-6pm daily Apr.-May, 8am-6:30pm daily Sept.-Oct., 8am-7:30pm daily June-Aug.) is located two miles north of Cherokee, North Carolina.

Clingmans Dome Visitor Contact Station (10am-6pm daily Apr.-Oct., 9:30am-5pm daily Nov.) is located at the Clingmans Dome trailhead 7 miles off US 44 on the Clingmans Dome Road.

In addition to the visitors centers located inside the park, the park service operates centers in gateway communities surrounding the Smokies. All these visitors centers sell maps, guides, and books. They are staffed with people who can answer questions and who have up-to-date information about weather and roads. They cannot help with reservations or backcountry permits, however.

The **Gatlinburg Welcome Center** (520 Parkway, 865/436-0504, 8am-7pm daily Apr.-Oct., 8:30am-5:30pm Nov.- daily Mar.) is located on the spur road between Pigeon Forge and Gatlinburg.

The **Sevierville Visitor Center** (3099 Winfield Dunn Pkwy., 865/932-4458, 9am-6pm daily) is located on Highway 66 between I-40 and Sevierville.

The **Townsend Visitor Center** (7906 E. Lamar Alexander Pkwy., 865/448-6134, 9am-5pm, June-Oct. daily 9am-6pm daily Jan.-May and Nov.-Dec.) is located on Highway 321 in Townsend. It is closed on Thanksgiving and Christmas Day.

There is a downloadable visitor guide available at www.nps.gov/grsm/planyourvisit/index.htm.

INFORMATION AND SERVICES

The national park publishes a free quarterly newspaper, *Smokies Guide*, which is available from any National Park Service (NPS)-affiliated visitors center. The newspaper includes information about seasonal hazards, road closures, and upcoming events.

To request general park information, contact the park headquarters at 865/436-1200. Campground and other reservations may be made at 877/444-6777 or www.recreation.gov. For backcountry campsites call 865/436-1231. You can order maps and guides at 888/898-9102.

A wide selection of brochures, guides, and books are available for purchase at visitors centers or online at www.smokiesinformation.org.

The park website (www.nps.gov/grsm) has a lot of information about attractions, activities, and current conditions. The website offers webcams that show current conditions at Look Rock and Purchase Knob within the park.

Pets

You may bring your pet to campgrounds and roadside stops as long as they are restrained at all times. Pets are not allowed on trails, except for the Gatlinburg and Oconaluftee River Trails.

Communications

Do not count on your cell phone working inside the park. While you are likely to get service in the gateway communities surrounding the park, most parts of the Smokies are outside of cell phone range. Campgrounds and visitors centers do have pay phones.

GETTING AROUND

Distances to various sites within the park are relatively short; it is just 34 miles from Cherokee, North Carolina, to Gatlinburg.

But the drives are not quick (nor should they be). National park roads are winding two-lane blacktops. It can take hours to drive from Gatlinburg to Newfound Gap due to traffic congestion and the steep and windy nature of the road. If you are keen on avoiding traffic jams, consider entering the park through either Townsend or Cosby, and start your day early.

PLANNING YOUR TIME

If you have only one day in the Smokies, choose between a day hike or a drive to Clingmans Dome. Make the choice based on your own capacity for hiking, the weather (Clingmans Dome is often enveloped in haze), and the season (avoid Clingmans Dome during peak visitation periods).

If you have a few days, go camping. Spend one day hiking, one day driving, and one day exploring Cades Cove. Ambitious hikers should make reservations at LeConte Lodge and plan a rest day between the hike in and the hike out to enjoy the peace and quiet at the top of the mountain.

Sights

★ Newfound Gap

This mountain pass, located at 5,048 feet, is one of the Smokies' greatest attractions. Named because it was not discovered until the 1850s, **Newfound Gap** is the lowest pass over the mountains. Today's visitors enjoy its refreshing cool air, its views, and the fact that you can straddle the state line between Tennessee and North Carolina. It was here, on September 2, 1940, that President Franklin D. Roosevelt dedicated the Great Smoky Mountains National Park.

There is a large parking lot here, with the best views facing southward into the Oconaluftee River Valley in North Carolina. The Appalachian Trail (AT), which travels the ridge of the mountains through the Smokies, crosses the road here at Newfound Gap. You can hike along the AT in either direction for as long as you like.

Clingmans Dome

Come to **Clingmans Dome** for the views. Here at the highest point in the park (6,643 feet), you can climb an observation tower that takes you up above the treetops. It is a stunning view and a refreshing experience, and afterward you can say that you were on the top of Ol' Smoky.

Clingmans Dome is the highest peak in the Smokies, and the third-highest peak in the eastern United States. Once called Smoky Dome because it is rounded like a dome, it is now called Clingmans after Thomas Lanier Clingman, a North Carolina attorney and politician who was involved in early attempts to measure and catalog mountain peaks.

The concrete observation tower atop Clingmans Dome dates to the 1960s. Immediately in front of the tower there are two steel-frame towers, a communications tower and a climactic data collection tower. On a clear day, the 360-degree view is truly awesome. Fontana Lake, Mount Mitchell, Knoxville, and Mount LeConte are just a few of the landmarks visible from the tower. Unfortunately, visibility from Clingmans Dome is often limited—often just 20 miles—by air pollution. Park officials blame coal-burning power plants in the southeastern United States for most of the pollution, which can also pose a health risk for people with breathing difficulties.

Another environmental problem evident at Clingmans Dome is the infestation of mature Fraser fir trees by the balsam woolly adelgid. The dry skeletons of these once-majestic evergreens haunt the mountainsides here. Fraser firs were the iconic champions of the unique spruce-fir forest that exists in the high elevations of the Smokies. But beginning in 1963, the adelgid, an aphid-like insect less than one millimeter long, arrived in the Smokies after coming to the United States from Europe, probably on nursery stock. Without any natural predators, the adelgids thrived on the sap of mature Fraser fir trees. Today, park officials estimate that some 70 percent of mature Fraser fir trees have been killed by the adelgids; the rest are infested. You can identify an infested tree by the white woolly mass covering its bark. Sometimes it causes the tree to look whitewashed.

Park rangers treat Fraser fir trees in developed areas and sites accessible by road with a soap solution sprayed from truck-mounted spray units. Other treatments to trees that the trucks can't reach include drenching the soil with the active ingredient in flea and tick medication for dogs. This has been very successful and is effective up to five years. The park rangers have also been releasing predatory beetles that feed exclusively on adelgids, but it will take years for the population of these beetles to have any effect on the adelgids. By 2011, the park had released more than half a million beetles. Preliminary monitoring has been encouraging. The park has also transplanted some firs to lower elevations in the park, where they can be protected and preserved in the event that scientists discover a way to guard against the microscopic predators.

When planning to visit Clingmans Dome, check the weather first. Remember that it is often much more cold and wet on top of Ol' Smoky than it is in the lowlands. On cloudy or overcast days, there will be no visibility at all.

Clingmans Dome is located at the end of a seven-mile spur road. It is a half-mile walk along a steep, but paved, footpath from the parking area to the base of the observation tower. The road to Clingmans Dome is closed December 1-March 31.

Mount LeConte

It is as if **Mount LeConte** keeps watch over the Smokies. The 6,593-foot peak stands sentry over the foothills; its size makes it easy to identify, even from a distance. Accessible only by foot, Mount LeConte is a destination for hikers who yearn for a sense of accomplishment. And what an accomplishment it is, with spectacular views and beautiful scenery along the way. The peak is also home to LeConte Lodge, the only indoor accommodations in the park.

ELKMONT

An old logging town that later became a summer resort community, **Elkmont** is now a campground and the starting point for several day hikes. The park has considered tearing down the deteriorating remains of summer cottages here, but for now they still stand—a reminder of the days before the park existed. Present-day vacationers can lay their heads at the 208-site Elkmont campground.

Elkmont is noted for the appearance here every June of synchronous fireflies. People come in droves to watch the insect show, which normally lasts about two weeks and begins around the second week of June. The park service offers trolley transportation to Elkmont during the firefly show.

Metcalf Bottoms

Metcalf Bottoms is a day-use area popular for picnicking and swimming. From here you can walk one mile to **Little Greenbrier School,** a 19th-century split-log schoolhouse with original furniture.

Just west of **Metcalf Bottoms** along the Little River Road are two water attractions. **The Sinks** is a waterfall with a pool so deep it once swallowed an entire derailed logging train, or so they say. Swimming here is not recommended, but it is nice to sit and watch the water crash over the falls.

Close to the intersection with Highway 73, which goes to Townsend, is the **Townsend Y,** probably the most popular swimming hole in the park. The river here is relatively wide and smooth, and the grassy bank is perfect for sunbathing.

★ CADES COVE

Historical and natural attractions lie side by side in **Cades Cove**, a flat mountain valley on the Townsend side of the park. It was a population center before the park was established.

There are indications that Cherokee and other Native Americans used Cades Cove for hunting and as a way to travel through the rough mountain terrain. But it is believed that whites were the first people to settle permanently in this fertile yet remote place. Early homesteaders came in the 1820s, and by 1850 the population was nearly 700. Families—with names such as Jobe, Oliver, Tipton, Shields, Burchfield, Cable, Sparkes, and Gregory—farmed, raised cattle, collected wild chestnuts, and hunted. They built churches, a school, a gristmill, and homes. Theirs was the hard yet happy life of the mountains.

In the 1920s and 1930s, the government came to buy up Cades Cove land for the park. Some of the remaining 600 residents agreed to the financial settlement and left the cove. Others took less money but retained the right to live in Cades Cove until they died. One man, John W. Oliver, took Tennessee to court, but he lost and moved out in 1937. During the 1940s, the population of Cades Cove dropped quickly. The school closed in 1944, and the post office was shuttered in 1947. By the end of the decade it was a ghost town, left to the imaginations of visitors yet to come.

Access to Cades Cove is along an 11-mile one-way loop road. Traffic moves slowly through this pastoral landscape, so plan on spending at least two hours on the loop. Two two-way lanes cross the cove and allow you to shorten or lengthen your drive.

The roads in Cades Cove are closed to vehicular traffic on Wednesday and Saturday mornings until 10am May-September. Exploring on foot or bike is a lovely way to experience the cove.

Historic Buildings

Cades Cove is home to more than 70 historic buildings, which makes it the best place in the park to learn about human inhabitation of the Smokies. Along the 11-mile loop you will have the opportunity to explore various homesteads, including the **John Oliver Place,** the **Henry Whitehead Place,** and the **Carter Shields Cabin.** Historic churches include the 1902 **Methodist Church,** the 1887 **Primitive Baptist Church,** and the 1915 **Missionary Baptist Church.**

At the extreme western end of the loop is the Cable Mill area, which you should

Cades Cove is home to many historic buildings.

Black Bears

Black bears are cute and photo worthy, but they are also wild animals. Attacks by black bears in the Smokies are rare, but they have happened. In May 2000, a 50-year-old schoolteacher from Cosby was attacked and killed by two bears in the Elkmont area of the Great Smoky Mountains National Park. In 2006, a six-year-old girl was killed near Benton Falls in the southern Cherokee National Forest; the girl's mother and two-year-old brother were injured in the same attack. A teenage boy lying in a hammock was injured by a bear in 2015. In May and June, before the summer crops are readily available, bear attacks are more likely to take place. If you see a bear in the woods, proceed with extreme caution and follow this advice from the National Park Service:

- If you see a bear, keep your eyes on it. Do not approach it. If your presence causes the bear to change its behavior (stops feeding, changes its travel direction, watches you, etc.), then you're too close. Being too close may promote aggressive behavior from the bear, such as running toward you, making loud noises, or swatting the ground. The bear is demanding more space. Don't run, but slowly back away, watching the bear. Try to increase the distance between you and the bear. The bear will probably do the same.
- If a bear persistently follows or approaches you without vocalizing or paw swatting, try changing your direction. If the bear continues to follow you, stand your ground. If the bear gets closer, talk loudly or shout at it. Act aggressively and try to intimidate the bear. Act together as a group if you have companions. Make yourselves look as large as possible (for example, move to higher ground). Throw nonfood objects such as rocks at the bear. Don't run and don't turn away from the bear. Don't leave food for the bear; this encourages further problems.
- Most injuries from black bear attacks are minor and result from a bear attempting to get at people's food. If the bear's behavior indicates that it is after your food and you're physically attacked, separate yourself from the food and slowly back away.
- If food isn't the lure and you're physically attacked, fight back aggressively with any available object—the bear may consider you as prey. Help protect others by reporting all bear incidents to a park ranger immediately. But prevention is the best course of action: Keep your distance from bears.

explore on foot. The gristmill here is original; it was built by John P. Cable in the 1870s. Outbuildings around the mill were moved here from other parts of the park. They include a cantilever barn, blacksmith shop, smokehouse, and the Gregg-Cable House, believed to be the first frame house built in the cove.

There is a parking lot, visitors center, and restrooms at the Cable Mill.

Wildlife

Deer are a common sight in Cades Cove. You may also see bear, river otter, elk, woodchuck, wild turkey, rabbit, and squirrel. Elusive animals of the cove include bobcat, raccoon, and gray and red fox.

Over the years, the park service has debated how to manage the Cades Cove environment. Since it is a "historical district," the objective is not to return the cove to nature but to preserve its open spaces and historic buildings. In the early years, the park service issued grazing permits, built large drainage ditches, and introduced nonnative fescue grass. More recently, they have rethought these policies. They are phasing out grazing and haying, resorting instead to prescribed burns to keep the cove open. Native grasses and wildflowers are being reintroduced, and drainage ditches are being plugged so that low-lying areas will return to being wetlands.

Rich Mountain

You can leave Cades Cove (but not enter it) along the one-way Rich Mountain Road, which climbs up and over Rich Mountain and deposits you in Tuckaleechee Cove, near Townsend. The road is steep and curvy, offering lovely views of the cove below. It is closed mid-November-mid-March.

Parsons Branch

Another exit from Cades Cove is **Parsons Branch** Road, a one-way seasonal road that departs the cove near the Cable Mill and heads through unspoiled mountains. After joining with Forge Creek Road, this route ends at Highway 129 and Calderwood Lake. It is 10 miles from Cades Cove to Highway 129.

From 129 you can drive east into North Carolina or west to Chilhowee and the Foothills Parkway in Blount County.

ABRAMS CREEK

Abrams Creek is a lovely and relatively uncrowded corner of the Smokies. Accessible by car only from Happy Valley Road, this is one part of the park you can enjoy without setting foot (or tire) in any of the traditional entry points.

Abrams Creek is the focal point of this recreation area. The creek is deep and wide enough for swimming along the picnic area and campground. It is a good place for fishing, too. From the campground, you can hike four miles to **Abrams Falls,** a 20-foot waterfall. Continue on past the falls another 2.5 miles, and you reach Cades Cove.

Foothills Parkway

An 18-mile limited-access scenic parkway, the Foothills Parkway's western portion connects Chilhowee Lake with Townsend. While strictly located outside the bounds of the national park, the parkway offers stunning views of the western reaches of the Smokies. It is lightly traveled and a good alternative to other more crowded scenic roads.

The parkway follows the ridge of Chilhowee Mountain. There is a campground, picnic area, and observation tower at **Look Rock.** Seemingly in an effort to confuse visitors, the parkway actually consists of two separate roadways. The eastern section, also called the Foothills Parkway, is a six-mile stretch that connects Cosby with I-40.

Fontana Dam

The tallest dam east of the Rocky Mountains, **Fontana Dam** was built in 36 short months starting in 1942. Spurred by World War II, crews worked in three shifts 24 hours a day on the construction. Fontana is some 480 feet tall and required a mind-boggling three million cubic yards of concrete. Completed, it had a power-generating capacity of 293,600 kilowatts.

The Appalachian Trail passes over the top of the dam, and you can, too. It is a mammoth concrete creation—equivalent to a 50-story skyscraper. The renovated **visitors center** (9am-6pm daily) is open May-November, but only when the U.S. Homeland Security threat level is below high (orange). There are picnic tables and an overlook around the dam. Of note to hikers are the restrooms with hot-water showers, dubbed the Fontana Hilton by through-hikers on the Appalachian Trail.

Fontana impounds the Little Tennessee River. The resulting **Fontana Lake** is popular for fishing, boating, and swimming. Fontana Village in North Carolina offers shopping, dining, and lodging options.

GREENBRIER

Greenbrier is a pleasant day-use area located on the banks of the Little Pigeon River. Greenbrier Cove, located where the Middle Prong runs into the Pigeon River, was a population center before the park was formed. Swimming and fishing are popular pursuits here today.

Greenbrier is accessible from Highway 321, which runs from Cosby to Gatlinburg. It is possible to get here without driving through Pigeon Forge or Gatlinburg, which is a plus for many visitors. It is a 3.2-mile drive along the Little Pigeon from Highway 321 to Greenbrier Cove. At the cove, the road forks. Turn left along the Middle Prong to find the trailheads for the Old Settlers Trail and the Ramsey

Cascades Trail. Turn right for picnic areas and a one-mile trail that leads you to historic homesteads and a cemetery.

COSBY

Here, **Cosby** refers to the recreation area at the northeast corner of the park, not the town that lies nearby, outside the bounds of the park. This is one of the least-visited areas in the park, offering hiking, waterfalls, camping, and swimming.

The Cosby Creek provides opportunities for swimming and wading. It is a 2.1-mile hike along the Gabes Mountain Trail to **Hen Wallow Falls.** Several other hiking trails pass through Cosby, including the Low Gap Trail, which climbs 2.5 miles to the Appalachian Trail.

OCONALUFTEE

This is North Carolina's main gateway to the park. Adjacent to the Oconaluftee Visitor Center is the **Mountain Farm Museum** (828/497-1900, sunrise-sunset daily, free), a village of original log structures collected from throughout the park. A historical highlight is seeing a log home built of American chestnut before the chestnut blight. About a half mile north of the Farm Museum is the **Mingus Mill** (no phone, 9am-5pm daily mid-Mar.-mid-Nov., plus Thanksgiving weekend, free), a water-powered gristmill that still operates. Watch corn ground into cornmeal.

About three miles north of **Oconaluftee** is Smokemont. Once a lumber company town, Smokemont is now a recreation area with hiking trails, a picnic area, and a campground.

Located near Bryson City, North Carolina, **Deep Creek** is a recreation area noted for its waterfalls. It is also the location of the Deep Creek and Indian Creek Trails, both of which allow mountain bikes.

A North Carolina attraction of special note is the **Blue Ridge Parkway,** a two-lane scenic blacktop highway that traverses Nantahala and Pisgah National Forests before heading north into Virginia.

CATALOOCHEE

Cataloochee is, in some respects, another Cades Cove. In other respects, it is quite different. A valley surrounded by mountains, Cataloochee was once the most populous community in what is now the national park. Its name is derived from the Cherokee word for the area, *Gadalutsi* (standing up in a row or wave upon wave).

Like Cades Cove, Cataloochee is a cove surrounded by wooded mountains. Historic buildings, including a school, churches, a barn, and several homesteads, provide a sense of human inhabitation. In 2001, the park service introduced a herd of elk in Cataloochee; elk are most likely to be seen in the early morning or evenings.

Unlike Cades Cove, Cataloochee is not crowded. The most obvious reason for this is that getting here is a bit of a challenge. The easiest way to get to Cataloochee is to take I-40 east into North Carolina. At exit 20, it's 11 miles along Cove Creek Road to Cataloochee. The last two miles of your journey are along a gravel road, which is fine for standard passenger vehicles but slow going nonetheless.

Those who make the journey to Cataloochee will be rewarded with scenes of an idyllic mountain valley and notable trout fishing, as well as facilities to camp, hike, and picnic.

Driving Tours

Taking a relaxing drive through the park is a great way to see its most prominent attractions. During weekends in the summer and October expect long lines of traffic on the most popular roads. Try to choose a weekday and strike out early to avoid crowds.

The mountain ascents and descents can strain your vehicle. Watch your engine temperature carefully, particularly in the summer, and use a low gear when coming down the mountain. Slow-moving vehicles should use pullouts.

Several park roads are closed in winter. If you plan to visit between November and April, call the park first to confirm closures.

As you drive through the park, you will see signs for **Quiet Walkways.** These trails are designed to encourage you to get out of your car and stroll for a few minutes through the forest. Some of the walkways are short—about a half mile—while others join up with longer trails. Walk as far as you like, and then turn back and return to your car the way you came.

NEWFOUND GAP ROAD

Journey through the mountain pass that early settlers used to reach the Tennessee side of the mountains. Newfound Gap Road travels 30 miles from Sugarlands Visitor Center to Oconaluftee in North Carolina. The road climbs some 3,000 feet, traveling through ecosystems including cove hardwood, pine-oak, and northern hardwood forests. At the top of the pass you will see an evergreen spruce-fir forest.

About two miles into your drive, you will find the **Campbell Overlook,** where you can see Mount LeConte and other large peaks. There is also a display that identifies the different types of forest found in the Smokies.

At 4.6 miles is the Chimney Tops Picnic Area, once a common place for bear sightings. If you see a bear, remember to keep your distance. Admire it, take photos with a zoom lens, but do not feed it. Less than a mile past the picnic area is a series of three overlooks giving you views of **Sugarland Mountain** and **Chimney Tops.** From here you can see some of the only virgin spruce forest left in the eastern United States.

After passing along the West Prong of the Little Pigeon River and entering into the harsh northern elevations of the Smokies, you will find **Morton Overlook,** situated at 4,837 feet. Here you can look down on the ribbon of asphalt that you just traveled.

Newfound Gap is located at mile 13.2 on your journey. This mountain pass offers spectacular views. Just 0.2 mile beyond Newfound Gap is the entrance to the 7-mile spur road that will take you to Clingmans Dome, the highest point in the park.

From this point, the road descends along the Oconaluftee Valley through the North Carolina side of the park. You will pass several more overlooks and quiet walkways. At mile 29 is the **Mingus Mill,** an old gristmill that operates from early spring through the fall. The drive ends at the **Oconaluftee Visitor Center,** located adjacent to the **Mountain Farm Museum.** This environmentally friendly building was the first in North Carolina built specifically as a full-service visitors center.

CADES COVE LOOP

Cades Cove is one of the most popular sites in the national park and a favorite place for exploring by car. Traffic along the one-way 11-mile loop road proceeds slowly, and there are frequent opportunities to stop and explore on foot. Beware that during peak visitation, it can take five hours to drive the loop—longer than it would take to walk it. Set out early in the day to have it more to yourself.

The drive begins at the **orientation shelter,** located near the Cades Cove campground and picnic area. If you don't already have one, pick up the detailed guide to Cades Cove here. The first homestead you arrive at is that of John Oliver. If it's crowded, drive on—there are more cabins later in the tour.

You will next pass Cades Cove's three extant churches. These beautiful buildings date from 1887 to 1915. Opposite the Missionary Baptist Church is Rich Mountain Road, a winding, steep road that goes to Townsend. It is closed during the winter.

At the extreme southwestern corner of the cove is the **Cable Mill** area. Here you will find restrooms and Cades Cove's, one of the more substantial visitors center. There is also a collection of historic buildings to explore on foot.

As you drive along the southern side of the cove, you will pass a series of homesteads, including the Dan Lawrence Place, Tipton Place, and the Carter Shields Cabin.

There are two north-south "lanes" that cut through the loop. If you have time, and traffic allows it, drive through one of them to see the broad, flat expanse of the cove more closely.

ROARING FORK AUTO NATURE TRAIL

This six-mile paved road departs from Gatlinburg. To find it, turn left at traffic light No. 8 in Gatlinburg and follow the signs to the park. As you enter the park, roll down your windows to feel the cooler and fresher air of the forest. Sights along the way include the **Noah "Bud" Ogle Place,** where you can get out and walk a short nature trail through the forest. Here you'll see parts of the homestead, including a tub mill and wooden flume.

Just past the Ogle Place, the road becomes one-way and winds for six miles along Roaring Fork, a fast-moving mountain stream. Along the way you will pass more historic structures and the trailhead for Grotto Falls, a popular and relatively easy hike. At the end of the drive is the waterfall **Place of a Thousand Drips,** which runs during wet weather.

Hiking

Hiking is the best way to experience the grandeur of the Smoky Mountains. On the trail you will feel, smell, and breathe the mountain air; see wildflowers and trees; and experience views inaccessible by road. Hiking destinations can be historic structures, crisp waterfalls, or one of the Smokies' seemingly enchanted highland balds. Or you may just wish to walk for walking's sake—to acquire a more intimate understanding of the forest and its inhabitants.

In total the Smokies have a whopping 850 miles of hiking trails! Not bad for a park known for its car-friendly access. Only Yellowstone and Yosemite have more miles of trails.

PLANNING YOUR HIKE

The Great Smoky Mountains Association publishes the best and most reliable guides to hiking in the Smokies. These guides provide detailed descriptions of hikes, elevations, hazards, and features you will see along the way. They are a worthwhile investment if you plan to do a lot of hiking. *Hiking Trails of the Smokies* is the authoritative volume. *Day Hikes in the Smokies* and *History Hikes in the Smokies* offer specialized focus.

You can buy the official NPS trail map for less than a dollar at any visitors center or download it for free (www.nps.gov/grsm/planyourvisit/hiking.htm). This map shows trail locations, distances, and the locations of backcountry campsites. The National Geographic/Trail Illustrated map of the Smokies, available at visitors centers and online, is worth the $12 investment, however. It includes much more detail and will hold up to the elements.

Guides and Gear

The best guide service in the Smokies is

Safe Hiking

Getting out of the car and onto your feet is one of the best ways to see the Smokies. When planning a day hike, take time to consider your safety. These commonsense precautions will ensure you have a memorable hike, for the right reasons.

Plan ahead. Using trail maps or guides, determine your route before you set out, and let someone know where you'll be headed and when you expect to be back. Cell phones rarely work on the trail.

Dress the part. Your clothes must protect you from the elements. Layering is a smart choice because temperatures can vary on the trail and weather conditions can change. Wear sturdy shoes with ankle support. Wear wool or fleece clothing (especially socks), not cotton, which holds water and can make you cold.

Wear ID. Whether it is a Road ID bracelet, a medic alert, or just carrying your driver's license, the information about who you are and what ER staff needs to know if you are injured should be easily accessible.

Don't overestimate your ability. Be conservative when planning your walk. Most people average about 1.5 miles per hour. If you have never hiked before, or if it's been a while, start with a day hike no longer than 5 miles. Be sure to give yourself enough time to wrap up before sunset, which can be as early as 5:30pm in winter (and as late as 9pm in summer).

Eat and drink for energy. Bring water and food, even if you don't think you'll need it. Eat before you're hungry and keep hydrated as you walk. Nuts, dried fruit, and chocolate are good energy foods, as are apples and oranges.

offered by **A Walk in the Woods** (4413 Scenic Dr. E., Gatlinburg, 865/436-8283, www.awalkinthewoods.com), run by husband-and-wife team Erik and Vesna Plakanis, naturalists and mountain (and park) enthusiasts. These helpful folks do it all: They lead day hikes and backpacking trips, they offer trip plans for backpackers too busy to do the advance legwork themselves, they shuttle hikers to trailheads or pick them up at their destination, and they offer special classes about birds, wildflowers, and medicinal plants of the Smokies. They also rent backpacking and other mountain gear, so you can try the whole thing out as a hobby before making an investment in expensive gear.

DAY HIKES

There are as many day hikes in the Smokies as there are days. The following are some of the most highly recommended choices.

Loop Hikes

RICH MOUNTAIN LOOP
(8.5 miles, moderate)

This loop offers lovely views of Cades Cove. In spring you may see mountain laurel, and in the fall the colors are spectacular. Park in the large lot at the start of the Cades Cove Loop Road. You will travel along the Rich Mountain Loop Trail (2.9 miles), Indian Grave Gap Trail (2.5 miles), and the Crooked Arm Ridge Trail (2.2 miles).

CUCUMBER GAP
(5.5 miles, easy)

Cucumber Gap explores the Elkmont area and follows the Little River. Expect beautiful wildflowers in spring. Park near the barricade at the start of Little River Trail above Elkmont campground. You will travel on Little River Trail (2.4 miles) before turning back along the Cucumber Gap Trail (2.4 miles) and Jakes Creek Trail (0.3 mile), which passes Elkmont's abandoned summer cottages. Return to your car along the road.

Waterfall Hikes

LAUREL FALLS
(2.6 miles round-trip, easy)

Laurel Falls may be the most popular hike in the Smokies. The pathway is paved all the way to the falls, and the trailhead is located a short drive east of Sugarlands along the Little River Road. If you walk another 0.75 mile past the falls, you will reach stands of old-growth forest. Parking is limited at the trailhead.

RAMSEY CASCADES

(8 miles round-trip, strenuous)

Ramsey Cascades takes you to a spectacular 100-foot waterfall. The last two miles of the hike are through old-growth forest. The trailhead is located near the Greenbrier day-use area of the park.

HEN WALLOW FALLS

(4.4 miles round-trip, moderate)

Hen Wallow Falls takes you to a 45-foot waterfall. The walk originates near the Cosby picnic area.

Hikes with a View

CHIMNEY TOPS

(4 miles round-trip, strenuous)

This is a difficult, but rewarding, hike that takes you to the rock formations known as the Chimneys. The trailhead is located almost seven miles south of Sugarlands Visitor Center along the Newfound Gap Road. The trails, once badly eroded, have been rebuilt for another generation of explorers.

ALUM CAVE BLUFF AND MOUNT LECONTE

(10 miles round-trip, strenuous)

Alum Cave Bluff and Mount LeConte are destinations for seasoned hikers. It is 2.3 miles from the trailhead to Alum Cave Bluffs and another 2.7 miles to Mount LeConte. (Don't be misled by the relatively short distances; this is a challenging hike.) Pause for views at Cliff Tops and Myrtle Point. The trailhead for this excursion is located 6.8 miles south of Sugarlands along the Newfound Gap Road. Like many trails in the Smokies, this one has been eroded from heavy use, rain, and the steep terrain. As of this writing it was undergoing reconstruction during the weekdays, but open on weekends. Check with a ranger before you head out.

★ ANDREW'S BALD

(3.6 miles round-trip, moderate)

Andrew's Bald is one of the Smokies' mysterious highland grassy meadows, called a bald. It is a lovely, magical place, great for relaxing in the sun or even playing a game of Frisbee or catch. The hike departs the Clingmans Dome parking area and travels Forney Ridge Trail.

CHARLIES BUNION

(8 miles round-trip, strenuous)

Charlies Bunion follows the Appalachian Trail along the ridge of the mountains. The trail departs Newfound Gap and provides lovely views along the way. It passes through the spruce-fir forest, where you can see evidence of the Fraser fir's demise.

Strolls

GATLINBURG TRAIL

(3.8 miles round-trip, easy)

This trail connects the city of Gatlinburg with Sugarlands Visitor Center and follows the West Prong of the Little Pigeon River. The path is paved. Leashed dogs and bicycles are allowed.

CADES COVE NATURE TRAIL

(0.75 mile round-trip, easy)

Cades Cove Nature Trail takes you through pine and oak forest. The trail departs from near the Henry Whitehead Place, just past the intersection with Parsons Branch Road. A trail guide ($0.50) available on-site points out notable plants and other sights.

BACKCOUNTRY CAMPING

Backcountry camping allows you to hike longer and reach more remote sites in the park. Backpackers can plan journeys of one, two, three, or more days, with nights spent at backcountry campsites and shelters. For many people, the self-sufficiency of carrying all that you need on your back is a joy. Twenty-four-hour immersion in the wilderness—sometimes without seeing another person—is equally appealing.

Preparation

Multiday hiking expeditions require planning. Consult reference guides and maps carefully. You can also call the volunteers at the **Backcountry Information Office** (865/436-1297, 9am-noon daily) for help planning your trip. As you plan your route, remember that 5-8 miles is a reasonable distance to cover each day. You'll be carrying a heavy pack and will need time at the beginning and end of each day to set up and break down camp.

Rules and Regulations

Every backcountry hiker is required to have a free permit and advance reservations from the park service. You can obtain these from most visitors centers and campgrounds, including Sugarlands, Cosby Campground Office, Greenbrier Ranger Station, Elkmont Campground, Cades Cove Campground Office, Abrams Creek Ranger Station, and Great Smoky Mountains Institute at Tremont.

All backcountry sites are near sources of water—although, depending on the weather, sometimes springs or creeks go dry. They each have a cleared area for your tent and an important cable system for hanging your food out of the reach of bears. Seventeen campsites and all of the Appalachian Trail shelters require advance reservations. These may be made up to a month ahead with the **Backcountry Reservation Office** (865/436-1231, 8am-6pm daily). Remember, camping is allowed at backcountry sites only.

Several rules apply at backcountry sites: You can stay at any one site for a maximum of three nights, and a maximum of one night at any backcountry shelter. No more than eight people can camp together at one site. Fires are prohibited, except at designated sites. Neither are you allowed to stake your tent at a shelter site. Due to quarantines, you should buy local firewood rather than bring some from outside the park.

Equipment

Certain equipment is essential for backcountry camping. You are advised to bring two flashlights, water, raingear, comfortable ankle-supporting shoes, high-energy food, and extra clothing. Always carry a map and compass, and know how to use them. A camp stove, water-purification tablets, and a spade for burying human waste are also very useful. Of course, you will also need to carry a sleeping bag and tent for the night.

In the higher elevations, you must be prepared for cold, wet weather. Expect snow as early as October and as late as April.

Leave No Trace

As you hike and camp in the backcountry, remember that it is up to you to leave the environment as you found it. Never cut, deface, or take any plant, animal, or historical feature. Don't use soap to wash your dishes or bathe in streams and rivers. Human feces should be buried at least six inches deep at least 100 feet from the nearest water source.

Perhaps the most important rule is that all food should be stored at least 10 feet off the ground and 4 feet from the nearest tree limb. All backcountry sites have special cable systems for this purpose. This keeps food out of the reach of bears, who are regular residents of the park.

Other Recreation

BIKING

There are no dedicated mountain biking trails in this national park. While you can bike on any park road, many are unsuitable because they are narrow, steep, and clogged with cars. The best biking experience is the 11-mile Cades Cove loop, which is closed to vehicular traffic until 10am on Wednesday and Saturday mornings May-September. You can rent bikes ($4-6 per hour) during the summer and fall from the **Cades Cove store** (865/448-9034, cadescovetrading.com), which is open March 5-May 31 and August 16-December 4 daily 9am-5pm, June 1-August 15 9am-9pm daily, with a 7am opening time on Wednesday and Saturday during the biking season.

Bikes are not allowed on park trails, with the exception of the Gatlinburg Trail, Oconaluftee River Trail, and the Deep Creek Trail. Less-traveled park roads that are usually good for biking are Greenbrier and Tremont Roads.

In the state of Tennessee, all children 16 years and younger are required to wear a helmet when they ride a bike. Of course, adults are encouraged to do so as well.

HORSEBACK RIDING

Four concessionaires offer horseback riding trips in the park, starting in mid-March and ending in November. These outfitters will rent you a horse for about $30 an hour. Overnight packages are available.

Tennessee outfitters are **Cades Cove Stables** (Cades Cove, 865/448-9009, www.cadescovestables.com), **Sugarlands Stables** (865/436-3535, www.sugarlandridingstables.com), and **Smoky Mountain Stables** (Gatlinburg, 865/436-5634, www.smokymountainridingstables.com). In North Carolina, **Smokemont Stables** (828/497-2373, www.smokemontridingstable.com) is located near Cherokee.

Horses are allowed on certain trails inside the park. The NPS trail map indicates horse trails, as well as backcountry campsites where horses are allowed. In addition, there are five drive-in horse camps that provide access to backcountry horse trails. These camps are located at Cades Cove, Big Creek, Cataloochee, Round Bottom, and Towstring, and are open April-mid-November. Reservations may be made by calling 877/444-6776 or visiting www.recreation.gov.

FISHING

All streams in the Smokies originate as mountain springs, burbling up along the high mountain ridge. At high elevations they flow quickly over steep, rocky beds. As more streams flow into one another, and the elevation drops, the streams widen and flow more slowly. They are no longer sheltered entirely by

Horseback is a great way to explore Cades Cove.

The Brookies Are Back

The Smokies' greatest fish story is that of the native brook trout. These beautiful fish, also called brookies or speckled trout, were once the only type of trout swimming in the Smokies' waters and are the only trout native to the area. They were high-elevation fish, found in fast-moving mountain streams as they dashed down mountainside. But developments in the early 20th century nearly wiped out the brook trout. From 1934 to 1974, officials stocked park streams with other types of trout, including rainbow and brown trout, which quickly took over previous brook trout habitats. In 1976, park officials banned fishing for brook trout to protect the disappearing species. They also made a policy decision that stocking fish was contrary to the mission of the park.

But the story does not end there. In 1986, the National Park Service, working alongside other agencies and nonprofits, started to reintroduce the native brook trout, as well as remove rainbow and brown trout from certain streams. Park fishery managers used a combination of electrofishing and chemicals to remove nonnative trout from stream segments that lie above waterfalls and other barriers that prevent upstream movement of fish.

The result of the reintroduction effort was that beginning in 2006, anglers were able to fish for and keep brook trout in all park streams for the first time in almost 30 years. The population of brook trout is being carefully monitored, and studies have shown that even with fishing, the population remains healthy and self-sustaining. For example, in 2007 officials found that brook trout were the only species of trout in 17 miles of streams, and they were coexisting with other types of trout in 69 additional miles.

Hurdles remain, of course, among them being the acidification of high-elevation mountain streams due to air pollution and climate change, which impact water temperature. But for now, chalk one up for the brookies.

the forest canopy, and they become warmer. By the time they reach the park boundaries, they are rivers.

The diversity of the Smokies' streams and rivers means a diversity of fish. The fast-moving headwaters at high elevations are the native habitat of brook trout, also called brookies, or speckled trout. As streams reach elevations lower than 3,000 feet, other types of trout begin to appear, such as nonnative rainbow and brown trout. Near the park boundaries, where waters are warmer and move more slowly, you will find these trout as well as bass, shiners, minnows, suckers, and darters.

Fishing in the Smokies is a sport, but it is also an opportunity to view wildlife and experience the rich ecosystem of mountain streams. Anglers, particularly those who venture away from roads and into more remote areas of the park, will enjoy the sounds of running water and the sights of salamanders, insects, mammals, and wildflowers.

Guides

Get helpful local knowledge or brush up on your technique with a fishing guide. **Smoky Mountain Anglers** (469 Brookside Village Way, Gatlinburg, 865/436-8746, www.smokymountainangler.com) offers full- and half-day guided fishing trips starting at $175. It also sells hand-tied and commercial flies, plus all the other gear an angler would need.

Rules and Regulations

Fishing is governed by rules that have been established to protect species and the environment. It is up to individual anglers to takes these rules to heart so that the fishery remains strong and the surrounding environment remains in balance.

Fishing is allowed in almost all streams and rivers in the park. The park service closes one or two each season due to active brook trout restoration activities; call ahead or check the NPS website to find out which streams are closed.

Anglers must be in possession of a valid

Tennessee or North Carolina fishing license, depending on where in the park they are fishing. The park service does not sell these licenses, but they are available online and from outfitters in Townsend, Gatlinburg, Cosby, and other gateway communities.

Live bait may not be used, and only single hooks are allowed. Fishing is allowed 30 minutes after official sunrise and must cease 30 minutes before official sunset. The daily limit is five fish, although up to 20 rock bass are allowed. Anglers must stop fishing as soon as they reach their bag limit. Smallmouth bass and brook, rainbow, and brown trout must be at least seven inches long to be kept. There is no size limit for rock bass.

As you fish, be a good park citizen. Pick up any trash you may find and don't move or disrupt rocks, which are where many fish lay their eggs.

SWIMMING

There is nothing as refreshing or enlivening as a dip in the icy-cold waters of a mountain stream. The *Y*, near the Townsend entrance to the park, is one of the most popular swimming holes in the park. Other good places to swim are at the Abrams Creek campground, the Greenbrier picnic area, and at Cosby.

Because swimming in rocky, fast-moving rivers can be dangerous, the park service officials frown on swimming. Despite this, many people do it. If you swim, remember that there are no lifeguards in the park, and that hidden rocks and ledges lurk beneath the surface of the water. Never dive into streams or rivers.

FESTIVALS AND EVENTS

Spring Wildflower Pilgrimage

Wildflowers in the Smokies are legendary, and every April they are in the spotlight at the **Spring Wildflower Pilgrimage** (www.springwildflowerpilgrimage.org). This five-day event organized by the Friends of the Great Smoky Mountains National Park consists of wildflower, fauna, and natural history walks, motorcades, photographic tours, art classes, and indoor seminars.

Pilgrimage events are very popular, and advance registration is almost always a must. Registration is $50 per day, $75 for two or more days for an adult, and $15 per day for high school and college students. Children under 12 are free with a registered adult. A detailed schedule is posted online, and reservations are accepted beginning in October the year before and closes a few days before the festival begins; after that you must register onsite.

Townsend Winter Heritage Festival

In 2007, Townsend and the Great Smoky Mountains National Park established the annual **Townsend Winter Heritage Festival** (800/525-6834, www.smokymountains.org). Featuring concerts, lectures, guided hikes, and other special events, the festival focuses on the music, food, history, and culture of people who once lived inside the park. It takes place in early February.

CLASSES

Great Smoky Mountains Institute at Tremont

The **Great Smoky Mountains Institute at Tremont** (9275 Tremont Rd., 865/448-6709, www.gsmit.org) offers residential environmental education programs year-round. They include naturalist certification and education, photography workshops, hiking weeks, family camping events, and programs for children and teachers.

Accommodations are in large air-conditioned and heated dormitories, and meals are served family-style in a large dining hall. Program fees apply, and reservations are essential.

Smoky Mountain Field School

A partnership between the University of Tennessee and the national park, the **Smoky Mountain Field School** (865/974-0150, www.smfs.utk.edu) offers workshops, hikes, and hands-on instruction. Programs range from daylong seminars on medicinal plants of the Smokies to a two-day program on fly-fishing. Other topics include orienteering, waterfalls of the Smokies, and salamanders in the park. Fees apply to all programs, and advance registration is required.

Ranger-Led Programs

The park service offers lectures, guided walks, and cultural presentations year-round. Check the park service website (www.nps.gov/grsm) for a schedule, or call a visitors center for more information.

Practicalities

ACCOMMODATIONS

There is one lodge inside the national park. ★ **LeConte Lodge** (Mt. LeConte, 865/429-5704, www.lecontelodge.com, adults $136, children $85, including dinner and breakfast), located at the peak of Mount LeConte, is a rustic inn accessible only by foot. While the amenities are sparse, the lodge is a palace for trail-worn hikers. It also offers two- and three-bedroom lodges for 8-13 people, with meals as an added option (prices range from $732-1,082, plus meals).

Accommodations are in rough-hewn log cabins scattered around the compound. Each guest gets a bunk bed with warm wool blankets. There are flush toilets, but no showers or electricity. Cabins are lighted with kerosene lamps and warmed with kerosene heaters.

The standard cabins sleep four or five people and are suitable for two couples or a family. LeConte Lodge does not put strangers in cabins together. Larger "lodges" that sleep up to 13 people are also available. Rental rates include breakfast and dinner, and LeConte's meals are famously filling—perfect after a day of fresh air and hiking. If you're a vegetarian, say so when you make your reservation so that arrangements can be made.

LeConte Lodge is open from mid-March-November. Even though you won't be there in the dead of winter, be prepared for cold temperatures and inclement weather. The temperatures here are often 20-30°F cooler than the lowlands, and it has never gotten above 80°F. During spring and fall, there is often snow on the ground and temperatures in the teens.

Reservations are available starting on October 1 for the next year. The lodge is almost always fully booked by November, although you might still find a vacancy for midweek dates during the spring or fall. If you can't get a room at the inn, there is a park service shelter nearby.

Guests are advised to pack a flashlight and hand towel. You should also pack an extra sweater or coat for the cold weather, plus snacks and water for the trail. Lunch is provided only to guests who are staying more than one night.

CAMPING

There are 10 developed campgrounds in Great Smokies, 5 on the Tennessee side of the park. None of the campgrounds have showers or hookups, and each campground has different size limits for RVs. You can make reservations up to six months in advance for sites at Elmont, Smokemont, Cosby, Cataloochee, and Cades Cove by calling 877/444-6777 or online at www.recreation.gov. All other sites are on a first-come, first-served basis.

A single campsite may be occupied by no more than six people in two tents or an RV and one tent.

Townsend Entrance

★ **Abrams Creek** (Mar.-Oct., $14) has 16 sites located along Abrams Creek and at the trailhead to Abrams Falls. Accessible only from the extreme western end of the park, this is usually one of the quietest campgrounds.

Located along the Foothills Parkway, which travels from Tellico Lake to Walland, **Look Rock** (May-Oct., $14) is the highest-elevation campground on the Tennessee side of the park. **Cades Cove** (year-round, $17-20) has 159 sites and is located at the head of the Cades Cove loop.

Gatlinburg Entrance

Elkmont (Mar.-Nov., $17-23) is the largest campground in the park. Its 220 sites are situated in a pleasant mountain valley along the Little River.

Cosby Entrance

From Cosby you can easily access two pleasant campgrounds. **Cosby** (Apr.-Oct., $14) has 157 sites along the Cosby Creek. **Big Creek** (Apr.-Oct., $14) is a tents-only campground with 12 sites. It is located just over the North Carolina line along Big Creek.

North Carolina

Other North Carolina sites are **Deep Creek** (Apr.-Oct., $17), located near Bryson City, and **Cataloochee** (Mar.-Oct., $20, reservations required), on the eastern end of the park. **Smokemont** (year-round, $17-20) is located about two-thirds of the way from Newfound Gap to Oconaluftee. **Balsam Mountain** (May-Oct., $14), which at more than 5,300 feet is the highest-elevation campground in the Smokies, is located on the remote Balsam Mountain Road and is accessible only from the eastern end of the Blue Ridge Parkway.

FOOD

There are no restaurants or concessions inside the park. The best way to eat is to pack a picnic and enjoy it at one of the many picnic grounds throughout the park. All picnic grounds include tables and fire grates.

HEALTH AND SAFETY

According to the park, motor vehicle accidents and drowning are the leading causes of death in the Smokies. Drive and swim with care. Pay attention to the road even when admiring the scenery. Do not climb on top of waterfalls, and do not go tubing inside the park. If you swim, don't try to show off, and never dive into the water—you cannot see underwater obstructions.

Venomous Snakes

Two species of venomous snakes live inside the park. Northern copperheads and timber rattlesnakes are particularly fond of rocky areas, including stone walls and buildings.

Insects

Look out for yellow jackets, a type of wasp with a feisty sting. Yellow jackets build their nests in the ground and get mad when you disturb them. People with allergies should bring epinephrine kits. Remove any rings from your fingers right away if you're stung on the hand.

Medical Care

LeConte Medical Center (865/446-7000) is located in Sevierville, 15 miles from Gatlinburg. **Blount Memorial Hospital** (865/983-7211) is in Maryville, 25 miles from Cades Cove.

Gateways to the Smokies

The most popular way to get to the Smokies is along the Sevier County corridor, which begins at exit 407 off I-40 and passes through Sevierville, Pigeon Forge, and Gatlinburg. These three communities long ago shed their quiet, rural roots to become pinnacles of hyperactive commercialism. It is hard to imagine a landscape so opposed to the peace and majesty of the national park.

In this land of plenty you will find pancake houses next to outlet malls, monster truck rides next to a Bible museum, and country music dinner theater next to helicopter rides. The "live black bear" attractions seem to have faded into history, but they have been replaced by a rain forest zoo, Christian-themed entertainment complexes, and a theme park owned and operated by Sevier County native Dolly Parton.

The cost of exuberant development is traffic jams, and Sevier County has plenty. It may be a short 15 miles from Sevierville to the park, but it will feel like far more as you stop dozens of times at traffic lights along the way. At least it makes your eventual arrival inside the cool, fresh air of the park that much more welcoming.

It may seem incongruous to pass through this corner of the world on the way to a national park. But there is a time in every person's life for mini golf, and back-to-school shopping is achieved quickly and inexpensively at outlet malls. Or celebrate your big day with a hot-air balloon ride over the foothills. The most open-minded among us might find themselves pleased at the opportunity to "live the nightmare" at Ripley's Haunted Adventure or pause, mesmerized, to watch a taffy machine in action.

If you don't want to join in the fun, then bypass these cities entirely by entering the park through one of the side doors: Townsend or Cosby. It's up to you, but you're missing a prime photo opportunity if you skip the tourist attractions.

GATLINBURG

Surrounded on three sides by the national park, Gatlinburg is the capital city of the Smokies. Once a quiet mountain hamlet where folks lived off the land, the "Burg" is now a busy tourist trap where anything goes. Anything may include new generations of ever more gargantuan hotels and condominiums, or new attractions that try to giggle, wow, or scare the money out of you. Anything is also the unrelenting commercial machine that peddles pancakes, taffy, T-shirts, and mountain-kitsch goodies to whoever passes by.

Gatlinburg is the Tennessee city closest to the Smokies, but the mountains seem oh so far away. If you came to the Smokies strictly to enjoy nature, this isn't where you want to stop. But if your idea of fun includes a little kitsch, then maybe you'll find it in your heart to spend an afternoon gorging on cotton candy and taking funny pictures with your traveling companions. Gatlinburg's scenery and family-friendly atmosphere have made it a popular wedding destination. You'll see wedding chapels and honeymoon deals offered around town.

Ripley's Aquarium of the Smokies

Exactly why you need an aquarium at the doorstep of one of the country's most biologically diverse mountain parks is hard to understand, but too much thought will ruin any trip to Gatlinburg. So if you've grown tired of the environment of the Smoky Mountains, trade it in for exotic ocean seascapes at the **Ripley's Aquarium of the Smokies** (9am-8pm Mon.-Thurs., 9am-10pm Fri.-Sun. Jan.-Feb., 9am-9pm Mon.-Thurs., 9am-10pm Fri.-Sun. Mar.-Memorial Day, 9am-10pm Mon.-Thurs., 9am-11pm Fri.-Sun. Memorial Day-Labor Day, 9am-9pm Mon.-Thurs., 9am-10pm Fri.-Sun. Labor Day-New Year's Day, 888/240-1358, www.ripleyaquariums.com/

gatlinburg/, adults $27, children 6-11 $16, children 2-5 $6, save $2 per ticket when purchased in advance on the website). Here you will see sharks, stingrays, crabs, and lots of colorful tropical fish. There are touch tanks and daily feeding demonstrations. A highlight is walking through an underwater tunnel where you are surrounded on three sides by aquarium tanks. Ripley's latest exhibit is "Perfect Predators: SHARKS!" Note: The cash only parking lot behind the aquarium is $6.

There are six other Ripley attractions in Gatlinburg: Ripley's Believe It or Not! Odditorium, Haunted Adventure, Moving Theater, Mirror Maze, Mini Golf, Guinness World Records Attraction. Combo passes to add these to an aquarium ticket at a discount are available.

★ Arrowmont

Gatlinburg has bulldozed much of its history, but a few remnants remain. One of the best enduring is **Arrowmont School of Arts and Crafts** (556 Parkway, 865/436-5860, www.arrowmont.org). Arrowmont began as a settlement school for mountain folks. It opened in 1912 as the Pi Beta Phi Settlement School, named for the Pi Beta Phi fraternity. In addition to providing an education for mountain children, the school promoted local handicrafts. In 1926, Arrowcraft Shop opened in Gatlinburg as a retail outlet for local crafts.

By the mid-1960s, Sevier County took over public education, and the settlement school turned its focus to crafts. In 1970, the main studio complex was built. Today, Arrowmont is known for its contemporary arts-and-crafts education. Adults from around the country come here for one- and two-week residential programs in clay, paper, metals, fiber, glass, enamels, weaving, basketry, sculpture, polymer clay, woodturning, and woodworking, among others.

Arrowmont Galleries (8:30am-5pm Mon.-Sat. year-round, free) hold more than 10 juried, invitational, themed, and media-oriented exhibitions each year. The art supply store and bookshop stocks tools, art materials, and other specialty items.

Visit artists at work at the Arrowmont School of Arts and Crafts.

Located next to Arrowmont's retail outlet is the **Ogle Cabin** (556 Parkway). Built of rough-hewn logs around 1807, this cabin was the first homestead in Gatlinburg. The location was chosen by William Ogle, but he died before his family could make the move from South Carolina to the mountains of East Tennessee. His widow, Martha Jane Huskey Ogle, and her seven children, together with her brother Peter Huskey and his family, moved to Gatlinburg—then called White Oak Flats—in 1807. The Ogle family remained in the cabin until about 1910, and in 1921 it was sold to the Pi Beta Phi fraternity, which converted it into a clinic and later a museum. Ogle and Huskey remain two of the most common names in Gatlinburg.

★ Great Smoky Mountains Arts and Crafts Community

Craft connoisseurs should head to the **Great Smoky Mountains Arts and Crafts**

Community (light No. 3A, E. Parkway/Hwy. 321 N., www.gatlinburgcrafts.com). The community started during the 1930s, when area artisans decided that instead of selling their wares in downtown Gatlinburg, they would invite tourists out to their studios and homes. During the early years, the community featured traditional, local artisans making brooms, furniture, candles, quilts, and more.

Nowadays, authentic country craftsmen share the stage with modern artisans who have adopted new styles and media. The community, strung along eight miles of back roads, is home to more than 100 different studios, gift shops, and restaurants.

Ogle's Broom Shop (670 Glades Rd., 865/430-4402, www.oglesbroomshop.com) is a third generation workshop making brooms, walking sticks, and canes. **The Chair Shop** (830 Cantrell Cir., 865/436-7413) sells custom-designed handmade rocking chairs. One of the most remarkable stories of the community is the **Cliff Dwellers Gallery** (668 Glades Rd., 865/436-6921, www.cliffdwellersgallery.com). This chalet-style gallery was built in downtown Gatlinburg in 1933 and served as a gallery and workshop for many years. In 1995, threatened with destruction, the building was moved to Glades Road to form part of the Great Smoky Mountains Arts and Crafts Community. It is owned cooperatively by 6 artists and carries the work of some 60 more.

The community is located three miles east of downtown Gatlinburg, along East Parkway (Highway 321 North). The route follows Glades Road and Buckhorn Road before running back into Highway 321. The Gatlinburg Trolley travels the route of the arts community. There are also parking areas and public restrooms along the way.

Because of the sheer number of galleries, think ahead about what you seek. Pick up a copy of the arts community brochure and map, which shows the exact location of each gallery and includes a brief description of what they sell. Or visit the community's website and search for galleries selling the kinds of items you prefer.

Attractions

Attractions are Gatlinburg's special variety of fun, so much so that the Attractions Association of Gatlinburg (www.attractions-gatlinburg.com) was formed to help keep them all straight. New attractions open each year, offering variations on the theme of mindless, family-friendly, fun activities.

Some attractions that stand out from the rest are the **Amazing Mirror Maze** (919 Parkway, 865/436-4415, 9am-midnight daily in season, 9am-10pm daily off season, adults and children 10 and up $10, children 3-9 $8), touted as the world's largest, and **Ripley's Believe It or Not Odditorium** (lights Nos. 7 and 8, Parkway, 865/436-5096, 10am-11pm daily, adults and children 12 and up $17, children 3-11 $10), where you can see some of the strangest and most extreme sights in the world, such as two-headed cows and shrunken heads. **Mysterious Mansion** (424 River Rd., 865/436-7007, 10am-11pm daily May-Oct., adults $11, children $8) is a classic haunted house, and **Motion Ride Movie Theater** (716 Parkway, Reagan Terrace Mall, 865/430-8985, 10am daily, five and older $12-17, children under eight must be accompanied by an adult) shows eight different movies during which the seats move in tandem with the on-screen action, making you feel like you're really in the cab of an 18-wheeler as it descends, without brakes, down the side of a mountain.

Other attractions in Gatlinburg fall in the category of higher-is-better. The **Space Needle** (115 Historic Nature Tr., 865/436-4629, 9am-11pm Mon.-Thurs., 9am-midnight Fri.-Sun., adults $9.50, children 5-12 $5, www.gatlinburgspaceneedle.com) is more than 400 feet tall and offers 360-degree views of scenic Gatlinburg and the surrounding mountains. As if the view were not enough, there is a high-tech arcade, virtual-reality roller coaster, and mini golf inside at the base of the needle.

The **Gatlinburg Sky Lift** (light No. 7, 765 Parkway, 865/436-4307, www.gatlinburgskylift.com, 9am-9pm daily Apr.-May, 9am-11pm daily June-Aug., daily 9am-10pm Sept.-Oct., as posted, weather permitting Nov.-Mar., adults $15, children 3-11 $11.25) is an old-fashioned attraction dating back to the 1950s. Take a seat in a chairlift and climb gently up 518 feet, enjoying views of Gatlinburg and the mountains along the way. This attraction is as near to a timeless pleasure as you'll find in Gatlinburg.

Festivals and Events

The **Craftsmen's Fair** (865/436-7479, www.craftsmenfair.com) takes place at the Gatlinburg Convention Center in July and October. For $7 admission, you can watch more than 180 craftspeople from around the country make traditional crafts such as baskets, pottery, brooms, and stained glass.

Shopping

The best arts-and-crafts shop in downtown Gatlinburg is **Arrowcraft** (576 Parkway, 865/436-4604, 10am-6pm daily, until 7pm during summer), a member of the Southern Highland Craft Guild and affiliate of Arrowmont School of Arts and Crafts. The gallery has a wide selection of crafts, from jewelry to pottery to handwoven clothing, all made by regional craftspeople.

For fishing gear, go to **Smoky Mountain Angler** (469 Brookside Village Way, Ste. 8, 865/436-8746, 8am-5pm Mon.-Sat. spring-fall, 10:30am-4pm Sun., 9am-4pm Mon.-Sat., Sun. 10:30am-4pm winter).

For a full-service outfitter to get you ready for day hikes or camping trips, go to **Nantahala Outdoor Center** (1138 Parkway, 865/277-8209, www.noc.com, 10am-6pm Sun.-Thurs., 10am-8pm Fri.-Sat.). Beyond the basics, this outfitter has climbing gear and clinics in fly-fishing, hiking, and bird-watching. They can also guide your river rafting or take you on a zip line.

Skiing

Yes. Skiing in the South. It is one of the outdoor pleasures of Gatlinburg. You can drive Ski Mountain Road up to **Ober Gatlinburg** (865/436-5423, www.obergatlinburg.com), but most people prefer to take the aerial tramway (adults $12, children 5-11 $9.50) that departs from 1001 Parkway.

Ober Gatlinburg's slopes are not spectacular, but they are good for beginners and the best you'll find in this neck of the woods. In addition to skiing (lift tickets: adults $36-65, seniors and children 7-11 $30-55), you can enjoy year-round ice-skating ($9), Wildlife Encounter ($7, $5 children), and amusements such as an arcade, carousel or chair swing ($3.50) alpine slide or scenic chairlift ($7), and Kiddie Land and Rides ($7).

Accommodations

There are more than 10,000 hotel rooms in and around Gatlinburg. That means even at the top of peak season, you will find a place to lay your head. Prices vary according to season; summertime and fall foliage (October) are peak periods, along with Christmas and New Year's.

While there are some high-end hostelries, Gatlinburg's specialty is affordable family-friendly lodging.

UNDER $100

Gatlinburg is chockablock with motels, particularly along River Road, the road that runs parallel to the Parkway. Some are chain motels, and others are independent. The **Riverhouse Motels** (610 River Rd., 865/436-7821, www.riverhousemotels.com, $49-183) has the most secluded riverfront rooms in town. Rooms have either two queen-size beds or one king, and many come with fireplaces (gas or wood burning) and balconies overlooking the river. Rates vary based on your choice of amenities and the season. Continental breakfast is included. The same management owns **the Riverhouse Motor Lodge** and Riverhouse at the Park (865/436-2070).

Located right on the Parkway, ★ **The Gatlinburg Inn** (755 Parkway, 865/436-5133, www.gatlinburginn.com, $69-159, family suites $119-229) was the third hotel to open in Gatlinburg. Today it holds on to an aura reminiscent of times gone by. The inn was built in 1937 by R. L. Maples Sr. His wife, Wilma Maples, continues to manage the hotel. The inn has 67 rooms and seven suites. There is a swimming pool and tennis courts, and a common sitting area at the front. Lady Bird Johnson, Liberace, Dinah Shore, Tennessee Ernie Ford, and J. C. Penney stayed here, and Boudleaux and Felice Bryant wrote the song "Rocky Top" in room 388. The Gatlinburg Inn is clean and comfortable, with decor (and maids' pink uniforms) frozen in the 1970s. All in all, it is a joyful retreat from the Parkway hustle and bustle, where the hospitality is still genuine. Its motto is "clean, quiet, and comfortable." The Gatlinburg Inn is open April-October. Infant cribs are available by request. No motorcycles or motor homes permitted.

$100-150

Located on River Road, **The Edgewater Inn** (402 River Rd., 865/436-4151, www.edgewater-hotel.com, $90-186) is a full-service hotel and conference center ideal for families or business travelers. Guests enjoy free continental breakfast, indoor and outdoor swimming pools, and in-room fireplaces, plus free parking and wireless Internet.

Situated in a 1930s home, **Laurel Springs Lodge** (204 Hill St., 865/430-9211, www.laurelspringslodge.com, $135-165 is a bed-and-breakfast with five guest rooms. Each room has a private bath, television, and fine linens. Mini-suites have a DVD/VCR and bathrobes. Breakfast is served each morning at 8am and features fresh, hearty home-style fare, although light options are also available. The inn is located within walking distance of many Gatlinburg attractions and restaurants.

Located just a few miles from the Greenbrier area of the Great Smoky Mountains National Park and five miles from Gatlinburg, ★ **Buckhorn Inn** (2140 Tudor Mountain Rd., 865/436-4668, www.buckhorninn.com, $125-285) is a peaceful and elegant retreat. Situated in the Great Smoky Mountains Arts and Crafts Community on 25 acres of land, the Buckhorn Inn has four types of accommodations. Standard rooms ($125-140) have king-size beds, phones, baths, and sitting areas. Premier rooms ($185-205) add a fireplace, private balcony, whirlpool tub, coffeemaker, and refrigerator. Private cottages ($185) offer the same amenities as a premier room but in a small private cottage. Private guesthouses ($195-285) are two-bedroom accommodations with full kitchens, fireplaces, living rooms, and ample outdoor spaces. All Buckhorn rooms are furnished in an elegant, yet homey, style. Comforts abound. Overnight guests enjoy breakfast in the sunny dining room, with views of Mount LeConte in the park. A four-course dinner is served nightly at an additional charge of $35 per person. The food at Buckhorn Inn is superb. You can pass the time walking the nature trail or strolling in Rachael's Labyrinth. Relax in the library or watch the view from the flagstone terrace. Children under 12 are not permitted at in the lodge but are welcomed in cottages and guesthouses. On weekends and holidays there is a two-night minimum stay. The innkeepers offer special packages for honeymooners, hikers, fly fishers, and others.

$150-200

Located on a mountainside far above Gatlinburg, **The Lodge at Buckberry Creek** (961 Campbell Lead Rd., 865/430-8030, www.buckberrylodge.com, $180-460) is an all-suite luxury lodge. Modeled after the Adirondack-style mountain lodge, with lots of exposed wood and rustic finishes, Buckberry feels a bit like an elite mountain club that you're lucky to be a member of. Guest suites have king-size beds, sitting areas, balconies, and kitchens. Fine dinners are served nightly in the restaurant, which is praised as one of the area's most upscale.

CHALETS AND CABINS

In addition to hotel rooms, Gatlinburg guests can stay in private cabins and "chalets." The term *chalet* traditionally referred to an A-frame-style vacation home, but now it encompasses just about every type of vacation apartment. Most chalets and cabins offer amenities like fireplaces, whirlpool tubs, full kitchens, and balconies. They are located on the hillsides and valleys surrounding Gatlinburg.

Rates range $500-1,200 weekly for one- and two-bedroom cabins. Large four- and five-bedroom properties can cost as much as $3,000 per week. Daily rates are often available and start around $120.

There are dozens of different chalet and cabin developments, and thousands of individual properties. The best way to make a reservation is to use a reservation service. The friendly folks at **Smoky Mountain Accommodations** (865/436-6943, www.smagatlinburg.com) can recommend a property that fits within your price range and meets your needs (e.g., kid friendly, close to the park, close to Gatlinburg, etc.). On the website you can look at pictures and read a description of each property.

Food

Restaurants in Gatlinburg serve pancakes. Also steaks, barbecue, burgers, and other crowd-pleasing country-style food. But lots of pancakes. Snack shops sell sweets, candy, doughnuts, and other temptations. There's even a Hard Rock Café here.

The Peddler Restaurant (820 River Rd., 865/436-5794, http://peddlergatlinburg.com, 5pm-10pm Sun.-Fri., 4:30pm-10pm Sat., $20-40) is Gatlinburg's best steak house, with a super salad bar. In addition to New York strip, prime rib, and filet mignon, you can order fresh trout, shrimp, or blackened chicken. The extra-large salad bar comes with dinners or is available for $13 on its own.

The fine folks who own The Peddler also operate **Park Grill Steakhouse** (1110 Parkway, 865/436-2300, www.parkgrillgatlinburg.com, opens lunch 11:30am daily, 4:30pm Sat., 5pm Sun.-Fri., $12-35), giving you another good option for a hearty meal.

For breakfast all day, the **Pancake Pantry** (628 Parkway, 865/436-4724, 7am-4pm daily June-Oct., 7am-3pm daily Nov.-May, $6-12) cannot be beat. Its 24 different varieties of pancakes share the menu with waffles, eggs, and other traditional hearty breakfast favorites, plus box picnic lunches if you want to take something into the park. Beginning at 11:30am daily, the Pantry offers sandwiches, soups, and salads. There's a Pancake Pantry in Nashville, too, and people across the state are loyal to this restaurant.

Follow Highway 321 north 1.5 miles to Newman Road to find ★ **Greenbrier Restaurant** (370 Newman Rd., 865/436-6318, www.greenbrierrestaurant.com, 4:30pm-9pm Sun.-Thurs., 4:30pm-10pm Fri.-Sat., $15-30), which serves dinner specialties, including steak and shrimp, and indulgent desserts. Vegetarian options include sautéed vegetables with provolone cheese and pasta Alfredo. There is a children's menu ($7-8).

Information

Gatlinburg operates two visitors information centers. The first (1011 Banner Rd., 865/436-0519, 8:30am-7pm daily Memorial Day-Oct. 31, 8am-5:30pm daily Nov.-May) is located along U.S. 441 before you arrive in the city. This is also a national park visitor information center, and it is a park-and-ride facility for the Gatlinburg Trolley.

The second (88 River Rd., 865/436-0535, 9am-5:30pm Sun.-Thurs., 9am-9:30pm Fri.-Sat. Jan.-Mar. 31, 8:30am-9pm Sun.-Thurs. 8:30am-9:30pm Fri.-Sat. Apr.-Dec. 31) is located at traffic light No. 5, right next to Ripley's Aquarium.

To request information, contact the **Gatlinburg Chamber of Commerce** (800/588-1817, www.gatlinburg.com).

Services

The **Anna Porter Public Library** (158 Profitt Rd., 865/436-5588) has free Internet access and a Smoky Mountain Collection where you can browse history books, guides, and nature reference books.

Gatlinburg's largest food store is **Food City** (1219 E. Parkway, 865/430-3116), located on Highway 321 opposite the Gatlinburg post office. **Parkway Liquor Store** (286 Parkway,

865/436-9635) sells wine, liquor, and pre-mixed cocktails.

Getting There and Around

Gatlinburg is easy to find, but traffic can be intense. Vehicles creep slowly along the Parkway, and you feel more like you're cruising than driving. Parking, when you find it, costs around $2 per hour or $8 a day.

The **Gatlinburg Trolleys** are the answer. Free parking is available at the Gatlinburg Welcome Center on the Spur, outside of town, and at the municipal garage located on Highway 321. From either stop you'll pay $0.50 for the trip into town, and the trolley will deposit you right in front of the aquarium. From there you can catch rides up River Road ($0.50), out Highway 321 to the Great Smoky Mountains Arts and Crafts Community ($1), or into the national park ($2), or purchase an all-day pass ($2). Exact change is required on all routes. Or you can hoof it—walking distances in Gatlinburg are short.

Trolley route maps are available from visitors centers, by download (www.gatlinburg.com/maps/), or by calling the Mass Transit Center at 865/436-3897 or www.gatlinburg-trolley.org.

If you are traveling through Gatlinburg only to get to the national park, skip it all by taking the **Gatlinburg Bypass.** The bypass veers off Highway 441 shortly after the Gatlinburg Welcome Center and climbs the mountainside overlooking Gatlinburg. It deposits you back on Highway 441 inside the national park.

PIGEON FORGE

Nothing can truly prepare you for **Pigeon Forge**. This long strip of highway that lies between Gatlinburg and Sevierville on the road to the Smokies takes tacky to the nth degree. You can see the evolution of lowbrow consumerism here, where roadside pit stops selling concrete lawn ornaments seem quaint next to the fruits of modern-day developers' machinations, some of which have been hit by postrecession foreclosures. Consider this: In 2008 Pigeon Forge welcomed its newest development—Belle Island, a massive $110 million Disney World-esque development with 95 retail shops, 126 hotel rooms, and four major restaurants. Located on an actual island, the development went belly-up and was demolished. But by 2013, it was redeveloped, and by 2015, the space, which now includes a 200-foot Ferris wheel, a Jimmy Buffett Margaritaville hotel and restaurant, and plenty of shopping and restaurants, is now completely at capacity, with no vacant real estate and no parking for visitors. That's Pigeon Forge; love it or hate it, you can't keep it down.

Before you discard Pigeon Forge, consider what it has going for it. The Dollywood theme park is truly something, with its legit roller coaster, mountain craft demonstrations, and musical performances. During the hot summer months, who can resist Dollywood's Splash Country, the crème de la crème of water parks? If shopping is on your list, then try on Pigeon Forge's myriad outlet malls. If you truly let go, then dive right in to all the rest: comedy barns, Elvis museums, indoor skydiving, bungee jumping, car museums, mini golf, and country music dinner theater.

★ Dollywood

There is no way around it: **Dollywood** (2700 Dollywood Parks Blvd., 800/365-5996, www.dollywood.com, adults $59, seniors 60 and older $54, children 4-11 $47) is just good clean fun. Owned and operated by Sevier County native Dolly Parton, the Dollywood theme park combines excellent rides with family-friendly entertainment. Mountain craft demonstrations keep Dolly's childhood alive. The park's wooden roller coaster, the Thunderhead, is thrilling and fun; at River Battle you get to aim and shoot water cannons at fellow riders; and the Blazing Fury takes you through an 1880s frontier town engulfed in flames. Dollywood also has plenty of less-thrilling attractions. The county fair has Ferris wheels and other classic amusements. Calico Falls Schoolhouse is a replica of a one-room mountain school, and the Dollywood

Express takes you on a five-mile railroad journey through the foothills of the Smokies. There is also a bald eagle sanctuary and the Southern Gospel Music Hall of Fame.

Dollywood also offers live music. Performers on various stages play bluegrass, country, gospel, and oldies. All shows are free with your admission to Dollywood.

Arts-and-crafts demonstrations are also a big part of Dollywood. You can watch glass-blowers at work, see lye soap being made, and observe candles being dipped. A blacksmith shop produces metalwork, and a woodcarver makes one-of-a-kind pieces of artwork.

As if this weren't enough, Dollywood puts on several major events each year, when special entertainment is offered. The Festival of Nations, held March-May, includes singers, dancers, and performers from around the world. Barbeque and Bluegrass, held during September, offers special concerts by bluegrass favorites, and Smoky Mountain Christmas in December is a remarkable display of lights. Other events are KidsFest (June-August) and Harvest Celebration (October-November).

For less than the price of two general admission tickets, you can buy a season pass to Dollywood. Many area residents choose this option so they can come back again and again, and so they won't feel compelled to cram everything Dollywood into a single visit.

Dollywood's doors open at 9am or 10am and close between 6pm and 9pm, depending on the season. Call ahead or check the website to find out what time the gates open on any particular day. Dollywood is closed January-March and, except during the peak of the summer, is closed some weekdays.

Dollywood's Splash Country (light No. 8, 1198 McCarter Hollow Rd., 865/429-9910, 10am-6pm daily mid-May-mid-Sept., closes at 7pm late June-July, adults $47, seniors 60 and older and children 4-11 $42) is a super-duper water park with 23 different rides and slides. Some are thrilling white-water adventures, and others are placid kid-friendly games. Swiftwater Run takes you round and round a tightening corkscrew until you're sent down the chute. The Cascades is an 8,000-square-foot lagoon-style pool with interactive elements ideal for younger children.

Plan to stay all day to get your money's worth. On top of the admission fee, you'll pay $8 for parking unless you have a gold season pass or gold super season pass. Guests are not permitted to bring coolers, food, or other picnic goods inside the park, although you can

Dollywood features thrilling coasters for adrenaline junkies.

leave the park and return later in the day. Food is available for purchase.

Dollywood's **DreamMore Resort** (2525 DreamMore Way, 800/365-5996, www.dollywoodsdreammore.com) opened as the resort's first on-property hotel, with a spa, pools, restaurant, and breathtaking views of the Smokies.

Children under 13 are not allowed in Splash Country without an adult.

Other Sights

Pigeon Forge's city park is **Patriot Park,** located behind the Old Mill. Named for the Patriot Bomber that is on permanent display, the park is the site of festivals, fairs, and other events.

You can't help but notice **WonderWorks** (Parkway, 865/868-1800, www.wonderworkstn.com, 9am-midnight daily, adults 13 and up $24, children 4-12 and seniors 55 and up $16), whose facade is turned completely upside down. The illusion is merely cosmetic, but it sets the stage for the over-the-top kid-friendly activities inside. WonderWorks includes a disaster zone where you can feel what it would be like to experience a major earthquake or hurricane. There is a gallery of optical illusions, and laser tag ($15 unlimited play or combo with entry, 1 game $3 extra). WonderWorks is also home to *Terry Evanswood Presents The Wonders of Magic* ($18, $14 if purchased in entry combo), a family-friendly magic show that is staged several times a day.

The **Hollywood Wax Museum** (106 Showplace Blvd., 865/428-5228, www.hollywoodwaxmuseum.com/pigeonforge, 9am-10pm daily, closes at midnight many weekends and during summer, adults $17.95, children $8.95, $1 discount if ordered online) was moved from Gatlinburg to Pigeon Forge. Look for the giant King Kong replica hanging from the building. Inside you'll see wax creations of other celebrities, both real and imagined. The museum is pure camp, but it's fun. Check the website for online discounts on tickets before you head over.

Entertainment

Gaudy stage entertainment is another Pigeon Forge hallmark. Massive theater complexes line the Parkway, surrounded by even more massive parking lots. **Country Tonite** (129 Showplace Blvd., 865/453-2003, www.countrytonitepf.com, adults $28.75, children 12 and up $23.75) is a country music show with patriotic music and gospel thrown in. **The Comedy Barn** (2775 Parkway, 865/428-5222,

WonderWorks is one of Pigeon Forge's oddities.

www.comedybarn.com, adults $30, child 3-11 $10) offers terribly hokey country-style comedy.

Memories Theatre (2141 Parkway, 865/428-7852, www.memoriestheatre.com, adults $27, seniors $25, teens $20, children 6-11 $5, children 5 and under free) is one of the longest-running shows in town, with perennial Elvis tribute shows plus tributes to other stars such as Tina Turner and Tim McGraw.

One of the most famous dinner theaters is the Dolly (as in Parton's) **Dixie Stampede** (3849 Parkway, 865/453-4400, www.dixie-stampede.com, adults $50-62, children 4-11 $28-34). Here guests are seated around a circular arena where actors and animals put on a rodeo-inspired dinner show. A four-course barbecue meal is served while you watch.

Feast on the fixin's—that's corn, fried chicken, "mashed taters," and more—while watching the comedy **Hatfield & McCoy Dinner Show** (119 Music Rd., 865/ 908-7469, www.hatfieldmccoydinnerfeud.com, 5pm and 8pm daily, adults $54.95, $19.95). The family-friendly show offers stunts and singin' and dancin'. In December there is a Christmas-themed option.

The Escape Game (131 The Island Dr., 865/868-3400, theescapegamepigeonforge.com, $31.99) is a national chain of entertainment for grownups who want to do something else besides hang out at the bar. You book your group for a scheduled hour-long adventure, like an interactive game of Clue. Together you work to solve the themed riddle and get out of the room. Different rooms accommodate different numbers of people. This is a more intellectual pursuit than Pigeon Forge's joke-filled dinner theaters, but lots of fun.

Shopping

Pigeon Forge once was a destination for outlet shopping; now it is more souvenirs than designer discounts. However, you'll still find some bargains at the **Shoppes of Pigeon Forge** (161 E. Wears Valley Rd.), you'll find Eddie Bauer, Burlington Brands, and Reebok Outlet Stores. Though it is technically located inside Sevierville's city limits, the **Tanger Outlet Sevierville** (1645 Parkway, Sevierville, 865/453-1053) is Pigeon Forge at heart. Five Oaks is the area's newest and largest outlet mall, with Old Navy, Gap, Van Heusen, Brooks Brothers, and Reebok, among many others. Many retailers relocated here from other outlet malls.

Most outlet malls open at 10am during the winter and 9am during summer. They usually stay open until sunset.

Pigeon Forge Pottery was a Pigeon Forge institution. In 1946, Douglas Ferguson established the business, and over the years he formed a reputation for excellent pottery. Visitors enjoyed watching craftspeople work when they visited the shop, and the pottery's famous black bears were collectors' items. Ferguson died in 2000, and the pottery was sold to the Old Mill. Today, **Pigeon River Pottery** (Old Mill Sq., 865/453-1104) sells beautiful handmade pottery in a variety of styles, but you won't find many of the designs that made the pottery famous in the first place. Check the seconds corner for discounted pieces.

Recreation

Pigeon Forge leads the United States in far-fetched extreme activities—the type of thing you'll be talking about after you get home.

Case in point: **Outdoor Gravity Park Pigeon Forge** (203 Sugar Hollow Rd., 865/366-2687, 10am-5pm Sun.-Thurs., 10am–6pm Fri.-Sat., $20). H2OGO and Fishpipe barrel are water and wild rides, such as rolling down a 1,000-foot hill in a hamster wheel-type ball, with water.

Indoor skydiving is a Pigeon Forge tradition. At **Flyaway** (3106 Parkway, 877/293-0639, www.flyawayindoorskydiving.com, 11am-6pm weekdays, 10am-7pm weekends, $34) you can "body fly" in a vertical wind tunnel. You'll get about 20 minutes of instruction, plus the use of a suit, helmet, and other safety gear. Then you'll get about three minutes of flying time inside the tunnel. What fun!

Finally, there is bungee jumping at **The Track** (2575 Parkway, 865/453-4777, www.pigeonforgetrack.com, $24). Jump from a 65-foot platform attached by a harness and elastic bungee cord. The Track also has bumper cars, go-karts, and an arcade.

Accommodations

There's no shortage of places to stay in Pigeon Forge, from cabins and chalets to campgrounds to budget motor lodges to resort-style hotels. This includes many major chains as well as independently owned condos through sites such as airbnb.com and vrbo.com.

★ **DreamMore Resort** (2525 DreamMore Way, 800/365-5996, www.dollywoodsdreammore.com, $149-475) is exactly the kind of onsite hotel befitting the Dollywood brand. You're greeted by a big porch with rocking chairs, a portrait of Dolly in a meadow, and Parton's signature butterflies on every possible surface. The 300-room resort has epic views of the Smokies, ideal for watching leaves change colors or fireworks bursting in the sky.

This is a true family-friendly destination, with indoor and outdoor pools, s'mores outside every night, storytelling at dinner at **Song & Hearth** (7am-11pm daily), a relaxing spa and salon, and shuttles to the theme park. The lobby has checkers and other games you can play with your kids and the pools are designed so that the kiddie pool isn't separated from the rest of the family: The idea is that you all have fun together. The food and drink here aren't the strong suit; they're decent but nothing special—the rest of hotel experience is though. The staff is as friendly as you imagine Dolly herself would be.

The cozy **Margaritaville Island Hotel at Pigeon Forge** (131 Island Dr., 844/434-6787, www.margaritavilleislandhotel.com, $239-499) on the Island at Pigeon Forge development combines Jimmy Buffet-style laid back attitude with Southern Appalachian hospitality. The 132-room hotel is in a bustling location, near the Ferris wheel and other entertainment. But the rooms themselves have a décor that elicits calm, as does the spa and the rooftop deck.

Pigeon Forge loves nothing more than a kitschy theme. So it should be no surprise that there's somewhere like **The Inn at Christmas Place** (119 Christmas Tree Ln., 888/920-4244, www.innatchristmasplace.com $94-329) exists. Every day is December 25. You have all

Dollywood's DreamMore Resort

the standard hotel amenities, such as a fitness center and wireless Internet, but you'll also get cookies (just like Santa) before you go to bed, Christmas carols, and a singing Santa.

Food

Like Gatlinburg, Pigeon Forge has a lot of family-friendly eateries, chain restaurants, and a lot of places to grab pancakes. Pigeon Forge has quirky liquor laws. You can get a drink in a restaurant, but there are no packaged liquor sales. While many restaurants serve alcohol, just as many do not. And it is likely that your bartender won't know much about your wine or how to mix an Old Fashioned.

The **Old Mill** (175 Old Mill Ave. at light No. 7, 865/428-0771, www.old-mill.com, 8am-9pm daily, $5-25) is a favorite for Southern-style dining. Come here for hearty meals all day—the dinner menu offers no fewer than five different Southern fried specialties: chicken, steak, pork chops, beef liver, and country ham.

Mel's Diner (119 Wears Valley Rd., 865/429-2184, www.melsdinerpf.com, 7am-midnight daily, $6-10) is a classic diner in the traditional sense, with affordable breakfasts (pancakes, of course), burgers, and other items from the grill, plus the iconic facade.

Family-style is the watchword at **Paula Deen's Family Kitchen** (131 The Island Dr., 865/366-1510, 7:30am-10pm Sun.-Thurs., 7:30am-11pm Fri.-Sat., adults $21.99, children $10.99). Choose multiple sides and entrées for your table; you're charged per person, and eat all you can. The menu is chock-full of southern favorites like pot roast, pork chops, and fried chicken. The restaurant is on the second floor. There's likely to be a wait but you can take your pager and roam the Island shops or the gift store on the first floor. The restaurant does not serve alcohol (But there's an **Old Smoky Tennessee Moonshine Distillery** (131 The Island Dr., olesmoky.com, 10am-11pm daily) should you want some hooch.).

Getting Around

Pigeon Forge and Sevierville have joined forces to offer the **Fun Time Trolley** (865/453-6444, www.pigeonforgetrolley.org). All trolleys originate at Patriot Park. An all-day pass can be purchased at the Fun Time Trolley office for $2.50. The **North Parkway Trolley** ($0.50) travels north through Pigeon Forge and continues on into the city of Sevierville. After traveling north to the Governor's Crossing and Walmart

Margaritaville Island Hotel at Pigeon Forge

areas, it turns south again and returns to Patriot Park. The **South Parkway Trolley** ($0.50) travels north to traffic light No. 6, then turns westbound onto Pine Mountain Road. It then travels to the south city limits, serving campgrounds in the area and the Dixie Stampede before returning to Patriot Park. The **Gatlinburg Welcome Center Trolley** ($0.75) travels nonstop to the Gatlinburg Welcome Center on the spur just outside the city. The **Dollywood Trolley** ($0.50) travels to and from Dollywood, including DreamMore. The **Splash Country Trolley** ($0.50) goes to and from Splash Country, also including DreamMore. The **Wears Valley Trolley** ($0.50) travels north on Teaster Lane through the Pigeon River Crossing/Riverview Mall area to traffic light No. 2 on the Parkway. From light No. 2 it goes to Community Center Drive, McGill Street, and then on to Wears Valley Road, continuing past campgrounds and other businesses to the city limits before returning to Patriot Park by the same route. The **Courthouse Trolley** ($0.50) travels north on Teaster Lane, passing through mall areas and entering the Parkway northbound at traffic light No. 2. It continues north into downtown Sevierville before turning around at the Sevier County Courthouse. Stops include Tanger Outlet Sevierville, Walmart, Kmart, and the River Place Shops.

Trolleys run daily 8am-midnight early March-October and 10am-10pm daily November-December. Exact fare is required, and fare is required to be paid each time someone boards unless they have purchased the $2.50 day pass. Parkway trolleys run every 20-25 minutes, Dollywood trolleys every 15-20 minutes, Wears Valley trolleys every 40-45 minutes, the Gatlinburg Welcome Center trolley every 20-25 minutes, and the Courthouse trolley runs every 25 minutes.

SEVIERVILLE

It used to be that the sprawl of malls, oversized theaters, restaurants, and tourist attractions was pretty much contained to Pigeon Forge. **Sevierville** (seh-VEER-vil), the Sevier County seat and first city on the journey from interstate to national park, was a laid-back place. But the lure of tapping into tourist dollars was too much, and Sevierville is beginning to look like a young Pigeon Forge. Shopping malls, giant flea markets, mini golf, and hotels now line the entire route along Highways 66 and 441. The old city center of Sevierville is just a dot on the map.

Sights

Sevier County's elegant Victorian courthouse dominates the Sevierville skyline. Stop here to see a life-size statue of a willowy young Dolly Parton, Sevier County's hometown girl.

Located at the Sevierville municipal airport, the **Tennessee Museum of Aviation** (135 Air Museum Way, 865/908-0171 or 866/286-8738, www.tnairmuseum.com, 10am-6pm Mon.-Sat., 1pm-6pm Sun., closes at 5pm Jan.-Feb. adults $12.75, seniors $9.75, children 6-12 $6.75, children under 6 free) is an enthusiast's dream. Glass-enclosed cases display memorabilia associated with Tennessee aviation, and the heated exhibit hangar houses airworthy planes, including two P-47D Thunderbolts and a Navy TBM Avenger. The aviation museum is located two miles outside of downtown Sevierville along Highway 411. Look for the signs to the airport and aviation museum.

Recreation

The Knoxville K-Jays moved east to Sevier County in 2000 and became the **Tennessee Smokies** (Hwy. 66, 865/286-2300, www.smokiesbaseball.com, field-level seats: adults $9.50, seniors and children $8.50, bleacher seats: adults $7.50, seniors and children $6.50, grass berm seating: $6). The Smokies, a AA Chicago Cubs affiliate, play in a stadium located right next to I-40 at exit 407. The regular season runs April-August. Smokies games are heavy on between-inning entertainment and promotions. Special no-alcohol seating areas are available. Reserved-seat tickets are $1 more if you buy them at the gate. Advance tickets are available online and in person at the Smokies box office.

For something totally different, sign up for a hot-air balloon ride with **Smoky Mountain Balloon Adventures** (865/622-1394, www.smokymtnballoons.com). For $295 per adult (less if you agree to join up with another group), you'll get 1-1.5 hours in a hot-air balloon, floating over the foothills of the Smokies. These are private balloon trips; you'll be with members of your own party and will only be put in with another group if you arrange it that way at the time of your reservation. Typically you'll meet at the **Starbucks** (646 Winfield Dunn Pkwy./Hwy. 66) in Sevierville and be shuttled to the launch site, but you'll get directions when you book. Launch sites vary based on wind and weather conditions. After your flight, you'll enjoy a toast with the captain, and you'll get a special certificate as a keepsake. Balloon flights are offered April-November. Most flights depart early in the morning or late in the afternoon and reach 1,500-2,000 feet above the ground.

The **Wilderness at the Smokies Resort** (1424 Old Knoxville Hwy., 877/325-9453, www.wildernessatthesmokies.com) is for families who want a little adrenaline on their vacation and didn't get it in Pigeon Forge. After all, one of its water park rides features a trap door launching pad and a gravity-powered loop-the-loop experience at 2.5 G (g-force). The resort has both "dry" amusement-park-type rides and both indoor and outdoor water parks, plus a conference center, hotel, and other resort amenities.

Food

One of Sevierville's most beloved restaurants is the ★ **Applewood Farmhouse Restaurant** (240 Apple Valley Rd., 865/428-1222, www.applewoodfarmhouserestaurant.com, 8am-9pm daily, $7-20), a country-cooking institution. Applewood is located next to the Apple Barn, a general store and cider press, where you can watch as apple cider and other goodies (from apples) are being made.

Getting Around

Traffic congestion is a problem in Sevierville. In 2006, officials opened State Route 448, which is supposed to speed up your journey through town. Traffic headed toward Pigeon Forge and the national park should remain on Highway 441 (the Parkway), but traffic headed in the other direction, toward the interstate, should follow the signs to the new Route 448 through town.

An even newer alternate route worth noting is Veteran's Drive, or Highway 449. This four-lane divided highway runs from Highway 411 to Pigeon Forge, bypassing the sprawl and traffic lights. You enter Pigeon Forge near Dollywood.

COSBY

Located on the northeastern side of the Great Smoky Mountains, **Cosby** is a rural town with services and accommodations for visitors. From the Cosby entrance to the park, you can explore Cosby campground and picnic area, hike to Henwallow Falls or Mount Cammerer, or join up with the Appalachian Trail.

Historically, Cosby was known as a moonshiners' town. Today, it is home to artists and craftspeople. Near Cosby, the town of Hartford is noted for white-water rafting, and Newport is a center for commerce in the area.

Arts and Crafts

Holloway's Country Home Quilts (3892 Cosby Hwy./Hwy. 321, 423/487-3866, www.hollowaysquilts.com) is a quilter's studio, quilting supply store, and place to purchase finished quilts and other mountain handicrafts. Holloway's is a cozy, welcoming place, jam-packed with goodies of interest to quilters and non-quilters alike. Pop in next door at the studio to see a quilter at work.

Look for the barn board building where the Cosby Highway intersects with Wilton Springs Road to find **Santa Cruz Woodworks** (2776 Cosby Hwy./Hwy. 321, 423/623-7856). Bob and Cindy Evans make solid wood cabinets, rocking chairs, birdhouses, trunks, and much more. Browse the shop or put in your custom order.

River Rafting

Near the town of Hartford, the Pigeon River is a popular venue for **white-water rafting.** The Upper Pigeon offers fast-paced Class III and IV rapids while the Lower Pigeon is placid and peaceful. Outfitters offer trips on both sections of river, but not every day. Since the Pigeon is a dam-controlled river, as are most in the state, trips are offered only when there is water on which to raft. Make your reservations in advance.

Outfitters including **Wildwater Ltd.** (866/319-8870, www.wildwaterrafting.com) and the **Nantahala Outdoor Center** (NOC) (828/785-5082, www.noc.com) offer journeys on both parts of the river. All outfitters are located along Old Hartford Road, at exit 477 off I-40. NOC also offers stand-up paddleboarding classes and a number of other water-based activities for all ages and ability levels. NOC is one of the country's top water-education centers. If you're the kind of traveler who plans vacations around access to white water, check out the offerings in advance.

Llama Trekking

For a truly upscale day hike or a luxurious backpacking expedition, consider llama trekking. Let the llamas carry your picnic or overnight gear while you walk comfortably to destinations in the Cherokee National Forest and Nantahala National Forest (llamas aren't permitted in the Great Smoky Mountains National Park). **English Mountain Llama Treks** (828/506-1017) in Newport offers day trips for $75-100 a person. Call for group rates or information on two-to-three day treks; all gear and food is provided. The former owner, Lucy Lowe, 828/622-9686 operates horse trail rides.

Accommodations

The nine-room **Christopher Place** (1500 Pinnacles Way, Newport, 423/623-6555, www.christopherplace.com, $130-330) is an intimate and elegant bed-and-breakfast. Located near Newport, atop English Mountain, this colonial-style resort with a European atmosphere is perfect for a romantic getaway. Guests may walk the extensive grounds, play tennis, work out in the fitness room, swim in the pool, or relax in the billiards room or library. You may also simply want to retreat to your suite, which is appointed with luxurious furnishings and private bath. Some rooms also have private balconies overlooking the mountains. Christopher Place guests enjoy a full breakfast as part of their room rate. Dinner is served nightly at the Mountain View Dining Room for an additional $40 per person. Reservations are required 24 hours in advance.

Not just a place to stay, the **French Broad Outpost Ranch** (461 Old River Rd., Del Rio, 423/487-3147, www.frenchbroadriver.com, $225-280 per adult, three, four, and seven night stays; check website for last-minute discounts) is a place to go. This dude ranch offers overnight accommodations in the Rough Cut, a Western-style lodge, and daily horseback riding, ranching, and white-water rafting excursions. Meals are included in the rates, which are $280 per adult per night during the high season and $225 in the low season. Slightly lower prices are offered for children, and weeklong packages are available. Prices include all of the activities in which you'll partake at the ranch. Rooms are rustic and designed to sleep families or groups. Meals are served family-style and feature hearty meat-and-potatoes fare.

Food

★ **Carver's Applehouse Restaurant** (3460 Cosby Hwy./Hwy. 321, 423/487-2710, 8am-8pm daily, $6-16) is country dining the way it ought to be. The dining room overlooks the Carver apple orchard, and the home-style fare is comforting and tasty. Each meal—breakfast, lunch, or dinner—comes with sweet-savory apple fritters and a glass of homemade apple cider. The apple-smoked barbecue is a standout, as is the chicken potpie. Other choices include steaks, chicken, and fresh mountain trout—grilled or fried. The breakfast menu is extensive, with eggs, pancakes, fried potatoes, and more.

Next door to the restaurant is a farmers market that sells fresh apples and other local specialties.

For fine dining, make reservations at least 24 hours in advance at the **Mountain View Restaurant** (1500 Pinnacles Way, 423/623-6555, 7pm-9pm, $40-50 Tues.-Sat.), the restaurant at upscale Christopher Place resort on English Mountain, near Newport. Dinner is served at 7pm, and diners must choose their entrée when they make their reservation the day before. The food is excellent, and the refined ambience perfect for that special occasion.

For a post-meal beverage, go to Christopher Place's **Marston's Library Pub** (1500 Pinnacles Way, 423/623-6555, 5:30pm-8pm Sun.-Mon., $12-15).

TOWNSEND

Located in the broad flat plain of Tuckaleechee Cove, **Townsend** is a world apart from Pigeon Forge and Gatlinburg. This park gateway, which provides quick access to Cades Cove and the Little River Road, seems to have the proportions just right: There is still a lot of undisturbed green space surrounding a few hotels, restaurants, and the only heritage center this side of the Smokies. Outfitters rent tubes for floating down the Little River, and Tuckaleechee Caverns are nearby for underground exploring.

Recent archaeological digs found evidence of human settlement in the Tuckaleechee Cove as many as 10,000 years ago. During the early 20th century, Townsend was the end of the railroad line; timber cut from forests inside what is now the national park was floated down the river and loaded onto railcars here in Townsend.

Sights

For an introduction to the history and culture of Townsend and the surrounding park area, visit the **Great Smoky Mountains Heritage Center** (123 Cromwell Dr., 865/448-0044, www.gsmheritagecenter.org, 10am-5pm Mon.-Sat., Sun. noon-5pm April-December, adults $6, seniors and children 6-17 $4). Exhibits here describe the remarkable archaeological finds made in Townsend and explain what scientists have learned from their discoveries. There are interactive exhibits about the lifestyles and culture of Native Americans who lived in the mountains, as well as the white settlers who carved out a life here beginning in the 1700s. Another exhibit, "Tennessee on the Move," describes just how hard it was to get around the mountains before paved roads and advanced automobiles. Outside, you can tour replicas of mountain cabins, a gristmill, cantilever barn, and smokehouse. There is an outdoor amphitheater and indoor auditorium for special events. The street address does not work well on a GPS. To get to the center from Townsend, drive toward the Smoky Mountains, through the stoplight, for 0.75 mile. The center will be on the right.

The **Little River Railroad and Lumber Museum** (Hwy. 321, 865/448-2211, www.littleriverrailroad.org, Mon.-Sat. 10am-5pm Sun. 1pm-5pm June-Aug. and Oct., Sat. 10am-5pm, Sun. 1pm-5pm Apr.-May, Sept. and Nov., call for an appointment Dec.-Mar., free) is more than another railroad museum. It is also a place to learn about the extensive logging that took place in the Smokies during the early 20th century. Originally called Tuckaleechee Cove, Townsend got its name from the founder of the Little River Railroad and Lumber Company, Col. W. B. Townsend. Exhibits here include antique railroad equipment and photographs from the era of railroads and logging in the Smokies.

Tuckaleechee Caverns (825 Cavern Rd., 865/448-2274, www.tuckaleecheecaverns.com, 10am-6pm daily, adults $16, children 5-11 $7) is the oldest tourist attraction in these parts. The caverns were known to Native Americans and early white settlers who would travel to the mouth of the caves on hot summer days to cool off. In the early 1950s, local residents W. E. Vananda and Harry Myers invested their savings into making the caves a tourist attraction, because no bank would loan to them. A year after the caverns first opened to the public, its greatest attraction—its underground Big Room—was discovered. The Big Room, part of the one-mile underground tour, is 300 feet by 400 feet, with ceilings of up to 150 feet high. The cave maintains a constant 58°F temperature, and it's open rain or shine.

Watch dulcimers and other mountain instruments being made at **Wood-n-Strings Dulcimer Shop** (7645 E. Lamar Alexander Pkwy., 865/448-6647, www.clemmerdulcimer.com, hours vary, call ahead). This music shop also hosts a free "Pickin' Porch" on Saturdays at 7pm during the summer. Call or check their website for a schedule.

Tubing

Tubing may be the lazy man's version of river rafting, but, boy, is it fun! Plunk your behind down in the middle of an inner tube and float on down the river. It's that simple.

Tubing is great for the whole family and the perfect way to cool off on a hot day (and there are plenty of hot days in Tennessee). Be sure to wear shoes and sunscreen; a pair of sturdy-bottomed shorts is also recommended.

There are several tubing outfitters in Townsend, including **Smoky Mountain River Rat** (205 Wears Valley Rd., 865/448-8888, www.smokymtnriverrat.com, May-Sept. 10am-6pm daily, but call to confirm times, $13). Outfitters transport you a mile or so up the river and let you float back down to the starting point.

Festivals and Events

On most Friday evenings May-August, the **Sunset Concert Series** (Great Smoky Mountains Heritage Center, 123 Cromwell Dr., 865/448-0044, www.gsmheritagecenter.org) offers live music in a lovely outdoor amphitheater.

Accommodations

Located right on the main highway in Townsend, **Highland Manor Inn** (7766 E. Lamar Alexander Pkwy., 800/213-9462, www.highlandmanor.com, $90-120) is a respectable motor inn with king- and queen-size rooms. All rooms have refrigerators, and guests receive free continental breakfast and use of the outdoor swimming pool and playground.

The 10-room **Richmont Inn** (220 Winterberry Ln., 865/448-6751, www.richmontinn.com, $180-305) offers guest rooms and suites, all named for notable Smoky Mountains people and decorated in a tasteful yet rustic style. Guests enjoy a full breakfast featuring homemade breads, plus healthy and hearty options. Evening dessert is served by candlelight with gourmet coffee. Both are served in the inn's dining room, with panoramic views of the mountains.

Dancing Bear Lodge (137 Apple Valley Way, 865/448-6000, www.dancingbearlodge.com, $115-325) offers both guest rooms and one- and two-bedroom cabins with a pronounced upscale edge. The lodge has a rustic feel—afforded by lots of wood finishes and botanical artwork—with refined touches like feather beds and hot tubs. Cabins feature full kitchens, wood-burning fireplaces, and private porches. Guests are invited to a top-notch continental breakfast each morning, and they may make reservations for dinner in the lodge restaurant, which features the only full bar in Townsend. Guests are also invited to lounge in front of the lodge fireplace in the lobby or on the porch overlooking the mountains.

The Smokies' most luxurious accommodations are, without a doubt, at ★ **Blackberry Farm** (1471 W. Millers Cove Rd., Walland, 865/380-2260, www.blackberryfarm.com, $895-2,595). A 4,200-acre working farm located in unblemished seclusion not far from Townsend, Blackberry Farm is a true upscale resort. A member of the Relais and Chateaux group of resorts and perennial member of the elite circle of top U.S. resorts, Blackberry Farm is a remarkable place to stay. While the refined elegance of meals and atmosphere seems far removed from the rustic, down-home character of the Smokies, the closeness to the land and unspoiled nature of the property bring guests straight to the marvelous beauty of this corner of the world.

Blackberry Farm has 69 guest accommodations, including rooms, suites, cottages, and houses. All rooms are carefully appointed and leave nothing to be desired. Rates include three meals a day, many of which are prepared with organic meats and produce raised right on the farm. The food served at Blackberry Farm is simply unparalleled in these parts and combines the best of regional ingredients with sophisticated culinary techniques.

Blackberry Farm may not be for most of us, but hats are off to those who can afford this special type of Smoky Mountains luxury.

Food

Miss Lily's Café (122 Depot St., 865/448-1924, www.misslilyscafe.com, 11am-9pm Mon.-Sat. earlier during off season, Sun. 10am-2pm, $7-22) serves Southern food, but with a freshness unknown at many country-cooking-style restaurants. Try the Yankee pot roast or fish and grits. Salads are fresh and filling. The pulled-pork sandwich is a favorite at lunch or dinner.

Miss Lily's Café is next door to the Lily Barn, a venue for weddings and other special events. The barn also sells daylilies, and the gardens are ideal for a picturesque stroll after dinner.

The First Frontier

Look for ★ to find recommended sights, activities, dining, and lodging.

Highlights

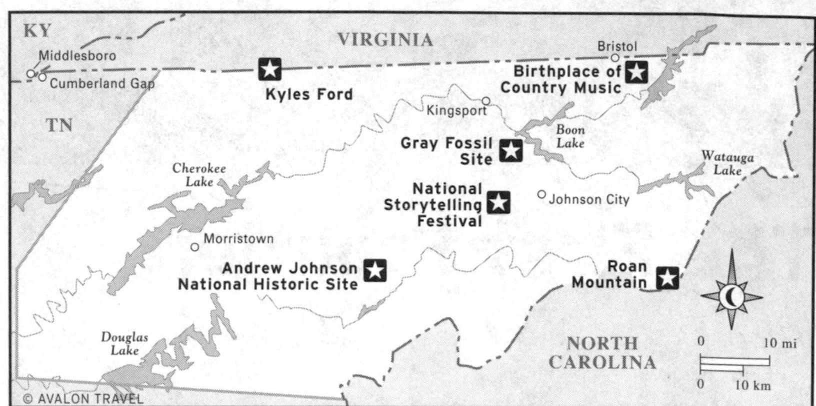

★ **Birthplace of Country Music Museum**: Hear about the now-giant genre's modest beginnings at this interactive museum (page 452).

★ **Gray Fossil Site**: This major fossil site is home to an interactive and educational museum of prehistoric Tennessee (page 459).

★ **Roan Mountain**: Roan Mountain lets you experience the natural beauty and majesty of the Southern mountains (page 468).

★ **National Storytelling Festival**: The world's best storytellers from African, European, Native American, and Appalachian traditions entertain at this annual event (page 474).

★ **Andrew Johnson National Historic Site**: The home and tailor shop of Andrew Johnson in Greeneville are a memorial to one of the most controversial commanders-in-chief in this country's history (page 476).

★ **Kyles Ford**: This small town on the Clinch River is representative of remote Appalachian communities. A top-notch country restaurant and eco village make it a worthy stop (page 482).

The mountains and valleys of Tennessee's northeastern tip were the first frontier of settlement during the 18th century.

Old towns and historic sites—including the birthplace of Davy Crockett, the tailor shop of an American president, and Tennessee's first capitol—are the legacy of this rich history. Modern-day cities, including Jonesborough and Elizabethton, have preserved their historic buildings and are now among the best places to soak in the atmosphere of early Tennessee.

The easternmost band of land in Tennessee is the Cherokee National Forest, and it is some of the most beautiful landscape in the state, with rhododendron gardens, cranberry bogs, and high mountain vistas. The Appalachian Trail and other hiking paths are ideal for exploring on foot; winding blacktop roads invite auto touring. Friendly mountain towns like Mountain City, Erwin, and Unicoi provide the essentials for exploring this still-wild part of Tennessee.

West of the mountains lie the Tri-Cities: Bristol, Kingsport, and Johnson City, each with its own unique character. Bristol straddles the state line with Virginia and is known as the place where the first country music stars were discovered (not to mention a big NASCAR, or National Association for Stock Car Auto Racing, track). Johnson City is home to East Tennessee State University and a state-of-the-art fossil museum. Kingsport, a leader in downtown revitalization, has a pleasant, walkable downtown district. Together, the Tri-Cities serve as the unofficial capital cities of the rugged mountain region of upper East Tennessee and southwest Virginia.

West of the Tri-Cities the landscape becomes a series of long valleys divided by steep ridges. Tucked into this ridge-and-valley landscape is the city of Greeneville, hometown of U.S. president Andrew Johnson. A staunch Unionist in a secessionist state, Johnson's story evinces the complexity of Civil War history in this border state. Rogersville is home to the oldest newspaper press in Tennessee. As you leave the cities and strike out over the countryside of this isolated and enchanting landscape, you realize that Tennessee's first frontier is also quite likely its last.

Previous: Chartered in 1794, Tusculum College is the oldest college in Tennessee; the Birthplace of Country Music Museum. **Above:** The Andrew Johnson Monument.

The First Frontier

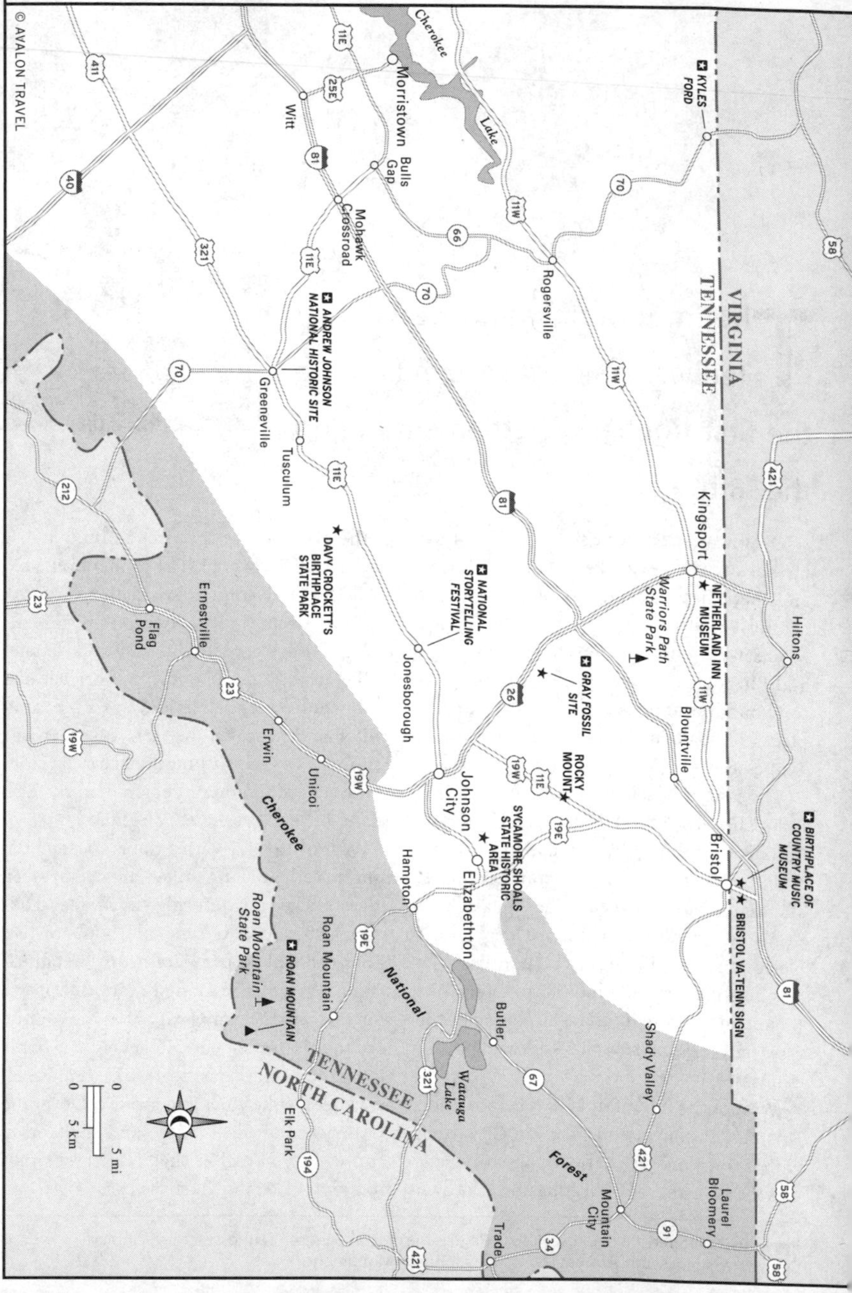

VIRGINIA
TENNESSEE
NORTH CAROLINA
Cherokee Lake
Cherokee National Forest
Watauga Lake
KYLES FORD
Morristown
Witt
Bulls Gap
Mohawk Crossroad
Rogersville
ANDREW JOHNSON NATIONAL HISTORIC SITE
Greeneville
Tusculum
DAVY CROCKETT'S BIRTHPLACE STATE PARK
NATIONAL STORYTELLING FESTIVAL
Jonesborough
Kingsport
NETHERLAND INN MUSEUM
Warriors Path State Park
GRAY FOSSIL SITE
Blountville
Hiltons
BIRTHPLACE OF COUNTRY MUSIC MUSEUM
Bristol
BRISTOL VA-TENN SIGN
ROCKY MOUNT
SYCAMORE SHOALS STATE HISTORIC AREA
Johnson City
Elizabethton
Hampton
Ernestville
Flag Pond
Erwin
Unicoi
Roan Mountain
Roan Mountain State Park
ROAN MOUNTAIN
Butler
Shady Valley
Elk Park
Mountain City
Laurel Bloomery
Trade
0 5 mi
0 5 km
411, 40, 321, 11E, 25E, 81, 66, 70, 11W, 58, 421, 212, 23, 19W, 26, 19E, 67, 194, 34, 91

The Tri-Cities

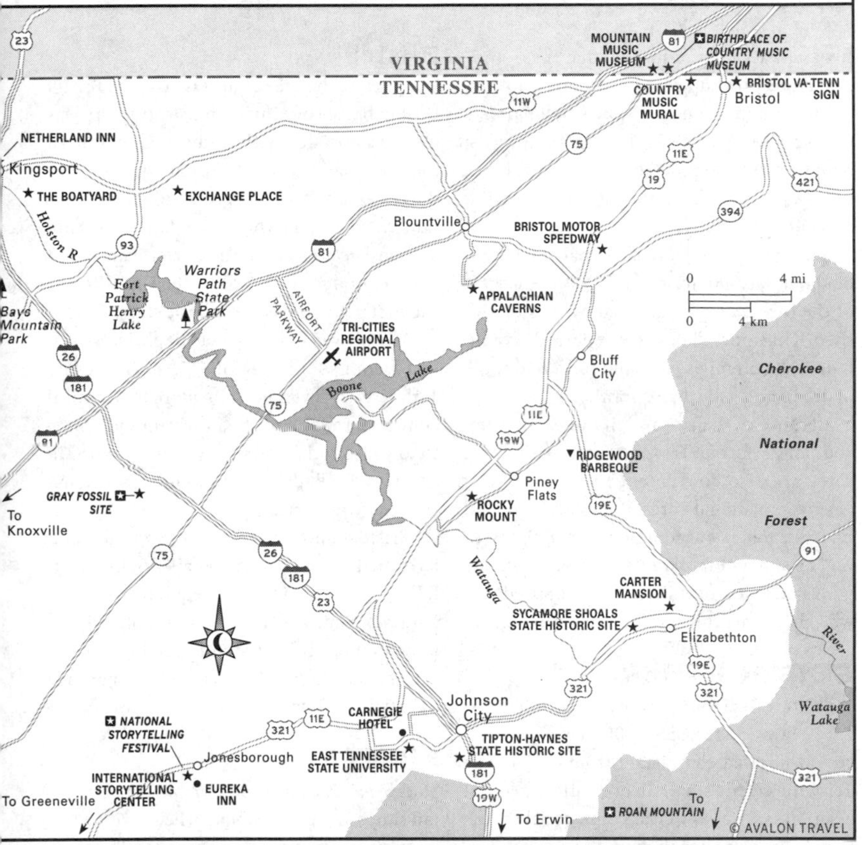

PLANNING YOUR TIME

If you want to see all of northeastern Tennessee, plan on staying at least a week. This is dense territory: It may look compact on a map, but narrow, windy roads and steep mountains and ridges make travel slow.

If you have less than a week, choose a subregion as your focus. The Tri-Cities offer the greatest diversity of attractions: motor speedways, historic sites, fossils, and live music. If you enjoy the outdoors, focus on the northern Cherokee National Forest; spend your time auto touring, hiking, and rafting along the Nolichucky River. The remote ridges and valleys in the western area of this region are an ideal destination if you want to leave the hustle and bustle behind and see some of the most remote territory in the state.

The Tri-Cities

It was an accident of history that three mid-size cities grew up so close to one another. Bristol and Johnson City were small hamlets until the railroads came through these parts; Kingsport was a quiet river port until it became a planned industrial city at the turn of the 20th century.

The Tri-Cities region has a total population of about 500,000. Johnson City is the largest of the three, closely followed by Bristol and then Kingsport. They are separated by no more than 30 miles each and form a triangle of urban and suburban sprawl.

Because of their proximity to each other, you can stay in one Tri-City and tour all three. They are also convenient to the northern Cherokee National Forest, Jonesborough, and Elizabethton. If you come for general sightseeing, be sure not to plan your trip to coincide with a major event at Bristol Motor Speedway, when hotels are full and the roads are clogged.

GETTING THERE

Tri-Cities Regional Airport (TRI or TCRA, 2525 Hwy. 75, 423/325-6000, www.triflight.com) is located equidistant from each of the Tri-Cities. This small airport offers general aviation services as well as commercial flights to hub airports in the region.

Three airlines serve the Tri-Cities. Allegiant Air has nonstop service from Orlando and Tampa Bay; Delta Connection flies from Atlanta and Cincinnati; and American flies from Charlotte to the Tri-Cities.

GETTING AROUND

Getting around the Tri-Cities is easy, although a little confusing thanks to the sheer number of roads. I-26 connects Kingsport and Johnson City, and I-81 connects Bristol with points south. U.S. 11E/19W, also called the Bristol Highway, connects Bristol and Johnson City. U.S. 11W connects Kingsport and Bristol.

Bristol

Long before the U.S. Congress declared Bristol the birthplace of country music, this city was closely associated with traditional mountain music. It was here in 1927 that a record producer named Ralph Peer came to record local musicians. During these now-famous Bristol sessions, Peer recorded the Carter Family and Jimmie Rodgers, who have been credited as the first popular country music stars.

Bristol was first named Sapling Grove, and from its founding in 1771 until the late 19th century it was nothing more than a rural country hamlet. But then the railroads came to town—Southern Railway and the Norfolk and Western Railroad—and a modern, industrial city was born.

Bristol famously straddles two states, and its main drag, appropriately called State Street, follows the state line between Tennessee and Virginia. South of the city is Bristol's biggest attraction, the Bristol Motor Speedway, which draws a quarter million people on major race days twice annually.

SIGHTS

State Street is a pleasant four-block row of retail shops and professional offices, with a few restaurants and bars along the way. The city's most famous landmark is the **Bristol VA-TENN Sign**, which spans the eastern end of the street. Erected in 1910, the first city slogan to appear was "Push—That's Bristol." In 1921, after a citywide contest was held, the slogan was changed to today's "A Good Place to Live." If you drive down State Street headed east, it is fun to watch the sign come into clearer and clearer focus as you approach.

Another Bristol landmark is the ***Country Music Mural***, painted in 1987, which depicts heroes of the city's country music story. The mural features the Carter Family, Jimmie Rodgers, and Ralph Peer, the record producer who orchestrated the 1927 Bristol Sessions.

The Bristol Sessions

By the mid-1920s, a genre of music variously called "old-time music," "old Southern tunes," "hill-country tunes," and "hillbilly music" was gaining popularity. The first fiddle record was made in 1922 and the first country vocal record made a year later. Early recording artists like Charley Oaks, Uncle Am Stuart, George Reneau, and Uncle Dave Macon made records that were distributed on a small scale by a Knoxville music promoter named Gus Nennsteil.

Soon major-label record executives sensed that something was happening down South. Beginning in 1926, record companies began to organize "field sessions" so artists could be recorded without having to make an expensive trip to New York. The sessions that took place in Bristol in July and August 1927 proved that country music—as it eventually came to be called—both sounded good and could be a commercial success.

It was Victor Talking Machine Company talent scout Ralph Peer who ran the Bristol sessions. He chose Bristol because it was the largest urban center in the Appalachian region. Peer, who had run previous field sessions for Victor and other music labels, set up his studio in a hat warehouse on State Street. Advertisements in the newspaper initially generated limited response, but when news emerged that artists were being paid up to $100 in cash on the spot and could earn more in royalties, Peer had to schedule night sessions to accommodate everyone.

By the end of the sessions, Peer had recorded 19 performers and 76 songs, including A. P., Sara, and Maybelle Carter singing "Bury Me Under the Weeping Willow," "Little Log Cabin By the Sea," "The Storms Are on the Ocean," "Single Girl, Married Girl," and "The Wandering Boy." Jimmie Rodgers, who heard about the sessions only because he was staying in a boardinghouse in town, recorded "The Soldier's Sweetheart" and "Sleep, Baby, Sleep." Other artists included a gospel quartet from Alcoa, Bristol's Tenneva Ramblers string band, and a Kentucky holiness preacher and his congregation.

As a result of the Bristol sessions, Jimmie Rodgers and the Carter Family became overnight commercial successes. Musicologists who look back on the sessions also note that Peer made little attempt to coach or influence the artists who came to record in 1927, so the entire session is a valuable portrayal of traditional American music of the period. In addition, the business model that Peer established, where performers were paid cash up front for recording and then earned royalties for each record sold, formed the basis of the modern recording industry.

Record labels continued to schedule field sessions around Tennessee in the succeeding years, hoping to replicate the success of Bristol in 1927. Victor returned to Bristol in 1928 and went to Nashville the same year; Columbia had sessions in Johnson City and Memphis in 1929, and Vocalion recorded in Knoxville in 1929 and 1930. The sessions led to a rich trove of recordings by diverse Tennessee artists.

The Great Depression and other economic and social forces put a close on field sessions by the early 1930s. But the genre that had been born in Bristol in 1927 was established, and music has never been the same.

The park at the foot of the mural is a venue for public concerts and the weekly State Street Farmers Market, which takes place May-October.

The **Bristol Train Station** (corner of E. State St. and Martin Luther King Blvd., 276/644-1573) was built in 1902 for less than $80,000. This handsome brick two-story train station was a busy passenger and freight depot from its construction until the 1970s. It was restored for Bristol's 150th anniversary in 2006. About 12 freight trains continue to pass through each day.

You can walk by and see the exterior of the **E. W. King Home** (www.bristolhistoricalassociation.com), which is located at the corner of Anderson and 7th Streets.

There is also a detailed self-guided walking tour of downtown Bristol available from the convention and visitors bureau. You can also rent an audio version of the tour, or listen to it on the chamber of commerce website.

MOUNTAIN MUSIC MUSEUM

In 1998, Bristol opened its first museum dedicated to the city's place in musical history. The **Mountain Music Museum** (626 State St., 423/573-2262, www.mountainmusicmuseum.org, 1pm-6:45pm Mon., 1pm-5pm Tues-Sat., adults $3, children 12 and under free) has a new location, allowing it to continue to share the area's musical roots closer to-downtown Bristol.

The exhibits include memorabilia from the Carter Family, hometown boy Tennessee Ernie Ford, Jimmie Rodgers, bluegrass legend Bill Monroe, the Stanley Brothers, Flatt & Scruggs, and several lesser-known Bristol artists and groups. The stories are told through vintage photographs, musical instruments, LP recordings, authentic stage costumes, and more. The gift shop has a good selection of traditional, bluegrass, and old-time music CDs.

TENNESSEE ERNIE FORD'S HOME

Bristol native Ernest Jennings Ford was a country and gospel star during the 1950s and 1960s. Ford got his start as a radio announcer in California after World War II, where he adopted the nickname "Tennessee Ernie" and the country character the Pea Picker. Ford recorded his first album in 1949 and made his Grand Ole Opry debut in 1950. He is known for his gravelly, deep voice and his rendition of "Sixteen Tons," a song about the hardships of coal mining. The chorus goes:

> You load 16 tons, and what do you get /
> Another day older and deeper in debt /
> St. Peter don't you call me, cause I can't
> go / I owe my soul to the company store

Ford was born and grew up in a small white house on Anderson Street, a few blocks away from downtown Bristol. His home was purchased and restored by the **Bristol Historical Association** (www.bristolhistoricalassociation.com), which now uses the building (1223 Anderson St.) for storage and meetings. Ford died in 1991 of liver disease, but the musician knew about plans to restore his home and was pleased by the honor.

★ BIRTHPLACE OF COUNTRY MUSIC MUSEUM

Less than a mile from Tennessee Ernie Ford's Home, but across the border into Virginia, is the **Birthplace of Country Music Museum** (520 Birthplace of Country Music Way Bristol, VA, 423/573-1927, www.birthplaceofcountrymusic.org, 10am-6pm Tues.-Sat., 1pm-5pm

the Birthplace of Country Music Museum

Sun., adults $13.95, children and seniors $11.55, kids under 5 free). Opened in 2014, after decades of hard work by a grassroots organization, the museum tells the story of the 1927 recordings through archival material and state-of-the-art displays. You'll read and hear the story of the region. Plan on spending at least two hours perusing the exhibits (and the museum store) of this traditional music. The museum also houses a research collection for those with academic interests in the history.

BRISTOL MOTOR SPEEDWAY

The **Bristol Motor Speedway** (151 Speedway Blvd., 423/989-6933, www.bristolmotorspeedway.com) looks like a spaceship that has landed on the countryside southeast of Bristol. The speedway is a massive building, arguably one of the largest arenas in the United States. It seats 160,000 people, and on major race days as many as 100,000 more crowd the grounds around the track to tailgate.

Bristol's race track was first developed in the early 1960s, and it would have been in nearby Piney Flats if the town hadn't banned alcohol sales on Sunday. The first race was the Volunteer 500, run in July 1961. Today Bristol is one of NASCAR's most beloved tracks, renowned for its 36-degree banking on both ends. It was sold to its current owner, Bruton Smith, for $26 million in 1996.

Going to the races is one of the most popular, and iconic, things to do while in Bristol. The track's main events take place in the spring and late summer, and attract a quarter million race fans. These events sell out in a matter of days and are a major commitment: Ticket prices start at $100, and you'll also need a place to stay. The best accommodations are in your own RV or trailer at one of the campgrounds immediately around the track. You can also get a hotel room around Bristol, but if you do so, be prepared to fight the traffic to and from the track every day.

If you can't make it to one of the major events, check out the schedule at the Bristol Dragway, also called **Thunder Valley**. Weekend events are held here March-September, and most will set you back a mere $5. Events include street fights, drag-bike events, and the National Hot Rod Association (NHRA)-rated Thunder Valley Nationals, usually in May. For a current schedule, contact the Dragway at 423/989-6933 or www.bristoldragway.com.

Even if you can't make a race event, it is worth your time to take a tour of the massive racetrack. Even non-race fans will enjoy

Speed is the name of the game at the Bristol Motor Speedway.

seeing such a major racetrack up close. During the hour-long tour of the facility, you will see the area where drivers stay when they come to Bristol, take a cruise down the drag strip, and circle the track itself. You'll also get a bird's-eye view of the track from track owner Bruton Smith's own suite.

Tours begin at the souvenir shop in the Bruton Smith building, a large white building next to the track. They depart every hour on the hour. Tours are offered Monday-Saturday, with the first tour at 9am and the last starting at 4pm. On Sunday, the tours start at 1pm and end at 4pm. No tours are given during the week preceding a major race event. A tour will run an adult $5 (much less than the $100 or $200 price tag for a seat at the main events). Call 423/989-6960 for tour information.

APPALACHIAN CAVERNS

Tour a cave and learn about the people who used it during the settlement period and the Civil War at **Appalachian Caverns** (420 Cave Hill Rd., Blountville, 423/323-2337, www.appacaverns.com, 9am-6pm Mon.-Sat., 1pm-5pm Sun., adults $12, seniors $10, children 4-11 $7.50, children 3 and under free). The hour-long regular tour is good for all audiences. Wild tours, where you get dirty, are also available and cost more than the regular admission.

Entertainment and Events

NIGHTLIFE

O'Mainnin's Pub and Grille (712 State St., 423/844-0049) has open-mic nights on Tuesday and live entertainment on weekends. **State Line Bar and Grill** (644 State St., 423/652-0792) has happy hour, ladies' nights, and DJ music for the dance floor.

THE ARTS

Bristol's historic **Paramount Center for the Arts** (518 State St., 423/274-8920, www.theparamountcenter.com) is the city's first venue for theater and concerts. Built in 1931 and restored in 1991, the Paramount is a historic site and a great venue for entertainment. The stage hosts concerts, plays, musicals, and more.

The Appalachian Cultural Music Association puts on free concerts most 7pm-9pm Mondays at the **Pickin' Porch** (620 State St., 423/573-2262, free, but a $5 donation is appreciated). Few things connect you to the legacy of this area more than listening to its music. Call for a schedule.

FESTIVALS AND EVENTS

Bristol's headline event of the year is the **Bristol Rhythm and Roots Reunion** (www.bristolrhythm.com, three-day pass $65-75), held in late September. Stages are set up along State Street, inside the Paramount Center, and in other venues downtown for the three-day weekend festival that draws fans from around the country. Musical styles include alternative country, bluegrass, roots, and blues. Headliners have included Ralph Stanley, Sam Bush, Doc Watson, and the Carolina Chocolate Drops.

Reserve your hotel room early since this is an increasingly popular event. Organizers offer shuttle buses to and from area hotels, so you can skip the driving once you get to town.

The **State Street Farmers Market** (801 State St., www.statestreetfarmersmarket.com) convenes in front of the *Country Music Mural* in downtown Bristol on Saturday mornings May-October, and Wednesday evenings July-September. In addition to local produce, the farmers market often has musicians performing live music.

Recreation

The **Bristol Pirates** (1501 Euclid Ave. Bristol, VA, 276/206-9946, www.milb.com), a farm team for the Pittsburgh, Pennsylvania, team with the same name, play at DeVault Memorial Stadium June-August. Tickets are a bargain at $4 for adults ($3 for kids). Box seats are just $6.

Accommodations

Bristol is the land of chain motels. Partly because I-81 passes right through town, and partly because of the heavy demand for rooms caused by the Bristol Motor Speedway, Bristol

Mountain Music In the Fold

While technically it's located across the state line in Virginia, it's impossible to talk about this part of Tennessee without mentioning **The Carter Family Fold** (3449 A. P. Carter Hwy., Hiltons, VA, 276/386-6054, www.carterfamilyfold.org), a music center and memorial to the music created by the Carter family. Established in the 1970s by Janette Carter, a daughter of A. P. and Sara Carter, the center's mission is to preserve old-time music.

The Carter Fold is in Poor Valley, north of Clinch Mountain in southwest Virginia. This humble, yet lovely, corner of the world is where Carters have lived for generations. The music center consists of the Carter Family Museum, which houses exhibits about the first family of country music; the one-room log cabin where A. P. Carter was born; and an outdoor amphitheater where live concerts are held on Saturday nights.

Action at the Carter Fold revolves around the Saturday-night concerts. You may not hear big names, but you will hear big sounds. This is mountain music the way it really is, without interference from slick record producers and music executives. There is lots of room up front for dancing. No alcohol is permitted; these are family-friendly affairs. Tickets are $10 for adults, $1 for children 6-11. Make sure you come early enough to tour the museum and the A. P. Carter Cabin.

Camping is allowed on the grounds of the music center. The closest hotels are in Bristol and Kingsport.

The Carter Fold is located just a few miles over the border, but getting there involves a 20-minute drive over winding back roads (as so much in this part of the state does). To get there, go to Gate City and then head east on Highway 58. Follow the green highway signs to the Carter Fold.

seems to have more than its share of standard-issue motels.

Be aware that while room rates around Bristol are generally low, during the weekends of the big race events, in March and August, hotels hike their prices by as much as 1,000 percent. On one trip, a nondescript Econo Lodge that was charging $38 on other days raised its price to more than $350 per night during an event.

The **Holiday Inn** (3005 Linden Dr., 276/466-4100, $95-120) is located at the Bristol Convention Center and offers more amenities than most Bristol motels, including a fitness room, business center, and airport shuttle. Nearby is the **Courtyard by Marriott** (3169 Linden Dr., 276/591-4400, $110-200), whose guests enjoy an indoor pool, on-site restaurant, fitness and business centers, and airport shuttle.

Over on the Tennessee side of the state line, **Hampton Inn** (3299 W. State St., 423/764-3600, $139-200) is located along Highway 11W, near the Bristol Regional Medical Center.

Food

Bristol's finest restaurant is **The Troutdale Dining Room** (412 6th St., 423/968-9099, www.thetroutdale.com, 5pm-close Tues.-Sat., $25-60). Located in an 1850 Victorian town house, the Troutdale has a superb menu that changes with the seasons. Dishes like veal scaloppine and pan-seared Hawaiian sea bass are impressive and well executed. The restaurant offers an array of trout dishes made with seafood from Troutdale's own 600-gallon fish tank. There's no batter-fried fish here, though—it's more in the vein of trout roulade and Akashi poached trout. There are daily and monthly specials, as well as a glorious six-course tasting menu ($100-plus) that is like heaven for your taste buds. Other features you can expect: exquisite service, a superior wine list, delectable desserts, and an unquestionable upscale atmosphere.

Just a few steps from State Street you can dine in an authentic burger bar, straight from the 1950s. **Burger Bar** (8 Piedmont Ave., 276/466-6200, 10:30am-7pm Mon.-Thurs., 10:30am-8pm Fri., 8am-close Sat., $3-8) may be where the legendary Hank Williams passed up his last meal (or so the story goes), but you won't go hungry here. Burgers are what its famous for, but the plate lunches and homemade desserts are also worth the trip. This is the type of place that is worth getting out of the big cities to experience.

For Italian food, choose **Valentino's** (1501 King College Rd., 423/968-7655, 11am-10:30pm Mon.-Sat., 11am-9:30pm Sun., $6-16), which serves pasta, pizza, calzones, subs, gyros, and salads.

If you're up for an adventure, or if barbecue is your calling, then make a detour to ★ **Ridgewood Barbeque** (900 Elizabethton Hwy./Old 19E, 423/538-7543, 11am-7:30pm Mon.-Thurs., 11am-2:30pm and 4:30pm-8:30pm Fri.-Sat., $7-12). Here the beef and pork barbecue is made the old-fashioned way—slowly—and the result is the most sublime barbecue within at least 100 miles. At the Ridgewood, there's no pork shoulder, only hams, which are smoked over hickory embers for nine hours before being cooled, thin sliced, and then heated on the grill and sauced with the Ridgewood's own sweet and tangy barbecue sauce. Pork and beef (barbecue aficionados scoff at beef) platters come smothered with hand-cut, home-fried french fries. Sandwiches are served on white-bread sandwich buns. Side dishes of tangy coleslaw and smoky baked beans are advisable, although not because you need added sustenance. Portion control is not something that is practiced at the Ridgewood.

The Ridgewood is well off the beaten track, but that hasn't limited its popularity, so expect to wait if you arrive at peak mealtimes. (Seating is also limited, so that contributes to the wait.) To find the Ridgewood, drive southeast from Bristol toward Blountville and Bluff City. From Bluff City, take Highway 19E/37 toward Elizabethton. Shortly after crossing the railroad tracks, look on your right for the nondescript two-lane Elizabethton Highway, also called Old 19E. It's easy to miss. Once you're on the Elizabethton Highway, the Ridgewood is located on your right in a low-slung strip mall with a red awning. Look for the cars in the parking lot.

Information

The **Bristol Convention and Visitors Bureau** (20 Volunteer Pkwy., 423/989-4850, www.bristolchamber.org, 8am-5:15pm Mon.-Wed., 8am-4pm Thurs.) publishes maps, guides, and a walking tour of the downtown. The office also serves as a visitors center.

The **Birthplace of Country Music Alliance** (www.birthplaceofcountrymusic.org) is the driving force behind a lot of the good things that are happening in Bristol. This organization is working on the establishment of a downtown museum, and they promote local musical events. In addition, they are an excellent resource for information about Bristol's musical heritage.

JOHNSON CITY

The largest city in Washington County, **Johnson City** was once an industrial city. It was founded in 1856 by Henry Johnson as a railroad depot called Johnson's Station. After the Civil War, iron ore furnaces here processed ore from the Cranberry Mines in North Carolina. Three railroads—including the Carolina, Clinchfield, and Ohio (CC&O)—passed through the city.

In 1903, a U.S. Veterans Administration rest home was built in Johnson City for Union Civil War veterans, and 10 years later a normal school was established. The Quillen College of Medicine, named for U.S. congressman James Quillen, was founded in 1974.

Downtown Johnson City still has a gritty, postindustrial feel, with lots of boarded-up buildings and empty streets. The city is enlivened by the presence of East Tennessee State University (ETSU), a state school with total enrollment of about 14,000. It includes the Quillen College of Medicine and also a College of Pharmacy that opened in 2007. ETSU's Appalachian Studies program is also of note. Its journal *Now and Then* is a biannual magazine devoted to the history and culture of Appalachia. The university campus lies southwest of the city center and provides several attractions for visitors.

East Tennessee State University

The **Carroll Reece Museum** (ETSU, 423/439-4392, www.etsu.edu/reece, 9am-4:30pm Mon.-Fri.), a regional art and history museum, was named for the late congressman B. Carroll Reece. The museum's permanent exhibit includes a feature on music of the Tri-Cities. An interactive computer kiosk allows you to see archival video footage of early performances by stars such as Jimmie Rodgers and the Carter Family. Other exhibit halls feature student work and changing exhibits. As of press time, the museum was under a $1.5 million capital improvement project, so call ahead.

James Quillen hailed from upper East Tennessee, and he represented the area for more than 30 years in the U.S. Congress. A noted conservative, Quillen introduced the first law outlawing desecration of the U.S. flag in 1968. The late congressman's papers and memorabilia are housed on the 4th floor of the Sherrod Library. The **Quillen Gallery** (Lake St. and Seehorn Rd., 423/439-1000, 8am-4:30pm Mon.-Fri., free) includes dozens of cases of photographs, plaques, and other memorabilia of the Republican's career in politics, including his collection of elephant statues. There is a room that has been furnished to look like the congressman's Washington office.

Also on the fourth floor of the library is the **Archives of Appalachia** (423/439-4338), a project of the Appalachian Studies Department. While not much to see, the archives are an important depository of documents and primary source material related to the culture, economics, and history of the Appalachian region.

ETSU has an arboretum, and you can take a tour of its giant trees, including a 200-year-old white oak in front of Sherrod Library. Collect a map of the giant trees from the Reece Museum, or contact the ETSU Arboretum (www.etsu.edu/arboretum).

If you visit ETSU, stop at the public safety office at the main entrance for a visitor's parking pass.

Quillen Veterans Administration Medical Center

The massive medical school and health center located adjacent to ETSU, the **Quillen Veterans Administration Medical Center**, has an interesting history. In 1903, it was established as a residential home for ailing Union Army veterans. Later it evolved into a facility for all veterans of war. At the time of the writing of the 1939 *WPA Guide to Tennessee*, Mountain Home, as the facility came to be known, was home to 3,500 patients, including 400 hospital cases and 2,000 permanently disabled residents. Mountain Home had its own post office, theater, and chapel, and residents here were trained in handicrafts.

In the 1960s, civic leaders in upper East Tennessee first started to discuss the need for a regional health center in the area. It took almost 20 years to make this dream a reality, and in 1978, the first class of students at the Quillen College of Medicine began courses. Today, the university's medical school is a leading health-care provider in the region.

Tipton-Haynes Historic Site

The **Tipton-Haynes Historic Site** (2620 S. Roan St., 423/926-3631, www.tipton-haynes.org, 9am-4pm Tues.-Sat. Mar.-Nov., adults $5, children 12 and under $2.50) consists of 11 historic buildings, a cave, and a wooded area. It represents several areas of early Tennessee history. Woodland Indians and Cherokee hunted buffalo that were drawn to the spring here. Later, the buffalo trail became an early stage road, and long hunters camped in the cave.

The home on the property took shape in 1784, when John Tipton, a Maryland native, built a log cabin here. Tipton is remembered in history because he was an outspoken opponent of the State of Franklin, the unofficial state established by overmountain settlers in 1783. When North Carolina authorities seized some of State of Franklin proponent John Sevier's slaves in 1788, they took them to Tipton's home. When Sevier tried to recover his slaves, a skirmish erupted. This so-called Battle of the Lost State of Franklin marked the end of the State of Franklin movement.

In 1837, the property changed hands from the Tipton to the Haynes family. Landon Carter Haynes, who added a Greek Revival portico, was a farmer, lawyer, newspaper editor, and a three-term member of the Tennessee General Assembly. Haynes was also a secessionist who departed to West Tennessee after the Civil War.

The Tipton-Haynes property was conveyed to the state in 1944-1945. It is maintained by the Tipton-Haynes Historical Association. Call ahead to arrange an appointment during the winter.

Hands On! Regional Museum

Travelers with children should take note of the **Hands On! Regional Museum** (315 E. Main St., 423/434-4263, www.handsonmuseum.org, 9am-5pm Tues.-Fri., 9am-6pm Sat., 1pm-5pm year-round, and 9am-5pm Mon. Mar., Jun., Aug. only, adults and children three years and up $8). This is an interactive museum of arts and sciences where children can fly an airplane, visit a coal mine, and walk through an ancient ark filled with exotic animals from around the world. In addition to its regular hours, the museum is also open 9am-5pm Mondays June-August.

Entertainment

There are two live-music venues that you shouldn't miss in Johnson City. The first, the **Down Home** (300 W. Main St., 423/929-9822, www.downhome.com), is this region's best venue for rock, folk, blues, and other roots-style music. Founded in 1976, the Down Home has now nurtured at least two generations of music lovers in upper East Tennessee.

The inside is polished wood on the floor and walls. There are about 160 seats—most of them in straight-back wooden chairs—so the atmosphere is intimate. There are shows here most every Thursday–Sunday night and open mics on Wednesday. The kitchen serves bar food and Tex-Mex Thursday–Sunday nights.

The Down Home is located on a nondescript block a short drive from downtown. A small marquee is about all you'll see from the road, so it's easy to miss it.

The second venue for live music in Johnson City is the **Acoustic Coffeehouse** (415 W. Walnut St., 423/434-9872, www.acousticcoffeehouse.net), which has live acts most nights of the week. The patio out front is a popular place to sit in nice weather, and this is also a good place to grab a cup of joe day or night.

Accommodations

★ **Carnegie Hotel** (1216 W. State of Franklin Rd., 423/979-6400, www.carnegiehotel.com, $135-260) is Johnson City's finest hotel. Located next door to ETSU, the hotel offers standard amenities plus special high-end touches like separate soaking tubs, daily newspapers, bathroom scales, and dry-cleaning service. An on-site restaurant, spa, and fitness room mean you may not ever have to leave the grounds if you don't want to. The Carnegie first opened in the 1890s and re-opened in 2000.

Food

Quite possibly the most popular restaurant in Johnson City, **The Firehouse** (627 W. Walnut St., 423/979-7377, 11am-9:30pm Mon.-Thurs., 11am-10pm Fri.-Sat., $7-18) serves hickory-smoked barbecue with traditional accompaniments like corn bread, coleslaw, and baked beans. You can also order non-barbecue items such as fish and sandwiches.

A popular choice for decent Italian food is **Alta Cucina** (1200 N. Roan St., 423/928-2092, www.altacucinajc.com, 11:30am-2pm and 5pm-10pm daily, lunch $6-13, dinner $12-30). The lunch menu includes hot and cold sandwiches, salads, pasta, pizza, calzone, stromboli, and other Italian favorites. Dinner specialties include fresh grilled seafood and steak, plus pastas. There is a full bar, and take-out is available.

Information

The **Johnson City Chamber of Commerce**

(603 E. Market St., 423/461-8000, www.johnsoncitytnchamber.com) provides visitor information.

AROUND JOHNSON CITY

Rocky Mount

The first territorial capitol of Tennessee, **Rocky Mount** (200 Hyder Hill Rd., Piney Flats, 423/538-7396, www.rockymountmuseum.com, 11am-5pm Tues.-Sat. Mar.-mid-Dec., other times by appointment, adults $8, seniors $7, children 5-17 $5) sits about five miles outside of Johnson City, on the road to Bristol. It was in this frontier homestead—the home of land surveyor William Cobb—that the governor of the Southwest Territory, William Blount, lived from October 1790 to March 1792. In a spare office here Blount organized the territory's first census and elections. In 1792 he moved to Blount Mansion in Knoxville, and the capitol moved with him.

Although the home seems rustic to us today, it was luxurious by the standards of the early Tennessee frontier. Glass windows, abundant provisions, and feather beds were some of the comforts Blount enjoyed at Rocky Mount.

Today, the home is primarily a living-history museum. Staff dress in period costumes and play Mr. and Mrs. Cobb, Governor Blount, and other members of the Cobb household and extended family. They also tend to farm animals, toil in the kitchen garden, and perform other daily tasks of frontier life. Inside, there is a museum and video that explore frontier life and the early political history of Tennessee.

★ Gray Fossil Site

Crews cutting a new road near Gray, Tennessee, in 2000 discovered fossilized animal bones, setting off a sequence of events that led to the opening in 2007 of the **Natural History Museum at the Gray Fossil Site** (1212 Suncrest Dr., 866/202-6223, www.grayfossilmuseum.org, 9am-5pm Tues.-Sat., adults $6, seniors $4, children 5-12 $3). The fossil find spawned the creation of a paleontology program at East Tennessee State University, which now leads the scientific investigation of the Gray site. So far, two new ancient animal species, a red panda and badger, have been discovered.

The Gray site encompasses more than five acres, and the best estimate is that it will take more than 100 years to fully excavate and study the fossils that lie here. It is so rich in fossil remains because 4.5-7 million years ago it was a water hole where beasts large and small came to drink and, in some cases, die.

The museum and outdoor displays are designed for children, but adults enjoy them, too. The museum describes the animal and plant life that surrounded the water hole. It also takes visitors through the tedious yet exciting process of discovery and analysis that scientists follow. Overall, the exhibits are captivating and creative.

Upstairs, you join a guide who takes you out to the site itself. Inside, you can peer into the laboratory where each bone fragment that is found is carefully cleaned, analyzed, preserved, and stored.

KINGSPORT

A city with industrial roots and a unique history, **Kingsport** is perhaps the most culturally sophisticated of the Tri-Cities. Located on the Holston River, Kingsport was an important shipping port for years before the city was born. The Long Island of the Holston, a large island that lies in the Holston River, was a site of political and spiritual importance to the Cherokee.

Downtown Kingsport is being revived, and it is a pleasant place to stroll. Attractions around the city include historic homes and one of the largest city parks in the state.

History

Kingsport is located along the route of a historic trail used by Indians, hunters, and early settlers. The **Long Island of the Holston**, a 3,000-plus-acre island in the Holston River, was important to the Cherokee, and it served as a neutral meeting ground for

Indians and settlers. The Long Island of the Holston Treaty was negotiated here in 1777. By 1809, the Cherokee had ceded the island and nearby lands to settlers, and the settlement on the Holston became known as Ross's Landing. The city of Kingsport was first chartered in 1822.

Kingsport was destined to remain a quiet river community until the early 20th century, when industrialists and city planners joined to establish a new, model city. This self-proclaimed "All-American City" was born around 1915 with the establishment of the Kingsport Improvement Corporation. The corporation, founded by the owners of the Carolina, Clinchfield and Ohio Railway (CC&O), had the job of planning and building a new industrial city.

Experts were hired to plan the city, design housing, make landscape designs, develop a school system, and install sewerage and sanitation facilities. Corporation lawyers drew up articles of incorporation in 1917.

But what really made Kingsport a success was the industry that it attracted. Tennessee Eastman was and is Kingsport's largest employer. Over the years, Eastman has produced photographic chemicals, war explosives, acetate yarn, polypropylene for outdoor signs, and polyester plastic for use in beverage bottles, among many other things. During World War II and beyond, Eastman was responsible for managing the Y-12 National Security Complex at Oak Ridge.

Like other small and midsize American cities, Kingsport has wrangled with problems like sprawl and the decline of its downtown over the years.

Sights

Central Kingsport is the city that was laid out by town planners and industrialists in the early 20th century. The oldest attractions in Kingsport are located slightly west of downtown, along the Holston River. A lovely nine-mile greenway connects the Holston River area with Historic Exchange Place on the east side of town.

HISTORIC DOWNTOWN

The planned nature of Kingsport is evident downtown. Broad Street is a wide, divided two-lane road with four blocks of storefronts, many of which still sport notable art deco architecture. The old depots for the Carolina, Clinchfield & Ohio railway stand along Main Street; the passenger depot is now a bank, and the freight depot houses the visitors bureau. At the other end of Broad Street is the **Church Circle**, a traffic circle that houses four churches. At the corner of Center and Commerce Streets is a mural that represents Kingsport's history. Students of architecture should follow the 1.8-mile walking tour developed by the Downtown Kingsport Association.

It has taken a lot of effort to make Kingsport's downtown what it is today. Like other towns of its size in Tennessee, Kingsport suffered during the 1970s and 1980s as businesses moved out of downtown and economic activity spread to the outlying areas, starting with the first shopping malls. But in 1974 a downtown association was formed, and over the past 30-plus years they have led the way in Kingsport's resurgence. They have been involved with projects ranging from the improvement of sidewalks to annual arts events.

THE BOATYARD

The oldest part of Kingsport is the Boatyard, located along the Holston River on the west side of town. The **Netherland Inn** (2144 Netherland Inn Rd., 423/765-0937, www.netherlandinn.com, 2pm-5pm Sat.-Sun. May-Oct., free) was a stagecoach stop, inn, and boatyard catering to travelers who came through this country by land or river. The inn, first built between 1802 and 1808 by William King, was named after Richard Netherland, who bought the property in 1818 and expanded it. Group tours may be arranged by appointment.

At the rear of the inn are several log homes, including a Daniel Boone cabin, which was moved here in order to preserve it. This is the symbolic beginning of the Daniel Boone Heritage Trail, which celebrates the wilderness trail that Boone and thousands of other early settlers used to enter the Tennessee frontier.

Across the road from the Netherland Inn is one end of Kingsport's greenway system. You can walk or bike nine miles from here to Exchange Place, on the other side of town.

The greenway passes the **Long Island of the Holston**. A site of political and spiritual importance to the Cherokee, and a place for meetings between the Cherokee and white settlers, the Long Island is now home to **Heritage Park**, which has walking trails, picnic tables, and historical markers. Parts of the island are residential, while a coal gasification plant belonging to Tennessee Eastman sits on the southern end of the island.

EXCHANGE PLACE

This 1850s homestead is a living-history museum and center for workshops, festivals, and other special events that celebrate traditional arts, crafts, and ways of life. **Exchange Place** (4812 Orebank Rd., 423/288-6071, www.exchangeplace.info, 2pm-4:30pm Sat.-Sun. May-Oct., adults $1, children under 12 $0.50) consists of about a dozen period buildings, most of them original to the property. They include the "saddlebag"-style log house, kitchen, springhouse, schoolroom, blacksmith shop, and barn. Across the road is an early-20th-century home that serves as the visitors center. Exchange Place got its name because its owner, John Preston, exchanged money for travelers who passed by on the stagecoach road from Virginia into Tennessee. He also exchanged goods.

Exchange Place is operated by a private nonprofit organization. Some of the funds needed to maintain the old buildings come from the proceeds of selling works completed by the Exchange Place Quilters and Overmountain Weavers, volunteers who weave and quilt.

Several special events are held here every year. They include the Spring Garden Fair at the end of April, the Fall Folk Arts Festival at the end of September, and Christmas activities in December.

Festivals and Events

The **Spring Garden Fair** (www.exchangeplace.info) kicks off the season in April at Exchange Place, a working farm and living-history museum. The Garden Fair features local and regional craftspeople, food, and music. The bookend to the fair is the **Fall Folk Arts Festival** in September, also held at Exchange Place.

Recreation

Kingsport has an extraordinary city park. **Bays Mountain Park** (853 Bays Mountain Park Rd., 423/229-9447, www.baysmountain.com, 8:30am-8pm Mon.-Sat., 11am-8pm Sun. March-Oct., 8:30am-5pm Mon.-Sat., 11am-5pm Sun. Nov.-Feb., $4 per car) is a 3,300-acre nature preserve that lies between Bays Mountain and the Holston River Mountain, southwest of downtown Kingsport. It takes about 15 minutes to drive to Bays Mountain from downtown. The park's attractions include a **nature center** (8:30am-5pm Mon.-Fri., noon-7pm Sat.-Sun. June-Aug., 8:30am-5pm Mon.-Fri., noon-7pm Sat.-Sun. Mar.-May and Sept.-Oct., Mon.-Fri. 8:30am-5pm, Sat.-Sun. 1pm-5pm Nov.-Feb.), with exhibits on plants, weather, space, and animals; a planetarium with regularly scheduled shows; star observatory; deer, wolf, bobcat, otter, and raptor habitats; farmstead cabin; and 25 miles of hiking trails. There are also service roads open to mountain bikers after they have paid a $2 registration fee. A barge cruises the Bays Mountain Reservoir on weekends year-round and daily June-August. Bays Mountain offers special naturalist-led programs nearly every day, ranging from wolf howls to moonlight barge rides. Check the website for current programs and schedules.

Warriors' Path State Park (490 Hemlock Rd., 423/239-8531) is located on the shores of Fort Patrick Henry Lake, as the Holston River is called south of the Fort Patrick Henry Dam. There are 12 miles of hiking trails, mountain bike paths, an Olympic-size swimming pool, an 18-hole golf course, and a 22-hole disc golf course in this 950-acre park. Boaters enjoy

Pal's Sudden Service

For once, it is not the Golden Arches that define fast food. At least not here. In the Tri-Cities, look for the large, turquoise, and garishly decorated fast-food chain known locally simply as **Pal's.**

Fred "Pal" Barger opened his first fast-food restaurant in Kingsport in 1956, after meeting Ray Kroc (of McDonald's fame) at a restaurant convention. The second Pal's opened in 1958. The chain expanded again in the 1990s and at the same time adopted its present slogan, "Great Food in a Flash." Now there are 20 Pal's from Morristown to Lebanon, Virginia. Many are drive-ins only.

Don't worry about driving past a Pal's; you can't miss them! The restaurants are painted a blinding shade of blue and come with a humongous wiener, drink, French fries, and burger as outdoor decorations. Pal's is beloved for its quart-size iced tea (sweetened, of course; this is the South), called the Big Tea, as well as for fast and accurate service. The Sauceburger, chipped ham, and Frenchie Fries are also well loved. In 2002, President George W. Bush gave Pal's Sudden Service the Baldridge National Quality Award.

cruising and fishing on the lake; paddle- and fishing boats are available for rent from the marina office. In addition, there is a 135-site campground with modern hot-water bathhouses and water and electrical hookups. Warriors' Path State Park is located southeast of downtown Kingsport, just a quick 15-minute drive from the city.

Accommodations

Located near the civic auditorium and close to downtown Kingsport, **Fox Manor B&B** (1612 Watauga St., 423/378-3844 or 888/200-5879, www.betterbedandbreakfasts.com/foxmanor, $110-150) is a 19th-century townhome that has been converted into a luxurious bed-and-breakfast. The five guest rooms are decorated with rich fabrics, deep woods, and top-notch furnishings. High-quality linens, fireplaces, ceiling fans, and private baths add to the appeal. Start the morning off right with breakfast served in an elegant dining room. Other common rooms include the library, with an English-style bar, and the cozy verandah.

Chain hotels in Kingsport include the **Days Inn Kingsport** (805 Lynn Garden Dr., 423/246-7126, $70-80), located very close to downtown. There is a free continental breakfast, in-room coffeemakers, hair dryers, microwaves, and refrigerators. There is an outdoor pool.

Located about midway between downtown and Exchange Place is a **Red Roof Inn** (100 Indian Center Ct., 423/378-4418, $80-90), a 122-room hotel with standard amenities and an above-average hot breakfast bar, plus an outdoor pool for those hot Tennessee summer days. This is a popular hotel for folks headed to the motor speedway. Ask for one of the renovated rooms.

Food

The **Café N'Orleans** (161 E. Main St., 423/245-5400, 11am-3pm Mon., 11am-8pm Tues.-Thurs., 11am-9pm Fri., 5pm-9pm Sat., $5-11) downtown offers gumbo, jambalaya, po'boys, and other Louisiana favorites.

Sandwiches are the specialty at **Deli Sandwich Factory** (1308 E. Stone Dr., 423/246-3354, www.delisandwichfactory.com, 10am-7pm Mon.-Sat., $3-7). The house specialty is the Kitchen Sink Sandwich, which features ham, smoked turkey, salami, corned beef, roast beef, and Swiss cheese.

For home-style Southern fare, head to **Mama's House Buffet** (2608 N. John B. Dennis Hwy., 423/247-5691, 11am-8pm Mon.-Thurs., 11am-8:30pm Fri.-Sat., 11am-6pm Sun., $6-10), which offers lunch and dinner daily, and breakfast on Wednesday and Saturday. The buffet features different meats and sides daily, but expect choices like sweet potatoes, meat loaf, bread dressing, pork loin, sliced ham, brown beans, and spaghetti and meatballs.

Broad Street BBQ (2921 E. Center St., 423/247-8646, 11am-8pm daily, $5-7) is one of Kingsport's most popular barbecue joints. Check out the full menu of barbecue choices, including hickory-smoked ribs, pulled pork, and barbecue chicken.

Kingsport's favorite seafood restaurant is **Riverfront Seafood Company** (1777 Netherland Inn Rd., 423/245-3474, 11am-9pm Mon.-Thurs., 11am-10pm Fri.-Sat., $7-20). Casual food here includes oyster, shrimp, white fish, and smoked turkey po'boys. At least a dozen types of fish are available, fried, grilled, or prepared specially according to house recipes. Crab legs and Maine lobster are also on the menu.

Information

Downtown Kingsport (140 W. Main St., 423/246-6550) promotes the city center and publishes a walking tour to historic sites. The **Kingsport Convention and Visitors Bureau** (400 Clinchfield St., Ste. 100, 423/392-8820, www.visitkingsport.com) has maps and brochures, and can help you organize tours and group events.

Northern Cherokee National Forest

The northern Cherokee National Forest covers 327,000 acres from the northern boundary of the Great Smoky Mountains National Park to the Virginia state line. It encompasses wilderness regions, state parks, and towns. Because it is a national forest and not a national park, commercial enterprises, including logging, are allowed.

The Appalachian Trail passes through this part of the Cherokee National Forest, giving you abundant opportunities for hiking, biking, camping, and other outdoor pursuits. The Nolichucky River is popular with white-water rafters, and the Watauga Lake offers boating and fishing prospects.

Sights include Roan Mountain's verdant rhododendron gardens, Shady Valley's cranberry bogs, and dramatic Backbone Rock. Thanks to the smattering of towns, including Erwin and Mountain City, there is enough "civilization" to make this countryside accessible and easy to explore. While it's outside of the bounds of the national forest, Elizabethton shares the characteristics of the region and offers a quaint downtown experience with shopping, restaurants, and historic homes.

It is less than a two-hour drive along I-40 to the ranger station in the forest from Knoxville.

Visitor Information

For information about the northern Cherokee National Forest, visit one of two ranger stations. The **Watauga Ranger District** (4400 Unicoi Dr., Unicoi, 423/735-1500, 8am-4:30pm Mon.-Fri.) is in the town of Unicoi and is the headquarters for the northernmost portion of the forest. The **Unaka/Nolichucky Ranger District** (4900 Asheville Hwy./Hwy. 70, Greeneville, 423/638-4109, 8am-4:30pm Mon.-Fri.) is headquartered outside of the bounds of the forest, in Greeneville. Both ranger stations offer maps, guides, and other helpful information about the forest.

LAUREL BLOOMERY

Laurel Bloomery is located in the extreme northeastern corner of Tennessee, the first town you will meet after crossing over the Virginia state line. Named for the mountain laurel that grows here and the iron smelters, or bloomers, that once raged here, Laurel Bloomery is now a peaceful mountain village. Every August, on the weekend before Labor Day, the town hosts an **Old Time Fiddlers' Convention** (276/236-8541, www.oldfiddlersconvention.com) at the Old Mill Music Park on Highway 91. The tradition of an annual music convention began here back in 1925,

Northern Cherokee National Forest

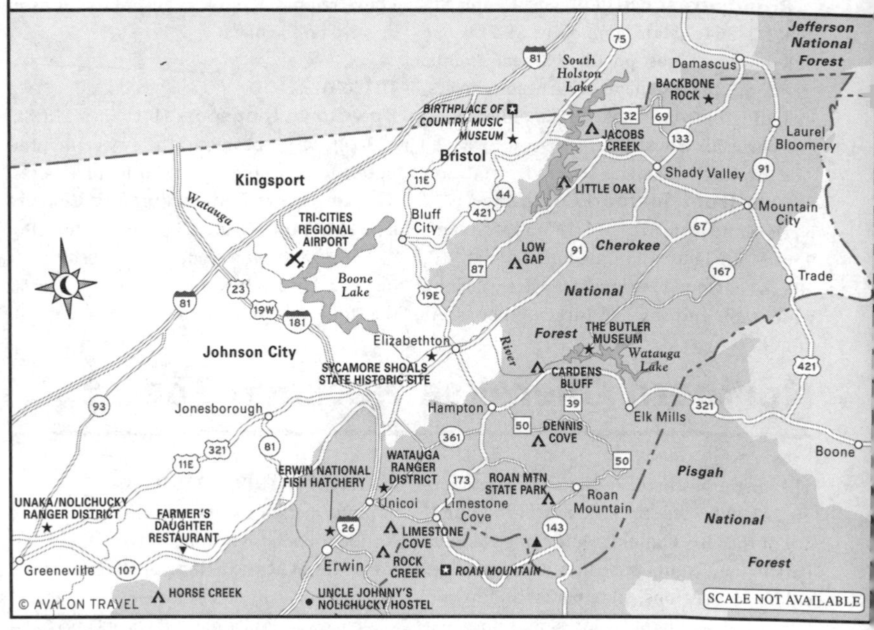

and this is one of the best places to come to hear real old-time music. The music usually gets started around 6pm and keeps rolling well into the night. Many conventioneers set up camp along the river for the weekend. Ticket prices range $6-12; camping is $80.

Gentry Creek Falls

Chain-effect waterfalls—one 30 and one 40 feet high—are located along Gentry Creek near Laurel Bloomery. It is a 2.5-mile hike to the falls from the trailhead, which is located on Gentry Creek Road a short ways off Highway 91. To get to **Gentry Creek Falls**, turn on Gentry Creek Road and drive for 0.7 mile. Turn right, following Gentry Creek Road, for another 1.8 miles. At this point the road becomes unpaved. Drive for 0.2 mile and turn right again, and follow the road another 1.8 miles to the trailhead. There is limited parking. For information, contact the Watauga Ranger District of the Cherokee National Forest at 423/735-1500.

BACKBONE ROCK

A remarkable natural and man-made landmark west of Laurel Bloomery, on the road between Damascus, Virginia, and Shady Valley, Tennessee, Backbone Rock is a rock formation that developed where the Beaverdam Creek flows past a spur of Holston Mountain. The rock is almost 100 feet tall in places and about 50 feet thick; it is called **Backbone Rock** because it resembles a spine. In 1901 a tunnel was drilled through the rock to make way for the railroad. Today, the road passes through this gap, known locally as the shortest tunnel in the world.

Get out of your car and hike the short path up and over the rock. The trail is steep and rocky, and children should be closely supervised along it. Another hike takes you to Backbone Falls.

There is a lovely creekside picnic area here, and the Beaverdam Creek invites you to wade or swim in its clear waters.

Camping in the Northern Cherokee National Forest

Campgrounds are located throughout the Unaka and Watauga Districts of the Cherokee National Forest and are a great way to really experience these great outdoors. All forest service campgrounds are available on a first-come, first-served basis only. They have potable water and toilets; some have warm-water showers.

- **Backbone Rock Recreation Area** is located near the Virginia state line. Its 11 campsites accommodate tents or trailers; only a few accommodate RVs. There are flush toilets and drinking water, but no showers or electrical hookups.
- **Cardens Bluff Campground** is a 43-site campground on Watauga Lake, which can accommodate tent and trailer campers, plus a few RVs. Amenities include showers, drinking water, and flush toilets. There are no electrical hookups.
- **Jacobs Creek Recreation Area** is located near the Virginia state line on the banks of South Holston Lake. Its 27 sites can accommodate tents or RVs. There are showers, drinking water, flush toilets, and a dump station.
- **Little Oak Campground**, also located on South Holston Lake, is a large campground with 70 tent and RV sites. It has showers, flush toilets, a dump station, and drinking water.
- **Rock Creek Recreation Area** near Erwin sits at the foot of Unaka Mountain. It has 37 campsites, 14 with electrical hookups. Day-use facilities include a swimming hole, bike trail, hiking paths, and picnic tables. Fees are $10 a day for tent sites with no electricity, $15 a day for single site with electric hookups, $30 a day for a double site with electric hookups; day-use fee is $2 a day per car. To find Rock Creek, take Rock Creek Road from Main Street in Erwin. It is three miles to the campground.
- **Dennis Cove Campground** near Hampton has 16 campsites, flush toilets, no hookups, and no showers. It is along Laurel Fork Creek, making it popular among anglers. To get here, take U.S. 19E through Hampton and turn right onto Dennis Cove Road. Drive up the mountain 4.5 miles; the campground is on your right.

Facilities include a picnic area and a primitive campground.

SHADY VALLEY

Located at 2,800 feet and surrounded by mountains is **Shady Valley**, a high-mountain cove that is best known for its wetlands. Bogs and white pine/hemlock forests once covered most of the valley; they flourished here due to the higher elevation and the influence of the last ice age. With human settlement, many of the bogs were drained to make way for agriculture.

Today, Shady Valley is a quiet collection of old and new homes on rolling farmland. The winding rural roads leading to the valley attract motorcyclists. The four-way intersection of highways constitutes the commercial center—there are three gas station/delis but little else. The town has erected an information board near the intersection, and here you'll find a map to at least four of Shady Grove's cranberry bogs. The easiest one to find is **Schoolyard Springs**, located a few hundred yards from the Shady Valley Elementary School. Local residents have built a boardwalk over and around the bog. Here you can watch the bog bubble up from below and listen to a symphony of birdsong. The effort to preserve Shady Valley's bogs has been led by the Nature Conservancy.

Shady Valley celebrates its cranberry bogs and much more with the annual **Cranberry Festival** (423/739-2131), held during the second full weekend in October. You could not imagine a more picturesque setting, what with the glorious fall leaves surrounding the valley like a giant-size stadium. The festival includes various cranberry-themed events, a parade, an arts-and-crafts auction, and other amusements. Shady Valley also holds an all-you-can-eat **Soup Supper** each March.

MOUNTAIN CITY

This small town of about 3,000 is the seat of Johnson County and a commercial hub for the northernmost mountains in Tennessee. The **Johnson County Welcome Center and Museum** (716 S. Shady St./Hwy. 421, 423/727-5800, www.johnsoncountychamber.org, 9am-5pm Mon.-Sat., 1pm-5pm Sun.) is a good stop for information and orientation. The museum houses local historical relics, and there are brochures, maps, and helpful people to offer assistance.

Recreation

Redtail Mountain is a high-end residential development near Mountain City. Its 18-hole, par 72 **golf course** (423/727-7931) is open to nonresidents. Greens fees are $59 Monday-Thursday and $79 Friday-Sunday, $39 daily after 3pm. Check for weekly specials like ladies' day and men's day.

Accommodations

The **Prospect Hill B&B Inn** (801 W. Main St./Hwy. 67, 423/727-0139, www.prospect-hill.com, $109-180) is a five-room inn housed in an 1889 brick Victorian-shingle home. Fully renovated and carefully restored, the inn's guest rooms have special features like whirlpool tubs, private balconies, and private entrances. All guests enjoy the mountain views from the porch and a hearty homemade breakfast. Rooms are furnished in a classic, tasteful style, with original artwork hanging in many of them. If you're looking for a romantic getaway, this is a good choice.

TRADE

Considered the oldest community in Tennessee, this mountain hamlet is located within spitting distance of the North Carolina state line. Named Trade because it was where settlers and Indians once met to trade, the town is now a quiet, rural settlement with lovely scenery all around. Highway 421, which connects **Trade** with Mountain City, is a winding, scenic route through the mountains. It is said that North Carolina fugitive Tom Dula, made famous by the folk song "Tom Dooley," hid out in Trade until a posse

Redtail Mountain Resort features an 18-hole golf course.

found him and arrested him for murdering his fiancée.

WATAUGA LAKE

The Tennessee Valley Authority was at work in this part of Tennessee, too. In 1949, TVA completed the Watauga Dam and created Watauga Lake, the highest-elevation lake in Tennessee. Even today, it is surprising to find a placid lake amid the Unaka mountain peaks in this landscape. The lake is picturesque, with clear, cool waters ideal for swimming and fishing.

Pontoon boats, fishing boats, and sailboats are available for rent from **Fish Springs Marina** (191 Fish Springs Rd., Hampton, 423/768-2336). An all-day rental will cost $180-215, plus fuel. Reservations are recommended, particularly on weekends.

When the lake was formed, the town of Butler was covered with water. "Old Butler" lies at the bottom of the lake, but "New Butler" remains on the shore. **The Butler Museum** (123 Selma Curtis Rd., 423/768-3880, www.thebutlermuseum.com, 1:30pm-4pm Sat.-Sun. and other times by appointment, requested donation) houses community artifacts taken from the post office, barber shop, and people's homes before it was flooded, and it records the way of life of more than 400 families in the Watauga River valley who were forced to move when the lake was made.

Downstream from Watauga Lake is Wilbur Lake, also called Horseshoe Lake. Wilbur Lake was created in 1912, when the Watauga Power Company dammed the Watauga River. The dam has been owned by TVA since 1945.

There are public canoe launches on Wilbur Lake, but no commercial recreation facilities. Because the water is so cold, only rainbow and brown trout are found in the waters. Both are stocked.

Accommodations

You can rent your own cabin overlooking the lake from **Cherokee Forest Mountain Cabins** (798 Grindstaff Rd., Butler, www.cabin4me.com, $170-210). These fully furnished homes away from home have fireplaces, hot tubs, full kitchens, and plenty of space to relax and unwind. Weekly rates are available.

Iron Mountain Inn (268 Moreland Dr., Butler, 423/768-2446, www.ironmountaininn.com, $350) is a four-room bed-and-breakfast located in a log cabin. The innkeepers offer a variety of special packages that focus on

Watauga Lake

pastimes including hiking, golf, fishing, and biking. There are also romantic getaways, holiday specials, and special midweek or off-season rates.

★ ROAN MOUNTAIN

Quite possibly the most lovely natural site in northeastern Tennessee, **Roan Mountain** is a high mountain ridge noted for its open balds and rhododendron gardens. Part of the Cherokee National Forest, Roan Mountain is a five-mile stretch of ridge that straddles the North Carolina-Tennessee state line and ranges from 6,286 feet at its peak to 5,500 feet at Carver's Gap. The 10-mile stretch of the Appalachian Trail that follows the crest of Roan Mountain is believed by some to be the most beautiful of the entire trail. Treeless mountain balds, including Jane's Bald, Grassy Bald, and Round Bald, open up sweeping views of the Blue Ridge Mountains. During June, the tall, bushy Catawba rhododendron bloom, creating a blanket of pink, white, and yellow flowers.

Visitors to the top of Roan Mountain can stop at the National Park Service information cabin for maps and directions. From the cabin you can take an easy, short walk along a paved track through the rhododendron gardens to an overlook. The Cloudland Trail is a 1.2-mile moderate hike to the Roan High Bluff Overlook.

Also nearby is **Dave Miller Homestead** (9am-5pm Wed.-Sun. Memorial Day-Labor Day, 9am-5pm Sat.-Sun. Oct., free), a 1909 farmhouse that has been restored to show traditional mountain life. On summer weekends, special storytelling, music, and arts-and-crafts programs keep it alive.

If you wish to make Roan Mountain your destination, then there is no better home base than **Roan Mountain State Park** (1015 Hwy. 143, 423/772-0190), located eight miles down the mountain. Park facilities include a museum, cabins, campground, swimming pool, and tennis courts. Even if you don't stay at the park, the **museum** (8am-4:30pm daily, free) in the visitors center is well worth a stop for its detailed look at the natural and human history of the nearby mountains.

The 30 fully equipped cabins ($70-170) are open year-round and provide kitchens, woodstoves, and outdoor grills. A campground ($20-70) has 107 sites, including 87 with RV water/electricity hookups.

ELIZABETHTON

The seat of Carter County, **Elizabethton** is one of the oldest incorporated towns in

Roan Mountain State Park

The 1770 Carter Mansion was luxury on the frontier in its day.

Tennessee. Its downtown is vibrant, and the important historic site of Sycamore Shoals is on the outskirts of town. The Doe River, which passes through the city, makes it a scenic spot.

Historic Downtown

Spanning the Doe River in downtown Elizabethton is the **Doe River Covered Bridge**, which crosses the Doe River at Hattie Avenue. This 1882 wooden bridge spans some 134 feet and rests on earth and limestone abutments. It was high enough to withstand floods, including the Great May Flood of 1901. It is now closed to vehicular traffic—a new concrete bridge spans the river at Elk Avenue—but remains open to foot and bike traffic. There is a pleasant park on the east bank of the river from which you can enjoy views of the bridge.

On the west bank, you can see a piece of early Tennessee history. It was in the early 1770s that the very first overmountain settlers began to establish farms in what is now northeastern Tennessee. The wilderness still belonged to the Cherokee, but the settlers could not resist the promise that it represented. By 1772, an estimated 80 farms were located along the Holston and Watauga Rivers.

The settlers soon realized they needed some form of local government. They were outside the bounds of the closest statethe Holston and Watauga Rivers.ugh to withstand floods, including, the settlers formed the Watauga Association, which allowed them to prosecute criminals and settle disputes. A part of the sycamore tree under which this association was formed is on display a few steps from the Doe River Covered Bridge.

Elizabethton has a number of historic homes, old businesses, and landmarks, including the tallest Fraser fir in the state of Tennessee. Get a copy of the brochure *Elizabethton Walking Tour* from the visitors bureau or the public library to explore further.

Carter Mansion

One of the first settlers in this area was John Carter, a trader who first moved into modern-day Tennessee in 1770. In 1772, he moved near the Watauga River, in present-day Elizabethton. John Carter was one of the signers of the Watauga Association agreement. John Carter's son, Landon, was also a political leader and businessman. Landon Carter's wife, Elizabeth, was Elizabcthton's namesake, and Carter County was named for him. The family home has been preserved and is now called the **Carter Mansion** (1013 Broad St., 423/543-6140 or 423/543-5808, tours 2 pm Wed.-Sun. May 15-Aug. 15, other times by appointment, free). The simple white wood-frame home may look homely, but it was luxury on the frontier. Its hand-carved crown molding, chair rail, and mantels are evidence of this. The home is managed by the Sycamore Shoals State Historic Site.

Port Rayon

As you drive into Elizabethton from the west, you cannot miss the large factory that sits along the banks of the Watauga River. This is the remains of the **Bemberg and Glanzstoff rayon factories**, which opened in the 1920s. In their heyday, these factories had their own rail depot, called Port Rayon, which brought members of their workforce to the factory every day. The factories experienced ups and downs throughout the Great Depression, World War II, and during the postwar years. At their peak in 1949, the factories employed some 6,000 people. Economic fluctuations, the cost of new environmental protection measures, and changing corporate structures caused the factories to downsize during the 1970s, 1980s, and 1990s. By 1998, there were just 250 people employed at the factory, now called North American Rayon Corporation. A massive fire broke out at North American Rayon in 2000. It took firefighters a week to fully put out the blaze, which led to the final closure and demolition of the factory.

Sycamore Shoals

Many of the most important events in early Tennessee history took place in the area of **Sycamore Shoals State Historic Site** (1651 Elk Ave., 423/543-5808), along the Watauga River, just a few miles outside of Elizabethton. It was near here in 1775 that the Cherokee agreed to sell 20 million acres of land to Richard Henderson in what is now known as the Transylvania Purchase. Fort Watauga, built as a defensive fort for early settlers along the Watauga River, was near here. And in an open glade next to the river, hundreds of overmountain men mustered in 1780 as they began their march to King's Mountain to fight the British during the Revolutionary War.

The historic site consists of a replica of Fort Watauga and a walking trail that takes you along the Watauga River to the areas where some of these momentous events are believed to have taken place. Inside the **visitors center** (8am-4:30pm Mon.-Sat., 1pm-4:30pm Sun., free) there is a museum and video.

Annual events at Sycamore Shoals include the staging of *The Wataugans* in July, the Muster at Fort Watauga in May, the Native American Festival in June, the Overmountain Victory Trail Celebration in September, and the Fort Watauga Knap-In in October.

Accommodations

The Doe River Inn (217 Academy St., 423/292-2848, up to $75) is set in an 1894 home near where early settlers forded the Doe River. There are two guest rooms in the house, or you can rent the two-bedroom cottage or one-bedroom carriage house, also on the property.

Food

The Coffee Company (444 E. Elk Ave., 423/542-3438, 7am-5pm Mon.-Sat. for coffee and desserts, kitchen is open 11am-3pm) is a coffee shop and bakery that also offers the best salads and sandwiches in town. Sandwiches include a grilled panini with meat or veggies, French dip, or pesto turkey. Salads feature fruit, meat, and vegetables.

Information

The best guide to Elizabethton is the walking tour, a substantial brochure available from the local tourism council and some downtown businesses. Pick up a copy at the **Elizabethton-Carter County Chamber of Commerce and Tourism Council** (500 Veterans Memorial Pkwy, 423/547-3850, https://www.tnvacation.com) or the **Elizabethton Public Library** (201 N. Sycamore St., 423/547-6360).

ERWIN

Gateway to the Cherokee wilderness and commercial center for largely rural Unicoi County, **Erwin** is a friendly and unpretentious town. Located along both I-26 and an active railroad line, Erwin is a place where things and people are on the move. A smattering of restaurants, hotels, and the only bona fide hostel in these parts make it a good home base for exploring the forest.

Erwin had a succession of names during its early history. First known as Unaka, it was changed to Longmire in 1840. Then it became Vanderbilt. In 1879, town officials agreed to name the city after D.came Vanderbilt. In 1879 Unaka,ilroad line, Erwin is a place where things and people are Mr. Ervin, a mistake by post office officials caused the name to be recorded as Erwin. Finally, a name stuck.

Unlikely industries keep Erwin afloat: State and federal fish hatcheries produce broodstock and fish, and National Fuel Services prepares enriched uranium for nuclear-powered navy ships. CSX Rail also has a depot and car repair center in Erwin.

For 40 years starting in 1917, Erwin was home to one of America's largest and most well-known manufacturers of hand-painted pottery. Southern Pottery, located a few miles outside of town, created dinnerware that was sold under the name Blue Ridge. Men shaped, finished, and fired the dishes while a decorating department of more than 500 area women painted designs on by hand. **Blue Ridge pottery** is now highly collectible.

The appeal of Blue Ridge pottery is the individual flair left behind by the painters. While the women worked from patterns, they painted by hand, and so each plate turned out just a little different than the next.

Sights

Erwin is home to two fish hatcheries, one operated by the state and one by the federal government. The **Erwin National Fish Hatchery** (520 Federal Hatchery Rd., 423/743-4712, 7:30am-4:30pm Mon-Fri., free) produces 10-12 million rainbow trout eggs annually, which are shipped to federal, state, and tribal fish hatcheries around the country. It is one of two federal rainbow trout broodstock facilities in the country. There is a small exhibit and display raceway for visitors. If you visit outside of working hours, there is an outdoor kiosk next to the display raceway.

The **Erwin State Trout Hatchery** (475 Banner Springs Rd, 423/743-4842, 7:30am-4:30pm Mon.-Fri., free) is one of the facilities that receives Erwin's trout eggs. This hatchery keeps the trout until they are big enough to be released into area streams and lakes. Visitors can walk up and down the raceways and look at the fish.

On the grounds of the Erwin National Fish Hatchery, in a building that once housed the fishery superintendent, is the **Unicoi County Heritage Museum** (529 Federal Hatchery Rd., 423/743-9449, 1pm-5pm daily May-Oct. 31, adults $2, children $1). The museum houses exhibits about Erwin and Unicoi County; it has a nice collection of Blue Ridge pottery from the old Southern Pottery plant in Erwin and displays about the Clinchfield Railroad, which is closely tied to the history of Erwin. At the rear of the museum is a nature trail with marked trees and other plants. A 30-minute recorded narrative is available to accompany the walk.

The heritage museum is housed in a white Victorian farmhouse built in 1903 as accommodation for the fish hatchery superintendent. In 1982, instead of demolishing the old house as ordered by the federal government, the local chamber of commerce petitioned for the old building to be saved and turned into a local history museum.

Erwin is surrounded by good **apple-growing country**. Farms in this area produce sweet, crisp apples that are sold in the fall. The **Unicoi County Chamber of Commerce** (100 Main St., 423/743-3000, www.unicoicounty.org) can provide you with a list of area farms that are open to the public.

Festivals and Events

The **Unicoi County Apple Festival** (www.unicoicounty.org) takes place in October and includes a gospel music showcase, apple contests, a show of Blue Ridge pottery, and free shuttle buses to the Unicoi County Heritage Museum.

Shopping

Alan Stegall keeps the tradition of pottery alive in Erwin. His shop, **Stegall's Pottery** (200 Nolichucky Ave., 423/743-3227), across from the public library, produces beautiful mugs, platters, and other stoneware.

Recreation

The Nolichucky River makes for an exciting, beautiful, and unpredictable rafting trip. River outfitters in Erwin offer trips along the Upper and Lower Nolichucky. With Class II-IV rapids, the river trip is exciting. It also offers a lovely journey down an otherwise inaccessible 3,000-foot river gorge. Due to the rapids, no one under 12 is allowed on the river. On average, a full-day river trip costs $60-80 per person.

Erwin-based outfitters include **Cherokee Adventures** (2000 Jonesborough Rd., 423/743-7733, www.cherokeeadventures.com) and **USA Raft** (1002 Jones Branch Rd., 423/743-7111, www.usaraft.com), also known as Mountain Adventure Guides.

Accommodations

Hikers and budget travelers love **Uncle Johnny's Nolichucky Hostel** (151 River Rd., 423/735-0548, www.unclejohnnys.net, $20-95). Located just two miles outside of Erwin along the Nolichucky River, the hostel is about 60 feet from the Appalachian Trail. Through-hikers fill up the hostel during the early spring months, but outdoor folks with lesser ambitions love it year-round. Guests at Uncle Johnny's choose from accommodations ranging from private cabins to communal bunkhouses. Rooms are heated, and there is a bathhouse with hot water, showers, and a sink for washing dishes. There is a definite outdoors feel here; the front desk sells just about every piece of gear a hiker might need, and the accommodations are rustic. But for a hiker, particularly one who is trying to complete the 2,170-mile Appalachian Trail, the digs are downright palatial.

There is a bike path into town and a fleet of bikes available to borrow. Uncle Johnny will also shuttle you into town. Most hikers head first for food60 feet from the Appalachian Trail. Through-hikers fill up the hostel duri and check their email at the local library. The Nolichucky Hostel is a good base even if you are not hiking the whole Appalachian Trail. Section hikers use it as a base, and others fashion great day hikes that end at the doorstep. Talk to Uncle Johnny for help planning your itinerary.

In addition to the hostel, there is a **Mountain Inn & Suites** (2002 Temple Hill Rd., 423/743-4100, $80-100) and a **Super 8** (1101 N. Buffalo St., 423/743-0200, $50-99).

Food

Located on Highway 107, midway between Erwin and Greeneville, is ★ **The Farmer's Daughter Restaurant** (7700 Erwin Hwy./Hwy. 107, 423/257-4650, 11:30am-8:30pm Fri.-Sat., 11:30am-5pm Sun., $12). This wood-paneled eatery is well worth the drive, particularly for those who relish home-style country cooking. The menu features a changing selection of main entrées, which are served with a smorgasbord of family-style side dishes: mashed potatoes, corn-bread salad, carrot soufflé, fried okra, creamed corn, and coleslaw. Entrées include dishes like fried chicken livers, fried chicken, chicken and dumplings, barbecue ribs, and country ham. Adult plates are $12.75, and plates for children (6-11 years) are $6.38. Children five years and younger eat free.

Ridges and Valleys

West of the Cherokee National Forest, the high mountains are replaced by a series of ridges and valleys. These ridges run parallel to the mountains—at a northeasterly keel—and cause roads and railways to follow a similar slantways track.

Some of these valleys are home to relatively large towns and busy roads. But as you head westward and push north toward the Kentucky state line, you enter into countryside that remains largely unblemished by widespread development. This area is an easy 90-minute drive east of Knoxville; take I-40 to Highway 11.

JONESBOROUGH

If this region of Tennessee is the state's first frontier, then Jonesborough is its first town. Established in 1779, while the frontier was still part of North Carolina, Jonesborough was named for Willie Jones, a North Carolina legislator who supported westward expansion. Jonesborough was the capital of the erstwhile State of Franklin and an important commercial and political hub in the years before Tennessee became a state. Other interesting historical connections are that Andrew Jackson practiced law in Jonesborough for several months in 1788, and that the first regularly published abolitionist newspaper was published in Jonesborough by Quaker Elihu Embree starting in 1820.

The best thing about Jonesborough today is that its history has been preserved. Way back in the 1970s, when other cities were building strip malls and highways, Jonesborough started to preserve its historic downtown. It was the first downtown district in Tennessee to be placed on the National Register of Historic Places. In 1973, the first National Storytelling Festival was held, and it continues to be one of Tennessee's most popular annual events.

Today, historic Jonesborough is one of the most vibrant small towns in the region for shopping and dining. Its downtown district is inviting and a pleasant place for a stroll. And since the International Storytelling Center opened here in 2002, visitors who miss the storytelling festival may still hear some great tales.

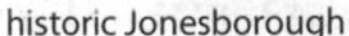
historic Jonesborough

The Lost State of Franklin

For about five years in the 1780s, settlers in what is now upper East Tennessee tried to establish a new American state called Franklin. The movement was spurred mostly by the feeling among many of these overmountain families that they were too far away from the government of North Carolina, and that North Carolina was not providing the law and order that they needed.

The State of Franklin movement met with opposition in North Carolina, which viewed it as an act of rebellion. More important, however, was the fact that many wealthy North Carolina land speculators held title to land over the mountains and that the existence of a separate state could invalidate their claims.

Despite the opposition from North Carolina and a few local settlers, the State of Franklin enjoyed some success. In December 1784, a convention met in Jonesborough and agreed that the North Carolina constitution would form the basis of Franklin's government, with a few minor alterations. A second convention a year later led to the adoption of the Holston Constitution, which provided for a unicameral legislature. At a third convention in March 1786, John Sevier was elected the governor of Franklin.

North Carolina continued to oppose the statehood movement in its western territories. Overmountain settlers themselves had mixed feelings about Franklin. North Carolina improved its government services in the frontier as conciliation, so some settlers no longer saw the need for a separate state government. But in the area south of the French Broad, the frontier of the day, residents appreciated the strong anti-Indian stance taken by Sevier and the Franklin government.

Support for the State of Franklin dwindled by early 1789. By this time the Cherokee had been pushed south of the Little Tennessee River, providing, at least for the time being, peace. John Sevier became a member of the North Carolina legislature from Greene County and retreated as an outspoken proponent of separate statehood.

No leader emerged to succeed Sevier, and the movement faded into history. Less than 10 years later, the lands over the mountain, now called Tennessee, were admitted as the 16th state.

Sights

The **Historic Jonesborough Visitors Center** and the **Jonesborough-Washington County History Museum** (117 Boone St., 423/753-1010, 8am-5pm Mon.-Fri., 10am-5pm Sat., 12:30pm-5pm Sun., free) share a building about one block from Main Street. Together, they make a good first stop for visitors to the town. The visitors center has maps and other information, while the museum houses artifacts and memorabilia about Tennessee's oldest town, including the oldest known photo of Jonesborough, which dates to 1850.

HISTORIC DOWNTOWN

Jonesborough's oldest frame building is the **Chester Inn** (116 W. Main St.). The Chester Inn was constructed in the late 1790s by William Chester, a medical doctor who capitalized on the new stage road that passed through town. Now owned by the state, the Chester Inn houses the offices of the National Storytelling Festival.

The **Christopher Taylor House** (124 W. Main St.) appears a bit out of place among Jonesborough's handsome frame and brick buildings. This log cabin, which once housed Andrew Jackson, was moved to Main Street and restored. It was built around 1778. Some say Andrew Jackson's ghost still haunts this house.

★ National Storytelling Festival

The **National Storytelling Festival** (800/952-8392, www.storytellingcenter.net) is Jonesborough's premier event. Taking place during the first weekend in October, the festival features multiple tents with storytellers from a diverse range of traditions and styles. Traditional mountain tellers share the stage with world performers from Africa, Asia, Europe, and South America. Native American, Irish, and African American storytelling traditions are showcased. Indeed, if you thought that storytelling was a dying art, you will be pleasantly surprised by the depth and relevance of the artists who perform at the festival.

The storytelling festival began in 1973, and today it attracts some 10,000 people each year. Weekend passes cost $165 for adults and $145 for children; single-day passes are also available. Registered attendees receive a detailed schedule for each tent, and you can simply choose which tellers you want to hear. Food is served in a food court and at area restaurants, or you can pack a picnic. The storytelling festival is a good experience for people of just about every walk of life, and it's considered to be one of Tennessee's best and most distinctive events.

Book a room very, very early if you hope to stay in Jonesborough proper during the festival (and be prepared to pay premium rates). The closest motel accommodations are in Johnson City. Erwin and Greeneville are not far away, and camping is available at Davy Crockett State Park.

If you can't make it to the national festival, you can still hear stories in Jonesborough. The **International Storytelling Center** (116 W. Main St., 423/753-2171, www.storytellingcenter.net, 2pm Tues. and 7:30pm Sat., matinees: adults $12, seniors, students, and children under 18 $11, evening tickets: adults $15, not recommended for children under 12) offers storytelling from the storyteller in residence May-November. While it lacks the electricity and excitement of the large-scale festival, it is still a wonderful way to pass some time and rediscover this classic art form. During the rest of the year, the center houses exhibits about storytelling. It also has a nice gift shop.

Recreation

For something a little different, take the family to **The Wetlands** (1523 Persimmon Ridge Rd., 423/753-1550, 10am-6pm Mon.-Sat., noon-6pm Sun. May-mid-Aug., weekends only mid-Aug.-Sept., adults $12, seniors and children 4-12 $9), a water park that includes flume rides, boardwalks, a wave pool, and much more. Check for exact opening dates, which normally coincide with local school calendars.

Accommodations

There are bed-and-breakfast-style inns and guesthouses in Jonesborough. On the highways leading to town you will find major chain motels.

The historic ★ **Eureka Inn** (127 W. Main St., 423/913-6100 or 877/734-6100, www.eurekajonesborough.com, $119-139) is your best choice for accommodations in Jonesborough. Built in 1797 and expanded 100 years later, this handsome hotel offers 16 guest rooms that blend old-fashioned atmosphere with modern comforts. Amenities include soundproof insulation, voice mail and dataports, private telephone lines, individual climate control, and cable TV. Private baths, high-speed wireless Internet, and a continental breakfast round out the offerings. The Eureka Inn is centrally located, and guests will enjoy use of the back garden, plus off-street private parking.

Many of Jonesborough's other bed-and-breakfasts are located in historic homes that line quiet side streets in town. Distinctive bed-and-breakfast-style accommodations are found at the **Blair-Moore House** (201 W. Main St., 423/753-0044, $150-185). This Greek Revival-style brick home has been fully restored and an English-style garden built in the rear. The two guest rooms and one suite have high ceilings, four-poster beds, and fine linens. Rooms also each have a private balcony, and bathroom with antique claw-foot tubs. The suite also has a walk-in shower. The homemade breakfast prepared by hostess Tami Moore is a real winner.

Housed in an elegant 1832 home on four acres, the **Febuary Hill Bed and Breakfast** (102 W. College St., 423/737-6501, $150-200) is named for a local family, not the month. This large and upscale home sits just a block from

Main Street atop a hill overlooking the town. Each room has a private bathroom.

Food

Jonesborough has a pleasing array of eateries. Located a few blocks from the historic downtown, the **Olde Town Pancake House** (142 Boone St., 423/913-8111, 7am-2pm Mon.-Thurs. and Sat., 7am-9pm Fri., 8am-2pm Sun., $8-12) is a classic breakfast eatery. There are dozens of varieties of pancakes, including buttermilk, buckwheat, and apple stack. In addition, choose from omelets, biscuits and gravy, or classic breakfasts of eggs, toast, and bacon. At lunch you can also order grilled sandwiches or burgers, and dinner specials include fried catfish and rib-eye steak.

Information

The **Historic Jonesborough Visitors Center** (117 Boone St., 866/401-4223, www.historicjonesborough.com, 8am-5pm Mon.-Fri., 10am-5pm Sat.-Sun.) provides free maps, a walking tour, and other information about the town.

GREENEVILLE

Founded in 1783 and named after Nathanial Greene, a Revolutionary War hero, Greeneville is the seat of Greene County. Two American heroes, Davy Crockett and U.S. president Andrew Johnson, are affiliated with the city and the county.

★ Andrew Johnson National Historic Site

America's 17th president called Greeneville home. Andrew Johnson was born in Raleigh, North Carolina, in 1808, but he spent the better part of his life in this Tennessee city. It was here that Johnson, a self-educated tailor, first showed promise as a debater and political leader. Three Johnson buildings remain in Greeneville, and together they make up the **Andrew Johnson National Historic Site** (121 Monument Ave., 423/638-3551, www.nps.gov/anjo, 9am-5pm daily, free). Johnson's Early Home is where he and his wife, Eliza McCardle, lived during the early years of their marriage. Next door is Johnson's old Tailor Shop, fully enclosed by the present-day visitors center, where Johnson sewed clothes and debated local politics with his customers and friends. About three blocks away is the Johnson Homestead, the grander home to which the Johnsons moved in 1851, and where they returned in 1869 after his term as president ended.

the homestead at the Andrew Johnson National Historic Site

Hunting for Quilts

As you drive through Tennessee, look for quilt squares on the sides of barns and other buildings. These aren't spontaneous displays of artwork; they are part of the **Appalachian Quilt Trail** (AQT), a program designed to encourage visitors to get off the interstate and explore the smaller roads and communities; i.e., "the scenic route."

The program began in 2004, when the first quilt panel was hung on a barn in Grainger County. Over the succeeding years, almost 800 quilt patterns have been hung. Though the program started in rural East Tennessee, it has grown to span across the entire state. In East Tennessee, however, the trail is most developed.

The squares are designed to highlight something unique to travelers who are drawn to take the path off the highway. The architecture of the rural South is something they aim to preserve. The squares also highlight artists, craftspeople, galleries, and farms with homemade wares for sale. Some of these goods are available at River Place on the Clinch and at local craft fairs across the state. AQT attempts to bring rural craftsmanship to a larger audience and encourage sustainable tourism and growth.

Download a guide from the AQT website at www.vacationaqt.com or pick one up at a Tennessee visitors center. The trail is diverse enough that you can choose a mini-trail that highlights a certain area, county, art form, or even quilt pattern.

Inside the Early Home are displays about Johnson's early life and family. The visitors center contains a museum about Johnson's political career, and inside the Tailor Shop you can see some of the tools Johnson would have used to sew clothes. Guided tours of the Homestead include several family bedrooms and the parlor, arranged as it would have been during Johnson's postpresidential years. As evidence of the unpopularity of Johnson's pro-Union views, the tour includes a section of unflattering graffiti on an interior wall, just some of what the Johnsons found upon their return to Greeneville in 1869.

In addition to these buildings, there is also a replica of the Raleigh, North Carolina, building where Johnson was born. This is located across the street from the Early Home and was erected in 1999. On a hill overlooking the town is Johnson's grave, over which are the words, "His Faith In the People Never Wavered."

The visitors center is open daily except holidays. Tours of the Homestead are offered hourly on the half hour; tours are free, but tickets for this tour must be obtained from the visitors center in advance.

Other Sights

Revolutionary War hero Nathanael Greene is not only the namesake of the county and town, but also the local history museum. Come to the **Nathanael Greene Museum** (101 W. McKee St., 423/636-1558, www.nathanaelgreenemuseum.com, 11am-4pm Tues.-Sat., open Mon. in the summer, free) for a closer look at the town's history, its notable buildings, and its hometown hero, Andrew Johnson.

Greeneville's most prominent home was built between 1815 and 1821 by Irish and enslaved African artisans. The **Dickson-Williams Mansion** (108 N. Irish St., reservations and information 423/787-0500, tours: 1pm Mon.-Sat., $10) was owned first by William Dickson, a wealthy landowner, merchant, and Greeneville's first postmaster. His daughter, Catherine Dickson Williams, was well known for entertaining esteemed guests, including the Marquis de Lafayette, Davy Crockett, and three presidents: Andrew Johnson, Andrew Jackson, and James K. Polk. Tours of the home are given Monday-Saturday at 1pm and cost $10 for adults and $5 for children 6-18.

Tours

Main Street Tours (310 S. Main St., 423/787-0500) offers a guided walking tour of Greeneville, which stops at historically and architecturally significant buildings, including the oldest jail in Tennessee and sites important to Andrew Johnson's history. The tours are offered April-October Monday-Saturday at 9:30am. Tickets, which cost $5, may be purchased at the General Morgan Inn.

In addition to these guided tours, local officials have developed two self-guided tours for visitors. One, titled "A Walk with the President," is a walking tour of Greeneville. The second includes 40 different auto tours of Greene County. Copies of either are available from **Greene County Partnership** (115 Academy St., 423/638-4111, www.greenecountypartnership.com).

Recreation

Kinser Park (650 Kinser Park Ln., 423/639-5912, www.kinserpark.com, Apr.-Oct., hours vary, call ahead) is a public park with a swimming pool; waterslide; putt-putt golf course; 18-hole golf course; volleyball, basketball, tennis, and other ball fields; and a 157-site campground.

Accommodations

Named for the Confederate outlaw and hero Gen. John Hunt Morgan, nicknamed "The Thunderbolt of the Confederacy," who was killed in Greeneville, the ★ **General Morgan Inn** (111 N. Main St., 423/787-1000, www.generalmorganinn.com, $105-159) is Greeneville's most distinctive hotel. First opened as the Grand Central Hotel in 1884, the General Morgan was restored and reopened in 1996. Its lobby has a high ceiling and elegant chandeliers; the refinement continues in the 52 guest rooms and suites, where you'll find luxury linens, marble vanities, wireless Internet, and iPod-compatible radios. Guests can also take advantage of business services and passes to a local gym.

Food

The denizens of Greeneville meet for lunch of club sandwiches and chicken salad at the **Tannery Downtown** (117 E. Depot St., 423/638-2772, Mon.-Fri. 10:30am-2pm, $5-6), located a few doors down from the Andrew Johnson visitors center.

For something more elegant, choose **Brumley's** (111 N. Main St., 423/787-1000, 11am-2pm, 5pm-9pm Mon.-Fri., 10am-2pm, 5pm-9pm Sat., 10am-2pm Sun., lunch $7-10, dinner $18-30) in the General Morgan Inn. The weekday soup and salad bar is popular with lunchtime diners, along with the smothered black beans and rice, roasted pork, and crab cakes. Dinner choices include baked sea bass and filet mignon.

Information

The **Greene County Partnership Tourism Council** (115 Academy St., 423/638-4111, www.greenecountypartnership.com) has maps and other guides to Greeneville and the rest of Greene County.

AROUND GREENEVILLE

Tusculum

About 10 miles east of Greeneville is Tusculum, a small college town. Tusculum College was chartered in 1794 and is the oldest college in Tennessee. In 1872, it admitted women, making it one of the first coeducational colleges in the United States. Nine buildings on the Tusculum campus have been placed on the National Register of Historic Places, including the **Andrew Johnson Presidential Library and Museum** (Tusculum College, 423/636-7348, NPS.gov/andrewjohnson, 9am-5pm Mon.-Fri., free). This is the official museum and library dedicated to Johnson, a Tusculum trustee, as designated by Congress. The museum houses political memorabilia, artifacts, and photographs emphasizing the daily life of the Johnson family, including the bed in which he died. His papers are also here and are used by researchers and historians.

The **Doak House Museum** (Tusculum College, 423/636-8554, http://doakhouse.tusculum.edu, 9am-5pm Mon.-Fri., adults $5, children $2), owned by the college, is the home that the Reverend Samuel Witherspoon Doak built beginning in 1818 for his father, Dr. Samuel Doak. Dr. Doak had been one of the first ministers on the Tennessee frontier. He preached to the overmountain men before they left on their journey to Kings Mountain in 1780. Dr. Doak moved to Washington County and established Salem Church and school in the early 1780s. The school became Washington College, a day and boarding school for young men. Boys from far and near traveled for the opportunity to learn Latin, mathematics, and other subjects.

The Doak House is where both Samuel Doak lived from 1818 until 1829, when the elder Doak died. The museum features a few articles of furniture original to the Doak home. The handsome redbrick building was lived in by members of the Doak family until the 1950s. There is also a replica of Doak's original schoolhouse on the property.

Limestone

Davy Crockett was not born on a mountaintop in Tennessee, as the song goes (guess it was a better rhyme); he was born in the rolling foothills, near where the Limestone River flows into the Nolichucky. His birthplace is near the present-day settlement of **Limestone**, about 15 minutes' drive from Greeneville. The cabin where Crockett was born is long gone, but a replica sits on the banks of the Nolichucky at the **Davy Crockett Birthplace State Park** (1245 Davy Crockett Park Rd., 423/257-2167), also home to a museum about this most famous Tennessean.

Crockett lived on the banks of the river with his parents for 10 years before the family decamped to Morristown to open a tavern. After he became a man, Crockett continued to move gradually westward, seemingly following the ever-migrating frontier of America. He is known to have lived in Greene, Hamblen, Lincoln, Franklin, Lawrence, and Obion Counties in Tennessee before he moved to Texas, where he was killed at the Alamo.

Crockett's folksy language and boasting stories turned him into one of the most enduring symbols of the frontiersman. A museum at the state park includes copies of all the known portraits of Crockett, memorabilia he inspired, plus information about what is known about this remarkable man. Crockett's most famous sayings include, "Let your

the Doak House Museum

tongue speak what your heart thinks," and "Be always sure you're right, then go ahead."

In addition to the sights related to all things Crockett, the state park has a campground with 88 sites, which are available on a first-come, first-served basis; about 2.5 miles of hiking trails; and a swimming pool, which is open Memorial Day-Labor Day.

ROGERSVILLE

A town of many firsts, **Rogersville** is a worthwhile destination. Tennessee's first newspaper was published here, and the city is home of the oldest courthouse, inn, and post office still in operation in Tennessee.

Rogersville was settled in about 1775. According to legend, some of those early settlers were Davy Crockett's grandparents. It was named after Joseph Rogers, an Irishman who received the land on which Rogersville sits as a wedding present from his father-in-law, Col. Thomas Amis.

Rogersville was on the Wilderness Road, the route that traveled from Bean Station to Cumberland Gap and into Kentucky. Beginning in the 1840s, the city was a transportation hub for native pink and red marble, which was used in construction of the Washington Monument in Washington DC, the South Carolina State Capitol, and the municipal buildings in Baltimore.

Today, Rogersville is a quiet yet relatively happening place. A handful of attractions, an inviting downtown district, and the nearby countryside, which is beautiful and rural, make this a small town worth remembering.

Historic Downtown

Take a few minutes to explore Rogersville's historic district. The **Hawkins County Courthouse** is the oldest original courthouse still in use in Tennessee. It was built in 1836 and was fashioned after Independence Hall in Philadelphia. Across the road from the courthouse is **Overton Lodge**, the oldest Masonic lodge in continuous operation in Tennessee. The lodge was chartered in 1805. The present building was constructed in 1839 as the first branch of the Bank of the State of Tennessee.

Also on the town square is the **Hale Springs Inn** (110 W. Main St.). Built in 1824, it is the oldest continually operating inn in Tennessee.

A few blocks north is the **Swift College Campus** (200 N. Depot St.). Swift College was a Northern Presbyterian college for African Americans and operated from 1883 to 1955. It was founded by Dr. William Henderson Franklin of Knoxville, who was the first black graduate of Maryville College. From 1955 to 1963, it was Hawkins County's African American high school. After integration, the lovely administration building was torn down. Remaining buildings are used by the Hawkins County Department of Education.

Price Public School (203 Spring St., 423/921-3888, www.swiftmuseum.org, 10am-2pm Mon.-Fri., noon-2pm Sat.) is a community center that was once Rogersville's African American school. Established in 1868, Price Public School educated blacks from 1870 until desegregation. The present building was constructed in 1922. If you go inside, you can view a room dedicated to Swift College and Price Public School.

A printed guide to historic Rogersville is available from the Rogersville Heritage Association (415 S. Depot St.) and the Rogersville-Hawkins County Chamber of Commerce (107 E. Main St.).

Tennessee Newspaper and Printing Museum

The *Knoxville Gazette* was first published in Rogersville in November 1791, before it was moved to Knoxville. George Roulstone and Robert Ferguson arrived in Rogersville on the invitation of Governor William Blount, and they named their newspaper in anticipation of the establishment of the new city to the south. But while Knoxville was getting off the ground, Roulstone and Ferguson published for about one year from Rogersville. When the time came to move, they moved the presses to Knoxville on a flatboat down the Holston River.

The Melungeon Mystery

Hancock County was one of the first parts of Tennessee to be settled by Europeans. A 1673 letter by early explorer Abraham Wood described his visit to the area: "Eight dayes jorny down this river lives a white people which have long beards and whiskers and weares clothing. . . ." These white people were also described by John Sevier in 1784, who reported that they seemed to have been living in the area for some time.

The word that came to be used to describe these mysterious early settlers was *Melungeon*. Even the origin of the word is unclear; it was initially thought to have derived from the French word *mélange* (mixture). Other research suggests it may be an Afro-Portuguese word meaning white person, and still other scholars believe it is from the Turkish language and means cursed soul.

When Anglo-European settlers arrived in the area, they conveniently decided that the Melungeons, who had olive complexions and dark hair, were people of color and promptly took their land. Discrimination and prejudice caused Melungeons and their descendants to retreat to some of the most rural and remote territory of the county.

Despite ongoing efforts to determine exactly how and when Melungeons arrived in Appalachia, there are still many questions about the origins of these very early Tennesseans. In the 1990s, a 30-member panel put together by Clinch Valley College of the University of Virginia spent four years researching Melungeons. The consensus, by no means definitive, was that they are of Middle Eastern or Mediterranean heritage. It is still debated how they came to Appalachia and whether they intermarried with Native Americans.

Despite the passage of time and increasing interest in Melungeon heritage, the story of the Melungeons remains one that is often told in whispers. A good source of information is the Melungeon Heritage Association (www.melungeon.org).

Rogersville's first newspaper is recalled at the **Tennessee Newspaper and Printing Museum** (415 S. Depot St., 423/272-1961, 10am-3pm Mon.-Thurs., free), located in the town's old train depot. It is best to call ahead and confirm hours.

The museum contains a re-created 19th-century print shop, original copies of more than two dozen newspapers that were printed here, and artifacts from the Pressman's Home. You can also see the last linotype machine used to set type for a Tennessee newspaper; the machine was used by the *Rogersville Review* until 1982.

Pressmen's Home

Located about 12 miles north of Rogersville are the abandoned remains of **Pressmen's Home**, a once-thriving community affiliated with the 125,000-member International Printing Pressmen and Assistants' Union (IPPAU). Rogersville native George Berry headed the union from 1907 until 1948, and it was due to his efforts that the substantial facility was built in remote upper East Tennessee.

Pressmen's Home covered 2,700 acres. It had its own phone and electrical system, post office, and farm. In addition to being the administrative headquarters of the IPPAU, Pressmen's Home was a retirement home, sanatorium, and printing trade school. For a time, Pressmen's Home was the largest training school of its kind in the world. New and experienced pressmen came here to learn offset-printing methods. It also offered a correspondence school.

Pressmen's Home operated from 1911 until 1966, when union officials decided they needed to return to a more cosmopolitan place. In 1967, the IPPAU headquarters moved to Washington DC. Not 10 years later, the IPPAU merged with another union and disappeared from the union registry.

Today, Pressmen's Home is abandoned, and the community has been renamed Camelot. It is not a very inviting place. A former country club and golf course on the property failed, and plans to turn it into a state prison and an environmental education center did not reach fruition. In 2008, fire destroyed what was left of the hotel. But if you drive north on Highway 70, and then turn left on Highway 94, you will soon see the still-imposing edifices of the remaining buildings.

Shopping

The **Local Artists Gallery** (124 E. Main St., 423/921-7656, www.rogersvillegallery.com) has a wide selection of arts and crafts, including paintings and prints, woodwork, pottery, textiles, and candles.

Accommodations

The **Hale Springs Inn** (110 E. Main St., 423/272-5171, www.halespringsinn.com, $125-165) was built in 1824 and reopened in 2009 following extensive renovations. The inn balances modern comfort with ambience befitting such a historic structure. This should be your first choice for accommodations in Rogersville.

Food

Rogersville has several coffee shops that double as cafés. **Miss Bea's Perks and Pies** (109 S. Church St., 423/272-6555, 7am-3pm Mon.-Fri., $4-5) has a repertoire of sandwiches, panini, wraps, and soups. Each day, It offers two soups and sandwiches for customers to choose from. Favorites are the turkey and artichoke panini, chicken and grape salad sandwich, and the stuffed-pepper soup. For breakfast, Miss Bea's offers stratas and biscuits, plus a variety of pastries. They also serve fresh-brewed specialty coffees.

Offering lunch-counter fare, daily lunch specials, and hearty breakfast platters, **Oh Henry's** (201 E. Main St., 423/272-0980, 6am-11pm Mon.-Sat., $4-12) is an institution in Rogersville. It's a down-home, no-frills, friendly type of place.

Information

The **Rogersville Heritage Association** (415 S. Depot St., 423/272-1961, www.rogersvilleheritage.org) does an admirable job of promoting the town and sharing its history with the world. You can also contact the **Rogersville-Hawkins County Chamber of Commerce** (107 E. Main St., 423/272-2186, www.rogersvillechamber.us).

★ KYLES FORD

The countryside north of Rogersville, in Hawkins and Hancock Counties, is some of

bridge over the Clinch River at Kyles Ford

Stop and rest at River Place in Kyles Ford.

the most rural and isolated in this region. If the northeastern tip of Tennessee is its first frontier, then this is the last.

It is the rugged landscape that keeps this area from changing. Long, steep valleys lie between Clinch and Powell Mountains. The Clinch River flows unimpeded from Virginia, cutting a wide valley, which is prone to flood. And narrow, two-lane roads wind around hills and over mountains. This is beautiful countryside, but only if you're willing to slow down and enjoy it.

As for a destination, head north along Highway 70 to **Kyles Ford,** a small settlement along the Clinch just a few miles from Virginia. In 2007, an exciting development project led by the Clinch River RC&D (Resource, Conservation, and Development Council), a rural organization serving Claiborne, Grainger, Hancock, Hawkins, and Union Counties, gave visitors a good reason to make the trip.

★ **River Place** (2788 Hwy. 70, 423/733-4400, www.clinchriverecotourism.com, 11am-7pm Mon.-Thurs., 7am-9pm Fri.-Sat., 9am-4pm Sun., $4-9), a general store and restaurant, is the cornerstone of the development project. This handsome riverfront building is a small grocery and the best restaurant in these parts. The food here is actually made from scratch (not just claimed to be the case); homemade biscuits, comfort casseroles, and sides like real mashed potatoes will please your palate. The matter of fact friendliness of the folks here will please your spirit. The slogan is: "Nothing fancy. Just food you want to eat."

Behind the cafstore ★ **River Place Cabins** (423/733-4400, www.clinchriverecotourism.com, $80-95 or $575 per week), four vacation cabins and an 1800s cottage now restored for guests. The vacation cabins were constructed in 2007 but look like they've been settled into the hillside for years. Interior wood paneling, quilts, and simple decor ease your mind and invite relaxation. The cabins overlook the Clinch River and have fully functioning kitchens, telephones, and central heat and air. There's no cell phone service, and you have to drive to the local library to check your email.

A few hundred yards down the road, on the other side of the river, the **Clinch River Conservation and Retreat Center** (3225 Hwy. 70, 423/733-4400) is an old farmhouse that has been restored and renovated to become an environmental retreat center and venue for reunions, meetings, and other gatherings.

Background

The Landscape

Tennessee is a long, narrow state. Shaped roughly like a parallelogram, it is 500 miles from east to west and 110 miles from north to south. Partly due to its unusual shape, Tennessee, along with Missouri, borders more states than any other in the country. Its neighbors are North Carolina, Virginia, Kentucky, Missouri, Arkansas, Mississippi, Alabama, and Georgia. Tennessee is the 36th-largest state in the United States, with a land mass of 41,234 square miles.

Like the rest of the United States, Tennessee was covered by a large shallow sea approximately 500 million years ago. As the sea dried up, the land that is now Tennessee turned swampy and eventually dry. The sea creatures that once lived in the sea died, their skeletons forming limestone. The plants and animals that lived in the swampy landscape died, eventually forming coal.

Beginning about 600 million years ago, the Appalachian Mountains were formed through plate movement. Once sharp and rocky, the Appalachians have been worn down over millions of years to the gentle, rounded slopes that now characterize the range.

GEOGRAPHY

If you ask a Tennessean where he is from, the answer is never as simple as "Tennessee." Tennessee is divided by the Tennessee River into three "Grand Divisions": East Tennessee, Middle Tennessee, and West Tennessee. These are even represented on the state flag and seal.

East Tennessee

East Tennessee is defined by the Appalachian Mountains and their foothills. This region was historically small farms and isolated mountain communities.

Within East Tennessee are two geographic regions. The Unaka Mountains are part of the Appalachian Mountain chain, which peak along the state's border with North Carolina. This zone includes the Great Smoky Mountains National Park. It is also where you will find Clingmans Dome, which at 6,643 feet above sea level is the highest point in Tennessee.

West of the Unaka Mountains is the Great Valley of East Tennessee, home to Knoxville and Chattanooga. This region is characterized by picturesque low ridges and a wide, fertile valley.

Middle Tennessee

Middle Tennessee is home to Tennessee's capital city, Nashville, and some of its most fertile farmland. Before the Civil War, great plantation mansions dotted the countryside south of Nashville.

Geographically, Middle Tennessee begins with the Cumberland Plateau, which rises to about 2,000 feet above sea level and lies west of East Tennessee's Great Valley. Despite its name, the plateau is not flat; there are a number of steep valleys in the plateau, the largest being the Sequatchie Valley.

The Highland Rim is a region of hills, valleys, and fertile farmland that lies west of the plateau. The largest physical region of Tennessee, the Highland Rim contains 10,650 square miles of land, or almost 25 percent of the state. Almost entirely surrounded by the Highland Rim is the Central Basin, a low, flat, and fertile region in north-central Tennessee. Nashville is located in the Central Basin.

West Tennessee

West Tennessee is more like the Deep South

Previous: Civil War era cannon overlooking Chattanooga from Point Park on Lookout Mountain; Tipton homestead in Cades Cove.

than the rest of the state. Mostly flat and rural, this was the epicenter of the state's cotton industry both before and after the Civil War. The Gulf Coastal Plain, an area of 9,000 square miles, is drained by the Mississippi River and its tributaries. Memphis lies in the southwestern corner of this area.

RIVERS AND LAKES

The largest river in Tennessee is the Mississippi River, which forms the western border of the state. The Hatchie River is among the smaller tributaries that drain West Tennessee and flow into the Mississippi.

The state's two most important rivers are the Cumberland and Tennessee Rivers. The Cumberland River flows through Nashville and along the north-central portion of the state. The Tennessee River flows in a *U* shape, first flowing south through East Tennessee, through Knoxville and Chattanooga, and then northward, defining the boundary between Middle and West Tennessee. Both the Cumberland and the Tennessee Rivers empty into the Ohio River, which flows to the Mississippi.

All but one of Tennessee's major lakes are artificial, having been created by the Tennessee Valley Authority (TVA) during the last century. The lone exception to this is Reelfoot Lake in northeastern Tennessee, which was formed from the 1811 New Madrid earthquake when the mouth of what had been Reelfoot Creek was closed off and the creek's water spread out to cover the surrounding land.

CLIMATE

Tennessee has a mild climate. The average temperature is 58°F; in winter, temperatures generally hover 30-40°F, and summer temperatures are 70-80°F. Summer days can feel very hot, however, particularly in Middle and West Tennessee. Of the state's three major cities, Memphis temperatures rise slightly higher than the others during the summer, and the city stays warmest in winter. Knoxville is the coolest city.

The state receives an average of 50 inches of rain per year, and only a few places in the Appalachian Mountains receive more than 10 inches of snow per year. Many parts of Tennessee receive little, if any, snow or ice precipitation annually. When they do, schools and streets close, as few cities own snow-removal equipment.

Heavy rains associated with tropical weather systems can sometimes affect the

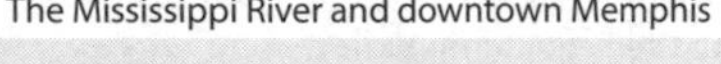
The Mississippi River and downtown Memphis

state, and winter weather can close roads in the higher elevations along the Cumberland Plateau and the Smoky Mountains.

Tornadoes

The Mid-South, including western and central Tennessee, is prone to tornadoes. The tornado season runs November-April, but can continue into the summer. The danger of tornadoes is compounded by the fact that they may strike after dark and that in many areas of the state, visibility is limited by hills and trees.

On Super Tuesday, February 5, 2008, a series of tornadoes struck Tennessee, killing 32 people, most of them in Sumner and Macon Counties north of Nashville. Of those who died, 20 were in mobile homes when the storm struck. The event, one of the most deadly natural disasters in Tennessee history, led to calls for better education and awareness.

The best way to avoid injury in a tornado is to monitor a weather radio and move quickly to a cellar, basement, or windowless interior room if a tornado is on the way.

Floods

The devastating flood in Nashville and Middle Tennessee in May 2010 brought the issue of global climate changes, combined with man-made development and water management, to the forefront of the minds of city planners and residents. The flood caused more than $1.5 billion of damage to the Music City, although it quickly rallied and rebuilt. Floods were also a concern in 2011 when the Mississippi threatened to cover parts of Memphis with water.

ENVIRONMENTAL ISSUES

Forestry

Beginning in the 1980s, the number of paper and wood chip mills in Tennessee grew dramatically. With no legislation regulating the clearing of forested land, some parts of Tennessee experienced widespread clear-cutting of old forests. Over the years, local environmental groups have fought for an overarching law that would insist on responsible forestry practices. While no such law has been passed, some stopgap measures have been put in place.

Strip Mining

Strip mines have a devastating environmental impact. In a strip mine, the surface of the earth above a seam of coal is removed, leaving scarred and bare earth. The most devastating type of strip mining is mountaintop removal, when the whole mountain is destroyed by explosives to get to the coal, which can lie as many as 800 feet below the surface.

Mountaintop removal and other types of strip mining have terrible consequences for drinking-water quality, animal and plant life, and the native culture of places that are affected. Dumping of debris from the removal process buries streams and fills valleys. When the coal companies are done, they pile dirt back up on the exposed mountains and drop exotic grass seed from above. In this way, they say, the mountain is restored. But while they may be able to approximate the shape of the old mountain, they cannot re-create the intricate web of life that once existed there.

Strip mining is most common in parts of Virginia, West Virginia, and Kentucky, but it takes place in Tennessee, too. Mining operations exist in Scott, Campbell, and Claiborne Counties in the northern Cumberland Plateau region. Residents and environmental activists fought to prevent mountaintop removal at Zeb Mountain in Scott and Campbell Counties but were unsuccessful.

Air Pollution

Car emissions, industrial pollution, and other activities cause air pollution. In Tennessee, exhaust from cars and trucks, plus the toxic emissions from coal-fired generating plants, are the biggest contributors to air pollution.

The air quality in the Great Smoky Mountains National Park is a serious concern for scientists. This is because so many people drive to this car-friendly national park. According to the park, the average visibility is 25 miles, compared to the national average of 93 miles. Some days, haze causes visibility to diminish to less than one mile. Some days, the level of ground-level ozone exceeds what is recommended for human exposure.

Air quality is typically worst during the hot summer months of July and August. The park service reports that average visibility in the southern Appalachians has decreased 40 percent in winter and 80 percent in summer since 1948.

Land Use

According to the Tennessee Environmental Council, the state has the seventh-highest rate of development in the United States. In fact, 80,000 acres of rural land are developed in Tennessee each year. The areas around Nashville and Knoxville have seen the greatest sprawl.

Urban and suburban sprawl leads to long driving times, increased air pollution, strain on scarce water resources, and the elimination of farmland, rural landscapes, and natural habitats. Smart growth policies, zoning issues, and better transportation solutions are some of the biggest challenges facing Tennessee at the moment.

Water Pollution

The cleanliness of Tennessee's rivers, lakes, and streams is monitored according to the standards of the Clean Water Act. The Tennessee Department of Environment and Conservation monitors the health of the state's rivers. In its last report, the agency reported that 25 percent of the state's river miles were category one, the cleanest, and 31 percent were in the dirtiest category. As for lakes and reservoirs, 21 percent of lake acres were classified as "impaired."

Most water pollution is caused by sedimentation and silt runoff from construction and agriculture. Habitat alteration, pathogens found in wastewater, and nutrients from fertilizers are also problems. Some pollution can be readily cleaned up, but so-called legacy pollutants, such as PCBs (polychlorinated biphenyl) and chlordane from old industrial sites, can remain present for years and can poison fish and other marine animals.

According to the state government, 41 percent of pollution in streams and rivers in 2006 came from agriculture, 19 percent from hydrologic modification, and 18 percent from municipal sources. For lakes, 72 percent of contaminants were legacy pollutants.

The state is supposed to post a warning when a river or stream is deemed too polluted for fishing, swimming, or other forms of use. For a listing of such bodies of water, contact the Water Pollution Control division of the Department of Environment and Conservation (615/532-0625), or the Tennessee Clean Water Network (www.tcwn.org).

Plants and Animals

Encyclopedias are written about Tennessee's rich and diverse menagerie of animals and plants. The eastern mountains are one of the most biologically diverse areas in the United States, and whole volumes are devoted to their flora and fauna.

Middle and West Tennessee share the more typical plants and animals of the Deep South. Western Tennessee's cypress swamps are rich depositories of plant and animal life, while the plains are important for agriculture.

WILDFLOWERS

In the spring and summer, wildflowers spring up along roadsides, mountain streams, and pastures. Look for the small yellow blooms of **St. John's wort** and the bushy purple crowns of **ironweed.** Delicate purple **bluebells** and white, pink, or purple **phlox** blanket cool stream banks and coves. Placid lakes and ponds come alive with the white-pink blooms of **water lily.**

Fields and gardens are decorated with the

Tennessee Pearls

The fast-running rivers of Tennessee are great for recreation, but they also are home to freshwater mussels, and these mussels sometimes create surprises: beautiful pearls.

Native Americans were the first to discover Tennessee's pearls; Indians harvested mussels for food and used the pearls in jewelry. Tennessee history knows many stories of simple folks who stumbled upon a pearl, getting an unexpected payday in the process. In one such story, Charles Bradford and James Johnson were looking for bait to go fishing in the Caney Fork River in the early 1880s. They had pulled up several mussels and found a large white pearl inside one of them. The boys sent the pearl to Tiffany's in New York and received a check for $83.

Stories such as this one fueled the Tennessee pearl industry for many years. The industry peaked between 1882 and 1914, when special musseling boats would ply the Tennessee and other rivers, dragging a "brail" (resembling an underwater rake) that captured river mussels. In more modern times, diving is the most popular way to harvest wild mussels from the watery depths.

Tennessee pearls were a variety of colors and shapes, and the mother-of-pearl from the mussel shells was used in button manufacturing during the early part of the 20th century, before plastic buttons became common.

Tennessee pearls declined following the establishment of the Tennessee Valley Authority and the damming of many rivers in the state. This is because dams caused rivers to flow more slowly, thus eliminating the fast-moving water habitat required by freshwater mussels. Pollution also hurt wild mussels, as did overfishing and the rise of pearl cultivation in Asia.

The Tennessee River Pearl Farm, near Camden, Tennessee, still harvests pearls from the river, although they are cultivated. Some of the pearls harvested here are fashioned into jewelry, but most are exported to Asia, where they are used in the cultivation of high-grade pearls.

The pearl was named the Tennessee state gem in 1979.

bracing yellow blooms of **sunflowers** and the bright-orange colors of **butterfly weed.** Cultivated lawns and gardens showcase delicate **roses** and elegant **irises,** the state flower of Tennessee.

TREES

Tennessee's official state tree is the **tulip poplar,** a fast-growing tree often used for timber. It blooms in May. **Flowering dogwoods** are celebrated with a springtime festival in Knoxville. The dogwood's vibrant flowers are actually white-colored leaves that surround a tight cluster of flowers in the center. Some dogwood "blooms" are pink. Throughout the state you will see **magnolia** trees, notable for their thick, heavy green leaves and large white blooms, as well as their sweet scent. The Vanderbilt University campus in Nashville is particularly fragrant when magnolias are in bloom.

In West Tennessee's wetlands and at Reelfoot Lake, look for **cypress** trees, easily identifiable by their rough, bumpy knees.

BIRDS

Field, swamp, house, chipping, and song **sparrows,** as they flit about and perch on tree limbs, are ubiquitous in the Volunteer State. Look for the red **cardinal,** the black-and-white **junco,** and the yellow **goldfinch.**

The **Carolina chickadee** puffs out its breast in winter, and the **blue jay** patrols bird feeders. The **mockingbird** is Tennessee's state bird; it mimics the calls of other birds and has a gray body and dark wings.

Unless you are unusually patient or light of foot, you're unlikely to see the nocturnal **Eastern screech owl** or its cousins, the great horned owl and barred owl, in the wild. Keep your eyes pinned on the sky for **hawks,** red-tailed, sharp-shinned, and Cooper's. **Bald eagles** winter at Reelfoot Lake and other protected locations in the state.

Wild turkeys are making a comeback; groups may be seen patrolling many state parks and natural areas. Look for the male's impressive feathers. Listen for the knocking of the **woodpeckers**—hairy, redheaded, downy, and pileated varieties.

Bodies of water are some of the best places to seek feathered friends. **Sandhill cranes** winter on the Hiwassee River in East Tennessee. Float down a river, and you may see a statuesque **great blue heron** hunting for food. **Wood ducks** and **mallards,** whose males have a striking green head, live around ponds and lakes.

LARGE MAMMALS

Many of the large, wild creatures of Tennessee are threatened. **Elk** and **bison,** which ranged here before settlement by Europeans, have been reintroduced at Land Between the Lakes and the Great Smoky Mountains National Park. Scruffy **feral pigs** live in scattered populations in East Tennessee. **Black bears,** the icon of the Smoky Mountains, have a shaggy black coat and sharp sense of smell. They can run and climb trees. **Coyotes** and **red fox** are lovely, quick, and adaptable. **Bobcats** are stealthy and elusive hunters that prefer the hours right before sunrise and right after sunset.

SMALL MAMMALS

Raccoons, with their bandit's mask and striped tail, are adorable until one has ruined your bird feeder or gotten into your garbage (or even bitten you, which has been known to happen). **Eastern cottontail** is the most common type of rabbit, and they prefer grasslands and cultivated areas. Look for the white of their stubby tail. **Eastern chipmunks** are small creatures that scurry along forest floors, pastureland, and city parks. **Eastern gray squirrels** are easier to see—they are larger and more ubiquitous.

Keep your eyes open for goldfinch.

AMPHIBIANS AND REPTILES

Listen for the "harumph" of the **bullfrog** or the night song of the **Cope's gray tree frog** near water. Salamanders and newts flourish in the damp, cool forests of the eastern mountains: look for the lizard-like **Eastern newt** and the **spotted salamander,** which can grow up to 10 inches. The largest of the salamanders is the **Eastern tiger salamander,** which comes in a rainbow of colors and patterns best left to your imagination. They grow up to 13 inches.

Snapping turtles live in rivers and streams, rarely coming on land. The **Eastern box turtle** prefers moist forests and grasslands. Most Tennessee snakes are harmless. The **garter snake** is the most common. It prefers areas that are cool and moist. **Green snakes** like bushes and low-hanging branches near the water.

Hemlocks Under Threat

First the American chestnut, then the Fraser fir, and now the hemlock: Nonnative insects have taken a terrible toll on the native trees of the Smokies. The dead trees visible throughout the spruce-fir forests at high elevations are testament to the loss of Fraser firs. Now park scientists and others are racing against time to protect hemlock trees.

The hemlock woolly adelgid is the culprit. Native to Asia, the adelgid feeds at the base of the hemlock needles, disrupting nutrient flow and eventually causing the tree to starve to death. Hemlock woolly adelgids were first discovered near Richmond, Virginia, in 1951. To date, they have spread through the eastern regions of the hemlock's native range. As of 2010, they were found in North Carolina, Georgia, Tennessee, Kentucky, Virginia, and South Carolina.

Hemlocks are beautiful, big trees. They can live to be more than 600 years old and can grow to heights of more than 165 feet. Hemlock trees grow in a variety of habitats and serve myriad purposes in the Smokies' ecosystem. By blocking out the sunlight, hemlocks keep mountain streams cool. Migratory birds such as the Blackburnian warbler and the wood thrush shelter in hemlock groves. Loss of hemlocks will have a negative effect on rivers and streams. Scientists are already seeing higher acidity in some streams where dead hemlock trees have fallen.

Scientists are using insecticidal soap to spray infested trees, but this method is labor intensive and works only for trees that are near roadsides or otherwise easily accessible. Applying insecticides around the soil of the trees is also an effective method, but it's prohibitively expensive for a park with millions of hemlock trees to protect.

Biological control—the introduction of a natural predator beetle to the woolly adelgid—is the most promising long-term preventative. Scientists have pinned their hopes on a poppy-seed-size predator beetle that, in its native Japan, eats only hemlock adelgids. Since 2002, the park has been releasing the predator beetle in the Smokies, and more than 350,000 have been released to date. The predator program got a boost in 2004 when the University of Tennessee opened a new beetle-rearing facility. However, the cost and limited supply of the beetles is the greatest hurdle.

A large number of hemlocks have already been lost, and park officials warn that the consequences of their deaths are only beginning to show. In addition to efforts to stop the spread of the adelgid, scientists are intent on saving enough hemlocks at different elevations in the park in order to save a representative gene pool, which could be used to repopulate the forest if the adelgid threat is ever fully contained.

History

THE FIRST TENNESSEANS

The first humans settled in what is now Tennessee 12,000-15,000 years ago. Descended from people who crossed into North America during the last ice age, these Paleo-Indians were nomads who hunted large game animals, including mammoth, mastodon, and caribou. Remains of these extinct mammals have been found in West Tennessee, and the Indians' arrowheads and spear points have been found all over the state. The ice age hunters camped in caves and under rock shelters but remained predominantly nomadic.

About 10,000 years ago, the climate and vegetation of the region changed. The deciduous forest that still covers large parts of the state replaced the evergreen forest of the fading ice age. Large game animals disappeared, and deer and elk arrived, attracted by the forests of hickory, chestnut, and beech. Descendants of the Paleo-Indians gradually abandoned the nomadic lifestyle of their ancestors and established settlements, often near rivers. They hunted deer, bear, and turkey;

gathered nuts and wild fruit; and harvested freshwater fish and mussels. They also took a few tentative steps toward cultivation by growing squash and gourds.

This Archaic Period was replaced by the Woodland Period about 3,000 years ago. The Woodland Indians adopted the bow and arrow for hunting and—at the end of their predominance—began cultivating maize and beans as staple crops. Ceramic pottery appeared, and ritualism took on a greater importance in the society. Pinson Mounds, burial mounds near Jackson in West Tennessee, date from this period, as does the wrongly named Old Stone Fort near Manchester, believed to have been built and used for ceremonies by the Woodland Indians of the area.

The development of a more complex culture continued, and at about AD 900 the Woodland culture gave way to the Mississippian Period, an era marked by population growth, an increase in trade and warfare, the rise of the chieftain, and cultural accomplishments. The Mississippian era is best known for the impressive large pyramid mounds that were left behind in places such as Etowah and Toqua in Tennessee and Moundville in Alabama. Mississippian Indians also created beautiful ornaments and symbolic objects including combs, pipes, and jewelry.

Europeans Arrive

Having conquered Peru, the Spanish nobleman Hernando de Soto embarked on a search for gold in the American southeast in 1539. De Soto's band wandered through Florida, Georgia, and the Carolinas before crossing into what is now Tennessee, probably in June 1540. His exact route is a source of controversy, but historians believe he made his way through parts of East Tennessee before heading back into Georgia. The popular myth that he camped on the Chickasaw Bluff—the site of Memphis today—in 1541 remains unproven.

It was more than 100 years until another European was reported in the Tennessee wilderness, although life for the natives was already changing. De Soto and his men brought firearms and disease, and there was news of other whites living to the east. Disease and warfare led to a decline in population for Tennessee's Indians during the presettlement period. As a result, Indian communities formed new tribes with each other: The Creek Confederacy and Choctaws were among the tribes that were formed. In Tennessee, the Shawnee moved south into the Cumberland River country—land previously claimed as hunting ground by the Chickasaw Nation. Also at this time, a new tribe came over the Smoky Mountains from North Carolina, possibly to escape encroachment of European settlers, to form what would become the most important Indian group in modern Tennessee: the Overhill Cherokee.

In 1673, European scouts entered Tennessee at its eastern and western ends. Englishmen James Needham, Gabriel Arthur, and eight hired Indian guides were the first European party to enter East Tennessee. Needham did not last long; he was killed by his Indian guides early in the outing. Arthur won over his traveling companions and joined them on war trips and hunts before returning to Virginia in 1674. Meanwhile, on the western end of the state, French explorers Father Jacques Marquette and trader Louis Joliet came down the Mississippi River and claimed the surrounding valley for the French.

Nine years later, Robert Cavelier de La Salle paused at the Chickasaw Bluff near present-day Memphis and built Fort Prudhomme as a temporary base. The fort was short-lived, but the site would be used by the French in years to come in their war against the Chickasaws and later in the French and Indian War.

The Long Hunters

The first Europeans to carve out a foothold in the unknown frontier of Tennessee were traders who made journeys into Indian territory to hunt and trade. These men disappeared for months at a time into the wilderness and were therefore known as long hunters. They left with European-made goods and returned with animal skins. They led pack trains of horses and donkeys over narrow, steep, and crooked mountain trails and through sometimes-hostile territory. It was a lonely, hard life, full of uncertainty. Some of the long hunters were no better than crooks; others were respected by both the Indians and Europeans.

The long hunters included men like Elisha Walden, Kasper Mansker, and Abraham Bledsoe. Daniel Boone, born in North Carolina, was in present-day Washington County in northeastern Tennessee when, in 1760, he carved on a beech tree that he had "cilled" a "bar" nearby. Thomas Sharp Spencer became known as Big Foot and is said to have spent the winter in a hollowed-out sycamore tree. Another trader, a Scotch-Irish man named James Adair, traded with the Indians for years and eventually wrote *A History of the American Indian,* published in London in 1775 and one of the first such accounts.

The animal skins and furs that were the aim of these men's exploits were eventually sold in Charleston and exported to Europe. In 1748 alone, South Carolina merchants exported more than 160,000 skins worth $250,000. The trade was profitable for merchants and, to a lesser extent, the traders themselves. But it was rarely profitable for the Indians, and it helped to wipe out much of Tennessee's native animal life.

The French and Indian War

In 1754, the contest between the French and the British for control of the New World boiled over into war. Indian alliances were seen as critical to success, and so the British set out to win the support of the Cherokee. They did this by agreeing to build a fort in the land over the mountain from North Carolina—territory that came to be known as the Overhill country. The Cherokee wanted the fort to protect their women and children from French or hostile-Indian attack while the men were away. The fort was begun in 1756 near the fork of the Little Tennessee and Tellico Rivers, and it was named Fort Loudoun after the commander of British forces in America. Twelve cannons were transported over the rough mountain terrain by horse to defend the fort from enemy attack.

The construction of Fort Loudoun did not prove to be the glue to hold the Cherokee and British together. In fact, it was not long before relations deteriorated to the point where the Cherokee chief Standing Turkey directed an attack on the fort. A siege ensued. Reinforcements were called for and dispatched, but the British colonel and 1,300 men turned back before reaching the fort. The English inside the fort were weakened by lack of food and surrendered. On August 9, 1760, 180 men, 60 women, and a few children marched out of Fort Loudoun, the first steps of a 140-mile journey to the nearest British fort. The group had been promised to be allowed to retreat peacefully, but on the first night of the journey the group was ambushed: killed were 3 officers, 23 privates, 3 women. The rest were taken prisoner. The Indians said they were inspired to violence upon finding that the British had failed to surrender all of their firepower as promised.

The Cherokee's action was soon avenged. A year later, Col. James Grant led a party into the Lower Cherokee territory, where they destroyed villages, burnt homes, and cut down fields of corn.

The French and Indian War ended in 1763, and in the Treaty of Paris the French withdrew any claims to lands east of the Mississippi. This result emboldened European settlers and land speculators who were drawn to the land of the Overhill country. The fact that the land still belonged to the Indians did not stop the movement west.

EARLY SETTLERS

The First Settlements

With the issue of French possession resolved, settlers began to filter into the Overhill country. Early settlers included William Bean, on the Holston River; Evan Shelby, at Sapling Grove (later Bristol); John Carter, in the Carter Valley; and Jacob Brown, on the

Nolichucky River. By 1771, the settlers at Wataugua and Nolichucky won a lease from the Cherokee, and the next year, they formed the Watauga Association, a quasi government and the first such in Tennessee territory.

The settlers' success in obtaining land concessions from the Indians was eclipsed in 1775 when the Transylvania Company, led by Richard Henderson of North Carolina, traded £10,000 of goods for 20 million acres of land in Kentucky and Tennessee. The agreement, negotiated at a treaty conference at Sycamore Shoals, was opposed by the Cherokee chief Dragging Canoe, who warned that the Cherokee were paving the way for their own extinction. Despite his warning, the treaty was signed.

Dragging Canoe remained the leader of the Cherokee's resistance to European settlement. In 1776, he orchestrated assaults on the white settlements of Watauga, Nolichucky, Long Island, and Carter's Valley. The offensive, called by some the Cherokee War, had limited success at first, but it ended in defeat for the natives. In 1777, the Cherokee signed a peace treaty with the settlers that ceded more land to the Europeans.

Dragging Canoe and others did not accept the treaty and left the Cherokee as a result. He and his followers moved south, near Chickamauga Creek, where they became known as the Chickamauga tribe. Over time, this tribe attracted other Indians whose common purpose was opposition to white settlement.

The Indians could not, however, overpower the increasing tide of European settlers, who brought superior firepower and greater numbers. Pressure on political leaders to free up more and more land for settlement made relations with the Indians and land agreements with them one of the most important features of political life on the frontier.

In the end, these leaders delivered. Europeans obtained Indian land in Tennessee through a series of treaties and purchases, beginning with the Sycamore Shoals purchase in 1775 and continuing until 1818, when the Chickasaw ceded all control to land west of the Mississippi. Negotiating on behalf of the settlers were leaders including William Blount, the territorial governor, and Andrew Jackson, the first U.S. president from Tennessee.

Indian Removal

Contact with Europeans had a significant impact on the Cherokee's way of life. Christian missionaries introduced education, and in the 1820s, Sequoyah developed a Cherokee alphabet, allowing the Indians to read and write in their own language. The Cherokee adopted some of the Europeans' farming practices, as well as some of their social practices, including slavery. Adoption of the European lifestyle was most common among the significant number of mixed-race Cherokee. In 1827, the Cherokee Nation was established, complete with a constitutional system of government and a capital in New Echota, Georgia. From 1828 until 1832, its newspaper, the *Cherokee Phoenix,* was published in both English and Cherokee.

The census of 1828 counted 15,000 Cherokee remaining in Tennessee. They owned 1,000 slaves, 22,400 head of cattle, 7,600 horses, 1,800 spinning wheels, 700 looms, 12 sawmills, 55 blacksmith shops, and 6 cotton gins.

Despite these beginnings of assimilation, or because of them, the Cherokee were not welcome to remain in the new territory. Settlers pushed for a strong policy that would lead to the Cherokee's removal, and they looked over the border to Georgia to see that it could be done. There, in 1832, authorities surveyed lands owned by Cherokee and disposed of them by lottery. Laws were passed to prohibit Indian assemblies and bar Indians from bringing suit in the state. The majority of Tennessee settlers, as well as Georgia officials, pushed for similar measures to be adopted in Tennessee.

The Cherokee were divided in their response: Some felt that moving west represented the best future for their tribe, while others wanted to stay and fight for their land and the Cherokee Nation. In the end, the Cherokee leaders lost hope of remaining, and on December 29, 1835, they signed the removal treaty. Under the agreement, the Cherokee were paid $5 million for all their lands east of the Mississippi, and they were required to move west within two years. When that time expired in 1838 and only a small number of the Cherokee had moved, the U.S. army evicted the rest by force.

Thousands of Cherokee died along the ensuing Trail of Tears, which followed four different routes through Tennessee and eventually into Oklahoma: A southern route extended from Chattanooga to Memphis, two northern routes headed into Kentucky and Missouri before turning southward into Oklahoma, and the fourth was a water route along the Tennessee and Mississippi Rivers. Harsh weather, food shortages, and the brutality of the journey cost thousands of Cherokee lives. In the end, out of the estimated 14,000 Cherokee who began the journey, more than 4,000 are believed to have died along the way.

Some Cherokee remained by hiding deep in the Great Smoky Mountains. Later, they were given land that became the Cherokee Reservation in North Carolina.

STATEHOOD

Almost as soon as settlers began living on the Tennessee frontier there were movements to form a government. Dissatisfied with the protection offered by North Carolina's distant government, settlers drew up their own governments as early as the 1780s. The Watauga Association and Cumberland Compact were early forms of government. In 1785, settlers in northeastern Tennessee seceded from North Carolina and established the State of Franklin. The experiment was short-lived but foretold that in the future the lands west of the Smoky Mountains would be their own state.

Before Tennessee could become a state, however, it was a territory of the United States. In 1789, North Carolina ratified its own constitution and in doing so ceded its western lands, the Tennessee country, to the U.S. government. These lands eventually became known as the Southwest Territory, and in 1790, President George Washington appointed William Blount its territorial governor.

Blount was a 41-year-old land speculator and businessman who had campaigned actively for the position. A veteran of the War for Independence, Blount knew George Washington and was one of the signers of the U.S. Constitution in 1787.

At the time of its establishment, the Southwest Territory was 43,000 square miles in area. The population of 35,000 was centered in two main areas: the northeastern corner and the Cumberland settlements near present-day Nashville.

Governor Blount moved quickly to establish a territorial government. In October 1790, he arrived in Washington County and established the state's first capitol in the home of William Cobb. This simple wood-frame house, known as Rocky Mount, would be the territory's capitol for the next 18 months before it moved to James White's Fort in Knoxville.

The territory's first election was held in 1793, and the resulting council met a year later. They established the town of Knoxville, created a tax rate, and chartered Greeneville and Blount Colleges. They also ordered a census in 1795, which showed a population of more than 77,000 people and support for statehood.

The territory had met the federal requirements for statehood, and so Blount and other territorial leaders set out to make Tennessee a state. They called a constitutional convention, and delegates spent three weeks writing Tennessee's first constitution. The first statewide poll elected John Sevier governor of the new state. Meanwhile, Tennessee's request to become a state was being debated in Washington, where finally, on June 1, 1796, President Washington signed the statehood bill and Tennessee became the 16th state in the Union.

Frontier Life

The new state of Tennessee attracted settlers who were drawn by cheap land and the opportunity it represented. Between 1790 and 1800, the state's population tripled, and by 1810, Tennessee's population had grown to 250,000. The expansion caused a shift in power as the middle and western parts of the state became more populated. The capital moved from Knoxville to Nashville in 1812.

Life during the early 19th century in Tennessee was largely rural. For the subsistence farmers who made up the majority of the state's population, life was a relentless cycle of hard work. Many families lived in one- or two-room cabins and spent their days growing food and the fibers needed to make their own clothes; raising animals that supplied farm power, meat, and hides; building or repairing buildings and tools; and cutting firewood in prodigious quantities.

Small-hold farmers often owned no slaves. Those who did only owned one or two and worked alongside them.

Children provided valuable labor on the Tennessee farm. Boys often plowed their first furrow at age nine, and girls of that age were expected to mind younger children, help cook, and learn the skills of midwifery, sewing, and gardening. While women's time was often consumed with child rearing, cooking, and sewing, the housewife worked in the field alongside her husband when she was needed.

Education and Religion

There were no public schools on the frontier, and the few private schools that existed were not accessible to the farming class. Religious missionaries were often the only people who could read and write in a community, and the first schools were established by churches. Presbyterian, Methodist, and Baptist ministers were the first to reach many settlements in Tennessee.

Settlements were spread out, and few had established churches. As a result, the camp meeting became entrenched in Tennessee culture. The homegrown spirituality of the camp meeting appealed to Tennesseans' independent spirit, which looked suspiciously at official religion and embraced the informal and deeply personal religion of the camp meeting.

The meetings were major events drawing between a few hundred and thousands of people. Wilma Dykeman writes:

From distances as far as 40, 50 and more miles, they came in wagons, carriages, a wide array of vehicles, and raised their tents. . . . They spent the summer days and nights surrounded by seemingly endless expanse of green forest, supplied with a bounty of cold pure water, breathing that acrid blue wood smoke from rows of campfires and the rich smells of food cooking over glowing red coals, listening to the greetings of old friends, the voices of children playing, crying, growing drowsy, a stamping of the horses, and the bedlam of the meeting itself once the services had begun.

Camp services were passionate and emotional, reaching a feverish pitch as men and women were overtaken by the spirit. Many camp meetings attracted both black and white participants.

The War of 1812

Tennesseans were among the "War Hawks" in Congress who advocated for war with Great Britain in 1812. The conflict was seen by many as an opportunity to rid their borders once and for all of Indians. The government asked for 2,800 volunteers, and 30,000 Tennesseans offered to enlist. This is when Tennessee's nickname as the Volunteer State was born.

Nashville lawyer, politician, and businessman Andrew Jackson was chosen as the leader of the Tennessee volunteers. Despite their shortage of supplies and lack of support from the War Department, Jackson's militia prevailed in a series of lopsided victories. Given command of the southern military district, Andrew Jackson led U.S. forces at the Battle of New Orleans on January 8, 1815. The ragtag group inflicted a crushing defeat on the British, and despite having occurred after the signing of the peace treaty with Great Britain, the battle was a victory that launched Jackson onto the road to the presidency.

Growth of Slavery

The state's first settlers planted the seed of slavery in Tennessee, and the state's westward expansion cemented the institution. In 1791, there were 3,400 blacks in Tennessee—about 10 percent of the general population. By 1810, blacks were more than 20 percent of Tennessee's people. The invention of the cotton gin and subsequent rise of King Cotton after the turn of the 19th century also caused a rapid expansion of slavery.

Slavery was most important in West Tennessee; eastern Tennessee, with its mountainous landscape and small farms, had the fewest slaves. In Middle Tennessee the slave population was concentrated in the central basin, in the counties of Davidson, Maury, Rutherford, and Williamson. By 1860, 40 percent of the state's slave population was in West Tennessee, with the greatest concentration in Shelby, Fayette, and Haywood Counties, where cotton was grown on plantations somewhat similar to those of the Deep South.

As slavery grew, slave markets were established in Nashville and Memphis. The ban on the interstate sale of slaves was virtually ignored.

From 1790, when the state was founded, until 1831, Tennessee's slave code was relatively lenient. The law recognized a slave as both a chattel and a person, and slaves were entitled to expect protection against the elements and other people. Owners could free their slaves for any reason, and many did, causing growth in Tennessee's free black population in the first half of the 1800s. These free blacks concentrated in eastern and Middle Tennessee, and particularly the cities of Nashville, Memphis, and Knoxville, where they worked as laborers and artisans.

There were vocal opponents to slavery in Tennessee, particularly in the eastern part of the state. The first newspaper in the United States devoted to emancipation was established in 1819 in Jonesborough by Elihu Embree. Charles Osborne, a Quaker minister, preached against slavery shortly after the turn of the 19th century in Tennessee. Emancipationists formed societies in counties that included Washington, Sullivan, Blount, Grainger, and Cocke. Many of these early abolitionists opposed slavery on religious grounds, arguing that it was incompatible with the spirit of Christianity.

These abolitionists often argued for the gradual end of slavery and sometimes advocated for the removal of freed slaves to Africa.

Slave Experiences

There was no single slave experience for Tennessee's slaves. On the farm, a slave's experience depended on the size of the farm, the type of crops that were grown, and the number of slaves on the farm.

Most Tennessee slaves lived on small- or medium-size farms. The 1860 census showed that only one person in the state owned more than 300 slaves, and 47 owned more than 100. More than 75 percent of all slave owners had fewer than 10 slaves. Work assignments varied, but almost all slaves were expected to contribute to their own subsistence by keeping a vegetable garden. Slaves with special skills in areas like carpentry, masonry, blacksmithing, or weaving were hired out.

Urban slaves were domestics, coachmen, house painters, laundresses, and midwives. In cities, many families owned just one or two slaves, and it was common for slaves to be hired out to others in order to provide a source of income for the slave owner. It became customary in some cities for a market day to be held on New Year's Day, when employers bargained for slave labor over the coming year.

Slaves sought to overcome their circumstances by building close-knit communities. These communities acted as surrogate families for slaves whose own spouse, parents, siblings, and children were often sold, causing lifelong separation.

Religion also served as a survival mechanism for Tennessee's slaves. Methodist and Baptist churches opened their doors to slaves, providing a space were slaves could be together. The musical tradition that resulted is today's gospel music. Religion also provided a vehicle for some slaves to learn how to read and write.

THE CIVIL WAR

In the 1830s, Tennessee's position on slavery hardened. The Virginia slave uprising led by Nat Turner frightened slave owners, who instituted patrols to search for runaway slaves and tightened codes on slave conduct. In 1834, the state constitution was amended to bar free blacks from voting, a sign of whites' increasing fear of the black people living in their midst.

The division between East and West Tennessee widened as many in the east were sympathetic with the antislavery forces that were growing in Northern states. In the west, the support for slavery was unrelenting.

Despite several strident secessionists, including Tennessee governor Isham Harris, Tennessee remained uncertain about secession. In February 1861, the state voted against a convention on secession. But with the attack on Fort Sumter two months later, followed by President Abraham Lincoln's call for volunteers to coerce the seceded states back to the Union, public opinion shifted. On June 8, 1861, Tennesseans voted 105,000 to 47,000 to secede.

A Border State

Tennessee was of great strategic importance during the Civil War. It sent an estimated 186,000 men to fight for the Confederacy, more than any other state. Another 31,000 are credited with having joined the Union army.

Tennessee had resources that both Union and Confederacy deemed important for victory, including agricultural and manufacturing industries, railroads, and rivers. And its geographic position as a long-border state made it nearly unavoidable.

Tennessee Battles

Some 454 battles and skirmishes were fought in Tennessee during the war. Most were small, but several key battles took place on Tennessee soil.

The first of these was the Union victory at Forts Henry and Donelson in January 1862. Gen. Ulysses S. Grant and 15,000 Union troops steamed up the Tennessee River and quickly captured Fort Henry. They then marched overland to Fort Donelson, and, 10 days later, this Confederate fort fell as well. The battle of Fort Donelson is where U. S.

view of the state capitol near the end of the Civil War

Grant earned his sobriquet: He was asked by the Confederate general the terms of capitulation, and he replied, "unconditional surrender."

The Battle of Shiloh was the bloodiest and largest confrontation in Tennessee. The battle took place near Pittsburgh Landing (the Federal name for the struggle), on the Mississippi River about 20 miles north of the Mississippi state line. More than 100,000 men took part in this battle, and there were more than 24,000 casualties.

The battle began with a surprise Confederate attack at dawn on April 6, 1862, a Sunday. For several hours, victory seemed in reach for the Southern troops, but the Union rallied and held. They built a strong defensive line covering Pittsburgh Landing, and on April 7 they took the offensive and swept the Confederates from the field. The Confederates' loss was devastating, and Shiloh represents a harbinger of the future bloodletting between Blue and Gray.

Another important Tennessee battle was at Stones River, near Murfreesboro, on December 31, 1862. Like at Shiloh, the early momentum here was with the Confederates, but victory belonged to the Union. The Battle of Chickamauga Creek, fought a few miles over the state line in Georgia, was a rare Confederate victory. It did not come cheaply, however, with 21,000 members of the Army of Tennessee killed.

Federal forces retreated and dug in near Chattanooga, while Confederates occupied the heights above the town. Union reinforcements led by General Grant drove the Confederates back into Georgia at Battle of Lookout Mountain, also known as the "Battle Above the Clouds," on November 25, 1863.

Wartime Occupation

Battles were only part of the wartime experience in Tennessee. The Civil War caused hardship for ordinary residents on a scale that many had never before seen. There was famine and poverty. Schools and churches were closed. Harassment and recrimination plagued the state, and fear was widespread.

In February 1863, one observer described the population of Memphis as "11,000 original whites, 5,000 slaves, and 19,000 newcomers of all kinds, including traders, fugitives, hangers-on, and negroes."

Memphis fell to the Union on June 6, 1862, and it was occupied for the remainder of the war. The city's experience during this wartime occupation reversed decades of growth and left a city that would struggle for years.

Those who could, fled the city. Many of those who remained stopped doing business (some of these because they refused to pledge allegiance to the Union and were not permitted). Northern traders entered the city and took over many industries, while blacks who abandoned nearby plantations flooded into the city.

While the military focused on punishing Confederate sympathizers, conditions in Memphis deteriorated. Crime and disorder abounded, and guerrilla bands developed to fight the Union occupation. The Federal commander responsible for the city was Maj. Gen. William T. Sherman, and he adopted a policy of collective responsibility, which held civilians responsible for guerrilla attacks in their neighborhoods. Sherman destroyed hundreds of homes, farms, and towns in the exercise of this policy.

The war was equally damaging in other parts of Tennessee. In Middle Tennessee, retreating Confederate soldiers after the fall of Fort Donelson demolished railroads and burned bridges so as not to leave them for the Union. Union troops also destroyed and appropriated the region's resources. Federals took horses, pigs, cows, corn, hay, cotton, fence rails, firearms, and tools. Sometimes this was carried out through official requisitions, but at other times it amounted to little more than pillaging.

Criminals took advantage of the loss of public order, and bands of thieves and bandits began roaming the countryside.

The experience in East Tennessee was different. Because of the region's widespread Union sympathies, it was the Confederacy that first occupied the eastern territory. During this time, hundreds of alleged Unionists were charged with treason and jailed. When the Confederates began conscripting men into military service in 1862, tensions in East Tennessee grew. Many East Tennesseans fled to Kentucky, and distrust, bitterness, and violence escalated. In September 1863, the tables turned, however, and the Confederates were replaced by the Federals, whose victories elsewhere enabled them to now focus on occupying friendly East Tennessee.

The Effects of the War

Tennessee lost most of a generation of young men to the Civil War. Infrastructure was destroyed, and thousands of farms, homes, and other properties were razed. The state's reputation on the national stage had been tarnished, and it would be decades until Tennessee had the political power that it enjoyed during the Age of Jackson. But while the war caused tremendous hardships for the state, it also led to the freeing of 275,000 black Tennesseans from slavery.

RECONSTRUCTION

Tennessee was no less divided during the years following the Civil War than it was during the conflict. The end to the war ushered in a period where former Unionists—now allied with the Radical Republicans in Congress—disenfranchised and otherwise marginalized former Confederates and others who had been sympathetic with the Southern cause.

They also pushed through laws that extended voting and other rights to the newly freed blacks, changes that led to a powerful backlash and the establishment of such shadowy groups as the Ku Klux Klan (KKK).

William G. "Parson" Brownlow of Knoxville, a vocal supporter of the Union, was elected governor of Tennessee in 1865. During the same year, the voters approved a constitutional amendment abolishing slavery, making Tennessee the only seceded state to abolish slavery by its own act. Brownlow and his supporters bent laws and manipulated loyalties in order to secure ratification of the 14th and 15th Amendments to the constitution, paving the way for Tennessee to be admitted back to the Union, the first Southern state to be readmitted following the war. Brownlow's success ensured that Tennessee would not experience

General Ulysses S. Grant (lower left-hand corner) visits Missionary Ridge, scene of a Civil War battle.

the congressionally mandated Reconstruction that other former Confederate states did.

Recognizing that the unpopularity of his positions among Tennessee's numerous former Confederates placed his political future in jeopardy, Brownlow and his supporters extended the right to vote to thousands of freedmen in February 1867. During the statewide vote a few months later, Brownlow and his followers were swept to victory, largely due to the support of black voters.

The quick rise to power of former enemies and the social changes caused by the end of slavery led some former Confederates to bitterness and frustration. In the summer of 1867, the Ku Klux Klan emerged as a political and terrorist movement to keep freedmen in their traditional place. Klan members initially concerned themselves principally with supporting former Confederates and their families, but they were soon known more for their attacks on black men and women. The KKK was strongest in Middle and West Tennessee, except for a small pocket near Bristol in East Tennessee.

Governor Brownlow responded strongly to the KKK's activities, and in 1869, he declared martial law in nine counties where the organization was most active. But when Brownlow left Tennessee shortly thereafter to fill a seat in the U.S. Senate, the KKK's grand wizard, former Confederate general Nathan Bedford Forrest, declared the group's mission accomplished and encouraged members to burn their robes. The KKK's influence quickly faded, only to reemerge 50 years later at Stone Mountain, Georgia.

Brownlow was replaced by Senate Speaker Dewitt C. Senter, who quickly struck a more moderate position than his predecessor by setting aside the law that had barred Confederate veterans from voting.

The greatest legacy of the Civil War was the emancipation of Tennessee's slaves. Following the war, many freed blacks left the countryside and moved to cities, including Memphis, Nashville, Chattanooga, and Knoxville, where they worked as skilled laborers, domestics, and more. Other blacks remained in the countryside, working as wage laborers on farms or sharecropping in exchange for occupancy on part of a former large-scale plantation.

The Freedmen's Bureau worked in Tennessee for a short period after the end of the war, and it succeeded in establishing schools for blacks. During this period the state's first black colleges were inaugurated: Fisk, Tennessee Central, LeMoyne, Roger Williams, Lane, and Knoxville.

As in other states, blacks in Tennessee enjoyed short-lived political power during Reconstruction. The right to vote and the concentration of blacks in certain urban areas paved the way for blacks to be elected to the Tennessee House of Representatives, beginning with Sampson Keeble of Nashville in 1872. In all, 13 blacks were elected as representatives between 1872 and 1887, including James C. Napier, Edward Shaw, and William Yardley, who also ran for governor.

Initially, these pioneers met mild acceptance from whites, but as time progressed whites became uncomfortable sharing political power with black people. By the 1890s, racist Jim Crow policies of segregation, poll taxes, secret ballots, literacy tests, and intimidation prevented blacks from holding elective office—and in many cases, voting—in Tennessee again until after the civil rights movement of the 1960s.

The Republican Party saw the end of its influence with the end of the Brownlow governorship. Democrats rejected the divisive policies of the Radical Republicans, sought to protect the racial order that set blacks at a disadvantage to whites, and were less concerned about the state's mounting debt than the Republicans.

Economic Recovery

The social and political upheaval caused by the Civil War was matched or exceeded by the economic catastrophe that it represented for the state. Farms and industry were damaged or destroyed, public infrastructure was razed, schools were closed, and the system of slavery that underpinned most of the state's economy was gone.

The economic setback was seen as an opportunity by proponents of the "New South," who advocated for an industrial and economic revival that would catapult the South to prosperity impossible under the agrarian and slavery-based antebellum economy. The New South movement was personified by carpetbagging Northern capitalists who moved to Tennessee and set up industries that would benefit from cheap labor and abundant natural resources. Many Tennesseans welcomed these newcomers and advocated for their fellow Tennesseans to put aside regional differences and welcome the Northern investors.

The result was an array of industries that were chartered during the years following the Civil War. Mining, foundries, machine shops, sawmills, gristmills, furniture factories, and textile and other manufacturing industries were established. Knoxville and Chattanooga improved quickly. Over the 10-year period from 1860 to 1870, Chattanooga's industrial works grew from employing 214 men to more than 2,000.

Memphis and Nashville also worked to attract industries. Memphis was on the cusp of a commercial and industrial boom in 1873 when yellow fever hit the city; the epidemic caused widespread death and hurt Memphis's economic recovery. In Nashville, new distilleries, sawmills, paper mills, stove factories, and an oil refinery led the way to industrialization.

Industry also settled in the small towns and countryside. The coal-rich region of the Cumberland Mountains was the site of major coal-mining operations. Copper mines were opened in Cleveland, flouring mills in Jackson, and textile factories in Tullahoma and other parts of the state.

Agriculture

A revolution was brewing in agriculture, too. Civil War veterans returned to small farms all over the state and resumed farming with implements largely unchanged for hundreds of years. Every task was achieved by hand, with the lone help of one or two farm animals.

But farm technology was beginning to change. Thirty years after the war, new labor-saving devices began to be put to use. These included early cotton pickers, reapers, and planters. Seed cleaners, corn shellers, and improved plows were made available. In 1871 the state formed the Bureau of Agriculture, whose employees prepared soil maps and studied the state's climate, population, and the prices of land. New methods such as crop diversification, crop rotation, cover crops, and the use of commercial fertilizers were introduced, and farmers were encouraged to use them.

Meanwhile, farmers themselves established a strong grassroots movement in the state. The Patrons of Husbandry, or the Grange, was organized shortly after the war to encourage members to improve farming methods and enhance their economic influence. Government encouraged county fair associations, which organized fairs where farmers could be awarded for their crops and encouraged to use new farming methods. The Farmers' Alliance and the Agricultural Wheel, both national organizations, grew in prominence in the 1880s and advocated currency reform, empowerment of farmers, and control of communication and transportation systems. The Alliance gave low-interest loans to farmers and encouraged cooperative selling.

While the Alliance and the Wheel were not political organizations as such, they supported candidates who adopted their views on agricultural matters. In 1890, the Alliance supported Democrat John P. Buchanan for governor, and he was successful. For their part, political elites did not take the farming movement or its leaders very seriously, ridiculing them as "hayseeds," "clodhoppers," and "wool-hat boys." In other places, rural and small-town residents resisted the Wheel and the Alliance, in part because they feared challenge of the status quo. As the Alliance became more radical in its views, the support in Tennessee dwindled, and by 1892 it had faded in many parts of the state.

While some blacks remained on farms as wage laborers or sharecroppers, many left for the cities, causing a labor shortage. Attempts to attract foreign or Northern immigrants to the state were unsuccessful. Tennessee's poor whites filled this labor shortage, now able to own or rent land for the first time.

Education

Despite popular attempts and pleas by some politicians for a sound education system, Tennessee lagged behind in public education during the postwar years. In 1873, the legislature passed a school law that set up a basic framework of school administration, but the state's debt and financial problems crippled the new system. Private funds stepped in—the Peabody Fund contributed to Tennessee's schools, including the old University of Nashville, renamed Peabody after its benefactor. Meanwhile, teachers' institutes were established during the 1880s in order to raise the level of instruction at Tennessee's public schools.

PROHIBITION

Prohibition was the first major issue Tennesseans faced in the new century. An 1877 law that forbade the sale of alcohol within four miles of a rural school had been used to great effect by Prohibitionists to restrict the sale and traffic of alcohol in towns all over the countryside. As the century turned, pressure mounted to extend the law, and public opinion in support of temperance grew, although it was never without contest from the powerful distillery industry. Finally, in 1909, the legislature passed the Manufacturer's Bill, which would halt the production of intoxicants in the state and overrode Governor Patterson's veto. When the United States followed suit with the 18th Amendment in 1920, Prohibition was old news in Tennessee.

WORLD WAR I

True to its nickname, Tennessee sent a large number of volunteer troops to fight in World War I. Most became part of the 30th "Old Hickory" Division, which entered the war on August 17, 1918. The most famous Tennessee veteran of World War I was Alvin C. York, a farm boy from the Cumberland Mountains who staged a one-man offensive against the German army after becoming separated from his own detachment. Reports say that York killed 20 German soldiers and persuaded 131 more to surrender.

WOMEN'S SUFFRAGE

The movement for women's suffrage had been established in Tennessee prior to the turn of the 20th century, and it gained influence as the century progressed. The Southern Woman Suffrage Conference was held in Memphis in 1906, and a statewide suffrage organization was established. State bills to give women the right to vote failed in 1913 and 1917, but support was gradually growing. In the summer of 1920, the 19th Amendment had been ratified by 35 states, and one more ratification was needed to make it law. Tennessee was one of five states yet to vote on the measure, and on August 9, Democratic Governor Albert H. Roberts called a special sitting of the legislature to consider the amendment.

Furious campaigning and public debate led up to the special sitting. The Senate easily ratified the amendment 25 to 4, but in the House of Representatives the vote was much closer: 49 to 47. Governor Roberts certified the result and notified the secretary of state: Tennessee had cast the deciding vote for women's suffrage.

AUSTIN PEAY

The 1920s were years of growth and development in Tennessee, thanks in part to the capable leadership of Austin Peay, elected governor in 1922. He reformed the state government, cut waste, and set out to improve the state's roads and schools. The improvements won Peay support from the state's rural residents, who benefited from better transportation and education. Spending on schools doubled during Peay's three terms as governor, and the school term increased from 127 to 155 days per year.

Peay also saw the importance of establishing parks: Reelfoot Lake State Park was established during his third term, finally ending fears of development in the area. Peay also supported establishment of the Great Smoky Mountains National Park, and he raised $1.5 million in a bond issue as the state's part toward the purchase of the land. Peay was dead by the time the park was opened in 1940, but it is largely to his credit that it was created.

THE DEPRESSION

The progress and hope of the 1920s was soon forgotten with the Great Depression. Tennessee's economic hard times started before the 1929 stock market crash. Farming in the state was hobbled by low prices and low returns during the 1920s. Farmers and laborers displaced by this trend sought work in new industries like the DuPont plant in Old Hickory, Eastman-Kodak in Kingsport, or the Aluminum Company of America in Blount County. But others, including many African Americans, left Tennessee for northern cities such as Chicago.

The Depression made bad things worse. Farmers tried to survive, turning to subsistence farming. In cities unemployed workers lined up for relief. Major bank failures in 1930 brought most financial business in the state to a halt.

President Franklin D. Roosevelt's New Deal provided some relief for Tennesseans. The Civilian Conservation Corps (CCC), Public Works Administration (PWA), and Civil Works Administration (CWA) were established in Tennessee. Through the CCC, more than 7,000 Tennesseans planted millions of pine seedlings, developed parks, and built fire towers. Through the PWA, more than 500 projects were undertaken, including bridges, housing, water systems, and roads. Hundreds of Tennesseans were employed by the CWA to clean public buildings, landscape roads, and do other work.

But no New Deal institution had more impact on Tennessee than the Tennessee Valley Authority. Architects of the TVA saw it as a way to improve agriculture along the Tennessee River, alleviate poverty, and produce electrical power. The dam system would also improve navigation along what was then an often dangerous river. The law establishing TVA was introduced by Senator George W. Norris of Nebraska and passed in 1933. Soon after, dams were under construction, and trade on the river increased due to improved navigability. Even more importantly, electric power was now so cheap that even Tennesseans in remote parts of the state could afford it. By 1945, TVA was the largest electrical utility in the nation, and new industries were attracted by cheap energy and improved transportation. Tourists also came to enjoy the so-called Great Lakes of the South.

The TVA story is not without its losers, however. TVA purchased or condemned more than one million acres of land and flooded 300,000 acres more, forcing 14,000 families to be displaced.

THE CRUMP MACHINE

The 1930s in Tennessee was the age of Ed Crump, Memphis's longtime mayor and political boss. The son of a former Confederate, Crump was born in Mississippi in 1874 and moved to Memphis when he was 17 years old. First elected in 1909 as a city councilman, Crump was a genius of human nature and organization. Able to assure statewide candidates the support of influential Shelby County, Crump's power extended beyond Memphis. His political power often required corruption, patronage, and the loss of individual freedoms. To get ahead, you had to pay homage to Boss Crump. He was particularly popular during the Depression, when constituents and others looked to Crump for much-needed relief.

Crump manipulated the votes in his home Shelby County by paying the $2 poll tax for cooperative voters. He allied with black leaders such as Robert Church Jr. to win support in the black community of Memphis.

WORLD WAR II

Tennessee, like the rest of the country, was changed by World War II. The war effort transformed the state's economy and led to a migration to the cities unprecedented in Tennessee's history. The tiny mountain town of Oak Ridge became the state's fifth-largest city almost overnight, and it is synonymous with the atomic bomb that was dropped on Hiroshima, Japan, at the final stage of the war.

More than 300,000 Tennesseans served in World War II and just under 6,000 died. During the war, Camps Forrest, Campbell, and Tyson served as prisoner-of-war camps. Several hundred war refugees settled in Tennessee, many in the Nashville area.

The war also sped up Tennessee's industrialization. Industrial centers in Memphis, Chattanooga, and Knoxville converted to war production, while new industries were established in smaller cities such as Kingsport. Agriculture was no longer Tennessee's most important economic activity. The industrial growth was a catalyst for urbanization. Nashville's population grew by 25 percent during the war, and Shelby County's by 35 percent. The war also finally saw the end of the Great Depression.

The war also brought women into the workplace in numbers that were then unprecedented; approximately one-third of the state's workers were female by the end of the war.

Tennesseans supported the war not only by volunteering to serve overseas, but on the home front as well. Families planted victory gardens, invested in war bonds, and supported soldiers.

Tennesseans served with distinction during the war. Cordell Hull, a native of Pickett County, was U.S. secretary of state for 12 years and is known as the Father of the United Nations for his role in drawing up the foundation of that institution.

Oak Ridge

No community was more transformed by the war than Oak Ridge. A remote area of countryside west of Knoxville in East Tennessee, Oak Ridge was home to 4,000 people, most of them farmers. The army was searching for a place to build the facilities to construct an atom bomb, and this 52,000-acre area fit the bill. In 1942, residents of Oak Ridge began to receive notices that they would have to leave because the government was taking their land. Clinton Laboratories, named after the nearest town, was built seemingly overnight. Housing was provided in dormitories, trailers, and "victory cottages." Scientists, engineers, and researchers moved in, together with blue-collar workers who were needed to labor at the facility, later named Oak Ridge National Laboratory.

Work proceeded on schedule inside the laboratory, and on August 6, 1945, shortly after 9am, the first atomic bomb was dropped over Hiroshima. Three days later the second bomb exploded over Nagasaki, and on August 14 Japan surrendered.

Oak Ridge, nicknamed the Secret City, remains today a key part of the U.S. nuclear system. While some degree of integration has taken place, Oak Ridge still has a different feel than most Tennessee towns, due in large part to the thousands of scientists and professionals who live there.

POSTWAR TENNESSEE

Tennessee's industrialization continued after the war. By 1960, there were more city dwellers than rural dwellers in the state, and Tennessee was ranked the 16th most industrialized state in the United States. Industry that had developed during the war transformed to peacetime operation.

Ex-servicemen were not content with the political machines that had controlled Tennessee politics for decades. In 1948 congressman Estes Kefauver won a U.S. Senate seat, defeating the candidate chosen by Memphis mayor Ed Crump. The defeat signaled an end to Crump's substantial influence in statewide elections. In 1953, Tennessee repealed the state poll tax, again limiting politicians' ability to manipulate the vote. The tide of change also swept in Senator Albert Gore

Sr. and Governor Frank Clement in 1952. Kefauver, Gore, and Clement were moderate Democrats of the New South.

CIVIL RIGHTS

The early gains for blacks during Reconstruction were lost during the decades that followed. Segregation, the threat of violence, poll taxes, and literacy tests discriminated against blacks in all spheres of life: economic, social, political, and educational. The fight to right these wrongs was waged by many brave Tennesseans.

Early civil rights victories in Tennessee included the 1905 successful boycott of Nashville's segregated streetcars and the creation of a competing black-owned streetcar company. In the 1920s in Chattanooga, blacks successfully defeated the Ku Klux Klan at the polls. Black institutions of learning persevered in educating young African Americans and developing a generation of leaders.

Following World War II, there was newfound energy in the fight for civil rights. Returning black servicemen who had fought for their country demanded greater equality, and the opportunities of the age raised the stakes of economic equality. In 1946, racially based violence targeted at a returned black serviceman in Columbia brought national attention to violence against black citizens and raised awareness of the need to protect blacks' civil rights.

The Highlander Folk School, founded in Grundy County and later moved to Cocke County, was an important training center for community activists and civil rights leaders in the 1950s. Founder Miles Horton believed in popular education and sought to bring black and white activists together to share experiences. Many leaders in the national civil rights movement, including Rev. Martin Luther King Jr. and Rosa Parks, attended the folk school.

In the 1950s, the first steps toward public school desegregation took place in Tennessee. Following a lawsuit filed by black parents, Clinton desegregated its schools in 1956 on order of a federal court judge. The integration began peacefully, but outside agitators arrived to organize resistance, and in the end Governor Frank Clement was forced to call in 600 National Guardsmen to diffuse the violent atmosphere. But the first black students were allowed to stay, and in May 1957, Bobby Cain became the first African American to graduate from an integrated public high school in the South.

In the fall of 1957, Nashville's public schools were desegregated. As many as half of the white students stayed home in protest, and one integrated school, Hattie Cotton School, was dynamited and partially destroyed. Other Tennessee cities desegregated at a slower pace, and by 1960, only 169 of Tennessee's almost 150,000 black children of school age attended integrated schools.

The Nashville lunch counter sit-ins of 1960 were an important milestone in both the local and national civil rights movements. Led by students from the city's black universities, the sit-ins eventually forced an end to racial segregation of the city's public services. Over two months hundreds of black students were arrested for sitting at white-only downtown lunch counters. Black consumers' boycott of downtown stores put additional pressure on the business community. On April 19, thousands of protesters marched in silence to the courthouse to confront city officials, and the next day Rev. Martin Luther King Jr. addressed Fisk University. On May 10, 1960, several downtown stores integrated their lunch counters, and Nashville became the first major city in the South to begin desegregating its public facilities.

As the civil rights movement continued, Tennesseans played an important part. Tennesseans were involved with organizing the Student Nonviolent Coordinating Committee and participated in the Freedom Rides, which sought to integrate buses across the south. In 1965, A. W. Willis Jr. of Memphis became the first African American representative elected to the state's General Assembly in more than 60 years. Three years later, Memphis's sanitation workers went on strike to protest discriminatory pay and work rules. Dr. King came to Memphis to support the striking workers. On April 4, 1968, King was assassinated by a sniper as he stood on the balcony of the Lorraine Motel in downtown Memphis.

MODERN TENNESSEE

The industrialization that began during World War II has continued in modern-day Tennessee. In 1980, Nissan built what was then the largest truck assembly plant in the world at Smyrna, Tennessee. In 1987, Saturn Corporation chose Spring Hill as the site for its $2.1 billion automobile plant.

At the same time, however, the state's older industries—including textiles and manufacturing—have suffered losses over the past three decades, due in part to the movement of industry outside of the United States.

During the 1950s and beyond, Tennessee developed a reputation as a hotbed of musical talent. Memphis's Elvis Presley may have invented rock 'n' roll, and his Graceland mansion remains one of the state's most enduring tourist attractions. The Grand Ole Opry in Nashville was representative of a second musical genre that came to call Tennessee home: country music.

Government and Economy

GOVERNMENT

Tennessee is governed by its constitution, unchanged since 1870, when it was revised in light of emancipation, the Civil War, and Reconstruction.

Tennessee has a governor who is elected to four-year terms, a legislature, and court system. The lieutenant governor is not elected statewide; he or she is chosen by the Senate and also serves as its Speaker.

The legislature, or General Assembly, is made up of the 99-member House of Representatives and the 33-member Senate. The Tennessee State Supreme Court is made of five members, no two of whom can be from the same Grand Division. The Tennessee Supreme Court chooses the state's attorney general.

The executive branch consists of 21 cabinet-level departments, which employ 39,000 state workers. Departments are led by a commissioner who is appointed by the governor and serves as a member of his cabinet.

Tennessee has 95 counties; the largest is Shelby County, which contains Memphis. The smallest county by size is Trousdale, with 113 square miles; the smallest population is in Pickett County.

The state has 11 electoral college votes in U.S. presidential elections.

Modern Politics

Like other Southern states, Tennessee has seen a gradual shift to the political right since the 1960s. The shift began in 1966 with Howard Baker's election to the U.S. Senate, and it continued with Tennessee's support for Republican presidential candidate Richard Nixon in 1968 and 1972. Despite a few exceptions, the shift has continued into the 21st century, although Nashville, Memphis, and other parts of Middle and West Tennessee remain Democratic territory.

East Tennessee holds the distinction as one of a handful of Southern territories that has consistently supported the Republican Party since the Civil War. Today, Republicans outpoll Democrats in this region by as much as three to one.

The statewide trend toward the Republican Party continued in 2008, with Tennessee being one of only a handful of states in which Democrat Barack Obama received a lesser proportion of votes than did Democrat Senator John Kerry four years earlier. State Republicans also succeeded in gaining control of both houses of the state legislature. The general shift to the right has continued in the governor's office. Previous governor Phil Bredesen is a Democrat, but he was succeeded by Republican Bill Haslam. Since 1967, no party has been able to keep the governor's seat for two terms.

Andrew Jackson may still be the most prominent Tennessean in American political history, but Tennessee politicians continue to play a role on the national stage. Albert Gore Jr., elected to the U.S. House of Representatives in 1976, served as vice president under Bill Clinton from 1992 until 2000, and he lost the hotly contested 2000 presidential contest to George W. Bush. Gore famously lost his home state to Bush, further evidence of Tennessee's move to the right. Gore went on to champion global climate change and win the Nobel Peace Prize, and he is often seen around Nashville.

Lamar Alexander, a former governor of Tennessee, was appointed secretary of education by President George H. W. Bush in 1990. Alexander—famous for his flannel shirts—ran unsuccessfully for president and was later elected senator from Tennessee. Bill Frist, a doctor, was also elected senator and rose to be the Republican majority leader during the presidency of George W. Bush, before quitting politics for medical philanthropy.

The most recent Tennessean to seek the Oval Office was former senator and *Law and Order* star Fred Thompson, now deceased, from Lewisburg in Middle Tennessee.

One of the most persistent political issues for Tennesseans in modern times has been the state's tax structure. The state first established a 2 percent sales tax in 1947, and it was increased incrementally over the years, eventually reaching 7 percent today. With local options, it is one of the highest sales tax rates in the country. (The state sales tax on food is 5.5 percent.) At the same time, the state has failed on more than one occasion—most recently during the second term of Republican governor Donald Sundquist in the late 1990s—to establish an income tax that would provide greater stability to the state's revenues.

Like much of the country, in 2008, Tennessee faced a serious budget crunch that led to the elimination of thousands of state jobs, cutbacks at state-funded universities, and the scaling back of the state health insurance program.

the state capitol and the downtown skyline in Nashville

ECONOMY

Tennessee has the 18th-largest economy in the United States. Important industries include health care, education, farming, electrical power, and tourism. In the past few years, most job growth has been recorded in the areas of leisure, hospitality, education, and health care. Manufacturing, mining, and construction jobs have declined. Despite the overall slowing in manufacturing, there was good news in 2008 when Volkswagen announced that it chose Chattanooga as home for a new, $1 billion plant. That plant was expected to bring 2,000 jobs to the state and it started to make progress on those goals. In 2015 it came to light that 11 million Volkswagens were using software to overstate fuel efficiency. These actions may impact the automakers' future success in the state.

Tennessee's unemployment rate fluctuates but generally sits a half point above the national average. In 2014, the jobless rate was about 5.7 percent.

About 17.6 percent of Tennessee families live in poverty, ranking the state 39th out of 50. The median household income in 2014 was $41,693, ranking it No. 45.

All of Tennessee's cities have poverty rates higher than the state or national average. The percentage of Memphis families living below the poverty level is the state's highest: 26.9 percent of Memphis families are poor. The U.S. Census calls Memphis one of the poorest cities in the nation. Knoxville's family poverty rate is 21.3 percent.

Agriculture

Farming accounts for 14.2 percent, or $38.5 billion, of the Tennessee economy. More than 42 percent of the state's land is used in farming; 63.6 percent of this is cropland.

Soybeans, tobacco, corn, and hay are among Tennessee's most important agricultural crops. Cattle and calf production, chicken farming, and cotton cultivation are also important parts of the farm economy.

Greene County, in northeastern Tennessee, is the leading county for all types of cow farming; Giles and Lincoln Counties, in the south-central part of the state, rank second and third. The leading cotton producer is Haywood County, followed by Crockett and Gibson, all three of which are located in West Tennessee. Other counties where agriculture figures largely into the economy are Obion, Dyer, Rutherford, and Robertson.

Tennessee ranks sixth among U.S. states

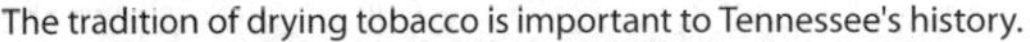

The tradition of drying tobacco is important to Tennessee's history.

for equine production, and walking or quarter horses account for more than half of the state's estimated 210,000 head of equine. The state ranks third for tomatoes, fourth for tobacco, and seventh for cotton.

Some farmers have begun converting to corn production in anticipation of a biofuel boom.

Tourism

According to the state tourism department, the industry generated $16.7 billion in economic activity in 2013. More than 175,000 Tennessee jobs are linked to tourism. The state credits the industry with generating more than $1.3 billion in state and local tax revenue.

People and Culture

DEMOGRAPHICS

Tennessee is home to 6.6 million people. Almost one quarter of these are 18 years and younger; about 13 percent are older than 65. Tennessee is 79 percent white and 17 percent black.

Memphis counts 656,861 residents and is the state's largest city. More than 63 percent of Memphians are African American, a greater proportion than is found in any other American city. Memphis has the youngest average age of the four major Tennessee cities.

Nashville's population is 644,014. Approximately 61 percent of Nashvillians are white, 28 percent are African American, and 10 percent are Latino or Hispanic. Nashville's foreign-born population tripled during the decade between 1990 and 2000, and 11 percent of the city's population was born outside of the United States. This includes large populations from Mexico, Vietnam, Laos, and Somalia. Nashville is also home to more than 11,000 Iraqi Kurds. Nashville is poised to supplant Memphis as the state's largest.

Knoxville, Tennessee's third-largest city, has a population of about 184,000. More than 173,000 people live in Chattanooga.

RELIGION

Tennessee is unquestionably part of the U.S. Bible Belt; the conservative Christian faith is both prevalent and prominent all over the state. According to the 2015 Census, 82 percent of Tennesseans call themselves Christians, and 39 percent of these identify as Baptist. The second-largest Christian denomination is Methodist. Nashville is the headquarters of the Southern Baptist Convention, the National Baptist Convention, and the United Methodist Church. Memphis is the headquarters of the mostly African American Church of God in Christ. However, the state's major cities do have growing populations that practice Judaism and Islam.

While Tennessee's urban centers are the home of church headquarters, religious fervor is strongest in the rural communities. Pentecostal churches have been known for rites such as speaking in tongues and snake handling, although these activities are not as widespread as they once were.

Non-Christians will feel most comfortable in urban areas, where numbers of religious minorities have grown in recent years and where the influence of the local churches is not as great.

One practical effect of Tennessee's Christian bent is that many counties and even cities are totally dry, while most bar the sale of alcohol on Sunday.

LANGUAGE

Tennesseans speak English, of a kind. The Tennessee drawl varies from the language of the upper South, spoken in East Tennessee and closely associated with the region's Scotch-Irish roots, and the language of West Tennessee, more akin to that of Mississippi and the lower South.

Little in Tennesseans' speech is distinct

"Beale Street Blues" by W.C. Handy with singer Teddy Tappan

to the state itself. Speech patterns heard in Tennessee are also heard in other states in the region.

Speech patterns that have been documented throughout the state, but that may be more prevalent in the east, include the following, outlined by Michael Montgomery of the University of South Carolina in the *Tennessee Encyclopedia of History and Culture.* Montgomery writes that Tennesseans tend to pronounce vowels in the words *pen* and *hem* as *pin* and *him;* they shift the accent to the beginning of words, so *Tennessee* becomes *TIN-i-see;* they clip or reduce the vowel in words like *ride* so it sounds more like *rad;* and vowels in other words are stretched, so that a single-syllable word like *bed* becomes *bay-ud.*

Tennessee speech patterns are not limited to word pronunciation. Tennesseans also speak with folksy and down-home language. Speakers often use colorful metaphors, and greater value is placed on the quality of expression than the perfection of grammar.

THE ARTS

Crafts

Many Tennessee craft traditions have their roots in the handmade housewares that rural families had to make for themselves, including things like quilts and coverlets, baskets, candles, and furniture. These items were fashioned out of materials that could be raised or harvested nearby, and colors were derived from natural dyes such as walnut hulls and indigo.

Many of the same crafts were produced by African Americans, who developed their own craft traditions, often with even fewer raw materials than their white counterparts. For example, African American quilts often used patterns and colors reflective of African culture. Blacksmiths were often African American, and these skilled artisans developed both practical and decorative pieces for white and black households.

As the lifestyles of Tennesseans changed and more household items were available in stores and by mail order, crafts were produced for sale. In 1929, the Southern Highland Handicraft Guild was formed and held its first meeting in Knoxville. In 1950 the guild merged with Southern Highlanders Inc., an organization established by the Tennessee Valley Authority, and the group's marketing and promotion efforts pushed westward toward the Cumberland Plateau and Nashville.

Today, artists from around the United States have settled in Tennessee to practice modern forms of traditional crafts of quilting, weaving, pottery, furniture making, and basket making, among others. While market forces have promoted a certain false folksiness among some artists, a great many of today's practicing artisans remain true to the mountain heritage that gave birth to the craft tradition in the first place.

Music

Tennessee may be more famous for its music than for anything else. The blues was born on Beale Street; the Grand Ole Opry popularized old-time mountain music; and the

Fisk Jubilee singers of Nashville introduced African American spirituals to the world. Rock 'n' roll traces its roots to Elvis Presley, Carl Perkins, Jerry Lee Lewis, and the city of Memphis.

The blues became popular in cities from New Orleans to St. Louis at the turn of the 20th century. But thanks in large part to composer and performer W. C. Handy, the musical form will be forever associated with Memphis and Beale Street. Early blues greats like Walter "Furry" Lewis, Booker T. Washington "Bukka" White, "Little Laura" Dukes, and Ma Rainey started in Memphis.

Sun Studio recorded some of the first commercial blues records in the 1950s, but the label is most famous for discovering Elvis Presley. Stax Records created a new sound, soul, in the late 1950s and early 1960s.

Country music was born in Bristol, Tennessee, where the earliest recordings of Jimmie Rodgers and the Carter Family were made in the 1920s. In the decades that followed, Nashville became the capital of country music, beginning thanks to radio station WSM and dozens of rural musicians who trekked to town to play on the radio. America was hungry for a type of music to call its own, and country music was it. First called "hillbilly music," country was popularized by barn-dance radio shows, including the Grand Ole Opry. Over the years, country music mellowed out, adopting the Nashville sound that softened its edges and made it palatable to a wider audience. The economic impact of the music industry on Nashville approached $9.7 billion in 2015, according to the Chamber of Commerce.

In 2013, the Bureau of Labor Statistics ranked Tennessee number one in the country for its concentration of musician jobs.

Dance

Clogging, or buck dancing, is a style of folk dance that originated with the Scotch-Irish settlers in the eastern mountains of Tennessee. Characterized by an erect upper body and a fast-paced toe-heel movement with the feet, traditional clogging is improvisational. Performers move at a very fast pace to the music of string bands.

Clogging was popularized during the 1940s and 1950s on television and radio shows that showcased country music. Modern clogging is often choreographed and performed with a partner.

Clogging can trace influences from Native American and African American styles of dance as well as the traditional dance of the British Isles.

Literature

The first literature inspired by Tennessee is not well known. *The Tennessean; A Novel, Founded on Facts* is a melodramatic novel written by Anne Newport Royall and published in 1827. Its plot brings readers along on a three-day journey from Nashville to Knoxville, and it is the first novel set in Tennessee. The first novel written by a Tennessean was *Woodville; or, The Anchoret Reclaimed. A Descriptive Tale,* written by Charles W. Todd and published in Knoxville in 1832.

Later Tennessee literature is better known. English novelist **Frances Hodgson Burnett** lived in New Market and then Knoxville in the 1860s and 1870s. While best known for her tales *Little Lord Fauntleroy* and *The Secret Garden,* Burnett penned several works set in Tennessee. In the 1920s, a group of writers at Vanderbilt University emerged under the leadership of John Crowe Ransom. The group's magazine, *The Fugitive,* was published 1922-1925. The Fugitives were succeeded by the Agrarians, who published their manifesto, *I'll Take My Stand,* in 1930. Writer **Robert Penn Warren** was a member of both the Fugitives and the Agrarians, and he went on to win the Pulitzer Prize for *All the King's Men,* about Governor Huey Long of Louisiana. Warren's novels *The Cave, Flood,* and *Meet Me in the Green Glen* are set in Tennessee.

Another award-winning Tennessee writer is **Peter Taylor,** who studied at Rhodes College and Vanderbilt University before moving to North Carolina and writing the Pulitzer Prize-winning *A Summons to Memphis* in 1986 and *In Tennessee Country* in 1994.

James Agee is another Pulitzer Prize winner. Raised in Knoxville, Agee wrote poetry, journalism, and screenplays before his winning *A Death in the Family* was published. Agee is also known for his singular work *Let Us Now Praise Famous Men,* with photographer Walker Evans, which documented the lives of poor whites during the Great Depression.

Few people knew Memphis-born writer and historian **Shelby Foote** until Ken Burns's landmark Civil War documentary. In addition to his seminal trilogy on the war, Foote wrote the novel *Shiloh* in 1952.

Women have also excelled as writers in Tennessee. **Anne Armstrong** published *The Seas of God* in 1915 and *This Day and Time* in 1930, both of which were set in her native East Tennessee. **Evelyn Scott** wrote *The Wave,* set during the Civil War, as well as an autobiography, *Escapade,* depicting the six years she and her common-law husband spent living in Brazil.

Perhaps the best-known female Tennessee writer is **Nikki Giovanni,** of Knoxville, who established herself as a poet of international importance with her 1968 *Black Feeling, Black Talk.* In recent years author **Ann Patchett** has built a national reputation, thanks to her articles about living in Nashville, covering everything from the real estate to the 2010 floods. Patchett, who wrote the acclaimed *State of Wonder* and *Bel Canto,* opened Parnassus Books, an independent bookstore, in Nashville in 2011.

No Tennessee writer is better known or more widely acclaimed than **Alex Haley,** whose *Roots* won the Pulitzer Prize and inspired a landmark film and television series. Haley's other works include *Queen,* which is based on the story of his grandmother, who worked and lived in Savannah, Tennessee, on the Tennessee River.

Knoxville native **Cormac McCarthy** is widely known for his works, including *All the Pretty Horses* and *The Road,* which were both made into films. But McCarthy had started out writing about his native East Tennessee in works such as *The Orchard Keeper* and *Suttree.*

Essentials

Getting There and Around

Most visitors to Tennessee drive their own cars. The highways are good, distances are manageable, and many, if not most, destinations in the state are not accessible by public transportation. Plus, the state is less than a day's drive from a large percentage of the population of the United States.

If you're coming to Nashville or Memphis for a weekend getaway or a conference, you likely can manage without a car. Otherwise, you will need your own wheels to get around.

AIR

International airports in Tennessee include Nashville International Airport (BNA) and Memphis International Airport (MEM). McGhee Tyson Airport (TYS) in Knoxville, Chattanooga Metropolitan Airport (CHA), and the Tri-Cities Regional Airport (TRI) in Blountville offer domestic service to hubs in the eastern United States. There are a few smaller regional airports.

RAIL

Only western Tennessee is easily accessible by passenger rail. Amtrak runs from Chicago to New Orleans, with stops in Memphis, Newbern-Dyersburg in West Tennessee, and Fulton on the border with Kentucky. The route, called The City of New Orleans, runs daily.

BUS

Greyhound fully serves Tennessee, with daily routes that crisscross the state in nearly every direction.

CAR

Tennessee is within one day's drive of 75 percent of the U.S. population, and most visitors to the state get here in their own cars. There are seven interstates that run into the state, from just about every direction you might want to come.

While urban centers, pit-stop motels, and population centers are all found along or very near interstates, some of Tennessee's most lovely landscapes are far from the stretches of multilane pavement (and worth the drive to get there). Because Nissan's U.S. headquarters are in Franklin, Tennessee, and because Nissan is a leader in electric cars, there are more places to pull over and charge an electric car than you might expect. Locally headquartered restaurant chain Cracker Barrel has a lot of charging stations in its parking lots.

Road Rules

Tennessee recognizes other states' driver's licenses and learner's permits. New residents are required to obtain a Tennessee license within 30 days of establishing residency, however.

Speed limits vary. On interstates limits range 55-75 miles per hour. Limits on primary and secondary routes vary based on local conditions. Travelers should pay special attention to slow zones around schools; speeding tickets in these areas often attract high penalties.

It is required by law that all drivers and passengers in a moving vehicle wear their seatbelts. Infants less than one year old must be restrained in a rear-facing car seat; children 1-3 years must be restrained in a front-facing car seat. A child of 4-8 years who is less than four feet, nine inches tall must have a booster seat.

Drunk driving is dangerous and against the law. It is illegal to drive in Tennessee with

Previous: old car on Beale Street; Memphis Suspension Railway to Mud Island.

a blood alcohol concentration of 0.08 percent or more.

Car Rentals

Rental cars are widely available throughout Tennessee. The greatest concentration of rental agencies are found at major airports, but there are also neighborhood and downtown locations. Most rental agencies require the renter to be at least 24 years old; some have an even higher age requirement.

Before renting a car, call you credit card company and primary car insurance provider to find out what kind of insurance you have on a rental. You can likely forego the expensive insurance packages offered by rental companies.

For the best rates on car rentals, book early. Most companies allow you to reserve a car in advance without paying a deposit.

Taxis

Taxis are available in major cities, including Memphis, Nashville, Knoxville, Chattanooga, and Clarksville. Taxi service in other parts of the state will be spotty and expensive.

Taxi stands are found in just a few locations, including airports and major tourist sites, such as Beale Street in Memphis. Otherwise you will have to call to summon a taxi.

Ride-Hailing

Ride booking services that use an app and contracted drivers in their own vehicles are becoming a popular solution in cities. **Lyft** (Lyft.com) is available in Memphis and Nashville. **Uber** (uber.com) serves Memphis, Nashville, Chattanooga, and Knoxville.

Traffic Reports

For current traffic and road reports, including weather-related closures, construction closures, and traffic jams, dial 511 from any mobile or landline phone. You can also log on to www.tn511.com.

RECREATIONAL VEHICLES

Recreational vehicles are an increasingly popular way to see Tennessee due to the prevalence of good campgrounds and the beautiful landscape of the state.

All state park campgrounds welcome RVs and provide utilities such as water, electricity, and a dump station. For people who enjoy the outdoors but do not want to forgo the basic comforts of home, RVs provide some real advantages. RVs range from little trailers that pop up to provide space for sleeping to monstrous homes on wheels. Gas mileage ranges 7-13 miles per gallon, depending on the size and age of the RV.

All RVers should have mercy on other drivers and pull over from time to time so that traffic can pass, especially on mountain roads that are steep and difficult for RVs to climb.

RV Rentals

You can rent an RV for a one-way or local trip from **Cruise America** (www.cruiseamerica.com), which has locations in Knoxville (6100 Western Ave., 865/450-5009), Nashville (201 Donelson Pk., 615/885-4281), and Memphis (10230 Hwy. 70, Lakeland, 901/867-0039). Renters should be 25 years or older. Rental rates vary depending on the size of the vehicle and other factors. They also charge for mileage, and you can buy kits that include sheets, towels, dishes, and other basic necessities.

Recreation

NATIONAL PARKS

Tennessee's most significant national park is the Great Smoky Mountains National Park, the most visited national park in the United States. This is the crown jewel of the state's natural areas and a major draw for visitors.

Other federal lands are more wild and less visited. The Big South Fork and Land Between the Lakes are uncrowded recreation areas along the northern border with Kentucky. The Cherokee National Forest flanks the Smokies on the north and south, creating an uninterrupted buffer of federally protected lands along the entire eastern mountain range.

STATE PARKS

Tennessee's state parks are glorious and one of the state's best calling cards. The state has 54 parks and 77 state natural areas, stretching from the Appalachian Mountains in the east to the banks of the Mississippi River in the west. State parks and natural areas encompass 185,000 acres throughout the state. In 2007, Tennessee's parks were judged the best in the nation by the National Recreation and Park Association. The commendation came after a long and bitter fight over user fees and state budget woes that led to the closure of 14 parks and the imposition of user fees at 23 parks between 2002 and 2006. The fight over the future of the state parks illustrated how valuable they are indeed; none of the parks have entrances fees.

Each state park includes basic amenities such as picnic facilities and day-use areas with public restrooms, water, and a park office of some kind. Most parks also have campgrounds, hiking trails, playgrounds, and facilities for sports such as volleyball, basketball, and baseball. A number of parks have swimming beaches, bicycle trails, areas for fishing or hunting, and backcountry campsites.

The park system includes 6 parks with inns, 12 with golf courses (and 2 disc golf sources), 8 with restaurants, and 4 with marinas for motorized boats. A number of parks also have cabins, ideal for families or other groups.

For travelers who enjoy the out-of-doors, the state parks are some of the best places in the state to visit. Despite persistent budget problems, the parks are generally well maintained. Accommodations are not luxurious, but they are clean and comfortable, and the natural beauty that exists in many of the parks is unparalleled. Camping in a state park sure beats the KOA any day.

Detailed information about fees, amenities, and services may be found on the state park website (http://state.tn.us/environment/parks). You can also request a published map and brochure. Enthusiasts may also want to subscribe to the *Tennessee Conservationist*, a magazine published by the State Department of Environment and Conservation.

HIKING

Opportunities to hike are abundant in Tennessee. State parks, national forests, national parks, and wildlife refuges are just a few of the areas where you will find places for a walk in the woods.

High-profile hiking trails such as the Appalachian Trail in the eastern mountains are indeed special. But lesser-known walks are often equally spectacular, and the best hike may well be the one closest to where you are right now.

Day hikes require just a few pieces of gear: comfortable and sturdy shoes; a day pack with water, food, and a map; and several layers of clothing, especially during volatile spring and fall months. In the winter, it's a good idea to bring a change of socks and extra layers of warm clothes.

Other gear is optional: A walking stick makes rough or steep terrain a bit easier, and a camera is always a nice idea.

Whenever you go hiking, tell someone where you're going and when you expect to be back. Do not expect cell phones to work on the trail.

Many state parks and the national parks in the eastern mountains welcome overnight hikers. Backpackers must carry lightweight tents, sleeping bags, food, and extra gear on their backs. They must also register in advance. You can sometimes reserve backcountry campsites. These campsites offer little more than a clearing for your tent and a ring of stones for your fire. Some are built near sources of water. Some trails have overnight shelters, especially nice in winter.

Hiking is one of the best ways to experience Tennessee's nature, and there are few better ways to spend a day or two.

BICYCLING

Bicycling is an increasingly popular pastime in Tennessee. Only in a handful of urban areas, and on some college campuses, is bicycling a form of regular transportation. But mountain and road biking is popular for staying fit and having fun. Many area parks offer BMX tracks.

Of course you can bicycle just about anywhere (but not on the interstates). Cities such as Nashville, Chattanooga, Knoxville, and Murfreesboro have greenways especially for bikers (and walkers). Dedicated mountain bike trails are popping up in parks across the state, including at Montgomery Bell State Park, Big Ridge State Park, and Meeman-Shelby Forest State Park. City parks in Memphis and Nashville also welcome bikers.

The **Tennessee Bicycle Racing Association** (www.tbra.org) promotes biking and is an umbrella organization for several local bike groups. The Tennessee Mountain Biking Alliance (www.mtbtn.org) promotes mountain biking and can put you in touch with mountain bikers in your neck of the woods. Local bike shops are also a good place to find out about good bike routes, local safety issues, and upcoming events.

FISHING

Fishing is tremendously popular in Tennessee. The lakes created by the Tennessee Valley Authority produced many opportunities to

hiking trails in Great Smoky Mountains National Park

fish. Smaller rivers and streams in all parts of the state are also good for fishing.

Some of the most common types of fish caught in Tennessee rivers and lakes are bass, trout, crappie, perch, pike, catfish, and carp. Various rivers and lakes are stocked regularly with fish.

Subject to a few exceptions, everyone who is 13 and older and who attempts to take fish from a body of water should have a valid Tennessee fishing license. License fees vary by type and duration: A one-day fishing license for a Tennessee state resident is $6.50; an annual fish-hunt license for a state resident is $34. Out-of-staters pay more: An annual license for all types of fish costs $99.

Annual licenses go on sale every year on February 18 and are good until the last day of February the following year.

You can buy a fishing license from county clerks, sporting goods stores, boat docks, and offices of the Tennessee Wildlife Resources Agency. You can buy a license online at http://wildlifelicense.com; licenses processed online are subject to a $3 or $4.25 processing fee depending on how the license is printed and fulfilled. You can also buy licenses by mail or over the phone by calling 888/814-8972.

Rules about limits, minimum sizes, and seasons are detailed and depend on the lake or stream. The Tennessee Wildlife Resources Agency (TWRA) publishes a comprehensive guide to fishing regulations every year. This guide includes fish stocking schedules, dam release timetables, detailed information about limits, and warnings about contaminants in certain types of Tennessee fish. You can request a copy of the guide from any TWRA office or download a copy online from www.tnwildlife.org.

TWRA offices are located in Crossville (931/484-9571 or 800/262-6704), Nashville (Ellington Agricultural Center, 615/781-6500 or 800/781-6622), Morristown (423/587-7037 or 800/332-0900), and Jackson (731/423-5725 or 800/372-3928).

PADDLING

The Volunteer State has some of the best paddling—kayaking, white-water rafting, canoeing, and stand-up paddleboarding—in the country. Chattanooga and the eastern part of the state, near the Ocoee, are most well known for their water-sports access. But, in truth, all of the state's major cities and many rural areas have opportunities for guide-led and independent paddling adventures.

Paddlers are required to have a U.S. Coast Guard-approved life preserver and whistle with them while on the water. In addition to the safety reasons for wearing one, there are fines for not complying with these regulations.

The Tennessee Scenic Rivers Association (TSRA) has been working to build more paddler access points across the state. Visit www.paddletsra.org for more details on their work. Other good resources include the Cumberland River Compact (www.cumberlandrivercompact.org) and the Tennessee Clean Water Network (www.tcwn.org).

Accommodations

Accommodations in Tennessee fall into three main categories, with little gray area in between.

HOTELS AND MOTELS

Chain motels are ubiquitous, particularly along interstates. These properties are entirely predictable; their amenities depend on the price tag and location. Most motel chains allow you to make reservations in advance by telephone or on the Internet. Most motels require a credit card number at the time of reservation, but they don't usually charge your card until you arrive. Always ask about the cancellation policy to avoid paying for a room that you do not ultimately need or use.

Savvy shoppers can save money on their hotel room. Shop around, and pay attention to price differentials based on location; if you're willing to be a few miles up the interstate from the city, you'll realize some significant savings. You may also be amazed by the power of the words "That rate seems high to me. Do you have anything better?" Employed regularly, this approach will usually save you a few bucks each night, at least.

Chain motels do not offer unique accommodations, and only the rarest among them is situated somewhere more charming than an asphalt parking lot. But for travelers who are looking for flexibility, familiarity, and a good deal, chain motels can fit the bill.

Independent motels and hotels range from no-brand roadside motels to upscale boutique hotels in urban centers. By their very nature, these properties are each a little different. Boutique hotels tend to be more expensive than chain hotels, but they also allow you to feel as if you are staying in a place with a history and character of its own. They may also offer personalized service that is not available at cookie-cutter motels.

BED-AND-BREAKFASTS

Bed-and-breakfasts are about as far from a chain motel as one can get. Usually located in small towns, rural areas, and quiet residential neighborhoods of major cities, bed-and-breakfasts are independent guesthouses. The quality of the offering depends entirely on the hosts, and the entire bed-and-breakfast experience often takes on the character and tone of the person in whose home you are sleeping. Good bed-and-breakfast hosts can sense the line between being welcoming and overly chatty, but some seem to struggle with this.

Bed-and-breakfasts offer a number of advantages over the typical motel. Their locations are often superior, the guest rooms have lots of character and charm, and a full and often homemade breakfast is included. Some bed-and-breakfasts are located in historic buildings, and many are furnished with antiques.

Reservations for bed-and-breakfasts are not as flexible as most motels. Many bed-and-breakfasts require a deposit, and many require payment in full before you arrive. Making payments can be a challenge, too; while some are equipped to process credit cards, others accept only checks and cash. Cancellation policies are also more stringent than most motels. All of this can make it hard for travelers who like to be flexible and leave things till the last minute. Additionally, if you're bringing children with you, be sure to check that your bed-and-breakfast allows children; some don't. If your travel plans are certain and you just can't bear another night in a bland hotel room, a bed-and-breakfast is the ideal alternative.

Bed-and-breakfast rates vary but generally range $90-150 per night based on double occupancy.

Bed and Breakfast Inns Online (www.bbonline.com) is a national listing service that includes a number of Tennessee bed-and-breakfasts.

HOSTELS

There are youth hostels in Nashville, Knoxville, and upper East Tennessee. Hostels provide dormitory-style accommodations at a fraction of the cost of a standard motel room. Bathroom and kitchen facilities are usually shared, and there are common rooms with couches, televisions, and Internet access. Hostels are usually favored by young and international travelers, and they are a good place to meet people.

PRIVATE RESIDENCES

Websites aggregators like **Vacation Rental By Owner** (vrbo.com) and Airbnb (airbnb.com) have become a popular way to find a room, apartment, or house to rent. Accommodations may be less expensive that traditional lodging, and often include parking and kitchens. You have fewer recourses if something goes wrong, however, so ask questions before you book.

Food

Throughout Tennessee, you will find restaurants that specialize in local and regional dishes. In urban centers, there is a wide variety of dining available, from international eateries to fine-dining restaurants.

Chain restaurants, including fast-food joints, are all over the state. But travelers owe it to themselves to eat in local restaurants for a taste of something more authentic.

MEAT-AND-THREES

Meat-and-threes, also called plate-lunch diners, are found throughout Tennessee, with the greatest concentration in Memphis and Nashville. The name is used to refer to the type of restaurant and the meal itself. These eateries serve the type of food that Tennesseans once cooked at home: main dish meats like baked chicken, meat loaf, fried catfish, and chicken and dumplings; side dishes (also called "vegetables"), including macaroni and cheese, mashed potatoes, greens, creamed corn, squash, and fried okra; breads, including corn bread, biscuits, and yeast rolls; and desserts like peach cobbler, Jell-O, and cream pies. Hands down, these diners are the best places to become acquainted, or renew your relationship, with Southern home cooking.

Plate-lunch diners focus on the midday meal. Most offer a different menu of meats and sides daily. Large restaurants may have as many as eight different main dishes to choose from; smaller diners may offer two or three. Some are set up cafeteria-style, and others employ servers. All offer a good value for the money and generally speedy food service.

Meat-and-threes exist in rural and urban communities, although in the countryside there's less fuss attached. They are simply where people go to eat.

The food served in these restaurants is generally hearty; health-conscious eaters should be careful. Vegetarians should also note that most vegetable dishes, like greens, are often cooked with meat.

REGIONAL SPECIALTIES

Barbecue

Memphis is the epicenter of Tennessee's barbecue culture. Here is hosted an annual festival dedicated to barbecue, and bona fide barbecue pits burn daily. In Memphis, they'll douse anything with barbecue sauce, hence the city's specialty: barbecue spaghetti.

Barbecue restaurants are usually humble places by appearances, with characters behind the counter and in the kitchen. Most swear by their own special barbecue recipe and guard it jealously. Nearly all good barbecue, however, requires time and patience, as the meat—usually pork—is smoked for hours and sometimes days over a fire. After the meat is cooked, it is tender and juicy and doused with barbecue sauce, which is tangy and sweet.

Pork barbecue is the most common, and it's often served pulled next to soft white bread. Barbecue chicken, turkey, ribs, bologna, and beef can also be found on many menus.

The Southern Foodways Alliance (SFA), part of the University of Mississippi's Center for the Study of Southern Culture, conducted an oral history project about Memphis and West Tennessee barbecue in the early 2000s. You can read transcripts of the interviews and see photos on the SFA website at www.southernfoodways.com.

Hot Chicken

Pan-fried "hot chicken" is one of Nashville's truly distinct culinary specialties. Breasts of spicy chicken are individually pan fried in cast-iron skillets at several holes-in-the-wall around Music City and interpreted on menus at higher-end restaurants. They are traditionally served on white bread with a pickle.

Don't come in a hurry; hot chicken takes time to prepare, and don't be overconfident with your tolerance for spice. Start with "mild" or "medium."

Catfish

Fried catfish is a food tradition that started along Tennessee's rivers, where river catfish are caught. Today, fried catfish served in restaurants is just as likely to come from a catfish farm. For real river catfish, look for restaurants located near rivers and lakes, such as those near Reelfoot Lake in northwestern Tennessee, or the City Fish Market in Brownsville.

Fried catfish (it's rarely served any way besides fried) is normally coated with a thin dusting of cornmeal, seasonings, and flour. On its own, the fish is relatively bland. Tangy tartar sauce, vinegar-based hot sauce, and traditional sides like coleslaw and baked beans enliven the flavor. Hush puppies are the traditional accompaniment.

FARMERS MARKETS

Farmers markets are popping up in more and more Tennessee communities. Knoxville, Nashville, Oak Ridge, and Memphis have large markets every Saturday (Nashville's operates daily). Chattanooga's is open in season on Sundays. Dozens of small towns and neighborhoods have their own weekly, seasonal markets. Jackson's is particularly vibrant.

There is a great deal of variety when it comes to the types of markets that exist. Some markets take place under tents, provide entertainment, and invite artisans to sell arts and crafts as well as food products. Other markets consist of little more than a bunch of farmers who have arranged the week's harvest on the back of their tailgates.

Regardless of the style, farmers markets are a great place to meet people and buy wholesome food.

The State Department of Agriculture (www.agriculture.state.tn.us) maintains a listing of all registered farmers markets, including locations and contact information.

Travel Tips

OPPORTUNITIES FOR STUDY

Tennessee is home to almost 50 colleges and universities, plus 13 public community colleges. The University of Tennessee, with campuses in Knoxville, Chattanooga, and Martin, is the largest. Other public colleges and universities include East Tennessee State University in Johnson City, Middle Tennessee State University in Murfreesboro, Tennessee State University in Nashville, and the University of Memphis. Private colleges include the historically black Fisk University in Nashville and Lemoyne-Owen College in Memphis; the University of the South at Sewanee, which is affiliated with the Episcopal Church; Memphis College of Art and Rhodes College in Memphis; and Vanderbilt University in Nashville. Each of these, plus the 31 other private institutions of higher learning, offer myriad short- and long-term education programs in fields as various as religious studies and medicine.

Several institutions of note offer workshops in arts and crafts. **The Appalachian Center for Craft** (Smithville, 931/372-3051, www.tntech.edu/craftcenter) is an affiliate of Tennessee Tech University and specializes in instruction in decorative arts and crafts. Full-time students can pursue a bachelor's degree in fine arts or a certificate in clay, fiber, glass, metal, or woodwork. The center also offers more than 100 different workshops each year. The school is set in scenic countryside on the Cumberland Plateau.

Perhaps one of the best-known craft schools in the entire United States, Gatlinburg's Arrowmont (865/436-5860, www.arrowmont.

org) offers dozens of short courses and weekend workshops annually. Arrowmont began as a settlement school for mountain folks, but today it is a center that combines traditional crafts with modern techniques and themes.

WOMEN TRAVELING ALONE

Women traveling alone in Tennessee may encounter a few people who don't understand why, but most people will simply leave you alone. Solo women might find themselves the object of unwanted attention, especially at bars and restaurants at night. But usually a firm "I'm not interested" will do the trick.

Anyone—man or woman—traveling alone in the outdoors should take special precautions. Backpackers and campers should always tell someone where they will be and when they expect to be back. Ideally, establish a check-in routine with someone back home, and beware of overly friendly strangers on the trail.

GAY AND LESBIAN TRAVELERS

Tennessee's gay, lesbian, bisexual, and transgender people have a mixed bag. On one hand, this is the Bible Belt, a state where not long ago a bill was introduced that would have banned teachers from even saying the word *gay* in the classroom. (This is often referred to as the "Don't Say Gay" bill.) On the other hand, there has been no better time to be gay in Tennessee. More and more social, civic, and political organizations are waking up to the gay community, and there are vibrant gay scenes in many Tennessee cities.

For gay travelers, this means that the experience on the road can vary tremendously. You may or may not be able to expect a warm welcome at the mom-and-pop diner out in the country, but you can find good gay nightlife and gay-friendly lodging in many cities.

The decision about how out to be on the road is entirely up to you, but be prepared for some harassment if you are open everywhere you go. The farther off the beaten track you travel, the less likely it is that the people you encounter have had many opportunities to get to know openly gay people. Some may be downright mean, but others probably won't even notice.

Several specific guidebooks and websites give helpful listings of gay-friendly hotels, restaurants, and bars. The Damron guides (www.damron.com) offer Tennessee listings; the International Gay and Lesbian Travel Association (IGLTA, www.iglta.org) is a trade organization with listings of gay-friendly hotels, tour operators, and much more. San Francisco-based Now, Voyager (www.nowvoyager.com) is a gay-owned and gay-operated travel agency that specializes in gay tours, vacation packages, and cruises.

You should also check out local gay and lesbian organizations and newspapers.

Nashville

Three different publications cover the gay, lesbian, bisexual, and transgender community in Nashville. *InsideOut Nashville* (www.insideoutnashville.com) is a free weekly; *Out and About* (www.outandaboutnewspaper.com) is a free monthly newsmagazine.

International Travel Inc. (4004 Hillsboro Rd., 615/385-1222) is a Nashville-based gay-friendly travel agency.

Memphis

The **Memphis Gay and Lesbian Community Center** (892 S. Cooper St., 901/278-6422, www.mglcc.org) is a clearinghouse of information for the gay and lesbian community. It has a directory of gay-friendly businesses, host social events, and promote tolerance and equality.

Mid-South Pride (www.midsouthpride.org) organizes Memphis Pride in June.

SENIOR TRAVELERS

Elderhostel (800/454-5768, www.elderhostel.org), which organizes educational tours for people over 55, offers tours in Memphis and Nashville.

For discounts and help with trip planning, try the **AARP** (800/687-2277, www.aarp.org), which offers a full-service travel agency, trip insurance, a motor club, and AARP Passport program, which provides you with senior discounts for hotels, car rentals, and other things.

Persons over 55 should always check for a senior citizen discount. Most attractions and some hotels and restaurants have special pricing for senior citizens.

TRAVELERS WITH DISABILITIES

More people with disabilities are traveling than ever before. The Americans with Disabilities Act requires most public buildings to make provisions for disabled people, although in practice accessibility may be spotty.

When you make your hotel reservations, always check that the hotel is prepared to accommodate you. Airlines will also make special arrangements for you if you request help in advance. To reduce stress, try to travel during off-peak times.

Several national organizations have information and advice about traveling with disabilities. **The Society for Accessible Travel and Hospitality** (www.sath.org) publishes links to major airlines' accessibility policies and publishes travel tips for people with all types of disabilities, including blindness, deafness, mobility disorders, diabetes, kidney disease, and arthritis. The society publishes *Open World*, a magazine about accessible travel.

Wheelchair Getaways (800/642-2042, www.wheelchairgetaways.com) is a national chain specializing in renting vans that are wheelchair accessible or otherwise designed for disabled drivers and travelers. Wheelchair Getaways has locations in Memphis (901/795-6533 or 866/762-165), Knoxville (865/622-6550 or 888/340-8267), and Nashville (615/451-2900 or 866/762-1656), and it will deliver to other locations in the state.

Avis offers **Avis Access**, a program for travelers with disabilities. Call the dedicated 24-hour toll-free number (888/879-4273) for help renting a car with features such as transfer boards, hand controls, spinner knobs, and swivel seats.

TRAVELING WITH CHILDREN

It is hard to imagine a state better suited for family vacations than Tennessee. The state parks provide numerous places to camp, hike, swim, fish, and explore, and cities have attractions like zoos, children's museums, aquariums, and trains.

Many hotels and inns offer special discounts for families, and casual restaurants almost always have a children's menu with lower-priced, kid-friendly choices.

FOREIGN TRAVELERS

Tennessee attracts a fair number of foreign visitors. Elvis, the international popularity of blues and country music, and the beauty of the eastern mountains bring people to the state from all over the globe.

Communication

Foreign travelers will find a warm welcome. Those in the tourist trade are used to dealing with all sorts of people and will be pleased that you have come from so far away to visit their home. If you are not a native English speaker, it may be difficult to understand the local accent at first. Just smile and ask the person to say it again, a bit slower. Good humor and a positive attitude will help at all times.

Visas and Officialdom

Most citizens of a foreign country require a visa to enter the United States. There are many types of visas, issued according to the purpose of your visit. Business and pleasure travelers apply for B-1 and B-2 visas, respectively. When you apply for your visa, you will be required to prove that the purpose of your trip is business, pleasure, or for medical treatment; that you plan to remain in the United States for a limited period; and that you have a place of residence outside the United States. Apply for your visa at the nearest U.S. embassy. For more information, contact the U.S. Citizenship and Immigration Service (www.uscis.gov).

Nationals of 38 countries may be able to

use the Visa Waiver Program, operated by Customs and Border Protection. Presently, these 38 countries are: Andorra, Australia, Austria, Belgium, Brunei, Chile, Czech Republic, Denmark (including Greenland and Faroe Islands), Estonia, Finland, France, Germany, Greece, Hungary, Iceland, Ireland, Italy, Japan, Latvia, Liechtenstein, Lithuania, Luxembourg, Malta, Monaco, the Netherlands (including Aruba, Bonaire, Curacao, Saba, and Sint Maarten), New Zealand, Norway, Portugal (including Azores and Madeira), San Marino, South Korea, Singapore, Slovakia, Slovenia, South Korea, Spain, Sweden, Switzerland, Taiwan, and the United Kingdom.

Take note that in recent years the United States has begun to require visa-waiver participants to have upgraded passports with digital photographs and machine-readable information. They have also introduced requirements that even visa-waiver citizens register in advance before arriving in the United States. For more information about the Visa Waiver Program, contact the Customs and Border Protection Agency (www.travel.state.gov).

All foreign travelers are now required to participate in U.S. Visit, a program operated by the Department of Homeland Security. Under the program, your fingerprints and photograph are taken—digitally and without ink—as you are being screened by the immigration officer.

Arrival

Nashville and Memphis are international airports with daily international flights. At the Nashville International Airport, you can exchange currency at SunTrust Bank near A/B concourse or at the Business Service Center (Wright Travel, 615/275-2658) near C/D concourse.

The Memphis airport is well equipped for foreign travelers. The lone international airline, Northwest/KLM Royal Dutch Airlines, provides interpreters for the Customs Clearance Facility and the boarding areas for international flights. It can accommodate Dutch-, German-, Arabic-, Spanish-, and French-speaking passengers.

International travel services are provided at the Business Service Center (Ticket Lobby B, 901/922-8090, 7am-7:30pm Mon.-Fri., 10am-7:30pm Sat., 11am-7:30pm Sun.). Here you can exchange currency, buy travel insurance, make telephone calls and send faxes, wire money, and buy traveler's checks. An additional kiosk is located in Concourse B near the international gates (gate B-36). Here you can buy travel insurance and exchange currency. The hours are 4:30pm-7:30pm daily.

Memphis International Airport is a "Transit Without Visa" port of entry. This means that foreign travelers whose flight will connect through Memphis on the way to another foreign destination beyond the United States no longer need a U.S. transit visa just to connect.

Health and Safety

DISEASES

West Nile Virus

West Nile virus was first recorded in humans in the United States in the early 2000s, and by 2007 nearly every state, including Tennessee, had reported confirmed cases of the disease. West Nile is spread by mosquitoes.

Summer is mosquito season in Tennessee. You can prevent mosquito breeding by eliminating standing water around your property. You can prevent mosquito bites by wearing an insect repellant containing 30-50 percent DEET. An alternative to DEET, picaridin, is available in 7 and 15 percent concentrations and would need to be applied more frequently. Wearing long-sleeved pants and shirts and not being outdoors during dusk and dawn are also ways to avoid exposure to mosquitoes.

Fever, chills, weakness, drowsiness, and fatigue are some of the symptoms of West Nile virus.

Lyme Disease

Lyme disease is a bacterial infection spread by deer ticks. The first indication you might have Lyme disease is the appearance of a red rash where you have been bitten by a tick. Following that, symptoms are flu-like. During late-stage Lyme disease, neurological effects are reported.

Ticks are external parasites that attach themselves to warm-blooded creatures like dogs, deer, and humans. Ticks suck blood from their host.

Tick bites are unpleasant enough, even if there is no infection of Lyme disease. After coming in from the woods, especially if you were walking off-trail, carefully inspect your body for ticks. If one has attached itself to you, remove it by carefully "unscrewing" it from your body with tweezers.

You can avoid ticks by wearing long sleeves and pants, tucking in your shirt, and wearing a hat. You can minimize your exposure to ticks by staying on trails and walking paths where you don't brush up against trees and branches.

White-Nose Syndrome

In 2006 in upstate New York, a caver noticed a substance on the noses of hibernating bats, as well as a few dead bats. The next year, more of both were found. Now bats dying of a fungus called "white-nose syndrome" have been found as far south as Tennessee.

Researchers are still trying to find out what causes the deadly (to bats, not people) fungus. Until then, certain caves may be closed to prevent the disease from spreading. Check individual cave listings before heading out.

Poison Ivy

If there is one plant that you should learn to identify, it is poison ivy. This woody vine grows in woods all around Tennessee. Touching it can leave you with a painful and terribly uncomfortable reaction.

Poison ivy is green, and the leaves grow in clusters of three. There are no thorns. Its berries are a gray-white color, and if the vine is climbing, you will notice root "hairs" on the vine. The following mnemonic might help: "Leaves of three, let it be; berries white, danger in sight."

An estimated 15-35 percent of people are not allergic to poison ivy. But after repeated exposure this protection is worn down. People who are allergic will experience more and more severe reactions with each episode of exposure.

Poison ivy is easily spread over your body by your hands, or from person to person through skin-to-skin contact. Never touch your eyes or face if you think you may have touched poison ivy, and always wash yourself with hot soapy water if you think you may have come into contact with the vine.

Treat poison ivy rashes with

over-the-counter itch creams. In severe cases, you may need to go to the doctor.

VENOMOUS SNAKES

The vast majority of snakes in Tennessee are nonvenomous. Only four species of venomous snakes exist there. Copperheads (northern and southern) live throughout the state, along with the timber rattlesnake. The pygmy rattlesnake lives in the Kentucky Lake region, and the cottonmouth water moccasin is found in wet areas in the western part of the state.

Venomous snakes of Tennessee can usually by identified by their elliptical (cat-eye) shaped pupils (not that you really want to get close enough to see that). Most also have thick bodies, blunt tails, and triangular-shaped heads.

MEDICAL SERVICES

Hospitals, medical centers, and doctors' offices are located throughout the state. Walk-in medical centers may be found in the yellow pages and are the best bet for minor needs while you're on vacation. In an emergency, proceed to the closest hospital or call 911.

The single most important thing you can have if you get sick while traveling is health insurance. Before you leave, check with your insurance provider about in-network doctors and medical facilities in the area where you'll be traveling.

Prescriptions

Always travel with your prescription drugs in their original container and with a copy of the prescription issued by your doctor. If you can, get refills before you leave. National chains of many drugstores exist across the state.

DRUGS

Tennessee's greatest drug problem is with methamphetamine, the highly addictive stimulant sometimes called "speed," "crank," and "ice," among other names. During the 1990s and 2000s, meth use spread quickly through rural America, including Tennessee. In 2004, Tennessee passed comprehensive legislation to combat meth. A year later, some 60 percent of Tennessee counties reported that meth remained their most serious drug problem.

The state's anti-meth strategy has been to aggressively seek out illegal meth labs, increase public education about meth use, and promote recovery programs. Despite the efforts, it is still difficult to eliminate meth use, partly because meth is relatively easy to manufacture in so-called labs, which can be built in homes, hotel rooms, trailers, and even vehicles.

Meth is a dangerous and highly addictive drug. It takes a terrible toll on the health of users, creates myriad family and social problems, and is among one of the most addictive drugs out there.

CRIME

Crime is a part of life anywhere, and travelers should take precautions to avoid being a victim of crime. Leave valuables at home and secure your hotel room and car at all times (including GPS devices, tablets, and other car-friendly technology). Always be aware of your surroundings, and don't allow yourself to be drawn into conversations with strangers in deserted, dark, or otherwise sketchy areas. Single travelers, especially women, should take special care to stay in well-lit and highly populated areas, especially at night.

Information and Services

MONEY

Banks

Dozens of local and regional banks are found throughout Tennessee. Most banks will cash traveler's checks, exchange currency, and send wire transfers. Banks are generally open weekdays 9am-4pm, although some are open later and on Saturday. Automatic teller machines (ATMs) are ubiquitous at grocery stores, live-music venues, and elsewhere, and many are compatible with bank cards bearing the Plus or Cirrus icons. Between fees charged by your own bank and the bank that owns the ATM you are using, expect to pay $2-5 extra to get cash from an ATM that does not belong to your own bank.

Sales Tax

Sales tax is charged on all goods, including food and groceries.

The sales tax you pay is split between the state and local governments. Tennessee's sales tax is 5 percent on food and groceries and 7 percent on all other goods. Cities and towns add an additional "local use tax" of 1.5-2.75 percent, making the tax as high as 9.25 percent in Nashville, Memphis, Knoxville, and Chattanooga.

Hotel Tax

There is no statewide tax on hotel rooms, but 45 different cities have established their own hotel tax, ranging 5-7 percent.

Cost

Tennessee routinely ranks favorably on cost-of-living indexes. Visitors can comfortably eat their fill in casual restaurants and coffee shops for $35 a day, although it is possible to spend much more if you prefer to eat in upscale restaurants.

The cost of accommodations varies widely, depending on the area you are visiting, the type of accommodations you are seeking, and when you are traveling. The most expensive hotel rooms are in urban centers. Rates go up during major events, on weekends, and during peak travel months in the summer. Cheaper accommodations will be found on the outskirts of town and along rural interstate routes. Budget travelers should consider camping.

If you are not coming in your own car, one of your most substantial expenses will be a rental car. Most rentals bottom out at $35 a day, and rates can be much higher if you don't reserve in advance or if you are renting only for a day or two.

Discounts

Most historic sites, museums, and attractions offer special discounts for senior citizens and children under 12. Some attractions also have discounts for students and members of the military. Even if you don't see any discount posted, it is worth asking if one exists.

Many chain hotels offer discounts for AAA members.

Bargaining

Consumer Reports magazine reported that you can often get a better hotel rate simply by asking for one. If the rate you are quoted sounds a little high, simply say that it is more than you were planning to spend and ask if it can offer a better rate. Many times, especially out of season, the answer will be yes. Your negotiations will be more successful if you are willing to walk away if the answer is no.

Tipping

You should tip waiters and waitresses 15-20 percent in a sit-down restaurant. You can tip 5-10 percent in a cafeteria or restaurant where you collect your own food from the counter.

Tip a bellhop or bag handler $1 per bag, or more if they went out of their way to help you.

TOURIST INFORMATION

The **Tennessee Department of Tourism Development** (615/741-2159, www.tnvacation.com) is a source of visitor information about Tennessee. It publishes an annual guide that contains hotel and attraction listings. The website has lots of links to local attractions and chambers of commerce.

Many cities have their own tourist organizations: Memphis, Nashville, Knoxville, Chattanooga, and Clarksville are among the Tennessee cities with a visitors bureau. In some rural areas, counties have teamed up to develop visitor information for the region. Other organizations, such as the National Park Service, Army Corps of Engineers, and the Tennessee State Parks, publish visitor information for certain attractions. Specific listings for visitor information are found throughout this book.

Several regional tourism organizations provide useful information and publications.

In West Tennessee there is the **Southwest Tennessee Tourism Association** (www.tast.tn.org) and the **Northwest Tennessee Tourism Association** (www.reelfootlakeoutdoors.com).

Middle Tennessee has the **Middle Tennessee Tourism Council** (www.middletennesseetourism.com), which covers the counties around Nashville; the **Upper Cumberland Tourism Association** (www.uppercumberland.org), which promotes the region surrounding the Cumberland River and the northern plateau; and the **South Central Tennessee Tourism Association** (www.sctta.net).

East Tennessee has several regional organizations. In southeast Tennessee, contact the **Tennessee Overhill Heritage Association** (www.tennesseeoverhill.com) or the **Southeast Tennessee Tourism Association** (www.southeasttennessee.com). Northeast Tennessee is represented by the **Northeast Tennessee Tourism Association** (www.netta.com). The area surrounding Knoxville and including the Smoky Mountains is served by the **Middle East Tennessee Tourism Council** (www.vacationeasttennessee.org).

If all else fails, contact the chamber of commerce for the county you will be visiting. Chambers of commerce will willingly mail you a sheaf of brochures and any visitor information that may exist. If you are already in town, stop by in person. You are sure to find someone who will be glad to help you.

Maps

Rand McNally publishes the best maps of Tennessee. In addition to the statewide map, Rand McNally publishes maps of Memphis, Nashville, Knoxville, Chattanooga, the Great Smoky Mountains National Park, Clarksville, Murfreesboro-Smyrna, and Gatlinburg-Pigeon Forge. You can buy Rand McNally maps from bookstores and through online sales outlets like Amazon.com. Rand McNally also sells downloadable PDF maps that you can view on your computer or print out.

For trail maps or topographical maps of parks and other natural areas, look for National Geographic's Trails Illustrated series.

The State Department of Transportation updates its official transportation map annually. Request a free copy at www.tdot.state.tn.us or by calling 615/741-2848. The official map is also available from many Tennessee welcome centers, chambers of commerce, and other tourism-related offices.

The state also creates maps of dozens of Tennessee cities and towns. All these maps are available for free download from the department of transportation website.

Hubbard Scientific (www.amep.com) produces beautiful raised-relief maps of Tennessee, the Great Smoky Mountains National Park, and other regions of the state. Found on display in some visitors centers, these maps make great wall art. They are also useful references, especially for the eastern parts of Tennessee where the landscape is mountainous.

Many GPS apps are now available for smartphones and other smart devices.

COMMUNICATION

Area Codes

Tennessee has seven different area codes. Memphis and vicinity use 901; the western plains are 731. The Heartland, including Clarksville, uses 931, while Nashville and the counties immediately north of the city are in 615 and 629. East Tennessee uses 423, except for Knoxville and eight surrounding counties, which are in 865.

Cell Phones

Cell phone signals are powerful and reliable in cities and along the interstates. In rural parts of the state you should not count on your cell phone, and in mountainous areas, such as the Cumberland Plateau and the Great Smoky Mountains National Park, forget about it altogether.

TIME ZONES

The eastern third of Tennessee lies in the Eastern time zone; Middle and West Tennessee are in the Central time zone, one hour earlier. The time zone line runs a slanted course from Signal Mountain in the south to the Big South Fork National River and Recreation Area in the north. The time zone line falls at mile marker 340 along I-40, just west of Rockwood and a few miles east of Crossville. Chattanooga, Dayton, Rockwood, Crossville, Rugby, Fall Creek Falls State Park, the Catoosa Wildlife Management Area, and Big South Fork lie close to or on the time zone line, and visitors to these areas should take special care to ensure they are on the right clock.

Resources

Suggested Reading

PHOTOGRAPHY AND ART

Escott, Colin. *The Grand Ole Opry: The Making of an American Icon.* Nashville: Center Street, 2006. An authorized (and somewhat sanitized) look at the Grand Ole Opry. Lots of pictures, reminiscences, and short sidebars make it an attractive coffee-table book.

McGuire, Jim. *Nashville Portraits: Legends of Country Music.* Guilford CT: The Lyons Press, 2007. Sixty stunning photographs of country music legends, including Johnny Cash, Waylon Jennings, Doc Watson, and Dolly Parton. The companion book to an eponymous traveling exhibit that debuted in 2007.

Sherraden, Jim, Paul Kingsbury, and Elek Horvath. *Hatch Show Print: The History of a Great American Poster Shop.* San Francisco: Chronicle Books, 2001. A fully illustrated, beautiful book about Hatch Show Print, the Nashville advertising and letterpress founded in 1897.

GUIDES

Brandt, Robert. *Touring the Middle Tennessee Backroads.* Winston-Salem, NC: John F. Blair Publisher, 1995. Brandt is a Nashville judge and self-professed "zealot" for Middle Tennessee. His guidebook details 15 driving tours through back roads in the heartland of Tennessee. Brandt's knowledge of local history and architecture cannot be surpassed, and his enthusiasm for his subject shines through the prose. While some of the entries are now dated, the guide remains an invaluable source of information about small towns in the region.

Hiking Trails of the Smokies. Gatlinburg TN: Great Smoky Mountains Natural History Association, 2001. The most comprehensive guide to hiking trails of the Smokies is small enough to fit in the glove compartment of your car. Descriptions give details of elevation, distance, and difficulty. They also describe the natural and historical features along the trail. The same publishers produce related guides of day hikes and history hikes.

Van West, Carroll. *Tennessee's Historical Landscapes: A Traveler's Guide.* Knoxville: University of Tennessee Press, 1995. The editor of the *Tennessee Historical Quarterly* and a professor of history at Middle Tennessee State University, Van West guides readers along highways and byways, pointing out historical structures and other signs of history along the way. A good traveling companion, especially for students of architecture and landscape.

The WPA Guide to Tennessee. Knoxville: University of Tennessee Press, 1986. The Works Progress Administration guide to Tennessee, written in 1939 and originally published by Viking Press, is a fascinating portrait of Depression-era Tennessee. Published as part of a New Deal project to employ writers and document the culture and character of the nation, the guide contains visitor information, historical sketches, and profiles of the state's literature, culture, agriculture, industry, and more. The guide, republished as part of Tennessee's "Homecoming '86," is a delightful traveling companion.

GENERAL HISTORY

Bergeron, Paul H. *Paths of the Past: Tennessee, 1770-1970.* Knoxville: University of Tennessee Press, 1979. This is a concise, straight-up history of Tennessee with a few illustrations and maps.

Corlew, Robert E. *Tennessee: A Short History.* Knoxville: University of Tennessee Press, 1990. The definitive survey of Tennessee history, this text was first written in 1969 and has been updated several times by writers, including Stanley J. Folmsbee and Enoch Mitchell. This is a useful reference guide for a serious reader.

Dykeman, Wilma. *Tennessee.* New York: W. W. Norton & Company and the American Association for State and Local History, 1984. Novelist and essayist Dykeman says more about the people of Tennessee and the events that shaped the modern state in this slim and highly readable volume than you would find in the most detailed and plodding historical account. It becomes a companion and a means through which to understand the Tennessee spirit and character.

SPECIALIZED HISTORY

Beifuss, Joan Turner. *At the River I Stand.* Brooklyn NY: Carlson Pub., 1985. This account of the Memphis garbage men's strike of 1968 is told from the ground up. It places the assassination of Dr. Martin Luther King Jr. in its immediate, if not historical, context.

Bond, Beverley G., and Janann Sherman. *Memphis: In Black and White.* Mount Pleasant SC: Arcadia Publishing, 2003. This lively history of Memphis pays special attention to the dynamics of race and class. The slim and easy-to-read volume contains interesting anecdotes and lots of illustrations. It is an excellent introduction to the city.

Branch, Taylor. *Parting the Waters: America in the King Years 1954-63.* New York: Simon and Schuster, 1989. The most authoritative account of the civil rights movement, told through the life of Dr. Martin Luther King Jr. The first in a three-volume account of the movement, *Parting the Waters* includes descriptions of the Nashville sit-ins of 1960. The final volume, *At Canaan's Edge,* includes King's assassination in Memphis.

Egerton, John. *Speak Now Against the Day: The Generation Before the Civil Rights Movement in the South.* Chapel Hill: University of North Carolina Press, 1995. Nashville native Egerton tells the relatively unacknowledged story of Southerners, white and black, who stood up against segregation and racial hatred during the years before the civil rights movement.

Egerton, John. *Visions of Utopia.* Knoxville: University of Tennessee Press, 1977. An accessible and fascinating portrait of three intentional Tennessee communities: Ruskin in Middle Tennessee, Nashoba in West Tennessee, and Rugby in East Tennessee. Egerton's usual sterling prose and sensitive observations make this volume well worth reading.

Honey, Michael. *Going Down Jericho Road: The Memphis Strike, Martin Luther King's Last Campaign.* New York: W. W. Norton & Co., 2007. Labor historian Honey depicts with academic detail and novelistic drama the Memphis Sanitation Strike of 1968. He documents Memphis of the late 1960s and the quest for economic justice that brought Dr. King to the city. King's assassination and its aftermath are depicted in devastating detail.

Irwin, John Rice. *The Museum of Appalachia Story.* Atglen, PA: Schiffer Publishing, 1978. An illustrated look at how one man's garage collection of ephemera became a Smithsonian affiliate.

Potter, Jerry O. *Sultana Tragedy: America's Greatest Maritime Disaster.* Gretna LA: Pelican Publishing Company, 1992. The definitive account of American's worst maritime disaster. The end of the Civil War and the assassination of Abraham Lincoln grabbed the headlines in April 1864, so much so that the sinking of the *Sultana* and the death of more than 1,800 men in the Mississippi River near Memphis went almost unnoticed. This book tells a tale more poignant and moving than the loss of the *Titanic.*

Sides, Hampton. *Hellhound on His Trail: The Stalking of Martin Luther King, Jr. and the International Hunt for His Assassin.* New York: Doubleday, 2004. A well-written, captivating account of MLK's murder and the efforts to nab his killer. Sides provides perspective on Memphis's troubled history.

Sword, Wiley. *The Confederacy's Last Hurrah: Spring Hill, Franklin and Nashville.* Lawrence: University Press of Kansas, 2004. This is a well-written and devastating account of John Bell Hood's disastrous campaign through Middle Tennessee during the waning months of the Confederacy. It was a campaign that cost the South more than 23,000 men. With unflinching honesty, Sword describes the opportunities lost and poor decisions made by General Hood.

BIOGRAPHY

James, Marquis. *The Raven: A Biography of Sam Houston.* Indianapolis: The Bobbs-Merrill Company, 1929. Possibly the most remarkable Tennessean in history, Sam Houston was raised by the Cherokee, memorized Homer's *Iliad,* and was twice elected governor of Tennessee before he headed west to the new American frontier to become president of the Texas Republic.

Leeming, David. *Amazing Grace: A Life of Beauford Delaney.* New York: Oxford University Press (USA), 1998. Beauford Delaney was a brilliant but often overlooked modernist painter who was born in Knoxville in 1901. African American and gay, Delaney later moved to New York, where he worked as an artist and moved in circles that included James Baldwin and Henry Miller.

Moore, Carmen. *Somebody's Angel Child: The Story of Bessie Smith.* New York: Thomas Cromwell Company, 1969. The illustrated story of Chattanooga native Bessie Smith's remarkable rise to, then fall from, the top of the music world.

MUSIC

Carlin, Richard. *Country Music.* New York: Black Dog and Leventhal Publishers, 2006. This is a highly illustrated, well-written, and useful reference for fans of country music. It profiles the people, places, and events that contributed to country's evolution. With lots of graphic elements and photographs, it is a good book to dip into.

Chapman, Marshall. *They Came to Nashville.* Nashville: Vanderbilt University Press, 2010. Singer-songwriter Chapman tells her tales, as well as those of many others, as they came to Music City and set about hitting the big time.

Escott, Colin. *Hank Williams: The Biography.* Boston: Back Bay Books, 2004. No country star had a bigger impact on Nashville's evolution to Music City than Hank Williams. This detailed history shares his failings, downfall, and remarkable legacy.

Gordon, Robert. *It Came from Memphis.* Boston: Faber and Faber, 1994. Memphis resident Gordon takes the back roads to tell the remarkable musical story that emerged from Memphis during the 1950s and 1960s. He paints a textured picture of the milieu from which rock 'n' roll eventually rose.

Guralnick, Peter. *Careless Love: The Unmaking of Elvis Presley.* Boston: Little, Brown and Company, 1999. Volume two of Guralnick's definitive biography of Elvis Presley. Guralnick writes in the introduction that he "knows of no sadder story" than Presley's life from 1958 until his death in 1977. The book unflinchingly examines the gradual unraveling of America's greatest pop star.

Guralnick, Peter. *Last Train to Memphis: The Rise of Elvis Presley.* Boston: Little, Brown and Company, 1994. Quite possibly the definitive biography of the King. In volume one, Guralnick re-creates Presley's first 24 years, including his childhood in Mississippi and Tennessee, his remarkable rise to fame, and the pivotal events of 1958, when he was drafted into the army and buried his beloved mother.

Handy, W. C. *Father of the Blues.* New York: The Macmillan Company, 1941. This memoir by Memphis's most famous blues man depicts the city during the first quarter of the 20th century. It is an entertaining and endearing read.

Kingsbury, Paul, ed. *Will the Circle Be Unbroken: Country Music in America.* London: DK Adult, 2006. An illustrated collection of articles by 43 writers, including several performing artists, this book is a useful reference on the genre's development from 1920 until the present.

Kossner, Michael. *How Nashville Became Music City: 50 Years of Music Row.* Milwaukee: Hal Leonard, 2006. Forget about the stars and the singers; this profile of country music focuses on the people you've never heard of: the executives, songwriters, and behind-the-scenes technicians who really make the music happen. It's an interesting read for fans who don't mind seeing how the sausage is made and a good introduction for people aspiring to be a part of it.

Raichelson, Richard M. *Beale Street Talks: A Walking Tour Down the Home of the Blues.* Memphis: Arcadia Records, 1999. A slim, well-written book that describes Beale Street as it was and Beale Street as it is. This is a handy companion for exploring the street.

Sharp, Tim. *Memphis Music: Before the Blues.* Mount Pleasant SC: Arcadia Publishing, 2007. Part of the Images of America series, this work includes rare and evocative photographs of Memphis people. The result is a painting of the backdrop on which the Memphis blues were born in the early 20th century.

Wolfe, Charles K. *Tennessee Strings.* Knoxville: University of Tennessee Press, 1977. The definitive survey of Tennessee musical history. This slim volume is easy to read.

Zimmerman, Peter Coats. *Tennessee Music: Its People and Places.* San Francisco: Miller Freeman Books, 1998. Tries, and succeeds, to do the impossible: tell the varied stories of Tennessee music all the way from Bristol to Memphis. Nicely illustrated.

REFERENCE

Abramson, Rudy, and Jean Haskell, eds. *Encyclopedia of Appalachia.* Knoxville: University of Tennessee Press, 2006. From language to food to history, this tome has 2,000 entries that will force readers to expand their conception of just what "Appalachia" is.

Van West, Carroll, ed. *The Tennessee Encyclopedia of History and Culture.* Nashville: Tennessee Historical Society and Rutledge Hill Press, 1998. Perhaps the most valuable tome on Tennessee, this 1,200-page encyclopedia covers the people, places, events, and movements that defined Tennessee history and the culture of its people. Dip in frequently, and you will be all the wiser.

FICTION

Agee, James. *A Death in the Family.* New York: Vintage, 1998. First published in 1958, this is the story of a Knoxville family whose domestic happiness is disrupted by the sudden death of the father. The story is largely autobiographical and features evocative descriptions of Knoxville in 1915. Winner of the Pulitzer Prize for fiction.

Burton, Linda, ed. *Stories from Tennessee.* Knoxville: University of Tennessee Press, 1983. An anthology of Tennessee literature, the volume begins with a story by David Crockett on hunting in Tennessee and concludes with works by 20th-century authors such as Shelby Foote, Cormac McCarthy, and Robert Drake.

Cawood, Chris. *Tennessee's Coal Creek War: Another Fight for Freedom.* Kingston TN: Magnolia Hill Press, 1995. For 18 months in the late 19th century, the National Guard occupied Coal Creek, now known as Lake City, to prevent labor unrest among coal miners. This historical novel is set during this so-called coal war of 1891.

Grisham, John. *The Firm.* Boston: G. K. Hall, 1992. Probably the most celebrated Memphis-set novel in recent years, especially following the success of the eponymous film. Mitchell McDeere takes on corrupt and criminal mob lawyers. It includes references to many city landmarks.

Haun, Mildred. *The Hawk's Done Gone and Other Stories.* Nashville: Vanderbilt University Press, 1968. A collection of stories set in the Smoky Mountains and told using dialect. This volume comes closer than any other to capturing the authentic language, culture, and way of life of East Tennessee's mountain residents during the early 20th century.

Hicks, Robert. *Widow of the South.* New York: Grand Central Publishing, 2006. Tour guides at Carton Plantation gripe about the poetic license taken with some facts in this fictional tale, but it offers a moving story of the Battle of Franklin and the high emotional costs of the Civil War.

Marshall, Catherine. *Christy.* New York: McGraw Hill, 1967. The fictional story of a young teacher, Christy Huddleston, who moves to the Smoky Mountains in 1912 to teach. The story is based on Catherine Marshall's own experience in the mountains. It was adapted into a drama and spawned a television miniseries.

McCarthy, Cormac. *Suttree.* New York: Random House, 1979. Cornelius Suttree is a fisherman who lives in a houseboat in Knoxville during the 1950s. This novel possesses McCarthy's typically clear language and robust characters, and tells a tale punctuated by violence and shocking events.

Neely, Jack. *From the Shadow Side and Other Stories of Knoxville.* Oak Ridge, TN: Tellico Books, 2003. Columnist for the Knoxville *Metropulse,* historian, and master storyteller Neely has done more to preserve Knoxville history than any other. This work builds on his previous volumes, *Secret History* and *Secret History II,* both of which are also worth seeking out.

Taylor, Peter. *Summons to Memphis.* New York: Knopf Publishing Group, 1986. Celebrated and award-winning Tennessee writer Peter Taylor won the Pulitzer Prize for fiction for this novel in 1986. Phillip Carver returns home to Tennessee at the request of his three older sisters to talk his father out of remarrying. In so doing, he is forced to confront a troubling family history. This is a classic of American literature, set in a South that is fading away.

Wright, Richard. *Black Boy*. New York: Chelsea House, 2006. The 1945 memoir of African American writer Wright recounts several years of residency in Memphis. His portrayal of segregation and racism in Memphis and Mississippi are still powerful today.

FOOD

Justus, Jennifer. *Nashville Eats: Hot Chicken, Buttermilk Biscuits, and 100 More Southern Recipes from Music City*. Stewart, Tabori & Chang, 2015. Compiled by a former newspaper reporter, this is the guide to making all the local foods you fall in love with on your trip.

Lewis, Edna, and Scott Peacock. *The Gift of Southern Cooking: Recipes and Revelations from Two Great American Cooks*. New York: Knopf Publishing Group, 2003. Grande dame of Southern food Lewis and son-of-the-soil chef Peacock joined forces on this seminal text of Southern cuisine. It demystifies, documents, and inspires. Ideal for those who really care about Southern foodways.

Lundy, Ronnie, ed. *Cornbread Nation 3*. Chapel Hill: University of North Carolina Press, 2006. The third in a series of collections on Southern food and cooking. Published in collaboration with the Southern Foodways Alliance, which is dedicated to preserving and celebrating Southern food traditions, the Cornbread Nation collection is an ode to food traditions large and small. Topics include paw-paws, corn, and pork. *Cornbread Nation 2* focused on barbecue. *Cornbread Nation 1* was edited by restaurateur and Southern food celebrant John Egerton.

Stern, Jane, and Michael Stern. *Southern Country Cooking from the Loveless Cafe: Biscuits, Hams, and Jams from Nashville's Favorite Café*. Nashville: Rutledge Hill Press, 2005. Road-food aficionados wrote the cookbook on Nashville's most famous pit stop: the Loveless Cafe. Located at the northern terminus of the Natchez Trace Parkway, the Loveless is quintessential Southern cooking: delectable biscuits, country ham, and homemade preserves. Now you can take some of that down-home flavor home with you.

Internet and Digital Resources

TOURIST INFORMATION

Chattanooga Convention and Visitors Bureau
www.chattanoogafun.com

The official tourism website for the Scenic City, this resource offers suggestions for where to stay, eat, and visit, with lots of tips on Chattanooga's outdoor activities.

Knoxville Tourism & Sports Corporation
www.knoxville.org

The official travel website for Knoxville features current news, a calendar of events, and links to the live stream of radio station WDVX, East Tennessee's finest. You can request visitor information through the site.

Memphis Convention and Visitors Bureau
www.memphistravel.com

The official travel website for Memphis has listings of hotels, attractions, and events. You can also download coupons, request a visitors guide, or book hotels. The bureau also offers a free smartphone app called Memphis Travel Guide.

Nashville Convention and Visitors Bureau
www.visitmusiccity.com
The official tourism website for Nashville, this site offers concert listings, hotel booking services, and useful visitor information. You can also order a visitors guide and money-saving coupons.

Oak Ridge
http://oakridgevisitor.com
Get the lowdown on visiting the Secret City from the official tourism website.

Tennessee Department of Tourism Development
www.tnvacation.com
On Tennessee's official tourism website you can request a visitors guide, search for upcoming events, or look up details about hundreds of attractions, hotels, and restaurants. This is a great resource for suggested scenic drives.

NEWS AND CULTURE

Eat Drink Smile
www.eat-drink-smile.com
A fun blog about what to eat (and drink) in Music City.

Knoxville Mercury
www.knoxmercury.com
A weekly alternative news magazine run by the nonprofit Knoxville History Project.

The Memphis Flyer
www.memphisflyer.com
Memphis's alternative weekly newspaper publishes entertainment listings and article archives on its website.

Memphis Magazine
www.memphismagazine.com
Good restaurant reviews and useful event listings. Subscriptions available online ($15 annually).

The Nashville Scene
www.nashvillescene.com
Nashville's alternative weekly has a great website. The dining guide is fabulous, the stories are interesting and archived, and the entertainment calendar is the best in town. Go to "Our Critics' Picks" for a rundown of the best shows in town. The annual manual, reader's choice awards, and other special editions are useful for newcomers and old-timers alike.

Nooga.com
www.nooga.com
Launched in 2011, this site offers local news and lifestyle happenings for Chattanooga.

RootsRated
http://rootsrated.com
A Chattanooga-based website featuring ideas on how to make the most of outdoor activities across the country.

The Tennessean
www.tennessean.com
Nashville's major newspaper posts news, entertainment, sports, and business stories online. Sign up for a daily newsletter of headlines from Music City or search the archives.

Visit Sevierville
Take virtual tours of Sevierville, or plan your own in real life, through this free mobile app.

PARKS AND RECREATION

NashVitality
Download this free app created by the Nashville mayor's office for GPS-specific information on where to get outdoors in Music City. The app includes water launches, bike trails, greenways, and more.

Outdoor Chattanooga
www.outdoorchattanooga.com

If your main reason for coming to Chattanooga is to bike, run, climb, paddle, or kayak, this is the website for you.

Tennessee State Parks
www.state.tn.us/environment/parks

An online directory of all Tennessee state parks, this site provides useful details, including campground descriptions, cabin rental information, and the lowdown on activities.

TVA Lake Info

This free mobile app lists recreational dam release schedules for across the state.

HISTORY

Tennessee Civil War 150

A free mobile app provides quick-hit history lessons about Civil War battle sites, plus information about visiting them.

Tennessee Encyclopedia of History and Culture
www.tennesseeencyclopedia.net

The online edition of an excellent reference book, this website is a great starting point on all topics Tennessee. Articles about people, places, and events are written by hundreds of experts. Online entries are updated regularly.

Index

A

B

C

INDEX

D

E

F

G

H

I

J

K

L

M

N

O

INDEX

S

T

U

VWXYZ

List of Maps

Acknowledgments

Even in the face of approaching deadlines, Dropbox folders filled with photographs, and marked-up maps littering the floor, I'm convinced I have the world's best job. I have a legitimate, work-related excuse to throw my tent in the station wagon, strap the paddleboard to the top, and head to Land Between the Lakes for a weekend. Or to call a few friends and ask them to help me check out Nashville's honky-tonks. Or taste-test the newest variety of MoonPie.

I'm grateful to many people who helped me synthesize what I've heard, seen, and experienced into something coherent that others could share. First and foremost, thanks go to DG Strong, who encouraged me to move back to Tennessee after many years away and who indulges (if not enables) my whims to drive for miles to see a haunted state park or try a new hot-chicken place. Joy Lusk showed me much to love in her hometown of Chattanooga, as did friends in Memphis, Knoxville, Oak Ridge, and other spots across the state.

Perhaps the only person who loves Music City as much as I do is Heather Middleton of the Nashville Convention and Visitors Corp. She's always available for brainstorming and, of course, providing photos (with the help of Dana W. McDowell). Convention and visitors bureau staffs across the state, including Jonathan Lyons, Tom Adkinson, Cindy Dupree and Molly Brown, Candace Davis, and Erin Donovan, were instrumental in helping me get up-to-date information and photographs that best illustrated the gems I experienced.

Lisa Arnett is a remarkable editorial assistant/sounding board, tracking down better photos than the ones I took and helping me ID additions in cities that are seeing significant growth. Lisa Friedman verified the alphabet soup of phone numbers and URLs without going cross-eyed.

I first worked with the crackerjack staff at Avalon Travel decades ago on *The Dog Lover's Companion to Chicago*. While other authors complain about their publishers, I've never felt like mine were anything less than essential partners in this process. Particular thanks, again, this time around to Lucie Ericksen, Albert Angulo, Elizabeth Hansen, Sierra Machado, and Kimberly Ehart. Many thanks to those who worked on previous editions of *Moon Tennessee* and *Moon Nashville*, including Susanna Henighan Potter and Jeff Bradley.

As always, I am grateful for the help and support of my family and friends, who tolerate my working long hours on "vacation" and dragging them to sightsee wherever we are, not to mention my soundtrack of bluegrass and country music and the ever-growing wardrobe of cowboy hats.

Photo Credits

Title page photo: © Dreamstime.com

page 6 © Chattanooga Convention & Visitors Bureau; page 7 © Dreamstime.com; page 8 (top left) © Dreamstime.com, (top right) © Clewisleake/Dreamstime.com, (bottom) © Chattanooga Convention & Visitors Bureau; page 9 (top) © Chattanooga Convention & Visitors Bureau, (bottom left) © daveallenphoto/123RF, (bottom right) © Alex McMahan Photography/Chattanooga Convention & Visitors Bureau; page 10 © Mike Slay; page 11 (top) © Doug Schweigert, (bottom left) © daveallenphoto/123RF, (bottom right) © Chattanooga Convention & Visitors Bureau; page 12 © Natalia Bratslavsky/Dreamstime.com; page 13 © Dreamstime.com; page 15 (top left) © dndavis/123RF, (top right) © Timothy Mainiero/123RF; page 17 © Dreamstime.com; page 18 © sean pavone/123RF; page 20 © Dreamstime.com; page 21 (top left) © Visit Knoxville, (top right) © Chattanooga Convention & Visitors Bureau; page 23 © Mtkitchn/Dreamstime.com; page 24 (top left) © Dreamstime.com, (top right) © Clewisleake/Dreamstime.com; page 25 (top) © Jack Kenner / Memphis Convention & Visitors Bureau, (bottom) © Andrea Zucker/ Memphis Convention & Visitors Bureau; page 27 © The Peabody Memphis; page 34 © Justin Fox Burks / Memphis Convention & Visitors Bureau; page 35 © Tennessee Department of Tourist Development; page 36 © Trey Clark for The Peabody Hotel; page 37 © Jack Kenner / Memphis Convention & Visitors Bureau; page 39 © Tennessee Department of Tourist Development; page 42 © Troy Glasgow / Memphis Convention & Visitors Bureau; page 44 © Andrea Zucker / Memphis Convention & Visitors Bureau; page 46 © Andrea Zucker / Memphis Convention & Visitors Bureau; page 49 © Brand USA / Memphis Convention & Visitors Bureau; page 54 © Jack Kenner / Memphis Convention & Visitors Bureau; page 56 © Andrea Zucker / Memphis Convention & Visitors Bureau; page 57 © Craig Thompson/ Memphis Convention & Visitors Bureau; page 60 © Craig Thompson / Memphis Convention & Visitors Bureau; page 62 © Craig Thompson/ Memphis Convention & Visitors Bureau; page 64 © Steve Roberts / Memphis Convention & Visitors Bureau; page 65 © Andrea Zucker / Memphis Convention & Visitors Bureau; page 68 © Craig Thompson / Memphis Convention & Visitors Bureau; page 79 (top) © Land Between the Lakes Staff, (bottom) © Margaret Littman; page 81 © Belinda Hofer | Dreamstime.com; page 84 © Tennessee Department of Tourist Development; page 90 © Brent Moore; page 91 © Tennessee Department of Tourist Development; page 93 © Matthew S. Howard; page 103 © Margaret Littman; page 106 © Ray Stainfield; page 109 © Kelly Best Bennett; page 113 © Garry Thompson; page 116 © Jake Warren; page 125 (top) © sean pavone/123rf.com, (bottom) © Tennessee Department of Tourist Development; page 127 © Clewisleake | Dreamstime.com; page 132 © Tennessee Department of Tourist Development; page 135 © Courtesy of The Johnny Cash Museum; page 137 © Tennessee Department of Tourist Development; page 141 © Margaret Littman; page 153 © Susanna Henighan Potter; page 154 © Andrea Behrends; page 160 © Live Nation; page 162 © Doyle & Debbie; page 173 © Courtesy of the Country Music Hall of Fame & Museum; page 175 © Nashville Convention & Visitors Corporation; page 180 © Nashville Paddle Co./Mickey Bernal; page 181 © Mike Strasinger/Nashville Sounds; page 183 © Nashville Contention & Visitors Corporation; page 200 (top) © B. Kim Hagar, (bottom) © George Dickel Tennessee Whisky; page 201 © The Battle of Franklin Trust Archives; page 209 © Margaret Littman; page 210 © Margaret Littman; page 223 © Courtesy of Franklin Theatre; page 235 © Paul Thomasson; page 236 © Susanna Henighan Potter; page 244 © Margaret Littman; page 247 © John I. Carney, Shelbyville Times-Gazette; page 251 © Hannah Coffey; page 254 © Susanna Henighan Potter; page 257 © Courtesy of Jack Daniel's; page 263 © Paul Thomasson; page 265 © Courtesy of Bonnaroo Music and Arts Festival; page 272 © Tennessee Department of Tourist Development; page 275 (top) © Cookeville-Putnam County CVB, (bottom) © Cookeville-Putnam County CVB; page 277 © Cookeville-Putnam County CVB; page 281 © Joel Kramer; page 283 © Chuck Sutherland; page 288 © Fentress County Chamber/World's Longest Yard Sale; page 291 © Rick Bennett; page 294 © Doug Schweigert; page 297 © Vicki S. Vaden; page 303 © Margaret Littman; page 305 © Jmaentz | Dreamstime.com; page 311 © Margaret Littman; page 315 © Kim Headrick; page 317 (top) © Tennessee Department of Tourist Development, (bottom) © Chattanooga Convention & Visitors Bureau; page 319 © Chattanooga Convention & Visitors Bureau; page 323 © Melinda Fawver/123RF; page 324 © Chattanooga Convention & Visitors Bureau; page 326 © Tennessee Department of Tourist Development; page 329 © Chattanooga Convention & Visitors Bureau; page 330 © Tennessee Department of Tourist Development; page 333 © Chattanooga Convention & Visitors Bureau; page 336 © Chattanooga Convention & Visitors Bureau;

page 349 © Ducktown Basin Museum; page 357 © Courtsey of The Lost Sea Adventure; page 361 (top) © Visit Knoxville, (bottom) © Visit Knoxville; page 363 © Visit Knoxville; page 366 © Visit Knoxville; page 369 © Visit Knoxville; page 371 © Visit Knoxville; page 378 © Visit Knoxville; page 387 © Margaret Littman; page 393 © Tennessee Department of Tourist Development; page 395 © Anderson County Tourism Council; page 398 © Michael Miller; page 401 © Tennessee Department of Tourist Development; page 403 © Pigeon Forge Department of Tourism; page 408 © Pigeon Forge Department of Tourism; page 413 © Tennessee Department of Tourist Development; page 422 © Tennessee Department of Tourist Development; page 428 © Katie Ries; page 434 © Courtesy of Dollywood; page 435 © Pigeon Forge Department of Tourism; page 437 © Courtesy of Dollywood; page 438 © Don Dudenbostel; page 445 (top) © Museums of Tusculum, (bottom) © Sarah Hauser, courtesy of The Birthplace of Country Music; page 447 © Courtesy of the Andrew Johnson National Historic Site; page 452 © Tennessee Department of Tourist Development; page 453 © U.S. Navy Photo by Mass Communications Specialist 2nd Class Kristopher Wilson; page 466 © Redtail Mountain Resort; page 467 © Matteo Torri; page 468 © daveallenphoto/123RF.com; page 469 © Susanna Henighan Potter; page 473 © Tennessee Department of Tourist Development; page 476 © Courtesy of the Andrew Johnson National Historic Site; page 479 © Museums of Tusculum; page 482 © Seth Gaines; page 483 © Stephani Richadson; page 484 (top) © Dreamstime.com, (bottom) © Dreamstime.com; page 490 © Brian Lasenby/123RF; page 498 © George R. Barnard/Courtesy NARA; page 500 © Author unknown, McClure's Magazin/WikiMedia; page 508 © Bruce Patten/123RF; page 509 © Zoran Simin/123RF; page 511 © Pace & Handy Music Co.; page 514 (top) © Pierre Jean Durieu | Dreamstime.com, (bottom) © Dreamstime.com

Also Available

MAP SYMBOLS

- Expressway
- Primary Road
- Secondary Road
- Unpaved Road
- Trail
- Ferry
- Railroad
- Pedestrian Walkway
- Stairs
- ★ Highlight
- ○ City/Town
- State Capital
- National Capital
- ★ Point of Interest
- • Accommodation
- ▼ Restaurant/Bar
- ▪ Other Location
- Λ Campground
- Airfield
- Airport
- ▲ Mountain
- Unique Natural Feature
- Waterfall
- Park
- Trailhead
- Skiing Area
- Golf Course
- Parking Area
- Archaeological Site
- Church
- Gas Station
- Glacier
- Mangrove
- Reef
- Swamp

CONVERSION TABLES

°C = (°F - 32) / 1.8
°F = (°C x 1.8) + 32
1 inch = 2.54 centimeters (cm)
1 foot = 0.304 meters (m)
1 yard = 0.914 meters
1 mile = 1.6093 kilometers (km)
1 km = 0.6214 miles
1 fathom = 1.8288 m
1 chain = 20.1168 m
1 furlong = 201.168 m
1 acre = 0.4047 hectares
1 sq km = 100 hectares
1 sq mile = 2.59 square km
1 ounce = 28.35 grams
1 pound = 0.4536 kilograms
1 short ton = 0.90718 metric ton
1 short ton = 2,000 pounds
1 long ton = 1.016 metric tons
1 long ton = 2,240 pounds
1 metric ton = 1,000 kilograms
1 quart = 0.94635 liters
1 US gallon = 3.7854 liters
1 Imperial gallon = 4.5459 liters
1 nautical mile = 1.852 km

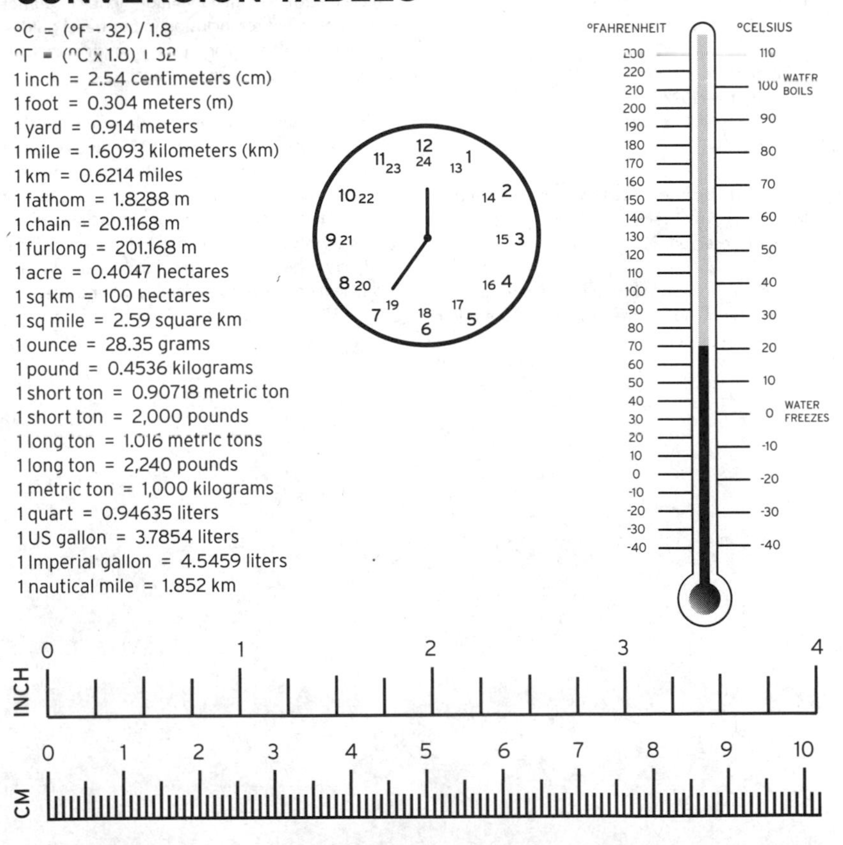

MOON TENNESSEE
Avalon Travel
a member of the Perseus Books Group
1700 Fourth Street
Berkeley, CA 94710, USA
www.moon.com

Editor: Kimberly Ehart
Series Manager: Kathryn Ettinger
Copy Editor: Rosemarie Leenerts
Graphics and Production Coordinator: Lucie Ericksen
Cover Design: Faceout Studios, Charles Brock
Interior Design: Domini Dragoone
Moon Logo: Tim McGrath
Map Editor: Albert Angulo
Cartographers: Brian Shotwell and Karin Dahl
Indexer: Greg Jewett

ISBN-13: 978-1-63121-262-8
ISSN: 1091-3343

Printing History
1st Edition — 1997
7th Edition — June 2016
5 4 3 2 1

Front cover photo: barn at Cades Cove, Great Smoky Mountains National Park © Jon Bilous / Alamy Stock Photo
Back cover photo: neon signs on historical Beale street, Memphis © Natalia Bratslavsky/123RF.com

Printed in Canada by Friesens